ESSENTIALS

OF

PROPERTY AND CASUALTY

INSURANCE

a complete guide to Pennsylvania licensure

by George E. Krauss, CPCU, CLU

This Manual Belongs to

Name

Address

Essentials of Property and Casualty Insurance *a complete guide to Pennsylvania licensure*

International Standard Book Number 0-9631842-0-2

Printed in the United States of America - Fourteenth Edition

PREFACE

This manual is part of a study program that has been approved for Pre-licensing Education (PE) in the state of Pennsylvania. Students may prepare in either of two formats. Traditional classroom study with a residential instructor or through independent self-study.

In the traditional classroom setting, your instructor will cover the material in this manual over a 24-hour period. This may be arranged in three consecutive days, or over several weeks. In either event, it is recommended that students complete the pre-assigned readings and exercises indicated in the front (xxii-xxiii) of this manual before attending the class. Students have also found it extremely helpful to use the companion software, EXAM MASTER to reinforce the learning process in traditional classroom study.

In the independent self-study format, students follow a recommended schedule and utilize the manual and its EXAM MASTER *Interactive* software. EXAM MASTER *Interactive* has the same powerful features of EXAM MASTER (practice exams, flash cards, glossary of terms, etc.), but adds several new features to promote learning in a self-study format. These new features include over 450 animated PowerPoint slides containing over 10 hours of audio summaries of key topics and concepts. EXAM MASTER *Interactive* includes an electronic manual with hyperlinked review questions. These are the same types of questions that are used in a classroom format to facilitate discussion. Students using the independent self-study option will receive a PE certificate after passing an on-site final exam that must be monitored by a disinterested third-party. The final exam is on the EXAM MASTER *Interactive* CD.

In addition to the introduction of pre-licensing education, several chapters of the study manual and software have been revised. Chapter Six has been updated to reflect the introduction of the ISO's Personal Auto '05 Policy and Chapter Seven has been revised to reflect changes brought about by the introduction of updated commercial policy forms. Chapter Ten has also been updated with the introduction of the mine subsidence insurance topic.

The study manual and software are structured in the same ten-chapter format as the state examination outline for ease in study. At the end of each chapter, exam-type questions have been prepared to assist retention. Each question has been thoroughly reviewed to ensure accuracy and exam relevance.

While every effort is made to ensure the accuracy of this manual, typographical and editorial errors may appear. Your constructive comments and criticisms are welcomed.

George E. Krauss, CPCU, CLU

GEORGE E. KRAUSS, CPCU, CLU
300 WEYMAN PLAZA - SUITE 280
PITTSBURGH, PA 15236

tel: 412-885-1210
fax: 412-885-1253
e-mail: gekrauss@magellangroupinc.com
www.magellangroupinc.com

Additional copies of this manual may be purchased at the above address or you may order through the mail or by Fax. An order form is included inside the back cover of this manual. For additional information on our products and services, please visit our home page at: www.magellangroupinc.com

TABLE OF CONTENTS

Topic **Chapter** **Page**

CHAPTER ONE - INSURANCE REGULATION

Topic	Chapter	Page
Introduction and Exam Strategies	xxi	xxiv
Purpose of Licensing	1	1
Application Process	1	1
Qualifications	1	1
Activities That Require Licensure	1	2
Persons to Be Licensed	1	2
Producer Powers	1	2
Nonresident Producers	1	3
Temporary Licenses	1	3
Managing and Exclusive General Agents	1	3
Contractual Relationship	1	3
Fiduciary Capacity	1	3
Co-mingling of Funds	1	3
License Restrictions	1	4
Name Restrictions	1	4
Producer Addresses	1	4
Fictitious or Assumed Name	1	4
Uniformity of Licenses	1	4
Restrictions of License Transfer	1	4
Change, Sale or Dissolution of an Agency	1	4
Criminal Charges	1	4
Waiver of Examination	1	5
Professional Designations	1	5
Nonresident Applicant	1	5
Temporary Licenses	1	5
Managers and Exclusive General Agents	1	5
Prohibited Acts	1	5
Company Certification	1	6
Limitations of License	1	6
Pennsylvania Continuing Education Requirements	1	6
Maintenance and Duration of Producer License	1	7
Disciplinary Actions	1	7
Suspension and Revocation	1	7
Disciplinary Procedures	1	8
State Regulations	1	8
Insurance Commissioner's General Duties and Powers	1	8
Pennsylvania Insurance Guaranty Assn Act	1	9
Company Regulation	1	9
Company Solvency	1	9
Rate Regulation	1	9
Unfair Claim Settlement Practices	1	9
Policy Forms	1	9
Agency Appointments	1	9
Unfair Claims Settlement Practices	1	10
Time Restrictions of Claim Issues	1	10
Producer Regulation	1	11
Unfair Trade Practices	1	11
Rebating	1	11
Misrepresentation	1	11
Twisting	1	11
False Advertising	1	11
Illegal Inducements	1	11
Boycott and Coercion	1	11
Defamation of Insurer	1	11

Topic	Chapter	Page
Unfair Discrimination	1	11
Producer Fees	1	12
Other Fees	1	12
Unfair Insurance Practices Act	1	12
Examination of Books and Records	1	13
Privacy of Consumer Financial Information Regulation	1	13
Insurance Fraud Regulation	1	14
Federal Regulation	1	15
Fair Credit Reporting Act	1	15
Fraud and False Statements	1	14
Major Lines of Insurance	1	15
Life, Accident and Health Policies	1	15
Ethical Conduct	1	18
Managing Ethical Issues	1	19
Insurance Regulations Practice Exam	1	23

CHAPTER TWO - GENERAL INSURANCE

Insurance Concepts	2	1
Risk Management	2	1
Risk	2	1
Exposure	2	1
Hazard	2	1
Physical Hazard	2	2
Moral Hazard	2	2
Morale Hazard	2	2
Peril	2	2
Loss	2	2
Insurance	2	2
Other Risk Management Concepts	2	2
Essential Elements of an Insurable Risk	2	3
Adverse Selection	2	3
Law of Large Numbers	2	3
Principle of Indemnity	2	3
Valued Policies	2	3
Doctrine of Insurable Interest	2	3
Reinsurance	2	4
Ceding Company	2	4
Assuming Company	2	4
Retention	2	4
Treaty Reinsurance	2	4
Facultative Reinsurance	2	4
Retrocession	2	4
Purpose of Reinsurance	2	4
Types of Insurers	2	5
Stock Companies	2	5
Mutual Companies	2	5
Fraternal Associations	2	5
Reciprocals	2	5
Lloyds	2	5
Private Insurers v. Government Insurers	2	5
Admitted or Authorized Companies	2	6
Nonadmitted or Unauthorized Companies	2	6
Domicile	2	6

Topic	Chapter	Page
Domestic Company	2	6
Foreign Company	2	6
Alien Company	2	6
Analysis of Financial Status	2	6
A.M. Best Company	2	7
Independent Rating Services	2	7
Insurance Department Examinations	2	7
National Association of Insurance Commissioners (NAIC)	2	7
Major Distribution Systems	2	8
Independent Agency System	2	8
Direct Writer System	2	8
Exclusive Agency or Captive Agency System	2	8
Direct Response System	2	8
Illustration of Major Distribution Systems	2	8
Management of Distribution Systems	2	9
Branch/Regional Office System	2	9
Managing General Agency System	2	9
Personal Producing General Agency System	2	9
Types of Insurance Producers	2	9
Agents	2	9
Independent Agents	2	9
Captive Agents or Exclusive Agents	2	9
Brokers	2	9
Company Representatives	2	9
Law of Agency	2	10
Presumption of Agency	2	10
Types of Authority	2	10
Express Authority	2	10
Implied Authority	2	10
Apparent Authority	2	10
Producer's Responsibilities to the Insured	2	11
Producer's Responsibility to the Insurance Company	2	11
Producer's Collection and Financial Responsibilities	2	11
Direct Billed Policies	2	11
Agency Billed Policies	2	11
Remittance of Premiums	2	11
Earned Premiums	2	11
Unearned Premiums	2	11
Premium Financing	2	11
Potential Liabilities and Exposures	2	12
Nature and Importance of Underwriting	2	12
Adverse Selection	2	12
Contract Elements	2	12
Offer & Acceptance	2	12
Consideration	2	12
Competent Parties	2	12
Legal Purpose	2	12
Distinct Characteristics of Insurance Contracts	2	13
Contracts of Adhesion	2	13
Aleatory Contracts	2	13
Personal Contracts	2	13
Unilateral Contracts	2	13
Conditional Contracts	2	13
Legal Interpretations Affecting the Insurance Contract	2	13
Ambiguities	2	13
Reasonable Expectations	2	13
Indemnity	2	13

Topic	Chapter	Page
Subrogation	2	13
Utmost Good Faith	2	14
Representations	2	14
Misrepresentations	2	14
Warranty	2	14
Affirmative Warranty	2	14
Continuing or Promissory Warranty	2	14
Implied Warranty	2	14
Concealment	2	14
Fraud	2	14
Waiver	2	14
Estoppel	2	14
General Insurance Practice Exam	2	17

CHAPTER THREE - PROPERTY AND CASUALTY INSURANCE BASICS

Insurable Interest	3	1
Underwriting	3	1
Adverse Selection	3	1
Field Underwriting	3	1
Profitability	3	2
Loss Ratio	3	2
Expense Ratio	3	2
Combined Ratio	3	2
Rating	3	2
Manual or Class Rating	3	2
Individual or Judgment Rating	3	2
Merit Rating	3	2
Loss Cost Rating	3	2
Hazards	3	3
Physical Hazard	3	3
Moral Hazard	3	3
Morale Hazard	3	3
Property Insurance v. Liability Insurance	3	3
Causes of Loss - Perils	3	4
Specified (Named Perils) v. Special Form (Open Perils)	3	4
Illustration of Named Peril Policy v. Special Form Policy	3	5
Direct Loss	3	5
Consequential or Indirect Losses	3	5
Blanket v. Specific Insurance	3	5
Blanket Insurance	3	5
Specific Insurance	3	5
Scheduled Insurance	3	5
Reporting Forms	3	6
Timely Reporting	3	6
Full Reporting (Honesty Clause)	3	6
Basic Types of Construction	3	6
Frame	3	6
Masonry	3	6
Other Categories of Construction	3	6
Loss Valuation	3	7
Actual Cash Value	3	7
Replacement Cost	3	7
Functional Replacement Cost	3	7
Market Value	3	7
Agreed Value	3	7
Stated Amount	3	7
Policy Structure	3	8
Definitions	3	8

Topic	Chapter	Page
Declarations Page	3	8
Insuring Agreement	3	8
Additional Coverage	3	8
Supplemental Payments	3	8
Conditions	3	8
Exclusions	3	9
Endorsements	3	9
Insured Status	3	9
Insured	3	9
Named Insured	3	9
Additional Insureds	3	9
First Named Insureds	3	9
Policy Period	3	10
Policy Territory	3	10
Deductibles	3	10
Dollar Deductible	3	10
Percentage Deductible	3	10
Time Deductible	3	10
Other Insurance	3	10
Nonconcurrency	3	10
Primary and Excess	3	11
Pro Rata	3	11
Contribution By Equal Shares	3	11
Policy Limits	3	11
Restoration of Limits	3	11
Coinsurance	3	12
Illustration of Coinsurance Formula and Examples	3	12
Liability Insurance	3	13
Tort Concepts	3	13
Intentional Torts/Intentional Acts	3	13
Unintentional Torts	3	13
Negligence	3	13
Proximate Cause	3	13
Common Law v. Statutory Law	3	13
Common Law Defenses	3	14
Contributory Negligence	3	14
Assumption of Risk	3	14
Intervening Cause	3	14
Statutory Defenses	3	14
Comparative Negligence	3	14
Statute of Limitations	3	14
Damages	3	14
Special Damages	3	14
General Damages	3	14
Compensatory Damages	3	14
Punitive Damages	3	14
Strict or Absolute Liability	3	15
Vicarious Liability	3	15
Limits Of Liability	3	15
Per Person Limits	3	15
Per Occurrence Limits	3	15
Aggregate Limits	3	15
Split Limits	3	15
Combined Single Limit	3	15
Insured's Provisions Or Duties	3	16

Topic	Chapter	Page
Duties After Loss	3	16
Transfer of Rights and Duties (Assignment)	3	16
Abandonment	3	17
Appraisal	3	17
Arbitration	3	17
Insurer's Provisions or Duties	3	17
Liberalization Clause	3	17
Transfer of Rights of Recovery (Subrogation)	3	18
Salvage	3	18
Claim Settlement Options	3	18
Duty To Defend	3	18
Unoccupancy and Vacancy	3	19
Illustration of an Overview of Unoccupancy and Vacancy	3	19
Third Party Provisions	3	20
Standard Mortgage Clause	3	20
Loss Payable Clause	3	20
No Benefit to Bailee	3	20
Related Pennsylvania Regulations	3	20
Binders	3	20
Pennsylvania Insurance Guaranty Association Act	3	21
Countersignature and Fees	3	21
Basic Property Insurance - Death of the Named Insured	3	21
Insurance Consultation Services Exemption Act	3	21
Cancellation and Nonrenewal	3	21
Cancellation Methods	3	21
Short Rate	3	21
Pro Rate	3	21
Illustration of Pennsylvania Cancellation and Nonrenewal Requirements	3	22
Standard Fire Policy	3	23
Friendly Fire v. Hostile Fire	3	23
Property and Casualty Insurance Basics Practice Exam	3	27

CHAPTER FOUR - DWELLING POLICY

Topic	Chapter	Page
Dwelling Policy	4	1
Illustration of the Dwelling Policy Coverage Forms	4	1
Coverage A - Dwelling Amount	4	2
Coverage B - Other Structures	4	2
Coverage C - Personal Property	4	2
Coverage D - Fair Rental Value	4	3
Coverage E - Additional Living Expenses	4	3
Illustration of Additional Living Expenses	4	3
Other Coverages	4	3
General Exclusions	4	5
Conditions	4	6
Coverage Forms	4	7
Dwelling Policy Basic Form DP 00 01	4	7
Dwelling Policy Broad Form DP 00 02	4	8
Dwelling Policy Special Form DP 00 03	4	9
Dwelling Policy Coverages and Loss Settlement Comparison	4	9
Endorsements	4	10
Automatic Increase In Insurance	4	10
Broad Theft Coverage	4	10
Dwelling Under Construction	4	10

Topic	Chapter	Page

Building Ordinance and Law Coverage	4	10
Sinkhole Collapse	4	10
Personal Liability	4	11
Standard Fire Policy Endorsement	4	11
Pennsylvania Notice	4	11
Water Backup and Sump Overflow - Pennsylvania	4	11
Pennsylvania Changes - Cancellation and Nonrenewal	4	11
Illustration of Dwelling Policy Cancellation Requirements - PA	4	11
Dwelling Policy Program Comparison	4	12
Dwelling Policy Practice Exam	4	15

CHAPTER FIVE - HOMEOWNERS POLICY

Homeowners Policy	5	1
Definitions	5	1
Homeowner Policy Structure	5	2
Illustration of Homeowner Policy Structure	5	2
Property Coverages - Section I	5	3
Coverage A - Dwelling Amount	5	3
Coverage B - Other Structures	5	3
Coverage C - Personal Property	5	3
Personal Property Not Covered	5	4
Coverage D - Loss of Use	5	4
Additional Coverages - Section I	5	4
Perils Insured Against	5	5
Homeowner Policy Program	5	6
Coverage Forms	5	6
Homeowner Form HO 00 02	5	6
Homeowner Form HO 00 03	5	6
Homeowner Form HO 00 04	5	6
Homeowner Form HO 00 05	5	6
Homeowner Form HO 00 06	5	7
Homeowner Form HO 00 08	5	7
Basic, Broad and Special Form Analysis	5	7
Section I - Exclusions	5	8
Section I - Property Exclusions	5	9
Section I - Property Conditions	5	9
Homeowner Coverage and Loss Settlement Comparison Illustration	5	10
Liability Coverage Section II	5	11
Coverage E - Personal Liability	5	11
Coverage F - Medical Payments to Others	5	11
Additional Coverages - Section II	5	11
Section II - Liability and Medical Payments Exclusions	5	12
Aircraft, Motor Vehicles and Watercraft Exclusion Illustration	5	13
Section II - Liability Conditions	5	14
Section I & II - General Conditions	5	15
Pennsylvania Homeowner Cancellation Requirements	5	15
Endorsements	5	16
Inflation Guard Endorsement (HO 04 66)	5	16
Business Pursuits (HO 24 71)	5	16
Permitted Incidental Occupancies (HO 00 42)	5	16
Scheduled Personal Property Endorsement (HO 04 61)	5	16
Limited Fungi, Wet or Dry Rot or Bacterial (HO 04 26 & HO 04 27)	5	16
Home Day Care Coverage Endorsement (HO 04 97)	5	17

Topic	Chapter	Page

Earthquake Endorsement (HO 04 54)	5	17
Personal Property Replacement Cost (HO 04 90)	5	17
Additional Residence Rented to Others (HO 24 70)	5	17
Watercraft Endorsement (HO 24 75)	5	17
Mobilehome Endorsement (HO 40 01)	5	17
Ordinance or Law Coverage (HO 04 77)	5	17
Personal Injury (HO 24 82)	5	17
Comparison of the Dwelling Fire and Homeowners Programs	5	18
Homeowners Policy Program Comparison	5	19
Homeowners Policy Practice Exam	5	23

CHAPTER SIX - AUTO INSURANCE

Pennsylvania Motor Vehicle Financial Responsibility Law	6	1
Required Limits of Liability	6	1
Bodily Injury Liability	6	1
Property Damage Liability	6	1
Tort Options	6	2
Limited Tort	6	2
Full Tort	6	2
First Party Benefits	6	2
Medical Benefits	6	2
Extraordinary Medical Benefits	6	2
Income Loss Benefits	6	2
Funeral Benefits	6	2
Accidental Death Benefits	6	2
Sources of First Party Benefits/Priority of Payments	6	3
Ineligible Claimants	6	3
Payments of Benefits	6	3
Statute of Limitations	6	3
Uninsured Motorists Insurance	6	4
Underinsured Motorists Insurance	6	4
Stacking	6	4
Rental Vehicles	6	4
Illustration of the Pennsylvania Motor Vehicle Responsibility Law	6	5
Other Provisions	6	5
Comprehensive Insurance	6	5
Collision Insurance	6	5
Discounts	6	5
Motor Vehicle Fraud	6	5
Personal Auto Policy	6	6
Illustration of the Personal Auto Policy Structure	6	6
Definitions	6	6
Eligible Vehicles Under the Personal Auto Policy	6	7
Newly Acquired Vehicles	6	7
Part A - Liability Coverage	6	7
Bodily Injury and Property Damage	6	7
Supplementary Payments	6	7
Liability Exclusions	6	8
Part B - Medical Payments	6	8
Part C - Uninsured Motorists Coverage	6	8
Underinsured Motorists	6	9
Underinsured Motorist Coverage Illustration	6	9

Topic	Chapter	Page

Part D - Coverage For Damage To Your Auto 6 10
Collision 6 10
Other Than Collision (OTC) 6 10
Deductibles 6 10
Transportation Expense 6 10
Exclusions 6 11
Part E - Duties After An Accident Or Loss 6 11
Part F - General Provisions 6 12
Illustration of the Personal Auto Cancellation Requirements 6 12
Endorsements 6 13
Extended Nonowned Coverage for Named Individuals 6 13
Joint Ownership Coverage 6 13
Miscellaneous Type Vehicles 6 13
Named Nonowner Endorsement 6 13
Towing and Labor 6 13
Amendments of Policy Provisions - Pennsylvania 6 14
First Party Benefits Coverage - Pennsylvania 6 14
Limited Tort Alternative Information Notice - Pennsylvania 6 14
Assigned Risk Plan 6 14
Commercial Auto Policy 6 15
Illustration of the Commercial Auto Policy 6 15
Definitions 6 15
Business Auto Coverage Form 6 16
Section I - Covered Autos 6 16
Section II - Liability Coverage 6 16
Liability Coverage Extensions 6 17
Liability Exclusions 6 17
Section III - Physical Damage Coverage 6 17
Comprehensive Coverage 6 17
Specific Perils Coverage 6 17
Collision Coverage 6 17
Physical Damage Coverage Extensions 6 17
Physical Damage Exclusions 6 17
Section IV - Business Auto Conditions 6 17
Section V - Definitions 6 17
Garage Coverage Form 6 18
Section I - Covered Autos 6 18
Section II - Garage Liability 6 18
Garage Liability Exclusions 6 18
Section III - Garagekeepers Coverage 6 18
Garagekeepers Exclusions 6 18
Truckers Coverage Form 6 19
Section I - Covered Autos 6 19
Section II - Truckers Liability Coverage 6 19
Section III - Trailer Interchange Coverage 6 19
Motor Carrier Form 6 20
Section I - Covered Autos 6 20
Section II - Motor Carrier Liability Coverage 6 20
Commercial Carrier Regulation 6 20
Illustration of Financial Responsibility 6 21
Commercial Auto Endorsements 6 21
Additional Insured - Lessor (CA 20 01) 6 21
Broad Form Products (CA 25 01) 6 21
Deductible Liability Coverage (CA 03 02) 6 21
Drive Other Car Coverage (CA 99 10) 6 22

Topic	Chapter	Page
Employees as Insureds (CA 99 33)	6	22
False Pretense Coverage (CA 25 03)	6	22
Hired Autos Specified as Owned Autos (CA 99 16)	6	22
Individual Named Insureds (CA 99 17)	6	22
Mobile Equipment (CA 20 15)	6	22
Truckers - Insurance for Non-Trucking Use (CA 23 09)	6	22
Pollution Liability Broadened Coverage for Covered Autos(CA 99 48)	6	23
Pollution Liability Broadened Coverage for Covered Autos(CA 99 55)	6	23
Pennsylvania Cancellation and Nonrenewal Requirements	6	23
Comparison of Personal Auto and Commercial Auto Programs	6	24
Auto Insurance Practice Exam	6	29

CHAPTER SEVEN - COMMERCIAL PACKAGE POLICY

Topic	Chapter	Page
Commercial Package Policy Overview	7	1
Commercial Package Policy (CPP) Format	7	1
Advantage of the Policy Package Concept	7	2
Common Policy Conditions	7	2
Illustration of the Commercial Package Policy Format	7	2
Commercial General Liability (CGL) Coverage Part	7	3
Illustration of the Commercial General Liability Coverage Part Format	7	3
Premises and Operations	7	3
Products and Completed Operations	7	3
Coverage Forms	7	4
Claims-Made v. Occurrence	7	4
Occurrence Coverage	7	4
Claims Made Coverage	7	4
Retroactive Date	7	4
Extended Reporting Periods (ERP)	7	4
Mini/Midi tail	7	4
Supplemental Extended Reporting Periods (SERP)	7	4
Claims Information	7	5
Laser Beam Endorsement	7	5
Illustration of Claims-Made Coverage Form	7	5
Commercial General Liability Coverages	7	6
Coverage A - Bodily Injury and Property Damage Liability	7	6
Coverage B - Personal and Advertising Injury Liability	7	6
Coverage C - Medical Payments	7	7
Supplemental Payments	7	7
Insured	7	7
Conditions	7	7
Limits of Liability	7	8
General Aggregate Limit	7	8
Products/Completed Operations Aggregate	7	8
Personal and Advertising Injury	7	8
Each Occurrence Limit	7	8
Damage To Premises Rented To You Limit	7	8
Medical Expense Limit	7	8
Illustration of Commercial General Liability Limits of Liability	7	8
Owners and Contractors Protective Liability Policy (OCP)	7	9
Pollution Liability	7	9
Pollution Liability Coverage Form	7	9
Pollution Liability Limited Coverage Form	7	9
Pollution Liability Extension Endorsement	7	9
Commercial Crime Coverage Part	7	9
Illustration of the Crime Coverage Part Format	7	10

Topic	Chapter	Page
Crime General Conditions	7	10
Crime General Exclusions	7	10
Crime General Definitions	7	10
Commercial Crime Coverage Forms	7	11
Loss Sustained Form	7	11
Discovery Form	7	11
Employee Theft	7	11
Forgery or Alteration	7	12
Inside the Premises - Theft of Money and Securities	7	12
Inside the Premises - Robbery & Safe Burglary of Other Property	7	12
Outside the Premises	7	12
Computer Fraud	7	12
Money Orders and Counterfeit Paper Currency	7	12
Funds Transfer Fraud	7	12
Extortion	7	12
Securities Deposited with Others	7	13
Guest's Property	7	13
Safe Depository	7	13
Lessees of Safe Deposit Boxes	7	13
Valuation Clause	7	13
Illustration of Commercial Crime Coverages	7	14
Boiler and Machinery Coverage Part	7	15
Illustration of the Boiler and Machinery Coverage Part	7	15
Equipment Breakdown Protection Coverage Form	7	16
Coverages Provided	7	16
Exclusions	7	17
Valuation	7	17
Suspension Provision	7	17
Deductibles	7	18
Commercial Property Coverage Part	7	19
Illustration of the Commercial Property Coverage Part Form	7	19
Building and Personal Property Form	7	20
Coverage A - Buildings	7	20
Coverage B - Business Personal Property	7	20
Coverage C - Personal Property of Others	7	20
Property Not Covered	7	20
Additional Coverages	7	21
Coverage Extensions	7	21
Limits of Insurance	7	21
Loss Conditions	7	21
Builders Risk Form	7	22
Business Income Coverage	7	23
Business Income	7	23
Illustration of the Coinsurance Requirements	7	23
Extra Expense	7	23
Civil Authority	7	23
Alterations and New Buildings	7	23
Extended Business Income	7	23
Optional Coverages	7	24
Maximum Period of Indemnity	7	24
Monthly Limit of Indemnity	7	24
Agreed Value Approach	7	24
Extended Period of Indemnity	7	24
Business Income From Dependent Properties	7	24
Contributing Locations	7	24
Recipient Locations	7	24

Topic	Chapter	Page
Leader Locations	7	24
Manufacturing Locations	7	24
Business Income Changes - Educational Institutions	7	24
Extra Expense Coverage Form	7	25
Leasehold Interest Coverage Form	7	25
Legal Liability Coverage Form	7	25
Glass Coverage Form	7	25
Condominium Forms	7	25
Condominium Association Coverage Form	7	25
Condominium Unit Owner's Coverage Form	7	25
Causes of Loss Forms	7	26
Basic Form	7	26
Broad Form	7	26
Special Form	7	26
Earthquake Form	7	26
Endorsements	7	26
Ordinance or Law	7	26
Peak Season Endorsement	7	26
Value Reporting Form	7	26
Inland Marine Coverage Part	7	27
Illustration of the Commercial Inland Marine Coverage Part	7	27
Inland Marine Conditions	7	28
Inland Marine Exclusions	7	28
Inland Marine Coverage Forms	7	28
Accounts Receivable Form	7	28
Commercial Articles Form	7	28
Equipment Dealers Form	7	29
Jewelers Block Form	7	29
Signs Form	7	29
Valuable Papers and Records Form	7	29
Other Inland Marine Coverages	7	29
Contractor's Equipment Form	7	29
Electronic Data Processing Form	7	29
Bailees' Customers Form	7	29
Installation Floater Form	7	29
Transportation Coverages	7	30
Common Carriers	7	30
Contract Carriers	7	30
Motor Truck Cargo Policy - Trucker's Form	7	30
Motor Truck Cargo Policy - Shipper's Form	7	30
Motor Truck Cargo Policy - Owner's Form	7	30
Transportation Policy - Annual Form	7	30
Transportation Policy - Trip Transit Form	7	30
Instrumentations of Transportation and Communication	7	30
Farm Coverage Part	7	31
Illustration of the Farm Coverage Part	7	31
Farm Property Coverage Form	7	31
Coverages A-G	7	32
Extensions	7	33
Farm Liability Coverage Form	7	33
Coverage H - Bodily Injury and Property Damage	7	33
Coverage I - Personal and Advertising Injury Liability	7	33
Coverage J - Medical Payments	7	34
Mobile Agricultural Machinery and Equipment Coverage Form	7	34
Livestock Coverage Form	7	34
Causes of Loss	7	34

Topic	Chapter	Page
Basic Form	7	34
Broad Form	7	34
Special Form	7	35
Conditions	7	35
Exclusions	7	36
Additional Coverages	7	36
Definitions	7	36
Pennsylvania Changes - Cancellation and Nonrenewal	7	38
Illustration of the Pennsylvania Commercial Cancellation Requirements	7	38
Commercial Package Policy Summary	7	39
Commercial Package Policy Practice Exam	7	43

CHAPTER EIGHT - BUSINESSOWNERS POLICY

Topic	Chapter	Page
Businessowners Policy	8	1
Eligible Risks	8	1
Ineligible Risks	8	1
Policy Structure	8	2
Illustration of the Businessowners Policy Structure	8	2
Declarations	8	2
Common Policy Conditions	8	2
Common Exclusions	8	3
Special Form	8	4
Common Exclusions	8	4
Covered Property	8	5
Businessowners Property Part Illustration	8	5
Coverage A - Buildings	8	5
Coverage B - Business Personal Property	8	6
Property Not Covered	8	6
Limitations	8	6
Additional Coverages	8	6
Debris Removal	8	6
Preservation of Property	8	6
Fire Department Service Charge	8	6
Collapse	8	6
Water Damage	8	6
Business Income	8	6
Extended Business Income	8	7
Extra Expense	8	7
Pollutants Clean Up and Removal	8	7
Civil Authority	8	7
Money Orders and Counterfeit Paper Coverage	8	7
Forgery and Alteration	8	7
Exterior Building Glass	8	7
Increased Cost of Construction	8	7
Glass Expenses	8	7
Fire Extinguisher Systems Recharge Expense	8	7
Coverage Extensions	8	8
Buildings Newly Acquired or Constructed	8	8
Personal Property at Newly Acquired Premises	8	8
Personal Property Off Premises	8	8
Outdoor Property	8	8
Valuable Papers and Records	8	8
Personal Effects	8	8
Accounts Receivable	8	8
Limits, Increases and Deductibles	8	8
Building Limit - Automatic Increase	8	8
Business Personal Property Limit - Seasonal Increase	8	8

Topic	Chapter	Page
Standard Deductible	8	8
Property Loss Conditions	8	9
Property General Conditions	8	9
Optional Coverages	8	10
Outdoor Signs	8	10
Crime Coverage	8	10
Employee Dishonesty	8	10
Mechanical Breakdown	8	10
Businessowner Liability Coverage Form	8	11
Business Liability	8	11
Supplemental Coverage Extensions	8	11
Medical Expenses	8	11
Liability and Medical Expense Conditions	8	12
Liability Exclusions	8	12
Definitions	8	13
Endorsements	8	14
Protective Safeguards (BP 04 30)	8	14
Utility Services - Direct Damage (BP 04 56)	8	14
Utility Services - Time Element (BP 04 57)	8	14
Hired Auto and Nonowned Auto (BP 04 04)	8	14
Pennsylvania Changes - Cancellation and Nonrenewal	8	14
Businessowners Policy Summary	8	15
Commercial Package Policy v. Businessowners Policy Illustration	8	16
Businessowners Policy Practice Exam	8	21

CHAPTER NINE - WORKERS COMPENSATION

Topic	Chapter	Page
Workers Compensation Overview	9	1
Workers Compensation Law	9	1
U. S. Longshore and Harbor Workers Compensation Law	9	1
Jones Act	9	2
Federal Employer's Liability Act	9	2
Federal Employees Compensation Act	9	2
Defense Base Act	9	2
Workers Compensation Policy	9	2
Illustration of Workers Compensation Policy Structure	9	2
Part One - Workers Compensation Insurance	9	3
Unlimited Medical Benefits	9	3
Income Benefits	9	3
Total Disability	9	3
Partial Disability	9	3
Permanent Partial Disability	9	3
Temporary Disability	9	3
Death Benefits	9	3
Rehabilitation Benefits	9	3
Part Two - Employers Liability	9	4
Part Three - Other States Insurance	9	4
Part Four - Duties If Injury Occurs	9	4
Part Five - Premium	9	4
Part Six - Conditions	9	4
Occupations Excluded	9	4
Subsequent Injury Fund	9	5
Special Considerations for Contractor and Subcontractor	9	5
Selected Endorsements	9	5
Voluntary Compensation	9	5
Foreign Coverage Endorsement	9	5
Premium Computations	9	6
Loss Cost Rating	9	6
Experience Rating	9	7

Topic	Chapter	Page
Premium Discount	9	7
Illustration of Experience Modification & Premium Discount	9	7
Participating Dividend Plans	9	7
Retrospective Rating	9	7
Other Sources of Coverage	9	7
Pennsylvania Workers Compensation Act (Act 44 of 1993)	9	8
Compliance	9	8
Notice/Recording Requirements	9	8
Compensation Exclusions	9	9
Reduction in Benefits	9	8
1996 Amendments to the Workers Compensation Law	9	9
Penalties	9	9
Workers Compensation Practice Exam	9	11

CHAPTER TEN - OTHER COVERAGES AND OPTIONS

Topic	Chapter	Page
Other Coverages and Options	10	1
Comprehensive Personal Liability Insurance	10	1
Personal Umbrella Policy	10	1
Commercial Umbrella Policy	10	2
Professional Liability Policies	10	2
Medical Malpractice	10	2
Legal Errors and Omissions	10	2
Agents and Brokers Errors and Omissions	10	2
Directors and Officer's Liability	10	3
Fiduciary Liability	10	3
Liquor Liability	10	3
Employment Practices Liability	10	3
Surplus Line Insurance	10	4
Surety Bonds	10	4
Parties to a Surety Bond	10	4
Bond Underwriting	10	5
Contract Bonds	10	5
Bid Bonds	10	5
Performance Bonds	10	5
Completion Bonds	10	5
Judicial Bonds	10	5
Judicial Bail Bonds	10	5
Appeal Bonds	10	5
Attachment Bonds	10	5
Injunction Bonds	10	5
Fiduciary Bonds	10	5
Miscellaneous Bonds	10	5
License or Permit Bond	10	5
Workers Compensation Bond	10	5
Motor Vehicle Bond	10	5
Ocean Marine Insurance	10	6
Hull Coverage	10	6
Cargo Coverage	10	6
Free Along Side (FAS)	10	6
Free On Board (FOB)	10	6
Cost and Freight (C&F)	10	6
Cost, Insurance and Freight (CIF)	10	6
Freight Coverage	10	6
Protection and Indemnity (P&I)	10	7
Implied Warranties	10	7
Coverage Forms	10	7
Loss Adjustment	10	7
Watercraft Insurance	10	8

Topic	Chapter	Page

Boatowners	10	8
Section I - Boatowners Property Coverage	10	8
Property Excluded	10	8
Section II - Boatowners Liability Coverage	10	8
Aviation Insurance	10	9
Airport Liability	10	9
Nonowned Aircraft	10	9
Air Meet Liability	10	9
Hangerkeepers Liability	10	9
National Flood Insurance Program	10	10
Eligibility	10	10
Emergency v. Regular	10	10
Perils Covered	10	10
Property Not Covered	10	10
Personal Article Floaters	10	11
Personal Effects Floaters	10	11
Personal Property Floaters	10	11
Difference In Conditions (DIC)	10	11
Residual Markets	10	11
Fair Access to Insurance Requirements (FAIR Plans)	10	11
Mine Subsidence Insurance	10	11
Alternative Funding Mechanisms	10	12
Risk Retention Groups	10	12
Risk Purchasing Groups	10	12
Self-insured	10	12
Pooling	10	12
Captives	10	12
Personal Umbrella Illustration	10	13
Other Insurance Coverages and Options Practice Exam	10	17
Chapter Answer Key	10	23
Some Final Thoughts	F	26

SPECIMEN PAGES

Standard Fire Policy 165 Lines	SP	1
Homeowner Special Form HO 00 03	SP	2
Personal Auto Policy	SP	26
Commercial Package Policy Common Policy Declarations	SP	39
Commercial Property Coverage Part Declarations Page	SP	40
Businessowners Policy	SP	41

INTRODUCTION

- **What is Pre-licensing Education (PE)?**

Effective June 4, 2003, Pennsylvania implemented a Pre-licensing Education (PE) requirement. Students may prepare in either of two formats. Traditional classroom study of 24-hours with a residential instructor or through an independent self-study program. Either format must be approved by the Pennsylvania Insurance Department. Students who successfully complete the course will be presented with a pre-licensing education certificate that they will have to present at the Thomson Prometric testing site to sit for their actual state exam.

- **What materials are needed to prepare for the Pre-licensing Education?**

In addition to this manual and EXAM MASTER, you should have a current Pennsylvania Licensing Information Bulletin. This bulletin provides complete details of all relevant data pertaining to the licensing process including the exam outline, examples of test questions and an application to register for the examination. **Please note** that this manual and software is revised annually to correspond with the new testing outlines. For example, the 2005 study guide and software editions are designed to be used for individuals taking their exam between July 1, 2005 and June 30, 2006 (next tentative scheduled revision). If you are taking your exam after June 30, 2006, it is recommended you purchase the most current edition of Essentials of Property and Casualty Insurance and its companion software. If you are preparing for the **Personal Lines Exam**, you should study: all of Chapter 1 through Chapter 5, Chapter 6 (pages 6-1 to 6-14), Chapter 10 (pages 10-1, 10-8, 10-10, and 10-11).

- **What is the best way to use this pre-licensing education study program?**

If you are attending a class, preview the material by following the 30-day programmed instructional guide (see following pages). First, read a chapter highlighting important concepts and topics. Make sure you pay attention to bolded or italicized words or phrases. Second, review the key terms and concepts at the end of the chapter. This feature is automated in EXAM MASTER under the flash card feature. Third, see if you can answer the review questions at the end of the chapter. These open-ended questions may also be used by your instructor in class to facilitate discussion. Finally, answer the questions in the practice exam at the end of the chapter. This feature is also automated in EXAM MASTER. Begin by taking the chapter exam in practice mode (answers supplied) in an open-book format. At the end of the practice exam, you will be given the option to view or print out your incorrect answers. Review the questions you answered incorrectly and retake the exam in test mode (answers not given until the exam is over). The test mode scores are maintained in memory so you can see how well you are doing in your preparation.

Individuals who have purchased the self-study pre-licensing program will have this study manual and EXAM MASTER *Interactive*. EXAM MASTER *Interactive* has the same powerful features of EXAM MASTER but adds several new features to promote learning in a self-study format. These new features include over 450 animated PowerPoint slides with audio summaries of key topics and concepts. Students can use this feature as a chapter preview before beginning their study or as a chapter review after completing a chapter. EXAM MASTER *Interactive* also includes an electronic manual with review questions hyperlinked to the answers. These are the same types of questions that are used in a classroom format to facilitate discussion. Students using the independent self-study option will receive a PE certificate after passing an on-site final exam that must be monitored by a disinterested third-party. The final exam is on the EXAM MASTER *Interactive* CD. Students will not be able to register for their state insurance exam until the day following receipt of their prelicensing education course completion certificate.

- **How does the computer examination work?**

The licensing exam is provided on a computer at an Thomson Prometric testing site. Students will be given an introductory lesson to become familiarized with the computer. The exam questions appear on the screen giving the student the option of recording the answer or to "mark" the answer for later review. At the end of the exam a pass/fail grade will appear on the screen and a hard copy will be presented to the student. Complete details on the computer examination, the location and related details will be included with the exam registration.

PROGRAMMED INSTRUCTIONAL GUIDE
(30 Day Schedule)

Preparation is the key factor for exam success. It is important that each student review the material in detail prior to attending a review class and/or taking the state exam. Some chapters are longer and more challenging to master (e.g., Chapters 3, 5, 6, and 7). In these cases, it is recommended that you study this material in small sections rather than attempting to comprehend a large amount of material at one time. The following is a recommended 30-day self-study guide, however, learners may wish to compress or expand preparation time based upon their individual experience.

DAY	CHAPTER	MATERIAL TO REVIEW	TIME
1	Chapter 1 Insurance Regulation	Read chapter	2 Hours
		Define key terms	1 Hour
2		Answer review questions	1 Hour
		Complete quiz/review chapter	1 Hour
3	Chapter 2 General Insurance	Read chapter	2 Hours
		Define key terms	1 Hour
4		Answer review questions	1 Hour
		Complete quiz/review chapter	1 Hour
5	Chapter 3 P&C Insurance Basics	Read chapter pages 3-1 to 3-12	2 Hours
		Define key terms/answer review questions 1-18	1 Hour
6		Read chapter pages 3-13 to 3-23	2 Hours
		Define key terms/answer review questions 19-42	1 Hour
7		Complete Quiz/Review Chapter	1 Hour
8	Chapter 4 Dwelling Policy	Read chapter	2 Hours
		Define key terms	1 Hour
9		Answer review questions	1 Hour
		Complete quiz/review chapter	1 Hour
10	Chapter 5 Homeowners Policy	Read chapter	3 Hours
		Define key terms	1 Hour
11		Answer review questions	1 Hour
		Complete quiz/review chapter	1 Hour
12	Chapter 6 Auto	Read chapter pages 6-1 to 6-14 (Personal Auto)	2 Hours
		Define key terms/Answer review questions 1 to 24	1 Hour
13		Read chapter pages 6-14 to 6-23 (Commercial Auto)	2 Hours
		Define key terms/Answer review questions 24 to 40	1 Hour
14		Complete quiz/review chapter	1 Hour

PROGRAMMED INSTRUCTIONAL GUIDE

(30 Day Schedule)

This marks your halfway point in your study process. With the exception of the last part of Chapter Six (Commercial Auto), you have studied about personal insurance exposures. Chapter Seven begins the introduction of commercial insurance. It is common to feel overwhelmed with the amount information contained in some of these chapters. For that reason it is important to study in small sections mastering the content before moving forward. You should also try to draw parallels between the new material you are studying and material you already know.

DAY	CHAPTER	MATERIAL TO REVIEW	TIME
15	Chapter 7 Commercial Package Policy	Read chapter pages 7-1 to 7-8 (CGL)	2 Hours
		Define key terms/Answer review questions 1 to 9	1 Hour
16		Read chapter pages 7-9 to 7-14 (Crime)	1 Hour
		Define key terms/Answer review questions 10 to 13	1 Hour
17		Read chapter pages 7-15 to 7-18 (Boiler & Machinery)	1 Hour
		Define key terms/Answer review questions 14 to 18	1 Hour
18		Read chapter pages 7-19 to 7-26 (Property)	2 Hours
		Define key terms/Answer review questions 19 to 30	1 Hour
19		Read chapter pages 7-26 to 7-30 (Inland Marine)	2 Hours
		Define key terms/answer review questions 30 to 33	1 Hour
20		Read chapter pages 7-31 to 7-38 (Farm)	2 Hours
		Define key terms/answer review questions 34 to 40	1 Hour
21		Complete quiz/review chapter	2 Hours
22	Chapter 8 Businessowners Policy	Read chapter	2 Hours
		Define key terms	1 Hour
23		Answer review questions	1 Hour
		Complete quiz/review chapter	1 Hour
24	Chapter 9 Workers Compensation	Read chapter	2 Hours
		Define key terms	1 Hour
25		Answer review questions	2 Hours
		Complete quiz/review chapter	1 Hour
26	Chapter 10 Other Coverages and Options	Read chapter	2 Hours
		Define key terms/Answer review questions	2 Hour
27		Complete quiz/review chapter	1 Hour
28	Chapters 1 to 5	Review chapter quizzes	3 Hours
29	Chapters 6 to 10	Review chapter quizzes	3 Hours
30	Chapters 1 to 10	Final exam/Review book	3 Hours

TEST TAKING STRATEGIES

- **Do Not Cram** - This examination can be arranged at any time up to ninety days from the date of your exam registration. Pace your study time over several weeks concentrating on areas you find most difficult. Study frequently in short time intervals of 45 to 60 minutes rather than longer sessions. Pay special attention to bolded or italicized words or phrases.

- **Test Yourself Frequently** - This manual contains over 400 multiple choice questions similar to ones that will appear on the state exam. Review each question that you have incorrectly answered or do not fully understand. If you are not consistently answering these questions correctly and understanding their intent, you will not pass the examination. If you are using EXAM MASTER software, each of the 800 plus multiple choice questions in its data bank will randomly be accessed to insure maximum preparation. The software will also tabulate your practice and final exam results.

- **Know The Material** - This manual follows the Pennsylvania Thomson Prometrics' outlines. It contains all the material needed to pass the examination. Students must prepare and master the content of this manual. Attempting to memorize questions is a prescription for failure. You must know the material and be able to apply it to the various question that may appear on the exam. Review concepts that are difficult or ones that require rote memorization (time periods, dollar amount, etc.) right before the exam.

- **The Examination - Read Carefully** - The combination Property Casualty examination consists of 150 questions weighted to reflect the percentages in the exam outline. You will need a 70% to pass this examination. The questions on the exam are objective multiple choice questions that will ask the student to choose the best possible answer. Some questions on the exam will include the word EXCEPT in the question. This type of question is asking the student to choose the answer that is unlike or dissimilar from the other three answers. Read each question carefully to avoid choosing an incorrect answer.

- **Time Management** - The examination is a 150 question test in which you will have 150 minutes to complete. The time element is typically not a problem, however, allocate no more than one minute per question.

- **Elimination Strategy** - Each of the multiple choice questions have four possible answers. Read each question carefully and choose the best one. If you are unsure, eliminate the unreasonable or irrelevant answers. This may sound too simple to be true, but some answers are obviously not relevant to the question and therefor can be eliminated.

- **Common Sense** - If a question appears and you do not know or cannot eliminate an answer, apply logic and/or common sense. Also, answer all questions since any unanswered question will be considered incorrect.

- **Arrive Early** - This may again sound simple but the last problem you want when taking an exam is to arrive late. It may be a good idea to drive by the testing facility to familiarize yourself with the location.

- **Final Review** - As a final review follow these steps prior to examination:

  - Review the "Some Final Thoughts" checklist on page 10-25.
  - Review all questions from the practice exams that you do not understand.
  - Review the examination outline to make sure you understand each topic.
  - Become familiar with the test site.
  - Follow your normal daily routine.
  - Get a good night's rest.
  - Eat your normal breakfast.
  - Arrive at the test site early.
  - Bring proper photo identification and your PE course completion certificate to the Thomson Prometric testing site.
  - Read the exam question including all answers carefully.
  - Apply the elimination and common sense strategy.
  - Answer all questions even if you must guess.
  - Think positive.

CHAPTER ONE

INSURANCE REGULATION

OVERVIEW

PURPOSE OF INSURANCE LICENSING

The purpose of licensing is to **ensure high standards of service** to the insuring public of this Commonwealth. The insurance department requires each individual seeking a producers license to meet certain minimum standards through a licensing process. Individuals may not conduct activities authorized by the producer license *until the license is received and all applicable agency appointments are processed.*

LICENSING APPLICATION PROCESS

An individual who does not have in effect a current license must complete an approved 24-hour prelicensing education course and pass the required state licensing exam. After passing the required state licensing examination, prospective producers must complete the applicant form IPL-01 and submit with fingerprints to the insurance department. Fingerprints may be electronically scanned for a fee at the Thomson Prometric Testing Center at time of examination.

Business entities such as **partnerships or corporations** may apply for a license if at least one qualifying partner or officer is licensed (i.e., active officer). Employees of the partnership or corporation must apply individually.

Individuals who have completed prelicensing education have **one year** to apply for a producer license. Individuals who pass their exam have **one year from the date of the exam** to have their producer license issued. Individuals who fail to comply with these time periods must complete prelicensing education and retake the state insurance examination.

QUALIFICATIONS FOR LICENSURE

Individuals may qualify for their **producer license** if they:

- Are 18 years of age
- Can read and write in English
- Maintain a business or legal address in Pennsylvania
- Complete a 24-hour self-study or classroom prelicensing education (PE) course
- Submit fingerprints for a criminal background check
- Have the professional competence, general fitness and integrity of character
- Pass the appropriate exam

An individual who is an employee of a public utility that conducts business in Pennsylvania may not be licensed.

ACTIVITIES REQUIRING LICENSURE

The insurance department **requires anyone acting as a producer to be properly licensed**. This means anyone soliciting insurance, giving advice, countersigning policies or collecting premiums away from a producer's office must be licensed. **Insurance agency employees who function exclusively in non-selling activities need not be licensed.**

Non-selling activities include:

- Discussing insurance matters in general, so long as no recommendation is made with respect to specific coverages, products or rates
- Receiving requests for coverage for transmittal to a certified producer
- Assisting with the completion of applications on the agency premises
- Passing on to the certified producer insurance inquiries of a particular nature
- Receiving payments delivered to the agency premises for coverage and issuing receipts on behalf of the producer or agency
- Arranging or making meeting appointments for a certified producer
- Collecting expiration data information from clients or potential clients

Officers, directors or employees of insurance organizations that provide underwriting, loss control, adjusting, risk manager or technical advice need not be licensed. Insurance licenses may not be transferred nor may they be delegated.

TYPES OF LICENSES ISSUED BY THE INSURANCE DEPARTMENT

The insurance department issues insurance licenses in the following four forms:

1) **PRODUCER LICENSE** is issued to individuals who sell insurance to the public. Producers are generally appointed by insurance companies and commonly act as the representative (the agent) of the insurer.

   Producers may also act as the representative of the prospective insured. When **producers represent the prospective insured they are acting as brokers**. In practice, producers commonly act in both capacities (agent or broker). The primary benefit of acting as a broker is the ability to place business with insurers that he or she (the producer) does not directly represent by means of an agency appointment. This transaction is known as **brokering business**. Before, June 4, 2003, Pennsylvania required agents (now called producers) who wanted to represent a prospective insured to have a brokers license. Today, that is no longer the case. Producers, by their actions and representations may represent the insurer, the prospective insured or both.

   Producers representing a consumer in a **fee arrangement** must execute a written agreement with the consumer prior to acting on his or her behalf. The written agreement must delineate the services to be provided and set forth full and complete disclosure of the fee to be paid to the producer by the consumers.

2) **NONRESIDENT PRODUCER LICENSE** is issued to a nonresident when the non-resident producer wants to sell insurance and collect commission in Pennsylvania. A nonresident is one who has neither a business nor a legal address in the Commonwealth of Pennsylvania. The insurance department may issue a nonresident producer license to the non-resident for the same lines of authorities (e.g., property & casualty) as the individual is licensed in his or her home state. The nonresident must submit to the insurance department a completed application or an updated copy of the individual's home state application indicating the lines of authority, proof of the individual's home state license and payment of the applicable fees.

3) **TEMPORARY LICENSE** is issued on a temporary basis to individuals, without the requirement for examination. **This normally occurs upon the death or incompetency of a producer, but is also available when individuals are serving in the armed services.** The insurance department recognizes the need to provide for an orderly transition in these circumstances, and thereby permits **the surviving spouse, surviving nonactive officer or partner, or legal representative** a temporary license to affect a sale of the agency or secure the required licenses by examination. **A temporary license is issued for a period not exceeding 180 days from the date of death or declaration of incompetence.** During this period, the temporary license permits the temporary producer to perform standard agency functions, such as processing endorsements and related correspondence and receiving commissions earned on business. The solicitation of new business is prohibited.

4) **MANAGERS AND EXCLUSIVE GENERAL AGENTS LICENSE** is issued to producers who conduct insurer type activities such as underwriting, policy issuance, and claims settlement. MGAs generally have specialized expertise.

FIDUCIARY CAPACITY

Every insurance producer in Pennsylvania is responsible in a fiduciary capacity for all funds received or collected. The general thrust of the law is to require producers to operate in an honest and faithful manner when entrusted with premium monies of insureds and prospective insureds.

Producers who maintain a bank account on premiums received (common in the commercial property casualty field) **must keep insurance premiums separate from personal monies** and shall, at all times, **maintain a complete and accurate accounting**. Producers who operate under an "account current system" shall, at all times, **maintain a balance at least equal to the net balance of premiums collected and unpaid to companies**. Producers who make immediate remittance of premiums to their companies need not maintain separate bank accounts. Immediate remittance means the payment to insurers shall be in the same form as the collection was received from the insured.

Producers are prohibited from co-mingling insurance premiums collected from applicants with personal monies without the expressed written consent of each insurer.

RESTRICTIONS PLACED ON PRODUCERS

NAME RESTRICTIONS - The insurance department will not issue a license if only the initials of the applicant's given name are used. The **license shall contain at least one full given name**. An abbreviated given name or a substitution for a true given name shall not be accepted. Producers must notify the insurance department of **any legal name change (marriage, divorce, etc.) within 30 days.**

ADDRESSES - Every producer holding a license must notify the insurance department of **a change in residence or business address within 30 days**. A similar notification must be given by producers to each insurer that has appointed that producer.

FICTITIOUS OR ASSUMED NAME - The insurance department will issue a license to an individual trading under a fictitious or assumed name. Individuals making application in these instances *must file the certificate with the Department of State* ***and*** *attach a copy of that certificate to the license application.*

UNIFORMITY OF LICENSES - Partnerships and corporations, including their qualifying active officers or qualifying active partners are required to be uniformly licensed with their respective organization. A "qualifying active officer" or "qualifying active partner" is the individual who holds a current producer license for the line of authority for which the corporation or partnership is applying.

RESTRICTIONS ON LICENSE - Licenses may not be delegated nor may they be transferred by power of attorney. They may only be acquired by passing the specific examination, by application for temporary license, by application as a qualified nonresident producer or by statutory waiver for qualified professional designations.

CHANGE, SALE OR DISSOLUTION OF AN AGENCY - Any agency that changes its name, or changes a qualifying active partner or qualifying active officer, must notify the insurance department **of the change, sale or dissolution within 30 days**.

CRIMINAL CONDUCT REPORTING - Any producer who has been charged with criminal conduct shall report the charges to the insurance department **within 30 days of being charged**. The licensee must provide the insurance department with a: copy of the criminal complaint, information or indictment; copy of the order resulting from a pretrial hearing if any; and, report of the final disposition of the charges. These documents must be provided to the insurance department within 30 days of their availability. The following chart illustrates the reasons and time periods required for producers to notify the insurance department.

REASON FOR NOTIFICATION - TRADE ISSUES	TIME PERIOD
Legal Name Change on License	30 Days
Address Change of Residence or Business	30 Days
Agency Change, Sale or Dissolution	30 Days
Criminal Conduct	30 Days

EXAMINATION WAIVERS

The insurance department may waive the mandatory prelicensing education requirement and the state licensing examination requirement for:

- **Certain professional designations** - A waiver of the property and casualty examination is granted for individuals who hold the Chartered Property Casualty Underwriter (CPCU) designation administered by The American Institute for CPCU. A similar waiver is provided to individuals who hold the Certified Insurance Counselor (CIC) designation administered by the Society of Certified Insurance Counselors.

- **Nonresident applicant** - An individual licensed in another state that is seeking to sell insurance in Pennsylvania. This waiver would also apply to an individual licensed in another state who is moving into Pennsylvania as a new resident.

- **Temporary licensee** - As cited earlier, an unlicensed individual may make application for a license on a temporary basis.

CIRCUMSTANCES FOR LICENSE APPLICATION REJECTION

In addition to failing the previously cited qualification requirements, the insurance department **may deny an application** if the applicant has provided incorrect or misleading information on an application; been denied or refused a license in another state; or, violated any section of the Commonwealth insurance laws.

CRIMINAL VIOLATIONS PREVENTING LICENSURE

An applicant for a producer license and/or a currently licensed producer may not:

- Provide incorrect, misleading or false information on a license application
- Violate an insurance department's laws or regulations or a subpoena/court order
- Obtain or attempt to obtain a license through misrepresentation or fraud
- Improperly withhold, misappropriate or convert (i.e., steal) money or property
- Intentionally misrepresent the terms of an insurance application or policy
- Admit to or been found to have committed an unfair insurance practice or fraud
- Use fraudulent, coercive or dishonest practices or demonstrated incompetence
- Have a producer's license or other financial services license denied or revoked
- Forge another person's name on an insurance application or similar document
- Cheat on an examination for an insurance producer license
- Knowingly accept insurance business that was sold by a unlicensed individual
- Fail to follow an administrative/court order imposing a child support obligation
- Fail to pay state income tax or comply with a related administrative/court order
- Commit a felony or its equivalent
- Commit a misdemeanor that involves the misuse or theft of money or property
- Transfer insurance coverage without the express consent of the insured
- Fail to notify the insurance department of a change in address within 30 days

INSURANCE COMPANY CERTIFICATION

Insurance companies are required to certify to the insurance department by making a reasonable inquiry to determine whether an appointed producer: has engaged in conduct that would disqualify the producer from a new certificate; has a financial indebtedness in his accounts to the inquiring company which demonstrates that producer's lack of general fitness and/or the producer's fiduciary responsibility, and; has pleaded guilty or nolo contendere, or has been found guilty of such crimes as would disqualify that producer from obtaining a license. This certification is typically conducted prior to the renewal of a producer's license, however, in the event the company becomes aware of activity as cited above, it shall notify the insurance department immediately.

LIMITATIONS PLACED ON PRODUCERS

Producers are limited to the type of license power authorized by the insurance department. For example, the series 16-01 examination for Life Insurance and Annuities corresponds to the license power 0100. Similarly, the series 16-02 for Accident and Health Insurance corresponds to license power 0300. Producers are restricted to soliciting insurance equivalent to the powers indicated on their licenses and may not receive commissions on policies unless they are properly licensed. Commission splitting or commission sharing with other licensed producers is proper as long as both have the authority for the same power. For example, a property casualty producer may split commissions on a property casualty policy with another property casualty producer, however, they would be prohibited from sharing commissions on a life policy unless they are both licensed for the life power.

CONTINUING EDUCATION (CE) REQUIREMENTS

Effective June 4, 2003 producers must complete 24-credit hours of continuing education for license renewal. The 24-credit hour requirement is aligned with the biennial (2 year) license renewal period. Producers can satisfy their CE requirements by completing national professional designation courses (e.g., CPCU, CLU, ChFC), self-study courses in either print or electronic format (e.g., CDs, Internet) or by lecture (i.e., credit hour is 50 minutes of class-room instruction). A Continuing education course must be approved in advance by the insurance department and will specify the number of approved CE hours.

A producer may carry forward excess CE credits hours up to a maximum of 24 credit hours from one licensing period to the next. Failure to comply with the continuing education requirement will result in the voluntary termination of the producer's license.

Producers initially appointed by an insurer may continue to be licensed without appointment if they meet continuing education requirements.

DURATION AND MAINTENANCE OF LICENSE

Producer licenses are issued for a two-year period (biennially). Producers wishing to have their license renewed will be required to complete Continuing Education (CE) programs as a condition to license renewal. Producers may complete CE up to the time of their license renewal. If a producer fails to renew his or her license by their renewal date, they will have 60 days to complete their CE and there will be no lapse in licensure. **After 60 days the producer will have up to one year from the date of his or her license renewal to complete CE, *however,* there will be a lapse in licensure.** Individuals who fail to renew their license after 1 year must complete 24 hours of Prelicensing Education (PE) and pass an exam as if they were a new producer.

EXEMPTIONS FROM CONTINUING EDUCATION REQUIREMENTS

The insurance department will exempt the following individuals from mandatory continuing education:

- A producer that has been continually licensed for the same lines of authority since December 31, 1970.
- A licensee that is a business entity.
- A licensee who has only a limited line of authority.
- A licensee who has a line of authority limited to restricted fraternal.
- A licensee who has a line of authority limited to limited line credit insurance.
- Nonresident producers who satisfy their home state's CE requirements.
- A licensee's line of authority is restricted to domestic mutual fire insurance and the license's appointment is with an insurer writing only coverage other than insurance upon automobiles.
- A producer who has good cause for exemption as approved by the Commissioner.

DISCIPLINARY ACTIONS - SUSPENSION AND REVOCATION

The insurance department may **fine, revoke, suspend or non-renew** a producer's license upon the finding of any of the following violations:

- Acting as a producer without a license.
- Advertising as a producer for an unauthorized company.
- Soliciting for fictitious or dead companies.
- Transacting business with an unlicensed producer.
- Larceny by producers.
- Fiduciary capacity of producers.
- Twisting, rebates and inducements.
- Misrepresentation of terms of policies and future dividends.

A violation of these activities is a misdemeanor, and upon conviction, the violator shall be sentenced to pay **a fine of not more than $5,000 for each and every violation**, and at the discretion of the court, to imprisonment in the county jail for a period of not more than six months, or both.

DISCIPLINARY PROCEDURE

The insurance department may initiate procedures and assess penalties as follows:

Administrative Hearing - An administrative hearing may be conducted to determine if a violation of applicable law has occurred. Following the hearing, the insurance department shall issue a written order resolving the factual issues presented and state what remedial action is necessary.

Administrative Penalty - Upon the determination that a violation has occurred, the department may issue an order requiring that person to cease and desist from engaging in such violation. The department may suspend or revoke the person's license.

Cease and Desist Orders - The insurance department may issue a cease and desist order requiring the person or insurer to stop the activity in question.

Injunction - If the alleged violator fails to comply with the order, an injunction may be filed with the Commonwealth Court of Pennsylvania in the county in which the violation occurred.

Civil Penalties - In addition to any other penalties imposed, the court, in an action filed by the insurance department, may impose the following civil penalties:

- A penalty of not more than $5,000 for each violation, not to exceed an aggregate of $50,000 in any six month period for any act or practice that the person knew, or should have known, was a violation.
- A penalty of not more than $1,000 for each violation, not to exceed an aggregate penalty of $10,000 in any six month period for any act or practice that the person did not know, nor reasonably should have known, was a violation.
- A penalty of not more than $10,000 for each violation of a cease and desist order, while such order is in effect.

Judicial Review - Any person aggrieved by the determination of an order may appeal to the Commonwealth Court within thirty days after the issuance of the order.

STATE REGULATION - COMMISSIONERS' DUTIES AND POWERS

The insurance department is an administrative department of the state government and is responsible for the regulation of all aspects of the insurance industry. The insurance department is administrated by the Insurance Commissioner who has the statutory responsibility to regulate the industry in the public's interest, balancing the needs of the consumer with those of the insurance industry to ensure and maintain a viable insurance market. The Insurance Commissioner is appointed by the Governor and empowered to enforce and execute the insurance laws of the Commonwealth. **These powers and duties include the right to:** staff the department; appoint deputies; conduct investigations; hold hearings and issue fines; suspensions or revocations of certificates or licenses. The Insurance Commissioner is charged with these responsibilities and requires detailed annual financial statements on all admitted insurance companies.

GUARANTEE FUNDS

Pennsylvania Insurance Guaranty Association Act provides a means of covering claims for certain property and casualty insurance policies. Coverage is provided to individuals who are insured with **admitted/authorized carriers** which subsequently become insolvent. Coverage is provided up to **$300,000 per covered claim and $10,000 per policy for a covered claim for the return of unearned premium**. Examples of policies covered under this Act include Homeowner, Dwelling Fire, Businessowner and Commercial Package policies. **The members of the association are subject to assessment to provide funds to carry out the purpose of this act.** This act **does not cover** life insurance, annuities, accident and health insurance, title insurance, credit insurance on accounts receivable, mortgage guaranty insurance, surety insurance, ocean marine insurance and workers compensation insurance. Producers are prohibited from advertising the existence of the Guarantee Association Act as a means to secure business.

REGULATION OF INSURANCE COMPANIES

Insurance companies are regulated by the insurance department under the direction of the Insurance Commissioner. The following are the **primary functions and objectives of state regulation**:

- **Company Solvency** is required by the Commissioner prior to, and while conducting business in the state. This includes the requirements to apply and be approved as a licensed company and to provide detailed information on company operations and financial stability. The Commissioner will conduct company audits and review data from the NAIC zone examinations and IRIS tests.

- **Rate Regulation** is performed by the Commissioner through detailed rate reviews. The Commissioner will prohibit rates that are excessive, inadequate or unfairly discriminatory. **Policy Forms** are the actual insurance policies and endorsements used by insurers. Most policy forms must be filed with the insurance department prior to their introduction. This requirement is to ensure the policy language and coverages are in the public's best interest.

  Please note that the provisions addressing rate regulation and policy forms do not apply to large commercial risks. Large commercial risks are ones in which the premiums exceed $25,000 annually (exclusive of workers compensation), the entity has at least 25 full-time employees and the entity uses an employee as the insurance buyer or retains a qualified risk manager or risk management consultant.

- **Agency Appointments** are written agreements between the producer and the insurance company under which the producer agrees to solicit, negotiate, and service insurance policies for compensation. These appointing companies must notify the insurance department of agency/producer appointments on a monthly basis and certify that the appointed producers are properly trained and qualified and have not violated any provision of the Pennsylvania Insurance Law.

UNFAIR CLAIMS SETTLEMENT PRACTICES

Unfair claims settlement practices refer to activities that the insurance department deems unfair in the settlement of claims. The following are **examples of unfair claims settlement practices:**

- Misrepresenting pertinent facts or policy provisions.
- Failure to acknowledge and act promptly upon written or oral communications.
- Failure to implement reasonable standards for the prompt investigation of claims.
- Failure to promptly, fairly and equitably settle claims.
- Refusing to pay claims without a reasonable investigation.
- Failing to affirm or deny coverage within a reasonable time.
- Not dealing in good faith for claims in which liability has become reasonably clear.
- Compelling individuals to institute litigation to recover amounts due.
- Attempting to settle a claim for less than the amount that a reasonable man would believe he is entitled to by reference to printed material related to the policy.
- Attempting to settle a claim on the basis of an altered application without the knowledge of the insured.
- Making claim payments without an accompanied statement setting forth coverages.
- Advising insureds and/or claimants the practice of appealing arbitration awards as an inducement to settle for a compromise or lesser amount.
- Delaying the investigation by requiring the insured or claimant to file a preliminary claim report and subsequently requesting a formal proof of loss; both of which submissions contain substantially the same information.
- Failing to promptly settle claims where liability has become reasonably clear under one portion of the coverage, as an inducement to influence settlements under other policy sections.
- Failure to promptly provide a reasonable explanation of policy coverage.
- Failure to maintain *complaint records of all* ***written complaints*** *over the* ***prior four years*** *indicating* ***total number*** *of complaints,* ***classification*** *by line,* ***nature and disposition***.

In addition to the above cited prohibited practices, insurers are required to comply with the following time restrictions on claim issues:

REASON FOR NOTIFICATION - CLAIMS ISSUES	TIME PERIOD
Acknowledge receipt of a claim (unless payment is made)	10 working days
Provide claim forms and reasonable assistance	10 working days
Respond to an insurance department inquiry	15 working days
Complete a claim investigation after notification	30 working days †
Accept or denial of claim after proof of loss is executed	15 working days †

† If the investigation cannot be completed within the time period indicated, every 45 days thereafter the insurer must provide the insured or claimant with a reasonable explanation for the delay and state when the decision on the claim will be expected.

REGULATION OF PRODUCERS

Producers are regulated by laws that address trade practices. The following are activities that are specifically prohibited:

Rebating is the illegal practice of a producer giving back to the insured monies or any form of consideration as an inducement to purchase insurance.

Misrepresentations are false statements that are relied upon as being truthful. Misrepresentation includes:

- **Twisting**, which is the illegal practice of misrepresenting policy provisions, or the making of incomplete comparisons as an inducement to terminate, lapse, forfeit or surrender one's policy for another of similar risks, and;

- **False Advertising**, which is using media with deliberate deceit to defraud.

- **Illegal Inducement** is any illegal act or activity that may induce or cause an individual to enter into an insurance contract.

Boycott and Coercion means the entering into an agreement to commit an act of boycott, coercion or intimidation resulting in or tending to result in the unreasonable restraint of trade or monopoly in the business of insurance.

Defamation of Insurer is the defaming of an insurance company by making false or derogatory statements as to the company's financial position.

Unfair Discrimination means:

- The unfair discrimination between individuals of the same class, and equal expectation of life, in the rates charged for any contract of life insurance, life annuity or in the dividends.

- Making or permitting any unfair discrimination between individuals of the same class, and of essentially the same hazards, in the amounts of premium, policy fees or rates charged for any policy or contract.

- Making or permitting any unfair discrimination between individuals of the same class, and essentially the same hazards, with regard to underwriting standards or eligibility requirements by reason of race, religion, nationality or ethnic group, age, sex, family size, occupation, place of residence or marital status. The terms underwriting standards and eligibility requirements do not include the promulgation of rates in accordance with the rate regulatory act of this Commonwealth.

  An example of unfair discrimination is **redlining**. This occurs when insurers discriminate based upon the location of the insured's home or business. Discrimination may be permitted when there is sound actuarial justification.

COMMISSIONS, CONSULTING AND REFERRAL FEES

Insurance producers may be compensated and/or pay referral fees as follows:

- **Commissions** - Insurance commissions are received by licensed producers for the sale and servicing of insurance products. Renewal commissions may be paid to an individual if the individual was licensed as a producer at the time of sale. Commissions may be shared between producers if both producers are licensed for the same lines of authority.

- **Consulting Fees** - Producers may charge a consulting fee in addition to a commission for the sale, solicitation or negotiation of **commercial business**. Written advance notice of the fee must be disclosed to the person and must be reasonable in relationship to the services provided. Fee many not be charged for the completion of an application for insurance.

- **Referral Fees** - Insurance entities and producers may pay a referral fee to an unlicensed individual if the referring person:

  1) does not discuss specific terms or conditions of the insurance contract, and
  2) in the case of referrals for insurance that is primarily personal, family or household use, the referring person receives a one-time nominal fee of a fixed dollar amount for each referral that is not dependent on whether the referral results in a sale.

UNFAIR INSURANCE PRACTICES ACT OF 1974

The purpose of this act is to regulate trade practices in the business of insurance by defining practices in this state which constitute unfair methods of competition or unfair or deceptive acts or practices. The following are **examples of unfair and/or deceptive trade practices:**

- Publishing false illustrations or sales presentations.
- Misrepresenting policy benefits, conditions or dividend projections.
- Misrepresenting dividends to be a share of surplus.
- Misrepresenting the name, title or class of any insurance policy.
- Circulating false and malicious information about a competitor.
- Misrepresentation to induce lapse, forfeiture, conversion or surrender.
- Misrepresenting the policy as being a share of stock.
- Deceptive advertising.
- Making false or derogatory statements of the financial condition of any person.
- Entering an agreement to boycott, coercion, intimidation or monopoly.
- Filing false statements of the financial condition of any person.
- Unfair discrimination.
- Rebating and inducements.

The purpose of the Unfair Insurance Practices Act is to regulate trade practices in the business of insurance. This includes both the sales and the claims practices as indicated in earlier in this Chapter. Penalties for violation under this Act are in addition to other penalties imposed.

PURPOSE OF EXAMINATION OF BOOKS AND RECORDS

The purpose of this regulation is to improve the insurance department's surveillance of the financial condition of insurers by requiring periodic examinations. This process permits the insurance department the right to conduct field and/or home office **audits at the insurance company's expense** in order to determine marketing conduct violations or to minimize insurer impairment and/or insolvency. Areas that are commonly examined by insurance department auditors include:

- **Claims Departments** - For example, the auditor may review an insurer's **claims reserves** (its potential liabilities) to determine if they are adequate and sufficient to pay incurred claims (its estimate of future claim payments). If claim reserves are inadequate, an insurer will have to increase its reserves and reduce its **policyholder's surplus** (the amount assets exceed liabilities).

- **Underwriting Departments** - For example, the auditor may review the policy forms and rates being used to determine if they are in compliance with their filings.

- **Marketing Departments** - For example, the auditor may review the advertising materials (e.g., brochures, form letters, circulars, illustrations, etc.) to ensure that they comply with insurance department requirements.

PRIVACY OF CONSUMER FINANCIAL INFORMATION REGULATION

Producers and insurers are required to adhere to Pennsylvania's Privacy of Consumer Financial Information Regulation as imposed by the Gramm-Leach-Bliley Act (GLBA). This regulation imposes the following obligations on producers and insurers:

1) **Privacy Notice Disclosure Requirement** - This requires insurance agencies and insurers to notify their customers with an initial and annual notice that describes the manner in which nonpublic personal information is collected, maintained and disseminated. **Nonpublic personal information** is any personal identifiable financial information that is available to the agent/insurer and not to the public. **Examples include**: salary, assets, health history, insurance coverage, premium payment history, bank account information, credit history, and data collected from an Internet cookie (an information-collecting device from a web server).

2) **Opt Out Notification Requirement** - This requires insurance agencies and insurers to permit customers to opt out or prohibit the insurance agency or insurer from disseminating nonpublic personal information to a non-affiliated third party.

3) **Data Security Requirement** - This requires insurance agencies and insurers to implement procedures to protect a customer's nonpublic personal information.

The purpose of this regulation is to protect the privacy of consumer financial information. Violation of Pennsylvania's Privacy of Consumer Financial Information Regulation is subject to penalties under the Unfair Insurance Practices Act.

INSURANCE FRAUD REGULATION

The Insurance Fraud Regulation was developed to minimize fraudulent insurance claims. The regulation addresses the following offenses:

- Filing a fraudulent motor vehicle claim with a state or local agency.
- Filing a fraudulent claim with an insurer.
- Acting as an accomplice or conspiring with another to file a fraudulent claim.
- Acting as an unlicensed producer or insurer with the intent to defraud.
- Knowingly receiving proceeds from insurance fraud.
- Using a health care facility to perpetrate insurance fraud.
- Using another person's financial responsibility/identification card to defraud.
- Being part of a "personal injury mill" based upon fraudulent insurance claims.
- Compensation by a health care provider to others to refer patients.
- Compensation by a lawyer to others for medical information on individuals.
- Compensation by a health care provider to others for medical information.
- Filing an application for insurance containing false material information.

In additional to criminal prosecution, individuals found guilty of the above cited offenses are subject to a civil penalty of up to:

- $5,000 for the first offense
- $10,000 for the second offense, and
- $15,000 for each subsequent offense.

Individuals may also be responsible for restitution.

To assist in the prosecution of fraudulent claims, persons are immune from civil or criminal liability arising from the supply or release of written or oral information to any authorized entity.

PENNSYLVANIA FRAUD NOTICE REQUIREMENT

Pennsylvania requires that all preprinted claims forms provided by an insurer to a claimant, that is required as a condition of payment, must contain a statement that clearly states in substance the following:

> "Any person who knowingly and with intent to defraud any insurance company or other person files an application for insurance or statement of claim containing any materially false information or conceals for the purpose of misleading, information concerning any fact material thereto commits a fraudulent insurance act, which is a crime and subjects such person to criminal and civil penalties."

The purpose of this regulation is to minimize insurance fraud.

FEDERAL REGULATIONS

Federal regulations apply to the business of insurance in the following areas:

1) **The Fair Credit Reporting Act (FCRA)** was **established to protect consumers** from unfair and inaccurate information contained in the files of credit reporting agencies. Insurance companies may wish to investigate the credit and background history of an applicant as part of its underwriting process. In these instances, notification to the insured is required at application and if coverage is declined, the applicant has a right to be informed of the name and address of the reporting agency. Any reporting agency that is negligent in complying with this Act will be liable to the consumer for actual damages and related court costs. The maximum penalty for fraudulent use of consumer information is $5,000, or one year in prison, or both.

2) **Fraud and False Statements** - This provision of the United States Code addresses individuals and organizations that engage in fraudulent conduct (e.g., making false material statements; willfully overvaluing property; misappropriating moneys, funds, premiums, credits or other property) **that affect interstate commerce**. In these instances, the individual and/or organization may be subject to a fine and/or imprisonment of up to 10 years. In the event the fraudulent conduct jeopardizes the safety and soundness of an insurer (e.g., causing conservation, rehabilitation or liquidation) the imprisonment is up to 15 years. In addition, the Attorney General may bring a civil action against any person who engages in such conduct and may be subject to a civil penalty of not more than $50,000 for each violation or the amount of compensation the person received or offered for the prohibited conduct, whichever is greater.

MAJOR CATEGORIES OF INSURANCE

Insurance is categorized into the following two major classes:

1) **Property and Casualty** - Property and casualty insurance is generally written together to protect an insured against common everyday exposures. Property insurance covers property that an individual owns. For example, an individual's home is covered by a property policy that will reimburse the individual if a loss occurs by certain perils (e.g., fire, lightning, windstorm, etc). Casualty insurance, which is commonly written in conjunction with property insurance, protects the insured in the event the insured is sued due to their negligence. For example, if a individual falls on an insured's sidewalk, the insured's Homeowners Policy will provide a legal defense (hire an attorney) and pay up to the policy's limit of insurance. Passing the Pennsylvania property and casualty licensing exam grants an individual the authority to sell these lines of coverage. This manual will address all these coverages in detail.

2) **Life, Accident and Health** - The other major category of insurance is life, accident and health insurance. Life insurance is used to insure a person's life in the event of death. Accident insurance is used to cover a person for accidents. Health insurance is used to covered a person's medical expenses. To sell these lines of coverage, an individual must pass the state life, accident and health exam.

MAJOR LIFE, ACCIDENT AND HEALTH POLICIES

Life, accident and health policies are sold to cover personal and business insurance needs. The following summarizes the most common life, accident and health policies.

LIFE INSURANCE POLICIES may be classified as permanent type policies or as a temporary type policy. **Permanent life insurance policies** provide protection for the life of the insured with level premiums and include a savings feature in the form of cash value. Permanent life insurance may be used to accumulate cash, to provide a death benefit, or specifically to fund estate tax and administration costs. Examples of permanent life policies include:

- **Continuous Premium Whole Life** is a level death benefit policy that requires continuous level premium payments to age 100, when the policy's cash value equals its face amount. It is a combination of decreasing term insurance and increasing cash value.

- **Limited Premium Whole Life** is similar to continuous premium Whole Life in that it provides a level death benefit; however, premiums are only paid for a specified period, at which time the policy becomes paid up for life. Examples of limited payment policies include 20-Pay Life and Life Paid-Up at Age 65.

- **Universal Life (UL)** is the generic trade name for Adjustable Premium Whole Life insurance. It is, in essence, a **combination of term insurance and a separate savings account** joined into one policy. This policy provides flexibility by permitting the insured the ability to choose the premium payment period and the time period the death benefit will be in force. Based upon these factors, a **planned premium** (also known as the target premium) is developed by the insurance company. Each premium payment will have mortality charges (either current charges or guaranteed maximum charges) deducted from the premium based upon the insured's current age. The balance of the premium is then deposited into a cash value account and credited at a current or guaranteed minimum interest rate. As the insured ages, a greater portion of the premium is used to pay mortality charges (based upon age and/or poor underwriting results) and a smaller portion is deposited in the cash value account. Universal Life insurance can be written on either an Option A - Level Death Benefit or Option B - Increasing Death Benefit basis.

- **Variable Life (VL)** insurance is a level fixed premium investment based product. It is, in essence, a **combination of decreasing term insurance and an investment fund**. The insured has the option of investing in various stock, bond or money market funds. Depending upon market performance, cash values may increase or decrease and no guarantee is provided. The **death benefit may not decrease below** the guaranteed minimum which is **the initial face amount**. Individuals selling variable life policies must also secure a securities license.

Temporary insurance or term insurance has fixed or guaranteed premiums and provides coverage for a specific term period. Coverage and premium amounts may be level, decreasing or increasing with age. Term policies have no cash value, consequently, premiums are substantially less than permanent insurance. Term insurance may be used to insure an outstanding mortgage, to cover the dependency period of children, or to cover a business debt obligation. Examples of term policies include Annually Renewable Term (ART), 5-Year Term and 10-Year Term.

ANNUITIES are used as a retirement planning vehicle to assure that income will be provided to the annuitant, free of investment concerns. Individuals choose the type of annuity (fixed or variable) and make flexible contributions that accumulate on a tax-deferred basis. Unlike life insurance, which provides for the immediate creation of an estate upon the death of the insured, **an annuity provides guaranteed income by the liquidation of the principal sum** in accordance with the terms of the various annuity contracts and provisions. The amount of periodic income received by the annuitant is determined by the contributions paid and/or accumulated, the age and sex of the annuitant and the type of annuity.

ACCIDENT AND HEALTH INSURANCE covers an insured for accidental injuries and illnesses. It includes:

- **Disability Income Insurance** is designed to replace a portion of income (commonly 66⅔%) that an individual loses when he or she is unable to work due to an accident or sickness. It pays after an **elimination period** (the time period after the accident or sickness that must expire before income benefits are paid) and for a **benefit period** (the time period income benefits are paid). Both periods (elimination and benefit) are chosen by the insured at time of application.

- **Medical Expense Insurance** provides coverage for basic medical expenses incurred by an individual. Higher limits of coverage are provided under a Major Medical Expense Policy. Coverage is typically provided in amounts up to $5,000,000, and in some cases, an unlimited dollar amount. A Major Medical Expense Policy covers all usual, customary and reasonable services. Coverage is on a blanket basis for both inpatient and outpatient services for hospital, medical and surgical expenses up to the dollar limit. The typical Comprehensive Major Medical Policy has an:

  - **Initial base deductible** (generally between $200 and $1,000)
  - **80%-20% coinsurance clause** (insurer pays 80% and insured pays 20%)
  - **Stop-loss provision** (limits the insured's annual out-of-pocket expenses)

  Medical expense plans are commonly written on a fee-for-service basis. This means the insured may choose his/her medical doctor or hospital and that the medical doctor of hospital will be reimbursed based upon the fees charged. An alternative to a fee-for-service plan is a prepaid plan. An example of a prepaid plan is an Health Maintenance Organization (HMO). HMOs limit the insured's choice of medical doctors and hospitals but generally provide broader coverages at a lower premium.

CREDIT LIFE INSURANCE provides coverage in **creditor-debtor relations** and is generally written on a group basis. Coverage amounts, premium charges and commissions payable are regulated by the insurance department. In these cases, the credit institution is named the policyholder and beneficiary for the outstanding balance of the loan. Proceeds payable in excess of the debt balance are payable to insured's beneficiary or estate. Group credit insurance is **based upon loan balance** and is generally written on a guaranteed or simplified underwriting basis.

TRAVEL ACCIDENT INSURANCE refers to policies that provide coverage in the event of injury or death while traveling as a fare paying passenger on a common carrier. These policies are sold at airports, but have also been marketed through the mail by major credit card carriers.

MANAGING ETHICAL BEHAVIOR

Ethical behavior relates to doing the right thing for all stakeholders (i.e., insured, insurer, producer). It is the attitudinal foundation that supports the very institution of insurance. It involves a deep personal reflection on individual behavior. In particular, the honesty, trustfulness, and personal responsibility that producers exhibit in their dealings with the public.

Producers are faced with ethical circumstances everyday. It is the responsibility of the producer to understand these ethical challenges and to "do the right thing". This is not only important for the consumer's benefit, but it is equally important for the producer and the represented insurer.

To manage ethical issues, a producer can ask himself the following basic questions.

1) **Is it legal?** - This is by far the easiest question to answer. Legal conduct is the minimum standard producers must adhere to. So, naturally, any conduct that would be illegal would also be unethical. For example, rebating, twisting, and illegal inducements are illegal, and therefore unethical.

2) **Is it fair?** - This question is a little more difficult to answer. Assume the following: you determined that your insured has a legitimate need for insurance; you determine that you have two products that can meet your insured's needs; one pays you a high commission, however, its coverages/values are lower than another product that pays you a lower commission. Which one do you recommend?

3) **Do I have a gut feeling that something is not right about this transaction?** In other words, can you live with your actions. One way to determine how you would feel is to ask yourself the following question: If my professional peers viewed this transaction in its entirety and knew all of the facts surrounding the transaction, would they consider it professional conduct?

4) **How would I feel if I were in the consumer's position?** Simple put, would you be satisfied or feel cheated.

The previously cited questions can be used as a guide to promote ethical conduct, however, producers can do more -- specifically, they can affiliate with a professional association. For example, professional property and casualty producers generally become affiliated with the Independent Insurance Agents and Brokers of America. And professional life, accident and health producers generally become affiliated with the National Association of Insurance and Financial Advisors (NAIFA). Both organizations subscribe to a code of professional ethics (see NAIFA's below) that assists in helping insurance producers to act in an ethical manner. In addition, professional associations commonly have monthly meetings that provide a forum for professional producers to meet, exchange ideas and foster professionalism.

Finally, this study manual gives you a wide range of circumstances where a producer's ethical conduct must be self-evaluated. Trade practice issues such as rebating, replacement, and disclosure, claims issues such as fair treatment in claims settlements, and practice issues such as recommendations on amounts and policy types are all critical facets of being a professional. Make sure that you reflect on these issues as you review this study manual.

NAIFA Code of Ethics

Preamble:

Those engaged in offering insurance and other related financial services occupy the unique position of liaison between the purchasers and the suppliers of insurance and closely related financial products. Inherent in this role is the combination of professional duty to the client and to the company, as well. Ethical balance is required to avoid any conflict between these two obligations. Therefore,

I Believe It To Be My Responsibility:

- To hold my profession in high esteem and strive to enhance its prestige.
- To fulfill the needs of may clients to the best of may ability.
- To maintain my clients' confidences.
- To render exemplary service to my clients and their beneficiaries.
- To adhere to professional standards of conduct in helping my clients to protect insurable obligations and attain their financial security objectives.
- To present accurately and honestly all facts essential to my clients' decisions.
- To perfect my skills and increase my knowledge through continuing education.
- To conduct my business in such a way that my example might help raise the professional standards of those in my profession.
- To keep informed with respect to applicable laws and regulations and to observe them in the practice of my profession.
- To cooperate with others whose services are constructively related to meeting the needs of my clients.

KEY TERMS AND CONCEPTS

The following terms were introduced in this chapter. You should know each word and concept and be able to apply them in everyday usage. To improve retention, it is recommended that you write out each key term and concept in your own words. This exercise will help you recognize and understand each term in its proper context.

Agency Appointment
Application Requirements
Claim Practices (time requirements)
Co-mingling of Funds
Company Regulation
Company Certification
Company Solvency
Complaint Records
Continuing Education (CE) Requirements
Consumer Privacy Regulation
Criminal Conduct Reporting
Disciplinary Procedures
Disciplinary Actions
Examination of Books and Records
Fair Credit Reporting Act
False Advertising
Fictitious or Assumed Names
Fiduciary Capacity
Illegal Inducements
Insurance Commissioner
Insurance Fraud Regulation
License Restrictions
Licensing Procedures
Licensure
Limitations of License
Maintenance and Durations
Managing General Agent
Misrepresentation
Nonrenewal of License
Nonresident
Pennsylvania Guaranty Association Act
Persons to be Licensed
Policy Forms
Policyholder's Surplus
Prelicensing Education (PE) Requirement
Producer License
Prohibited Acts
Purpose of Licensing
Rate Regulation
Rebating
Reserve
Standards for License Application
State Regulation
Suspension and Revocation of License
Temporary Licenses
Time restrictions for license application
Twisting
Unfair Claim Settlement Practices
Unfair Insurance Practices Act
Unfair Discrimination
Uniformity of Licenses
Waiver of Examination

REVIEW QUESTIONS

Before attempting to answer the end chapter practice questions, you should ask yourself if you can answer the following questions. It is recommended that you write out each review question in your own words. This exercise will help you apply the key terms and concepts that you've learned to form relationships with different topics.

1. Explain the purpose and process of licensing. (1-1)
2. Explain the qualifications for licensing. (1-1)
3. Identify 4 activities that require a license. (1-2)
4. Identify and explain the 4 types of licenses issued by the insurance department. (1-2)
5. Explain a producer's fiduciary responsibility. (1-3)
6. Explain the name and address restrictions placed on producers. (1-4)
7. Indicate the time periods that producers must notify the department in the event of name, address change or charge on criminal conduct. (1-4)
8. Indicate 5 prohibited acts that will cause a producer's license to be suspended or revoked. (1-5)
9. Explain the continuing education requirements including the number of credit hours for producers. (1-7)
10. Explain how a producer license is maintained? (1-7)
11. Explain the disciplinary procedure that governs producers. (1-8)
12. Explain the duties and responsibilities of the insurance commissioner. (1-8)
13. Explain the function of the Pennsylvania Insurance Guaranty Association. (1-9)
14. Explain the purpose of the Unfair Claims Settlement Practices Act and include 5 examples. (1-10)
15. Define and give an example of rebating, twisting and illegal inducements. (1-11)
16. Who may receive commissions? (1-12)
17. May a producer charge a fee in addition to receiving a commission? (1-12)
18. May a fee be paid to a unlicensed individual? (1-12)
19. Explain the purpose of the Unfair Insurance Practices Act and include 5 examples. (1-12)

20. What is the purpose of the insurance department's right to examine books and records? (1-12)

21. Explain the Privacy of Consumer Financial Information Regulation. (1-13)

22. Explain the Insurance Fraud Regulation. (1-13)

23. Identify two major categories of insurance. (1-17)

24. Identify and briefly explain 5 common life insurance policies. (1-16)

25. Explain the purpose of an annuity policy. (1-17)

26. Identify and briefly explain 2 primary health insurance policies. (1-17)

27. Explain ethical behavior and how an individual can manage ethical issues. (1-18)

28. Identify the 3 primary stakeholders that ethical conduct may affect. (1-18)

29. Identify 4 basic questions a producer can ask himself or herself to determine if conduct is ethical. (1-18)

30. Is there a difference between unethical conduct and illegal behavior? (1-18)

31. How can peers in a professional association help affect an individual's conduct? (1-18)

32. What are the benefits of belonging to a professional association? (1-19)

33. How does a code of professional ethics assist the producer in being ethical? (1-19)

34. Identify 10 common goals that may be found in a code of professional ethics. (1-19)

35. Identify 16 claims settlement activities that would be both unethical and illegal. (1-10)

36. Identify 14 producer activities that would be both unethical and illegal. (1-12)

37. Identify 8 insurance fraud activities that would be both unethical and illegal. (1-14)

PRACTICE EXAM ONE

ON

INSURANCE REGULATION

1. **All of the following are prohibited insurance practices EXCEPT:**

   A) Misrepresentation and defamation.
   B) Deceptive advertising.
   C) Direct mail marketing.
   D) Rebates and inducements. Ref. 1-12

2. **Which of the following activities would require an individual to be licensed?**

   A) Collecting expiration data information from clients or potential clients.
   B) Collecting premiums at an insured's office.
   C) Assisting with the completion of applications on the agency premises.
   D) Arranging or making meeting appointments for a producer. Ref. 1-2

3. **All of the following are true of complaint records EXCEPT:**

   A) It must be maintained for the preceding four years.
   B) It must include all written complaints.
   C) It must include all telephone and verbal complaints.
   D) It must document complaints by line, nature and disposition. Ref. 1-10

4. **Which of the following criminal activities would NOT be sufficient violation to warrant rejection, termination or nonrenewal of a producer's license?**

   A) Cheating on an insurance exam.
   B) Failing to pay child support.
   C) Theft of money.
   D) Failure to stop at a red light. Ref. 1-5

5. **All of the following are characteristics of a licensed insurance company EXCEPT:**

   A) Must pass state required minimum financial standards.
   B) Must agree to abide by statutory regulation.
   C) May utilize policy forms and rates prior to department approval.
   D) Must certify that their producers are qualified in the business of insurance.
   Ref. 1-6 & 1-9

6. **An applicant for an producer's license must be at least:**

   A) 16 years old.
   B) 18 years old.
   C) 19 years old.
   D) 21 years old. Ref. 1-1

7. The maximum fine per violation for soliciting insurance without a license is:

A) $ 300.
B) $ 500.
C) $1000.
D) $5000. Ref. 1-7

8. Which of the following is NOT a requirement necessary to qualify as a new resident producer in Pennsylvania?

A) Pass the exam required by statute.
B) Maintain a business or legal address in Pennsylvania.
C) Complete a 24-hour pre-licensing course.
D) Post a fidelity bond. Ref. 1-1

9. All of the following applicants may be denied a producer license EXCEPT:

A) An individual who owes state income tax.
B) An individual who provides false or incomplete information.
C) An applicant unable to read and write in English.
D) An individual who sells stocks. Ref. 1-1 & 1-5

10. A producer, when acting as a representative of the consumer must:

A) Place coverage through another producer.
B) Place coverage with a non-admitted insurer.
C) Execute a written contract with an attorney.
D) Execute a written contract with a consumer. Ref. 1-2

11. A producer who represents the consumer is acting as an:

A) Insurance solicitor.
B) Insurance adjuster.
C) Insurance agent.
D) Insurance broker. Ref. 1-2

12. Producers may co-mingle business monies with personal monies:

A) Never.
B) At any time if permitted by the insured.
C) Only if each represented company provides prior written consent.
D) Only if permitted in writing by the Insurance Commissioner. Ref. 1-3

13. A Temporary License permits an executor or administrator of a deceased producer's estate to do all the following EXCEPT:

A) Receive commissions.
B) Process normal correspondence.
C) Solicit new business.
D) Attempt to sell the agency. Ref. 1-3

14. The practice of giving back to an insured a portion of the commissions earned on the sale of a policy is:

A) Permitted under the Unfair Insurance Practice Act.
B) A good business practice.
C) A Rebate.
D) Twisting. Ref. 1-11

15. A licensed producer must notify the insurance department within 30 days of being:

A) Convicted of a serious offense that reflects upon the producer's honesty.
B) Charged of criminal conduct.
C) Sued for breach of contract.
D) Ordered to pay damages arising from the producer's negligence. Ref. 1-4

16. All of the following characterize the process of complaints filed with the insurance department against producers and companies EXCEPT:

A) May involve a formal hearing in Harrisburg.
B) Is usually investigated by the insurance department's local office.
C) May be appealed to Commonwealth Court.
D) Is usually investigated by a local District Attorney. Ref. 1-8

17. A Temporary License may be issued to approved individuals for a period of:

A) 180 days.
B) One year.
C) Two years.
D) Unlimited duration. Ref. 1-3

18. All of the following are true of an agency appointment EXCEPT:

A) It is a written agreement between the agency and the insurance company under which the agency agrees to solicit, negotiate, and service insurance policies for compensation.
B) The appointing company is required to certify to the insurance department that the agency producers are qualified and properly trained.
C) The appointing company is required to certify to the insurance department that the producer has not violated any provision of the Pennsylvania Insurance Law.
D) Individuals employed by appointed agencies may initiate sales activities upon successful completion of their state exam. Ref. 1-1 & 1-9

19. Which of the following individuals would be required to be licensed?

A) A risk manager who supervises a major corporation's insurance program.
B) A loss control representative who identifies hazards at the insured's business.
C) A premium auditor who verifies a business' payroll for insurance purposes.
D) An insurance consultant who shares commissions with an producer. Ref. 1-2 & 1-6

20. Which of the following activities would require an agency employee to be licensed?

A) Discussing insurance in general if no recommendations are made with respect to rates.
B) Assisting with the completion of applications.
C) Collecting expiration date information from clients.
D) Counseling an applicant on a product. Ref. 1-1 & 1-2

21. A producer license may be issued to all of the following EXCEPT:

A) A sole proprietor.
B) A member of a partnership or corporation.
C) An individual trading under an assumed or fictitious name.
D) A trustee. Ref. 1-1 & 1-3

22. All of the following are true of the Pennsylvania Insurance Guaranty Association Act EXCEPT:

A) Provides a means of covering claims for certain property and casualty policies.
B) Provides coverage for accident & health, workers compensation and surety losses.
C) Coverage is provided up to $300,000 per claim.
D) Coverage is provided to individuals who were insured with admitted and authorized carriers. Ref. 1-9

23. An insurance company adjuster must acknowledge receipt of a claim:

A) Immediately.
B) Within 5 working days in all instances.
C) Within 10 working days in all instances.
D) Within 10 working days unless payment is made within that time period. Ref. 1-10

24. The Unfair Insurance Practices Act:

A) Advises producers and insurers of fair and acceptable trade practices.
B) Regulates the activities of producers in the excess and surplus lines.
C) Regulates trade practices by defining practices which constitute unfair methods of competition and/or deceptive practices.
D) Advises the public on fair insurance practices. Ref. 1-10 & 1-12

25. All of the following would be considered an Unfair Claims Practice EXCEPT:

A) Failure to acknowledge written or oral communications.
B) Failure to deny or affirm coverage.
C) Dealing with the insured or claimant in good faith.
D) Refusing to pay covered claims. Ref. 1-10

26. The Property Casualty Licensing Examination may be waived for all of the following EXCEPT:

A) An individual applying for a Temporary License.
B) An attorney.
C) Individuals holding the professional designation of CPCU.
D) A qualified nonresident applicant. Ref. 1-3 & 1-5

27. Producers are permitted to share or split commissions if:

A) There is a written agreement between the two.
B) Both producers are licensed for the same powers.
C) The insured knows of the arrangement.
D) The insurance department knows of the arrangement. Ref. 1-7

28. A producer who has both his business and legal address outside the Commonwealth of Pennsylvania is considered:

A) An alien producer.
B) A domestic producer.
C) A nonresident producer.
D) A foreign producer. Ref. 1-3

29. The primary purpose of licensing is:

A) To provide a source of income to producers.
B) To ensure high standards to the insuring public of Pennsylvania.
C) To permit insurers to pay commissions.
D) To provide a source of revenue for the insurance department. Ref. 1-1

30. All of the following are true regarding premiums collected from a policyholder EXCEPT:

A) Producers may not co-mingle business monies with personal monies unless each insurer provides the producer written permission.
B) Producers who make immediate remittance of premiums collected, in the same form as received from the policyholder, need not maintain a separate business account.
C) If a producer holds a policyholder's funds, they must be maintained in a separate account.
D) If a producer receives cash from a policyholder, he may deposit the money into his personal bank account and write a check to the insurance company. Ref. 1-3

31. Which of the following activities would NOT be interpreted as acting as a producer?

A) Making a sales presentation.
B) Countersigning a policy.
C) Collecting premiums at an insured's place of business.
D) Collecting expiration data information from potential clients. Ref. 1-2

32. Producers are required to notify the insurance department within:

A) Within 30 days of being sued.
B) Within 30 days of being fined.
C) Within 30 days pleading guilty or nolo contendere to criminal conduct.
D) Within 30 days of being charged with criminal conduct. Ref. 1-4

33. What act was established to protect individuals from possible abuses of information contained in their credit files?

A) Trade Practices Act of 1974.
B) Fair Credit Reporting Act.
C) Federal Trade Commission Act.
D) McCarran-Ferguson Act. Ref. 1-15

34. All of the following are true of Pennsylvania's Continuing Education (CE) requirement EXCEPT:

A) A licensed producer must complete 24 credit hours for each licensing period.
B) Producers who fail to complete CE will have their license suspended.
C) Attorneys are exempt from continuing education.
D) Licensed producers have a continuing education requirement. Ref. 1-6 & 1-7

35. The business of insurance is regulated in Pennsylvania by:

A) The Governor.
B) The Insurance Superintendent.
C) The Insurance Commissioner.
D) The Attorney General. Ref. 1-8

36. All of the following individuals are required to be licensed EXCEPT:

A) An employee of the insurance agency making a sales presentation.
B) An individual contacting an insurer representing a client seeking coverage.
C) A Customer Service Representative advising a prospect on coverages.
D) A Risk Manager managing the loss exposures of a corporation. Ref. 1-2

37. A Managing General Agent:

A) Acts as a solicitor for a producer.
B) Generally has specialized expertise.
C) Produces life, accident and health business.
D) Acts as a public insurance adjuster. Ref. 1-3

38. A producer, when acting as a representative of the consumer must:

A) Place coverage through another producer.
B) Place coverage with a non-admitted insurer.
C) Execute a written contract with an attorney.
D) Execute a written contract with a consumer. Ref. 1-2

ANSWER KEY

1-C	2-B	3-C	4-D	5-C	6-B	7-D	8-D	9-D	10-D
11-D	12-C	13-C	14-C	15-B	16-D	17-A	18-D	19-D	20-D
21-D	22-B	23-D	24-C	25-C	26-B	27-B	28-C	29-B	30-D
31-D	32-D	33-B	34-C	35-C	36-D	37-B	38-D		

NOTES

CHAPTER TWO

GENERAL INSURANCE

OVERVIEW

This chapter focuses on basic concepts and principles which are common to all lines of insurance. To properly understand general insurance, the following terms and concepts must be mastered, as each concept will be applied in future chapters.

RISK MANAGEMENT

Risk Management is the process of treating and managing loss exposures. It includes the following five steps:

1) **Identify and analyze** loss exposures. This step would include the use of insurance applications, inspection reports, loss records and financial statements to identify and analyze potential loss exposures.
2) **Examine the alternative risk management techniques**. Risk can be either:
   - ***Controlled*** through loss avoidance, prevention, reduction or separation; or
   - ***Financed*** through the purchase of insurance, by self-insurance or by retention. Risk may also be transferred by contract (see the following page for additional examples). Typically, an insured will use both alternatives.
3) **Select the best risk reduction techniques**. For example, should a business install a sprinkler system, or if it is self insured, how much should it retain.
4) **Implement the techniques**. This means placing the plan into effect.
5) **Monitor the plan**. This includes making changes to meet risk management needs.

The task of managing risk typically begins with the individual who observes exposures in everyday life. From an insurance perspective, risk management is practiced by producers and in particular, insurance company underwriters. The key risk management terms and concepts include the following:

Risk is the exposure or uncertainty of loss. It can be classified as either **pure risk** or **speculative risk**. **Pure risk** is the type of exposure that has **two possible outcomes**, loss or no loss. A pure loss exposure has no opportunity for financial gain. **Speculative risk** is the type of exposure that includes the loss and no loss outcomes of pure risk, but **adds a third possible outcome**, that of financial gain. Insurers attempt to avoid speculative type risk.

Exposure is the possibility of loss. It is the condition of being unprotected. Insurance company underwriters seek to minimize their exposure to loss. The terms risk and exposure are used interchangeably.

- **Hazard** is **any condition or exposure that increases the possibility of loss**. For example, a business that maintains large amounts of cash overnight may attract a burglar or entice an employee to steal. Similarly, buildings that store combustible material have a greater likelihood of fire than those that do not. Hazards are commonly **classified in three categories:**

1) **Physical Hazards** are actual physical features. For example, a dwelling with bad electrical wiring or oily rags stored in the basement.

2) **Moral Hazards** are practices or behavior patterns such as poor finances or prior criminal history that increase the possibility of loss. For example, an insured who is behind on his mortgage starts his home on fire to collect on the insurance.

3) **Morale Hazards** refer to carelessness or absent-mindedness. For example, an insured fails to lock his car doors when holiday shopping, since he is insured.

Insurance company underwriters, who review applications for insurance, attempt to eliminate or minimize hazards and/or speculative type risk.

Peril is a **cause of loss**. For example, death is the peril insured against in a life insurance policy; the loss of income is the peril insured against in a disability insurance policy and fire is the peril insured against in a fire insurance policy. Policies are written as either **named peril policies**, which specifically **list the perils** insured against in the policies, or; **special or "all risk/open peril" policies**, which specifically **list the exclusions** from coverages.

Loss is the **reduction in the value of an asset**. For example, a fire to a house reduces its value to its owner. Similarly, death to an individual eliminates the future earnings capacity to the deceased's family.

Insurance is a method of **spreading risk of loss from one to many**. It is a **risk transfer** accomplished by the collecting and pooling of premiums to pay future losses. The treatment and management of risk may be financed through the purchase of insurance or controlled through other methods to manage risk.

OTHER METHODS AVAILABLE TO MANAGE RISK

In addition to financing an exposure with the purchase of insurance, risk may be managed by:

- **Avoidance of Risk**, by eliminating the exposure to loss by not acquiring the exposure or by selling the exposure. An example would be not driving an auto or not producing a product that may injure someone. The avoidance method is generally not practical in personal insurance.

- **Retention of Risk**, by assuming exposure to loss by selecting higher deductibles or by a self-insurance program.

- **Sharing of Risk**, by assuming a coinsurer position in property policies.

- **Reduction of Risk**, by reducing the severity of loss. An example would be the installation of a sprinkler system, the use of smoke detectors or automobile airbags.

- **Transfer of Risk**, by contract. This may be accomplished by a lease arrangement or by subcontracting work to another entity.

Each of the above are commonly used in the treatment of loss exposures.

ESSENTIAL ELEMENTS OF AN INSURABLE RISK

Insurance companies seek to insure pure loss exposures. In developing an underwriting policy, insurance companies consider the following as the essential elements of an insurance risk:

- The loss must be **definable**, so to determine the time and amount of the loss.
- The loss must be **accidental**, so to minimize fraud and to promote public policy.
- The probability of loss must be **predictable**, so to competitively set rates.
- The **law of large numbers should apply**, so to project losses for various policies.
- The loss must be large enough to **create financial hardship**, or no one will buy.
- The insurance **premium must be reasonable**, or the policy will not be purchased.
- The loss must **not be catastrophic** in nature, so a company is not financially ruined.

ADVERSE SELECTION

Adverse selection occurs when applicants for insurance have a greater bias to an exposure than a random sampling of the population. **It is the tendency of poorer risks to seek insurance.** For example, an individual may not choose to buy insurance until they believe they are exposed to a loss. Insurance company underwriters attempt to minimize adverse selection by carefully underwriting insurance applications.

LAW OF LARGE NUMBERS

The Law of Large Numbers **is a law of statistical probability used in the rate making process**. The basic principle of this law states that the **larger the number of occurrences** exposed to a similar type of exposure (homogeneous), the **more predictable future losses will become**. For example, the probability of predicting a coin flip is fifty percent. If the coin was flipped a small number of times (5 or 10 flips), the totals may not reflect the 50/50 chance. However, as the number of events increase, the outcome will more accurately follow the 50/50 probability.

PRINCIPLE OF INDEMNITY

The principle of indemnity is the concept of "making one whole" by **restoring or reimbursing one to the extent of their loss**. This concept is utilized extensively in the underwriting and adjusting of property casualty policies. Life insurance policies, unlike indemnity contracts, are **valued contracts** and **agree to pay the amount stated in the policy in the event of a total loss**. The principle of indemnity is closely related to the insurable interest concept discussed below. Both attempt to avoid wagering and/or moral hazards that would be against public policy if this concept were not enforced.

DOCTRINE OF INSURABLE INTEREST

Insurable interest is the interest one has in property or life **that may cause one the possibility of financial loss**. It is a basic requirement of an insurance contract. For example, an individual would have an insurable interest in the home, auto or business that they owned. Similarly, a mortgage company, a finance company or a bank may also have an insurable interest in the same property reflecting its interest in the property. **Property and casualty contracts require an insurable interest to exist at the time of loss.**

REINSURANCE

Reinsurance is the contractual process **used by insurance companies to insure its loss exposures** (i.e., claims that may have to be paid on policies written) and its assets (i.e., profits from prior years). In the reinsurance process, insurance companies retain losses up to a specified dollar amount or percentage of losses (like deductible), allowing the reinsurance company to pay losses in excess of that dollar amount or percentage. The following defines important terms related to reinsurance:

- **Ceding Company** is the **original insurer that reinsures its loss exposures**. Commonly, an insurance company will reinsure its loss exposures to minimize the negative effects of catastrophic losses. This can occur when a company has a high concentration of risks in a certain geographic region. For example, property, such as homes and businesses in Florida, is highly susceptible to large losses due to hurricanes and high winds. Similarly, insurers may choose to limit large losses on individual risks. Because of these types of exposures, insurance companies will generally enter into a reinsurance agreement with a reinsurance company to minimize severe losses due to these exposures. A ceding company may also be referred to as the primary insurer or the direct writer.

- **Assuming Company** is the reinsurance company that **assumes the exposure** from the ceding company. Following the example cited above, property insurers in Florida have a great need for reinsurance because of the wind peril. These insurers (the ceding company) will attempt to negotiate a reinsurance agreement with the reinsurer (the assuming company) to cover claims in excess of a stated amount.

- **Retention** refers to the **exposure retained** by the ceding company. This retention of liability may be expressed as a dollar amount, a percentage of the original amount of insurance or as a combination of both. Once again, following the above example, the ceding company may decide to retain its first $100,000 on each loss with the assuming company paying claims in excess of this amount. The retention amount is similar to a deductible.

- **Treaty Reinsurance**, also known as **automatic reinsurance**, is a type of reinsurance whereby the ceding company agrees to cede business to the reinsurer, who in turn agrees to accept the risks. Treaty reinsurance would be used to insure standard risk exposures that fall within the treaty limits.

- **Facultative Reinsurance** is another type of reinsurance that requires an **individual reinsurance** agreement on each individual risk. Facultative reinsurance would be used to insure risk exposures which fall outside the treaty reinsurance agreement.

- **Retrocession** is the process of **reinsuring reinsurance**. This process spreads the risk of loss to larger groups. For example, the assuming company may choose to insure its reinsurance. The organization that reinsures the reinsurance company is called the Retrocessionaire.

The **purpose of reinsurance** is to promote the growth and stability of the insurance business through the sharing of risk exposures. **Insurance companies purchase reinsurance** for risk reduction and loss sharing, stabilization of loss experience, increased capacity, unearned premium reserve relief, catastrophic protection, underwriting assistance and retirement from a line or territory.

TYPES OF INSURERS

Insurance companies are organized in one of the following legal structures:

- **Stock companies** are **owned by stockholders** who have the usual rights of ownership, including the right of voting and incurring profits or losses. Examples of stock companies include Travelers and Chubb.
- **Mutual companies** do not have stockholders but **are owned by the policyholders** who share profits in the form of dividends. Mutuals are classified as either: **Assessment Mutuals**, which may assess policyholders additional amounts if premiums are insufficient for operations; or **Non-assessment Mutuals**, which cannot assess policyholders if premiums are insufficient for operations. Most insurers today are nonassessment mutuals. Mutual policyholders also have voting rights. Examples of mutual companies include State Farm and Amica Mutual.
- **Fraternals** are **benevolent societies** that include lodges and related associations that originally provided organized welfare plans for their members. Over the years, fraternals organized **formal insurance plans and provided primarily life and health insurance products to their members**. Because of the charitable nature of these organizations, fraternals are exempt from federal income and state taxes. An example of fraternals would be Greater Beneficial Union of Pittsburgh and Modern Woodmen of America.
- **Reciprocals** are unincorporated associations in which members, called **subscribers, insure one another**. The reciprocal is managed by an attorney-in-fact who solicits new subscribers, collects premiums, adjusts losses, and processes related administrative functions. An example of a reciprocal would be the Erie Insurance Exchange and Farmers Insurance Exchange.
- **Lloyds** associations **are groups of individuals or corporations who share in the making of insurance contracts**. For example, Lloyd's of London is a society of individual underwriters who accept insurance risks for their personal profit or loss. Each underwriter is aligned with a syndicate. In the United States, Lloyds associations pattern themselves after Lloyd's of London.

PRIVATE INSURERS VERSUS GOVERNMENT INSURERS

Private insurers are organizations owned and operated by private citizens. They can be classified as either proprietary, which include stock companies, or co-operative, which include mutuals or reciprocals. Private insurers will insure most coverage types, however, they exclude risk exposures that are considered uninsurable. Examples would be war, unemployment or flood.

Government insurers are organizations owned and operated by the government. They can be classified in two broad categories: insurers who write coverages that are **commercially uninsurable**, such as war, flood or unemployment, and; insurers who write coverages that are **commercially insurable** and, as such, compete with the private insurers. For example, Social Security coverages and Workers Compensation. Typically, the government only insures risks that are either catastrophic or cyclical in nature.

ADMITTED VERSUS NONADMITTED COMPANY

An admitted or authorized company is one that **is authorized by the insurance department** to conduct business. A license is issued to an admitted company. **Producers are required to do business with admitted companies.**

A **nonadmitted or unauthorized company** is one that **is not authorized or admitted by the insurance department to conduct business**. A nonadmitted company may not qualify or may choose not to do business within that state. **Business may be placed by a producer** with a nonadmitted company in the property and casualty field for hard to place risks. **Individuals who accept business from a producer for placement with an unlicensed insurer are known as surplus lines agents.** These individuals must be licensed as a producer and pass a surplus lines exam. This area of the insurance business is known as excess and surplus lines business.

Business placed with admitted or authorized companies is covered by the Pennsylvania Insurance Guaranty Association Act. This Act protects policyholders in the event an admitted company becomes insolvent. In these cases, claims are covered up to a limit of $300,000 per claim. **Business placed in nonadmitted or unauthorized insurance companies is not covered by this Act.**

DOMICILE

Domicile refers to the **legal address of a company**. It is generally the place where the company's home office is located. Insurance companies are as classified as:

- **Domestic companies**, which are **domiciled in your state**. For example CIGNA, Erie and Harleysville are domestic companies because their domicile is in the state of Pennsylvania.

- **Foreign companies**, which are **domiciled outside of the Commonwealth of Pennsylvania** but within the United States. For example, Prudential is domiciled in New Jersey, Metropolitan in New York and Travelers and Hartford are in Connecticut. All of these companies are considered foreign to Pennsylvania.

- **Alien companies**, which are **domiciled outside the United States**. For example, Nippon Life is domiciled in Japan; Allianz is domiciled in Germany.

ANALYSIS OF FINANCIAL STATUS

A primary goal of insurance regulation is the financial soundness of the insurance industry. Each insurance department conducts extensive audits and reviews to ensure integrity in the financial analysis of insurance companies. This process is important so that regulators, producers and the insuring public in general is aware of the financial soundness of the insurers they are regulating, marketing or placing their trust in. The following are the various independent organizations which provide detailed evaluations enabling the public to observe and monitor a company's resources:

A. M. Best Company is the oldest and largest insurance company rating service providing extensive financial information on over 3700 insurance companies. The information is based upon Underwriting Performance, Management Economy, Reserve Adequacy, Adequacy of Net Resources and Soundness of Investments. The Best's Rating Guide, which is published annually, rates companies with an alphabetical rating, along with a financial size classification. The following provides a general overview of the A.M. Best Company rating classifications:

Alphabetical Rating		Category	Financial Size Categories
A ++	A+	Superior	The financial size category rating is based upon a company's reported policyholder's surplus and is grouped from the smallest financial category which is class I (up to $1,000,000) to the largest financial category which is class XV ($2,000,000,000 and above). Policyholder's surplus is in effect the owner's equity and provides the insurer with a surplus fund in the event the insurer suffers adverse results.
A	A -	Excellent	
B ++	B +	Very Good	
B	B -	Good	
C ++	C +	Fair	
C	C -	Marginal	
D		Below Minimum Standards	
E		Under State Supervision	
F		In Liquidation	

As a general rule, the highest alphabetical rating A++ and the highest financial category rating XV is viewed as most favorable. In addition to the major capitalized alphabetical ratings, A.M. Best also utilizes various small letter modifiers to qualify a company. For example, the letter "w" indicates the company is on a watch list because of some decline in performance. The A. M. Best rating is the most commonly used reference in determining the financial stability of a company or group of companies. Other rating services which provide similar information on insurers include:

- **Standard & Poor's** rates insurers from AAA to D.
- **Moody's** rates insurers from Aaa (Exceptional) to C (Lowest).
- **Duff & Phelps** rates insurers from AAA to CCC.
- **Weiss Research** rates insurers from A (Excellent) to E (Very Weak).

Additional supervision is provided in the following areas:

Insurance Department Examinations are periodically performed on insurance companies. If the department believes financial problems exist, it has the power and responsibility to initiate steps to promote the solvency of the company. These actions may include restrictions on writing new business, directives on managing the company or in extreme cases, ordering the liquidation of the company.

National Association of Insurance Commissioners (NAIC) is an organization of Insurance Commissioners from each state. Although the organization has no regulatory authority, it is active in the formation of uniform recommendations which are generally adopted by each state. The NAIC conducts Zone Examinations and maintains an Insurance Regulatory Information System (IRIS) to review insurance company operations and sets minimum Insurance Regulatory standards and ratios.

MAJOR DISTRIBUTION SYSTEMS

Independent Agency System is comprised of insurance producers who are **independent contractors** who enter into agency and marketing arrangements with various insurance companies. Under their agency agreement, the producer may place business with any company and has complete control and **ownership of their expirations** (policy data). Examples of companies that are part of the independent agency system include Travelers, Hartford, and Fireman's Fund.

Direct Writer System is comprised of insurance producers who are **employees of the insurance company** they represent and market the products of that one company. The **ownership of the expirations is usually vested with the company**. USAA, GEICO and Amica Mutual are examples of direct writers.

Exclusive Agency or Captive Agency System is comprised of insurance producers who are **independent contractors** but agree to market the products of **one exclusive company**. In most cases, exclusive producers do not have control over ownership of their expirations. Many nationally known insurers, such as State Farm and Nationwide, fall into this category.

Direct Response System does not use insurance producers, but markets products through the mail, television, magazines and most recently the Internet. These organizations are generally located in a centralized location servicing a large geographical area. Many traditional insurers are branching into this distribution system.

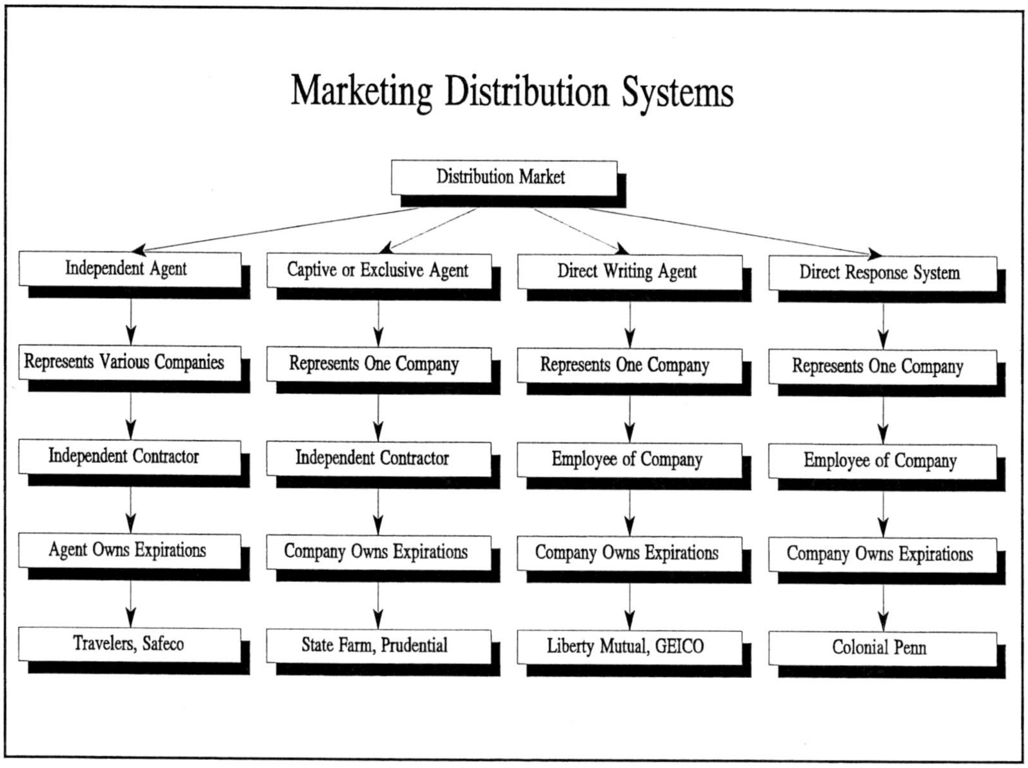

MANAGEMENT OF DISTRIBUTION SYSTEM

Insurance companies must provide some form of supervision to assure quality and success in the distribution process. The following supervisory producer systems provide technical support and producer evaluation:

Branch/Regional Office System is composed of **company employees** who staff strategically located offices throughout the country. The size of these offices range from small service offices with several employees, to large operations with complete marketing, underwriting and claims personnel.

Managing General Agency System is composed of **insurance agencies** that perform many of the functions of the branch office system. The MGA usually appoints and supervises producers under their direction, and may service some of the underwriting and claim functions normally handled by company branches. MGA's are typically appointed by insurers because they have some form of unique or specialized knowledge.

Personal Producing General Agency System is similar to the Managing General Agent, however, the PPGA does not appoint producers. The **PPGA is a personal producing life producer** whose primary objective is to sell insurance. The PPGA does not appoint or supervise producers. PPGAs are typically appointed by insurers because of his or her ability to sell high volumes of insurance.

TYPES OF INSURANCE PRODUCERS

The term **Producer** refers to individuals who sell insurance to the public. Pennsylvania issues a producer license to individual to sell insurance. Producers are also commonly referred to as agents or brokers. Producers that act as **agents** are classified as either:

- **Independent Agents** (independent contractors) who enter into agency and marketing arrangements with various insurance companies. Under their agency agreement, the agent may place business with any insurance company and has complete **control and ownership of their expirations**.

- **Captive Agents** or **Exclusive Agents** are also independent contractors but agree to market the products of **one exclusive company**. In most cases, exclusive agents do not have control over ownership of their expirations.

Producers acting as agents represent the insurance company.

Producers may also act as the representative of the prospective insured. When **producers represent the prospective insured they are acting as brokers**. In practice, producers commonly act in both capacities (agent or broker). The primary benefit of acting as a broker is the ability to place business with insurers that he or she (the producer) does not directly represent by means of an agency appointment. This transaction is known as **brokered business**. Please note that before, June 4, 2003, Pennsylvania required agents who wanted to represent a prospective insured to have a brokers license. Today that is no longer the case. Producers, by their actions and representations may represent the insurer, the prospective insured or both.

LAW OF AGENCY

Agency is the **legal relationship** that exists when one party acts on behalf of another party. This relationship **consists of a principal**, the insurance company, **and its authorized representative**, the agent. When an agent performs within the scope of his authority, the acts of the agent bind the principal. Moreover, the knowledge of the agent is considered the knowledge of the principal. For example, if an agent has knowledge that a hazard exists and does not communicate this to the insurer, the insurer may not at a later date deny coverage based upon their lack of knowledge. **The knowledge of the agent is the knowledge of the company**.

PRESUMPTION OF AGENCY

Situations may arise where an agent acts outside his authority and a **presumption of agency** occurs. For example, if a company provides materials such as stationary or business cards to an unauthorized individual (not licensed or not formally approved by the company), and that individual binds or contracts with another party, the insurance company will be bound by the unauthorized acts of the individual.

Since agency has far reaching consequences, it requires a high degree of trust between the agent and insurance company.

TYPES OF AUTHORITY

Producers may be granted or may assume authority in any of the following three forms:

- **Express Authority** is specific authority that **may be either verbal or written**. It is the authority defined in the producer's agreement setting forth the specific powers and functions of the producer.

- **Implied Authority** is authority that is not specifically defined in the producer's agreement, but **is an extension of a producer's standard duties**. This would include general customs and business practices. For example, it is implied that a producer who sells insurance would also be permitted to service his clients.

- **Apparent Authority** is the **authority the public perceives the producer to have** based upon the producer's actions. Apparent authority is not given to the producer, but is based upon the insured's reasonable belief that the producer has the authority. For example, if a producer leads an insured to believe coverage is in force, and the insured relies upon the producer's representations, the insurance company may be prohibited from denying coverage. Similarly, if an producer consistently permits an insured to pay his premium after the due date, the insurance company may be estopped from denying a claim that occurs after the due date. Apparent authority is sometimes referred to as authority by estoppel.

PRODUCER'S RESPONSIBILITIES TO THE INSURED OR APPLICANT

The producer's responsibilities to the insured or applicant includes: a **fiduciary responsibility** to perform honestly and faithfully and; a **professional responsibility** to carry out the insured's instructions by performing duties in a timely and professional manner. This includes a continual effort to increase knowledge and skill. It should be noted that because of today's litigious society, producers have an ever-increasing responsibility to adhere to the highest professional standards of conduct.

PRODUCER'S RESPONSIBILITY TO THE INSURANCE COMPANY

The producer's responsibility to the insurer includes the duty to **perform honestly and in accordance with the producer's agreement**. For example, the producer must render agency accounts and premiums within prescribed time limits, adhere to company underwriting guidelines, use reasonable care in his business practice and communicate information about insurance applicants. For example, if a producer becomes aware of adverse underwriting information on an applicant, the producer has a duty to convey that information to the company. As a general rule, producers have a duty to their principal which includes **obedience, loyalty, reasonable care, accounting and communication**.

PRODUCER'S COLLECTION AND FINANCIAL RESPONSIBILITY

These topics refer to the fiduciary activities, duties and responsibilities of producers. The law requires producers to operate in an honest and trustworthy manner. The following are commonly used terms and definitions related to the premium collection process:

- **Direct Billed Policies** are policies that are **billed directly to the insured and collected by the insurance company**. In the direct billing process, the producer's commission is usually paid to the producer at the end of each month. Direct billing eliminates the producer's involvement in the collection of premiums.
- **Agency Billed Policies** are policies that are **billed by the producer to the insured**. In these instances, the **producer subtracts his commission** directly from the policy premium and remits the net balance to the company. This form of billing is common in the commercial property and casualty field.
- **Remittance of Premiums** refers to the requirement of remitting premiums due the company in a timely manner and in accordance with the producer's contract.
- **Earned Premiums** represent the **portion of the policy premium that has been used** in the course of a policy term. The balance is the unearned premium.
- **Unearned Premiums** represent the **portion of the policy premium that has not been used** in the course of the policy term. The balance is the earned premium.
- **Premium Financing** refers to the financing of policy premiums. If an insured is unable to pay the amount required by the company, the policy may be financed like an installment loan agreement.

POTENTIAL LIABILITIES AND EXPOSURES

Producers have both a professional and fiduciary responsibility to their principal (either insured or insurer). These responsibilities require as a minimum duty an obligation to follow instructions. Generally, a producer expands their duties to include **advising, securing, maintaining and recommending coverages**. Because of these responsibilities, producers are exposed to possible legal action for their activities. The following are some **practices that producers should maintain to minimize this exposure**: carefully underwriting business, paying particular attention to recommending proper coverages; advising the insured of the introduction of new products; maintaining quality notes and records; following company guidelines and directives; increasing skill and knowledge. In addition to the recommendations indicated above, producers should maintain adequate errors and omissions insurance to protect themselves and their agency against this exposure.

NATURE AND IMPORTANCE OF UNDERWRITING

Underwriting refers to the broad range of duties and functions performed by producers and company employees in the risk selection process. This includes the formation of underwriting policy with its primary goal of developing profitable business. An important function of the underwriting department is to minimize **adverse selection**. This is a process that occurs when applicants for insurance have a greater bias to an exposure than a random sampling of the population. It is the **tendency of poorer risks to seek insurance**. For example, a businessowner is more likely to seek insurance for crime exposures after experiencing a robbery or theft. Underwriters attempt to eliminate or minimize adverse selection by carefully evaluating applicants for insurance. Underwriting is responsible for the selection and classification of risk, the determination of rate, and the continual monitoring of business.

ELEMENTS OF A CONTRACT

The following are the elements of a contract. **If one of these elements is missing, it is void (no legal effect) and as such, no contract exists.**

- **Agreement (offer & acceptance)** refers to the *offer by one party* and the *acceptance by a second party*. A counteroffer by the second party voids the initial offer. Both offer and acceptance must be communicated to each other and must not be under any undue influence, fraud or duress.
- **Consideration** refers to the *price paid or the bargaining elements* of the agreement. In an insurance contract, the insured's consideration is the *representations made at application and the premium paid*. The consideration an insurer gives is its *promise to perform in accordance with the policy provisions*.
- **Competent Parties** refers to *legal capacity*. That is, neither party being restricted by minority (age 18), insanity or intoxication.
- **Legal Purpose** refers to the *lawful purpose* of the contract. That is, the contract is free from illegality and consistent with public policy.

Since an insurance policy is a legal contract, it is subject to the law of contracts.

DISTINCT CHARACTERISTICS OF AN INSURANCE CONTRACT

Insurance contracts consist of the following unique features:

Contracts of Adhesion are contracts that are drawn up by one party (the insurance company) and presented to a second party (the insured) to be "adhered to" or rejected. Because the second party has no opportunity to alter or change the conditions of the contract, **all ambiguous areas are found in favor of the second party**. Insurance policies are contracts of adhesion.

Aleatory Contracts are contracts in which the insured may recover at some future time a substantial larger value than the premium payments made. Aleatory contracts are based upon the occurrence of **a future event of unequal bargaining value**. An insurance policy is an aleatory contract.

Personal Contracts refer to the personal nature between parties **requiring the highest degree of good faith**. Insurance contracts are personal contracts and, therefore, cannot be transferred to another party.

Unilateral Contracts refer to contracts in which **an act** (payment of premium) **is exchanged for a promise** (payment of claims in the event of loss). Insurance contracts are unilateral contracts.

Conditional Contracts refer to contracts which are contingent upon certain acts by the insured and/or claimant. For example, the payment of the premium is a condition precedent to coverage.

LEGAL INTERPRETATIONS AFFECTING THE INSURANCE CONTRACT

The following address how insurance contracts are interpreted:

Ambiguities, if found in a contract of adhesion, **are interpreted against the party that wrote the contract**. Since insurance policies are contracts of adhesion, any unclear language or policy provision is interpreted against the insurance company and in the insured's favor.

- **Reasonable expectations** is a doctrine which states that an insured is entitled to the coverage under a policy that he or she might reasonably expect it to provide, particularly if it is a mass marketed contract. Exclusions and/or limitations must be conspicuously displayed.

Indemnity is the principle of **restoring or reimbursing one to the extent of their loss**. The principle of indemnity is used extensively in the property and casualty fields. Closely related to the principle of indemnity is the concept of subrogation. **Subrogation** refers to the company's right to subrogate against third parties who, because of their negligence, cause the company to pay a claim. For example, if a negligent party causes property damage, the insurance company will indemnify the insured to the extent of their loss and seek payment from the negligent third party.

Utmost Good Faith means the dealing in accordance with standards of **honesty and sincerity**. Insurance is a contract of utmost good faith.

- **Representations** are either oral or written statements made by the applicant with the intention of securing insurance coverage.

- **Misrepresentations** are false statements that were relied upon by the insurer in issuing coverage. A misrepresentation will generally not affect a policy unless it is a material misrepresentation. A **material misrepresentation** is a misrepresentation that if originally known by the insurer would cause that insurer to reject coverage, based upon that fact. If an insurer discovers a material misrepresentation by the insured, the contract is voidable at the insurer's option.

- **Warranty** refers to **statements or promises** contained in an insurance contract that **would void the policy if untrue**. Courts do not strictly interpret warranties as such and may construe them as representations. The following are **three types of warranties:**

  1) **Affirmative Warranty** requires certain facts to be affirmed or true at policy inception.
  2) **Continuing or Promissory Warranty** requires certain facts to be promised and continued during the policy term. The failure to maintain a continuing or promissory warranty may void the policy.
  3) **Implied Warranty** is a type of warranty that is found in most sales contracts. That is, the product is legal, merchantable and fit for public use. Implied warranties are also found in "wet marine" (ocean going) coverages and include the seaworthiness of the vessel, that the ship will not deviate from its intended course, and that the cargo is of legal purpose.

- **Concealment** refers to the applicant's **failure to divulge facts**. If an applicant is **silent to a material fact**, the concealment may result in coverage being denied.

- **Fraud** is the deliberate deceit with the intent to take property of another. In insurance, fraud typically occurs when an insured or claimant makes false statements or misrepresents certain facts in an effort to be compensated under an insurance policy.

Waiver is the intentional and the **voluntary relinquishment of a known right.** A company may waive its rights by not enforcing a policy provision.

Estoppel prohibits or stops a company from citing its standard policy defenses because of the actions or inactions of the company and/or its agents. Estoppel occurs when a false representation is made by one party, that is relied upon by a second party, causing that second party to be financially injured, suffer harm or prejudice if the representations are not binding. It requires the following three elements: **(1) A false representation made by one party** (the agent or company), **(2) Reliance upon those representations by a second party** (the insured), causing that second party to **(3) be financially injured, suffer harm or prejudice**, if the representations are not binding. For example, if an agent or company leads an insured to believe coverage exists and the insured relies upon those representations, the courts will generally estop the insurance company from denying coverage.

KEY TERMS AND CONCEPTS

The following terms were introduced in this chapter. You should know each word and concept and be able to apply them in everyday usage. To improve retention, it is recommended that you write out each key term and concept in your own words. This exercise will help you recognize and understand each term in its proper context.

A. M. Best Company
Adhesion
Admitted or Authorized Companies
Adverse Selection
Agency
Agency Billed Policies
Agreement (Offer & Acceptance)
Aleatory
Alien Company
Ambiguities
Apparent Authority
Assuming Company
Branch Office System
Ceding Company
Characteristics of Insurance Contracts
Competent Parties
Concealment
Conditional Contracts
Consideration
Direct Billed Policies
Direct Response System
Direct Writer System
Doctrine of Insurable Interest
Domestic Company
Earned Premiums
Elements of a Legal Contract
Essential Elements of an Insurable Risk
Estoppel
Exclusive or Captive Agency System
Exposure
Express Authority
Facultative Reinsurance
Financial Status
Foreign Company
Fraternal Associations
Fraud
Government Insurers
Hazard(s)
Implied Authority
Indemnity
Independent Agency System
Insurance
Law of Large Numbers
Legal Interpretations Affecting Insurance
Legal Purpose
Lloyds
Loss
Managing General Agency System
Marketing Distribution Systems
Material Misrepresentations
Misrepresentations
Mutual Companies
Named Peril Policies
National Assn. of Ins. Commissioners
Nonadmitted or Unauthorized Companies
Open Peril Policies
Other Independent Rating Services
Other Methods Available to Manage Risk
Peril
Personal Contracts
Personal Producing General Agent
Potential Agent Liabilities and Exposures
Premium Financing
Presumption of Agency
Principle of Indemnity
Private Insurers
Producer's Collection Responsibilities
Producer's Responsibilities to Insured
Producer's Responsibility to Insurer
Producers
Pure Risk
Purpose of Reinsurance
Reasonable Expectations
Reciprocals
Reinsurance
Remittance of Premiums
Representations
Retention
Risk
Risk Management
Special Policies
Speculative Risk
Stock Companies
Subrogation
Treaty Reinsurance
Unearned Premiums
Unilateral Contracts
Utmost Good Faith
Valued Policies
Void/Voidable
Waiver
Warranty Types

REVIEW QUESTIONS

Before attempting to answer the end chapter practice questions, you should ask yourself if you can answer the following questions. It is recommended that you write out each review question in your own words. This exercise will help you apply the key terms and concepts that you've learned to form relationships with different topics.

1. What is risk management? (2-1)
2. Identify the 5 steps of the risk management process. (2-1)
3. Identify and explain 2 types of risk. (2-1)
4. Identify and define the 3 types of hazard. (2-1)
5. Identify, explain and give one example of the 5 other methods available to manage risk. (2-2)
6. Identify and explain the 7 essential elements of an insurable risk. (2-3)
7. What is adverse selection? (2-3)
8. What is insurable interest? (2-3)
9. What is indemnity? (2-3)
10. Explain reinsurance and define ceding, assuming, retention, treaty and facultative. (2-4)
11. Identify and explain the 5 different types of insurers. (2-5)
12. Explain the difference between domestic, foreign and alien companies. (2-6)
13. Identify and explain 4 insurance distribution systems. (2-8)
14. What is agency? (2-10)
15. Identify and explain the 4 elements of a contract. (2-12)
16. Define the terms adhesion and aleatory.(2-13)
17. How do representations differ from misrepresentations? (2-14)
18. How do misrepresentations differ from material misrepresentations? (2-14)
19. How does waiver differ from estoppel. (2-14)

PRACTICE EXAM TWO

ON

GENERAL INSURANCE

1. **Risk may be defined as:**

   A) The exposure or uncertainty of loss.
   B) The perils listed in the policy.
   C) The premium paid by the insured.
   D) None of the above. Ref. 2-1

2. **Risk exposures may be classified as either:**

   A) No risk and some risk.
   B) Pure risk and speculative risk.
   C) Named perils and listed perils.
   D) None of the above. Ref. 2-1

3. **Which of the following is the type of risk exposure that insurance companies seek to insure? It has two possible outcomes.**

   A) No risk exposures.
   B) Speculative risk exposures.
   C) All risk exposures.
   D) Pure risk exposures. Ref. 2-1

4. **Insurance may be described as:**

   A) The retention of risk.
   B) The elimination of risk by control techniques.
   C) The spreading of risk by the collection of premiums to finance future losses.
   D) None of the above. Ref. 2-2

5. **In addition to insurance, risk exposures may be managed by:**

   A) Avoidance of risk.
   B) Retention of risk.
   C) Reduction of risk.
   D) All of the above. Ref. 2-2

6. **All of the following are essential elements of an insurable risk EXCEPT:**

   A) The law of large numbers must apply.
   B) Losses must be predictable.
   C) Losses must be intentional.
   D) Premium costs must be affordable. Ref. 2-3

7. **All of the following are true of insurable interest EXCEPT:**

A) It is the interest one has in property that may cause the possibility of financial loss.
B) In property and casualty insurance, it is required to exist at the time of loss.
C) It cannot exist in business relationships.
D) A mortgage company has an insurable interest in mortgaged property. Ref. 2-3

8. **The Principle of Indemnity as found in some insurance contracts:**

A) Indemnifies an insured in excess of their loss.
B) Reduces lawsuits.
C) Restores or reimburses one to the extent of their loss.
D) Requires a contribution by equal shares. Ref. 2-3

9. **An insurance company domiciled in the state of Pennsylvania is considered:**

A) Foreign.
B) Alien.
C) Domestic.
D) Surplus. Ref. 2-6

10. **All of the following are characteristics of a licensed or admitted insurance company EXCEPT:**

A) Must pass state required minimum financial standards.
B) Must agree to abide by statutory regulation.
C) Accepts surplus and excess lines business.
D) Produces business through local branches and agents. Ref. 2-6

11. **Which of the following does NOT assemble and review detailed information on the financial condition of insurance companies?**

A) The Insurance Department.
B) The A.M. Best Company.
C) The National Association of Insurance Commissioners (NAIC).
D) The Independent Insurance Agents and Brokers of America (IIABA). Ref. 2-6 & 2-7

12. **The principle of insurance that restores one to approximately the same condition that they enjoyed prior to their loss is:**

A) Valued contracts.
B) Subrogation.
C) Retention.
D) Indemnification. Ref. 2-3

13. An association of subscribers which insures one another and is managed by an Attorney-in-fact is called a:

A) Lloyds association.
B) Mutual company.
C) Fraternal organization.
D) Reciprocal. Ref. 2-5

14. All of the following are characteristics of reinsurance EXCEPT:

A) The original insurer is the ceding company.
B) Reinsurance is a contractual process used to spread loss exposures.
C) Facultative and Treaty are two common reinsurance arrangements.
D) Reinsurance is used only with casualty exposures. Ref. 2-4

15. Reinsurance may be arranged in which of the following reinsurance forms?

A) Retention.
B) Treaty or facultative.
C) Assuming or ceding.
D) Retrocession. Ref. 2-4

16. What reinsurance arrangement automatically accepts exposures from a ceding company?

A) Facultative.
B) Retrocessionaire.
C) Treaty.
D) Ceding. Ref. 2-4

17. All of the following are distributors of insurance EXCEPT:

A) The Direct Writer System.
B) The Independent Agency System.
C) The Employer Administered System.
D) The Exclusive Agency System. Ref. 2-8

18. An insurance company domiciled outside the United States would be considered:

A) Alien.
B) Excess.
C) Domestic.
D) Foreign. Ref. 2-6

19. All of the following are characteristics of the Law of Agency EXCEPT:

A) It is the legal relationship that exists when one acts for another.
B) It is a fiduciary relationship consisting of a principal and an agent.
C) When agency is legally formed, the agent binds the principal to their actions.
D) The knowledge of the agent is not imputed to the principal. Ref. 2-10

20. All of the following are types of authority that a producer may be granted, or may assume EXCEPT:

A) Express authority.
B) Implied authority.
C) Apparent authority.
D) Waiver authority. Ref. 2-10

21. The voluntary relinquishment of a known right is:

A) Estoppel.
B) Waiver.
C) Subrogation.
D) None of the above. Ref. 2-4

22. The type of authority that is specifically defined in a producer's agreement is:

A) Implied authority.
B) Express authority.
C) Apparent authority.
D) Waiver authority. Ref. 2-10

23. All of following are reflective of the fiduciary or professional responsibility of an producer EXCEPT:

A) Performs in an honest and good faith manner.
B) Recommends coverages that are proper and within the needs of the insured.
C) Performs risk management services that reduces the insured's premium costs.
D) Splits the commission with the insured. Ref. 2-11

24. Which one of the following occurrences would least likely create an errors and omissions exposure for a producer?

A) Failure to process an application in a timely manner.
B) Failure to upgrade coverages to reflect inflation or other known factors.
C) Failure to provide coverage for an exposure that is concealed by the insured.
D) Failure to recommend proper coverage. Ref. 2-12

25. All of the following are examples of the underwriting process EXCEPT:

A) Completing and reviewing the application for insurance.
B) Classifying and rating of the risk.
C) Paying the insured a fair settlement after a loss occurs.
D) Monitoring of business. Ref. 2-12

26. Insurance companies attempt to minimize and if possible eliminate the process of adverse selection. Which of the following describes adverse selection?

A) A process that occurs when applicants for insurance have a greater bias to an exposure than a random sampling of the population.
B) A process that enables insurance companies to predict losses.
C) Insuring only excellent risks.
D) The process of insuring risk exposures with a reinsurance company.
Ref. 2-3 & 2-12

27. How will a court of law interpret an insurance contract that contains policy language that is ambiguous?

A) Find in favor of the company since the insured should have read the policy.
B) Find in favor of the insured since the insured had no duty to read the policy.
C) Find in favor of both insured and company by apportioning each party's fault at 50% of the total verdict amount.
D) Find in favor of the insured since the policy is a contract of adhesion. Ref. 2-13

28. All of the following are essential elements of a contract EXCEPT:

A) Consideration.
B) Legal purpose.
C) Incompetent parties.
D) Agreement (offer and acceptance). Ref. 2-12

29. What term describes the statements made by an individual at application?

A) Warranty.
B) Concealment.
C) Misrepresentations.
D) Representations. Ref. 2-14

30. An insurance contract feature that permits all ambiguous areas to be construed in favor of the insured is:

A) Aleatory.
B) Adhesion.
C) Utmost good faith.
D) Fraud. Ref. 2-13

31. All of the following are characteristics of insurance contracts EXCEPT:

A) Aleatory.
B) Personal contract.
C) Adhesion.
D) Bilateral contract. Ref. 2-13

32. The legal right of an insurance company to seek reimbursement from a negligent third party is:

A) Parol Evidence Rule.
B) Warranty.
C) Subrogation.
D) Adhesion. Ref. 2-13

33. Warranties refer to statements or promises contained in some insurance contracts that may void the contract if untrue. Warranties fall into three main types. Which of the following is NOT one of these warranty types?

A) Affirmative warranty.
B) Continuing or promissory warranty.
C) Implied warranty.
D) Guaranteed warranty. Ref. 2-14

34. What term describes the failure to disclose a fact to the application for insurance?

A) Representation.
B) Misrepresentation.
C) Concealment.
D) Aleatory. Ref. 2-14

35. Under an insurance contract, both the insured and insurer give up something of value which is called:

A) Reasonable expectations.
B) Consideration.
C) Subrogation.
D) Estoppel. Ref. 2-12

ANSWER KEY

1-A	2-B	3-D	4-C	5-D	6-C	7-C	8-C	9-C	10-C
11-D	12-D	13-D	14-D	15-B	16-C	17-C	18-A	19-D	20-D
21-B	22-B	23-D	24-C	25-C	26-A	27-D	28-C	29-D	30-B
31-D	32-C	33-D	34-C	35-B					

CHAPTER THREE

PROPERTY AND CASUALTY INSURANCE BASICS

OVERVIEW

This chapter introduces the basic insurance concepts and principles which are the very foundation of today's insurance policy. These topics will generally reappear in every insurance contract.

INSURABLE INTEREST

Insurable interest is the interest one has in life or property that may cause one the possibility of financial loss. It is **a basic requirement of an insurance policy**. The primary reason for this requirement is to avoid the possibility of speculative wagering on another's property in which one has no interest. For example, an individual may not collect insurance proceeds on a property unless that person owned the property or had an insurable interest in that property. In property and casualty insurance an **insurable interest must exist at the time of loss** for coverage to be afforded.

UNDERWRITING

Underwriting refers to the broad range of duties and functions performed by producers and company underwriters during risk selection. The **underwriting process includes** the gathering of information, the making of an underwriting decision, and the continual monitoring of business to promote profitability. Information during the underwriting process is gathered from a producer's application, motor vehicle reports (MVR), consumer credit companies such as Equifax, and financial sources such as Dun and Bradstreet. After the initial underwriting is completed, the underwriter may:

- Issue the policy as applied for.
- Issue the policy subject to certain exclusions or limitations.
- Reject the application.

A major underwriting objective is to minimize the possibility of **adverse selection**. This occurs when applicants for insurance have a greater bias to an exposure than a random sampling of the population. It is the **tendency of poorer risks to seek insurance**. For example, a businessowner in a high crime area of a city may aggressively seek insurance for crime exposures, whereas, a similar businessowner in a low crime area of the same city may not. Insurance companies expect losses to occur based upon a random sampling. Underwriters attempt to eliminate or minimize adverse selection by carefully evaluating the applicants for insurance. Insurance companies rely on their agents to conduct **field underwriting** as a means to further minimize their loss exposures. Field underwriting includes interviewing applicants for coverage and may involve the physical inspection of property to be insured. The primary goal of field underwriting is to screen out undesirable risks before coverage is bound and submitted to the underwriter.

PROFITABILITY

Insurance companies closely monitor their premium writings and expenses to judge the underwriting success of their operations. A **loss ratio** is the ratio of **losses incurred to premiums earned**. This term is used extensively in the property and casualty business as an indication of profitability. A loss ratio of 60 is usually considered break even with lower ratios preferable. An **expense ratio** is the ratio of **expenses incurred** by the company (producer commissions, office rent, employee salaries, etc.) in producing the business **to premiums earned**. An expense ratio in the 35-40 range is normal with lower ratios preferable. A **combined ratio** is the **combination or sum of the loss and expense ratios**. If the combined ratio exceeds 100, the company is paying out more in total expenses (losses and expenses) than premium revenue earned, and thus incurring an underwriting loss. The combined ratio is used extensively by the property and casualty companies to reflect profit level. A lower combined ratio indicates a more profitable insurance company.

RATING

Rating is the process by which an insurance company determines a price for the exposure it is underwriting. In property insurance, the **rate** is the price charged per exposure unit. The **exposure unit** is a measure of loss potential. The **rate per unit is multiplied by the number of units** to determine the **premium** the applicant pays for the policy. For example, if the rate per hundred of insurance is $1.25 and the insured purchases $100,000 in coverage, the premium is $1,250. In Workers Compensation insurance, the exposure unit is based upon a rate per hundred of payroll. In general liability insurance, **a rate is multiplied by a rate exposure** to equal the premium. The **rate exposure**, which is also known as the **premium base**, reflects the size of the business. Common rate exposures for liability insurance include square foot area, gross sales or payroll. Rates may be classified as follows:

- **Manual or Class Rating** applies to large homogeneous groups. Most personal lines policies and many commercial lines policies are class or manual rated.

- **Individual or Judgment Rating** applies to a specific nonstandard risk. This type of rating is used almost exclusively in commercial insurance and only rated by an experienced underwriter after an extensive underwriting analysis of the risk.

- **Merit Rating** applies schedules and experience to a specific risk. For example, a manual rated Homeowner Policy may be merit rated for home protective devices.

- **Loss Cost Rating** utilizes loss costs published by a rating bureau permitting insurers to apply their own expense costs. The sum of the loss costs and expense costs make up the final rate.

Insurance underwriters analyze various factors which may effect the final premium rate of a risk. For example, construction (brick v. frame), fire protection (proximity to a fire department or hydrant) age, and type of occupancy are important in rating property risks. Similarly, location of garaging, usage (business v. pleasure) and age of drivers is important in rating automobile risks. ***Basically, anything that increases the frequency or severity of loss will create an increase in premium.***

HAZARDS

A hazard is any condition or exposure that **increases the possibility of loss**. They are generally classified as:

- **Physical Hazards**, which are physical in nature and include such conditions as the storing of explosive materials within a building, or defective stairs which may cause a fall.
- **Moral Hazards**, which are conditions that increase the likelihood of loss such as an applicant with a poor financial history or one with an extensive police record.
- **Morale Hazards**, which reflects an indifference or an "I don't care" attitude, since the insured is covered.

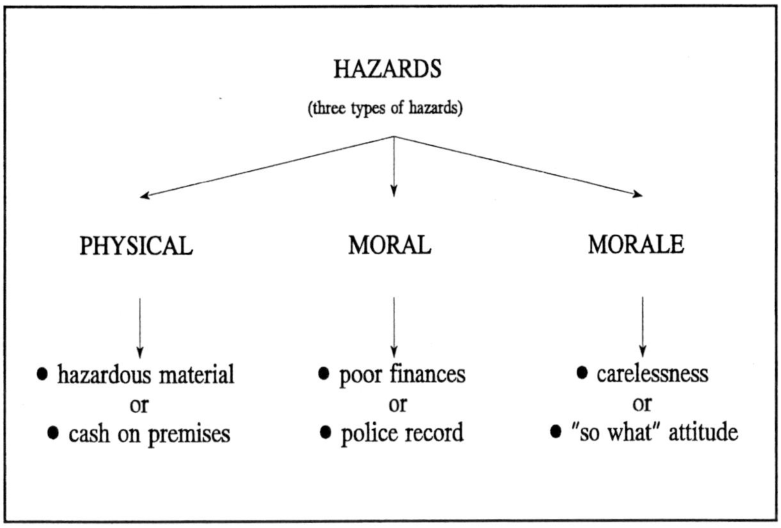

The underwriting process attempts to minimize, and if possible, eliminate these types of hazards.

PROPERTY INSURANCE v. LIABILITY INSURANCE

Insurance coverages are classified into two broad categories. **Property insurance** which covers real and/or personal property and **liability insurance** which covers an insured's legal liability. For example, a property policy will cover a house and contents if damaged by fire, lightning, etc., whereas, a liability policy will cover the homeowner if a visitor slips and falls on the premises and initiates a lawsuit. Similar examples are available for commercial exposures. **Property policies consist of two parties**, the insured who is the first party, and the insurer who is the second party. **Liability policies introduce a third party, the claimant**. Hence, liability policies are sometimes referred to as third party coverage since it protects the insured for claims brought by third party claimants.

The following pages will address first party property insurance with third party liability insurance being addressed later in this chapter.

CAUSES OF LOSS - PERILS

Causes of loss are the perils of the policy. For example, fire, lightning, and explosion are all causes of loss. Property insurance policies are written on a **Basic Form, Broad Form or Special Form** basis, with the Basic Form being the most limited and the Special Form being the most comprehensive. The following chart illustrates the Commercial Property Coverage Part causes of loss forms. These causes of loss forms will be reviewed in chapter seven. Similar perils are also insured under the Dwelling Policy (Chapter Four), the Homeowners Policy (Chapter Five) and the Businessowners Policy (Chapter Eight).

CAUSES OF LOSS FORMS

Named Perils	**Basic**	**Broad**	**Special†**
Fire	●	●	●
Lightning	●	●	●
Explosion	●	●	●
Windstorm & Hail	●	●	●
Smoke	●	●	●
Aircraft or Vehicles	●	●	●
Riot or Civil Commotion	●	●	●
Vandalism	●	●	●
Sprinkler Leakage	●	●	●
Sinkhole Collapse	●	●	●
Volcanic Action	●	●	●
Falling Objects		●	●
Weight of Snow, Ice or Sleet		●	●
Water Damage (accidental discharge)		●	●
Special/Open Peril Coverage			●†

† Special Form (Open Peril) policies provide coverage for risk of direct physical loss unless specifically excluded.

The basic causes of loss form offers the fewest coverage perils and charges the lowest premium. Whereas, the special causes of loss form offers the most perils and charges the highest premium. Causes of loss forms, which are incorporated into policies, are classified as either Specified Named Peril policies (Basic or Broad Form) or as Special Form policies. These causes of loss forms will appear in all property policies with minor variations.

SPECIFIED (NAMED PERILS) v. SPECIAL FORM (OPEN PERILS)

Specified Peril or Named Peril is the type of policy that specifically **lists the perils insured against in the policy**. If the cause of loss is listed in the policy, coverage applies. Conversely, Special Form or Open Peril policies **list the exclusions from coverage**. Under this approach, if the cause of loss is excluded, no coverage applies. The following chart illustrates the difference between these two types of policies.

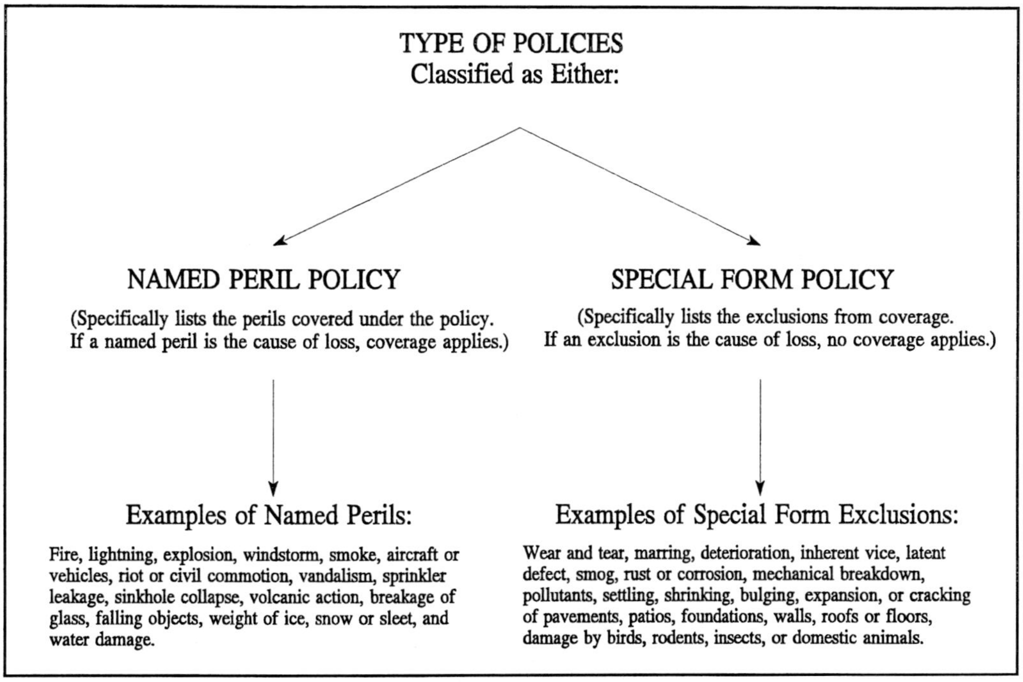

DIRECT LOSSES v. INDIRECT (CONSEQUENTIAL) LOSSES

Direct losses are **losses that are the direct physical result of an insured peril**. Fire (including water to extinguish it) and vandalism are examples of direct losses. It is the type of loss that has actual physical damage to the property or the actual loss of the property. Indirect or consequential losses **are losses that are the result of a direct loss**. For example, if an individual's home or business were damaged by fire (a direct loss), that individual or business owner would incur the consequential loss of renting another place to reside or conduct business. Coverages for indirect or consequential type losses are automatically provided under some policies.

BLANKET v. SPECIFIC v. SCHEDULED INSURANCE

The terms blanket, specific and scheduled insurance refer to ways of writing property insurance and the application of policy limits. Property insurance can written as follows:

- **Blanket insurance** is a single amount of insurance that's provided to all locations. For example, a business may have a single blanket limit covering several locations.
- **Specific insurance** provides a single amount for a specific location.
- **Scheduled insurance** is a variation of blanket and specific insurance. When property is scheduled, specific amounts are provided for each item or location.

A policy will be issued with at least one limit of insurance, and in most cases, more than one. For example, a Homeowners Policy will contain a specific limit on the dwelling, a blanket limit on the contents, and commonly a scheduled limit for valuable articles. Blanket, specific and scheduled insurance are common ways to insure property.

REPORTING FORMS

Reporting Forms **are used to vary the amount of coverage in force** to reflect fluctuations in property. By using reporting forms, coverages can closely mirror the exposure and avoid the problem of overinsurance or underinsurance. For example, a **seasonal business** may have wide swings in the amount of inventory at different times of the year. Similarly, a **building under construction** would also have variations from beginning of construction to completion. Reporting forms would be used to cover these types of exposures. The following topics address important features of reporting forms:

- **Timely Reporting** requires the timely reporting of changes in values. In the event an updated reporting form is not filed or filed late, the previously filed report will be considered in effect. Because of the possibility of penalties being applied, the use of reporting forms requires close monitoring.

- **Full Reporting (Honesty Clause)** penalizes the insured if values are under reported. In these instances, the company will pay the pro rated portion of reported values to actual values. For example, if the reported values were $75,000 of inventory, and at the time of loss it was discovered that the actual value of inventory was $100,000, the insured would be penalized 25% for under reporting and paid 75% of the loss. The full reporting requirement is also known as the honesty clause.

BASIC TYPES OF CONSTRUCTION

An important element in the underwriting and rating of property insurance is the determination of the type of construction. **This is important for several reasons. First**, determining the type of construction allows the underwriter to *assign a rating factor* used in calculating the policy premium. For example, frame buildings are generally charged a higher premium than masonry buildings. This is due to the higher possibility of total loss caused by fire on frame construction in comparison to masonry construction. **Second**, the type of construction may be a *factor in the eventual decision* to accept the risk. For example, damage to aluminum siding and metal roofs is higher in areas of the country which are susceptible to high winds and hail storms. Consequently, underwriters may choose to avoid these types of exposures in those areas or require high deductibles. The following are the basic construction types encountered in the risk selection process:

- **Frame** construction means buildings where the exterior walls are wood or other similar combustible materials. This would include, aluminum siding, stucco and brick veneer. Premiums are generally higher for frame construction.

- **Masonry** construction means buildings where the exterior walls are of masonry materials such as adobe, brick, concrete, concrete block, stone, tile, or similar material. Premiums are generally lower for masonry construction.

Other categories of construction include: **Joisted Masonry** (walls are masonry & floors are wood), **Noncombustible** (metal); **Masonry Noncombustible** (walls are masonry & floors are noncombustible); and **Fire Resistive** (exterior walls & floors are resistive to fire). Fire resistive material must have a fire rating of at least 2 hours.

LOSS VALUATION

The insured has the option of choosing a policy with one of several loss valuation provisions at the time of application. These loss valuation provisions address how the insured property will be valued at the time of loss. The following are the primary ways a property may be valued for insurance purposes:

- **Actual Cash Value (ACV)** is a basic concept that reinforces the previously discussed topic of indemnity. It is defined as **replacement cost less depreciation**. For example, if a property has a current replacement value of $100,000 and has depreciated 40% due to age and use, the actual cash value of the property would be $60,000. Originally, all property was insured on an actual cash value basis. Today, actual cash value policies are generally written on older buildings with newer buildings written on a replacement cost basis.

- **Replacement Cost** is contrary to the basic concept of indemnity since it may provide the insured with a loss settlement or betterment in excess of the property's actual cash value. Replacement cost is defined as the **cost to replace with like kind and quality at today's replacement cost, without any deduction for depreciation**. It is replacing old damaged property with new replacement property. Today, most real property is insured on a replacement cost basis.

- **Functional Replacement Cost** is a variation of replacement cost. Its permits the insurer to **replace damaged property with a functional equivalent**. For example, if a building is damaged by fire, the insurer may replace plaster walls with sheet rock walls or replace a slate roof with an asphalt shingle roof. Functional replacement cost is utilized when there is a wide disparity between a building's replacement cost and its market value. It is written without a coinsurance clause.

- **Market Value** is the price one would pay **based upon free market conditions**. With few exceptions, property insurance is generally written on either an actual cash value basis or replacement cost basis. Seldom is a property policy written on a market value basis.

- **Agreed Value** coverage is an alternative method of writing property coverage. When agreed value coverage is written, the coinsurance clause is suspended as the **insured and insurer agree to the amount of coverage to be written for the policy term**. Coverage is provided up to the agreed value amount. If the option is not extended at expiration, the coinsurance provision is reinstated.

- **Stated Amount** establishes coverage amounts on property at policy inception, however, unlike agreed value which pays the agreed value, stated amount *pays the insured the least of* (1) the stated amount, (2) the actual cash value, or (3) the cost of repair. Stated amount coverage is a valued policy approach used to insure certain exposures such as antique autos or customized cars.

POLICY STRUCTURE

A property casualty policy is comprised of the following major components:

- **Definitions** clarify terms as used in the policy. For example, a policy will define such terms as **"bodily injury", "business", "insured", and "insured location"**. The purpose of the definitions section of a policy is to clearly set forth the meaning of terms as used in the policy. Words which are defined are typically in quotations or are bolded. See SP-2 and SP-3 for additional examples and exact policy language.

- **Declarations or Declarations Page** indicates the named insured and address, policy term, the amount of insurance, policy forms, deductible, premium and related information that is specific to the insured. In Workers Compensation policies, the Declaration Page is called the Information Page. The Declaration Page **personalizes the policy** and is typically computer generated. See SP-39 and SP-40 for examples.

- The **Insuring Agreement** is the **contractual clause of the policy** setting forth the agreement between the insured and the insurance company. It provides coverage for the insured in return for the premium and compliance with all applicable policy provisions. Insurance policies may have more than one insuring agreement. For example the Homeowners Policy contains a property insuring agreement (SP-2) and a liability insuring agreement (SP-17). For additional examples see SP-27 and SP-41.

- **Additional Coverage and Supplemental Payments** provide coverage beyond the principal policy coverages. For example, the additional coverages in a Homeowner Policy includes property coverage for debris removal; reasonable repairs; damage to trees, shrubs and other plants; fire department service charge; property removed; and credit card, fund transfer card, forgery and counterfeit money (SP-7). Supplemental Payments or Additional Liability Coverage are secondary benefits that extend coverage for expenses associated with the litigation process. Examples include claim expenses, first aid expenses, damage to property of others, and loss assessment. Both Additional Coverage and Supplemental Payments typically have dollar limitations. See SP-21, SP-27 and SP-43 for examples.

- **Conditions** set forth the **rules, duties, provisions and obligations of the insured and insurance company**. Examples include the duty of the insured to pay the premium and to report losses promptly and cooperate in the adjustment process. Similarly, the insurer is required to adjust losses in accordance with the policy. Other conditions address possible problem areas. For example, the appraisal condition addresses value disputes that may occur at the time of loss. Another common policy provision is the other insurance condition which addresses how claims will be settled if multiple policies are in effect at the time of loss. The conditions of a policy attempt to eliminate or minimize these problem areas. See SP-14, SP-22, SP-24, SP-36, SP-37, SP-38, SP-41 and SP-80 for examples of policy conditions.

- **Exclusions** eliminate coverage for specific occurrences **that are deemed uninsurable** or not calculated in the policy premium. Examples include intentional acts, war, flood, nuclear radiation, smog, inherent vice, latent defect, rust and corrosion. Similarly, **activities or conditions which are in the control of the insured** are also generally excluded. For example, wear and tear, marring and deterioration. Finally, **property which can be better insured under another policy** is also generally excluded. For example, autos are excluded from homeowner policies and personal property is excluded from auto policies. See SP-13, SP-27, SP-31 and SP-34 for additional examples.

- **Endorsements** are **used to change a policy's original terms, conditions or coverages**. An endorsement may be included at the time of policy issuance or added later in the policy term. Typically, endorsements add or delete coverage, or correct names and addresses. For example, the Homeowner Policy may be endorsed to insure personal property for specific scheduled amounts above the special limits indicated in the policy. See SP-4 for homeowner special limits.

Insurance policies are comprised of these same basic components. The major difference being, that each specific policy type excludes from coverage perils that are generally insured under a separate specific policy. After a policy has been underwritten, it is physically produced and included in a policy jacket for delivery to the insured. Please note, the major components of a policy include the **D**eclarations, **I**nsuring agreement, **C**onditions and **E**xclusions. The acronym **DICE** may assist you in the study process.

COMMON PROVISIONS

INSURED STATUS

An important factor in the application of coverages centers around the definition of an insured. For example, under a Homeowners Policy, an insured not only means the person(s) named on the declaration page, but it includes resident relatives and individuals under the age of 21 who are in the care of any insured (See SP-2). The following terms further define who may be an insured under the policy:

- **Insured** refers to anyone who may be covered by the policy. As indicated above, an insured may include individuals who are not named in the policy, such as resident relatives, minor children or nonrelated individuals who are carrying out a task at the insured's direction.

- **Named Insured** is the individual(s) or business named in the policy declarations.

- **Additional Insureds** refers to individuals or businesses that are not named as an insured in the declarations, but added by endorsement to the policy. For example, a subcontractor may request to be added to a general contractor's general liability policy. Similarly, a distributor may ask a manufacturer to be added to the manufacturer's products liability policy.

- **First Named Insured** refers to the individual, partnership, joint venture, corporation or association to whom insurance policies are issued. **The first named insured is responsible for carrying on the day-to-day functions of the insured, such as** *paying premiums, reporting losses or cancelling the policy.*

POLICY PERIOD

The policy period is the time period as indicated in the Declarations Page during which coverage will be provided. Generally, a policy **begins and expires at 12:01 a.m. Standard Time on the location and date indicated in the declarations**. Policy periods are most often one year in duration, however, six month policies are not uncommon. Finally, some policies cover the time period it takes to complete a task. For example, transit policies which insure cargo, covers the duration of a single trip. See SP-17 and SP-36 for examples.

POLICY TERRITORY

The policy territory **defines the location where coverage will be provided**. For example, the Homeowner Policy covers both property and liability losses on a worldwide basis, whereas, the Personal Auto Policy, Commercial Auto Policy and the Commercial General Liability limit the coverage territory to the United States, Canada and Puerto Rico. See SP-37, SP-41 and SP-61.

DEDUCTIBLES

The deductible **is the initial amount, or the first dollar cost paid or absorbed**, by the insured in the event of loss. Deductible types include:

- **Dollar deductible**, which is expressed in a dollar amount. For example, a $250 or $500 deductible. This is the most common type of deductible.

- **Percentage deductible**, which is expressed as a percent of the amount of insurance, the value of the insured property, or the amount of loss. A percentage deductible is commonly used in earthquake coverage and some property policies.

- **Time deductible**, which is expressed in a number of days which must elapse prior to coverage being afforded. For example, the personal auto policy provides coverage for transportation expenses (up to $20 per day to a maximum of $600) if the insured's vehicle is stolen. **The payment does not begin until 48 hours after the theft.** See SP-33 for complete policy language.

OTHER INSURANCE

Policies include other insurance provisions which **address the apportionment of coverages in the event more than one policy is written on the same risk at the time of loss**. This may occur by design, or in some cases, by oversight. Coverage that is written to cover the same property, but not on the same coverage basis is **nonconcurrent** coverage. Coverage that is written to cover the same property and same coverage basis is **concurrent coverage**. As a general rule, when concurrent coverage (same property and coverage basis) applies, a loss will be prorated (see following page). When nonconcurrency applies, coverage is excess. Specific types of other insurance provisions include: 1) primary insurance, 2) excess insurance, 3) proration of coverage, or 4) contribution by equal shares. Each policy will state how it coordinates with other policies. The following defines these four concepts:

STRICT OR ABSOLUTE LIABILITY

Strict or Absolute liability is a legal doctrine that allocates liability without regard to fault or negligence. All that has to be proven is that the individual or organization was responsible for the activity that caused the harm or injury. **Strict liability is commonly applied in product liability** cases where a defect must be proven. An example would be where an automobile was delivered to an individual with defective brakes. The manufacturer would be held strictly liable if it were proved the brakes were defective and injury resulted. **Absolute liability is imposed when conduct is of a hazardous nature**. For example, a business utilizing wild animals or explosives would be held absolutely liable for injuries or damage incurred by these hazardous activities.

VICARIOUS LIABILITY

Vicarious liability is a legal doctrine in which **liability is imputed from one to another**. Such situations extend liability from the actual wrongdoer to any person or organization responsible for the actions of the wrongdoer. For example, a business is responsible for the actions of its employees.

LIMITS OF LIABILITY

Limits of liability refers to the specific amount indicated in a dollar figure that **limits an insurer's exposure to loss**. The term "limits of liability" is used primarily to describe liability limits (third party claimants) versus policy limits (first party insureds) described earlier in this chapter. Liability limits include:

- **Per Person Limits** of liability **limit the amount of coverage for each person**, regardless of the overall or aggregate limit. For example, if an auto policy has a $15,000 per person limit and an accident occurs injuring 3 passengers, the maximum amount payable is $15,000 per person or $45,000 total.

- **Per Occurrence Limits** of liability **limit the amount of coverage for each occurrence**, regardless of the number of persons injured. For example, if an auto policy has a $30,000 per occurrence limit and an accident occurs injuring 3 passengers, the maximum amount payable for that single occurrence is $30,000.

- **Aggregate Limits** of liability **limit the amount of coverage to a maximum overall limit for the policy period**. Aggregate limits may be written a *per location* (maximum payable at that location) or *per project* basis (maximum payable on that project).

- **Split Limits** of liability **specify different amounts of coverage for different types of losses**. For example, the minimum requirement to satisfy the financial responsibility law for automobile insurance in Pennsylvania is $15,000/$30,000-/$5,000. This means $15,000 for bodily injury liability per person, $30,000 bodily injury liability per accident, and $5,000 property damage liability per accident.

- **Combined Single Limit** combines **both bodily injury and property damage into one single limit of protection**. This is in contrast to split limits of liability.

INSURED'S PROVISIONS OR DUTIES

The insured is required to perform certain duties to ensure coverage will be afforded at the time of loss. **These duties include** paying the premium, giving prompt notice of claim, protecting the property from further damage, preparing an inventory of damaged property, and providing a sworn proof of loss. These duties are found in the Conditions Section of the various policies. See SP-14, SP-36 and SP-57. Additional duties address assignment and abandonment provisions which are reviewed in the following section.

DUTIES AFTER LOSS

The insured is required under the **property conditions** of a policy to perform certain duties after loss. Specifically, to:

- Give immediate notice of loss to their producer or insurer.
- Notify the police in case of loss by theft.
- Notify the credit card or fund transfer card company of loss by theft.
- Protect the property from further damage and make reasonable repairs necessary to protect the property, and to keep an accurate record of expenditures.
- Prepare an inventory of damaged property showing quality, description, actual cash value and amount of loss.
- Exhibit the damage as often as reasonably required, and submit to examination under oath.
- Submit to the company a signed sworn proof of loss within 60 days of request.

See SP-1, SP-14, and SP-57 for examples. Similar duties are required under the **liability conditions** as follows:

- Give written notice of loss to their producer or insurer.
- Promptly forward every notice, demand and summons relating to the accident.
- Assist the insurance company in making settlement by attending hearings or trials.
- Submit to the company a signed sworn proof of loss within 60 days of request.

These claim procedures are common to all insurance policies and are set forth in detail in the Conditions Section of each policy. See SP-22 and SP-36.

TRANSFER OF RIGHTS AND DUTIES (ASSIGNMENT)

The **transfer of rights and duties provision prohibits** the insured from transferring or assigning the policy to another individual without the written consent of the insurer. For example, if you sell your home, you cannot transfer or assign your Homeowners Policy to the new purchasers of your house, unless the insurance company gives you approval for the transfer. Since insurance is a personal contract, the insurance company has the right to underwrite each individual before it assumes the risk of loss. See SP-24 and SP-38.

ABANDONMENT

The **abandonment provision prohibits** the insured from abandoning the property to the insurance company and claiming a total loss. For example, if a home is damaged by fire, the homeowner cannot abandon the home and demand policy limits. See SP-1 and SP-16.

APPRAISAL

The appraisal condition is a common provision found in property policies. It provides that in the event the insured and insurer cannot agree to the value of damaged property, that **either party may make a demand for appraisal**. In these cases, each party selects an appraiser, who in turn selects an impartial umpire. If neither party can agree on an impartial umpire, either party may request the choice be made by a judge of a court. Each appraiser submits their estimate of damage. A decision of any two is final. The appraisal process promotes claim settlement and helps in reducing legal expenses. When appraisal is demanded, **each party pays the cost of their own appraiser with other costs being shared equally**. See SP-16.

ARBITRATION

The arbitration condition is a common provision found in liability policies. It provides that in the event the insured and insurer cannot agree on the amount of loss, that **either party may demand for arbitration**. In these cases, each party appoints an arbitrator, who in turn selects an impartial competent umpire. Each arbitrator submits his settlement of damages. A decision made by any two is final. The arbitration process promotes claim settlement and helps in reducing legal expenses. See SP-32.

INSURER'S PROVISIONS OR DUTIES

The insurer is required to perform certain duties to the insured after the payment of the premium. **These duties include** paying all losses in accordance with the conditions of the policy and Pennsylvania's Claims Settlement Practices Act, canceling policies only by advance written notice as permitted by the state insurance department, and returning all premiums due the insured because of cancellation. These duties are found in the Conditions Section of various policies. See SP-15.

LIBERALIZATION CLAUSE

The liberalization clause is a common insurance policy condition. It provides that in the event the **insurer broadens coverage without an additional premium charge,** the broadened coverage will apply to all insureds immediately. For example, if a company adopts a policy form which covers property excluded under the predecessor policy form, this broadened coverage will apply to all insureds, including those whose policy had not yet renewed. See SP-23.

TRANSFER OF RIGHTS OF RECOVERY (SUBROGATION)

The transfer of rights of recovery refers to the **insurance company's right to subrogate against third parties who, because of their negligence, cause the insurance company to pay a claim**. In these instances, the insured transfers their rights of recovery to the insurance company in return for immediate settlement of their claim. For example, if a television set causes a house fire, the homeowner's insurer will reimburse the homeowner, and subrogate (seek payment) against the manufacturer of the defective television set. See SP-37. Please note that subrogation may be waived (not pursued) if a **waiver of subrogation** is executed in writing before a loss occurs. This means that the insured and insurer will not bring an action against a negligent third-party that caused the insurer to pay a claim.

SALVAGE

Salvage refers to **property which is taken by the insurer to reduce its loss after a claim is paid**. For example, if a vehicle is damaged to the point where it is considered a total loss, the insurer will pay the insured the ACV and then take legal possession of the vehicle. The insurer will then sell the damaged vehicle to reduce its loss. Similar salvage examples apply to property losses.

CLAIM SETTLEMENT OPTIONS

An insurer has several claim settlement options it may exercise at the time of loss. These claim settlement options include:

1) Pay the value of the lost or damaged property;
2) Pay the cost of repairing or replacing the lost or damaged property;
3) Take all or part of the property at an agreed or appraised value; or
4) Repair, rebuild or replace the property with other property of like kind and quality.

The insurer may choose to repair or replace the damaged property with like kind and quality rather than paying a cash settlement. This typically occurs when the insurer believes it can have the repair work completed at a lower cost than having the insured's contractor complete the work. The insurer must notify the insured of these intentions within 15 working days of receiving a sworn proof of loss.

DUTY TO DEFEND

The duty to defend is a liability policy provision. It **requires the insurance company to investigate and defend any claim or lawsuit brought against an insured**. This clause in effect creates two important and separate duties which are at the very heart of liability insurance. That is, the duty to defend and the duty to indemnify. Under the duty to defend, a distinct and separate obligation, apart from the insurer's duty to indemnify is created. This duty is broad and extends to claims which are clearly, or even arguably within the scope of coverage. Any doubts regarding the insurer's duty to defend under the policy must be resolved in favor of the insured. In the event a claim falls potentially within the scope of coverage or the policy is potentially in effect on the date of the loss, the insurer has a duty to defend.

UNOCCUPANCY AND VACANCY

The terms unoccupancy and vacancy are two different and important terms which may have an effect upon a claim settlement.

- **Unoccupancy** means the absence of people from the insured home or building, whereas, **vacancy** means the absence of both people and furniture. For example, if an insured goes on vacation for a month, the home is considered **unoccupied (contents but no people)** during the one month period. Unoccupancy will generally not affect the coverage provided under most policies.

- **Vacancy (no contents and no people)** provides a greater exposure for loss, hence, coverage is excluded outright for certain perils or the loss settlement is reduced by a certain percentage after a specific time period. The following chart provides an overview of the effect of an unoccupied and vacant risk on four of the most common policies used today. For complete policy language refer to policy forms.

<table>
<tr><th>Name of Policy</th><th>Unoccupied</th><th>Vacant ‡</th></tr>
<tr><td>Dwelling</td><td rowspan="2">No effect †</td><td rowspan="2">If vacant over 60 consecutive days, no coverage applies to loss caused by Vandalism & Malicious Mischief, Accidental Discharge, Damage by Burglars or Glass Breakage.</td></tr>
<tr><td>Homeowner</td></tr>
<tr><td>Commercial Property</td><td rowspan="2">No effect †</td><td rowspan="2">If vacant over 60 consecutive days, no coverage applies to loss caused by: Vandalism & Malicious Mischief; Building Glass Breakage; Water Damage; Theft or Attempted Theft.

All other covered losses are reduced by 15%.</td></tr>
<tr><td>Businessowners</td></tr>
<tr><td colspan="3">† Although unoccupancy will not affect coverage, failure to maintain heat will eliminate coverage due to freezing and subsequent water damage.
‡ Buildings under construction are not considered vacant.</td></tr>
</table>

SPECIAL NOTE: Unoccupancy status requires more than just some contents within a home or building. Technically, a residential home must contain enough basic contents to support its intended use (e.g., food, utilities, bed, etc.). In a commercial policy, an owner occupant or tenant occupant must have enough business personal property to conduct customary operations. In the event the commercial building is owner occupied, at least 31% of the total square footage of the building must be rented and/or occupied for customary operations, otherwise it will be considered as vacant.

THIRD PARTY PROVISIONS

Third party provisions address the rights of third parties in the insurance contract. These third parties include mortgage companies, that may have a secured interest in a home, a financing company which may have an unsecured interest in an automobile, or a bailee who may seek coverage under a policy. The following addresses these third party provisions:

- **Standard Mortgage Clause** is a basic provision of all property policies *covering real property*. It **reflects the legitimate interest that mortgage holders have in real property in which they have a financial interest**. Mortgage holders are entitled to receive payment for losses and may act in the absence of the insured. For example, if an insured does not pay his or her homeowners insurance premium on time, the mortgage company may pay the premium or secure replacement coverage. Similarly, if the insured fails to adhere to the loss conditions (i.e., cooperate with the insurer in a claims investigation), the mortgage company may act for the insured to protect it's interest in the damaged property. Please note that fraudulent conduct upon the part of an insured will not void the mortgage holders right to recover. For example, if the insured burns down his home, the insurer is required to pay-off the mortgage balance. Mortgagees (i.e., mortgage holder) must be notified of cancellation. See SP-1 & SP-16.

- **Loss Payable Clause** is a basic provision of all property policies *covering personal property* such as automobiles and leased equipment. It **reflects the legitimate interest that the finance company has in personal property in which it has a financial interest**. Loss payees will be named on the check issued by the insurer to reflect their legitimate interest in the damaged property. Loss payees (i.e., finance company) must be notified of cancellation.

- **No Benefit to Bailee** provision is a basic condition of all property policies. **Its purpose is to exclude any assignment or granting of any policy provision to any person or organization holding, storing or moving property for a fee**. A bailee is any person who takes another's property for service or storage. For example, if an insured has clothes serviced at a cleaners, no coverage may be assigned under the insured's Homeowners Policy to benefit that cleaner/bailee. This means the insured's Homeowners Policy will not cover the liability of a bailee for property in the bailee's possession.

RELATED PENNSYLVANIA REGULATIONS

The following are Pennsylvania regulations addressing various aspects of the property and casualty field:

- **Binders** are temporary insurance contracts. These contracts may be made orally or in writing **for a period not exceeding 30 days**. In practice, agents bind coverage orally and immediately issue standard binder forms to the insured and insurer evidencing coverage.

- **Pennsylvania Insurance Guaranty Association Act** provides a means of covering claims for certain property and casualty insurance policies. Protection is provided to insureds who are covered by **admitted/authorized carriers** that subsequently become insolvent. Coverage is provided up to **$300,000 per covered claim and $10,000 per policy for a covered claim for the return of unearned premium**. All admitted property and casualty insurers must belong to the association. **The members of the association are subject to assessment to provide funds to carry out the purpose of this act**. This act does not cover life insurance, annuities, accident and health insurance, title insurance, credit insurance on accounts receivable, mortgage guaranty insurance, surety insurance, ocean marine insurance and Workers Compensation insurance. Producers **are prohibited from advertising the existence of the state guarantee fund** for the purpose of sales, solicitation or inducement to purchase any form of insurance covered by this act.

- **Countersignature and fees** addresses the requirement that all policies written by resident producers must be countersigned by a resident producer. An exception to this requirement is home office or departmental issued policies if such policies are issued on applications procured and submitted by licensed resident producers who receive commissions. Policies written by nonresident producers to cover domestic exposures do not require a resident producer's signature. Fees may be charged on commercial business, however, they must be reasonable for the services performed. **No fee is permitted for placing business in the Pennsylvania FAIR Plan or Pennsylvania Automobile Assigned Risk Plan.**

- **Basic Property Insurance - Death of the Named Insured** provision limits the insurer's ability to cancel a risk due to the death of the insured occupant. It requires basic property insurance to remain in effect for: **1) 180 days after the insured's death,** *or* **2) until the end of the policy period,** *whichever is later.* This provision is incorporated in basic property policies including the Dwelling Policy and Homeowner Policy.

- **Insurance Consultation Services Exemption Act** provides that the insurer, its agents, employees or service contractors are not liable for damages from injury, death or loss occurring as a result of any act or omission relating to surveys, consultations or inspections. **This Act does not apply if** the injury, death or loss occurred during the actual performance of the services or if the acts or omissions are judicially determined to constitute a crime, actual malice or gross negligence.

- **Terrorism Risk Insurance Act (TRIA) of 2002** is a federal program that provides up to $100 billion in the event of terrorism attack. The federal government pays 90% of the insured losses in excess of the insurer's deductible. Federal participation is triggered when the Secretary of Treasury, Secretary of State and the Attorney General certifies an act of terrorism. To qualify under TRIA, the certified act must (1) be a violent act, (2) result in damage in the US or to a US air carrier or ship, (3) be committed by someone acting on behalf of any foreign interest, and (4) result in aggregate losses in excess of $5 million. Terrorism coverage is required to be offered to all commercial policyholders by endorsement.

CANCELLATION AND NONRENEWAL

As a general rule, insurance policies permit cancellation and/or nonrenewal by **advance written notice** which may be either mailed or delivered in person to the insured. Policies may be cancelled by the insured or by the insurer. When this occurs, policies are cancelled as either:

- **Short rate**, meaning the insured requested the cancellation. In these instances, a penalty will be charged against the return premium; or

- **Pro rate**, meaning the insurer requested the cancellation. In these instances, the actual proportion of the unearned premium will be returned to the insured.

Policies which are issued by the company that are not taken and are returned are cancelled **flat rate**, meaning no premium is exchanged and no coverage provided.

The following are the advance cancellation and nonrenewal notice requirements for Pennsylvania:

PENNSYLVANIA CANCELLATION AND NONRENEWAL REQUIREMENTS *			
	15 Days	**30 Days**	**60 Days**
Homeowner Policy † **Dwelling Policy** (owner occupied) †			
Nonpayment of premium		●	
Material misrepresentation/increase in hazards		●	
Personal Auto Policy			
In effect for less than 60 days or any driver whose license is revoked/suspended within one year of issuance.	●		
Nonpayment of premium	●		
Material misrepresentation			●
Commercial Policies **Dwelling Policy** (nonowner occupied)			
In effect for less than 60 days		●	
In effect more than 60 days			
Nonpayment of premium	●		
Material misrepresentation	●		
Underwriting reasons ‡			●

† After policy is in effect for 60 days cancellation/nonrenewal is only permitted due to increase in hazard.
‡ Increase in risk factors, loss of reinsurance and failure to comply with policy conditions.
* See specific policy chapters for respective detailed cancellation/nonrenewal provisions.

Furthermore, cancellation and nonrenewal notices for property policies must include a notification advising the insured of the availability of the FAIR Plan.

OVERVIEW

STANDARD FIRE POLICY

The Standard Fire Policy and its predecessor policies were developed by the fire insurance industry as a means of providing uniform fire coverages. These policy forms were eventually standardized into the 1943 New York Standard Fire Policy. The policy lists the applicable conditions in a 165 line format and requires the attachment of additional forms which address important aspects of coverage. Today, the Standard Fire Policy has been replaced with the introduction of the Homeowner Policy, the Dwelling Policy, the Businessowners Policy and the Commercial Property Policy. Although the Standard Fire Policy itself has been phased out of day-to-day use by most insurance companies, its conditions and policy provisions have become the basis of most property policies. In addition, *Pennsylvania law requires that all property policies issued in this Commonwealth contain policy language which, at a minimum, is equal to the policy language of the Standard Fire Policy*. For these reasons it is important to understand the Standard Fire Policy. See specimen page SP-1 for an illustration of the 165 line Standard Fire Policy format.

FRIENDLY FIRE V. HOSTILE FIRE

The peril of **fire** is not defined in the Standard Fire Policy, or any of its successor policies, however, its meaning has been well established by courts. The usual definition is "**oxidation sufficiently rapid to cause a flame or glow.**" This is important since the definition excludes such occurrences as charring and scorching. Fire is defined into the following two classes:

- **Friendly Fire**, which is a deliberately ignited flame or glow that **stays within its intended confines**. Examples of friendly fire include fire within heating, cooking or lighting units.

- **Hostile Fire**, which is fire that **escapes its intended confines**. Examples of hostile fire include damage caused by a log rolling out of a fireplace or a hot ash which falls from a cigarette. Although not specifically stated, the **Standard Fire Policy only provides coverage for hostile fire.**

Please note that although the Standard Fire Policy has been basically phased out of everyday use, successor policies have adopted most of its provisions. In fact, the Dwelling Policy Basic Form (see Chapter Four) closely mirrors the Standard Fire Policy.

KEY TERMS AND CONCEPTS

The following terms were introduced in this chapter. You should know each word and concept and be able to apply them in everyday usage. To improve retention, it is recommended that you write out each key term and concept in your own words.

Abandonment
Actual Cash Value
Additional Insureds
Additional/Supplemental Coverages
Aggregate Limits
Agreed Value Approach
Appraisal
Arbitration
Assumption of Risk
Binders
Blanket v. Specific Insurance
Cancellation and Nonrenewal
Cancellation Method
Cause of Loss
Claims Procedures
Class or Manual Rating
Coinsurance
Combined Single Limit
Comparative Negligence
Compensatory Damages
Concealment
Conditions
Consequential or Indirect Loss
Contribution by Equal Shares
Contributory Negligence
Countersignature and Fees
Declarations
Deductibles
Definitions
Direct Loss
Duties of the Insured
Duties of the Insurer
Endorsements
Exclusions
First Named Insured
Frame
Friendly Fire
Full Reporting (Honesty Clause)
Functional Replacement Cost
General Damages
Hazards
Hostile Fire
Individual or Judgment Rating
Insurable Interest
Insured
Insuring Agreement
Intentional Torts/Intentional Acts
Intervening Cause
Liberalization Clause
Limits of Liability
Loss Cost Rating
Loss Payable Clause
Loss Ratios
Market Value
Masonry
Merit Rating
Named Insured
Named Perils v. Special Form
No Benefit to Bailee
Nonconcurrency
Other Insurance
Pennsylvania Insurance Guarantee Act
Per Occurrence Limits
Per Person Limits
Policy Period
Policy Territory
Primary and Excess
Pro Rata
Property Insurance v. Liability Insurance
Punitive Damages
Rating
Replacement Cost
Reporting Forms
Restoration of Limits
Salvage
Short Rate
Special Damages
Split Limits
Standard Fire Policy
Standard Mortgage Clause
Stated Value
Statute of Limitations
Statutory Defenses
Strict or Absolute Liability
Timely Reporting and Full Reporting
Transfer of Rights & Duties-Assignment
Transfer of Rights & Recovery-Subrogation
Types of Construction
Underwriting
Unintentional Torts/Negligence
Unoccupancy
Vacancy
Vicarious Liability
Waiving Coinsurance

REVIEW QUESTIONS

Before attempting to answer the end chapter practice questions, you should ask yourself if you can answer the following questions. It is recommended that you write out each review question in your own words. This exercise will help you apply the key terms and concepts that you've learned to form relationships with different topics.

1. What is the purpose of underwriting? (3-1)

2. Explain loss, expense and combined ratios. (3-2)

3. Explain manual, judgment, merit and loss cost rating. (3-2)

4. Identify and explain 3 types of hazards. (3-3)

5. What is third party insurance and how does it differ from two party insurance? (3-3)

6. What are causes of loss? (3-4)

7. How does a named peril policy differ from a special form policy? (3-4)

8. How do direct losses differ from indirect losses? (3-5)

9. What are reporting forms and when are they used? (3-6)

10. Why is the type of construction important to underwriters? (3-6)

11. How does the loss valuation provision actual cash value differ from replacement cost? (3-7)

12. How does the loss valuation provision replacement cost differ from functional replacement cost? (3-7)

13. What is the purpose of the conditions of a policy and name 3 common conditions? 3-8)

14. What is the purpose of the exclusion of a policy and name 5 common exclusions? 3-9)

15. Identify and explain the 4 types of insured status. (3-9)

16. Identify and explain the 4 types of other insurance provisions found in policies. (3-10)

17. Explain the difference between policy limits and sublimits. (3-11)

18. What is the primary purpose of coinsurance and state the formula? (3-12)

19. What are torts and are they covered under liability policies? (3-13)

20. What are the 4 primary elements of a negligent act? (3-13)

21. How does common law differ from statutory law? (3-13)

22. Identify and explain 3 common law defenses. (3-14)

23. Identify and explain 2 statutory defenses. (3-14)

24. Identify and explain 4 types of damages. (3-14)

25. What is strict or absolute liability? (3-15)

26. What is vicarious liability? (3-15)

27. Identify and explain 5 types of limits of liability. (3-15)

28. Identify and explain 5 duties of an insured after a property loss. (3-16)

29. Identify and explain 4 duties of an insured after a liability loss. (3-16)

30. Explain the transfer of rights and duties provision. (3-16)

31. Explain the abandonment provision. (3-17)

32. How does appraisal differ arbitration? (3-17)

33. Explain the liberalization clause. (3-17)

34. Explain the transfer of rights provision. (3-18)

35. What is salvage? (3-18)

36. What are 3 property claim settlement options available to insurers after a loss? (3-18)

37. What is the duty to defend provision? (3-18)

38. How does unoccupany differ from vacancy? (3-18)

39. What affect does vacancy have on a dwelling or homeowner policy? (3-19)

40. What affect does vacancy have on a commercial property or businessowners policy? (3-19)

41. Explain the no benefit to bailee clause. (3-20)

42. What is the Pennsylvania Insurance Guaranty Association Act? (3-21)

PRACTICE EXAM THREE

ON

PROPERTY AND CASUALTY INSURANCE BASICS

1. **Hazards are exposures that may cause or increase the likelihood that a loss will occur. Which of the following describes a type of hazard?**

   A) Physical hazard.
   B) Moral hazard.
   C) Morale hazard.
   D) All of the above. Ref. 3-3

2. **All of the following would be considered a hazard EXCEPT:**

   A) Trash and debris in the basement of a home.
   B) Properly stored paint and related solvents.
   C) Broken steps and hand railings.
   D) Overloaded electrical wiring. Ref. 3-3

3. **Illegal gambling or the illegal use of narcotics would be an example of a:**

   A) Physical hazard.
   B) Moral hazard.
   C) Morale hazard.
   D) Psychology hazard. Ref. 3-3

4. **The perils covered in a policy may be described as:**

   A) Something that increases the possibility of loss.
   B) The certainty of a loss.
   C) The cause of a loss.
   D) The uncertainty of loss. Ref. 3-4

5. **Negligence may be defined as:**

   A) Any crime.
   B) Failure to use reasonable or prudent care.
   C) An intentional act that results in injury.
   D) An unintentional act that results in injury. Ref. 3-13

6. **All of the following are Common Law Defenses EXCEPT:**

   A) Contributory negligence.
   B) Intervening cause.
   C) Statute of limitations.
   D) Assumption of risk. Ref. 3-14

7. **Which of the following describes Contributory Negligence?**

A) Negligence that is apportioned between parties.
B) Any degree of negligence by the injured party may bar recovery.
C) The time period in which a lawsuit must be filed.
D) The voluntary assumption of exposure to risk. Ref. 3-14

8. **Which of the following describes the Common Law Defense of Assumption of Risk?**

A) Negligence that is apportioned between parties.
B) Any degree of negligence by the injured may bar recovery.
C) The time period in which a lawsuit must be filed.
D) The voluntary assumption of exposure to risk. Ref. 3-14

9. **Which of the following describes the Common Law Defense of Intervening Cause?**

A) The time period in which lawsuits must be filed.
B) An interruption in the required chain of events.
C) The voluntary assumption of exposure to risk.
D) The voluntary relinquishment of a known right. Ref. 3-14

10. **Which of the following is a Statutory Defense?**

A) Contributory negligence.
B) Comparative negligence.
C) Intervening cause.
D) Assumption of risk. Ref. 3-14

11. **Which of the following describes Comparative Negligence?**

A) Negligence that is apportioned between parties.
B) Any degree of negligence may bar recovery.
C) The time period in which a lawsuit must be filed.
D) The voluntary assumption of exposure to risk. Ref. 3-14

12. **Vicarious liability may be defined as:**

A) The time period in which a lawsuit must be filed.
B) The preservation of the rights of a deceased to claim damages for the wrongful death.
C) Liability which is imputed from one to another.
D) The voluntary assumption of exposure to loss. Ref. 3-15

13. **Negligent liability is the failure to exercise the care that a reasonable or prudent person would under similar circumstances. All of the following are elements of negligent liability EXCEPT:**

A) A legal duty and a breach of that duty.
B) Resulting injury or damage to another person.
C) Proximate cause.
D) Absolute cause. Ref. 3-13

14. All the following legal defenses may eliminate or reduce a person's legal liability EXCEPT:

A) Assumption of risk.
B) Comparative negligence.
C) Intervening cause.
D) Strict liability. Ref. 3-14

15. The type of liability that is imposed regardless of fault or negligence is:

A) Comparative negligence.
B) Strict or absolute liability.
C) Intentional liability.
D) Contributory negligence. Ref. 3-14

16. Which of the following definitions best describes Special (Open Peril) coverage?

A) Only perils listed in the policy are covered.
B) Provides coverage for direct loss unless specifically excluded.
C) Provides coverage for "all risks".
D) None of the above. Ref. 3-4

17. Which of the following definitions best describes Specific (Named Peril) Coverage?

A) Only perils listed in the policy are covered.
B) Provides coverage for direct physical loss unless specifically excluded.
C) Provides coverage for "all risks".
D) None of the above. Ref. 3-4

18. Which of the following definitions best describes a direct loss?

A) Consequential damages to a building.
B) Actual physical damage to an insured risk.
C) Any covered peril is a direct loss.
D) An unintentional act. Ref. 3-5

19. Which of the following would be an example of a direct loss?

A) Loss of business income due to a covered peril.
B) Additional living expenses due to fire.
C) Fire to a house.
D) Extra expense incurred due to a covered peril. Ref. 3-5

20. All of the following are direct losses EXCEPT:

A) Windstorm to a house.
B) Lightning to an apartment building.
C) Loss of rental income to the apartment if it becomes uninhabitable due to a covered peril.
D) Vandalism to a building. Ref. 3-5

21. Which of the following definitions best describes an indirect or consequential loss?

A) Actual physical damage to an insured risk.
B) The results or consequences of a direct loss.
C) The named perils of the policy.
D) The intentional damage to covered property. Ref. 3-5

22. Which one of the following is NOT a common means of writing property insurance?

A) Specific coverage.
B) Blanket coverage.
C) Scheduled coverage.
D) Manuscript coverage. Ref. 3-5

23. Which of the following best describes scheduled limits?

A) Specific coverage to one location.
B) Specific coverage to several specific locations.
C) Specific single blanket coverage to all locations.
D) Specific coverage at one location. Ref. 3-5

24. All of the following are characteristics of Reporting Forms EXCEPT:

A) To report accurate values for insurance.
B) Used when business has fluctuating inventories.
C) To provide excess insurance.
D) Requires timely reporting. Ref. 3-6

25. All the following are true of timely reporting requirements of reporting forms EXCEPT:

A) A penalty may apply for failure of timely reporting.
B) If reports are not processed timely, the most recent report may be used.
C) Reporting forms contain a full reporting (honesty) clause.
D) Reporting requirements may be waived by the insured. Ref. 3-6

26. The primary purpose of the full reporting or honesty clause is to:

A) Promote proper values and proper coverage amounts.
B) Provide excess coverage for inventories.
C) Eliminate correspondence between the insured and company.
D) All of the above. Ref. 3-6

27. Which of the following is NOT required of an insured after a loss?

A) Notify the insurer as soon as possible.
B) Protect property from further loss.
C) Notify a public adjuster.
D) Notify police in case of theft. Ref. 3-16

28. Which of the following is NOT a part of the claims process?

A) Appraisal.
B) Subrogation.
C) Arbitration.
D) Aleatory. Ref. 3-17 & 3-18

29. Property insurance policies contain a valuation clause that determines how exposures are to be valued. All of the following are methods to value property EXCEPT:

A) Excluded value.
B) Replacement value.
C) Actual cash value (ACV).
D) Market value. Ref. 3-7

30. Actual Cash Value (ACV) is:

A) Arbitration value.
B) Replacement cost minus depreciation.
C) Market value minus depreciation.
D) Determined in a court of law. Ref. 3-7

31. The valuation type that after a loss occurs will replace damaged property with like kind and quality at today's cost is:

A) Market value.
B) Actual cash value (ACV).
C) Replacement value.
D) Guaranteed value. Ref. 3-7

32. Which of the following is a common provision found in liability policies that promotes claim settlements and helps in reducing legal expenses?

A) Subrogation.
B) Adhesion.
C) Arbitration.
D) Abandonment. Ref. 3-17 & 3-18

33. All of the following are true of insurable interest EXCEPT:

A) It is the interest one has in property or in one's life.
B) In property and casualty insurance it is required to exist at the time of loss.
C) In property and casualty insurance it is only required to exist at time of application.
D) It reduces the possibility of the speculative wagering on another's property. Ref. 3-1

34. Which of the following is true of the Contribution by Equal Shares provision?

A) Losses are paid equally by all policies.
B) After one policy is exhausted, all other policies cease payment.
C) Contributions are proportional based upon face amount.
D) Losses are paid equally until one policy is exhausted, requiring the second policy to pay until the claim is satisfied or the second policy is exhausted. Ref. 3-11

35. Which of the following are the four primary components that make up the typical property casualty insurance policy?

A) Declarations, Insuring agreement, Conditions, and Exemptions.
B) Declarations, Implied agreement, Conditions, and Exclusions.
C) Declarations, Insuring agreement, Conditions, and Exclusions.
D) Definitions, Insuring agreement, Conditions, and Exclusions.

Ref. 3-9

36. Which of the following policy structure components describes insurance terms?

A) Definitions.
B) Declarations.
C) Insuring Agreement.
D) Exclusions.

Ref. 3-8 & 3-9

37. Which of the following policy structure components indicates the named insured, address, policy and related specifics about the risk insured?

A) Endorsements.
B) Declarations.
C) Insuring Agreement.
D) Exclusions.

Ref. 3-8 & 3-9

38. Which of the following policy structure components specifically eliminates coverage?

A) Definitions.
B) Declarations.
C) Insuring Agreement.
D) Exclusions.

Ref. 3-8 & 3-9

39. Which of the following policy structure components alters the initial policy declarations?

A) Definitions.
B) Conditions.
C) Insuring Agreement.
D) Endorsements.

Ref. 3-8 & 3-9

40. Which of the following policy structure components sets forth the insured's and insurer's rights and duties?

A) Conditions.
B) Declarations.
C) Insuring Agreement.
D) Exclusions.

Ref. 3-8 & 3-9

41. Which of the following policy structure components provides coverages in addition to the covered perils of the policy?

A) Conditions.
B) Declarations.
C) Supplementary coverages.
D) Definitions.

Ref. 3-8 & 3-9

42. Which of the following describes a deductible?

A) The amount paid if underinsured.
B) The amount waived for compliance of the coinsurance provisions.
C) The first dollar cost absorbed by the insured in the event of a covered loss.
D) None of the above. Ref. 3-10

43. All of the following are true of the coinsurance clause EXCEPT:

A) Penalizes the insured for not satisfying the coinsurance requirement.
B) Usually requires insurance to 80% of the property's ACV or replacement cost.
C) It offers the insured a reduced rate if coinsurance is satisfied.
D) Guarantees full payment regardless of the limit of insurance. Ref. 3-12

44. A primary purpose of the coinsurance requirement is to:

A) Make the insured a co-insurer.
B) Promote adequate amounts of insurance coverage.
C) Eliminate the necessity of determining the ACV.
D) Make the insured a self insurer. Ref. 3-12

45. Which of the following describes the relationship to determine the loss settlement under a typical coinsurance clause?

A) Insurance carried over insurance required times loss amount.
B) Insurance required over insurance carried times loss amount.
C) 80% of insurance amount times loss.
D) None of the above. Ref. 3-12

46. Determine the loss payment of the following situation with an 80% coinsurance clause: Building value $100,000 - Coverage amount $40,000 - Loss amount $10,000.

A) $10,000
B) 5,000
C) 40,000
D) 80,000 Ref. 3-12

47. Determine the loss payment of the following situation with an 80% coinsurance clause: Building value $100,000 - Coverage amount $60,000 - Loss amount $10,000.

A) $10,000
B) 5,000
C) 7,500
D) 80,000 Ref. 3-12

48. Determine the loss payment of the following situation with an 80% coinsurance clause: Building value $100,000 - Coverage amount $80,000 - Loss amount $90,000.

A) $10,000
B) 5,000
C) 40,000
D) 80,000 Ref. 3-12

49. Which of the following describes the Agreed Value method of insuring property?

A) A predetermined value is placed on the risk and the coinsurance clause is waived.
B) Insurance carried over insurance required times the loss amount.
C) Provides special "all risk" type coverage regardless of the coinsurance clause.
D) Insurance required over insurance carried times loss amount. Ref. 3-7

50. Policies that cover the same property but on a different coverage basis is:

A) Similar coverage.
B) Concurrent coverage.
C) Nonconcurrent coverage.
D) Open Peril coverage. Ref. 3-10

51. Excess coverage would apply to a loss after:

A) Agreed value coverage.
B) Primary coverage.
C) Named peril coverage.
D) Special form coverage. Ref. 3-11

52. The Pro-Rata Clause provides:

A) Proportional coverage to losses when two or more policies apply.
B) Excess liability coverage to losses when two or more policies apply.
C) Primary coverage to losses.
D) Contributions by equal shares when two or more policies apply. Ref. 3-11

53. The insured under a contract of insurance includes:

A) Only the named insured as listed in the declarations.
B) Anyone who may be covered by the insurance.
C) Only the owners of the property insured.
D) None of the above. Ref. 3-9

54. All of the following are true statements concerning first named insureds EXCEPT:

A) First named insured is the primary person responsible for contractual duties.
B) First named insured is responsible for paying insurance premiums.
C) First named insured is responsible for pursuing subrogation.
D) First named insured is responsible for cancelling the policy. Ref. 3-9

55. Which of the following describes a Combined Single Limit of Liability?

A) The liability limit which is divided between BI and PD resulting from any one accident.
B) The liability limit which combines BI and PD resulting from any one accident.
C) The liability limit which only provides medical coverage.
D) None of the above. Ref. 3-15

56. A Per Person Limit of Liability refers to:

A) The maximum limit of liability per accident.
B) The maximum limit of liability per person per accident.
C) The excess limit of liability per accident.
D) None of the above. Ref. 3-15

57. An Aggregate Limit of Liability refers to:

A) The maximum limit of liability per contract term.
B) The maximum limit of liability per person per accident.
C) The excess limit of liability per accident.
D) None of the above. Ref. 3-15

58. The Split Limits of 100,000/300,000/50,000 means:

A) BI of 100,000 per person/300,000 per accident/PD of 50,000 per accident.
B) PD of 100,000 per accident/300,000 per accident/BI of 50,000 per person.
C) MP of 100,000 per accident/300,000 per accident/BI/ of 50,000 per person.
D) None of the above. Ref. 3-15

59. Which of the following are duties of the insured?

A) Pay the premium.
B) Provide prompt notice of loss.
C) Protect property from further damage.
D) All of the above. Ref. 3-16

60. All of the following are duties of the insurer EXCEPT:

A) Pay losses according to provisions of the policy.
B) Advise the insured in writing of cancellation.
C) Return premiums due the insured.
D) Reject losses without proper notification. Ref. 3-17

61. The Transfer of Rights and Duties (assignment) under a typical property policy:

A) Is never permitted.
B) Is only permitted with the written consent of the insured.
C) Is only permitted with the written consent of the insurer.
D) Is only permitted with the written consent of the Insurance Commissioner. Ref 3-16

62. The Transfer of Rights of Recovery (subrogation) under a typical property policy provides for all of the following EXCEPT:

A) Provides for the insurer the authority to bring legal action against negligent third parties only to the extent of the insured loss.
B) Subrogation is closely related to the Principle of Indemnity.
C) Subrogation eliminates the possibility of the insured collecting twice.
D) Subrogation is only a provision of commercial policies. Ref. 3-18

63. **All of the following are examples of the underwriting process EXCEPT:**

A) Completing and reviewing the application for insurance.
B) Classifying and rating of the risk.
C) Paying the insured a fair settlement after a loss occurs.
D) Developing an inspection report and property value. Ref. 3-1

64. **What ratio is commonly referred to when attempting to determine the overall profit or loss of a property and casualty company?**

A) Expense ratio.
B) Profit ratio.
C) Loss ratio.
D) Combined ratio. Ref. 3-2

65. **Which of the following insurance companies, based upon its combined ratio would be considered the most profitable:**

A) Company A with a combined ratio of 99.
B) Company B with a combined ratio of 107.
C) Company C with a combined ratio of 96.
D) Company D with a combined ratio of 131. Ref. 3-2

66. **Reporting forms as used in property insurance are characterized by all of the following EXCEPT:**

A) Reporting forms are used to report accurate values for insurance.
B) Reporting forms are generally used when businesses have fluctuating inventories.
C) Reporting forms are generally used to provide excess insurance.
D) Reporting forms require timely reporting of values. Ref. 3-6

ANSWER KEY

1-D	2-B	3-B	4-C	5-B	6-C	7-B	8-D	9-B	10-B
11-A	12-C	13-D	14-D	15-B	16-B	17-A	18-B	19-C	20-C
21-B	22-D	23-B	24-C	25-D	26-A	27-C	28-D	29-A	30-B
31-C	32-C	33-C	34-D	35-C	36-A	37-B	38-D	39-D	40-A
41-C	42-C	43-D	44-B	45-A	46-B	47-C	48-D	49-A	50-C
51-B	52-A	53-B	54-C	55-B	56-B	57-A	58-A	59-D	60-D
61-C	62-D	63-C	64-D	65-C	66-C				

CHAPTER FOUR
DWELLING POLICY

OVERVIEW

DWELLING 2002 POLICY

The Dwelling Policy provides insurance coverage for **residential rental properties up to four units**, or **occupied by no more than five roomers or boarders**. Certain incidental occupancies, such as offices and studios, are permitted. **Risks written under this program generally are ones which do not qualify for the broader coverages of the Homeowner Policy** (see Chapter Five). The unendorsed Dwelling Policy provides property coverages indicated by the coverage letters A, B, C and D. Additional coverages may be added by endorsement. These additional coverages include automatic increase coverage, theft coverage and personal liability coverage. The insured property *can be tenant or owner occupied, however, the vast majority of dwelling policies are tenant occupied.* A Dwelling Policy may be written on a **Basic Form (DP 00 01), Broad Form (DP 00 02) or Special Form (DP 00 03)** basis as illustrated below.

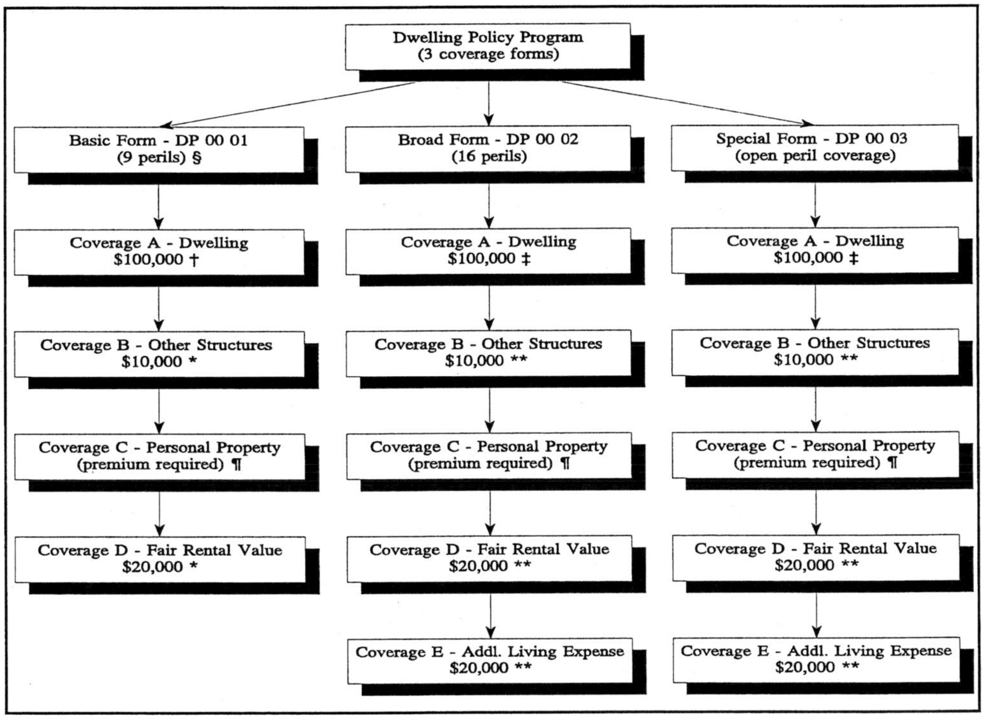

§ Includes Fire, EC & VMM.
† Illustrated amount of $100,000 is reduced by 20% on Basic Form if Other Coverages are elected.
‡ Illustrated amount of $100,000 is unaffected on Broad & Special Forms by the 10% Other Coverage election.
* Illustrated amount of $20,000 (20% of Coverage A) is reduced if Other Coverages option is elected.
** Illustrated amount of $20,000 (20% of Coverage A) is additional insurance for Other Coverage.
¶ If Coverage C - Personal Property premium is paid, 10% of Coverage C limit may be applied for Improvements, Alterations and Additions under Other Coverages. If this option is elected, it reduces Coverage C limit on Basic Form and is additional insurance on Broad and Special Forms. Also, all dwelling forms limit off premises coverage for personal property up to 10% of the Coverage C limit.

COVERAGE A - DWELLING

Coverage A - Dwelling provides **coverage for the dwelling, including structures attached to the dwelling** at the described premises as shown in the declarations. Materials and supplies located on or next to the residence premises used to construct, alter or repair the dwelling or other structure is covered along with building and outdoor equipment (if not insured elsewhere) used to service the dwelling.

COVERAGE B - OTHER STRUCTURES

Coverage B - Other Structures provides **coverage for other structures on the described location that are set apart by clear space**. An example would be a detached garage or storage building. Other structures used in part or in whole for commercial, manufacturing, farming purposes, or rented to anyone other than a tenant of the dwelling, are not covered **except for use as a private passenger garage or to store manufacturing or farming property.** The insured may carry a coverage limit under Coverage B - Other Structures and pay the required premium or choose to elect the Other Coverage option of 10% of Coverage A - Dwelling amount. See Other Coverages on page 4-3 for additional explanation.

COVERAGE C - PERSONAL PROPERTY

Coverage C - Personal Property provides **coverage for personal property usual to the occupancy of a dwelling owned by the insured** or members of the insured's family, while residing at the described location. **At the insured's request**, coverage will be provided for personal property owned by a guest or servant. Coverage will also be provided for personal property for **up to 30 days if a new principal residence is acquired**. Under Coverage C - Personal Property, off premises coverage is limited to 10% of the limit of Coverage C, **except for rowboats and canoes which are specifically excluded**. Rowboats and canoes *located on the premises are covered if loss is caused by a covered peril.* Coverage C - Personal Property **excludes or limits the following personal property:**

- Accounts, bank notes, bills, bullion, coins, currency, deeds, evidence of debt, gold other than goldware, letters of credit, manuscripts, medals, notes other than bank notes, passports, personal records, platinum, securities, silver other than silverware, tickets, stamps, credit cards, electronic fund or access cards.
- Animals, birds and fish.
- Aircraft/parts **except model/hobby aircraft not used to carry people or cargo**.
- Motor vehicles and their equipment or accessories, **other than motorized equipment to service the described location**.
- Watercraft, **other than rowboats and canoes;** Hovercraft and their parts.
- Data, including data stored, books, drawings, records, electronic data processing tapes, wires, discs and software media. Coverage is provided for the cost of **blank recording media and programs available on the retail market**.
- Water, steam, or gravemarkers including mausoleums.

Coverage C - Personal Property coverage requires the selection of a limit of liability and the payment of the appropriate premium.

COVERAGE D - FAIR RENTAL VALUE

Coverage D - Fair Rental Value provides coverage for **the fair rental value in the event the dwelling at the described location becomes uninhabitable due to an insured peril**. For example, if a two unit rental property is damaged by fire and its fair rental value is $500 per month per unit, the insured will receive $1,000 per month. The insured may carry a coverage limit under Fair Rental Value and pay the required premium or choose to elect the Other Coverage option of 20% of Coverage A - Dwelling amount.

COVERAGE E - ADDITIONAL LIVING EXPENSE

Coverage E - Additional Living Expense provides coverage for **necessary increases in living expenses incurred by the insured in the event the dwelling at the described location becomes uninhabitable due to an insured peril**. This coverage only applies if the insured is a resident of the dwelling. The following is an illustration of how the Additional Living Expense coverage is applied:

ADDITIONAL LIVING EXPENSE ILLUSTRATION			
Expense	Normal Monthly Expenses	New Monthly Expenses	Additional Monthly Expenses
Rent	$700	$1,025	$325
Gas	100	120	20
Water	30	50	20
Electricity	145	175	30
Telephone	15	45	30
Food	200	350	150
Totals	**$1,190**	**$1,765**	**$575**
Number of months apartment is uninhabitable			**3**
Amount payable to insured under Additional Living Expense			**$1,725**

The insured may carry a coverage limit for additional living expenses and pay the required premium or choose to elect the Other Coverage option of 20% of Coverage A - Dwelling. This Other Coverage option does not apply to the Dwelling Basic Form.

OTHER COVERAGES

Other Coverages are automatically provided under each Dwelling Policy at no additional cost. The other coverages include the following:

- **Other Structures** coverage permits the insured to **apply up to 10% of the Coverage A amount to other structures described** in Coverage B. Use of this amount **does not reduce the Coverage A** limit of liability.*

- **Debris Removal** coverage reimburses the insured for reasonable expenses incurred by the insured **for the removal of debris caused by a covered peril**. Debris removal is included in the limit of liability applying to the damaged property.

- **Improvements, Alterations and Additions** provides coverage to a tenant of the described location, for damage to property made to the rental unit. An example would be a built-in book shelf installed by the tenant which is damaged by an insured peril. Under this coverage the insured may **apply up to 10% of the Coverage C limit** for loss to **improvements, alterations and additions**. Use of this coverage **does not reduce the Coverage C** limit of liability.*

- **Worldwide Coverage** permits the insured to **apply up to 10% of the Coverage C amount for personal property** covered by an insured peril **except** for rowboats and canoes while anywhere in the world. Use of this coverage **reduces the Coverage C limit of liability**.

- **Rental Value and Additional Living Expense** permits the insured to **apply up to 10% of the Coverage A** amount for loss of rental value and additional living expenses.** Use of this amount **does not reduce the Coverage A** limit of liability.

- **Reasonable Repairs** coverage reimburses the insured for expenses incurred by the insured for reasonable repairs. Reasonable repair coverage is **included in the limit of liability** applying to the damaged property.

- **Property Removal** extends coverage for property removed from the premises because of endangerment from an insured peril, for **not more than 30 days on broad and special form coverage, and 5 days on basic form** coverage. This coverage does not change the limit of liability applying to the property removed.

- **Trees, Shrubs and Other Plants** provides up to 5% of Coverage A subject to a **$500 limit per tree, per shrub and per other plant** on the described location for loss **caused by** fire, lightning, explosion, riot, civil commotion, aircraft, vehicles not owned or operated by the insured or a resident of the described location, or VMM including damage during a burglary or attempted burglary, but not theft of the property. This coverage is **additional insurance and is only provided under the Broad and Special Forms**.

- **Fire Department Service Charge** provides up to **$500 for liability** assumed by the insured for fire department service charges to protect covered property. This coverage is **additional insurance and no deductible applies** to this coverage.

- **Ordinance and Law** provides up to 10% of the Coverage A limit for any increase in a loss that is the result of a building ordinance or law.†

- **Collapse** provides coverage for the direct physical loss to covered property caused by: perils insured against in Coverage C (see broad form perils); hidden decay; hidden insect damage; weight of contents, equipment, animals or people, and; use of defective building materials or methods in construction, remodeling or renovation. Collapse does not include settling, cracking, or bulging expansion.†

- **Glass or Safety Glazing Material** provides coverage for breakage of glass and safety glazing materials (60 day vacancy applies).†

* **Application of Other Coverage provisions reduces amounts payable on Basic Form.**
** **Additional Living Expense is only provided on Broad and Special Forms.**
† **Ordinance/Law, Collapse and Glass are only provided under the Broad and Special Forms.**

GENERAL EXCLUSIONS

Exclusions apply to specific perils, persons, property, locations or occurrences listed in the policy that eliminate coverage. The following are the applicable Dwelling Policy general exclusions. **They appear in all property policies.**

- **Ordinance or law**, meaning enforcement of any ordinance or law requiring or regulating the construction, demolition, remodeling or repair of property including the removal of any debris. For example, if an older dwelling is damaged by a covered peril and new building codes require improvements in the reconstruction process, those improvements are not covered under the policy. This exclusion can be eliminated by endorsement. Please note the base Dwelling Policy provides up to 10% of the Coverage A amount for this exposure.

- **Earth movement**, meaning earthquake, including tremors, landslide, mine subsidence or mudflow. Direct loss caused by fire or explosion resulting from earth movement is covered. For example, no coverage would apply if the insured dwelling was damaged by earthquake or mine subsidence, however, if a gas line broke during an earthquake or because of mine subsidence causing a fire that damages the dwelling, coverage would apply to the ensuing fire damage. The peril of earthquake can be insured by endorsement.

- **Water damage**, meaning flood, surface water or the backing up of sewers or drains. Direct loss caused by fire or explosion resulting from water damage is covered. For example, no coverage would apply if the insured dwelling was damaged by flood, however, if a gas line broke during a flood causing a fire that damages the dwelling, coverage would apply to the ensuing fire damage. The peril of flood can be insured under a Flood Policy (see Chapter 10).

- **Power failure**, meaning the failure of power taking place off the described location, but if a peril ensues on the premises, the ensuing peril is covered. For example, if a utility power station fails causing loss of electricity, no coverage applies to food spoilage at the described location. However, if the water pipes freeze and break causing water damage to the dwelling, coverage applies. This example does not apply to the basic form.

- **Neglect**, meaning failure of the insured to use reasonable steps to save and protect property from further damage. For example, if a fire damages the dwelling the insured must attempt to save and protect the property. In the event the insured fails to do so, the insurance company is not responsible for the loss.

- **War**, including undeclared war, insurrection and rebellion. This exclusion eliminates coverage in the event a war damages covered property.

- **Nuclear hazard** as defined in the nuclear hazard clause. This clause eliminates coverage for nuclear hazards and clarifies that a loss caused by nuclear reaction will not be considered fire, explosion or smoke.

- **Intentional loss**, meaning acts carried out by an insured with purpose and knowledge of their consequences.

- **Governmental Action** which eliminates coverage for damage caused by a governmental authority except when attempting to stop the spread of fire.

The following are excluded for Coverages A & B, **however, any ensuing loss to property not excluded is covered**:

- **Weather conditions** that are concurrent with any general exclusion. For example, if an earthquake causes structural damage to a dwelling at the same time heavy winds and rain drives water into the dwelling, no coverage applies.
- **Acts or decisions** as a person/member of any organization or governmental body. For example, if an individual monitoring a dam accidentally releases too much water into a river causing flooding, no coverage applies.
- **Faulty, inadequate or defective** planning, design, workmanship and maintenance. For example, if a contractor designs a drainage system which causes the earth to move a dwelling off its foundation, no coverage applies.

These exclusions will appear in every special form policy.

CONDITIONS

The conditions part of the policy **sets forth the duties and rights of both insured and insurer**. The following are the conditions of the Dwelling Policy. **Almost all of the following items were discussed in chapter three**. They will continue to reappear in other policies with slight variations.

- **Policy Period** defines the term of insurance coverage. It is the period in which the loss must occur for coverage to apply. For example, if a loss occurs on 6/30/05, and the policy period is 1/1/05 to 1/1/06, this policy will respond regardless if the claim is reported during the policy period or after the policy period.
- **Insurable Interest and Limit of Liability** condition provides that coverage is afforded to the insureds who have an insurable interest in the property at the time of loss, and for no more than the policy limit.
- **Concealment or Fraud** condition voids coverage for material misrepresentations (typically made at the time of application) and/or fraudulent statements (typically made at the time of loss).
- **Your Duties After Loss** condition sets forth the insured's duties to give prompt notice to the company, to protect the property from further damage, to make reasonable and necessary repairs, to prepare an inventory of damaged property, to show the damaged property and provide the company with records as requested, and to submit to the company within 60 days after requested the insured's sworn proof of loss setting forth damages.
- **Loss Settlement** condition addresses how claims will be adjusted. Under the **basic form**, both personal property and dwelling losses are adjusted at actual cash value with no coinsurance requirement. Actual cash value means replacement cost minus depreciation. Under the **broad and special forms**, personal property, awnings, carpeting, household appliances, outdoor antennas/outdoor equipment and structures which are not buildings are adjusted on an actual cash value basis. However, the dwelling is adjusted on a replacement cost basis. Replacement cost means replacement with like kind and quality at today's cost. Under the broad and special form, the insured is required to carry coverage equal to 80% of the dwelling's value at the time of loss to avoid a loss adjustment penalty. In the event the dwelling is underinsured, the insurance company will pay the greater of the actual cash value or the proportionate cost to repair the damaged property.

- **Loss to a Pair or Set** condition permits the insurer the right to restore the part damaged or lost to its value prior to loss, or to pay the difference between its ACV of the property before and after the loss.
- **Glass Replacement** condition requires the **replacement with safety glazing material** when required by ordinance or law.
- **Appraisal** condition sets forth the rights of both the insured and insurer to demand an appraisal if loss values cannot be agreed upon.
- **Other Insurance** condition (1) prorates losses by face amounts if more than one policy is in effect at the time of loss and is (2) excess if a warranty applies.
- **Subrogation** permits the insurer to recover from negligent third parties.
- **Suit Against Us** requires compliance with policy conditions, including the initiation of legal actions within two years of loss.
- **Our Option** condition permits the insurer the right to repair or replace damaged property rather than make a claim payment. The insurer may exercise this option if they give the insured written notice within 15 days of receipt of the insured's proof of loss.
- **Loss Payment** condition requires payment within 60 days of receipt of proof of loss, appraisal or judgment.
- **Abandonment of Property** condition prohibits the insured from abandoning the property to the insurer and claiming a total loss.
- **Mortgage Clause** addresses the rights of the mortgagee, including the right to be named on loss drafts and the right to act for the insured to protect its interest.
- **No Benefit to Bailee** condition prohibits assignment of coverage that benefits any organization holding property for a fee.
- **Cancellation** condition permits cancellation by advance written notice.
- **Liberalization Clause** broadens coverage when new forms are introduced, at no additional premium.
- **Waiver or Change of Policy Provisions** requires changes to be in writing.
- **Assignment** of the policy is prohibited without approval of the insurer.
- **Death** condition makes the insured's legal representative an insured. It also requires the insurer to cover the property for: **(1) 180 days after the insured's death,** *or* **(2) until the end of the policy period,** *whichever is later.*
- **Nuclear Hazard Clause** describes and specifically excludes nuclear hazards.
- **Recovered Property** requires both insured and insurer to notify each other of any recovered property.
- **Volcanic Eruption Period** defines multiple volcanic eruptions within a 72 hour period to be considered as one occurrence.

DWELLING POLICY BASIC FORM - DP 00 01

Dwelling Policy Basic Form provides basic form coverage on a named peril basis with losses adjusted on an actual cash value basis. This means depreciation will be applied against the replacement cost of the damaged property in determining a loss settlement. **This policy closely resembles the Standard Fire Policy** discussed in Chapter Three. The following perils are provided under the basic form:

- **Fire and lightning.**
- **Internal explosion.**

The insured may pay an additional premium to obtain the following extended coverages (EC) and/or Vandalism or Malicious Mischief (V&MM):

- **Windstorm and hail**, excluding awnings, antennas, signs, trees, shrubs, canoes.
- **Explosion.**
- **Riot and civil commotion.**
- **Aircraft.**
- **Vehicles**, excluding loss to fences and driveways caused by the insured or resident.
- **Smoke.**
- **Volcanic eruption**, other than loss caused by earthquake, land shock or tremors.
- **Vandalism or Malicious Mischief, excluding** loss to glass and safety glazing material constituting part of the building **(except for glass block)**; for pilferage, theft or burglary; to property on the described location if the dwelling has been **vacant for more than 60 consecutive days prior to loss**. A dwelling under construction is not considered vacant.

Please note that in most instances the basic form is written with the EC and VMM coverages.

DWELLING POLICY BROAD FORM - DP 00 02

Dwelling Policy Broad Form provides broad form coverage on a named peril basis with the following additional perils provided:

- **Damage by burglars**, meaning damage caused by burglars in an attempt to steal property. If the dwelling has been **vacant for more than 60 consecutive days prior to the loss**, no coverage applies to this peril.
- **Falling objects,** meaning damage done to the dwelling exterior caused by a falling object. *Coverage does not apply to interior damage caused by a falling object unless the falling object caused exterior damage first.*
- **Weight of ice and snow**, excluding awnings, fences, pavements and retaining walls. For example, if a heavy snow causes a roof to collapse, coverage would be provided. However, if a heavy snow causes an awning or fence to collapse, no coverage applies.
- **Accidental discharge or overflow of water or steam** from within a plumbing system. Coverage does not apply to the system or appliance from which the water leaked, nor is there coverage due to freezing if the dwelling was **vacant for more than 60 consecutive days prior to the loss**.
- **Sudden and accidental tearing apart, cracking, burning or bulging** from within a plumbing system.
- **Freezing**, unless the insured has failed to use care or maintain heat.
- **Sudden and accidental damage from artificially generated electrical current**, excluding loss to tubes, transistors or similar electronic components.

The Dwelling Policy Broad Form is a replacement cost form and requires the insured to carry coverage equal to 80% of the dwelling's replacement cost at the time of loss to avoid a loss settlement penalty.

DWELLING POLICY SPECIAL FORM - DP 00 03

The Dwelling Policy Special Form provides special form coverage that goes beyond the named peril coverage of the basic and broad forms. This means coverage will be provided for **risk of direct physical loss unless specifically excluded**. The following are the special form exclusions:

- Freezing, **unless the insured has used reasonable care or maintained heat.**
- Freezing, thawing, pressure or weight of water or ice to a fence, pavement, patio, swimming pool, foundation, retaining wall, bulkhead, pier, wharf or dock.
- Theft of any property **which is not actually part of the building**.
- Theft **to a dwelling or structure under construction**.
- Wind, hail, ice, snow, or sleet damage to: outdoor radio and television antennas; lawns, trees, shrubs or plants; and rowboats and canoes.
- Vandalism and Malicious mischief, theft or breakage of glass and safety glazing materials **if the dwelling has been vacant for more than 60 consecutive days** immediately prior to loss.
- Continuous or repeated **seepage from water systems**.
- Wear and tear; marring; deterioration; inherent vice; latent defect; mechanical breakdown; smog; rust or other corrosion; mold, wet or dry rot; smoke from agricultural smudging or industrial operations; discharge, dispersal, seepage, migration release of pollutants; settling, shrinking, bulging or expansion, including resultant cracking of pavements, patios, foundations, walls, floors, roofs, or ceilings; birds, vermin, rodents, insects or domestic animals. **If any of these cause water to escape from** a plumbing, heating or air conditioning system or household appliance, the **coverage for water damage is provided**. The company **covers the cost to tear out and replace any part of the building** necessary to repair the system or appliance, but **does not cover the system or appliance itself**.

The same 80% replacement cost loss adjustment provision that applies to the Dwelling Policy Broad Form applies to the Dwelling Policy Special Form.

<table>
<tr><th colspan="5">DWELLING POLICY COVERAGES and LOSS SETTLEMENT COMPARISON</th></tr>
<tr><th rowspan="2">Policy Coverage Forms</th><th colspan="2">Coverage A & B</th><th>Other Coverages</th><th rowspan="2">Used to Insure</th></tr>
<tr><th>Peril Coverage</th><th>Loss Settlement</th><th>Other Structures
Fair Rental Value
Add'l Living Expenses †</th></tr>
<tr><td>Basic Form DP 00 01</td><td>Named</td><td>ACV</td><td>If elected reduces Coverage A limit by 20%</td><td rowspan="3">Used primarily to insure dwellings which do not qualify under the Homeowners Program</td></tr>
<tr><td>Broad Form DP 00 02 *</td><td>Named</td><td>RC</td><td rowspan="2">If elected is additional insurance of 20% of Coverage A limit</td></tr>
<tr><td>Special Form DP 00 03 *</td><td>Special</td><td>RC</td></tr>
<tr><td colspan="5">* Under the Broad and Special Form, coverage equal to 80% of the dwelling's replacement value must be maintained in order to avoid a loss settlement penalty.
† Does not apply to the Basic Form.</td></tr>
</table>

ENDORSEMENTS

The following are endorsements which are commonly attached to a Dwelling Policy.

- **Automatic Increase in Insurance** provides for increases in coverage amounts to reflect increase in inflation. This endorsement provides an annual increase of 4%, 6% or 8% on Coverages A and B. For example, if a dwelling was insured for $100,000 at policy inception, and the insured chose the 8% automatic increase in insurance endorsement, the policy will have increased to $108,000 by the end of the policy year.

- **Broad Theft Coverage** may be added to all dwelling policies. The peril theft is defined as theft, attempted theft and vandalism and malicious mischief damage resulting from the theft act. Coverage **applies to owner occupied dwellings** subject to the following limitations:

  - $200 on money, bank notes, bullion, gold (other than goldware), silver (other than silverware), platinum, coins and medals;
  - $1,500 on securities, accounts, deeds, evidences of debt, letters of credit, manuscripts, passports, personal records, tickets and stamps;
  - $1,500 on watercraft including trailers, furnishings and outboard motors;
  - $1,500 on trailers not used with watercraft;
  - $1,500 on jewelry, watches and furs, precious and semi-precious stones;
  - $2,500 on firearms; and
  - $2,500 on silverware and goldware including trophies made of this material.

  Property excluded from coverage includes: Aircraft and parts; motor vehicles and accessories; property held for as a sample or for sale; animals; birds, and fish; credit cards or fund transfer cards; and property separately insured.

  Broad Form Theft **offers both on-premises and off-premises coverages** with a separate limit of liability. This endorsement is very similar to the theft limitation provided under the Homeowner Policy.

- **Dwelling Under Construction** provides coverage for the named insured for dwellings under construction and by endorsement permits the naming of additional insureds, such as contractors. The premium under this endorsement is calculated at 65% of the completed value premium. This type endorsement will also be available with other policies.

- **Building Ordinance and Law Coverage** provides coverage if, at the time of loss, stricter building ordinances require construction different than originally designed. It also provides coverage for demolition if the building is beyond reconstruction due to a covered peril. This type endorsement will also be available with other policies.

- **Sinkhole Collapse** provides coverage for sudden settlement or collapse of the earth supporting the property if caused by subterranean voids created by the action of water on limestone or similar rock formation. This type endorsement will also be available with other policies.

- **Personal Liability Supplement Coverages "L" and "M"** provides Liability and Medical Payments to Others in the event a claim or suit is brought against an insured by a third party for damages because of bodily injury or property damage caused by an occurrence. Under Coverage L - Liability, the insurer will **provide a legal defense and pay up to the limit of liability for damages for which the insured is legally liable**. Defense costs and related interest charges levied on a verdict are paid in addition to the policy's limit of liability. Under Coverage M - Medical Payments to Others, the insurer will **pay medical payments regardless of fault up** to the medical payments limit.

  The Personal Liability Supplement may be added to any Dwelling Policy form to create a package policy (property and liability). Coverage limits are a minimum $100,000 for personal liability, and $1,000 for medical payments. Liability coverages and exclusions are similar to the exclusions found in the liability section of the Homeowner Policy. (See Chapter 5)

- **Standard Fire Policy Endorsement** requires the 165 line Standard Fire Policy Provisions be attached to all policies. The endorsement in effect prohibits any new policy language to be more restrictive than the 165 line fire policy.

- **Pennsylvania Notice (HO-291)** advises the insured that the insurance company, as a condition to issue or renew insurance coverage, may conduct surveys, consultations or inspections of the premises to reduce the likelihood of loss.

- **Water Back Up and Sump Overflow - Pennsylvania** provides coverage of up to $5,000 for direct physical loss to covered property damaged by water which backs up through sewers or drains or water which overflows from a sump even if caused by mechanical breakdown. A $250 deductible applies to this cause of loss.

- **Pennsylvania Changes - Cancellation and Nonrenewal** is the state mandated endorsement requiring advance written notice as follows:

PENNSYLVANIA DWELLING POLICY CANCELLATION REQUIREMENTS

Nonowner Occupied Dwelling Policies

Cancellation by the company is permitted with advance written notice:

If the policy has been in effect for less than 60 days:

- At least 30 days advance written notice is required.

If the policy has been in effect for more than 60 days:

- At least 15 days advance written notice for material misrepresentation and nonpayment of premium.
- At least 60 days advance written notice is required for increased risk factors, loss of reinsurance, failure to comply with policy conditions, or any other reason deemed by the insurance commissioner.

Cancellation by the named insured is permitted by:

- Giving advance written notice of the date cancellation will take effect.

Owner Occupied Dwelling Policies

- 30 days advance notice is required in all instances

DWELLING POLICY COMPARISON

NAMED PERIL	**Basic†**	**Broad**	**Special**
Fire, Lightning or Internal Explosion	●	●	●
Windstorm or Hail	●	●	●
Explosion	●	●	●
Riot or Civil Commotion	●	●	●
Aircraft	●	●	●
Vehicles	●	●	●
Smoke	●	●	●
Volcanic Eruption	●	●	●
Vandalism & Malicious Mischief	●	●	●
Damage by Burglars		●	●
Falling Objects		●	●
Weight of Ice and Snow		●	●
Accidental Discharge		●	●
Sudden/Accidental Tearing Apart/Cracking/Bulging		●	●
Freezing		●	●
Artificially Generated Electrical Current		●	●
Special Open Perils Coverage			●
† Includes EC & V&MM			

OTHER COVERAGES	**Basic**	**Broad**	**Special**
Other Structures	-10%	+10%	+10%
Debris Removal	●	●	●
Improvements/Alterations	-10%	+10%	+10%
Worldwide Contents Coverage (add'l premium required)	-10%	-10%	-10%
Rental Value	-20%	+20%	+20%
Additional Living Expenses		+20%	+20%
Reasonable Repairs	●	●	●
Property Removed	5 days	30 days	30 days
Trees, Shrubs and Plants		$500	$500
Fire Department Service	$500	$500	$500
Ordinance and Law		+10%	+10%
Collapse		●	●
Glass		●	●

PERSONAL PROPERTY NOT COVERED - Accounts, bills, bullion, deeds, manuscripts, money and securities, animals, birds, fish, aircraft and parts, motor vehicles other than motorized equipment to service the described location, watercraft other than rowboats and canoes, data including books, drawings, and electronic data processing media.

GENERAL EXCLUSIONS - Ordinance or law, earth movement, water damage, power failure, neglect, war and nuclear hazard, governmental action, intentional loss, weather conditions, acts or decisions and faulty, inadequate or defective planning.

SPECIAL PROPERTY EXCLUSIONS - Freezing, unless the insured has used reasonable care or maintained heat; freezing, thawing, pressure or weight of water or ice to a fence, pavement, patio, swimming pool, foundation, retaining wall, bulkhead, pier, wharf or dock; theft to any property which is not actually part of the building; theft to a dwelling or structure under construction; wind, hail, ice, snow, or sleet to outdoor radio and television antennas, lawns, trees, shrubs or plants; vandalism and malicious mischief, theft or breakage of glass and safety glazing materials if the dwelling has been vacant for more than 60 consecutive days immediately prior to loss; continuous or repeated seepage from water systems; wear and tear; marring; deterioration; inherent vice; latent defect; mechanical breakdown; smog, rust or other corrosion; mold, wet or dry rot; smoke from agricultural smudging or industrial operations; discharge, disposal, seepage, migration release of pollutants; settling, shrinking, bulging or expansion including resultant cracking of pavements, patios, foundations, walls, floors, roofs, or ceilings; birds, vermin, rodents, insects or domestic animals. If any of these cause water to escape from a plumbing, heating, or air conditioning system or household appliance, the coverage for water damage is provided. The insurer covers the cost to tear out and replace any part of the building necessary to repair the system or appliance, but does not cover the system or appliance itself.

KEY TERMS AND CONCEPTS

The following terms were introduced in this chapter. You should know each word and concept and be able to apply them in everyday usage. To improve retention, it is recommended that you write out each key term and concept in your own words.

Appraisal
Automatic Increase Endorsement
Broad Form Theft
Collapse
Concealment or Fraud
Conditions
Coverage A - Dwelling
Coverage B - Other Structures
Coverage C - Personal Property
Coverage D - Fair Rental Value
Coverage E - Additional Living Expenses
Debris Removal
Dwelling Policy Basic Form
Dwelling Policy Broad Form
Dwelling Policy Program
Dwelling Policy Special Form
Dwelling Under Construction
Earth Movement
Fire Department Service Charge
General Exclusions
Glass Or Safety Glazing Material
Improvements, Alterations & Additions
Intentional Loss
Loss Settlement
Loss to Pair or Set
Neglect
No Benefit to Bailee
Nuclear Hazard
Ordinance or Law
Ordinance or Law Endorsement
Other Coverages
Other Insurance
Pennsylvania Cancellation/Nonrenewal
Pennsylvania Notice (HO-291)
Personal Liability Supplement L & M
Personal Property not Covered
Power Failure
Property Removal
Reasonable Repairs
Rental Value/Additional Living Expense
Sinkhole Collapse
Standard Fire Policy Endorsement
Subrogation
Theft Endorsement
Trees, Shrubs & Other Plants
Vacancy Exposure
War
Water Backup and Sump Overflow
Worldwide Coverage

REVIEW QUESTIONS

Before attempting to answer the end chapter practice questions, you should ask yourself if you can answer the following questions. It is recommended that you write out each review question in your own words. This exercise will help you apply the key terms and concepts that you've learned to form relationships with different topics.

1. What types of properties are eligible under the Dwelling Policy? (4-1)

2. What does Coverage A - Dwelling Amount cover? (4-2)

3. What does Coverage B - Other Structures cover and give 4 examples? (4-2)

4. What does Coverage C - Personal Property cover? (4-2)

5. Identify and give examples of 6 categories of personal property that are not covered under the Dwelling Policy. (4-2)

6. What does Coverage D - Fair Rental Value cover? (4-3)

7. What does Coverage E - Additional Living Expense cover? (4-3)

8. Identify and explain the 12 Other Coverages provided under the Dwelling Policy. (4-4)

9. Identify and explain the 8 General Exclusions of the Dwelling Policy. (4-5)

10. Damage to trees, shrubs and plants is covered up to $500 if caused by what 8 perils? (4-4)

11. Explain the loss settlement provisions of the Dwelling Policy's Basic, Broad and Special forms. (4-6)

12. What do the perils vandalism or malicious mischief, damage by burglars, and accidental discharge or overflow of water have in common? (4-8)

13. Explain how liability coverage is provided under the Dwelling Policy. (4-11)

14. Under the Dwelling Policy's Basic Form, name the 2 coverages which if elected reduces the Coverage A - Dwelling Amount. (4-1)

15. Under the Dwelling Policy's Broad and Special Forms, name 2 coverages that provide an additional 20% coverage each. (4-1)

16. What important peril is excluded under the Dwelling Policy's Basic and Broad form and limited under the Dwelling Policy's Special form? (4-9 & 4-10)

PRACTICE EXAM FOUR

ON

THE DWELLING POLICY

1. **All of the following are characteristics of the Dwelling Policy EXCEPT:**

    A) Dwellings up to four units are eligible.
    B) The Dwelling Policy is used primarily to insure residential type exposures.
    C) The Dwelling Policy is used primarily to insure mercantile type exposures.
    D) Incidental occupancy of limited service type exposure is permitted. Ref. 4-1

2. **Under the Dwelling Policy's Broad and Special Forms, trees, shrubs and plants would be covered for damage caused by which peril?**

    A) Windstorm.
    B) Theft.
    C) Hail.
    D) Lightning. Ref. 4-4

3. **Under the Dwelling Policy, charges for fire department services are covered up to:**

    A) $100.
    B) $250.
    C) $500.
    D) $1,000. Ref. 4-4

4. **Which of the following would provide coverage to a garage not attached to the primary insured dwelling?**

    A) Coverage A - Dwelling.
    B) Coverage B - Other Structures.
    C) Coverage C - Personal Property.
    D) Coverage D - Loss of Fair Rental Value.
    E) Coverage E - Additional Living Expense. Ref. 4-2

5. **Which of the following would provide coverage to contents damaged in a fire?**

    A) Coverage A - Dwelling.
    B) Coverage B - Other Structures.
    C) Coverage C - Personal Property.
    D) Coverage D - Loss of Fair Rental Value.
    E) Coverage E - Additional Living Expense. Ref. 4-2

6. **All of the following claim losses would be excluded under the Dwelling Policy's Special Form EXCEPT:**

A) Theft of cash.
B) Theft of building materials.
C) Theft of a rowboat.
D) Theft of a stained glass window. Ref. 4-2 & 4-9

7. **Which of the following would provide coverage to the primary structure at the insured premises?**

A) Coverage A - Dwelling.
B) Coverage B - Other Structures.
C) Coverage C - Personal Property.
D) Coverage D - Loss of Fair Rental Value.
E) Coverage E - Additional Living Expense. Ref. 4-2

8. **Which of the following would provide coverage for additional living expenses incurred by the owner occupant in the event a covered peril made the premises uninhabitable (applicable only to forms DP 00 02 and DP 00 03)?**

A) Coverage A - Dwelling.
B) Coverage B - Other Structures.
C) Coverage C - Personal Property.
D) Coverage D - Loss of Fair Rental Value.
E) Coverage E - Additional Living Expense. Ref. 4-3

9. **All of the following are Other Coverages under the Dwelling Policy EXCEPT:**

A) Other Structures.
B) Debris Removal.
C) Reasonable Repairs.
D) Power Failure. Ref. 4-3, 4-4 & 4-6

10. **The Dwelling Policy's Basic Form DP 00 01 may be expanded to cover eight additional perils by adding:**

A) Broad Form Theft.
B) Personal Liability Supplement.
C) EC and V&MM.
D) Building Ordinance and Law. Ref. 4-7, 4-8, 4-10 & 4-11

11. **Which of the following is true if a dwelling is vacant for 60 or more consecutive days?**

A) Loss by Vandalism and Malicious Mischief is covered.
B) Loss by Vandalism and Malicious Mischief is excluded.
C) Damage to the dwelling caused by mine subsidence is covered.
D) Damage to building glass is covered. Ref. 4-8

12. **Under the Dwelling Policy's Broad and Special Forms, trees, shrubs and plants are covered for specified perils up to what individual dollar amount limitation?**

A) $100.
B) $300.
C) $500.
D) $1,000. Ref. 4-4

13. **All of the following are excluded losses under a Dwelling Policy EXCEPT:**

A) Damage to an other structure used for manufacturing purposes.
B) Damage to accounts, bills, bullion, currency, deeds, and debt instruments.
C) Damage to the dwelling caused by an internal explosion.
D) Damage to the dwelling caused by surface water. Ref. 4-2, 4-5 & 4-8

14. **To avoid a co-insurance penalty under the Dwelling Policy's Broad and Special Forms, the insured must carry coverage equal to 80% of a dwelling's replacement cost:**

A) At no time.
B) When the policy is written.
C) When the loss occurs.
D) When the claim is reported. Ref. 4-6

15. **Which of the following is true of the loss settlement provision of the Dwelling Policy's Basic Form:**

A) There is no insurance to value requirement.
B) There is a market value requirement.
C) There is an 80% insurance to value replacement requirement.
D) There is an 100% insurance to value replacement requirement. Ref. 4-6

16. **All of the following would be eligible for a Dwelling Policy EXCEPT:**

A) A four unit tenant occupied apartment building.
B) A one unit owner occupied building.
C) A hardware store.
D) A duplex with an accountant's office as an incidental occupant. Ref. 4-1

17. **The Broad Form DP 00 02 provides additional perils to the more limited basic form DP 00 01. All of the following are examples of these additional perils EXCEPT:**

A) Falling objects.
B) Damage caused by burglars.
C) Damage to animals, birds or fish.
D) Weight of ice and snow. Ref. 4-8

18. **Which of the following claims would be covered under the Dwelling Policy?**

A) Personal property damage caused by latent defect, rust, vermin or deterioration.
B) Fire to construction material on the premises for repairs.
C) Dwelling damage caused by settling, cracking and shrinking of foundation.
D) Theft of a riding lawnmower used to service the premises. Ref. 4-12

19. If an insured elects to apply the Other Coverages - Other Structures option that is applicable under the Dwelling Policy Basic Form, Coverage A will:

A) Be reduced by 20%.
B) Be increased by 20%.
C) Have no effect on the policy's limits of liability.
D) Is only applicable if the insured pays the additional premium. Ref. 4- 1 & 4-3

20. Under the Dwelling Policy, Coverage C - Personal Property is:

A) Automatically included as an Other Coverage.
B) Only provided when the insured pays the premium for the coverage.
C) Limited to 50% of the Coverage A - Dwelling Amount.
D) A prohibited coverage under all forms. Ref. 4-2

21. All of the following claim losses would be excluded under the Dwelling Policy EXCEPT:

A) Fire damage to a garage located on the insured premises used as a repair shop.
B) Death of the insured's dog due to smoke inhalation.
C) Theft of the insured's automobile stolen from the detached garaged.
D) Fire damage to the insured's rowboat located in the attached garage. Ref. 4-2

22. Under the Dwelling Policy, personal property located off-premises is limited to:

A) 10% of Coverage A - Dwelling Amount.
B) 10% of Coverage B - Other Structures.
C) 10% of Coverage C - Personal Property.
D) 100% of Coverage C - Personal Property. Ref. 4-2

23. A building owner, insured under a Dwelling Policy Broad Form (DP 00 02), turns off the heat in the insured building during the winter months. If the building's water pipes freeze and break causing damage:

A) The loss is excluded under all forms.
B) The loss is covered under all forms.
C) The loss is covered under the Special Form DP 00 03.
D) The loss can be insured by endorsement. Ref. 4-8

ANSWER KEY

1-C	2-D	3-C	4-B	5-C	6-D	7-A	8-E	9-D	10-C
11-B	12-C	13-C	14-C	15-A	16-C	17-C	18-B	19-A	20-B
21-D	22-C	23-A							

CHAPTER FIVE

HOMEOWNERS POLICY

OVERVIEW

HOMEOWNERS 2000 POLICY (Pennsylvania '01 Edition)

The Homeowners Policy provides insurance coverage for **owner occupied private residential exposures**. Eligible risks include **one to four family structures, apartment units, and condominium units**. The one to four family structures may not have more than two boarders or roomers per family. The apartment and condominium units may not have more than one additional family or two boarders or roomers. Certain incidental occupancies for office and studio use are permitted subject to limitations and exclusions.

DEFINITIONS

Definitions define terms as used in the policy. The purpose is to clarify and set forth the meaning of policy terms. The following are the Homeowner Policy definitions:

- **Aircraft, Hovercraft and Motor Vehicle Liability** is excluded except for the limited coverage provided by exception (see page 5-12 for exceptions).

- **Bodily Injury** is bodily harm, sickness or disease including required care, loss of services and death that results.

- **Business means trade, profession or occupation**, however, certain business activities are covered. They include: up to $2,000 in compensation; volunteer activities in which only expense reimbursement is received; home day care activity in which no compensation is received other than mutual exchange of services; home day care activity of a relative without compensation restriction.

- **Insured** is anyone who may be granted coverage under the policy. This means **the named insured; resident relatives** (including anyone related to the named insured by blood, marriage or adoption); **individuals under the age of 21 in the care of an insured** (such as a foster child or ward); **students enrolled full time in school** under the age of 24; **individuals and organizations authorized by the insured to use or supervise their watercraft, vehicles** (not requiring a license) **or animals** (pets). For example, if the insured permits an individual to operate his boat, use his riding lawnmower on the insured's premises, or watch his dog, that individual would be covered under the insured's Homeowner Policy.

- **Insured Location** means the **residence premises as shown in the declarations**; **vacant land owned by the insured**, including land where the insured is constructing a new home (land used for business purposes is excluded); **premises rented to the insured** (a hotel room or wedding hall); and **cemetery plots or burial vaults**.

- **Occurrence** means an accident, including continuous or repeated exposure to substantially the same general harmful conditions that result, during the policy period, in bodily injury or property damage.

- **Property Damage** means physical injury to, destruction of, or the loss of tangible property.

- **Residence Employee** is an employee whose duties are related to the maintenance of the residence (domestics) or one who performs similar duties.

- **Residence Premises** means the one to four family dwelling, other structures and grounds as indicated in the declarations. See SP-3 for an illustration of definitions.

HOMEOWNER POLICY STRUCTURE

The Homeowner Policy is divided into **two main parts**. **Section I provides property coverage** for the dwelling, other structures, personal property and loss of use. This is indicated in the policy by the **coverage letters A, B, C & D**. **Section II of the policy provides liability insurance and medical payments to third parties**. This is indicated in the policy by the **letters E & F**.

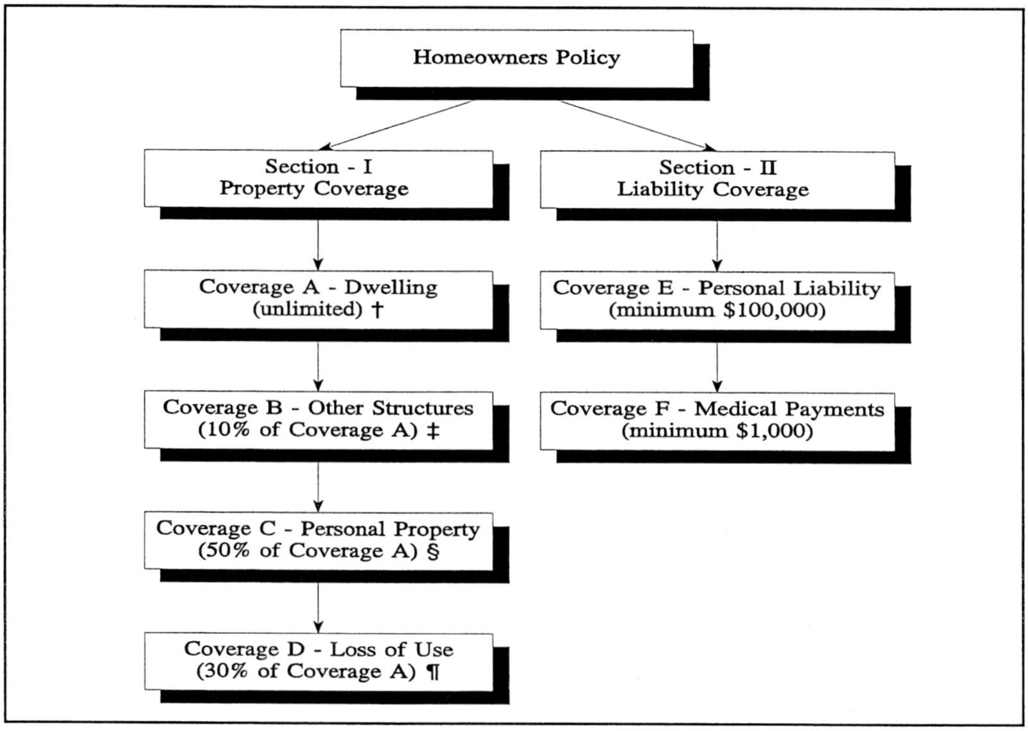

† Only limited by individual company's underwriting guidelines. No coverage limit is provided for the apartment unit coverage (HO 00 04) and $5,000 is provided for condominium unit owners (HO 00 06).

‡ Reduced to 5% on three-unit and four-unit dwellings.

§ Reduced to 30% on a three-unit dwelling and 25% on a four-unit dwelling.

¶ Reduced to 10% of the Coverage A amount for the Modified Form (HO 00 08). Apartment unit coverage (HO 00 04) is 30% of the Coverage C amount and condominium unit owners (HO 00 06) is 50% of the Coverage C amount.

COVERAGE A - DWELLING

Coverage A - Dwelling amount provides coverage for the **dwelling, including structures attached to the dwelling at the described premises** as shown in the declarations. **Materials and supplies** located on or next to the residence premises and used to construct, alter or repair the dwelling or other structure are covered with the following exception. Theft coverage would not apply to the building materials **until the insured has completed the construction and occupied the dwelling**. This requirement (completion and occupancy) does not apply if the insured is making renovations (room addition, etc.) to the residence already occupied.

COVERAGE B - OTHER STRUCTURES

Coverage B - Other Structures provides coverage for **other structures on the residence premises that are set apart by clear space**. Examples of other structures include detached garages, storage sheds, flag poles, fences and swimming pools. The coverage amount applicable to **Coverage B is 10% of Coverage A**. This is a blanket amount. Other structures **used for business are excluded**, except when the other structure is used as a private passenger garage or to store business property owned by the insured or tenant. (See SP-4)

COVERAGE C - PERSONAL PROPERTY

Coverage C - Personal Property provides coverage for **personal property owned or used by the insured anywhere in the world**. At the request of the insured, coverage is provided to personal property of others (e.g. guest), while on the residence premises occupied by the insured. Coverage is also provided to **personal property at a newly acquired principal residence for 30 days**. The coverage amount applicable to **Coverage C is generally 50% of Coverage A**. The following special limits of liability apply to each specific category of personal property (See SP-4):

- $ 200 on money, bank notes, gold, silver, platinum, scrip, stored or smart cards
- $1,500 on securities, accounts, deeds, manuscripts, passports, tickets and stamps
- $1,500 on watercraft including trailers, equipment and motors ***(premises only)***
- $1,500 on trailers not used with watercraft ***(premises only)***
- $1,500 on loss **by theft** of jewelry, watches, furs and precious stones
- $2,500 on loss **by theft** of firearms and related equipment
- $2,500 on loss **by theft** of silverware, goldware and pewterware
- $2,500 on business property located at the residence premises
- $ 500 on business property located away from the premises
- $1,500 on adaptable electronic apparatus **that is in or on a motor vehicle**
- $1,500 on adaptable electronic apparatus **away from the residence premises** and **used solely for business purposes**, while **not in or upon a motor vehicle**

Personal property usually located at a secondary residence ***(a weekend home or cabin)*** **is limited to 10% of Coverage C or $1,000, whichever is greater.**

Personal Property Not Covered - The following classes of personal property are not covered under the Homeowner Policy:

- Articles separately insured. For example, personal property scheduled on the HO 04 61 endorsement is not covered under Coverage C - Personal Property.
- Animals, birds or fish.
- Motor vehicles requiring motor vehicle registration and equipment, accessories, tapes, discs and other media operated solely by the vehicle's electrical system whether or not in or on the motor vehicle.
- Aircraft and parts except for model aircraft.
- Property of roomers and tenants not related to the insured.
- Property in an apartment regularly held for rent.
- Property rented or held for rental off the premises.
- Books, drawings, tapes and discs used in business (retail software is covered).
- Water or steam that is lost (e.g., water lost due to a broken pipe).

COVERAGE D - LOSS OF USE

Coverage D - Loss of Use refers to the **additional expenses incurred in the event the dwelling becomes uninhabitable due to an insured peril**. Loss of use provides coverage in two areas. **First**, for any necessary increases in living expenses incurred and **second**, for the fair rental value of the home. **The coverage amount applicable for Coverage D - Loss of Use is** 30% of the Coverage A amount on homeowner policies HO 00 02, HO 00 03 and HO 00 05; 10% of the Coverage A amount on the HO 00 08; 30% of the Coverage C amount on HO 00 04; and 50% of the Coverage C amount on the HO 00 06. Homeowner Loss of Use is calculated the same as the dwelling policy Coverages D and E. See page 4-3 for illustration.

ADDITIONAL COVERAGES - SECTION I

Additional Coverages are in addition to the basic peril coverage. They include:

- **Debris Removal** up to an additional 5% if the limit of insurance is exhausted. For example, if Coverage A - Dwelling is insured for $100,000 and *is totally destroyed by fire*, an additional $5,000 may be applied to cover debris removal. **Debris removal of trees** is also covered up to $1,000 ($500 per tree) if the:

  1) **Trees were felled by** windstorm or hail, or a Coverage C peril ***and*** the trees damaged a covered structure.
  2) **Governor of Pennsylvania declares** the area to be a disaster area.
  3) **Trees block a driveway or ramp for the handicapped** even if there is no damage to a covered structure.

- **Reasonable Repairs** incurred to protect property. For example, if high winds cause roof shingles to blow off a dwelling, the insured may have a roofer place a tarp over the damaged area and do reasonable and necessary repairs.
- **Trees, Shrubs and Other Plants** up to 5% of Coverage A subject to a **$500 limit per tree, per shrub and per other plant** on the residence premises **for loss by** fire or lightning, explosion, riot or civil commotion, aircraft, non-owned vehicles, V&MM and theft. **This is additional insurance.**

- **Fire Department Service Charge** of up to $500 for liability assumed by agreement for fire department charges to protect property. **This is additional insurance and no deductible applies.**
- **Property Removal** up to 30 days, to protect the property from further damage. For example, if a fire causes damage to a home, and the insured moves the property to protect it from further possible damage, it is covered up to 30 days.
- **Credit Card**, fund transfer card, forgery and counterfeit money, up to $500.
- **Loss Assessment** up to $1,000 for any assessment charged to the insured as the owner of the residence premises. *This protects owners of condominium units in the event the condominium association's property insurance is inadequate.*
- **Collapse** is the direct physical loss to covered property involving collapse of the building caused by: perils insured against in Coverage C; hidden decay; hidden insect damage; vermin damage; weight of contents, equipment, animals or people; weight of rain that collects on a roof; use of defective building materials or methods in construction, remodeling or renovation. For collapse coverage to apply, a falling down or a caving in of part of the building that makes it unfit for its current intended purpose must occur. Collapse does not include settling, cracking, shrinking, bulging or expansion. Collapse coverage does not apply to decks, awnings, fences, pavements, swimming pools, septic tanks, retaining walls and piers unless the loss is a direct result of a collapse of building.
- **Glass or Safety Glazing Material**, when not vacant beyond 60 days.
- **Landlord's Furnishings** up to $2,500 for loss by insured perils, **except theft**, to appliances, carpeting and other household furnishings in a residence premises apartment regularly rented or held for rent.
- **Ordinance and Law** provides up to 10% of the Coverage A limit for any increase in a loss that is the result of a building ordinance or law.
- **Grave Markers** up to $5,000.

PERILS INSURED AGAINST

The Homeowner Policy provides coverage for **direct physical loss to the property described in Coverages A, B and C as follows:**

- **Fire or lightning.**
- **Windstorm or hail.**
- **Explosion.**
- **Riot and civil commotion.**
- **Aircraft.**
- **Vehicles**, excluding loss to fences/driveways caused by an insured. This exception does not apply to the Special Form HO-3 or Comprehensive Form HO-5.
- **Smoke**, meaning sudden and accidental damage (i.e., a furnace malfunctions).
- **Vandalism and malicious mischief** (60 day vacancy applies).
- **Theft**, meaning theft from a known place or location. This peril does not apply to *trailers or watercraft off premises*, nor does it apply to a student's property at a residence, *if that student has been absent for longer than 60 consecutive days.*
- **Falling objects** (damage to interior only applies if there is exterior damage).
- **Weight of ice, snow and sleet**, excluding awnings, fences, etc.
- **Accidental discharge of water or steam** (60 day vacancy applies).

- **Sudden and accidental tearing apart, cracking, burning or bulging** of a steam or hot water heating system, air conditioning system or appliance for heating.
- **Freezing**, unless the insured has failed to maintain heat at all times.
- **Sudden and accidental discharge from artificially generated electrical current**, excluding tubes, transistors, electronic components or circuitry.
- **Volcanic eruption**, meaning lava flow, lava ash, airborne shock waves *but excluding earthquake, land shock waves or tremors*. See specimen pages SP-11 and SP-12 for illustration of policy perils insured against.

HOMEOWNER POLICY PROGRAM

The Homeowner Forms HO 00 02, HO 00 03, HO 00 05 and HO 00 08 are used to **insure one to four family owner occupied structures** and provide Coverages A, B, C, D, E and F. The HO 00 04 **contents form** is used to insure **apartment units** and the HO 00 06 **unit owners form** is used to insure **condominium units**. Both HO 00 04 and HO 00 06 are similar with minor variations in coverages. Under the HO 00 04, up to 10% of the Coverage C amount may be applied to improvements, alterations and additions to the unit. Under the HO 00 06, a $5,000 limit applies to Coverage A for building coverage. A separate commercial policy is used to insure the apartment and/or condominium building itself.

Homeowner Form HO 00 02 provides **broad form named peril coverages** for owner occupants of 1-4 family dwellings. This policy form is written on a replacement cost basis requiring the insured to carry insurance equal to 80% of the replacement value of the dwelling at the time of loss to avoid an underinsurance penalty.

Homeowner Form HO 00 03 provides **special form coverages for owner** occupants of one to four family dwellings. The special form coverage only applies to Coverage A and Coverage B. This policy form is also written on a replacement cost basis requiring the insured to carry insurance equal to 80% of the replacement value of the dwelling at the time of loss. **The only difference between the Homeowner Form HO 00 02 and the Homeowner Form HO 00 03** is that the Homeowner Form HO 00 03 provides Special Form coverage on Coverages A and B. All other provisions are identical.

Homeowner Form HO 00 04 provides **contents broad form named peril coverages** for tenant occupants of apartments. Coverage is similar to the HO 00 02 form with no coverage on the dwelling. The HO 00 04 form is written to insure the tenant's personal property and, therefor, **has no insurance to value requirement**.

Homeowners Form HO 00 05 provides **special form coverages for owner** occupants of one to four family dwellings. The special form coverage applies to Coverages A, B and C. This policy form is also written on a replacement cost basis requiring the insured to carry insurance equal to 80% of the replacement value of the dwelling at the time of loss. **The only difference between the Homeowner Form HO 00 05 and the Homeowner Form HO 00 03** is that the Homeowner Form HO 00 05 provides special form coverage on Coverages A, B and C, whereas, the Homeowners Form HO 00 03 only provides special form coverage to Coverages A and B. All other provisions are identical.

Homeowner Form HO 00 06 provides **unit owners broad form named peril** coverages to owner occupants of condominiums. Coverage is similar to the HO 00 04 form with minor variations (limited real property coverage) to reflect the coordination of coverages between the unit owner's HO 00 06 and the condominium association's commercial policy. The HO 00 06 is written to insure the owner's personal property and, therefor, **has no insurance to value requirement.**

Homeowner Form HO 00 08 provides **modified named peril coverage** to owner occupants of one to four family dwellings. This policy is **used primarily to insure older homes** which have wide disparities between replacement value and market value. Unlike the HO 00 02, HO 00 03 and HO 00 05 forms, the HO 00 08:

- **Does not require coverage equal to 80% of the replacement value of the dwelling at the time of loss.** This form permits the insured the option of selecting the amount of coverage desired with no insurance to value requirement. Under the HO 00 08, Coverage A - Dwelling and Coverage B - Other Structures are adjusted on a functional replacement cost basis. Coverage C - Personal Property is adjusted on an actual cash value basis.

- **The perils insured against are significantly fewer with the HO 00 08 than the HO 00 02, HO 00 03 and HO 00 05 forms.** For example, **coverage is excluded for** falling objects, weight of ice and snow, accidental discharge, rupture of heating and air conditioning systems, freezing, and artificially generated currents. Furthermore, **the peril of theft is limited to $1,000** and several other additional coverages are limited or excluded.

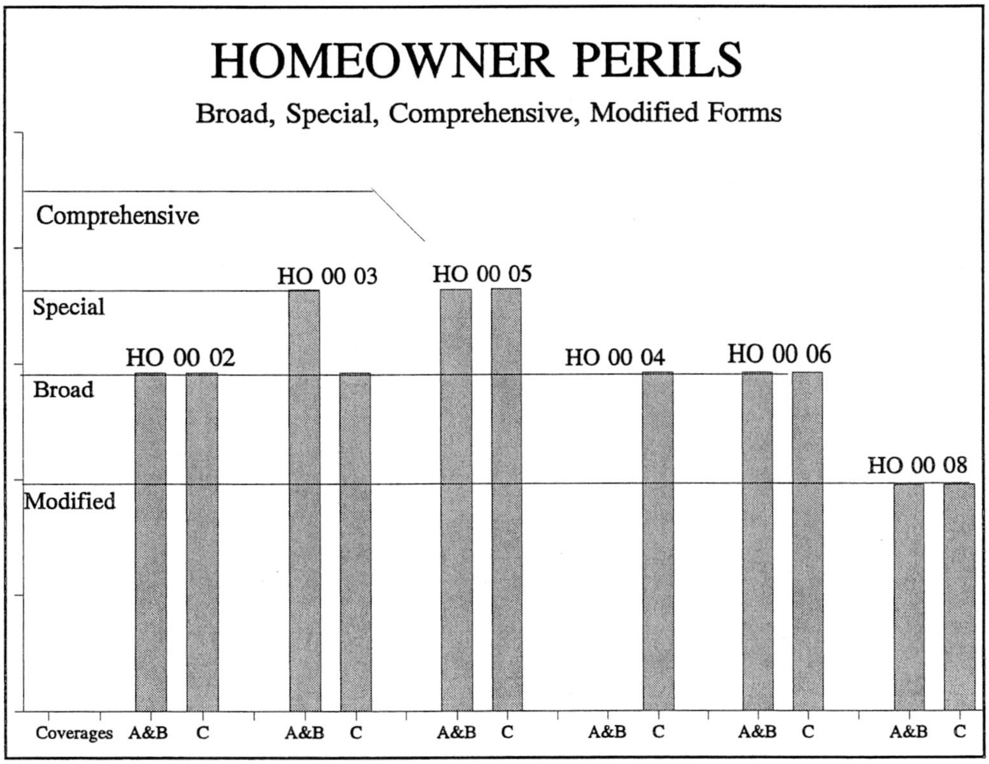

All of the above forms have identical Section II - Liability Coverages.

SECTION I - EXCLUSIONS

The following are the applicable Homeowner Policy exclusions. **Please note that most of these exclusions and limitations are identical to the Dwelling Policy.**

- **Ordinance or law**, meaning enforcement of any ordinance or law requiring or regulating the construction, demolition, remodeling or repair of property including the removal of any debris. This exclusion can be eliminated by endorsement. Please note that under Additional Coverages, 10% of Coverage A may be applied to cover losses for this exposure.

- **Earth movement**, meaning earthquake, including tremors, landslide, mine subsidence or mudflow. Direct loss caused by fire or explosion resulting from earth movement is covered. Earthquake coverage can be added by endorsement.

- **Water damage**, meaning flood, surface water or the backing up of sewers or drains. Direct loss caused by fire or explosion resulting from water damage is covered. The peril of flood can be insured under a Flood Policy.

- **Power failure**, meaning the failure of power taking place off the described location, but if a peril ensues on the premises, the ensuing peril is covered.

- **Neglect**, meaning failure of the insured to use reasonable steps to save and protect property from further damage.

- **War**, including undeclared war, insurrection and rebellion.

- **Nuclear hazard** as defined in the nuclear hazard clause. This clause eliminates coverage for loss caused by nuclear hazards and clarifies that a loss caused by nuclear reaction will not be considered fire, explosion or smoke.

- **Governmental Action** which eliminates coverage for damage caused by a governmental authority, except when attempting to stop the spread of fire.

- **Intentional loss**, meaning acts carried out with purpose and knowledge of the consequences. See specimen page SP-14 for an illustration of Section I - Exclusions.

Special Form Exclusions - The following are special form exclusions applicable to Coverages A & B, however, any ensuing loss to property not excluded is covered:

- **Weather conditions** that are concurrent with any general exclusion. For example, if an earthquake causes structural damage to a dwelling (an excluded peril) at the same time a windstorm (a covered peril), drives rain water into the dwelling, no coverage applies.

- **Acts or decisions** of a person/member of any organization or governmental body. For example, if an individual monitoring a dam accidentally releases too much water (a negligent act) into a river causing flooding (an excluded peril), no coverage applies.

- **Faulty, inadequate or defective** planning, design, workmanship and maintenance. For example, if a contractor designs a faulty or defective drainage system (a negligent act) which causes the earth to move a dwelling off its foundation (an excluded peril), no coverage applies.

SECTION I - PROPERTY EXCLUSIONS

The following property exclusions apply to all policy forms for damaged caused by:

- **Freezing** of plumbing, heating and air conditioning systems **if the insured failed to maintain heat in the building**
- Freezing or thawing of fences, pavements, patios, swimming pools, foundations, retaining walls or piers
- **Theft of building materials** on a dwelling under construction, **unless finished and occupied**
- Vandalism and malicious mischief or glass breakage **(60 day vacancy applies)**
- Wear and tear, marring and deterioration
- Inherent vice, latent defect and mechanical breakdown
- Smog, rust, mold **(unless hidden & caused by accidental discharge)** or wet rot
- Release of contaminants
- Settling, cracking, shrinking, bulging, or expansion of pavements, patios, foundations, retaining walls, floors or ceilings
- Birds, vermin, rodents, insects or animals owned or kept by an insured

If any of these cause water damage **not otherwise excluded**, from a plumbing, heating, air conditioning, or automatic fire protective system or household appliance, the insurer covers the loss caused by the water including the cost of tearing out and replacing any part of a building necessary to repair the system or appliance. The insurer does not cover loss to the system or appliance from which the water escaped.

CONDITIONS - SECTION I PROPERTY

The following conditions address policy provisions affecting claim settlement:

- **Insurable Interest and Limit of Liability** condition provides that coverage is afforded to insureds who have an **insurable interest in the property at the time of loss**, and for no more than the policy limit.
- **Your Duties After Loss** condition sets forth the insured's duties to give **prompt notice** to the insurer, **notify the police** in the event of theft, **notify the credit card company** of theft of credit cards, to **protect the property from further damage**, to **make reasonable and necessary repairs**, to **prepare an inventory** of damaged property, to show the damaged property and provide the insurer with records as requested and to **submit to the insurer within 60 days** after requested, the insured's **sworn proof of loss setting forth damages**.
- **Loss to a Pair or Set** condition permits the insurer the right to restore the part damaged or lost to its value prior to loss, or pay the difference between the ACV of the property before and after the loss. For example, if two earrings are valued at $1,000 before a loss, and the remaining one valued at $400 after one is stolen, the insurer will pay the difference. In this case, $600.
- **Glass Replacement** condition requires replacement with safety glazing material when required by ordinance or law.
- **Appraisal** condition sets forth the rights of both insured and insurer to demand an appraisal if property/loss values cannot be agreed upon.

- **Loss Settlement** condition addresses how claims will be adjusted. For example, personal property, awnings, carpeting, appliances and antennas are adjusted on **an ACV basis**, whereas, buildings (Coverages A and B) are adjusted **at replacement cost without depreciation**, if the insured has at the time of loss maintained coverage equal to at least 80% of the current replacement cost of the building. **In the event the dwelling is underinsured**, the insurer **will pay the greater of** the ACV or the proportionate cost to repair the damaged property.
- **Other Insurance** conditions prorates coverage if more than one policy is covering the insured property. See page 3-11 for illustration.
- **Other Service Agreement** condition makes the Homeowners Policy excess over other service agreements.
- **Suit Against Us** requires the compliance with policy conditions, including the initiation of **legal actions within two year of loss.**
- **Our Option** condition permits the insurer to repair or replace damaged property rather than making a claim payment. To exercise this option, written notice must be given to the insured within 15 days of receipt of the insured's proof of loss.
- **Loss Payment** condition requires payment within 60 days of receipt of proof of loss, appraisal or judgment.
- **Abandonment of Property** condition prohibits the insured from abandoning the property and claiming a total loss. For example, an insured may not abandon or discard property after a fire, since the insurance company may exercise its option to repair the property or salvage the damaged property.
- **Mortgage Clause** addresses the rights of the insured and mortgagee.
- **No Benefit to Bailee** condition prohibits any assignment of coverage that benefits any organization holding property for a fee. For example, if an insured has clothes serviced at a cleaners, no coverage may be assigned under the Homeowners Policy to benefit the cleaner/bailee.
- **Nuclear Hazard Clause** describes and excludes nuclear reactions or hazards.
- **Recovered Property** condition requires the insured to return recovered property for which the insurer has made payment.
- **Volcanic Eruption Period** is defined to include all eruptions occurring within a 72 hour period (See specimen page SP-14).

HOMEOWNER COVERAGE and LOSS SETTLEMENT COMPARISON

Policy Coverages	Coverage A & B		Coverage C		Used to Insure
	Peril Coverage	Loss Settlement	Peril Coverage	Loss Settlement	
HO 00 02	Named	RC	Named	ACV *	Average House
HO 00 03	Special	RC	Named	ACV *	Newer House
HO 00 04	N/A	N/A	Named	ACV *	Apartment Unit
HO 00 05	Special	RC	Special	ACV *	Newer House
HO 00 06	Named	RC	Named	ACV *	Condo Unit
HO 00 08	Named	FRC ‡	Named	ACV	Older House

* Personal Property Replacement Cost Endorsement (HO 04 90) may be added to all forms but HO 00 08.
‡ Adjusted on a Functional Replacement Cost basis.

LIABILITY COVERAGES - SECTION II

Liability coverages of the Homeowner Policy are listed under Section II of the policy. They are indicated in the policy by coverage letters E & F. (See SP-17)

COVERAGE E - PERSONAL LIABILITY

Coverage E - Personal Liability provides coverage in the event a claim or suit is brought against an insured for damages because of bodily injury or property damage caused by an occurrence. The insurance company will **provide a legal defense and pay up to the limit of liability for damages for which the insured is legally liable**. Defense costs and related interest charges levied on a verdict are paid in addition to the policy's limit of liability. (See SP-17)

COVERAGE F - MEDICAL PAYMENTS TO OTHERS

Coverage F - Medical Payments to Others provides coverage in the event an individual is injured and requires medical treatment. This **coverage does not apply to the insured or residents of the household**. Medical payments **may be made up to three years** from the date incurred or medically ascertained (See SP-17).

ADDITIONAL COVERAGES - SECTION II

Additional coverages are provided in addition to the perils of the policy. They include the following liability coverages (See SP-21):

- **Claim Expense**, meaning expenses incurred by the insured such as premiums on bonds, loss of earnings up to $250 per day for claims assistance, and interest on post-judgment verdicts.

- **First Aid Expense** meaning **immediate assistance** to aid others who are injured. For example, if a guest is injured at the insured premises, the insured may make voluntary payments for first aid, ambulance and related expenses.

- **Damage to Property of Others** up to $1,000, excluding amounts:

  - Recovered under Section I
  - Caused intentionally by an insured who is 13 years of age or older
  - To property owned by the insured or rented to a tenant or
  - Arising out of business pursuit

- **Loss Assessment** up to $1,000 for each act, for assessments charged. *This protects individuals who own condominium units in the event the condominium association's commercial general liability insurance is inadequate.*

SECTION II - LIABILITY AND MEDICAL PAYMENTS EXCLUSIONS

The following liability and medical payment exclusions apply to any occurrence:

- **Expected or intended by the insured**. For example, no coverage would apply to an insured who on purpose and with intent to injure, strikes another person. Please note that if the insured physically injures a person while attempting to protect himself, herself or another person, and or property, coverage applies.

- **Arising out of business pursuits**. For example, if an insured is operating a business from his or her home and a customer falls and is injured, no coverage would apply. Please note that an insured who is under the age of 21 and involved in a part-time or occasional business with no employees is covered. For example, if the insured's 15 year old son has a paper route and accidentally injures an individual while delivering newspapers, coverage applies. Please note that liability and medical payments coverage for business activities are generally excluded and may be covered by endorsement.

- **Arising out of the rental of any part of any premises**. ***This exclusion does not apply to the:***

  - Occasional rental of insured's home
  - Rental of a second unit or room
  - Rental of a garage as a private passenger garage or
  - Rental of part of the insured's home as a office, school or studio

  For example, liability and medical payments coverage would apply if the insured rented out his home for a month while on an extended vacation (occasional rental). Similarly, liability coverage would apply if the insured rented his garage or part of his home as a office or studio.

- **Arising out of the failure to render professional services**. For example, if an accountant is working out of his home and he makes an accounting error causing him to be sued by a client, no coverage would apply.

- **Arising out of a premises that is not an insured location**. Insured locations include:

  - The residence premises, temporary residences (e.g., hotel, camp ground)
  - Vacant land and
  - An occasionally rented premises (e.g., wedding hall, picnic grove)

  Any other location that is not an insured location is excluded from coverage.

- **Arising out of the ownership, maintenance or use of aircraft, motor vehicles and watercraft** subject to the following exceptions and limitations:

CLASS	USAGE, TYPE or SIZE REQUIREMENTS	COVERED
Aircraft	Aircraft (except model aircraft not carrying people/property)	No
Motorized Vehicles	Requiring motor vehicle registration	No
	Off road vehicles not subject to motor vehicle registration & not on insured premises (dirt bikes, ATVs, snowmobiles) *	No
	Off road vehicles not subject to motor vehicle registration and used to service the residence premises (riding lawnmowers, garden tractors, snow plows)	Yes
	Golf carts at a golfing facility and at a residential community as long as the golf cart does not exceed 4 persons and 25 mph. This coverage also applies when crossing public roads at these facilities.	Yes
	Motorized wheelchairs if the operator is handicapped	Yes
	Hovercraft/Flarecraft	No
Watercraft	Inboard or inboard-outdrive power (owned)	No
	Inboard or inboard-outdrive power of 50 HP or less not owned by the insured (borrowed or rented) †	Yes
	Inboard or inboard-outdrive power of more than 50 HP not owned or rented by the insured (borrowed) †	Yes
	Outboard motor power of 25 HP or less (owned, borrowed or rented) †	Yes
	Outboard motor power of more than 25 HP not owned by the insured (borrowed or rented) †	Yes
	Sailing boats less than 26 feet in length (owned, borrowed or rented) †	Yes
	Sailing boats 26 feet or more in length not owned or rented by an insured (borrowed) †	Yes

Outboard motors of more than 25 HP are covered if acquired by the insured prior to the beginning of the policy period or declared in writing with 45 days of acquisition. Coverage would also apply if the insured acquired (owned) the outboard motor during the policy period until the policy period expires, at which time it must be declared.

* May be covered by a Homeowner Policy endorsement or Personal Auto Policy endorsement, or by a separate recreational policy.

† Watercraft beyond HP size limitations may be covered by Homeowner Policy Watercraft endorsement (HO 00 75) or by a separate Boat Policy.

SPECIAL NOTE: This exclusion is rather complex. To help you in the study process, try to remember what is covered. For example: **model** aircraft; **vehicles used to service the premises** *that are not subject to motor vehicle registration* (e.g., riding lawnmower, segway or snowplow); **golf carts** *at a golf course or residential community*; **vehicles designed for the handicapped** (e.g., wheelchairs); **owned** watercraft powered by an outboard motor up to 25 HP and owned sailing vessels under 26 feet; **rented** watercraft up to 50 HP; **borrowed** watercraft regardless of size; and **watercraft in storage.**

- The **entrustment of an aircraft, motor vehicle or watercraft**. This exclusion eliminates coverage when an individual has the insured's permission to use the aircraft, motor vehicle or watercraft subject to the above exclusion exceptions.

- **Vicarious liability**, whether or not statutorily imposed, for actions of a child or minor. Vicarious liability **is liability that is imputed from one to another**. An example would be in an employment situation in which an employer is responsible for the acts of its employees. This exclusion eliminates coverage whether or not there is a law which makes the parents responsible for the actions of a child. For example, if the insured's 16 year old son vandalizes a high school causing $25,000 in damages, and a local law makes the parents responsible for these actions, the Homeowner Policy will not apply.

- Arising out of the **transmission of a communicable disease** by an insured. For example, if an insured transmits meningitis (a communicable disease), the Homeowner Policy will not apply.

- Arising out of **sexual molestation, corporal punishment** or **physical/mental abuse**. For example, if an insured sexually molests, physically punishes or mentally abuses an individual, no coverage applies.

- Arising out of the **sale, manufacture or use of a controlled substance**. For example, if an insured sells or manufactures a drug which injures an individual, no coverage applies.

See specimen pages SP-18 through SP-21 for illustration of Section II - Exclusions.

CONDITIONS - SECTION II LIABILITY

- **Limits of Liability** limits total liability to the amount shown in declarations.
- **Severability of Insurance** means insurance applies separately to each insured and will not increase the limit of liability. In other words, an insured cannot stack coverage.
- **Duties After Loss**, meaning cooperating with the insurer.
- **Duties of the Injured Person**, meaning cooperating with the insurer.
- **Payment of Claims** is not an admission of liability. In other words, if an insurer pays a third party the Medical Payment to Others limit of $1,000, it is not an admission of liability if the claimant eventually files a lawsuit for negligence.
- **Suit Against Us** requires compliance prior to legal action.
- **Bankruptcy** of an insured will not relieve the insurer of its obligation. In other words, if the insured declares bankruptcy, the insurer is still responsible to pay up to the limits of liability under the policy.
- **Other Insurance** condition addresses the allocation of coverage amounts if two or more policies are in effect at the time of loss. (See specimen page SP-22)

GENERAL CONDITIONS - SECTION I & II

The conditions part of the policy sets forth the duties and rights of both the insured and insurer. The following are the general conditions of the Homeowner Policy:

- **Policy period** defines the term of coverage. For example, a loss must occur during the policy period for coverage to apply.

- **Concealment and Fraud** provision voids coverage if the insured engaged in fraudulent conduct or made material misrepresentations. For example, if the insured submits a false claim, coverage does not apply.

- **Liberalization Clause** broadens coverage immediately when new policy changes are introduced at no additional premium. For example, if an the insurer introduces a new policy form with broader coverage and does not charge for that change in coverage, the insured is automatically granted that broader coverage immediately, even before the actual new policy is renewed. This is conditioned on no additional premium being charged.

- **Waivers or Changes of Policy Provisions** requires waivers/changes be in writing.

- **Assignment** is prohibited without the approval of the insurer. For example, if the insured sold his home, he may not assign (transfer) his Homeowners Policy as part of the transaction.

- **Subrogation** permits recovery against negligent third parties. For example, if the insured purchased a product and while using the product it caused the home to catch on fire, the insurer will pay the claim and subrogate (pursue in court) the manufacturer of the product.

- **Death** of an insured makes the insured's legal representative an insured under the policy. This provision also requires the insurance company to insure the property for: **1) 180 days after the insured's death,** *or* **2) until the end of the policy period,** *whichever is later.*

PENNSYLVANIA HOMEOWNER CANCELLATION REQUIREMENTS

Cancellation by the insurance company is permitted for:

- Nonpayment of premium
- Material misrepresentations or fraudulent statements
- Substantial change or increase in hazard from the date of policy issue
- Substantial increase in hazard caused by the insured's willful or negligent acts

In all instances, the insured must be given *30 days advance written notice.*

Cancellation by the insured is permitted by returning the policy to the insurance company or by giving written notice of the date of cancellation.

ENDORSEMENTS - The following are common homeowner endorsements:

- **Inflation Guard Endorsement (HO 04 66)** increases Coverages A, B, C & D to reflect the increase in costs due to inflation. For an additional premium, the coverages are increased on a prorated basis during the policy term. Inflation guard coverage may be written to increase at 4%, 6% or 8% of Coverage A.

- **Business Pursuits (HO 24 71)** eliminates liability exclusions for individuals who conduct certain business activities arising out of a business **in which the insured is not an owner or partner**. This endorsement extends Section II Liability to cover bodily injury and property damage at the insured's residence or away from the employer's premises after hours. Examples of individuals who may have a need for this coverage include clerical office employees, sales representatives, collectors, messengers and teachers. Teachers may obtain coverage for corporal punishment. Exclusions apply to the maintenance, use or entrustment by the insured to others of draft or saddle animals, aircraft, motorized land conveyances and watercraft when used for instructional purposes.

- **Permitted Incidental Occupancies - Residence Premises (HO 00 42)** endorsement deletes the standard business exclusions that are found in the Homeowners Policy. Liability coverage is provided for business activities such as an office or studio **on the residence premises**. When this endorsement is used, property insurance limits are available for Coverage B - Other Structures (if not endorsed, other structures are excluded if used for business). In addition, premises business furnishings and equipment is increased to the Coverage C limit.

- **Scheduled Personal Property Endorsement (HO 04 61)** provides coverage for personal property (jewelry, furs, silverware and other valuable articles) that have values in excess of the policy limits. This endorsement **provides special form "open peril" coverage to scheduled property with no deductible**.

  Please note that in the event an insured acquires an article of a class of property already covered, the additional property is covered up to 25% of the insurance for that class or $10,000, whichever is less. For this automatic coverage to be provided, all newly acquired property must be reported within 30 days (except fine arts which have 90 days) of acquisition and the appropriate premium must be paid. For example, if an insured has $10,000 of jewelry scheduled and decides to purchase a $2,500 ring, that $2,500 ring is automatically covered for up to 30 days for the broader peril coverage (mysterious disappearance, loss of ring) of the Scheduled Personal Property Endorsement. If however, the insured did not have jewelry scheduled, the $1,500 theft special limit would apply.

- **Limited Fungi, Wet or Dry Rot or Bacteria (HO 04 26) & (HO 04 27)** adds limited coverage for loss caused by mold related claims (fungi,wet/dry rot or bacteria). Separate annual aggregate limits of insurance for either property coverage (tear-out and repair, remediation, testing) or liability coverage (third-party alleges illness from mold) are indicated in the endorsement.

- **Home Day Care Coverage Endorsement (HO 04 97)** deletes the standard business exclusions that are found in the Homeowners Policy. **The endorsement is rated based upon the number of persons receiving day care services.** The number is listed on the endorsement. Liability coverage is provided for a home day care business on the residence premises. Property insurance limits are available for Coverage B - Other Structures (if not endorsed, other structures are excluded if used for business) and premises business furnishings and equipment is increased to the Coverage C limit. Although this endorsement provides liability and medical payments coverage, **exclusions apply to**:

  - Corporal punishment (spanking, etc.);
  - Sexual abuse; and,
  - Maintenance, use or entrustment by the insured to others of draft or saddle animals, aircraft, motorized land conveyances and watercraft when used for instructional purposes. Injury to any non-resident employee of the day care center is also excluded.

  This endorsement also includes an aggregate limit of liability.

- **Earthquake Endorsement (HO 04 54)** provides coverage in the event an earthquake causes loss to the dwelling.

- **Personal Property Replacement Cost (HO 04 90)** coverage provides full replacement cost coverage on personal property in place of actual cash value coverage. This means that in the event of loss to personal property, the loss will be adjusted on a replacement basis at today's cost without depreciation for age and use. Limitations apply to artifacts, antiques and memorabilia.

- **Additional Residence Rented To Others (HO 24 70)** extends the Homeowner Section II - liability coverage to additional residences rented to others. The endorsement provides for a listing of locations and **no one residence may contain more than four families**.

- **Watercraft (HO 24 75)** eliminates the liability exclusions for individuals who own certain watercraft. This endorsement provides coverage for scheduled watercraft with inboard or inboard-outdrive power, outboard motors in excess of 25 HP, or any sailing vessel in excess of 26 feet.

- **Mobilehome (MH 40 01)** coverage may be endorsed to a HO 00 02 or HO 00 03 policy form. To qualify for this coverage, the mobilehome must be used for year round living, and must be at least 10 feet wide and 40 feet long.

- **Ordinance or Law Coverage (HO 04 77)** provides additional coverage if, at the time of loss, stricter building ordinances require construction different than originally designed. It also provides coverage for demolition if the building is beyond reconstruction due to a covered peril.

- **Personal Injury (HO 24 82)** modifies the bodily injury definition to include libel, slander, malicious prosecution and invasion of privacy.

COMPARISON of the DWELLING FIRE and HOMEOWNERS PROGRAMS		
Category	**Dwelling Program**	**Homeowner Program**
Eligibility	Owner or tenant occupied residential rental properties up to four units, or occupied by no more than five roomers or boarders. Certain incidental occupancies, such as offices and studios, are permitted. Risks written under this program generally are ones which do not qualify for the broader coverages of the Homeowner Policy Program.	Owner occupied private residential exposures. Eligible risks include one to four family structures, apartment units, and condominium units. The one to four family structures may not have more than two boarders or roomers per family. The apartment and condominium units may not have more than one additional family or two boarders or roomers. Certain incidental occupancies, such as offices and studios, are permitted.
Application of Coverage Amounts	The unendorsed Dwelling Policy provides property coverages indicated by the coverage letters: A - Dwelling B - Other Structures C - Personal Property D - Fair Rental Value E - Additional Living Expense The insured must choose an insurance amount for all coverages although a percentage of the dwelling amount applies to Coverages B, D & E under the Other Coverages section. Personal liability and medical payments are not provided but may be added by endorsement.	The Homeowner Policy is divided into two main parts. Section I provides property coverages indicated by the coverage letters: A - Dwelling B - Other Structures (10% of Cov. A) C - Personal Property (50% of Cov. A) D - Loss of Use (30% of Cov. A) The insured chooses a Coverage A amount and Coverages B, C & D are issued based upon stated percentages. Section II of the policy provides liability insurance and medical payments to third parties. This is indicated in the policy by the coverage letters: E - Personal Liability F - Medical Payments
Coverage Forms	Basic Form (DP 00 01) Broad Form (DP 00 02) Special Form (DP 00 03) Theft is not provided but may be added by endorsement.	HO 00 02 (broad form), HO 00 03 (special form), HO 00 05 (comprehensive form) and HO 00 08 (modified form) are used to insure one to four family owner occupied structures. HO 00 04 (broad form) or HO 00 06 (broad form) are used to insure apartment unit and condominium units.
Policy Conditions	Policy conditions addressing: duties after loss; and general exclusions for ordinance or law, earth movement, water damage, power failure, neglect, war and nuclear hazard, governmental action, intentional loss, weather conditions, acts or decisions and faulty, inadequate or defective planning are basically the same. The vacancy condition under both the Homeowners Policy and Dwelling Policy is 60 days.	

HOMEOWNERS 2000 POLICY PROGRAM COMPARISON

NAMED PERILS	HO-2	HO-3	HO-4	HO-5	HO-6	HO-8
Fire or Lightning	●	●	●	●	●	●
Windstorm or Hail	●	●	●	●	●	●
Explosion	●	●	●	●	●	●
Riot or Civil Commotion	●	●	●	●	●	●
Aircraft	●	●	●	●	●	●
Vehicles	●	●	●	●	●	●
Smoke	●	●	●	●	●	●
Vandalism & Malicious Mischief	●	●	●	●	●	●†
Theft	●	●	●	●	●	●†
Falling Objects	●	●	●	●	●	
Weight of Ice and Snow	●	●	●	●	●	
Accidental Discharge	●	●	●	●	●	
Rupture of Heating/AC Systems	●	●	●	●	●	
Freezing	●	●	●	●	●	
Artificially Generated Elec. Current	●	●	●	●	●	
Volcanic Eruption	●	●	●	●	●	
Special Peril Coverage (A&B‡)		●‡		●		

ADDITIONAL COVERAGES

Claims Expense (e.g., premiums on bonds, $250/day loss of earnings, postjudgment interest).
First Aid Expense meaning immediate assistance to aid injured (e.g. first aid, ambulance costs).
Property Damage to Others up to $1,000.
Loss Assessment up to $1,000 for assessments charged.
Debris Removal additional 5% if limit of insurance is exhausted & $500 for trees (limitations apply).
Reasonable Repairs incurred to protect property (e.g., board up broken windows).
Trees and Shrubs up to 5% of Coverage A limited to $500/tree or shrub (limited perils apply).†
Fire Department Charge up to $500.
Property Removal up to 30 days when protecting property from a covered peril.
Credit Card, Forgery and Counterfeit Money is limited to $500.
Collapse caused by hidden decay, insect damage, content weight and Coverage C perils.†
Glass/Safety Glazing Material†
Landlord's Furnishings up to $2,500, excluding theft to appliances. (N/A to HO4, HO6 & HO8).
Ordinance and Law of up to 10% of the Coverage A limit.
Grave Markers up to $5,000

LIMITATIONS ON PERSONAL PROPERTY

$ 200 on money, bank notes, gold, silver, platinum medals, scrip, value and smart cards.
$1,500 on securities, accounts, deeds, tickets and stamps.
$1,500 on watercraft including trailers, equipment and motors.
$1,500 on trailers not used with watercraft.
$1,500 on loss by theft of jewelry, watches, furs and precious stones.†
$2,500 on loss by theft of firearms and related equipment.†
$2,500 on loss by theft of silverware, goldware and pewterware.†
$2,500 on business property located at the residence premises.
$ 500 on business property located away from the premises.
$1,500 on adaptable electronic apparatus that is in or on a motor vehicle or away from the residence premises and used solely for business purposes while not in or upon a motor vehicle.

Personal property located at a secondary residence is limited to 10% of coverage "C" or $1,000, whichever is greater.

† Limited or excluded under the HO-8 Policy.

PERSONAL PROPERTY NOT COVERED - Articles separately described; animals, birds, or fish; motor vehicles subject to motor vehicle registration and their parts; aircraft or parts; property of roomers not related to the insured; property in an apartment held for rent except amounts indicated in Additional Coverages; property rented to others off premises; business data; credit cards excepts for amounts indicated in Additional Coverages.

GENERAL EXCLUSIONS - Flood, war, earth movement, etc. (same as Dwelling Policy)

SPECIAL FORM EXCLUSIONS - Wear & tear, inherent vice, etc. (similar to Dwelling Policy)

KEY TERMS AND CONCEPTS

The following terms were introduced in this chapter. You should know each word and concept and be able to apply them in everyday usage. To improve retention, it is recommended that you write out each key term and concept in your own words.

Business
Business Pursuits Endorsement
Claim Expense
Coverage A - Dwelling
Coverage B - Other Structures
Coverage C - Personal Property
Coverage D - Loss of Use
Coverage E - Personal Liability
Coverage F - Medical Payments
Damage To Property of Others.
Earthquake Coverage
First Aid Expense
Home Day Care Business Coverage
Homeowners Form HO 00 02
Homeowners Form HO 00 03
Homeowners Form HO 00 04
Homeowners Form HO 00 05
Homeowners Form HO 00 06
Homeowners Form HO 00 08
Homeowners Policy Program
Inflation Guard Endorsement
Insured
Insured Location
Loss Assessment
Loss Settlement
Mobilehome Endorsement
Motor Vehicles
Ordinance or Law Endorsement
Permitted Incidental Occupancies End's.
Personal Injury Endorsement
Personal Property Limitations
Personal Property Not Covered
Personal Property Replacement Cost
Section I - Additional Coverages
Section I - Conditions
Section I - Exclusions
Section I - Property Coverages
Section I - Property Exclusions
Section II - Additional Coverages
Section II - Conditions
Section II - Liability Coverages
Section II - Liability Exclusions
Vicarious Liability
Watercraft
Watercraft Endorsement

REVIEW QUESTIONS

Before attempting to answer the end chapter practice questions, you should ask yourself if you can answer the following questions. It is recommended that you write out each review question in your own words. This exercise will help you apply the key terms and concepts that you've learned to form relationships with different topics.

1. What types of properties are eligible under the Homeowners Policy? (5-1)
2. What types of activities constitute a business? (5-1)
3. Identify 4 categories of individuals who may be granted insured status. (5-1)
4. Identify 4 locations that are considered insured locations. (5-1)
5. Identify the components of Section I and Section II of the Homeowner Policy. (5-2)
6. When are building materials and supplies covered? (5-3)
7. Under Coverage B - Other Structures, what condition totally eliminates coverage? (5-3)
8. Identify 5 classes of personal property and their sublimits. (5-3)
9. Identify 3 classes of personal property that may not be limited by their dollar sublimit. (5-3)
10. Identify 8 classes of personal property not covered under the Homeowners Policy. 5-4
11. Identify and explain the 11 Additional Coverages provided under Section I of the Homeowners Policy. (5-4 & 5-5)
12. Identify and explain the 2 major coverages provided under Section II of the Homeowners Policy. (5-11)
13. Identify and explain the 4 Additional Coverages provided under Section II of the Homeowners Policy. (5-11)
14. Identify and explain 10 Section II exclusions. (5-11 & 5-12)
15. Identify 4 motorized vehicles and 3 watercraft that are covered under Section II of the Homeowners Policy. (5-13)
16. Explain the automatic coverage including time limitations applicable to the Scheduled Personal Property Endorsement. (5-16)
17. Explain how the Home Day Care Coverage Endorsement is rated. (5-17)
18. What benefit does the Personal Property Replacement Cost Endorsement offer? (5-16)
19. What endorsement may be used to extend liability coverage to another location? (5-17)
20. Explain the coverages that are provided under the Personal Injury endorsement? (5-17)

NOTES

PRACTICE EXAM FIVE

ON

THE HOMEOWNERS POLICY

1. **All of the following are characteristics of the Homeowners Policy EXCEPT:**

   A) Provides coverage for owner occupied private residential exposures.
   B) Provides a wide range of property and liability coverages.
   C) Provides unlimited liability coverage for watercraft.
   D) Provides incidental occupancy for certain limited business exposures. Ref. 5-1

2. **All of the following would be considered an insured under a Homeowners Policy EXCEPT:**

   A) Individuals named in the policy declarations.
   B) Residents of the household who are relatives of the insured.
   C) The divorced wife of the insured living in another state.
   D) Individuals under the age of 21 and in the care of the insured. Ref. 5-1

3. **All of the following are insured locations under a Homeowners Policy EXCEPT:**

   A) Vacant land.
   B) Land used for business purposes.
   C) Premises rented to the insured.
   D) The residence premises as indicated in the declarations. Ref. 5-1

4. **All of the following are true of Coverage B - Other Structures EXCEPT:**

   A) Coverage B - Other Structures must be added by endorsement.
   B) The other structure must be separated by clear space from the primary insured dwelling.
   C) Coverage B - Other Structures is a blanket limit of insurance.
   D) An example of an other structure would be a detached garage. Ref. 5-3

5. **Coverage C - Personal Property of the Homeowners Policy provides:**

   A) Coverage only to loss at the residence premises.
   B) Coverage only to loss at the residence premises and secondary premises.
   C) Coverage only to scheduled personal property.
   D) Coverage worldwide. Ref. 5-3

6. **All of the following are true of the special limits of liability on personal property under all Homeowner Forms EXCEPT:**

   A) Money and bank notes for $200.
   B) Securities, accounts, deeds, tickets and stamps for $1,500.
   C) Business property located at the residence premises for $2,500.
   D) Personal property coverage is unlimited. Ref. 5-3

7. Under the Homeowners Policy, all of the following are classes of property NOT covered EXCEPT:

A) Articles separately described and insured.
B) Animals, birds and fish.
C) Motorized vehicles not used to maintain the residence premises.
D) Personal computer equipment on the residence premises. Ref. 5-3 & 5-4

8. All of the following are Section I Coverages of the Homeowner Policy EXCEPT:

A) Dwelling.
B) Other structures.
C) Personal property.
D) Personal liability. Ref. 5-3 & 5-4

9. All of the following are true of Coverage D - Loss Of Use of the Homeowner Policy EXCEPT:

A) Loss of use refers to the additional expenses incurred by the insured in the event the property becomes uninhabitable by an insured peril.
B) Provides coverage at 100% of Coverage A.
C) Provides coverage to the insured for additional living expenses incurred by the insured.
D) Provides coverage to the insured for loss of rent if a second unit in the insured residence is rented. Ref. 5-4

10. Which of the following coverages provides for indirect or consequential losses?

A) Coverage A - Dwelling.
B) Coverage B - Other Structures.
C) Coverage C - Personal Property.
D) Coverage D - Loss Of Use. Ref. 5-4

11. All of the following are Additional Coverages under the Homeowner Policy EXCEPT:

A) Debris removal.
B) Coverage for trees, shrubs and other plants.
C) A detached garage.
D) Fire department service charge. Ref. 5-4 & 5-5

12. All of the following are true of Coverage E - Personal Liability of the Homeowner Policy EXCEPT:

A) Provides coverage in the event a claim or lawsuit is brought against an insured.
B) Provides a legal defense even if groundless or fraudulent.
C) Provides a legal defense for an error that is caused by the insured in his law practice.
D) Provides a legal defense and pays legal costs in addition to judgment. Ref. 5-11

13. Which of the following is true of Coverage F - Medical Payments of the Homeowner Policy?

A) Provides coverages to the named insured.
B) Provides coverage to a guest who falls on the premises and incurs medical expenses.
C) Encourages lawsuits.
D) Is a Section I Coverage. Ref. 5-11

14. All of the following are Section II - Additional Coverages of the Homeowner Policy EXCEPT:

A) Claim expense.
B) Debris removal.
C) First aid expense incurred by the insured to assist injured parties.
D) Damage to property of others. Ref. 5-11

15. Which of the following Homeowner Forms provides named peril coverage to the dwelling, other structures and personal property?

A) Broad Form HO 00 02.
B) Special Form HO 00 03.
C) Contents Broad Form HO 00 04.
D) Comprehensive Form HO 00 05. Ref. 5-6 & 5-7

16. Which of the following Homeowner Forms provides special form coverage to the dwelling and other structures and named peril coverage to personal property?

A) Broad Form HO 00 02.
B) Special Form HO 00 03.
C) Contents Form HO 00 04.
D) Unit Owners Form HO 00 06. Ref. 5-6 & 5-7

17. Which of the following Homeowner Forms provides named peril coverage to the personal property to individuals who rent an apartment?

A) Broad Form HO 00 02.
B) Special Form HO 00 03.
C) Contents Form HO 00 04.
D) Unit Owners Form HO 00 06. Ref. 5-6 & 5-7

18. Which of the following Homeowner Forms provides named peril coverage to the personal property of individuals who own a condominium unit?

A) Broad Form HO 00 02.
B) Special Form HO 00 03.
C) Contents Form HO 00 04.
D) Unit Owners Form HO 00 06. Ref. 5-6 & 5-7

19. **Which of the following forms requires the insured to maintain coverages equal to 80% of the dwelling's replacement cost?**

A) Modified Form HO 00 08.
B) Broad Form HO 00 02, Special Form HO 00 03 & Comprehensive Form HO 00 05.
C) Contents Form HO 00 04.
D) Unit Owners Form HO 00 06. Ref. 5-6 & 5-7

20. **Which of the following describes the HO 00 03 Special Form coverage that is applicable to the dwelling and other structures?**

A) Coverage is provided if named in the policy.
B) Coverage is provided for direct physical loss unless specifically excluded.
C) Coverage is provided for "All Risks".
D) Coverage is provided if named in the policy unless eliminated. Ref. 5-6 & 5-7

21. **Which of the following Homeowner Forms may be recommended to individuals who own homes that are older and have unusually high replacement values in comparison to its market value?**

A) Modified Form HO 00 08.
B) Unit Owners Form HO 00 06.
C) Contents Form HO 00 04.
D) Special Form HO 00 03. Ref. 5-6 & 5-7

22. **Which of the Homeowner Forms provides special form coverage to Coverage A - Dwelling, Coverage B - Other Structures and Coverage C - Personal Property:**

A) Broad Form HO 00 02.
B) Special Form HO 00 03
C) Comprehensive Form HO 00 05.
D) Modified Form HO 00 08. Ref. 5-6 & 5-7

23. **All of the following are true of the Homeowner Policy EXCEPT:**

A) Money is covered up to $200.
B) Benefits are only paid to insureds.
C) Different forms have different loss settlement provisions.
D) Personal property is covered worldwide. Ref. 5-3, 5-10 & 5-11

24. **All of the following are Section I - Exclusions of the Homeowners Policy EXCEPT:**

A) Intentional loss.
B) War.
C) Surface water.
D) Off premises power failure which causes an on premises covered loss. Ref. 5-8

25. All of the following are true of the Homeowner Form HO 00 08 EXCEPT:

A) Buildings are adjusted on a functional replacement cost basis.
B) The named perils of the policy are fewer in number than other homeowner forms.
C) It may be recommended for dwellings with wide disparities between replacement value and market value.
D) Theft coverage is provided up to the limit of personal property Coverage C.

Ref. 5-7

26. All of the following are Section II Liability Exclusions EXCEPT:

A) Liability arising out of the negligent maintenance of the insured premises.
B) Liability arising out of an intentional or expected act.
C) Liability arising out of or failure to render professional services.
D) Liability arising out of the entrustment of aircraft and motor vehicles.

Ref. 5-12

27. Which of the following endorsements provides replacement cost coverage to Coverage C - Personal Property of the Homeowner Policy?

A) Inflation guard endorsement.
B) Personal property replacement cost endorsement.
C) Scheduled personal property endorsement.
D) Business pursuits endorsement.

Ref. 5-16 & 5-17

28. Which of the following provides coverage for direct physical loss, unless specifically excluded, to Coverage C - Personal Property of the Homeowner Policy?

A) Comprehensive Form HO 00 05.
B) Personal property replacement cost endorsement.
C) Scheduled personal property endorsement.
D) Special Form HO 00 03.

Ref. 5-6

29. Which of the following endorsements is used to insure Coverage C - Personal Property for values beyond the limitations of the Homeowner Policy?

A) Special personal property endorsement.
B) Personal property replacement cost endorsement.
C) Scheduled personal property endorsement.
D) Business pursuits endorsement.

Ref. 5-16 & 5-17

30. A homeowner seeking the broadest coverages available would choose:

A) Broad Form HO 00 02.
B) Special Form HO 00 03.
C) Comprehensive Form HO 00 05.
D) Unit Owners Form HO 00 06.

Ref. 5-6 & 5-19

31. All of the following are examples of coverage of the Personal Injury Endorsement of the Homeowner Policy EXCEPT:

A) Libel.
B) Slander.
C) Statements about an individual that are derogatory but true.
D) Invasion of privacy. Ref. 5-17

32. All of the following are true of the Mobilehome Endorsement EXCEPT:

A) May be endorsed to Homeowner Forms HO 00 02 and HO 00 03.
B) The mobilehome must be resided in year round.
C) Must be written as a separate mobilehome policy.
D) The mobilehome must be at least 10 feet wide and 40 feet long. Ref. 5-17

33. All of the following are true of the Inflation Guard Endorsement of the Homeowner Policy EXCEPT:

A) Inflation guard coverage is written to increase as a percent of the dwelling amount.
B) Inflation guard coverage is written to increase as a percent of the consumer price index.
C) Coverage increases during the policy term.
D) Coverage increases apply to Coverages A, B, C and D. Ref. 5-16

34. All of the following would be eligible for a Homeowners Policy EXCEPT:

A) A mobilehome with appropriate mobilehome endorsement.
B) A residence where the homeowner performs incidental business activities.
C) A commercial farm.
D) A four unit dwelling. Ref. 5-1

35. What minimum coverage amount should a homeowner carry if he purchased a home five years ago for $85,000, that today has a replacement cost of $100,000?

A) $100,000.
B) $ 80,000.
C) $ 64,000.
D) $108,000. Ref. 5-6

36. Which of the following occurrences are insured against under the Homeowners Policy?

A) Water damage caused from frozen pipes at a vacant dwelling, if the insured has maintained heat.
B) Flood.
C) Earth movement.
D) Power interruption off the premises. Ref. 5-5

37. Under a Broad Form Homeowner Policy, the peril volcanic eruption includes all of the following EXCEPT:

A) Lava.
B) Airborne shock waves.
C) Tremors
D) Ash. Ref. 5-6

38. All of the following would be covered under Section II of the Homeowners Policy EXCEPT:

A) The postman, while delivering mail, falls because of defective steps.
B) The named insured's dog attacks a neighbor.
C) The named insured's son damages the driveway and fence while operating a licensed vehicle.
D) The named insured's 10 year old adopted son, while on vacation in Canada, strikes another child with a rock. Ref. 5-11 - 5-13

39. Which one of the following circumstances is NOT covered under Section II - Liability of the Homeowners Policy:

A) A riding lawnmower used by the named insured to service the residence premises.
B) A boat in storage in the named insured's garage.
C) A motorized wheelchair used by the named insured's who is disabled.
D) A dirt bike driven by the named insured's son at a public park. Ref. 5-12 & 5-13

40. An insured's 16 year old son vandalizes a local high school causing $1,000 in damages. In this case:

A) The Homeowner Policy's limit of $1,000 applies.
B) The Homeowner Policy provides coverage by endorsement.
C) The Homeowner Policy provides no coverage.
D) It is covered under the vicarious liability provision. Ref. 5-14

41. Under a Homeowners Policy, a theft of an insured's credit cards requires all of the following EXCEPT:

A) Notification to the police.
B) Notification to the credit card company.
C) Notification to the credit bureau.
D) Notification to the insurance company. Ref. 5-9

42. Under Section II of a Homeowners Policy, a watercraft with an inboard motor is covered:

A) If under 75 horsepower.
B) If over 75 horsepower.
C) If being transported on a trailer.
D) If in storage. Ref. 5-13

43. Under a Homeowner Policy, theft of building materials is:

A) Always covered.
B) Never covered.
C) Covered if the insured is building a new house.
D) Covered if the insured is remodeling the house in which he resides. Ref. 5-3

44. A disabled insured, while operating his motorized wheelchair injures a small child. In this case:

A) The Homeowner Policy provides liability coverage.
B) The Homeowner Policy excludes liability coverage.
C) The Homeowner Policy only provides liability coverage by endorsement.
D) The Homeowner Policy limits liability coverage to $1,000. Ref. 5-13

45. Under an unendorsed Homeowner Policy, Coverage C - Personal Property is:

A) Adjusted on a replacement cost basis.
B) Adjusted on an actual cash value basis.
C) Adjusted on a functional replacement cost basis.
D) Adjusted on an agreed value basis. Ref. 5-10

46. Under a Homeowner Policy, Coverage C - Personal Property is generally issued at:

A) 10% of Coverage A.
B) 50% of Coverage A.
C) 70% of Coverage A.
D) 100% of Coverage A. Ref. 5-3

ANSWER KEY

1-C	2-C	3-B	4-A	5-D	6-D	7-D	8-D	9-B	10-D
11-C	12-C	13-B	14-B	15-A	16-B	17-C	18-D	19-B	20-B
21-A	22-C	23-B	24-D	25-D	26-A	27-B	28-A	29-C	30-C
31-C	32-C	33-B	34-C	35-B	36-A	37-C	38-C	39-D	40-C
41-C	42-D	43-D	44-A	45-B	46-B				

CHAPTER SIX
AUTO INSURANCE

OVERVIEW

This chapter addresses the personal and the commercial automobile insurance needs of individuals and businesses. The Personal Auto Policy, which is reviewed first, and the Commercial Auto Policy, which is reviewed second, are very similar from a coverage viewpoint. Differences between the two policies center on policy structure, use, and the statutory laws which affect both policies. Please note that the Commercial Auto Policy may be written as a separate policy as explained in this chapter, or as a coverage part under the Commercial Package Policy (CPP). See Chapter Seven on how the commercial auto can be written under the CPP.

PENNSYLVANIA MOTOR VEHICLE FINANCIAL RESPONSIBILITY LAW

The Pennsylvania Motor Vehicle Financial Responsibility Law (PMVFRL) was amended by Act 6 on July 1, 1990. This amendment to the law was made in an effort to reduce the high cost of automobile insurance and curtail the number of individuals who were driving without auto coverage. Under the Act, **an owner of a vehicle is required to show "financial responsibility" at the time of registration.** Financial responsibility is defined as the ability to respond to liability on account of accidents arising out of the maintenance or use of a motor vehicle. **Minimum limits of liability are required as follows:** $15,000 for injury to one person in any one accident; $30,000 for injury to two or more persons in any one accident; and $5,000 for damage to property of others in any one accident. **Financial responsibility may be demonstrated by** the purchase of automobile liability insurance, or through the posting of a bond, or being qualified as self-insured.

Under the PMVFRL, the insured is given the option to accept or reject various coverages (tort option, uninsured motorist, underinsured motorist, stacked coverage). The following is an overview of these coverages and the PMVFRL:

REQUIRED LIMITS OF LIABILITY include:

- **Bodily Injury Liability** of a required minimum of $15,000 per person and $30,000 per accident. Bodily injury liability pays others when the insured is responsible for causing injuries and includes medical and rehabilitation expenses, and noneconomic damages such as pain and suffering; and,

- **Property Damage Liability** of a required minimum of $5,000. Some insurance companies combine the two types of liability insurance with one dollar amount for both injuries and property damage with the required minimum amount of $35,000. Property damage liability pays others when the insured is responsible for damaging their property.

These types of benefits are paid to third parties in the event the insured is involved in an automobile accident and determined to be legally liable. The minimum limits indicated above are generally written at much higher amounts.

TORT OPTION SELECTIONS

Financial responsibility requirements mandate that each insurer notify its insureds of the choice of two options that will **govern their right to sue**. The **limited tort** option **limits the insured's right to sue** to specific out-of-pocket expenses, except in cases involving serious injury or death, in which case, the insured can sue for pain and suffering. **Serious injury** is any injury resulting in death, serious impairment of bodily function or permanent, serious disfigurement. **Specific or "special damages"** include medical expenses, loss of income along with the cost to repair the damaged vehicle. Under the limited tort option, the insured can only collect out-of-pocket damages, unless serious injury or death occurs.

The other option available is the **full tort** option which **does not restrict an individual's right to sue**. For example, if an individual chose the full tort option and was involved in an accident, they could collect both specific damages (medical expenses, loss of income, etc.) **plus noneconomic damages such as pain and suffering, regardless if the injury was serious or not**. Although individuals choosing limited tort coverage receive a premium reduction in comparison to full tort coverage, most individuals have opted for full tort coverage.

FIRST PARTY BENEFITS

First party benefits are benefits that are payable to an insured. They include:

- **Medical Benefits** with a **required minimum of $5,000** with options up to $100,000. Medical benefits are reasonable and necessary medical and rehabilitative services and **are paid regardless of fault**.

- **Extraordinary Medical Benefits**, which are medical and rehabilitation expenses in excess of $100,000. **This coverage is optional** and may be purchased in $100,000 increments up to $1,100,000. **After the first 18 months following an accident payments are limited to $50,000 per year**.

- **Income Loss Benefits**, which pays loss of income to an insured who is injured in an auto accident. **This coverage is optional** and limited to 80% of loss of gross income up to $2,500 per month and up to a maximum of $50,000. A **5 day waiting period applies**.

- **Funeral Benefits**, which pays the funeral, burial or cremation expenses if an insured dies in a car crash within 24 months from the date of the accident. **This coverage is optional** and pays up to $2,500.

- **Accidental Death Benefit**, which pays when an insured or a family member dies in a motor vehicle accident within 24 months from the date of accident. **This coverage is optional** with varying amounts up to $25,000.

Insureds may choose individual options as indicated above or select an **optional combination benefit** of up to **$177,500 of benefits in the aggregate** or benefits payable **up to three years from the date of the accident**. These benefits are subject to a $25,000 limit on accidental death and $2,500 on funeral benefits.

SOURCES OF FIRST PARTY BENEFITS/PRIORITY OF PAYMENTS

First parties injured in an automobile accident recover benefits in the following priority:

1) **For a named insured**, the policy on which he or she is the named insured.
2) **For an insured**, the policy covering the insured.
3) **For the occupants of an insured motor vehicle**, if not a named insured as in (1) above, or an insured as in (2) above, the policy on that motor vehicle.
4) **For a person who is not an occupant of a motor vehicle**, the policy on any motor vehicle involved in the accident. Parked or unoccupied motor vehicles involved in an accident are not considered motor vehicles for purpose of involvement unless it was parked so as to cause unreasonable risk of injury.

Individuals covered under more than one policy will be covered by the first insurer who receives the claim first under the priorities set above. That insurer will be wholly responsible and is entitled to recover contribution on a pro rata basis from any insurer for benefits paid and costs of claim processing.

INELIGIBLE CLAIMANTS

Ineligible claimants for first party benefits includes individuals who:

- Own a currently registered motor vehicle and do not have financial responsibility;
- Operate or occupy a recreational vehicle not intended for highway use;
- Operate or occupy a motorcycle, motor-driven cycle, motorized pedacycle, or like type vehicle required to be registered;
- Intentionally injure or attempt to injure oneself or another; *(e.g., road rage)*
- Are injured while committing a felony; *(e.g., carjacking)*
- Are injured while seeking to elude lawful apprehension or arrest by a law enforcement official.

Benefits may not be denied solely because the driver of the insured motor vehicle is determined to be under the influence of drugs or intoxicating beverages.

PAYMENTS OF BENEFITS

First payments are overdue if not paid within 30 days after the insurer receives reasonable proof of the amount of the benefits. Overdue benefits are subject to an interest charge at 12% per annum from the date the benefits become overdue. If first party benefits are not made, a lawsuit must be filed within **four years from the date of accident**. If first party benefits were paid, a lawsuit for further benefits must be filed within **four years from the date of the last payment**. Minors entitled to benefits must file a lawsuit within **four years from the date of the injured minor's attainment of age 18**.

Insurance subject to Pennsylvania's Motor Vehicle Financial Responsibility Law is primary to other coverages, **except for Workers Compensation**. Other coverages in effect under a group contract or under other programs are considered excess and not in duplication of any valid first party benefits or Workers Compensation.

UNINSURED MOTORIST (UM) v. UNDERINSURED MOTORIST (UIM)

Every automobile liability policy issued must offer Uninsured Motorist (UM) and Underinsured Motorist (UIM) coverage. Each coverage applies as follows:

- **Uninsured Motorist (UM) insurance** pays for bodily injuries caused by an uninsured motorist *(one with no insurance)*. This coverage is optional and coverage must be rejected by the insured to eliminate coverage. If not rejected, coverage will be provided with minimum amounts of $15,000 for injuries per person and $30,000 in the aggregate.

- **Underinsured Motorist (UIM) insurance** pays for injuries caused by a motorist whose insurance is inadequate *(limits are too low)* to pay what the insured is due. This coverage is optional and coverage must be rejected by the insured to eliminate coverage. If not rejected, coverage will be provided with minimum amounts of $15,000 for injuries per person and $30,000 in the aggregate.

Uninsured Motorist (UM) and Underinsured Motorist (UIM) coverage is typically written in the same amount as the limits elected for bodily injury. However, a named insured may request in writing lower limits for Uninsured Motorist (UM) and Underinsured Motorist (UIM) than the bodily injury limits.

STACKING

Stacking means that in the same type of accident, coverage limits would be the **sum of the uninsured** or **underinsured motorist coverage** limits **for all of the autos** insured under a policy. For example, if a husband and wife own two automobiles with $100,000 UM/UIM limits and choose stacking, each will be covered up to $200,000 in the event of a UM/UIM claim. The insured may waive stacking by signing a stacking waiver which results in a premium savings. **Stacking does not apply to other first party benefits.**

Where multiple policies apply, payment is made in the following order of recovery:

1) A policy covering a motor vehicle occupied by the insured at the time of accident.
2) A policy covering a motor vehicle not involved in the accident with respect to which the injured person is an insured.

Individuals covered under more than one policy will be covered by the first insurer who receives the claim first under the priorities set above. That insurer will be wholly responsible and is entitled to recover contribution on a pro rata basis from any insurer for benefits paid and costs of claim processing.

RENTAL VEHICLES

Every motor vehicle policy issued in Pennsylvania is required to contain a notice as to whether the policy covers or limits collision damage to rental vehicles. This is indicated on the policy declarations page.

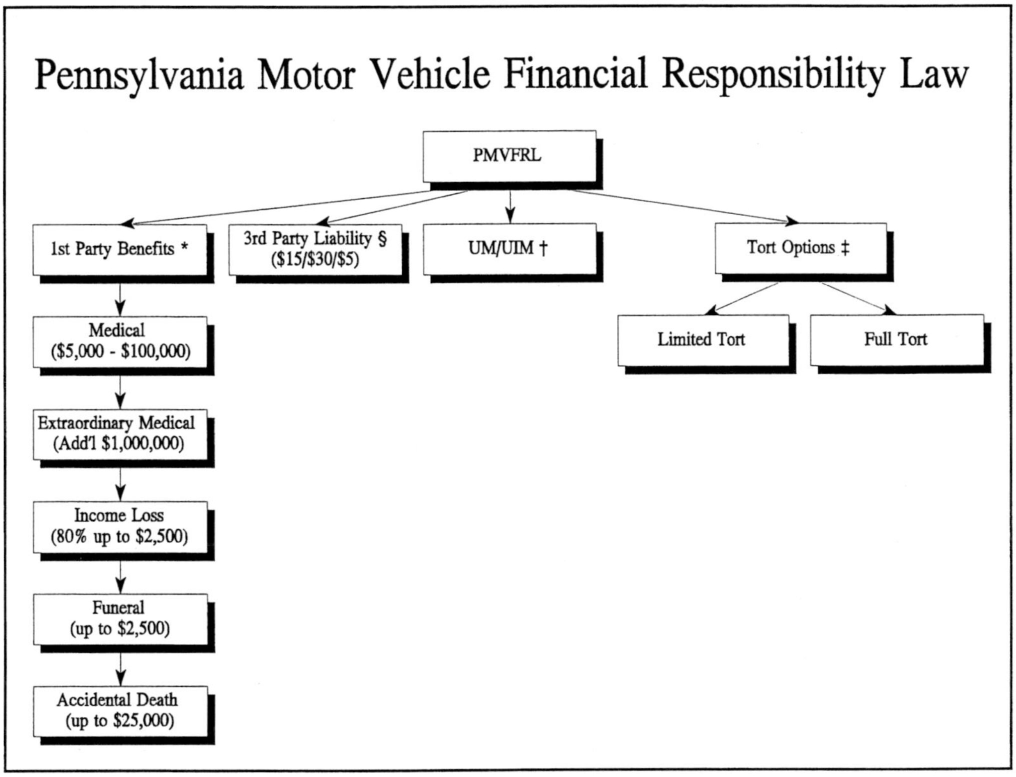

* First-party benefits cover an insured, or an occupant or a pedestrian with no auto insurance.

§ Third-party benefits cover an insured for their negligent acts. (minimum limits of $15/$30/$5)

† Uninsured Motorist and Underinsured Motorist coverage pays the insured for injuries sustained in an accident where the negligent or financially irresponsible driver is either uninsured (no coverage at all) or carries coverage that is insufficient (underinsurance).

‡ Limited tort option restricts the insured's rights to sue to specific out-of-pocket expenses, except in the event of serious injury or death. The full tort option is an unrestricted right to sue.

OTHER PROVISIONS

In addition to the requirements and benefits mandated above, the Pennsylvania Motor Vehicle Financial Responsibility Law requires the following provisions:

- **Comprehensive insurance** (referred to as "Other Than Collision" in the Personal Auto Policy) pays for theft or damage to an insured's car from hazards including fire, flood or vandalism. This coverage is optional but typically required by a bank or other lender for a car loan.

- **Collision insurance** pays for damage to an insured's car from a crash with another object or vehicle. This coverage is optional but typically required by a bank or other lender for a car loan. **A $500 deductible is standard**.

- **Discounts** for passive seat belts, air bags, anti-theft devices, and drivers age 55 or older who have completed approved courses are available.

- **Motor vehicle fraud** provisions were introduced to minimize insurance fraud and include the requirement for anti-fraud plans, a motor vehicle insurance fraud index bureau and penalties for fraud and failure to implement the anti-fraud plans.

PERSONAL AUTO '05 POLICY

The Personal Auto Policy provides liability and physical damage coverages. The liability coverage protects the insured for legal liability. The physical damage coverage protects the insured's vehicle. The Personal Auto Policy is designed to cover four wheel motor vehicles that are either owned or leased. The Personal Auto Policy is structured as follows:

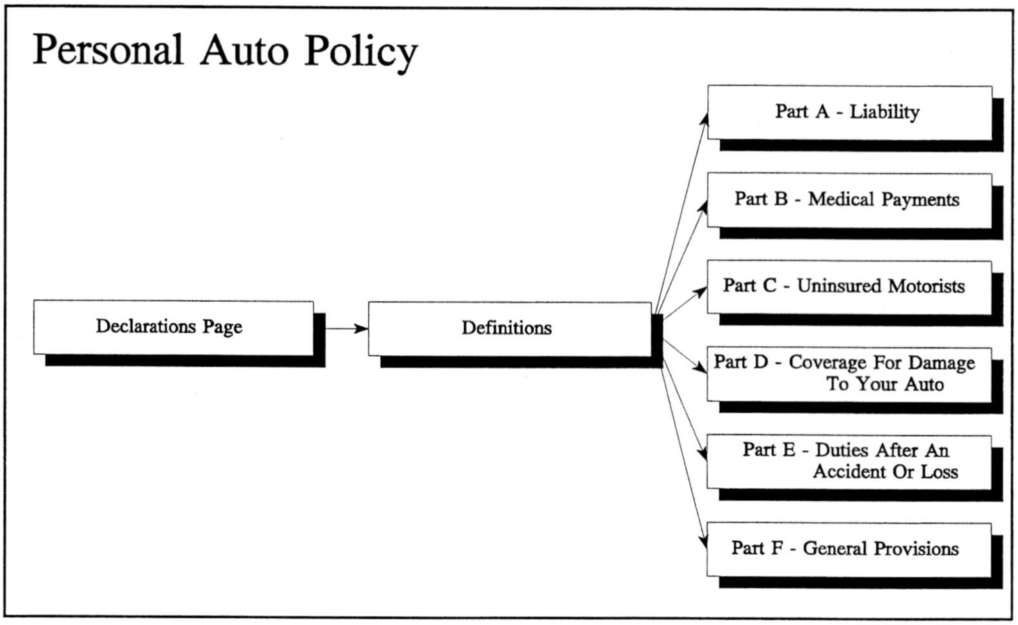

DEFINITIONS

Definitions define terms as used in the policy. The purpose is to clarify and set forth the meaning of terms. The following are the Personal Auto Policy Definitions:

- **You and your** refer to the named insured as shown in the declarations and the spouse if a resident of the same household.
- **We, us and our** refer to the company providing insurance.
- **Bodily injury** means bodily harm, sickness or disease, including death that results.
- **Business** includes trade, profession or occupation.
- **Family member** is a person related to the named insured by blood, marriage or adoption (including a foster child or ward) who is a resident of your household.
- **Occupying** means in, upon, getting in, on, out or off.
- **Property damage** means physical injury to, destruction of or loss of use of tangible property.
- **Trailer** means a vehicle designed to be pulled by a private passenger auto, pickup or van, or a farm wagon or farm implement while towed by a private passenger auto, pickup or van.
- **Your covered auto** means **any vehicle shown in the declarations** or any of the following types of vehicles on the date you become the owner:

1) **A private passenger auto.**

2) **A pickup or van not exceeding 9,000 pounds in Gross Vehicle Weight and is not principally used in any business** *other than farming or ranching*. In other words, a pickup or van that is used for farming or ranching or for incidental business use falls within the definition of a covered auto. Pickups or vans used principally for business should be insured under a commercial auto policy.

3) **A newly acquired auto** (i.e., replacement or additional auto) is granted:

   - The **broadest coverage** that applies to any vehicle insured under the policy. Additional autos are subject to a 14-day notification requirement from date of acquisition.
   - **Retroactive physical damage coverage** if no physical damage coverage is provided on the current policy subject to a 4-day notification requirement from date of acquisition. This is subject to a $500 deductible.

4) **Any trailer you own.** *(e.g., a boat trailer or utility trailer)*

5) **Any auto or trailer you do not own** while used as a temporary substitute for any other vehicle described in this definition which is out of normal use because of breakdown, repair, servicing, loss or destruction. *(e.g., a "loaner vehicle" used while the insured's auto is being repaired)* See SP-26

PART A - LIABILITY COVERAGE

Part A - Liability Coverage of the Personal Auto Policy provides coverage for bodily injury or property damage up to the limit of liability *for which an insured becomes legally responsible because of an auto accident.* **Defense costs and related interest charges levied on the verdict are paid in addition to the policy's limit of liability**. Persons insured for liability coverage include:

- The named insured and family members;
- Any person permitted to use a covered auto;
- Any person or organization legally responsible for the acts of a person using a covered auto. For example, if an insured is on a business trip and is involved in an accident, the insured's employer is afforded coverage.

SUPPLEMENTARY PAYMENTS

Supplementary Payments *are amounts paid in addition to the limit of liability* and includes:

- Up to $250 toward the cost of bail bonds required because of an accident.
- Premiums on appeal or attachment bonds in any suit the insurer defends.
- Interest accruing on judgments.
- Up to $200 per day for loss of earnings for assisting in legal proceedings.
- Other reasonable expenses incurred by the insured. See SP-27.

LIABILITY EXCLUSIONS

Liability exclusions eliminate coverage:

- For any insured who **intentionally** causes bodily injury or property damage.
- For damage to **property owned or being transported** by that insured.
- For damage to **property rented to, used by or in the care** of that insured.
- For bodily injury occurring in the course of employment. *(exception for domestics)*
- For bodily injury occurring while **carrying individuals or property for a fee**. *(car pool sharing is permitted)*
- Engaging in the **business of selling, repairing, storing or parking** autos.
- For any insured using any vehicle while employed or engaged in any business, except for farming, ranching and limited business use.
- For any insured using a vehicle without the reasonable belief that they are permitted to occupy that vehicle. *(e.g., theft)*
- For bodily injury or property damage for which the legally liable insured is also covered under a nuclear energy policy.
- For the ownership, maintenance or use of any motorized vehicle with **less than four wheels or designed mainly for use off roads**.
- For the ownership, maintenance or use of any vehicle, other than a covered auto, which is owned by or **regularly furnished to a family member**.
- For any vehicle located inside a racing facility for the purpose of racing.

PART B - MEDICAL PAYMENTS COVERAGE

Part B - Medical Payments Coverage provides reasonable and necessary medical and funeral expenses resulting from accidental bodily injury. Coverage applies to insureds, and is extended to occupants or pedestrians who are not covered under a Personal Auto Policy. Coverage applies on a per person, per accident basis for injuries **incurred within three years** from the date of accident. Medical payments, which are paid regardless of fault, are excluded to persons while occupying a:

- Vehicle with **less than four wheels**. *(i.e., motorcycle, snowmobile, or jet ski)*
- Covered auto when used to **carry people for a fee**. *(i.e., taxi)*
- **Vehicle used as a residence**. *(i.e., camper located at lake front)*
- Vehicle without having a reasonable belief that the insured is **entitled to occupy the vehicle** *(i.e., thief)*
- Vehicle while **at work if workers compensation benefits are required**.
- Vehicle located inside a racing facility for the purpose of racing.

Coverage does not apply to any person while occupying or being struck by a vehicle in the course of work, or from war and nuclear risks.

PART C - UNINSURED MOTORISTS COVERAGE

Part C - Uninsured Motorists provides coverage for bodily injury which an insured person is legally entitled to recover from an owner or operator of a vehicle **that is financially irresponsible, whose insurance company becomes insolvent, or an accident caused by a hit and run driver.**

An Uninsured Motor Vehicle is defined as any vehicle or trailer of any type:

- To which no bodily injury liability policy or bond applies at the time of accident.
- To which a bodily injury liability policy or bond applies, but the insurance or bonding company denies coverage or becomes insolvent.
- Which is a hit-and-run vehicle whose operator or owner cannot be identified, and hits an insured, a covered auto, or a vehicle an insured is occupying; or causes an accident without hitting an insured, a covered auto or a vehicle an insured is occupying. The facts of a non-contact accident must be proven.

Uninsured motor vehicles do not include: any vehicle or equipment owned by or furnished for the regular use of family members; owned or operated by a self-insurer; owned by any governmental agency; operated on rails or crawler trends; designed mainly for off road use; or while located at or used as a residence. Similar Part B - Medical Payments exclusions also apply to uninsured motorist coverage. See SP-30.

UNDERINSURED MOTORISTS

Underinsured Motorists provides coverage for bodily injury which an insured person is legally entitled to recover from the owner or operator of a vehicle **that is underinsured**. For example, an accident occurs between "Motorist A" with underinsured motorist (UIM) limits of $100,000 and "Motorist B" with the minimum liability limits of $15,000/$30,000/$5,000. It is determined that "Motorist B" is at fault. The following charts illustrates how each policy will respond in three different accident examples:

	Accident 1	Accident 2	Accident 3
Bodily Injury Damage Amount	$10,000	$100,000	$150,000
Motorist A	0	$85,000	$100,000
Motorist B	$10,000	$15,000	$15,000
Underinsurance Coverage Triggered	No *	Yes †	Yes ‡

* UIM is not triggered in the accident since Motorist B's liability ($15,000) is adequate to cover Motorist A's bodily injury claim of $10,000.

† UIM is triggered in the accident since Motorist B's liability ($15,000) is inadequate to cover Motorist A's bodily injury claim of $100,000. In this case Motorist A's UIM coverage pays the difference of $85,000.

‡ UIM is triggered in the accident since Motorist B's liability ($15,000) is inadequate to cover Motorist A's bodily injury claim of $150,000. In this case Motorist A's UIM coverage pays its limit of $100,000. The balance of the $35,000 claim is not covered by insurance.

Uninsured motorists described earlier in this chapter **and underinsured motorist** coverage illustrated above **are mutually exclusive remedies**.

PART D - COVERAGE FOR DAMAGE TO YOUR AUTO

Part D - Coverage For Damage To Your Auto provides coverage for direct and accidental physical damage to your auto *including the payment of applicable sales tax for stolen or damaged property*. Coverage is provided in the following two areas:

1) **Collision coverage**, meaning the upset of your covered auto or its impact with another object. Examples include crashing an auto into another vehicle, wall, tree, etc., or the overturning of the auto while driving too fast for conditions. Policies which have collision coverage will pay for this direct and accidental physical damage, and;

2) **Other Than Collision (OTC)**, meaning any type of loss that is not collision. The following losses are listed in the policy as being examples of OTC:

   - Missiles (i.e., rocks thrown by a tire from a roadbed) or falling objects.
   - Fire.
   - Theft or larceny.
   - Explosion or earthquake.
   - Windstorm.
   - Hail, water or flood.
   - Malicious mischief or vandalism.
   - Riot or civil commotion.
   - Contact with a bird or animal. (commonly a deer)
   - Breakage of glass.

   Common examples of losses covered under OTC include vehicle theft, vandalism, fire, flood and glass breakage.

Under prior Auto Policy Forms, **Other Than Collision (OTC)** coverage was referred to as **comprehensive** coverage. Although the term comprehensive has been deleted from the current Personal Auto Policy, it is commonly used to mean other than collision. See SP-32.

DEDUCTIBLES

Deductibles are the first dollar amounts paid by an insured in the event of loss. Under the Personal Auto Policy, deductibles apply separately to collision and other than collision coverage. Typically, collision is written at $500 with other than collision written at a lower deductible amount of $250.

TRANSPORTATION EXPENSE

The Personal Auto Policy provides temporary transportation expense of up to $20 per day and to a maximum of $600 in the event the insured incurs expenses in following instances: **First**, if a covered auto is stolen, the policy will pay beginning 48 hours after the theft and ending when the vehicle is returned to use or the loss is paid; and **second**, if the covered auto is damaged and it is insured for collision and/or other than collision, the policy will pay beginning 24 hours after the damage is incurred. See SP-33.

EXCLUSIONS

Coverage for Part D - Damage To Your Auto excludes physical damage losses:

- To a covered auto while carrying people or property for a fee.
- Due to wear and tear, freezing, mechanical breakdown or road wear to tires.
- Due to nuclear contamination, war, insurrection or revolution.
- To electronic equipment that reproduces, receives or transmits audio, visual or data signals that is **not permanently installed in the auto.** Equipment such as CB radios/scanners, navigational systems, internet access systems, personal computers, video entertainment systems, telephones, and TVs **are covered if they are permanently installed in the auto.** Disks and tapes are excluded.
- To a camper body or trailer owned by the insured and not declared in the policy. If newly acquired during the policy term, these coverages are automatic.
- To a nonowned auto or temporary substitute auto when used by an insured without a reasonable belief that he or she is entitled to use the vehicle.
- To TV antennas, awnings or equipment used to create additional living facilities.
- To any custom furnishings such as special carpeting, furniture, bars, TVs, cooking facilities, height extending roofs, and custom murals, paintings or decals.
- To equipment used for the detection of the location of radar or laser.
- To any nonowned vehicle while being maintained, employed or engaged in the automobile business including selling, repairing, servicing or parking.
- For any vehicle located inside a racing facility for the purpose of racing.

The above exclusions are business related (carrying people for a fee/being in the auto business), of a maintenance nature (wear and tear/freezing/mechanical breakdown), catastrophic (nuclear contamination), or beyond the intent of the personal auto policy (awnings, cooking facilities, height extending roofs, etc.). Vehicles stolen or damaged are adjusted at ACV or the cost to repair or replace, whichever is less. In addition, a **$1,000 limitation applies to after-market sound reproduction equipment** that is permanently installed in the auto in locations not used by the auto manufacturer. A **$1,500 limitation also applies to non-owned trailers**.

PART E - DUTIES AFTER AN ACCIDENT OR LOSS

Part E - Duties After An Accident Or Loss are conditions of the policy and require the insured to cooperate during the claim process by:

- Providing prompt notice of how, when, and where the accident or loss occurred and include names and addresses of all parties.
- Cooperating with the insurance company in the claims process, including the prompt forwarding of all legal notices and related papers, and submitting to physical exams and examinations under oath.
- Authorizing the company to obtain medical reports and other pertinent records.
- Promptly notifying the police if a hit-and-run driver is involved in an accident.
- Taking reasonable steps to protect your covered auto from further damage.
- Notifying the police in the event your covered auto is stolen.
- Permitting the insurance company to inspect and appraise damaged property.

These are the standard duties required of an insured after a loss.

PART F - GENERAL PROVISIONS

Part F - General Provisions is the final section of the Personal Auto Policy and sets forth the general provisions as follows:

- **Bankruptcy** or insolvency of the insured will not relieve a company of any obligations under the policy. For example, if the insured declares bankruptcy, the insurance company must fulfill its obligations under the policy.
- **Changes** provision requires any changes to be made by endorsement in writing.
- **Fraud** provision bars recovery if the insured has engaged in fraudulent statements. For example, if the insured claims his vehicle was stolen when in fact it was destroyed by the insured, no coverage applies.
- **Legal action against us** requires compliance prior to the initiation of legal action. This means that the insured must file a proof of loss and cooperate prior to initiating legal actions.
- **Our right to recover payment** provides subrogation rights. This permits the insurance company to seek payments from negligent third parties.
- **Policy period and territory** limits coverage to the policy term and to the United States, its territories or possessions, Puerto Rico and Canada.
- **Termination or nonrenewal** permits cancellation by advance written notice. **In Pennsylvania**, cancellation is permitted as follows:

PERSONAL AUTO CANCELLATION REQUIREMENTS

Cancellation by the company is permitted with advance written notice of:

At least 15 days:

- For nonpayment; or,
- If the policy was in effect for less than 60 days; or,
- If the driver's license of named insured has been revoked or suspended within one year of issuance; or, if the policy has been in effect longer than one year, since the last anniversary of the original date.

At least 60 days:

- If the policy is obtained through material misrepresentation.

Cancellation by the insured is permitted by:

- Returning the policy to the company; or
- Giving advance written notice of the date cancellation will take effect.

All cancellation notices must notify the insured of the eligibility of coverage through the Pennsylvania Automobile Insurance Plan.

The above are the standard General Provisions found in policies. They were addressed in Chapter Three and appear in a similar format in other policies. The specific policy language is listed in full on SP-36 and SP-37.

ENDORSEMENTS

The following are common endorsements that are used to alter the Personal Auto Policy:

- **Extended Nonowned Coverage for Named Individuals** extends the liability and medical payments coverages of the Personal Auto Policy to cover individuals named in the endorsement **while using or occupying a nonowned auto, which is furnished and available for the insured's regular use for any type** of business purposes. For example, an insured who is regularly furnished a company vehicle would not be covered for his personal use of that vehicle under his Personal Auto Policy. This coverage **only applies to individuals specifically named in the endorsement**. This means that spouses and/or other family members must be named for coverage to be provided.

- **Joint Ownership Coverage** modifies the policy language to permit coverage for joint owners in nontraditional households. This endorsement provides coverage between individuals other than husband and wife, and/or members who are not of same household.

- **Miscellaneous Type Vehicles** endorsement alters the definition of a covered auto to include motorcycles, dune buggies, golf carts and motor homes.

- **Named Nonowner Endorsement** is issued to individuals who do not own a personal auto but have personal auto exposures. The need for this endorsement generally occurs in the following two instances:

  1) An individuals **does not own an auto, but drives borrowed or rented vehicles**. For example, an individual who routinely borrows a vehicle or periodically rents an auto may be found to be legally responsible for an accident. A similar exposure may exist for individuals who drive a company vehicle and do not have a personal auto policy.

  2) An individual is **seeking a personal umbrella policy**. In this case the insurance company underwriting the umbrella will require underlying coverage for personal automobile exposures. Named Nonowner coverage **only applies to individuals specifically named in the endorsement**. This means that spouses and/or other family members must be named for coverage to be provided.

  In addition to the above cited reasons, individuals may also be held legally responsible for an automobile claim if the individual or a family member causes an auto accident by distracting a driver or some similar occurrence.

- **Towing and Labor** provides coverage limits of $25, $50 or $75 for towing and labor costs incurred each time an auto becomes disabled.

- **Amendments of Policy Provisions - Pennsylvania** is an endorsement which modifies the ISO Personal Auto Policy. These are Pennsylvania specific changes and they have been incorporated into the body of this chapter.

- **First Party Benefits Coverage - Pennsylvania** is an endorsement which modifies the ISO Personal Auto Policy. These are Pennsylvania specific changes and they have been incorporated into the body of this chapter.

- **Limited Tort Alternative Information Notice - Pennsylvania** advises the insured that even if he elects limited tort coverage, he may sue for non economic (pain and suffering) damages as if the individual damaged had elected the full tort alternative whenever the person at fault:

    1) Is convicted or accepts Accelerated Rehabilitative Disposition for driving under the influence of alcohol or a controlled substance.
    2) Is operating a motor vehicle registered in another state (e.g., Ohio).
    3) Intended to injure himself or another person.
    4) Has not maintained financial responsibility as required by the Pennsylvania Motor Vehicle Financial Responsibility Law.
    5) Is in the designing, manufacturing, repairing, servicing or otherwise maintaining of motor vehicles arising out of a defect caused by the business acts or omissions (e.g., repair shop). This does not apply to a defect in a motor vehicle which is operated by the business.
    6) Caused the insured to be injured while an occupant of a motor vehicle other than a private passenger auto (e.g., commercial vehicle).

ASSIGNED RISK PLAN

The Assigned Risk Plan *(also known as the Automobile Insurance Plan)* was developed to provide coverage to individuals who are unable to secure insurance through the voluntary auto market. The plan sets auto rates and provides for an equitable apportionment of assigned risks and clean risks among insurers based upon their premium writings. Assigned risk insureds are assigned to designated carriers for a maximum period of 36 months, however, they may leave the plan if they can secure coverage in the voluntary market. Following the 36 month period, the designated carrier may voluntarily choose to continue the coverage, otherwise the insured must reapply to the plan.

Coverage in the Assigned Risk Plan may be secured through any agent or broker who is certified by the plan as a producer. The same minimum limits of $15,000/-$30,000/$5,000, First Party Benefits and tort options which apply to the voluntary market also apply to the Assigned Risk Plan. Self insurers are not required to participate in the Assigned Risk Plan.

All cancellation notices must notify the insured of the eligibility of coverage through the Assigned Risk Plan.

OVERVIEW

COMMERCIAL AUTO POLICY

The Commercial Auto Policy **provides coverage for businesses which own, use or service automobiles or trucks**. These organizations have three kinds of automobile exposures. They are, **truckers** which move cargo, **garages** which service the auto business, and **other businesses which use automobiles and/or trucks**. The Commercial Auto Coverage Policy consists of:

- **Auto Declarations Page**.
- **One or More Auto Coverage Forms**.
- **Other Endorsements**.

Five different coverage forms which are set forth on the following pages have been designed to insure the various commercial vehicle exposures faced by business organizations. Please note that the Business Auto Coverage Form may be written as a separate Business Auto Physical Damage Form (without liability) providing physical damage coverage only. Section III of the Business Auto Form addresses this coverage.

The following is an illustration of the Commercial Auto Coverage Policy structure:

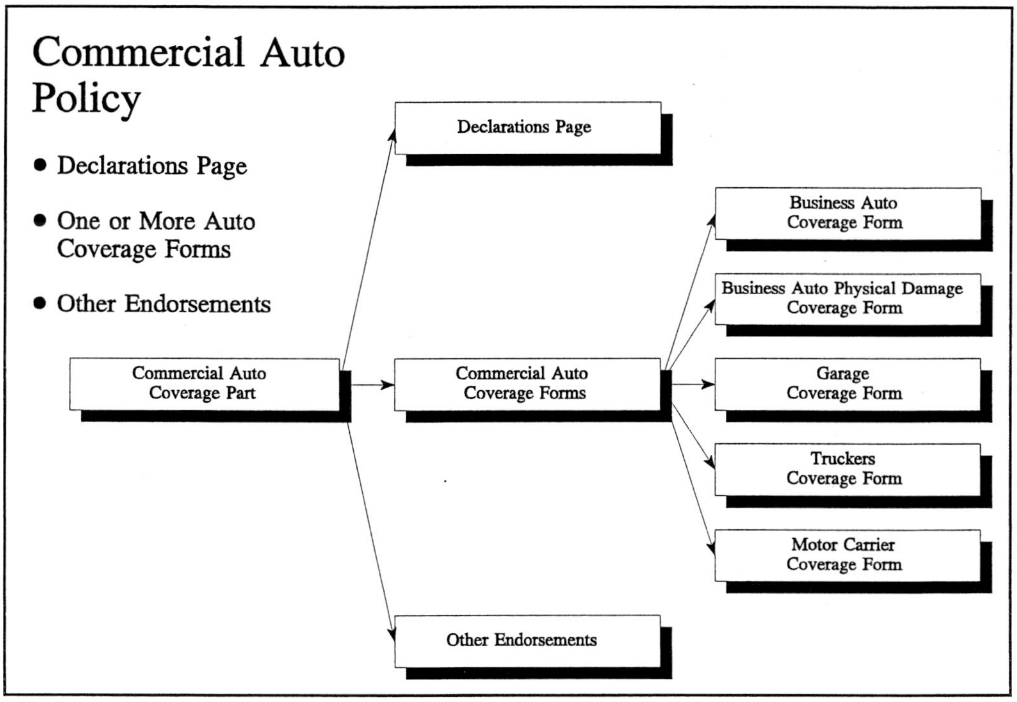

DEFINITIONS

Definitions define terms as used in the policy. The following are the Commercial Auto Policy Definitions:

- **Accident** includes a continuous and repeated exposure to the same conditions resulting in bodily injury or property damage.
- **Auto** means a land motor vehicle, trailer or semitrailer, designed for travel on public roads **but not including mobile equipment**.

- **Covered Pollution Cost or Expense** definition limits coverage to pollutant cost and expenses caused by the release of fuels or lubricants from a manufacturer's automobile or truck part. *This definition does not include pollution cost or expenses incurred resulting from an accident while transporting these types of products.* In other words, if a tanker truck is involved in a motor vehicle accident, coverage will apply to clean up oil from the truck's motor but not from the oil it is transporting. Coverage for tanker trucks and related type vehicles are available by endorsement.
- **Insured contract** means a lease, a sidetrack or easement agreements, or an agreement required by ordinance.
- **Loss** means direct or accident loss or damage.
- **Mobile equipment** means: bulldozers, farm machinery, forklifts and other vehicles designed for off road use; vehicles used to maintain the insured premises; vehicles with crawler treads; road construction equipment; cherry pickers and similar devices; street cleaning and resurfacing equipment.
- **Pollutants** means any solid, liquid, gaseous, or thermal irritant or contaminant including smoke, vapor, soot, fumes, acids, alkalis, chemicals and waste.
- **Trailer** includes semitrailers.

BUSINESS AUTO COVERAGE FORM

Business Auto Coverage Form **is used to insure owned, leased, hired or borrowed business autos**. The form is divided into the following five sections:

- **SECTION I - COVERED AUTOS**, meaning coverage applies to the autos as identified in the declarations according to the following symbols:

  #1 - Any auto.
  #2 - Owned autos only.
  #3 - Owned private passengers autos only.
  #4 - Owned autos other than private passenger auto.
  #5 - Owned autos subject to no-fault benefits.
  #6 - Owned autos subject to compulsory uninsured motorists laws.
  #7 - Specifically described only.
  #8 - Hired autos only.
  #9 - Nonowned autos only.

  Newly acquired autos are automatically covered until the end of the policy term if symbols #1 to #6 are entered next to a coverage. If symbol #7 is indicated, coverage is automatically provided for 30 days.

- **SECTION II - LIABILITY COVERAGE** agrees to pay the insured's legal obligation for damages caused by a covered accident, resulting in bodily injury or property damage, and to defend, investigate and settle all suits. An insured under the policy includes the named insured and anyone using the vehicle with permission, subject to certain exclusions. Also covered for liability are: trailers with load capacity of up to 2,000 pounds, mobile equipment while being carried or towed by a covered auto, and a temporary substitute auto for any vehicle which is out of service because of breakdown, repair, loss or destruction.

Supplementary Payments include: costs incurred by the insured; up to $2,000 for cost of bail bonds; cost of release attachment bonds; reasonable expenses including up to $250 per day to assist in the claims process; taxes levied against the insured and interest charges in the defense of the suit; and interest which accrues after entry of the judgment. Any out of state auto will automatically have that state's statutory required limits of liability. **Liability Exclusions** eliminate coverage for bodily injury and/or property arising out of intentional acts, contractual liability, except insured contracts, workers compensation exposures, damage to property transported and in the care, custody and control of the insured, handling of property, movement of property by mechanical devices not attached to a covered vehicle (e.g., forklift), completed operations, the release of pollutants (e.g., from tanker trucks), war and racing activities.

- **SECTION III - PHYSICAL DAMAGE COVERAGE** agrees to pay for loss to a covered auto under the following three coverage agreements:

  1) **Comprehensive Coverage**, which applies to loss from any cause, except collision with another object, or the overturn of the vehicle.

  2) **Specific Perils Coverage**, which applies to the specific perils of fire, lightning, explosion, theft, windstorm, hail, earthquake, flood, V&MM, or the sinking, burning, collision or derailment of any conveyance transporting the covered auto. This is an alternative to comprehensive coverage.

  3) **Collision Coverage**, which applies to collision with another object or overturn of the vehicle.

  Towing and Labor, which reimburses the insured for necessary towing and labor costs as the result of their vehicle being disabled may also be added.

  Physical Damage Coverage Extensions automatically include **transportation expenses** incurred as the result of theft, and pays up to $20 per day to a maximum of $600 for expenses incurred beginning 48 hours after the theft and ending when the vehicle is returned or the loss is paid. This extension only applies to either comprehensive or specified causes of loss coverage. **Physical Damage Exclusions** eliminate coverage arising out of nuclear hazards, war risks, racing activities, wear and tear, freezing, mechanical breakdown, loss to tapes, records, discs, radar devices, and related accessories. Sound reproduction equipment is covered if permanently installed in the vehicle. Vehicles stolen or damaged are adjusted at ACV or the cost to repair or replace, whichever is less.

- **SECTION IV - BUSINESS AUTO CONDITIONS** set forth the provisions of the policy and include appraisal, insured's duties in the case of loss, legal actions against the insurer, transfer of rights and subrogation. The **General Conditions** of the policy include bankruptcy, concealment, misrepresentation or fraud, liberalization, no benefit to bailee, other insurance, premium audit, policy territory and period conditions.

- **SECTION V - DEFINITIONS** define terms and include accident, auto, bodily injury, insured and insured contract. (See 6-15 & 6-16)

GARAGE COVERAGE FORM

The Garage Coverage Form modifies the Business Auto Coverage Form to **cover garage operations** by addressing the unique exposures of **service stations, auto dealers, parking garages, repair shops** and similar type risks. Its format is similar to the Business Auto Form, with the addition of a new coverage (Section III - Garagekeepers Coverage). It is divided into the following six sections:

- **SECTION I - COVERED AUTOS**, meaning coverage applies to the autos as identified in the declarations according to the following symbols:

  #21 - through #28 correspond to the Business Auto Coverage Form.
  #29 - Non-owned autos used in the garage business.
  #30 - Autos left for service, repair, storage or safekeeping.
  #31 - Dealers' autos and autos held for sale by non-dealers or trailer dealers.

- **SECTION II - GARAGE LIABILITY** agrees to pay the insured's legal obligation for damages caused by a covered accident, resulting in bodily injury or property damage and to defend, investigate and settle all suits. An insured under the policy includes the named insured and anyone using the vehicle with permission subject to certain exclusions. Garage liability is broader than the business auto liability since coverage is provided for premises operations, completed operations, and product liability. **Garage liability extensions** are the same as in the Business Auto Form. **Garage liability exclusions** are similar to the Business Auto Coverage Form with additional exclusions for:

  - Property damage to the garages' defective products (tire, batteries, etc.);
  - Work performed (failure to properly align tires or properly repaint an auto);
  - Product recall (due to the installation of a defective product);
  - Loss of use for failure to perform (failure to complete repairs as promised);
  - Bodily injury and property damage due to liquor liability (this eliminates coverage to service stations (mini marts) which may also sell alcohol).

  Please note that coverage may apply to subsequent damage. For example, if a garage improperly repairs a vehicle's brakes, no coverage applies. However, if the defective brakes cause an accident, coverage applies.

- **SECTION III - GARAGEKEEPERS COVERAGE** provides legal liability for damage to a customer's auto or property *in the insured's care, custody and control* while the insured is attending, servicing, parking or storing the property. Under the form, **the garage owner must be legally liable for coverage to be afforded**. As an option, the garage owner may purchase **direct coverage** which provides coverage regardless of fault. This direct coverage can be arranged on a **primary basis** (pays first) or on an **excess basis** (excess over the insured's Personal Auto Policy). Garagekeepers Coverage is written on a comprehensive, specified causes of loss or collision basis. **Garagekeepers extensions** are the same as in the Business Auto Form. **Garagekeepers exclusions** eliminate coverage arising out of contractual obligations, theft by an insured or employee, defective parts and faulty work.

Sections IV, V and VI of the Garage Form are similar to the Business Auto Form.

TRUCKERS COVERAGE FORM

The Truckers Coverage Form modifies the Business Auto Coverage Form to **cover trucking operations**. A trucker is a person or organization in the business of transporting goods, materials or commodities *for another*. **It does not cover air, water, or rail carriers or their employees.** The Truckers Coverage format is similar to the Business Auto Form and is divided into the following six sections:

- **SECTION I - COVERED AUTOS**, meaning coverage applies to covered autos as identified in the declarations according to the following symbols:

  #41 - Any auto.
  #42 - Owned autos only.
  #43 - Owned commercial autos only.
  #44 - Owned autos subject to no fault.
  #45 - Owned autos subject to compulsory uninsured motorists law.
  #46 - Specifically described autos only.
  #47 - Hired autos only.
  #48 - Trailers in your possession *under a written trailer interchange agreement.*
  #49 - Your trailers in the possession of anyone else under a written trailer interchange agreement.
  #50 - Nonowned autos only.

- **SECTION II - TRUCKERS LIABILITY COVERAGE** agrees to pay the insured's legal obligation for damages caused by a covered accident, resulting in bodily injury or property damage and to defend, investigate and settle all suits. An insured under the policy includes the named insured and anyone using the vehicle with permission subject to certain exclusions. **Truckers liability extensions** are the same as in the Business Auto and Garage Forms. **Truckers liability exclusions** are similar to the Business Auto Coverage Form.

- **SECTION III - TRAILER INTERCHANGE COVERAGE** agrees to pay the insured's legal liability for **loss or damage to nonowned trailers and equipment**. This exposure occurs when a trucker interchanges his own trailer for a nonowned trailer. Trailer interchange insurance, which is written on a comprehensive coverage, specified causes of loss coverage or collision coverage, insures this exposure. **Trailer interchange extensions** are the same as in the Truckers liability coverage. **Trailer interchange exclusions** are similar to the physical damage exclusions in the Business Auto and Garage Forms.

  An exposure not covered under the Trailer Interchange Coverage occurs when independent truck owners are hired by truckers to move goods. In these instances, the independent trucker is normally covered under the Truckers' Policy while moving cargo, however, no coverage would apply after the cargo is delivered. Coverage for this exposure is available by endorsement as explained in the commercial auto endorsement section.

Sections IV, V and VI of the Truckers Form is similar to the Business Auto Form.

MOTOR CARRIER FORM

The Motor Carrier Form is **an alternative to the Truckers Coverage Form**. It was developed as the result of reduced regulatory authority of the Interstate Commerce Commission and the increased activity of private carriers in the trucking industry. A motor carrier is a person or organization providing transportation by auto *in the furtherance of a much wider commercial enterprise*. This form is generally used to insure trucking operations that are larger than ones covered under the Truckers Form. The Motor Carrier Form does not cover air, water, or rail carriers or their employees and is commonly used to cover common and private motor carriers.

- **SECTION I - COVERED AUTOS**, meaning coverage applies to covered autos as identified in the declarations according to the following symbols:

  #61 - Any auto.
  #62 - Owned autos only.
  #63 - Owned private passenger type autos only. (not included in Truckers Form)
  #64 - Owned commercial autos only.
  #65 - Owned autos subject to no fault.
  #66 - Owned autos subject to a compulsory uninsured motorists law.
  #67 - Specifically described autos.
  #68 - Hired autos only.
  #69 - Trailers in your possession *under a written trailer or equipment interchange agreement*.
  #70 - Your trailers in the possession of anyone else under a written trailer interchange agreement.
  #71 - Nonowned autos only.

- **SECTION II - MOTOR CARRIER LIABILITY COVERAGE** agrees to pay the insured's legal obligation for damages caused by a covered accident, resulting in bodily injury or property damage and to defend, investigate and settle all suits. An insured under the policy includes the named insured and anyone using the vehicle with permission subject to certain exclusions. **Motor Carrier liability extensions** are the same as in the Business Auto and Truckers Forms. **Motor Carrier liability exclusions** are similar to the Business Auto Form.

Section III - Trailer Interchange Coverage, Section IV - Physical Damage, Section V - Truckers Conditions; and Section VI - Definitions are all similar to the Truckers Form.

COMMERCIAL CARRIER REGULATION

The purpose of the Commercial Carrier Regulation is to protect the public's interest by creating financial responsibility requirements which apply to commercial carriers. Commercial carriers are classified as either **common carriers**, which offer their services to the public at large, or **contract carriers**, which agree to service specific clients based upon prearranged agreements. These carriers may **prove financial responsibility by purchasing insurance, being bonded or by self insuring.** The following are the required limits for commercial carriers:

FINANCIAL RESPONSIBILITY

The Department of Transportation's Bureau of Motor Carrier Safety regulates the financial responsibility requirements under the provisions of the Motor Carrier Act of 1980.

The Motor Carrier Act of 1980 applies to vehicles in excess of 10,000 pounds that haul cargo over state lines and/or transport hazardous material. Tow trucks also fall under this act. The following are the four types of carriages and their minimum liability requirements:

- $ 750,000 for transporting non hazardous property.
- $5,000,000 for transporting hazardous substances such as radioactive materials.
- $1,000,000 for transporting oil and hazardous wastes in portable tanks.
- $5,000,000 for transporting explosives and poison gases.

Coverage under the Motor Carrier Act is generally obtained by attaching the **Endorsement for Motor Carrier Policies of Insurance for Public Liability (MCS-90)** to the Truckers Coverage Form. *This endorsement makes the insurance company absolutely liable to claimants in the event the insured is found to be responsible for an accident.* For example, if an accident occurs that is not covered under the policy, the insurer is required to pay the claim, afterwhich, it may seek reimbursement from the trucking company. This endorsement acts as a financial guarantee to the public.

Cancellation of this endorsement requires 30 days advance written notice to the Interstate Commerce Commission (ICC) and 35 days advance written notice to the other party.

COMMERCIAL AUTO ENDORSEMENTS

The following are endorsements which may be added to the Commercial Auto Policy:

- **Additional Insured -- Lessor (CA 20 01)** is used when a vehicle is under a long term lease. It establishes an insurable interest between the lessor (the finance company) and the lessee (the insured).

- **Broad Form Products (CA 25 01)** is a Garage Policy endorsement which eliminates the defective products exclusion. Under the unendorsed Garage Policy, no coverage would apply in the event a garage sold a customer a defective product, such as a tire or battery. This endorsement covers the amount of property damage to the insured's (garage owner) product. A $250 deductible applies per occurrence.

- **Deductible Liability Coverage (CA 03 02)** allows the insured to elect deductibles for bodily injury and property damage either separately or combined. These deductibles can be structured on a per-claim or per-occurrence basis.

- **Drive Other Car (DOC) Coverage (CA 99 10)** extends business auto coverage to non business (personal) exposures of **named individuals who may not own an automobile**. This typically occurs to individuals who are furnished company autos, but do not own or carry personal auto insurance. For example, if an individual is assigned a company vehicle, carries no personal auto insurance, and is involved in an accident while renting a vehicle on vacation or while borrowing a vehicle for personal use, no coverage would apply under the unendorsed business auto coverage. To remedy this gap, individuals who are furnished company vehicles and who do not have a personal auto policy should have Drive Other Car Coverage endorsed onto their employer's Business Auto Policy. This coverage only applies to the named individual and his spouse (resident relatives are excluded). Drive Other Car coverage may also be secured by purchasing a Named Nonowner Policy under the Personal Auto Policy.

- **Employees as Insureds (CA 99 33)** extends business auto coverage to employees who use their personal auto in the course of business. This endorsement provides the employee with excess liability coverage above the employee's Personal Auto Policy liability.

- **False Pretense Coverage (CA 25 03)** is a Garage Policy endorsement which provides coverage in the event the garage releases a vehicle under false pretense.

- **Hired Autos Specified as Owned Autos (CA 99 16)** is used to specify hired autos as owned autos. The need for this endorsement typically arises when a leased auto is required to have primary insurance. This endorsement does not contain a loss payable or cancellation clause.

- **Individual Named Insureds (CA 99 17)** extends business auto coverage to non business (personal) exposures of the individual named insureds who may not own an automobile. This endorsement is **intended to provide personal auto coverage to individuals who are sole proprietors** and who do not have a Personal Auto Policy.

- **Mobile Equipment (CA 20 15)** provides auto coverages (liability, medical payments, uninsured motorist, and physical damage coverage) to mobile equipment.

- **Truckers - Insurance for Non-Trucking Use (CA 23 09)** provides coverage to independent truck owners who are hired by truckers to move goods. In these instances, the independent trucker is normally covered under the Truckers' Policy while moving cargo, however, no coverage would apply after the cargo is delivered. This commonly occurs when the independent trucker is either picking up cargo at a terminal or returning from delivering cargo. In these instances, the trucker would be either:

  - **Deadheading** (driving the tractor and trailer without a load); or
  - **Bobtailing** (operating a tractor without a trailer).

  To fill this void, independent truckers need a Truckers - Insurance for Non-Trucking Use Endorsement. This coverage is also referred to as **Bobtail Liability**.

- **Pollution Liability - Broadened Coverage For Covered Autos (CA 99 48)** eliminates the pollution exclusion thereby providing coverage for bodily injury or property damage resulting from the transportation, handling, storage or disposal of pollutants. This endorsement does not apply to liability assumed under a contract or agreement.

- **Pollution Liability - Broadened Coverage For Covered Autos (CA 99 55)** this Garage Policy endorsement provides the same basic coverage that is applicable to above endorsement (CA 99 48), however, it only applies to the covered auto section of the Garage Policy.

PENNSYLVANIA CHANGES - CANCELLATION AND NONRENEWAL

Cancellation or nonrenewal of the Commercial Auto Policy in Pennsylvania is mandated requiring advance written notice as follows:

COMMERCIAL AUTO POLICY CANCELLATION REQUIREMENTS

Cancellation by the company is permitted with advance written notice:

If the policy has been in effect for less than 60 days:

- At least 30 days advance written notice is required.

If the policy has been in effect for more than 60 days:

- At least 15 days advance written notice for material misrepresentation and nonpayment of premium.
- At least 60 days advance written notice is required for increased risk factors, loss of reinsurance, failure to comply with policy conditions, or any other reason deemed by the insurance commissioner.

Cancellation by the first named insured is permitted by:

- Giving advance written notice of the date cancellation will take effect.

All cancellation and/or nonrenewal notices must notify the insured of the eligibility of coverage through the Assigned Risk Plan.

COMPARISON of PERSONAL AUTO and COMMERCIAL AUTO PROGRAMS		
Category	**Personal Auto Policy**	**Commercial Auto Policy**
Eligibility	Private passenger auto, pickup or van that is less than 9,000 pounds and not used as a delivery vehicle in a business	Any land motor vehicle, trailer or semi-trailer designed for travel on public roads but not including mobile equipment
Policy Form(s)	**One Form**	**Five Forms Used to Cover Three Exposures**
	Personal Auto Policy - Used to cover personal exposures of individuals and families Coverage for business exposure is subject to eligibility requirements (see above) Insurers will surcharge for business usage	Business Auto / Business Auto PD: Used to cover owned, leased, hired or borrowed business autos Garage †: Used to cover garage operations of service stations, auto dealers, parking garages, repair shops and similar type risks Truckers: Used to cover trucking operations; A trucker transports goods for another Motor Carrier: Used to cover trucking operations as alternative to the Truckers Form; A motor carrier transports goods in the furtherance of a much wider commercial enterprise; This form is commonly used to cover common and private carriers
Liability	**One Coverage**	**One Coverage**
	Pays third party when insured negligently operates vehicle	Pays third party when insured negligently operates vehicle
Physical Damage	**Two Coverages**	**Three Coverages**
	Pays insured for physical damage loss to vehicle 1) Other Than Collision (OTC) 2) Collision	Pays insured for physical damage loss to vehicle 1) Comprehensive (same as OTC) 2) Specific Named Perils (alternative to comprehensive) 3) Collision
MVFRL	Applies	Applies
Motor Carrier Act	N/A	Applies

† Garage Policy may include Garagekeepers coverage which provides legal liability for damage to a customer's auto or property in the insured's care, custody and control while the insured is attending, servicing, parking or storing the property. May be written on a primary or excess basis.

KEY TERMS AND CONCEPTS

The following terms were introduced in this chapter. You should know each word and concept and be able to apply them in everyday usage. To improve retention, it is recommended that you write out each key term and concept in your own words.

Accidental Death Insurance
Assigned Risk Plan
Bodily Injury Liability
Business Auto Form(s)
Collision
Commercial Auto Coverage Part
Commercial Carriers Regulations
Comprehensive Coverage
Deductibles
Discounts
Drive Other Car Coverage (CA 99 10)
Employees as Insureds (CA 99 33)
Extended Non-owner Liability
Extraordinary Medical Benefit Insurance
False Pretense Coverage (CA 25 03)
First Party Benefits
Full Tort
Funeral Benefit Insurance
Garage Form
Garagekeepers Coverage
Hired Autos Specified as Owned Autos
Income Loss Insurance
Individual Named Insureds (CA 99 17)
Joint Ownership Coverage
Liability Exclusions
Limited Tort
Medical Expense Insurance
Miscellaneous Type Vehicles
Mobile Equipment Endorsement (CA 20 15)
Motor Carriers Form
Motor Vehicle Fraud
Named Non-owned Endorsement
Newly Acquired Additional Vehicle
Newly Acquired Replacement Vehicle
Other Than Collision (OTC)
Part A - Liability Coverage
Part B - Medical Payments
Part C - Uninsured Motorists
Part D - Coverage For Damage To Your Auto
Part E - Duties After An Accident Or Loss
Part F - General Duties
Personal Auto Policy
Physical Damage Exclusions
Pollution Liability Endorsement (CA 99 48)
Pollution Liability Endorsement (CA 99 55)
Private Passenger Auto
Property Damage Liability
Required Limits of Liability
Stacking Waiver
Supplementary Payments
The Motor Carrier Act of 1980
Tort Option Selection
Towing and Labor
Transportation Expense
Trucker Form
Truckers Insurance for Non-Trucking
Underinsured Motorists Insurance
Uninsured Motor Vehicle
Uninsured Motorists Insurance
Your Covered Auto

REVIEW QUESTIONS

Before attempting to answer the end chapter practice questions, you should ask yourself if you can answer the following questions. It is recommended that you write out each review question in your own words. This exercise will help you apply the key terms and concepts that you've learned to form relationships with different topics.

1. What are the required minimum limits of liability under PMVFRL? (6-1)
2. How does full tort differ from limited tort? (6-2)
3. Identify and explain the 5 first party benefits. (6-2)
4. Identify the 6 categories of ineligible claimants for first party benefits. (6-3)
5. Explain how workers compensation and the PMVFRL are coordinated. (6-3)
6. Explain stacking and identify the coverages which may be stacked. (6-4)
7. Explain the time restrictions that apply to newly acquired autos. (6-5)
8. Identify and explain 3 categories of individuals or organizations that may be granted coverage under the Personal Auto Policy. (6-6)
9. Identify and explain 5 Supplementary Payments provided under the Personal Auto Policy. (6-7)
10. Identify 6 Liability exclusions found in the Personal Auto Policy. (6-8)
11. Identify 6 Medical Payments exclusions found in the Personal Auto Policy. (6-8)
12. What is an uninsured motor vehicle? (6-9)
13. What is Underinsured Motorist Coverage? (6-9)
14. When is Underinsured Motorist Coverage triggered? (6-9)
15. What are the 2 coverages available under Part D - Coverage For Damage To Your Auto of the Personal Auto Policy? (6-10)
16. How does Collision differ from Other Than Collision? (6-10)
17. Identify 10 perils covered under OTC. (6-10)
18. When does Transportation Expense pay and what are the dollar limits? (6-10)
19. Identify 10 physical damage exclusions found in the Personal Auto Policy. (6-11)
20. Identify and explain a dollar limitation that applies to physical damage losses. (6-11)
21. What is the coverage territory of the Personal Auto Policy? (6-12)

22. What primary benefit does the Personal Auto Policy endorsement Extended No-owned Coverage for Named Individuals provide? (6-12)

23. Identify and explain the 6 exceptions under the PMVFRL which grants individuals who choose limited tort an unrestricted right to sue for pain and suffering. (6-14)

24. Explain how Pennsylvania's Automobile Insurance Plan functions. (6-14)

25. Identify the 3 kinds of automobile exposures that may be covered under the Commercial Auto Policy. (6-15)

26. Explain if the discharge of pollutants are covered under Commercial Auto Policy. (6-16 & 6-21)

27. Identify 5 types of mobile equipment and indicate if or how it can be insured under the Commercial Auto Policy. (6-16 & 6-22)

28. Identify 4 types of businesses that have a need for the Garage Coverage Form. (6-18)

29. What does Garage Liability cover? (6-18)

30. What does Garagekeepers cover? (6-18)

31. How does the Truckers Form differ from the Motor Carriers Form? (6-19 & 6-20)

32. What is the Motor Carrier Act of 1980? (6-21)

33. What are the 4 minimum liability limits required under the Motor Carrier Act of 1980? (6-21)

34. What is the Endorsement for Motor Carrier Policies of Insurance for Public Liability (MCS-90)? (6-21)

35. What is the unique feature of the Endorsement for Motor Carrier Policies of Insurance for Public Liability (MCS-90)? (6-21)

36. What is DOC and who may need it? (6-22)

37. From an eligibility standpoint, how does the Personal Auto Policy differ form a Commercial Auto Policy? (6-24)

38. From a policy form(s) and exposure standpoint, how does the Personal Auto Policy differ from a Commercial Auto Policy? (6-24)

39. From a Liability Coverage standpoint, how does the Personal Auto Policy differ from a Commercial Auto Policy? (6-24)

40. From a physical damage standpoint, how does the Personal Auto Policy differ from a Commercial Auto Policy? (6-24)

41. Does the PMVFRL and Motor Carrier Act apply to vehicles covered under a Personal Auto Policy and Commercial Auto Policy? (6-24)

NOTES

PRACTICE EXAM SIX

ON

AUTO INSURANCE

1. Which of the following is true of the Pennsylvania Motor Vehicle Financial Responsibility Law as amended by Act 6?

A) That every applicant for registration of a vehicle subject to the law is informed that failure to prove financial responsibility when required could result in loss of registration or driver's license.
B) That coverage include liability insurance with minimum financial responsibility limits, liability insurance with first party benefits and uninsured and underinsured motorists coverage.
C) That an assigned risk plan, an assigned claims plan, and a catastrophic plan be created.
D) Only "Full Tort" coverage is available. Ref. 6-1 & 6-2

2. All of the following are true of the Pennsylvania Motor Vehicle Financial Responsibility Law as amended by Act 6 EXCEPT:

A) You must elect between "Full Tort" coverage and "Limited Tort" coverage.
B) If you elect the "Limited Tort" coverage option your premium is lower than the "Full Tort" coverage option.
C) If you elect the "Full Tort" coverage option your premium will be higher than "Limited Tort" coverage option.
D) The enactment of Act 6 to the Pennsylvania Motor Vehicle Financial Responsibility Law provided the insuring public with fewer options. Ref. 6-1 & 6-2

3. Which of the following is the required minimum liability insurance limit under the Pennsylvania Motor Vehicle Financial Responsibility Law as amended by Act 6?

A) $ 5,000 per person/$30,000 per accident/$10,000 property damage.
B) $15,000 per person/$30,000 per accident/$ 5,000 property damage.
C) $25,000 per person/$50,000 per accident/$10,000 property damage.
D) $30,000 per person/$75,000 per accident/$20,000 property damage. Ref. 6-1

4. All of the following are true of first party benefits under the Pennsylvania Motor Vehicle Financial Responsibility Law as amended by Act 6 EXCEPT:

A) Medical Expense Benefits of a required minimum of $5,000 with an option up to $100,000.
B) Extraordinary Medical Benefits is an option that pays medical and rehabilitation benefits up to a limit of $1,100,000.
C) Income Loss, Funeral Benefits and Accidental Death Insurance are options.
D) Medical Expense Benefits are required at a minimum amount of $10,000. Ref. 6-2

5. All of the following are true of the Pennsylvania Motor Vehicle Financial Responsibility Law as amended by ACT 6 EXCEPT:

A) Uninsured Motorist Insurance is optional.
B) Underinsured Motorist Insurance is mandatory.
C) Comprehensive and Collision Insurance is optional but normally required by a bank or lender of a car loan.
D) If you own more than one vehicle, you may waive your option to "Stack" limits on Uninsured and Underinsured Motorists Insurance. Ref. 6-4 & 6-5

6. First Party Benefits must be provided to all registered vehicles in Pennsylvania with certain exceptions. All of the following are exceptions to the law EXCEPT:

A) Recreational vehicles not intended for highway use.
B) Motorcycles.
C) Motorized pedacycles or similar vehicles are ineligible for this coverage.
D) High performance vehicles. Ref. 6-3

7. All of the following are eligible vehicles under the Personal Auto Policy EXCEPT:

A) Four wheel motor vehicles owned or leased.
B) A vehicle rented to another and used to carry passengers for a fee.
C) Any private passenger automobile.
D) Pickups or vans used for business. Ref. 6-6 & 6-7

8. All of the following would be considered an insured under the Personal Auto Policy EXCEPT:

A) A spouse having a different residence address.
B) A son or daughter of the insured using the car at college in another state.
C) A friend who has the insured's permission to use the auto.
D) A spouse having the same residence address. Ref. 6-6

9. In the Personal Auto Policy, Your Covered Auto means all of the following EXCEPT:

A) A trailer owned by the named insured.
B) Only vehicles shown in the Declarations.
C) A newly acquired auto for 14 days.
D) A pickup or van not exceeding 9,000 pounds. Ref. 6-7

10. Part A - Liability Coverage of the Personal Auto Policy provides coverage for:

A) Bodily Injury and Property Damage for which any insured becomes legally responsible because of an auto accident.
B) Only Bodily Injury for which any insured becomes legally responsible because of an auto accident.
C) Only Property Damage for which any insured becomes legally responsible because of an auto accident.
D) None of the above. Ref. 6-7

11. All of the following are true of the Transportation Expense Coverage under the Personal Auto Policy EXCEPT:

A) This coverage only applies if the vehicle is stolen.
B) It pays up to $20 per day to cover transportation expenses incurred by the insured.
C) It will cover transportation expenses incurred by the insured by a collision loss, if collision coverage is provided under the policy.
D) $600 is the maximum amount of transportation expense coverage. Ref. 6-10

12. All of the following are Exclusions to PART A - Liability Coverage EXCEPT:

A) Damage to property owned or being transported by that person.
B) Bodily Injury for which an insured becomes legally responsible because of an auto accident.
C) Damage to property rented to, used by, or in the care of that person.
D) Liability coverage to individuals using a vehicle without a reasonable belief that person is entitled to do so. Ref. 6-8

13. Which of the following is true of PART C - Uninsured Motorists Coverage?

A) Pays for bodily injury which an insured person is legally entitled to recover from the owner or operator of an uninsured motor vehicle because of accidental bodily injury.
B) Pays for bodily injury which an insured person is legally entitled to recover.
C) Pays for damage only to underinsured vehicles.
D) Pay for damage to any vehicle. Ref. 6-8 & 6-9

14. All of the following would be considered an uninsured motor vehicle EXCEPT:

A) A vehicle not covered by a bodily injury liability policy or bond.
B) A vehicle covered by a bodily injury liability policy or bonding company that denies coverage or becomes insolvent.
C) A hit-and-run vehicle whose driver cannot be identified.
D) A vehicle with minimum limits of $15,000/$30,000/$5,000. Ref. 6-9

15. All of the following are true of the Assigned Risk Plan EXCEPT:

A) It provides a market to individuals who are unable to secure coverage from the voluntary market.
B) Self insurers must participate.
C) All individuals who write auto insurance in Pennsylvania are required to participate in the plan.
D) The plan provides for an equitable apportionment of risks. Ref. 6-14

16. Which of the following is true of PART D - Coverage For Damage To Your Auto?

A) It may provide Collision coverage.
B) It may provide Other Than Collision coverage.
C) It pays for direct and accidental loss to a covered auto, any nonowned auto, including equipment minus any applicable deductible.
D) All of the above. Ref. 6-10

17. Which of the following is true of Collision coverage?

A) It is the upset of a covered auto or its impact with another vehicle or object.
B) Examples of Collision include missiles or falling objects.
C) Examples of Collision include fire, theft or larceny.
D) Examples of Collision include explosion, earthquake or windstorm. Ref. 6-5 & 6-10

18. All of the following are true of Other Than Collision (OTC) coverage EXCEPT:

A) It is the upset of a covered auto or its impact with another vehicle object.
B) Examples of OTC include contact with a bird or an animal or glass breakage.
C) Examples of OTC include malicious mischief or vandalism.
D) Examples of OTC include riot and civil commotion.
E) Examples of OTC include hail, water and flood. Ref. 6-5 & 6-10

19. An insured is arrested for driving under the influence of alcohol and placed in the County Jail. In this example, the Personal Auto Policy:

A) Pays nothing.
B) Pays up to $100 for the cost of bail bonds.
C) Pays up to $200 for the cost of bail bonds.
D) Pays up to $250 for the cost of bail bonds. Ref.6-7

20. All of the following are Exclusions to PART D - Coverage For Damage To Your Auto EXCEPT:

A) Loss to a covered auto used to carry persons or property for a fee.
B) Damage to the front end due to a collision with a tree.
C) Damage due to wear and tear, freezing, mechanical/electrical breakdown.
D) Radioactive contamination and war. Ref. 6-11

21. Which of the following are Exclusions to PART D - Coverage For Damage To Your Auto?

A) Loss to equipment designed for reproductive sound that is not permanently installed.
B) Loss to tapes or records designed for use with reproductive sound equipment.
C) Loss to citizen band radios, two way mobile radios, telephones or scanning monitor receivers unless permanently installed.
D) All of the above. Ref. 6-11

22. Under the Supplemental Payments section of the Personal Auto Policy, an insured attending a trial at the insurance company's request may be reimbursed for loss of earnings up to:

A) $100 per day.
B) $200 per day.
C) $300 per day.
D) $400 per day. Ref. 6-7

23. Which of the following is a PART F - General Provision?

A) Fraud meaning making false statements.
B) Legal Actions Against Us meaning that all terms of the policy must be complied with before legal actions may be commenced.
C) Our Right To Recovery meaning rights of subrogation.
D) All of the above. Ref. 6-12

24. Under the Pennsylvania Motor Vehicle Financial Responsibility Law, the extraordinary medical benefits are limited to $50,000 per year after:

A) 6 months following an accident.
B) 12 months following an accident.
C) 18 months following an accident.
D) 24 months following an accident. Ref. 6-2

25. The Personal Auto Policy endorsement which modifies the policy language to address the needs of the nontraditional household is:

A) Named Nonowner Endorsement.
B) Extended Nonowned Coverage for Named Individuals.
C) Rental Reimbursement.
D) Joint Ownership Coverage. Ref. 6-13

26. All of the following are PART E - Duties After an Accident or Loss under the Personal Auto Policy EXCEPT:

A) The insurance company must be notified promptly of how, when and where the accident or loss happened.
B) A person seeking coverage does not have to cooperate.
C) A person seeking coverage must cooperate with the company in the investigation, settlement or defense and must promptly forward related legal notices.
D) Submit to examinations and permit the company the right to obtain medical records and related pertinent records. Ref. 6-11

27. Bill's Auto Policy provides limits of 100/300/50. He is in an accident and found liable for bodily injury to Tom in the amount of $80,000 and to Mary in the amount of $90,000. Bill's policy will pay:

A) $170,000 plus defense costs.
B) $170,000.
C) $100,000 plus defense costs.
D) $100,000. Ref. 6-7

28. While driving on the Pennsylvania Turnpike, Jim's auto strikes a deer. In order for coverage to be afforded, Jim's Personal Auto Policy must have:

A) Collision.
B) Other Than Collision.
C) First Party Benefits.
D) Uninsured Motorists. Ref. 6-10

29. Financial Responsibility as defined under the Pennsylvania Motor Vehicle Financial Responsibility Law means:

A) The ability to respond to liability on account of accidents arising out of the maintenance or use of a motor vehicle.
B) The ability to respond to property damage on account of an occurrence.
C) The ability to respond to physical damage on account of an incident.
D) The ability to pay claims arising out of personal pursuits. Ref. 6-1

30. Under Pennsylvania's limited tort option:

A) The insured's right to sue is limited to specific out-of-pocket expenses, except for serious injury or death.
B) The insured's right to sue is unrestricted.
C) The insured's right to sue is exclusively limited to specific out-of-pocket expenses.
D) Premiums are higher than the full tort option. Ref. 6-2

31. All of the following are true of Named Nonowner Coverage EXCEPT:

A) This coverage is issued to individuals who do not own an automobile but may borrow or rent vehicles.
B) The Named Nonowner Coverage is an endorsement to the Personal Auto Policy.
C) An individual with a company auto would never have a need for Named Nonowner Coverage.
D) Named Nonowner Coverage may include liability, medical payments and uninsured motorists coverage. Ref. 6-13

32. Sally carries Underinsured Motorist coverage of $100,000. She is involved in an accident with Tom who has minimum limits of $15,000/$30,000/$5,000. If Tom is found to be 100% negligent for Sally's bodily injury, Tom's policy will pay:

A) $5,000.
B) $10,000.
C) $15,000.
D) $30,000. Ref. 6-9

33. Using the same information as above, how much would Sally receive if her bodily injuries amounted to $75,000:

A) Only $30,000 from Tom's policy since this is the limit of liability.
B) Only $50,000 from Tom's policy since this is the total limit of liability.
C) $15,000 from Tom's policy for his per person limit of liability and $60,000 from Sally's policy under her Underinsured Motorist coverage.
D) $75,000 from Sally's Underinsured Motorist coverage. Ref. 6-9

34. All of the following are automobile coverage forms that may be included in the Commercial Auto Coverage Part EXCEPT:

A) Business Auto Coverage Form.
B) Garage Coverage Form.
C) Mobile Equipment Coverage Form.
D) Truckers Coverage Form. Ref. 6-15

35. All of the following are true of the Business Auto Coverage Form EXCEPT:

A) Eligible vehicles include owned, leased, hired or borrowed vehicles.
B) It may be written as either a monoline policy or as part of a packaged policy.
C) The Business Auto Coverage Form is divided into five sections addressing covered autos, liability coverage, physical damage coverage, business auto conditions and definitions.
D) It includes Bobtail Liability. Ref. 6-16, 6-17 & 6-22

36. Business Auto Section I addresses covered autos. Which of the following numerical symbols when indicated on the Declarations Page will provide the broadest coverage?

A) Symbol #1 Any Auto.
B) Symbol #2 Owned Autos Only.
C) Symbol #3 Owned Private Passenger Autos Only.
D) Symbol #4 Owned Autos Other Than Private Passenger Autos. Ref. 6-16

37. Business Auto Section I addresses covered autos. Which of the following numerical symbols when indicated on the Declarations Page will provide the narrowest coverage?

A) Symbol #1 Any Auto.
B) Symbol #7 Specifically Described Autos Only.
C) Symbol #8 Hired Autos Only.
D) Symbol #9 Non-owned Autos only. Ref. 6-16

38. All of the following are excluded under Section III Physical Damage of the Business Auto Coverage Form EXCEPT:

A) Mechanical breakdown.
B) Wear and tear.
C) Nuclear hazards.
D) Transportation expenses incurred as the result of a theft. Ref. 6-17

39. All of the following are true of the Business Auto Section II Liability Coverage EXCEPT:

A) Liability may be written on either split limits or with a single limit of liability.
B) The insurer agrees to provide a legal defense.
C) The insurer agrees to pay the insured's legal obligation up to the policy limits for covered accidents resulting in bodily injury or property damage. Ref. 6-16 & 6-17
D) Coverage is provided for BI or PD which is expected or intended by the insured.

40. Under the Business Auto Section III Physical Damage Coverage, the term Comprehensive means:

A) Coverage for loss from any cause except collision with another object or overturn of a vehicle.
B) Coverage for towing and labor costs which are incurred when a covered auto is disabled.
C) Coverage for loss caused by impact with another object or the overturn of the auto.
D) Coverage for specific causes of loss, meaning fire, lightning, explosion, theft, windstorm, hail, earthquake, flood, vandalism, mischief, or the sinking, burning, collision, or derailment of any conveyance transporting the covered auto. Ref. 6-17

41. All of the following are true of Garage Coverage Section II Liability EXCEPT:

A) It provides premises operations coverage.
B) It provides product liability coverage.
C) It provides completed operations coverage.
D) It provides personal liability coverage. Ref. 6-18

42. Under the Business Auto Section III Physical Damage Coverage, the term Specific Perils means:

A) Loss from any cause except collision with another object or overturn of a vehicle.
B) Coverage for specific causes of loss, meaning fire, lightning, explosion, theft, windstorm, hail, earthquake, flood, vandalism, mischief, or the sinking, burning, collision, or derailment of any conveyance transporting the covered auto.
C) Coverage for towing and labor costs incurred when a covered auto is disabled.
D) Coverage for loss caused by collision with another object or the overturn of the auto.
Ref. 6-17

43. All of the following are examples of occurrences that may be covered under Comprehensive Coverage of the Business Auto coverage EXCEPT:

A) Collision with an animal or bird.
B) Collision with a tree or bridge.
C) Collision with a falling object.
D) Glass breakage. Ref. 6-17

44. Which of the following is NOT a Business Auto Section III Physical Damage Exclusion?

A) Loss to sound reproductive equipment unless permanently installed.
B) Loss to tapes, records and other devices for use with sound reproductive equipment.
C) Loss caused by the result of wear and tear, freezing and mechanical breakdown.
D) Loss caused by impact with another vehicle. Ref. 6-17

45. All of the following endorsements may be endorsed to Business Auto Policy EXCEPT:

A) Individual Named Insureds.
B) Drive Other Car Coverage.
C) Inflation Guard Coverage.
D) Employees as Additional Insured. Ref. 6-21 & 6-22

46. All of the following are true of the Garage Coverage Policy EXCEPT:

A) Eligible risks include auto dealers, repair shops, service stations and parking garages.
B) It may be written as either a monoline policy or as part of the CPP.
C) It provides liability coverage equal to the Business Auto Coverage.
D) It is designed to meet the specific needs of the automobile business. Ref. 6-18

47. Under the Business Auto Section III Physical Damage Coverage, the term Collision means:

A) Loss from any cause except collision with another object or overturn of a vehicle.
B) Coverage for specific causes of loss meaning fire, lightning, explosion, theft, windstorm, hail, earthquake, flood, vandalism, mischief, of the sinking, burning, collision, or derailment of any conveyance transporting the covered auto.
C) Coverage for towing and labor costs which are incurred when a covered auto is disabled.
D) Coverage for loss caused by impact with another object or the overturn of the auto.
Ref. 6-17

48. All of the following are Garage Coverage Section II Liability Exclusions EXCEPT:

A) Damage to property in the insured's care custody and control.
B) Damage caused by improper brake adjustments that cause an auto accident.
C) Coverage to workers injured on the job and covered under workers compensation.
D) Liability while racing, engaging in stunting activities or demolition contests. Ref 6-18

49. All of the following are true of Garage Coverage Policy Section III Garagekeepers Coverage EXCEPT:

A) It is legal liability coverage for damage to a customer's auto.
B) Coverage is excluded for theft of tape decks and sound equipment by an employee.
C) It is the same type of liability provided under the Business Auto Coverage.
D) It provides coverage for autos in the care of servicing, garage or parking operations.
Ref. 6-18

50. All of the following are true of the Truckers Policy EXCEPT:

A) Eligible risks include firms engaged in the business of transporting goods and materials.
B) Coverage is similar to the Business Auto Coverage.
C) A Trailer Interchange Endorsement is used when trucks interchange trailers.
D) Truckers are required to carry a Garage Policy. Ref. 6-19

51. All of the following are true of Commercial Carrier Regulations EXCEPT:

A) Commercial Carrier Regulations were enacted to protect the public's interest.
B) The only way to fulfill the Commercial Carrier Regulations is through the purchase of insurance.
C) Common Carriers are included in the regulation.
D) Under the Commercial Carrier Regulations, operators of commercial vehicles must maintain specified minimum limits. Ref. 6-20 & 6-21

52. Which of the following is NOT true of the Endorsement for Motor Carrier Policies of Insurance for Public Liability (MCS-90)?

A) Coverage is generally obtained by attaching the (MCS-90) endorsement to the Truckers Coverage Form.
B) This endorsement makes the insurance company absolutely liable to claimants.
C) Cancellation of this endorsement requires 30 days advance written notice to the ICC.
D) An insurer may not seek reimbursement from the insured after paying a noncovered claim.

Ref. 6-21

53. All of the following are true of Federal Regulation of Motor Carriers EXCEPT:

A) Minimum limit of $5,000,000 is required for transporting radioactive materials.
B) Minimum limit of $5,000,000 is required for transporting explosives.
C) Minimum limit of $500,000 is required for transporting oil.
D) Minimum limit of $750,000 is required for transportation of nonhazardous property.

Ref. 6-20 & 6-21

54. Insurance subject to the Pennsylvania Motor Vehicle Financial Responsibility Law is primary to all other coverage EXCEPT:

A) Personal umbrella policy.
B) Commercial umbrella policy.
C) Workers Compensation policy.
D) Excess liability policy.

Ref. 6-3

55. The primary benefit of selecting the full tort option from the insured's perspective is:

A) Their limited ability to sue.
B) Their unrestricted ability to sue for pain and suffering.
C) Their limited ability to collect special damages.
D) Their limited ability to sue for pain and suffering.

Ref. 6-2

ANSWER KEY

1-A	2-D	3-B	4-D	5-B	6-D	7-B	8-A	9-B	10-A
11-A	12-B	13-A	14-D	15-B	16-D	17-A	18-A	19-A	20-B
21-D	22-B	23-D	24-C	25-D	26-B	27-A	28-B	29-A	30-A
31-C	32-C	33-C	34-C	35-D	36-A	37-B	38-D	39-D	40-A
41-D	42-B	43-B	44-D	45-C	46-C	47-D	48-B	49-C	50-D
51-B	52-D	53-C	54-C	55-B					

CHAPTER SEVEN

COMMERCIAL PACKAGE POLICY

OVERVIEW

The Commercial Package Policy (CPP) was introduced in 1986 to replace the Special Multiple Peril Policy (SMP) and other related monoline policies. This program was developed by the Insurance Services Office (ISO) to provide standardized forms with a simplified rating approach. The policy language and format was updated to provide a package policy that included many of the common coverages needed to insure the large commercial client. The only type of risk prohibited under the CPP is the homeowner type exposure. **Eligible risks include** service stations; auto repair facilities; auto, motor home or mobile home dealers; parking lots or garage operators; warehouses; office and apartment buildings; petrochemical plants; electric generating stations; and other large commercial exposures. Smaller commercial risks for exposures such as main street businesses and small apartment or office buildings are generally insured under the businessowner policy. This policy will be discussed in the following chapter.

COMMERCIAL PACKAGE POLICY FORMAT

The Commercial Package Policy is comprised of the following essential elements:

- **Common Policy Declarations Page** includes the standard information such as the named insured, mailing address, policy period, etc., but also includes the premium charge for each specific coverage part.
- **Common Policy Conditions** are similar to the conditions found in other policies.
- **Interline Endorsements** are endorsements common to several coverage parts. For example, Pennsylvania's Cancellation and Nonrenewal provisions.
- **Two or more coverage parts.** The Commercial Package Policy allows the insured to choose from seven coverage parts. This provides the insured flexibility in designing a specific insurance program.

The Commercial Coverage Parts may be written as a package policy (more than one part) or as a monoline commercial policy (only one part). The following are the seven coverage parts which may be included in the Commercial Package Policy:

- **General Liability Coverage Part.**
- **Crime Coverage Part.**
- **Boiler and Machinery Coverage Part.**
- **Auto Coverage Part.**
- **Property Coverage Part.**
- **Inland Marine Coverage Part.**
- **Farm Coverage Part.**

The illustration on the following page provides an overview of the CPP format.

ADVANTAGE OF THE POLICY PACKAGE CONCEPT

The package policy concept offers **several advantages to all parties**. For example, the **insurer will have reduced administrative expenses** by producing one policy versus multiple policies. The **insured will have fewer policies to maintain**. This coupled with the fact that various coverage parts are written with the same company **minimizes the possibility of coverage gaps**. Finally, the producer is able to offer multiple coverage parts at a premium discount in one policy which **promotes customer satisfaction**.

COMMON POLICY CONDITIONS

Common Policy Conditions addresses the duties of the insured and insurer and include:

- **Cancellation** condition requires advance written notice of cancellation.
- **Changes** condition authorizes the first named insured to make policy changes.
- **Examination of books** condition permits the insurance company the right to examine the books and records of the insured up to three years from expiration.
- **Inspections and surveys** condition permits the company the right to inspect and survey the property for insurance values or related risk exposures.
- **Premiums** condition requires the payment or return of premiums.
- **Transfer of rights** condition prohibits the transferring of the policy without the insurer's consent.

Commercial Package Policy (CPP) Format

- Common Declarations
- Common Policy Conditions
- Interline Endorsements
- Two or More Coverage Parts (each with own Declarations Page)

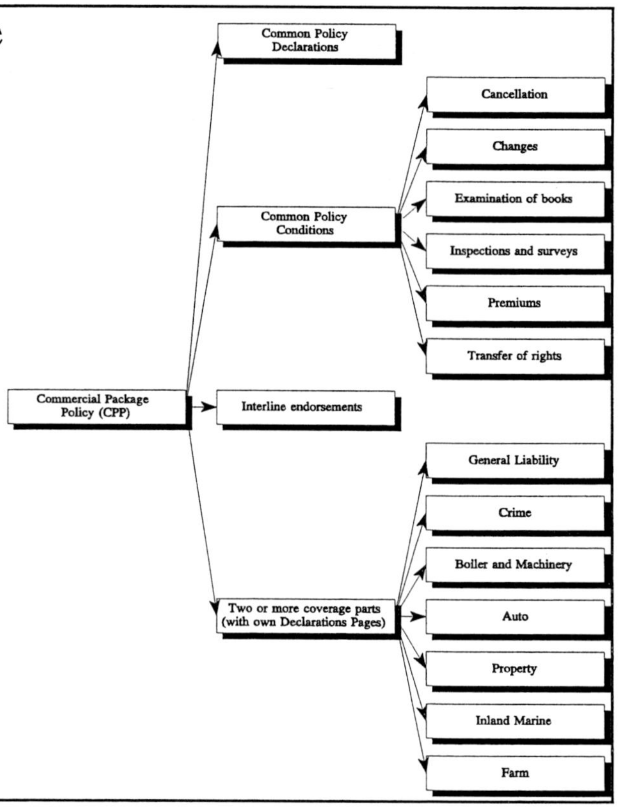

The following pages provide an overview and an illustration of the General Liability Coverage Part. This is the first of the seven CPP coverage parts.

OVERVIEW

COMMERCIAL GENERAL LIABILITY COVERAGE PART

The Commercial General Liability (CGL) Coverage Part **covers an insured's legal liability** arising out of injuries or damages suffered by the public, tenants and/or customers. Its policy structure is as follows:

- **A Declarations Page**.
- **A General Liability Coverage Form** ***(either occurrence or claims-made)*** - The CGL form covers Bodily Injury and Property Damage (Coverage A), Personal and Advertising Injury (Coverage B), and Medical Payments (Coverage C).
- **A Broad Form Nuclear Energy Exclusion Endorsement** - This endorsement specifically excludes coverage for bodily injury or property damage caused by nuclear material related to the operations of any nuclear facility.
- **Any other required endorsements** - This would include state endorsements.

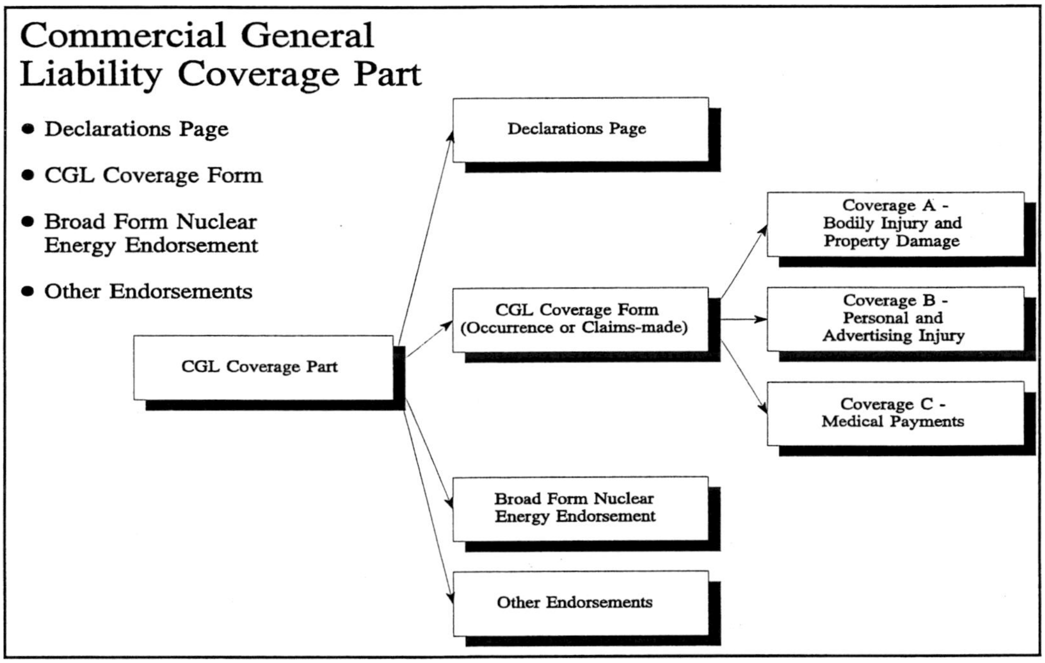

The Commercial General Liability Coverage Part consists of the following **two major sublines**. Each may be endorsed to exclude high risk type exposures.

1) **Premises and operations** provides coverage for **exposures at the insured's business location**. Examples include a customer slipping and falling on a wet floor or the improper preparing of food causing a customer to become ill. Both are negligent acts occurring at the premises and resulting from the business operations.

2) **Products and completed operations** provides coverage for **exposures away from the insured's business location**. Examples include a customer being injured by a defective product, such as an electrical appliance, or the improper installation of a furnace by a heating contractor. Both are negligent acts occurring away from the insured's premises and resulting from a product or a completed operation.

OCCURRENCE versus CLAIMS-MADE

The Commercial General Liability Coverage Part may be **written on either an occurrence or claims-made basis**. These coverage forms are basically the same. The major difference is the policy language which determines how a claim is triggered. The following addresses these CGL coverage forms:

Occurrence coverage applies to injury or damage **that occurs during the policy period,** *regardless of when the claim is reported to the company*. For example, if an individual is injured by a business' product on 6/30/05, and the policy's term is 1/1/05 to 1/1/06, this policy will respond regardless if the claim is reported during the policy period or after the policy period. Under occurrence forms, the policy that responds is the policy in effect at the time of the occurrence. Most liability insurance including automobile liability, homeowners liability, and businessowners liability are occurrence type coverages.

Claims-Made coverage applies to claims **occurring on or after the retroactive date** *and* **made during the claims-made policy period**, *even if the injury or damage occurred many years before the current policy term*. For example, if an individual is injured by a business' product on 6/1/05, the claim may not be made until several years after the injury. Under a claims-made form, the policy in force when the claim is made provides coverage, regardless if another claims-made policy was in effect when the loss occurred. A Claims-made form is commonly required by insurers when a business manufacturers a hazardous product. Claims-made forms contain the following features:

- **Retroactive Date** determines or **defines when coverage begins**. For example, when a claims-made policy is first written, the retroactive date is usually the policy's effective date. As successive claims-made policies are written, the original retroactive date is generally maintained. Retroactive dates are also used when an occurrence policy is renewed by a claims-made policy. **If no retroactive date is indicated, the insured is granted full prior acts coverage**.

- **Extended Reporting Periods (ERP)** are used to provide coverage for claims that may be reported after the end of a claims-made policy period. This is referred to as "tail coverage." The **Basic Extended Reporting Period (BERP) is provided automatically without an additional premium** as part of the policy and consists of two parts: (1) **Mini tail**, which covers claims reported **within 60 days of policy termination;** and (2) **Midi tail**, which covers claims reported **within 5 years of policy termination** provided the occurrence is reported within 60 days of termination of the coverage part.

- A **Supplemental Extended Reporting Period (SERP)**, which extends the reporting period indefinitely is also available, however, the **named insured must request it in writing within 60 days of policy termination**. Coverage is of an unlimited duration and at an extra charge, not to exceed 200% of the annual premium for the coverage part. **This endorsement only applies to claims which occurred during the policy period or within 60 days after policy termination**. Supplemental reporting period coverage is typically purchased when a business is ceasing operations, yet wishes to maintain coverage.

- **Claims Information** - Under a claims-made form, the first named insured is entitled to claims information of **reported occurrences including claim payments and reserves pertaining to the policy issued over the three previous years**. This information must be provided to the first named insured:

  1) **Within 30 days of policy termination** if the insurer is canceling or nonrenewing the policy; or,
  2) **Within 60 days of the end of the policy period if the insured makes a written request**. In this case, the insurer must provide the information within 45 days of receiving the demand.

A **Laser Beam Endorsement** may be added to the policy to exclude coverage for specific accidents, products, work or locations.

ILLUSTRATION OF CLAIMS-MADE COVERAGE FORM

Claims-Made Policy Form	**Basic Extended Reporting Period (two parts) ‡**		**Supplemental Extended Reporting Period ‡**
Policy Period	Mini Tail Period	Midi Tail Period	SERP
7-1-04† to 7-1-05	7-1-05 to 8-30-05	7-1-05 to 7-1-10	7-1-05 - forward
Claims-made coverage applies to **claims occurring on or after the retroactive date† and made during the policy period**, even if the injury or damage occurred many years before the current policy term.	Mini tail covers claims reported **within 60 days of policy terminat-ion;** and	**Midi tail**, covers claims reported **within 5 years of policy termination** provided the occurrence is reported within 60 days of termination of the coverage part.	A **Supplemental Extended Reporting Period** extends the reporting period indefinitely, however, the **named insured must request it in writing with-in 60 days of policy termination**. Coverage is of an unlimited duration and an at extra charge, not to exceed 200% of the annual premium for the coverage part. **This endorsement only applies to claims which occurred during the policy period or within 60 days after policy termination.**
This coverage is included in the basic policy premium.			Requires additional premium

† The retroactive date is typically the effective date of the initial claims-made policy and will generally remain as such as successive claims-made policies are renewed.

‡ The Basic Extended Reporting Period (BERP) and Supplemental Extended Reporting Period (SERP) is generally utilized when a business is terminating its operations, yet wishes to maintain coverage. It may also be utilized when a claims-made policy is renewed with an occurrence form policy.

COMMERCIAL GENERAL LIABILITY COVERAGES

The Commercial General Liability Coverage Part **covers an insured's legal liability** arising out of injuries or damages suffered by the public, tenants and/or customers. It includes the following three coverages:

COVERAGE A - BODILY INJURY AND PROPERTY DAMAGE covers all sums the insured becomes legally obligated to pay. This insurance does not apply to:

- Expected or intended injury.
- Contractual liability **except insured contracts such as** lease or easement agreements, elevator maintenance agreements, sidetrack agreements and contracts required by ordinance.
- Liquor liability if the insured is in the business of manufacturing, distribution or sale of alcohol. **(host liquor liability is provided)**
- Workers Compensation, Employers Liability and similar laws.
- Pollution, **except fluids that escape from mobile equipment.**
- Aircraft, Auto or Watercraft. **This exclusion does not apply to liability arising from:**
  - Watercraft on shore and on the insured's premises;
  - Nonowned watercraft under 26 feet & not used to carry people/cargo for a fee;
  - Parking an auto not owned, rented or loaned to an insured on or next to the insured's own or rented premises;
  - Liability assumed for any insured contract for the ownership maintenance or use of watercraft or aircraft;
  - The operation of cherry pickers or similar devices; or,
  - The operation of air compressors, pumps or spraying and cleaning equipment.
- Mobile Equipment meaning liability arising out of its transportation.
- War Risks.
- Damage to Property the insured owns, rents or occupies, or property in the insured's care, custody or control. (limited fire legal liability coverage is provided)
- Property damage to the insured's products arising out of any part of the product.
- Property damage to the insured's work.
- Damage to impaired property.
- Damage claimed due to product recalls, work deficiencies or electronic data.

COVERAGE B - PERSONAL AND ADVERTISING INJURY covers damages the insured becomes legally obligated to pay for personal injury exposures and advertising injury. Under this coverage, **personal injury** means slander, libel, invasion of privacy, false arrest or detention, malicious prosecution, and wrongful entry or eviction. **Advertising injury** means slander, libel, violation of privacy, copyright infringement, or misappropriation of advertising ideas. **Exclusions apply to:**

- Any oral or written publication *that the insured knows is false.*
- Assumed liability under a contract.
- Breach of contract.
- Failure of goods to perform as advertised including incorrect description or price.
- Infringement of copyright, patent, trademark or trade secret.
- An offense committed by an insured whose business is advertising, broadcasting publishing or Internet provider (including electronic chatrooms or bulletin boards).

COVERAGE C - MEDICAL PAYMENTS covers medical expenses caused by an accident, regardless of fault. **Medical Payment exclusions apply to persons:**

- Hired to work or covered under Workers Compensation;
- Taking part in athletic activities (physical exercises of games, sports or contests);
- Arising out of war or any act, condition or incident of war, declared or undeclared.

SUPPLEMENTAL PAYMENTS pay additional sums or secondary benefits beyond the basic Coverages A or B. These Supplemental Payments include:

- All expenses incurred by the insured (e.g., legal cost for attorney fees);
- All costs taxed against the insured in a suit (e.g., filing fees to process documents);
- Reasonable claims costs including up to $250 per day (e.g., for loss of earnings);
- Cost of bonds to release attachment (e.g., court attaches insured's auto after accident);
- Bail bonds up to $250 (e.g., insured may have to post bond to be released from jail);
- Postjudgment interest on a verdict (e.g., interest from verdict date until payment).

Legal defense costs **are paid in addition to the policy limit of liability**.

WHO IS AN INSURED addresses who qualifies for coverage. It includes:

- The person or organization (partnership/corporation) designated in the declarations;
- **Sole proprietors**, and **partners** of partnerships including **their spouses**; other entities (e.g., Limited Liability Companies) including their **executives, officers and directors** for **business activities**;
- The **insured's employees** while working within the scope of their employment;
- The insured's real estate manager if not an employee of the insured;
- Any person or organization with custody of the insured's property if the insured dies, but only for liability;
- Individuals using registered mobile equipment on public highways;
- Organizations (except partnerships or joint ventures) the insured acquires or forms for up to 90 days.

CONDITIONS are the duties of the insured and insurer and include the following:

- **Duties in the event of occurrence/claim/suit**, meaning prompt notice and co-operating with the company;
- **Legal action** against insurer requires the claimant to follow policy provisions prior to initiating legal actions;
- **Other insurance** addresses primary, excess pro-rating of losses;
- **Representations** meaning the policy is based upon the insured's representations;
- **Premium audit** addresses the duties of the insured and insurer and the rules affecting premium audit;
- **Transfer of rights of recovery** addresses subrogation;
- **When we do not renew** addresses the insurance company's duty to give advance written notice of nonrenewing coverage.

DEFINITIONS define or clarify terms within the policy. They include: advertising injury, auto, bodily injury, coverage territory, employee, executive officer, impaired property, insured contract, leased worker, loading or unloading, mobile equipment, occurrence, personal injury, products-completed operations, property damage, suit, temporary worker, your product and your work. These terms are defined on page 8-13 in the Businessowners Liability section.

LIMITS OF LIABILITY

Limits of Liability refers to the amount of insurance that will be paid under the policy subject to specific limits as follows:

- **General Aggregate Limit** represents the annual maximum that will be paid for coverages A & B, *except for products and completed operations which is subject to a separate annual aggregate limit.*
- **Products/Completed Operations Aggregate** represents the maximum that will be paid under coverage A.
- **Personal and Advertising Injury** represents the maximum that will be paid under coverage B. This is a subline subject to the overall general aggregate limit.
- **Each Occurrence Limit** represents the maximum that will be payable under coverage A or C. This is subject to either the general aggregate or products/completed operations aggregate, whichever is applicable.
- **Damage To Premises Rented To You** (previously Fire Legal Liability) represents the maximum limit that will be paid under Coverage A for damages, because of property damages to premises rented to the insured arising out of any one fire. This is subject to an occurrence and aggregate limit.
- **Medical Expense Limit** represents the maximum limit that will be paid under Coverage C for all medical expenses, because of bodily injury sustained by any one person. This is subject to an occurrence and aggregate limit.

Illustration of Commercial General Liability Limits of Liability

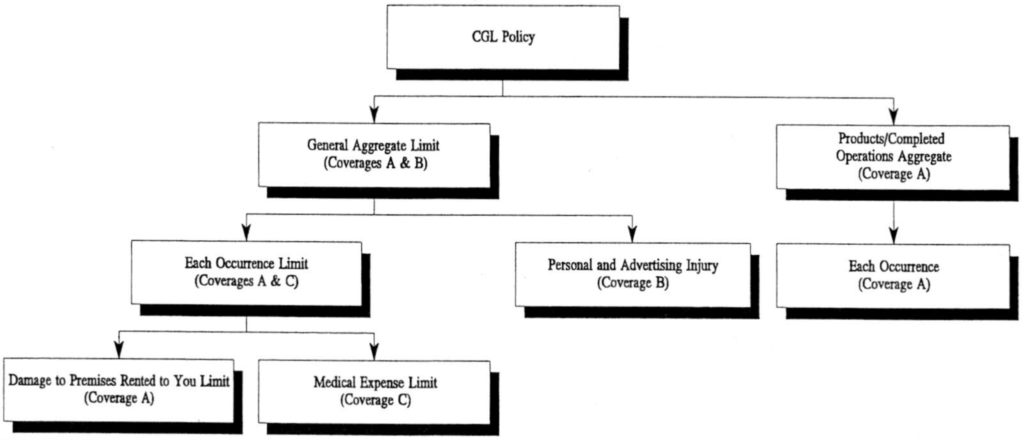

OWNERS AND CONTRACTORS PROTECTIVE LIABILITY POLICY (OCP)

This coverage protects an owner, operator or contractor against loss caused by the negligence of a hired contractor or subcontractor. For example, an insured owner may request or require a contractor to secure this coverage as a condition to perform work. This is an alternative to naming the owner as an additional insured under the contractor's policy. Under the OCP approach, the owner is assured that the policy limits will not be diluted or impaired by previous losses.

POLLUTION LIABILITY

The Commercial General Liability Coverage Part **contains an exclusion for pollution losses, which is far reaching**. Since many businesses have an exposure to various types of pollutants, coverage **may be bought back** through the following forms:

- **Pollution Liability Coverage Form** provides coverage for *bodily injury or property damage* caused by a pollution incident **including clean-up costs**. A pollution incident is defined as an emission, discharge, release or escape of pollutants onto land, the atmosphere, or any body of water provided that incident results in environmental damage. This coverage provides **both on-site and off-site coverage**. The incident **must commence after the retroactive date** and must be from a site in the declarations page or in the policy territory. The Pollution Liability Coverage Form **has a limit of liability separate from the CGL's limits of liability.** The obligation to pay must be mandated by a statutory authority of the United States or Canada.

- **Pollution Liability Limited Coverage Form** provides the same type of coverage as indicated in the Pollution Liability Coverage Form, **with the exception that it only applies to on-site pollution incidents.**

- **Pollution Liability Extension Endorsement** modifies the basic CGL by deleting the pollution exclusion for *bodily injury and property damage*. Although this endorsement gives back coverage for bodily injury and property damage, **it does not modify the exclusion for clean up costs.**

OVERVIEW

COMMERCIAL CRIME COVERAGE PART

The Commercial Crime Coverage Part **pays an owner of a business for the loss of covered property due to its wrongful taking by another**. The Commercial Crime Part may be written as either a coverage part within the CPP or as a separate mono-line policy. The coverage part consists of the following:

- **A Declarations Page**
- **A General Provisions Form** which contains the specific conditions, exclusions and definitions applicable to the crime part
- **One or More Crime Coverages** which are activated by indicating coverage limits in the Declaration Page
- **Other Endorsements**

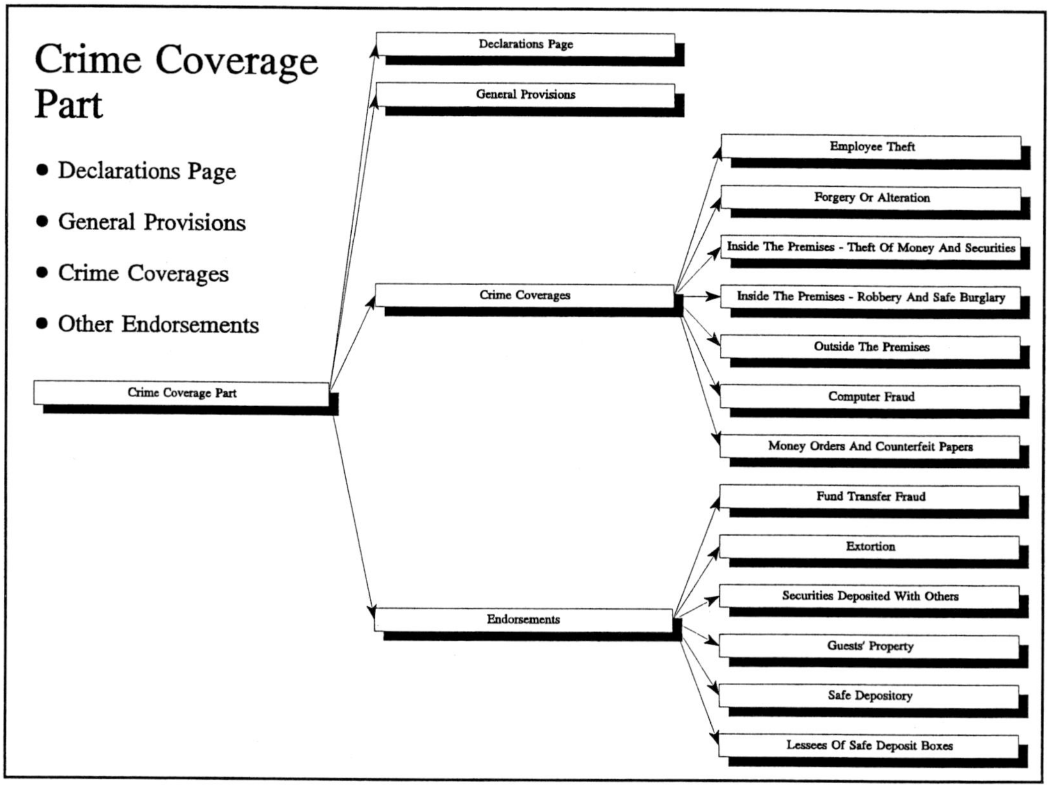

CONDITIONS

Conditions under the Crime Part is similar to those found in other commercial forms and include the policy period, territory (i.e., U.S., its territories, Puerto Rico and Canada) insured's duties at the time of loss, legal actions, subrogation, etc.

EXCLUSIONS

The Crime Part excludes any loss resulting from the named insured's or partner's involvement, governmental action, indirect loss, nuclear hazards, war, inventory shortages, accounting or arithmetic errors, and legal expenses relating to a crime loss.

DEFINITIONS sets forth the meaning of the policy terms. They include:

- **Burglary**, meaning the taking of property from within the premises by unlawful entering as **evidenced by marks of forcible entry or exit.**
- **Safe Burglary**, meaning the taking of property from within a locked safe or vault by a person of unlawful entry as **evidenced by a visible sign to the safe or vault**. It also means the removal of the safe from the premises.
- **Robbery**, meaning the unlawful taking of property from the care and custody of a person by the **threat of bodily harm**.
- **Extortion,** meaning the surrendering of property away from the premises by means of **threat communicated to the insured**.
- **Theft**, meaning the unlawful taking of money, securities or other property.

The property subject to loss under the Crime Coverage includes:

- **Money**, meaning currency, coins, bank notes, travelers checks, registered checks and money orders held for sale.
- **Securities**, meaning negotiable and nonnegotiable instruments including tokens, tickets, stamps and evidences of debt in relation to charge cards.
- **Other Property**, meaning any tangible property other than money and securities that has intrinsic value, but excluding property listed as not covered.

The Crime Coverage excludes certain specific kinds of property that is to be insured under other insurance forms. For example, motor vehicles, trailers, semi-trailers and its equipment are specifically listed as property not covered.

CRIME COVERAGE FORMS

Crime coverage may be written to cover commercial or governmental exposures. The form used (either Loss Sustained or Discovery) addresses which policy will respond to a covered loss. Other than that distinction, both forms are the same. The following provides an overview of these two coverage forms:

1) **Loss Sustained Form** covers **losses that are sustained during the policy period and discovered within one year of policy expiration**. If coverage is renewed or replaced, this extended period to discover loss terminates.

2) **Discovery Form** is similar to the claims-made CGL Policy. Under the Crime Discovery Form, a retroactive date is commonly indicated in the Declarations Page. In the event no retroactive date is indicated, the policy effective date becomes the retroactive date by default. For coverage to apply, the **loss must occur on or after this date and be discovered during the Discovery Form period, or within 60 days of its expiration**. If coverage is renewed or replaced, this 60 day extended period to discover loss terminates.

CRIME COVERAGE

Crime Coverage is used to insure property **in the event property is taken or converted by burglary, safe burglary, robbery, forgery, computer fraud, extortion or theft.** The property covered is categorized as money, securities or other property. Crime Coverage may be written as a single coverage (i.e., Employee Theft) or combined with other coverages (e.g., Employee Theft, Forgery or Alteration, Computer Fraud, etc.). The following are the Crime Coverages:

1) **EMPLOYEE THEFT** covers losses resulting from employee theft. Property covered under Employee Theft includes **money, securities, and other property**. Coverage is written on a blanket basis (i.e. all employees) but may be endorsed to a named scheduled (i.e., named employees) or position scheduled (i.e., employee position) basis. Coverage may also be endorsed to cover theft or conversion of funds from employee benefit plans such as 401(k) Plans, Pension Plans or Health and Welfare Plans.

2) **FORGERY OR ALTERATION** covers the insured worldwide for **loss of money** resulting from **forgery and alteration of outgoing checks, drafts, or promissory notes**. Defense coverage is also provided if the named insured is sued for failure to honor a financial instrument (e.g., check) if believed to be a forgery.

3) **INSIDE THE PREMISES - THEFT OF MONEY AND SECURITIES** covers **loss of money and securities** inside the premises or banking premises resulting directly from **theft, disappearance or destruction**. Merchandise and stock is not covered. This coverage also applies to damage of the premises or its exterior resulting from actual or attempted theft of money and securities and to loss or damage to a locked safe, vault, cash register, cash box or cash drawer located inside the premises resulting from any actual or attempted theft.

4) **INSIDE THE PREMISES - ROBBERY OR SAFE BURGLARY OF OTHER PROPERTY** covers **loss or damage to other property** inside the premises resulting from an **actual or attempted robbery of a custodian or inside the premises in a safe or vault resulting from an actual or attempted safe burglary**. This coverage also pays for loss for damage to the premises or its exterior resulting from an actual or attempted robbery or safe burglary of other property and loss of or damage to a locked safe or vault located inside the premises resulting from an actual or attempted robbery or safe burglary.

5) **OUTSIDE THE PREMISES** covers **loss of money and securities** outside the premises in the care and custody of a messenger or an armored motor vehicle company resulting directly from **theft, disappearance or destruction**. This coverage will also pay for loss or damage to other property outside the premises in the care or custody of a messenger or an armored motor vehicle company resulting directly from an actual or attempted robbery.

6) **COMPUTER FRAUD** covers the insured worldwide for **loss of or damage to money, securities and other property** resulting directly from the use of any computer to fraudulently cause a transfer of that property from inside the premises or banking premises to a person other than a messenger outside those premises or to a place outside those premises.

7) **MONEY ORDERS AND COUNTERFEIT PAPER CURRENCY** covers loss resulting directly from your having accepted in good faith in exchange for merchandise money or services, money orders issued by any post office, express company or bank that are not paid upon presentation or counterfeit paper currency that is acquired during the regular course of business.

Other crime coverages that may be added by endorsement include:

- **FUNDS TRANSFER FRAUD** covers losses resulting from fraudulent instructions received by a financial institution to pay money from an insured's transfer account to someone else; and,

- **EXTORTION** covers payments made in response to threats of bodily harm directed against the insured, its employees, directors or those persons' relatives who are captured or allegedly captured.

- **SECURITIES DEPOSITED WITH OTHERS** covers **securities** for theft, disappearance and destruction when deposited with a custodian, such as a bank or broker, or while the securities are being transported by the custodian. Each custodian must be scheduled in the endorsement and a separate limit of liability applies to each.

- **GUEST'S PROPERTY** covers a guest's property against loss caused by an **innkeeper's negligence**. Coverage applies to property in a safety deposit box and to property inside the premises. Each innkeeper must be scheduled in the endorsement and a separate limit of liability applies to each. Coverage also applies to legal expenses incurred in defending a suit that results from the insured's refusal to pay for loss to a guest's property. Coverage does not apply to vehicles or articles for sale (e.g., samples).

- **SAFE DEPOSITORY** covers an individual's property at a depository *other than a financial institution* in two areas:

  1) To loss of **property** caused by the **depository's negligence**. Coverage also applies to legal expenses incurred in defending a suit that results from the insured's refusal to pay for loss of property.

  2) To loss of property **other than money** resulting from destruction, damage, or actual or attempted robbery or burglary, **regardless if the insured is legally liable**. Coverage also applies to resulting damage to the premises or its exterior, and to a locked safe, vault, or safe deposit box, provided the insured is the owner or is liable for the damage.

  Each depository must be scheduled in the endorsement and a separate limit of liability applies to each.

- **LESSEES OF SAFE DEPOSIT BOXES** covers two categories of property:

  1) **Securities** for theft, disappearance and destruction while inside the depository premises; and

  2) **Property other than money and securities** while inside the depository premises for burglary, robbery and vandalism.

  Each bank or other depository must be scheduled in the endorsement and a separate limit of liability applies to each.

Commercial Crime coverage **includes a valuation clause** that establishes the loss of money to be paid at face value, the loss of securities to be paid at closing value when loss is realized, and loss of property other than money and securities to be paid at actual cash value. A **special limit of $5,000 applies per occurrence** for loss to precious metals and stones, pearls, furs, manuscripts, drawings and records, including the cost to reproduce the information contained within. Finally, **acts of employees are excluded** from crime coverage, except for Employee Theft which specifically covers this exposure.

ILLUSTRATION OF COMMERCIAL CRIME COVERAGES

Title	Covered Property	Cause of Loss
Employee Theft	All property	Employee theft
Forgery and Alteration	Money	Forgery or alteration of checks, drafts, etc.
Inside the Premises - Theft of Money and Securities	Money and securities inside the premises or at a banking premises Damage to the premises or its exterior resulting from actual or attempted theft of money and securities Loss or damage to a locked safe, vault, cash register, cash box or cash drawer located inside the premises resulting from any actual or attempted theft	Theft, disappearance and destruction
Inside the Premises - Robbery or Safe Burglary of Other Property	Damage to property inside the premises resulting from an actual or attempted robbery of a custodian or inside the premises in a safe or vault resulting from an actual or attempted safe burglary Damage to the premises or its exterior resulting from an actual or attempted robbery Safe burglary of other property and loss or damage to a locked safe or vault located inside the premises resulting from actual or attempted robbery or safe burglary	Robbery and safe burglary
Outside the Premises	Loss of money and securities outside the premises in the care and custody of a messenger or an armored motor vehicle company resulting directly from theft, disappearance or destruction Loss or damage to other property outside the premises in the care or custody of a messenger or an armored motor vehicle company resulting directly from an actual or attempted robbery	Theft, disappearance and destruction
Computer Fraud	All property	Computer fraud
Money Orders and Counterfeit Paper Currency	Money	Acceptance of fraudulent money orders or counterfeit paper currency
Funds Transfer Fraud	Money	Fraud
Extortion	All Property	Extortion
Securities Deposited with Others	Securities	Theft, disappearance and destruction
Guest's Property	All property, except vehicles & articles for sale	Negligence
Safe Depository	1) Property 2) Property other than money	1) Negligence 2) Destruction, damage, robbery or burglary
Lessees of Safe Deposit Boxes	1) Securities 2) Property other than money and securities	1) Theft, disappearance and destruction 2) Burglary, robbery and vandalism
Special limits of $5,000 applies per occurrence for loss to precious metals and stones, pearls, furs, manuscripts, drawings and records, including the cost to reproduce the information contained within.		

OVERVIEW

BOILER AND MACHINERY

Boiler and Machinery insurance is equipment breakdown insurance. It was originally used to cover losses to boilers and machinery in industrialized settings. Over the years, boiler and machinery coverage has evolved to cover more common exposures found in all types of business settings. Today, it is an integral part of a commercial risk management program and centers on minimizing loss through prevention.

BOILER AND MACHINERY COVERAGE PART

The Boiler and Machinery Coverage Part provides coverage for organizations that own or use a wide range of machinery. Examples of eligible equipment include: air-conditioning and refrigeration units; boilers and pressure vessels; computer-controlled machinery; electrical equipment; elevators and escalators; fans, motors and pumps; medical equipment; security and fire detection systems; and washers and other laundry equipment. Boiler and machinery coverage pays for direct damage to covered property caused by a covered cause of loss. Although this type of machinery is covered for certain perils under the Building and Personal Property Form (which will be discussed later in this chapter), no coverage applies to certain perils or mechanical breakdown. Boiler and machinery coverage fills that important gap. The Boiler and Machinery Coverage Part consists of the following:

- Boiler and Machinery Declarations Page.
- Equipment Breakdown Form.
- Other Endorsements.

The following is an illustration of the Boiler and Machinery Coverage Part structure:

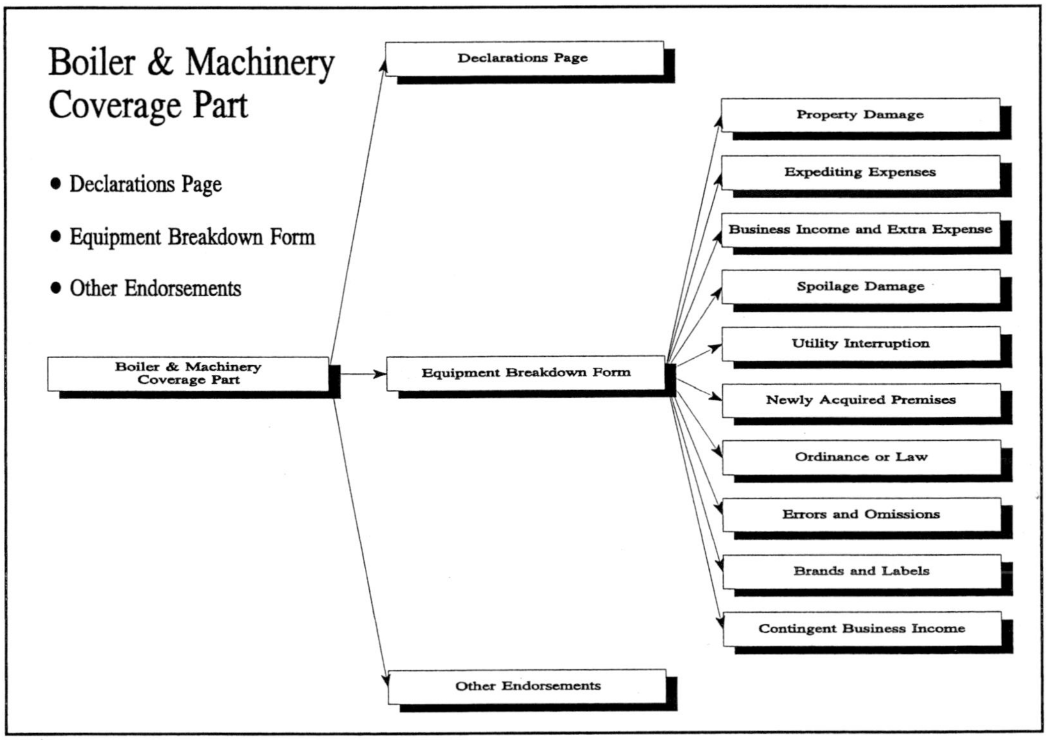

EQUIPMENT BREAKDOWN PROTECTION COVERAGE FORM

The Equipment Breakdown Protection Coverage Form agrees to pay for direct damage to covered property caused by a covered cause of loss. The **covered cause of loss is a breakdown to covered equipment**.

Breakdown means:

- Failure of pressure or vacuum equipment;
- Mechanical failure including rupture or bursting caused by centrifugal force; or
- Electrical failure including arcing.

Breakdown does not include:

- Malfunction including misalignment, cleaning or modification;
- Defects, erasures, errors, viruses in computer programs;
- Leakage of any valve, fitting, shaft seal, joint or connection;
- Damage to any vacuum tube, gas tube or brusk;
- The functioning of any safety or protection device; or
- The cracking of any part of an internal combustion gas turbine.

COVERAGES PROVIDED

The Equipment Breakdown Protection Coverage Form includes the following if either a limit or the word "INCLUDED" is shown for that coverage in the Declarations.

- **Equipment** that operates under internal pressure, vacuum, electric or mechanical means (that is above ground) and communications and computer equipment (excluding data or media);
- **Loss of Property** in the insured's care, custody and control;
- **Expediting Expenses** meaning temporary repairs to expedite permanent repairs;
- **Business Income and Extra Expense** during the period of restoration. If media is damaged, this coverage is limited to 30 days or $25,000, whichever is less.
- **Spoilage Damage** due to lack of or excess power, light, heat, steam or cooling.
- **Utility Interruption** extends the insured's loss of business income, extra expense or spoilage damage to the insured's utility in the event of a breakdown.
- **Newly Acquired Premises** grants coverage to newly acquired premises for a specified time period indicated in the Declarations (e.g., 90 days).
- **Ordinance or Law Coverage** pays the increases in loss necessitated by the enforcement of any ordinance or law.
- **Errors and Omissions** grants coverage in the event the insured makes an error or omission in describing the property to be insured. This coverage does not apply if the insured intentionally misrepresents the values in a reporting form.
- **Brands and Labels** coverage pays the insured to stamp the word "salvage" on the merchandise or containers or to remove the brands or labels. The insurer will then take the damaged merchandise for salvage.
- **Contingent Business Income and Extra Expense** extends business income and extra expense to a non-owned business that is indicated in the Declarations.

EXCLUSIONS

Equipment Breakdown Protection Coverage Form excludes the following:

- Ordinance or Law (if not caused by breakdown)
- Earth Movement (i.e., earthquake, landslide, mine subsidence)
- Water (i.e., flood, surface water, etc.)
- Nuclear Hazard (i.e., radio active contamination)
- War or Military Action (i.e., civil war, insurrection, etc.)
- Fire or combustion explosion
- Damage to covered equipment during testing
- Deterioration, corrosion, erosion, wear and tear (resulting damage is covered)
- Neglect by the insured

LIMITATIONS

Unless a higher limit or "INCLUDED" is shown in the Declarations, the most the insurer will pay for direct damage as a direct result of a breakdown to covered equipment is $25,000 for:

- Ammonia Contamination
- Consequential Loss
- Data and Media
- Hazardous Substance
- Water Damage

VALUATION

Property is insured on a replacement cost basis, *however, if damaged property is not repaired or replaced* ***within 24 months*** *after the breakdown, settlement is at the smaller of ACV or the cost to repair or replace.* If the insured elects or if the insurer requires that the repair or replacement of damaged property be done in a manner that improves the environment, increases efficiency or enhances safety, while maintaining the existing function, the insurer **will pay up to an additional 25%** of the limit of insurance.

SUSPENSION PROVISION

Coverage under a Boiler and Machinery Coverage Part **may be suspended if the insurance company discovers that covered equipment is exposed to a dangerous condition**. This typically occurs when the insurer's loss control representative is conducting an inspection of the insured object. The representative may immediately suspend the insurance by delivering or mailing a written notice of suspension to the insured's last known address or where the covered equipment is located. Coverage may be subsequently reinstated by endorsement after compliance with the loss control representative's recommendations.

DEDUCTIBLES

A **separate deductible applies for each applicable coverage** *unless*: **1)** a deductible is shown as **combined** in the Declarations; or, **2)** more than one covered equipment is involved in one breakdown, then only the highest deductible will apply.

SELECTED ENDORSEMENTS

The Equipment Breakdown Protection Coverage Form may include the following endorsements:

- **Business Interruption - Report of Values (BM 15 31)** is used to report values (e.g., net sales, commissions, expenses, etc) to determine the premium charge when business interruption coverage is indicated in the Declarations. The insured is required to report these values to the insurer **within three months of the report date** indicated in the Declarations and every anniversary thereafter. In the event the insured does not report the values as required, a 100% co-insurance provision applies.

- **Refrigeration Interruption Coverage (BM 15 39)** provides coverage for spoilage damage to refrigerated property as described in the endorsement schedule. A limit of insurance, deductible and waiting period is indicated on the endorsement.

- **Refrigeration Interruption Coverage - Report of Values (BM 15 40)** is used to report values to determine the premium charge when refrigeration interruption coverage is endorse to the policy. The insured is required to report these values to the insurer **within three months of the report date** indicated in the endorsement and every anniversary thereafter. In the event the insured does not report the values as required, a 100% coinsurance provision applies.

- **Turbine Units Explosion Coverage (BM 99 52)** replaces the definitions of "Breakdown" and "Covered Equipment." This endorsement is used to cover turbines and related equipment.

- **Pressure or Vacuum Equipment (BM 99 55)** replaces the definition of "Covered Equipment." This endorsement is used to cover any equipment built to operate under internal pressure or vacuum.

- **Production Machinery Exclusion (BM 99 57)** amends the definition of "Covered Equipment." Its purpose is to limit covered equipment. The endorsement states that covered equipment *does not* mean or include production or process machines or apparatus that processes, forms, shapes or cuts raw materials.

OVERVIEW

COMMERCIAL PROPERTY COVERAGE PART

The Commercial Property Coverage Part **provides coverage for various business property exposures**. It consists of the following elements and policy structure:

- **Commercial Property Declarations Page.**
- **Commercial Property Conditions Form**, which includes concealment and fraud, control of property, duplicate coverage, legal actions, liberalization, no benefit to bailee, other insurance, pro rata liability, policy period, territory, transfer of rights and subrogation.
- **One or More Coverage Forms** meaning any of the eight property coverage forms.
- **One or More Causes of Loss Forms** (Basic, Broad, Special or Earthquake)
- **Other Endorsements**.

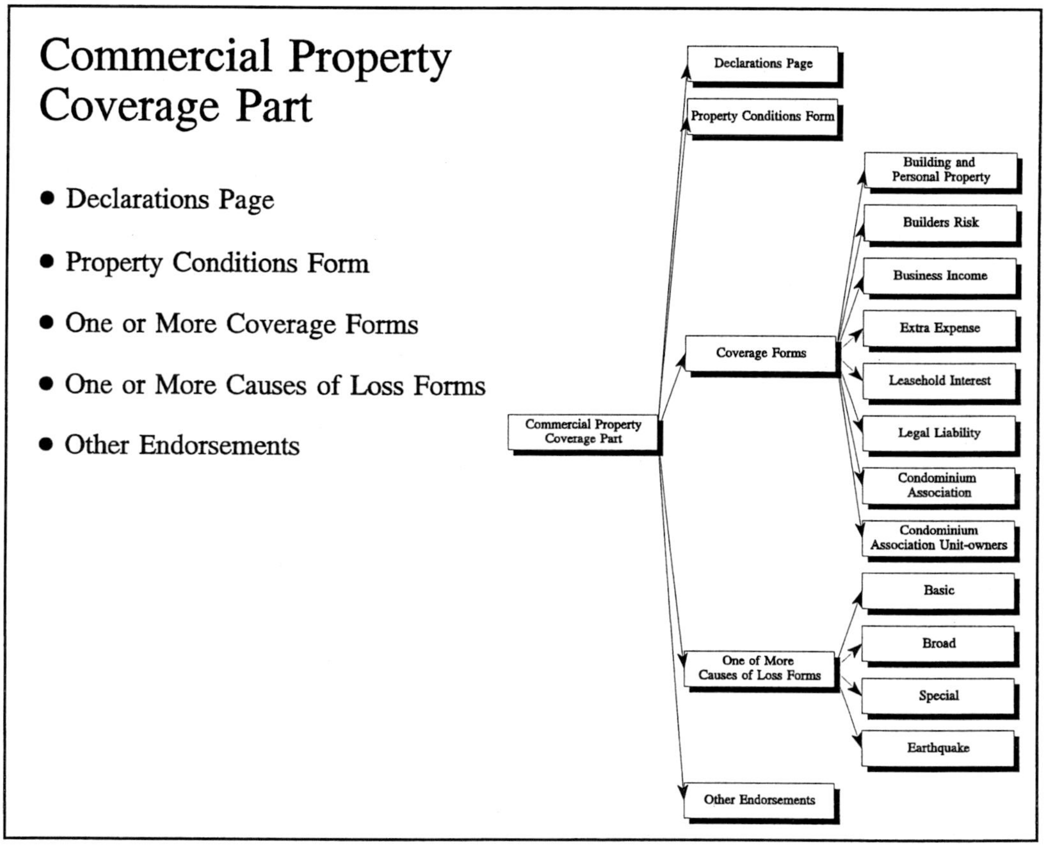

The following are the eight coverage forms of the Commercial Property Coverage Part.

BUILDING AND PERSONAL PROPERTY FORM

Building and Personal Property Form (BPP) may be **used to insure all types of commercial property except those classified as builders risk or condominiums**. These are separate forms to address these unique property exposures. Property forms must be combined with a causes of loss form to provide coverage for:

COVERAGE A - BUILDINGS covers the buildings **meaning the buildings and structures described in the declarations and including**:

- Completed additions, such as an office addition to a building.
- Permanently installed fixtures and equipment, such as signs, intercoms, blinds, etc.
- The insured's personal property for use as a landlord.
- Outdoor fixtures such as lights, awnings, mailboxes, flag poles, etc.
- Personal property owned by the insured **used to service the business premises**, such as fire extinguishers, outdoor furniture, lawnmowers, snowplows, floor coverings, and appliances used for heating, refrigeration, or ventilation.

If not insured elsewhere, coverage is provided for additions and alterations while under construction, and materials, equipment, supplies and temporary structures on or within 100 feet of the described premises used for additions or alterations.

COVERAGE B - BUSINESS PERSONAL PROPERTY includes property owned by the insured and used in business, such as furniture, fixtures, machinery or stock, the insured's use interest as tenant in improvements and betterments, and leased personal property such as computers or copiers. Business personal property that is in or on the buildings at the described premises or in the open, or in a vehicle within 100 feet of the described premises is covered as business personal property.

COVERAGE C - PERSONAL PROPERTY OF OTHERS, meaning the property of others in the insured's care, custody and control and located within the insured building or within 100 feet of the described premises.

The building and personal property form does not cover:

- Accounts, bills, currency, deeds, food stamps, money, notes and securities;
- Animals, unless owned by others and boarded by the insured or animals as stock within a building;
- Automobiles for sale;
- Bridges, roadways, walks, patios or other paved surfaces;
- Contraband or property in the course of illegal transportation or trade;
- Cost of excavating, grading, or backfilling;
- Foundations of buildings, structures, machinery or boilers if their foundations are below the basement floor or floor foundation;
- Land, water or crops;
- Personal property while airborne or waterborne;
- Bulkheads, pilings, piers, wharves or docks;
- Property specifically described under another policy;
- Retaining walls that are not part of a building;
- Underground pipes, flues and drains;
- Cost to research or restore information on valuable papers;
- Licensed vehicles and self-propelled machines (airplanes and watercraft);
- Property located outside a building (grain, crops, fences, radio and TV antennas).

ADDITIONAL COVERAGES are within the limits of insurance. They include:

- **Debris Removal** up to 25% of the amount of loss;
- **Preservation of Property** (saving property from loss) *applies for 30 days;*
- **Fire Department Service** charge of up to $1,000;
- **Pollution Clean Up and Removal** of up to $10,000;
- **Increased Cost of Construction** of up to $10,000 or 5% of the building limit.
- **Electronic Data** coverage to restore destroyed or corrupted data up to $2,500;
- **Fungus, wet rot, dry rot and bacteria** coverage up to $15,000.

COVERAGE EXTENSIONS are in addition to the limits of insurance if the insured maintains the policy's coinsurance requirement. They include:

- **Newly acquired property** up to $250,000 of Coverage A and $100,000 of Coverage B *(applies for 30 days);*
- **Personal effects of the insured/property of others** up to $2,500 per premises;
- **Valuable papers and records** up to $2,500 at each described premises;
- **Property off-premises** up to $10,000 (other than stock at a temporary location);
- **Outdoor property** up to $1,000 with a $250 per tree/shrub/plant limit. Outdoor property means fences, radio/television antennas (including satellite dishes), detached signs, trees/shrubs/plants (other than stock) and debris removal *for the perils of fire, lightning, explosion, riot or civil commotion or aircraft;*
- **Non-Owned Detached Trailers** up to $5,000.

LIMITS OF INSURANCE set forth the maximum amount paid in the declarations. In addition, **special sublimits apply to**:

- **Debris removal** up to $10,000 per location (applies after the 25% additional coverage is exhausted);
- **Outdoor signs** attached to buildings are covered up to $1,000 per occurrence.

LOSS CONDITIONS address the provisions affecting a loss. They include:

- **Abandonment** prohibits the insured from abandoning property as a total loss.
- **Appraisal** permits either insured or company to demand an appraisal of a loss.
- **Duties in the Event of Loss** means to notify the company, protect property, etc.
- **Loss Payment** permits the insurer, at its option, to pay, repair or rebuild the damaged or loss of property. Payment will be made within 15 days of proof of loss.
- **Recovered Property** means that both insured and carrier must notify each other.
- **Vacancy** beyond 60 days excludes coverage caused by: **vandalism; sprinkler leakage** (unless care is exercised); **building glass breakage**; **water damage; theft or attempted theft**. All other covered perils are reduced 15%.

  Special Note: Under the commercial property forms, **vacancy is triggered if a tenant** does not have sufficient business personal property to conduct customary operations. In the event the commercial building is owner occupied, at least 31% of the total square footage of the building must be rented and/or occupied for customary operations, otherwise it will be considered as vacant.

- **Valuation** will be determined **at actual cash value**. This means that at the time of loss the insurer will determine the property's (either building or personal property) replacement cost and subtract depreciation to determine its actual cash value for loss settlement. Other categories of property are settled as follows:

- **Losses up to $2,500 will be settled at replacement cost** if the insured complied with the coinsurance requirement. This provision does not apply to awnings, floor coverings, appliances, and outdoor equipment or furniture.

- **Stock** sold but not delivered will be valued at selling price less discounts. For example, if an appliance store sells a washing machine for $300 and it is destroyed before it is shipped to the customer, the appliance store recovers the selling price ($300) not the price it paid to acquire it from the wholesaler.

- **Glass** at replacement cost.

- **Tenant's improvements and betterments at actual cash value** if repairs are made promptly. If repairs are not made promptly, at a proportion of original value based upon time to expiration of lease.

- **Valuable Papers and Records**, including electronic or magnetic media at the **cost of blank media and labor** to transcribe or copy the records. This does not apply to prepackaged software.

A **coinsurance provision** is common to the Building and Personal Property Coverage Form. This provision, which was reviewed in detail in Chapter Three requires the insured to carry insurance equal to a specified percentage (typically 80%) of the property's actual cash value or replacement value. See page 3-11 and 3-12 for complete discussion on this important policy condition.

BUILDERS RISK FORM

Builders Risk Form **provides coverage to buildings under construction**. It is similar to the Building and Personal Property Form with the exception that it applies to buildings under construction. **Coverage begins on the date of construction and ceases**:

- Whenever the property is accepted by the purchaser.
- Ninety days after construction is completed.
- Sixty days after the constructed building is occupied or put into its intended use.
- When the insured's interest in the property ceases.

This coverage may be written on a reporting form basis. See page 3-6 and page 7-26 for additional information on reporting forms.

BUSINESS INCOME COVERAGE FORM

Business Income Coverage **provides income to a business following a suspension of operations due to a direct physical loss or damage to property at the described premises caused by a covered cause of loss.** Coverage is provided during the **period of restoration** *which begins 72 hours after the time of direct physical loss and ends when the property can be repaired, replaced or rebuilt.* The Business Income Form provides the following coverages:

- **Business Income**, means the actual loss of business income. It is defined as net income plus continuing operating expenses including payroll. Business income coverage is typically written subject to a 50% coinsurance provision as follows:

COINSURANCE EXAMPLE

Coinsurance percentage †	50 percent
Annual net income plus all expenses	$1,000,000
Limit of insurance	$250,000
Amount of loss	$100,000

Coinsurance Formula and Example				
Amount Carried / Amount Required	Times	Loss	Equals	Settlement
$250,000 / $500,000	X	$100,000	=	$50,000

† If a coinsurance percentage of 50% or more is shown as a declarations entry, business income insurance is extended as additional insurance without coinsurance to apply to newly acquired locations, except fairs or exhibits for up to $100,000.

In the above cited example, the business owner purchased an inadequate amount of business income insurance. The coinsurance formula used in this example is the same basic formula discussed in Chapter 3.

- **Extra Expense**, meaning the extra expenses incurred by the business to continue operations. This coverage can be purchased separately (see Extra Expense Coverage Form on page 7-25) in the event a business has no need for business income. The 72 hour time deductible does not apply to extra expense losses.
- **Civil Authority**, meaning prohibited by a civil authority to use the described premises as the result of a direct loss to property. For example, if an explosion occurred, causing a civil authority to close down a part of a city, and causing the insured to have a loss of business income and/or extra expense, coverage would be provided. **Coverage is provided up to 3 consecutive weeks and is subject to a 72 hour time deductible.**
- **Alterations and New Buildings**, meaning the loss of income resulting from a direct loss to new buildings and structures and to the alterations and additions of those buildings and structures. This also applies to machinery and building materials located within 100 feet of the described premises.
- **Extended Business Income** for a **maximum period of 30 days**. This coverage provides a readjustment period in consideration of loss customers.

BUSINESS INCOME OPTIONS

Business income options **permit the insured to waive the business income co-insurance provision** and select any of the following four alternatives:

1) **Maximum Period of Indemnity** limits the loss period covered to 120 days immediately after loss.
2) **Monthly Limit of Indemnity** limits the loss amount during each period of 30 consecutive days to that amount of insurance multiplied by the fraction shown in the declarations. The insured selects a limit of liability of a one-third, one-fourth or one-sixth option. This fractional option in effect provides 3, 4, or 6 months of coverage. For example, if the insured chooses a $200,000 limit with a ¼ option, this means that the insurer will pay up to $50,000 per month for four months, at which time the limit of liability is exhausted. See following example:

EXAMPLE OF MONTHLY LIMIT OF INDEMNITY			
30 Day Periods	**Actual Loss**	**Amount Paid by Insurer**	**Amount Paid by Insured**
Days 1 - 30	$45,000	$45,000†	$0
Days 31 - 60	$50,000	$50,000	$0
Days 61 - 90	$60,000	$50,000	$10,000‡
Days 91 - 120	$20,000	$20,000†	$0

† Insured cannot collect amount above actual loss.
‡ Insured underestimated actual loss and is paid $50,000 monthly limit.

3) **Agreed Value Approach** permits the insured to agree to specified amounts.
4) **Extended Period of Indemnity** permits the insured to readjust to a business income loss. This is the same additional coverage as the extended business income coverage. A declaration entry indicating the number of days of coverage activates this insurance.

BUSINESS INCOME ENDORSEMENTS

The Business Income Form may be endorsed to cover dependent property exposures. These dependent properties are categorized into four classes:

1) **Contributing locations**, which the insured depends upon for materials and services.
2) **Recipient locations**, which accept the insured's products.
3) **Leader locations**, which attract customers to the insured's business.
4) **Manufacturing locations**, which manufacturers products for delivery to the insured's customers under a sales contract.

Technical schools and colleges may also insure their business income loss exposures with the **Business Income Changes - Educational Institutions** endorsement. This endorsement **insures a school or college for loss of tuition and/or fees due to a covered peril**. Coverage may be written on a **limited basis**, which provides tuition and fees coverage, or on a **broad basis**, which includes loss of income from related school activities, such as bookstores and athletic events.

EXTRA EXPENSE COVERAGE FORM

Extra Expense Coverage Form **provides coverage to an insured for extra expenses incurred by a direct loss**. This is the same coverage as provided under the Business Income Form, but is offered as a separate coverage for businesses that are service related (e.g., banks, insurance agencies, accounting firms, etc.). Additional Coverages under the Extra Expense Form include alterations and new buildings and civil authority. Extra expense for dependent properties may be endorsed to the coverage form.

LEASEHOLD INTEREST COVERAGE FORM

Leasehold Interest Coverage Form **protects the lessee from loss in the event the business has a favorable lease arrangement that cannot be reproduced**. For example, if a lessee negotiates a very favorable lease (e.g., $10 per square foot) and the rental space is destroyed by fire, the lessee may have to rent space at a substantially higher current market rate (e.g., $25 per square foot). A lessee can insure the favorable (low cost) lease he negotiated by purchasing leasehold interest insurance. Coverage is provided for the tenant's lease interest (i.e., tenant's interest until lease expires), improvements and betterments, prepaid rent and bonus payments.

LEGAL LIABILITY COVERAGE FORM

Legal Liability Coverage Form **protects the insured against legal liability due to the damage of property of others in the insured's care, custody and control**. Coverage only applies if the insured is legally liable (negligent) for the loss.

CONDOMINIUM ASSOCIATION COVERAGE FORM

Condominium Association Coverage Form provides coverage for the building and personal property for Condominium Associations. Coverages are similar to the Commercial Building and Personal Property Form. Depending upon the condominium association's agreement, coverage may include fixtures, improvements and alterations, and appliances used for cooking, refrigeration, heating and security.

CONDOMINIUM UNIT OWNER'S COVERAGE FORM

Condominium Unit Owner's Coverage Form provides coverage for the unit owner of commercial condominiums. Building coverage is not provided. This coverage complements the Condominium Association Coverage Form.

Condominium Forms **address the unique ownership provisions of shared ownerships**. In the event a loss occurs and coverage is applicable to both the Association's form and the Unit Owner's form, the Association's form is primary.

CAUSES OF LOSS FORMS

Causes of Loss Forms specify the degree of peril coverage applicable to property forms. There are four commercial property causes of loss forms:

1) **BASIC FORM** coverage for the perils of fire, lightning, explosion, windstorm, hail, smoke, aircraft or vehicle, vandalism, sprinkler leakage, sinkhole collapse, and volcanic action.

2) **BROAD FORM** coverage includes the 11 basic coverage perils listed above and adds *falling objects*, *weight of snow, ice or sleet*, and *water damage*. **Additional coverages** includes *collapse* caused by hidden decay, hidden insect or vermin damage, weight of people, personal or rain or use of defective materials.

3) **SPECIAL FORM** coverage provides coverage for direct physical loss, unless specifically excluded. **Exclusions** include smog, wear, tear, loss of use or market, insects, birds, rodents or other animals, release of contaminants or pollutants, settling, cracking, shrinking, rain, snow or sleet to personal property in the open, smoke vapor or gas from agricultural or industrial operations, rust, corrosion, fungus, decay, deterioration, inherent vice, damage due to dampness or dryness, marring and scratching, dishonest acts of insureds and/or employees, voluntary parting of property, collapse except as provided as an additional coverage, weather conditions, acts or decisions, and faulty, inadequate or defective planning. Since the Special Form provides theft coverage, an important additional peril over the Broad Form, **special limitations** apply to furs, jewelry, dies and molds of $2,500, and stamps, tickets and letters of credit of $250.

   General Exclusions are common to the basic, broad and special form. They include ordinance or law, earth movement, governmental action, nuclear hazard, utility services, war/military action, water (i.e., flood), fungus, wet rot or bacteria.

4) **EARTHQUAKE FORM** coverage **must be written with one of the three other causes of loss forms** and adds the following two perils: earthquake and volcanic eruption. Additional **exclusions** include loss or damage resulting from artificially generated electric current, fire and explosion, landslide and mudflow.

ENDORSEMENTS common to the Commercial Property Coverage Part include:

- **Ordinance or Law** endorsement provides coverage in the event a loss occurs and recent ordinances and/or laws require additional construction.
- **Peak Season Endorsement** increases business property during specific periods.
- **Spoilage Coverage Endorsement** provides coverage for the loss to perishable stock. Examples of products susceptible to spoilage include: fruit, dairy, poultry, and seafood products. Coverage options apply to spoilage caused by power failure either on or off premises or for equipment or mechanical failure.
- **Value Reporting Form** addresses the various reporting valuation methods that may be utilized in writing commercial property insurance. The insured has five period options {DR (Daily); WR (Weekly); MR (Monthly); QR (Quarterly); or PR (Policy Year)} to report values.

OVERVIEW

COMMERCIAL INLAND MARINE COVERAGE PART

The need for Commercial Inland Marine Coverages grew out of a demand to insure property, such as cargo, that was being transported from ocean going vessels to destinations inland or within a country. Hence, the term inland marine and the related coverages evolved. Inland marine insurance may be **written to include virtually any type of risk that may be transported** and has been expanded to include **instruments of communications and transportation**. Examples of instruments of communications and transportation include tunnels, bridges, piers, pipelines, transmission lines and towers, and radio and television equipment. The Inland Marine Coverage Part is usually written on a scheduled "Open Peril" basis. Inland marine coverages may be written in a standardized format under the ISO Inland Marine Coverage Part or as a nonstandardized Inland Marine Policy. The following addresses the elements and structure of the standardized ISO Inland Marine Coverage Part:

- **Commercial Inland Marine Declarations Page.**
- **Commercial Inland Marine Conditions** which includes provisions addressing abandonment, appraisal, duties in the event of loss, insurance under two or more coverages, loss payment, other insurance, pair, set or parts clause, privilege to adjust with the owner, recovery or salvage, reinstatement of limits and rights of recovery.
- **One or more Commercial Inland Marine Coverage Forms**
- **Other Endorsements.**

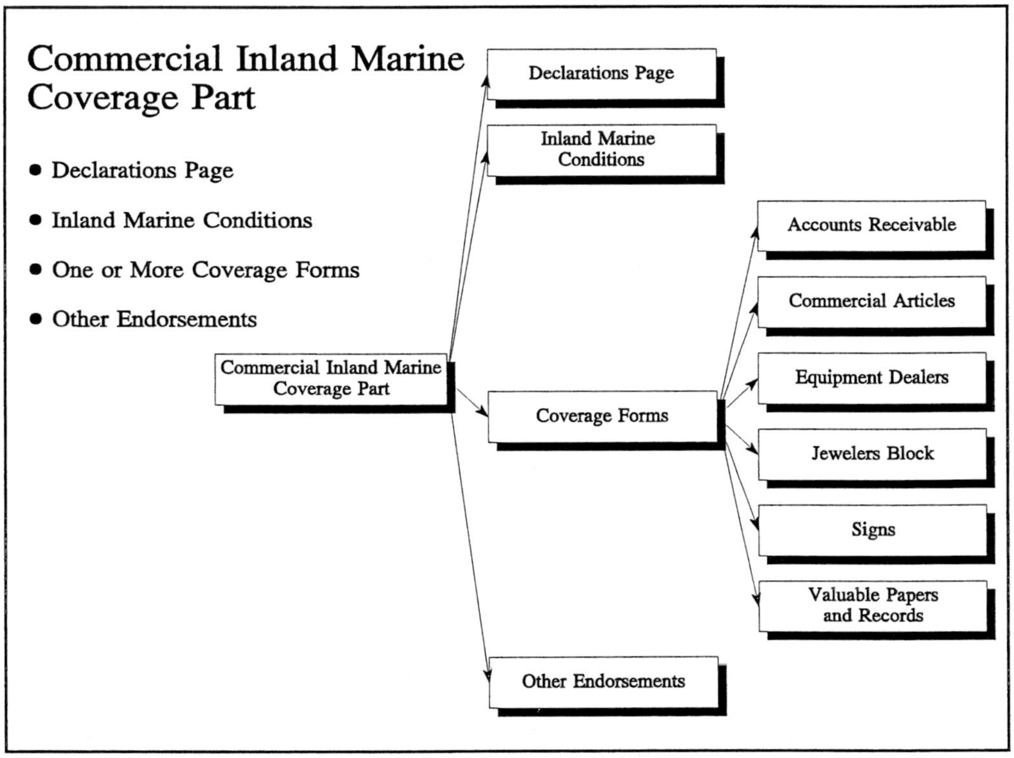

GENERAL CONDITIONS

The General Conditions under the Inland Marine Conditions address concealment, fraud or misrepresentation, legal actions, no benefit to bailee, policy period and valuation. Valuation is the actual cash value or replacement value, whichever is less.

EXCLUSIONS

Exclusions under the Inland Marine Coverage Part are similar in all Inland Marine Coverage Forms. They include earthquake, government action, nuclear hazards, war, flood or surface water, marring, scratching or exposure to light, loss of use, dishonest acts by the insured, accounting errors and inventory shortage.

INLAND MARINE COVERAGE FORMS

Inland Marine Coverage Forms **provide coverage for virtually any type of risk that may be transported**. These inland marine insurance exposures may be insured through standardized/filed forms under the Commercial Inland Marine Coverage Part or through nonstandardized/nonfiled forms under other inland policies. Inland marine exposure categories are classified by the Nationwide Marine Definitions and approved by the National Association of Insurance Commissioners as:

- Imports.
- Exports.
- Domestic Shipments.
- Instrumentalities of Transportation or Communications (e.g., bridges, tunnels, piers, pipelines, radio towers, and TV towers).
- Personal Property Floater Risks.
- Commercial Property Floater Risks.

Although property for the most part is insured under the Building and Personal Property Form, the inland marine coverage is specific and generally written on a Special Form basis. Losses are subject to coinsurance based upon the percentage indicated in the Declarations. **The following are six standard Commercial Inland Marine Coverage Forms:**

1) **Accounts Receivable Form** covers sums of money due the insured from customers which become uncollectible due to loss, damage or destruction of accounts receivable records. It also covers the cost to reestablish the account receivable records and interest charges on any loan required to offset amounts the insured is unable to collect pending the payment from the insurance company.

2) **Commercial Articles Form** covers property such as cameras, musical instruments and related equipment which is used commercially. Similar property of others in the care, custody and control of the insured is also covered.

3) **Equipment Dealers Form** covers a dealer's stock in trade, such as construction, agricultural and other mobile equipment. Similar property of others in the care, custody and control of the dealer is also covered.

4) **Jewelers Block Form** covers the jeweler's stock in trade, such as jewelry, precious and semi-precious stones and precious metals. Similar property of others in the care, custody and control of the jeweler is also covered.

5) **Signs Form** covers signs neon, fluorescent, automatic or mechanical electric signs and lamps. It does not cover ordinary wood signs or billboards even if illuminated by electric lights. Similar property of others in the care, custody and control of the insured is also covered.

6) **Valuable Papers and Records Form** covers the reconstruction cost to generate records such as blueprints, deeds or historical records that were destroyed due to a covered loss. Property of others in the care, custody and control of the insured is also covered.

OTHER INLAND MARINE COVERAGES

In addition to the six standardized/filed Commercial Inland Marine Coverage Forms discussed, the following are **four nonstandardized/nonfiled inland marine forms:**

1) **Contractor's Equipment Form** covers various types of equipment used by contractors such as bulldozers, backhoes, tractors, cranes, etc. The form is written on a special or named peril basis and a coinsurance provision generally applies.

2) **Electrical Data Processing Form** covers electronic data processing equipment, data processing media, extra expenses and business interruption incurred in the loss of media. Coverage is generally written on a special form basis. Examples of the types of losses covered under the EDP form include losses resulting from electrical and magnetic damage, mechanical breakdown, or temperature and humidity changes. A coinsurance provision generally applies.

3) **Bailees' Customers Form** covers a customer's property while in the insured business' control for such activities as cleaning, repairing or servicing. Whenever property is delivered for service a bailment has occurred. The person who transfers their property for service is the **bailor** and the business who accepts the property is the **bailee**. Since property policies have the no benefit to bailee exclusion and general liability policies have the care custody and control exclusion, no coverage is provided under those respective policies in the event the property is damaged, hence the need for the Bailee's Customers Form. Dry cleaners and laundryowners would have a need for this type of form.

4) **Installation Floater Form** covers property such as turbines, transformers and air conditioning equipment during transit or installation at the construction or installation site. It may be written on a special form or named peril basis.

TRANSPORTATION COVERAGES

Transportation exposures exist whenever property is transported. This coverage is needed since the Commercial Property Part and the Businessowners Policy (discussed in the following Chapter) provided limited coverage for property while in transit. Business property is commonly transported by either common or contract carriers.

- **Common carriers**, who offer their services to the public at large are legally liable for damage to property they are transporting. They are responsible for the safe delivery of goods and thus own a high degree of care. **Exceptions apply to losses caused by:** acts of God (earthquakes, floods, etc); acts of public enemy (war); exercise of public authority (confiscated cargo); shipper's fault (negligent packaging); and inherent vice (perishables). A common carrier issues a **Bill of Lading** which evidences receipt of property for shipment and title of property. Common carriers may limit their liability by issuing a **Released Bill of Lading** which limits their liability to a specified maximum dollar amount per shipment or per pound in the event of claim.

- **Contract carriers**, who agree to service specific clients based upon a pre-arranged agreement are only liable when they are negligent. For example, a common carrier would be responsible if property were stolen from a locked truck, whereas, a contract carrier would not be responsible. This distinction places a higher standard of care on common carriers. Property in transit may be covered in any of the following policy forms:

Motor Truck Cargo Policy - Trucker's Form provides *liability coverage* to cover cargo of others which is being transported for hire by truckers. In other words, the trucker is covered if he is negligent in transporting goods of others.

Motor Truck Cargo Policy - Shipper's Form provides *property coverage* to cover the owners' goods which are being shipped by a common carrier or contract carrier. In other words, the shipper's goods are covered while being transported by a common or contract carrier.

Motor Truck Cargo Policy - Owner's Form provides *property coverage* to cover the truck owner's goods while being transported in their trucks. In other words, the truck owner's goods are covered when they are transported in their own trucks.

Transportation Policy - Annual Form provides *property coverage* for a businesses that is shipping incoming and outgoing goods on an annual basis.

Transportation Policy - Trip Transit Form provides *property coverage* for a business that is shipping goods for one specific trip.

TRANSPORTATION EXCLUSIONS

Transportation policies generally exclude the following: contamination or deterioration, dishonesty by the insured, voluntary parting of property, labor disturbances, loss of use, changes or extremes of temperature or humidity and wear and tear.

OVERVIEW

FARM COVERAGE PART

The Farm Coverage Part was developed to address the unique exposures that occur when insuring farming type risks. Specifically, the merging of business and residential exposures under one policy. Although farming exposures can be insured under independently filed farm and ranchowners policies, this section will address the ISO's Farm Coverage Part. **Eligible risks under this form include**: 1) growing and marketing of field crops, fruits, mushrooms, nuts, or vegetables, flowers, greenhouse or nursery stock or sod; 2) raising or keeping of bees, fur bearing animals, livestock (except commercial feed lots), poultry, or worms; and 3) conducting of aquiculture. The Farm Coverage Part consists of the following elements.

- **One or More Farm Declarations Pages**
- **One or More Farm Coverage Forms** (four forms)
- **Other Endorsements**

The Farm Coverage Part includes a property, liability, mobile agricultural and/or a livestock form(s). Basic, broad and special causes of loss provisions are included in the property form and indicated by an entry on the farm property declarations page. The following is an illustration of the Farm Coverage Policy structure:

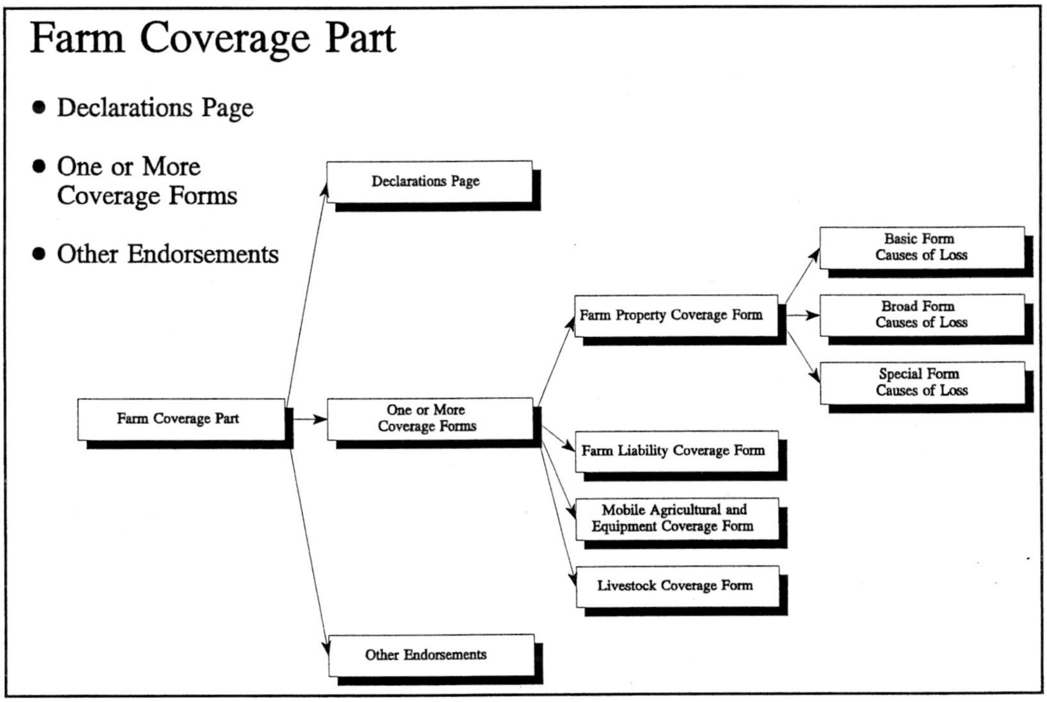

FARM PROPERTY COVERAGE FORM

Farm Property Coverage Form is structured similar to the Homeowner Policy's coverages A, B. C, D, with the addition of farm coverages E, F, and G. It includes the following coverage:

COVERAGE A - DWELLING is similar to the homeowner coverage with a *special limitation of $1,000 for antennas or satellite dishes.*

COVERAGE B - OTHER PRIVATE STRUCTURES is similar to the homeowners coverage. *Buildings used for farming must be scheduled under Coverage G.*

COVERAGE C - HOUSEHOLD PERSONAL PROPERTY *only applies to non farming personal property*. The following sets forth the special limits of liability:

- $ 200 on money, bank notes, gold, silver and platinum medals
- $1,500 on securities, accounts, deeds, manuscripts, passports, tickets/stamps
- $1,500 on watercraft including trailers, equipment and motors *(premises only)*
- $1,500 on trailers not used with watercraft *(premises only)*
- $2,500 on loss **by theft** of jewelry, watches, furs and precious stones
- $3,000 on loss **by theft** of firearms
- $2,500 on loss **by theft** of silverware, goldware and pewterware
- $5,000 on grave markers
- $2,500 on business property located at the residence premises
- $ 500 on business property located away from the premises
- $1,500 on adaptable electronic apparatus that is in or on a motor vehicle
- $1,500 on adaptable electronic apparatus away from the residence premises and used solely for business purposes, while not in or upon a motor vehicle

COVERAGE D - LOSS OF USE is similar to Homeowners Policy.

COVERAGE E - SCHEDULED FARM PERSONAL PROPERTY includes: grain, hay, farm products, poultry (excluding turkeys unless specified), computers related to farm management, miscellaneous equipment (i.e., tools), livestock (excluding live-stock in transit or at stock-yards), other animals, bees, worms, fish and portable structures. Coverage E - Scheduled Farm Personal Property **does not cover** crops, trees, household personal property, etc. In addition, **special limits apply as follows:**

- Hay, straw, or fodder (feed) in the open is limited to $10,000 per stack
- Poultry is limited to market value
- Miscellaneous farm equipment is limited $3,000 per item
- Livestock not specifically insured **is limited to the least of the following amounts**: 120% of the amount obtained by dividing the total insurance on the class & type of animal by the number of head of that class & type at time of loss; the ACV of the animal destroyed; or $2,000. Finally, each horse, mule, or head of cattle under 1 year of age at time of loss will be counted as ½ head.

Under Coverage E - Scheduled Farm Personal Property, each class of property (e.g., livestock, grain, etc.) to be covered is indicated by an amount in the declarations. As an alternative to this scheduled approach, farm personal property may also insured on a blanket basis under Coverage F.

COVERAGE F - UNSCHEDULED FARM PERSONAL PROPERTY includes equipment, supplies and products of farming operations. Specifically, feed, seed, fertilizer, livestock, poultry, grain, bees, fish, worms, produce and agricultural machinery, vehicles, and equipment. Unscheduled livestock is limited to $2,000 on any horse, mule or head of cattle and $1,000 if under one year of age at time of loss. This coverage is subject to an 80% coinsurance requirement.

COVERAGE G - BARNS, OUTBUILDINGS & OTHER FARM STRUCTURES includes farming structures such as barns, silos, fences and outdoor radio and television equipment. This coverage is subject to an 80% coinsurance requirement.

EXTENSIONS of coverages under the Farm Property Coverage Form includes:

- Trees, if the loss is caused by specified perils, up to a limit of $500 per tree
- Non-farm contents in a freezer up to a limit of $500
- Building additions & alterations under the tenant form to 10% of Coverage C
- Farm products (grain, hay, etc.) in the open up to 10% of Coverage F
- Damage to power and light poles up to a limit of $1,000 per occurrence
- New farm structures up to a limit of $100,000 if reported within 60 days
- Newly acquired farm machinery, vehicles & equipment up to a limit of $100,000
- Replacement farm machinery, vehicles & equipment up to a limit of $75,000
- Newly acquired livestock up to 25% of the Coverage E if reported within 30 days
- Newly acquired equipment up to $75,000 if reported within 30 days
- Grain and hay away from insured location up to 10% of Coverage E
- Miscellaneous equipment away from insured location up to 25% of Coverage E
- Farm personal property in the custody of a common carrier to a limit of $1,000

FARM LIABILITY COVERAGE FORM

Farm Liability Coverage Form is similar to the Homeowners Section II coverage for personal exposures and the Commercial General Liability policy for the business coverage. The Farm Liability Coverage Form includes:

COVERAGE H - BODILY INJURY AND PROPERTY DAMAGE covers an insured's legal liability (including defense costs) arising out of bodily injury or property damage. **Exclusions** include liability arising out of intentional acts, contractual liability, pollutants, aircraft and motor vehicles, watercraft, transportation of mobile equipment, business pursuits other than farming, professional services, rental of any residence, communicable diseases, workers compensation, impaired property and product recall. **Custom farming** (farming operations performed for an agreed charge at a farm (e.g., neighbor's farm) that is not an insured location) **is excluded if gross receipts exceed $5,000 in the 12 month period preceding loss.** This exposure can be endorsed if gross receipts exceed the $5,000 limit.

COVERAGE I - PERSONAL AND ADVERTISING INJURY LIABILITY covers an insured for personal injury (i.e., slander, libel, false arrest) and advertising injury (i.e., infringement of copyright or title) exposures. **Exclusions** include intentional acts, contractual liability, breach of contract, failure of goods to perform, any offense committed by an insured who is in the broadcasting business.

Additional coverages under Coverage H and I include reasonable costs incurred in assisting in the claims process up to $250 per day, cost of bonds and attachments, bail bonds to $250, interest costs accrued on the verdict, and up to $1,000 per occurrence for damage to the property of others.

COVERAGE J - MEDICAL PAYMENTS provides coverage for medical expenses caused by an accident, regardless of fault. **Exclusions** include medical payments to any insured or hired person, any person taking part in athletics or any act of war.

MOBILE AGRICULTURAL MACHINERY/EQUIPMENT COVERAGE FORM

Mobile Agricultural Machinery and Equipment Coverage Form provides Open Peril coverage to mobile agricultural machinery and equipment (e.g., tractors, combines, bailers, etc.). This coverage is provided under the Farm Property Coverage Form but may written separately to satisfy individual needs.

LIVESTOCK COVERAGE FORM

Livestock Coverage Form provides coverage for livestock. **Livestock means** cattle, sheep, swine, goats, horses, mules and donkeys. Coverage for livestock is provided under the Farm Property Coverage Form, however, an individual Livestock Coverage Form may be written to satisfy specific needs. Coverage is written on a limit of insurance per animal or a limit of insurance per class basis. Newly acquired livestock is covered up to 30 days subject to a limit of 25% of the livestock limit of insurance.

CAUSES OF LOSS

The Farm Property Coverage Form includes a description of the Basic, Broad and Special covered causes of loss. The applicable coverage is activated by an entry on the Farm Property Coverage Declarations as one of the following forms:

BASIC FORM covers the perils of fire, lightning, explosion, windstorm, hail, smoke, riot or civil commotion, aircraft or vehicle, vandalism, theft, sinkhole collapse and volcanic action. **Collision coverage is provided for Coverages E and F in the event of collision causing:** damage to machinery; death of livestock (including livestock killed on a public road or due to overturn of a vehicle); and damage to other farm personal property. Livestock is also covered for loss due to earthquake or flood.

BROAD FORM covers the perils listed above, **but adds electrocution of livestock**, **attacks on livestock** by dogs or wild animals, **accidental shooting of livestock**, **drowning of livestock (except for swine under 30 days old)**, **accidental death due to loading or unloading of livestock**, breakage of glass, falling objects, weight of ice, snow or sleet, sudden or accidental tearing apart of a hot water, air conditioning, automatic protective system or appliance for heating water, accidental discharge of water, freezing of plumbing, heating or air conditioning systems, sudden or accidental damage from artificially generated electrical systems.

SPECIAL FORM covers direct physical loss. **Exclusions include:**

- Fire, *if caused by curing tobacco*
- Collapse except as provided in additional coverages
- Windstorm or hail damage to dairy/farm products or watercraft left in the open
- Rain, snow or sleet damage to personal property left in the open
- Freezing or thawing to foundations, pavements, fences, or swimming pools
- Discharge or overflow or freezing if the insured failed to maintain heat
- *Explosion to alcohol stills, boilers, and steam pipes in farm buildings*
- Theft of property from the part of the residence rented
- Theft of building material prior to occupancy
- Theft of trailers or watercraft away from the premises
- Inventory shortages
- Voluntary parting of property
- Unauthorized instructions to transfer monies
- Vandalism and glass breakage if vacant beyond 30 days
- Dishonest acts of the insured or employees
- Artificially generated electrical currents
- Smoke and vapor from industrial operations
- Wear, tear, rust, corrosion, fungus, hidden decay, dryness, marring, scratching, weather conditions, faulty design and planning

FARM CAUSES OF LOSS FORMS

Named Perils	Basic	Broad	Special
Fire or Lightning	•	•	•
Windstorm or Hail	•	•	•
Explosion	•	•	•
Riot or Civil Commotion	•	•	•
Aircraft	•	•	•
Vehicles	•	•	•
Vandalism	•	•	•
Theft	•	•	•
Sinkhole Collapse	•	•	•
Volcanic Action	•	•	•
Collision (coverage E & F only)	•	•	•
Earthquake Loss to Livestock	•	•	•
Flood Loss to Livestock	•	•	•
Electrocution of Livestock		•	•
Accidental Shooting of Livestock		•	•
Drowning of Livestock		•	•
Loading/Unloading of Livestock		•	•
Breakage of Glass		•	•
Falling Objects		•	•
Weight of Ice and Snow		•	•
Sudden and Accidental Tearing Apart		•	•
Accident Discharge of Water		•	•
Freezing		•	•
Accidental Damage from Electrical Current		•	•
Special/Open Peril Coverage			•

CONDITIONS - The Conditions under the Farm Coverage Part are the standard commercial conditions and include provisions for abandonment, appraisal, duties in the event of loss, insurance under two or more coverages, legal action, pay the value of the loss, other insurance, pair or set clause, recovery or salvage and rights of recovery. ***If a building or structure is vacant or unoccupied beyond a period of 120 consecutive days***, the limits of insurance applicable to the building and its contents are reduced by 50%.

EXCLUSIONS - Exclusions include ordinance or law, earth movement, governmental action, nuclear hazard, power failure off premises, war and military action, and water, meaning flood and surface water.

ADDITIONAL COVERAGES - Additional coverages include debris removal, reasonable repairs, removal, fire department charges, removal of trees, credit card and transfer funds coverage up to $500, cost of restoring farm records up to $2,000, extra expense and collapse.

DEFINITIONS

The following addresses terms and definitions that are specific to the Farm Coverage Part:

- **Business** means a trade, profession, occupation, enterprise or activity, *other than farming or custom farming*, which is engaged in for the purpose of monetary or other compensation.

- **Business Property** means property pertaining to any trade, profession or occupation *other than farming*.

- **Custom Farming** means performance of specific planting, cultivating, harvesting or similar specific farming operations by an insured at a farm that is not an insured location. *Custom farming does not mean:* operations conducted at a premises rented, leased, or controlled by an insured; operations for which no compensation in money or goods is received; or a neighborly exchange of services.

- **Dwelling** means a building used principally for family residential purposes, and includes mobile homes and modular and prefabricated homes. *Dwelling does not* mean a building used in such agricultural operations as storage of farm produce, livestock or poultry.

- **Farming** means the operation of an agricultural or aquacultural enterprise, and includes the operation of roadside stands, on the named insured's farm premises, maintained solely for the sale of farm products produces principally by the named insured. *Unless specifically indicated in the Declarations, farming does not include* retail activity other than that described or mechanized processing operations.

- **Farm Personal Property** means equipment, supplies and products of farming or ranching operations, including but not limited to feed, seed, fertilizer, livestock, other animals, poultry, grain, bees, fish, worms, produce and agricultural machinery, vehicles and equipment.

- **Insured** under the Property Form means the named insured and, if the named insured is an individual it includes resident relatives and any other person under the age of 21 who is in the care of any insured. **Under the Liability Form** it means partnerships and corporation designated in the declarations, sole proprietors, and partners of partnerships including their spouses, other entities (e.g., Limited Liability Companies) including their executives, officers and directors for business activities, the named insured's employees while working within the scope of their employment, the named insured's real estate manager if not an employee of the insured, individuals using the insured's vehicles with his or her consent that are covered under this policy but only while on the insured location.

- **Insured Location** under the Property Form means any location, including its private approaches, described in the Declarations. **Under the Liability Form** it means the farm premises (including grounds and private approaches) and residence premises shown in the Declarations; the part of other premises, or of other structures and grounds, that is used by the insured as a residence and acquired by the insured during the present annual policy period for his or her use as a residence; any part of premises not owned by any insured but where an insured is temporarily residing; vacant land owned by or rented to an insured; land, owned by or rented to an insured, on which a dwelling is being constructed for occupancy by an insured, or by an insured's farm employees or residence employees or a building or structure is being constructed for use of an insured in farming operation; individual or family cemetery plots or burial vaults of an insured; any part of premises occasionally rented to any insured for other than business purposes; and any farm premises (including its grounds and private approaches) that the insured or the insured's spouse acquires during the present annual policy period.

- **Livestock** means cattle, sheep, swine, goats, horses, mules and donkeys.

- **Mobile Equipment** means bulldozers, forklifts and tractors designed for use principally off public roads; other farm machinery designed for use principally off public roads and as implements for cultivating or harvesting; vehicles that travel on crawler treads, except that snowmobiles are mobile equipment only while on an insured location or any premises own or rent to an insured; vehicles whether self-propelled or not, on which are permanently mounted power cranes, shovels, loaders, diggers or drill or road construction or resurfacing equipment such as graders, scrapers or rollers; vehicles that are maintained primarily to provide mobility to permanently attached equipment of air compressors, pumps and generators, including spraying, welding, building cleaning, geophysical exploration, lighting and well servicing equipment or cherry pickers and similar devices used to raise or lower workers.

- **Motor Vehicle** means a motorized land vehicle, trailer or semitrailer designed for travel on public roads or used on public roads; a motorized golf cart, snowmobile or other motorized land vehicle owned by an insured and designed for recreational use off public roads, while off an insured location; or any vehicle, including any attached machinery or equipment, while being towed by or carried on a vehicle included in this definition. *Motor vehicle does not mean*: mobile equipment, a boat, camp trailer, home trailer or utility trailer unless it is being towed by or carried on a motorized land vehicle included in this definition; a motorized golf cart while used for golfing purposes.

- **Unoccupancy or unoccupied** means the condition of a dwelling (except while being constructed) not being lived in; or any other building or structure (except while being constructed) not being used even if it contains furnishings or other property customary to its intended use or occupancy.

- **Vacancy or vacant** means the condition of a building or structure (except while being constructed) not containing sufficient furnishings or other property customary to its intended use or occupancy.

OVERVIEW

COMMERCIAL AUTO COVERAGE PART

The Commercial Auto Coverage Part provides coverage for businesses which own, use or service automobiles or trucks. This coverage part may be included in the Commercial Package Policy or it may be written as a separate monoline policy. Since this coverage was fully reviewed in Chapter Six as a separate monoline Commercial Auto Policy, it will not be repeated in this chapter. See pages 6-15 to 6-23 for complete information on this coverage part.

PENNSYLVANIA COMMERCIAL CANCELLATION REQUIREMENTS

Cancellation by the company is permitted with advance written notice:

If the policy has been in effect for less than 60 days:

- At least 30 days advance written notice is required.

If the policy has been in effect for more than 60 days:

- At least 15 days advance written notice for material misrepresentation and nonpayment of premium.
- At least 60 days advance written notice is required for increased risk factors, loss of reinsurance, failure to comply with policy conditions, or any other reason deemed by the insurance commissioner.

Cancellation by the first named insured is permitted by:

- Giving advance written notice of the date cancellation will take effect.

COMMERCIAL PACKAGE POLICY SUMMARY

(Common Policy Declarations and Conditions)
(Seven Coverage Parts)

CPP =

— **General Liability Coverage Part** — **2 Coverage Forms**

- Occurrence
- Claims-made

— **Crime Coverage Part** — **2 Coverage Forms**

- Loss Sustained
- Discovery
  - Employee Theft
  - Forgery and Alteration
  - Inside the Premises - Theft of Money and Securities
  - Inside the Premises - Robbery and Safe Burglary
  - Outside the Premises
  - Computer Fraud
  - Money Orders and Counterfeit Currency
  - Funds Transfer Fraud
  - Extortion
  - Securities Deposited with Others
  - Guest's Property
  - Safe Depository
  - Lessees of Safe Deposit Boxes

— **Boiler and Machinery Coverage Part** — **1 Coverage Form**

- Equipment Breakdown Protection Coverage

— **Commercial Auto Coverage Part** — **5 Coverage Forms**

- Business Auto
- Business Auto Physical Damage
- Garage
- Truckers
- Motor Carriers

— **Property Coverage Part** — **8 Coverage Forms**

- Building and Personal Property
- Builders Risk
- Business Income
- Extra Expense
- Leasehold Interest
- Legal Liability
- Condominium Association
- Condominium Unit-owners

— **Inland Marine Coverage Part** — **6 Coverage Forms**

- Accounts Receivable
- Commercial Articles
- Equipment Dealers
- Jewelers Block
- Signs
- Valuable Papers and Records

— **Farm Coverage Part** — **4 Coverage Forms**

- Farm Property
- Farm Liability
- Mobile Agricultural Machinery and Equipment
- Livestock

KEY TERMS AND CONCEPTS

The following terms were introduced in this chapter. You should know each word and concept and be able to apply them in everyday usage. To improve retention, it is recommended that you write out each key term and concept in your own words.

Accounts Receivable Form
Bailees' Customers Form
Basic Form
Bill of Lading
Bodily Injury/Property Damage Liability
Boiler and Machinery Part
Broad Form
Builders Risk Form
Building and Personal Property Form
Business Income Form
CGL Coverage Part
Claims-made v. Occurrence
Commercial Articles Form
Commercial Crime Coverage Part
Commercial Package Policy Format
Commercial Property Coverage Part
Common Carrier
Common Policy Conditions
Computer Fraud
Condominium Association Form
Condominium Unit Owners' Form
Contract Carrier
Contractors Equipment Form
Contributing Locations
Crime Exclusions
Custom Farming
Discovery Form
Earthquake Form
Electronic Data Processing Form
Employee Theft
Equipment Breakdown Coverage
Extended Reporting Periods (ERP)
Extortion
Extra Expense Form
Farm Coverage Part
Farm Liability Coverages
Farm Property Basic Cause of Losses
Farm Property Broad Cause of Losses
Farm Property Special Cause of Losses
Forgery and Alterations
Funds Transfer Fraud
Guests' Property
Indirect Loss Endorsements
Inland Marine Coverage Part
Inside Premises-Robbery or Safe Burglary
Inside Premises-Theft of Money/Securities
Installation Floater Form
Jewelers Block Form
Laser Beam Endorsement
Leader Locations
Leasehold Interest Form
Lessees of Safe Deposit Boxes
Legal Liability Form
Limits of Liability
Livestock Coverage Form
Loss Sustained Form
Manufacturing Locations
Medical Payments
Mobile Agricultural Machinery
Money Orders/Counterfeit Paper Currency
Motor Truck Cargo Policies
Optional Business Income Coverages (4)
Outside the Premises
Owners and Contractors Protective (OCP)
Personal and Advertising Liability
Pollution Liability Coverage Form
Pollution Liability Extension Endorsement
Pollution Liability Limited Form
Premises and Operations
Products and Completed Operations
Recipient Locations
Released Bill of Lading
Retroactive Date
Safe Depository
Securities Deposited with Others
Sign Form
Special Form
Supplemental Extended Reporting Period
Supplemental Payments
Transportation Coverages
Utility Interruption
Valuable Papers and Records Form

REVIEW QUESTIONS

Before attempting to answer the end chapter practice questions, you should ask yourself if you can answer the following questions. It is recommended that you write out each review question in your own words. This exercise will help you apply the key terms and concepts that you've learned to form relationships with different topics.

1. Identify and briefly describe the 7 coverage parts of the CPP. (7-1)
2. Identify 4 advantages of the CPP concept. (7-1)
3. Identify the 2 major sublines of the CGL Coverage Part and give 2 examples of each subline. (7-3)
4. What is the major difference between the Occurrence and Claims-made CGL forms?
5. Identify and explain 3 unique features of the Claims-made Form. (7-4)
6. Identify and explain the 3 primary coverages of the CGL Form. (7-6)
7. Identify and explain 5 Supplemental Payments under the CGL Part. (7-7)
8. Identify 5 individuals or organizations that may be granted insured status under the CGL part. (7-7)
9. Identify and explain 5 limits of liability under the CGL Part. (7-8)
10. Under the Crime Coverage Part, how does burglary differ from safe burglary? (7-10)
11. Under the Crime Coverage Part, how does robbery differ from theft? (7-10)
12. Under the Crime Coverage Part, how does money differ from securities? (7-11)
13. Identify 2 individuals not covered under the Crime Coverage Form Employee Theft. (7-10)
14. Identify 2 perils that are covered under the Boiler and Machinery Coverage Part and not covered under the Commercial Property Part. (7-14)
15. Explain "Breakdown" as defined under the Equipment Breakdown Form. (7-16)
16. Under the Equipment Breakdown Form, explain how losses to objects are settled including any time limitation. (7-17)
17. Identify and explain 3 endorsements that may be added to the Equipment Breakdown Form. (7-18)
18. Identify 8 coverage forms that may be added to the Commercial Property Part. (7-19)
19. Identify and explain the 3 coverages of the Building and Personal Property Form. (7-20)

20. Identify 10 of the 16 categories of property not covered under the Building and Personal Property Form. (7-20)

21. Identify 4 Additional Coverages of the Building and Personal Property Form. (7-21)

22. Identify 5 Coverage Extensions of the Building and Personal Property Form. (7-21)

23. Identify 2 sublimits that apply to the Building and Personal Property Form. (7-21)

24. Identify 5 coverages that apply to the Business Income Coverage Form. (7-23)

25. Identify 4 Optional Coverages of the Business Income Coverage Form. (7-24)

26. Identify and explain the 4 Endorsements of Business Income Coverage Form. (7-24)

27. What is Extra Expense coverage? (7-25)

28. How does the Legal Liability Coverage Form differ from the Bailee Customer Form? (7-25 & 7-30)

29. How does the Condominium Association Form differ from the Condominium Unit Owner's Form? (7-25)

30. Identify and explain 4 Endorsements that may be added to the Commercial Property Coverage Part. (7-26)

31. Identify 6 classes of property that may be insured under the Inland Marine Coverage Forms. (7-28)

32. Identify 6 standard ISO Inland Marine Coverage Forms and 4 nonstandardized Inland Marine Forms. (7-28 & 7-29)

33. Identify and explain the 3 Motor Truck Cargo Policy Forms and 2 Transportation Policy Forms. (7-30)

34. Identify the 4 Farm Forms. (7-31 & 7-33)

35. Identify the 7 Coverages provided under the Farm Property Form. (7-32 & 7-33)

36. Identify the 4 special limits that apply to Coverage E - Scheduled Farm Personal Property. (7-32)

37. Identify 5 Farm Property Coverage Extensions. (7-33)

38. What special limitation applies under the Farm Liability Form. (7-33)

39. Identify 3 perils that are unique to farming that are covered under the Farm Basic Cause of Loss Form that are not covered under the Building and Personal Property Basic Cause of Loss Form. (7-26 & 7-34)

40. Identify 5 perils that are provided under the Farm Broad Cause of Loss Form that are not provided under the Farm Basic Cause of Loss Form. (7-35)

PRACTICE EXAM SEVEN

ON

COMMERCIAL PACKAGE POLICY

1. **Which of the following is NOT included in the common policy declarations of the Commercial Package Policy?**

   A) Policy number.
   B) Description of the insured business.
   C) Coverage Extensions.
   D) Schedule of coverage parts and related premiums. Ref. 7-1

2. **All of the following are common policy conditions of the Commercial Package Policy EXCEPT:**

   A) Cancellation.
   B) Identity of insured and address.
   C) Transfer of rights.
   D) Examination of books. Ref. 7-2

3. **The Commercial General Liability Coverage Part may be issued:**

   A) As part of the Dwelling Policy Program.
   B) Only as a monoline policy.
   C) Only as a part of the Commercial Package Policy.
   D) As either a monoline or package policy. Ref. 7-3

4. **The Commercial General Liability Coverage Part must include all of the following EXCEPT:**

   A) A Commercial General Liability Declarations Page.
   B) A Professional Liability Coverage Form.
   C) A General Liability Coverage Part.
   D) The Broad Form Nuclear Energy Liability Exclusion Endorsement. Ref. 7-3

5. **The Commercial General Liability Coverage Part may be written on:**

   A) A scheduled basis.
   B) Only on an occurrence basis.
   C) A scheduled or occurrence basis.
   D) On either a claims-made or occurrence basis. Ref. 7-4

6. **Occurrence Coverage under the CGL may be described as:**

   A) Coverage which applies to injury or damage that occurs during the policy period, regardless of when the claim is reported to the company.
   B) Occurrence coverage is only provided by the Commercial General Liability Part.
   C) Occurrence coverage applies to injury that occurs anywhere in the world.
   D) Coverage which applies to claims occurring on or after the retroactive date and made during the policy period. Ref. 7-4

7. **All of the following are true of Claims-made Coverage EXCEPT:**

A) Claims-made coverage applies to claims which are made on or after the retroactive date and during the policy period.
B) A Retroactive Date is generally indicated in Claims-made coverage.
C) A Supplemental Extended Reporting Period is provided at no additional cost.
D) A Basic Extended Reporting Period is provided in Claims-made coverage. Ref. 7-4

8. **Which of the following describes a Retroactive Date?**

A) The Retroactive Date is the last day of coverage.
B) The Retroactive Date defines when coverage begins.
C) The Retroactive Date is indicated in occurrence form policies.
D) The Retroactive Date provides tail coverage. Ref. 7-4

9. **Which of the following describes Extended Reporting Periods of the Claims-made Coverage?**

A) Extended Reporting Periods determine when coverage begins.
B) Extended Reporting Periods provide tail coverage after the end of the policy period.
C) Extended Reporting Periods are the same as the Retroactive date.
D) Extended Reporting Periods do not provide tail coverage. Ref. 7-4

10. **Retroactive Dates and Extended Reporting Periods have all of the following common characteristics EXCEPT:**

A) They are used to minimize coverage gaps when transferring liability policies.
B) The Basic Extended Reporting Period is of an unlimited duration.
C) The Retroactive Date determines when coverage begins.
D) Extended Reporting Periods provide tail coverage after the end of the policy period. Ref. 7-4

11. **The Commercial General Liability Coverage Part A - Bodily Injury and Property Damage Liability provides coverage for which of the following major coverages?**

A) Personal liability.
B) Employers liability.
C) Liquor liability.
D) Premises/operations and products/completed operations. Ref. 7-3 & 7-6

12. **The Commercial General Liability Coverage A - Bodily Injury and Property Damage Liability excludes all of the following EXCEPT:**

A) Injury or damage expected or intended by an insured.
B) Liability imposed in an alcoholic beverage business.
C) Bodily injury from the insured's defective products.
D) Obligations under Workers Compensation. Ref. 7-6

13. The Commercial General Liability Coverage B - Personal and Advertising Injury Liability provides:

A) Premises/operations coverage.
B) Products/completed operations coverage.
C) Liquor liability coverage.
D) Copyright infringement coverage. Ref. 7-6

14. All of the following are Commercial General Liability Coverage B - Personal and Advertising Injury Liability exclusions EXCEPT:

A) Oral or written publications that are known to be false.
B) Offenses committed by an insured in the advertising, broadcasting, publishing or telecasting business.
C) Oral or written material that was first published prior to inception of the policy period.
D) Oral or written statements which are true but negatively reflect upon a third party.
Ref. 7-6

15. All of the following are true of the Commercial General Liability Coverage C - Medical Payments EXCEPT:

A) Provides coverage for medical payments caused by an accident.
B) Provides medical payments coverage for accidents occurring because of the insured's operations or occurring on his premises.
C) Requires the injured person to submit to examinations of the insurer's choice.
D) Provides pro-rated coverage with the applicable Workers Compensation coverage.
Ref. 7-7

16. All of the following are exclusions of the Commercial General Liability Coverage C - Medical Payments EXCEPT:

A) Injuries to the insured.
B) Injuries to third parties.
C) Injuries due to war.
D) Injuries due to participation in athletics. Ref. 7-7

17. All of the following are Commercial General Liability Supplementary Payments EXCEPT:

A) Expenses incurred by the insured including costs taxed against the insured in a lawsuit.
B) Medical payments to third parties injured on the premises.
C) Post-judgment interest charges.
D) Cost of bonds to release attachments. Ref. 7-7

18. All of the following are true of the limits of liability of the Supplementary Payments of Commercial General Liability EXCEPT:

A) Defense costs are included to the policy limits.
B) Supplementary payments are paid in addition to the applicable policy limits.
C) Defense costs are unlimited.
D) Defense costs are excluded from the policy limits. Ref. 7-7

19. All of the following are limits of liability that are indicated on the CGL Declarations Page EXCEPT:

A) A general aggregate.
B) Personal liability per person.
C) Personal and advertising injury per person or organization.
D) Fire damage limit per fire.
E) Medical expense limit per person. Ref. 7-7 & 7-8

20. Under the CGL, Advertising Injury means all of the following EXCEPT:

A) Misuse of a title or slogan.
B) Misappropriation of advertising ideas or style of business.
C) Failure of goods to perform as advertised.
D) Infringement of copyright, title or slogan. Ref. 7-6

21. Under the CGL, an Insured Contract means all of the following EXCEPT:

A) A contract that is to indemnify an architect for professional services.
B) A lease of premises.
C) A sidetrack agreement.
D) An elevator maintenance agreement. Ref. 7-6

22. Under the CGL, Personal Injury means all of the following EXCEPT:

A) Oral or written material that slanders or libels a person or organization.
B) False arrest, detention or imprisonment.
C) Malicious prosecution.
D) Oral or written material made by a broadcaster that slanders or libels a person.
E) Wrongful entry or eviction. Ref. 7-6

23. All of the following are true of pollution liability under the CGL EXCEPT:

A) It is carefully underwritten because of the volatile nature of pollution exposures.
B) The CGL may be endorsed to provide pollution coverage.
C) It is a standard coverage in all Claims-made and Occurrence Forms.
D) It is excluded under the CGL Form. Ref. 7-6 & 7-9

24. All of the following are true of the Commercial Crime Coverage Part EXCEPT:

A) It may be written as a monoline policy or part of the CPP.
B) Coverage may be written to cover either commercial or governmental exposures.
C) The insured may purchase several of the crime coverages under one policy.
D) The Crime Coverage Part has limited flexibility. Ref. 7-10 & 7-11

25. **All of the following are general exclusions of the Commercial Crime Coverage Part EXCEPT:**

A) Losses resulting from nuclear hazards.
B) Losses resulting from acts committed by the named insured.
C) Losses resulting from government seizure or destruction by government authority.
D) Losses resulting from acts committed by third parties. Ref. 7-10

26. **Under the Commercial Crime Coverage Part, Burglary means:**

A) The surrendering of property away from the premises by means of threat communicated to the insured.
B) The taking of property from inside the premises by unlawful entering, as evidenced by marks of forcible entry or exit.
C) The taking of property from the care and custody of a person by the threat of bodily harm.
D) The taking of property from within a locked safe or vault by a person of unlawful entry, as evidenced by visible signs to the safe or vault. It also means the removal of the safe from the premises. Ref. 7-10

27. **Under the Commercial Crime Coverage Part, Extortion means:**

A) The surrendering of property away from the premises by means of threat communicated to the insured.
B) The taking of property from inside the premises by unlawful entering, as evidenced by marks of forcible entry or exit.
C) The taking of property from the care and custody of a person by the threat of bodily harm.
D) The taking of property from within a locked safe or vault by a person of unlawful entry, as evidenced by visible signs to the safe or vault. It also means the removal of the safe from the premises. Ref. 7-10

28. **Under the Commercial Crime Coverage Part, Safe Burglary means:**

A) The surrendering of property away from the premises by means of threat communicated to the insured.
B) The taking of property from inside the premises by unlawful entering, as evidenced by marks of forcible entry or exit.
C) The taking of property from the care and custody of a person by the threat of bodily harm.
D) The taking of property from within a locked safe or vault by a person of unlawful entry, as evidenced by visible signs to the safe or vault. It also means the removal of the safe from the premises. Ref. 7-10

29. **All of the following are true of the Commercial Crime Coverage - Forgery or Alteration EXCEPT:**

A) It provides coverage for losses resulting from forgery or alterations of outgoing drafts, checks, promissory notes or similar instruments.
B) It provides coverage for loss of money due to forgery or alterations.
C) It provides coverage if employees forge or alter checks or drafts.
D) Coverage is provided worldwide. Ref. 7-12

30. All of the following are true of the Commercial Crime Coverage - Employee Theft EXCEPT:

A) It covers loss to money and securities and property other than money and securities caused by a dishonest employee.
B) It provides coverage if the named insured's partner absconds with funds.
C) It may be written on either a scheduled or blanket basis.
D) It is one of the most common forms of crime coverage. Ref. 7-11

31. Under the Commercial Crime Coverage Part, Robbery means:

A) The surrendering of property away from the premises by means of threat communicated to the insured.
B) The taking of property from inside the premises by unlawful entering, as evidenced by marks of forcible entry or exit.
C) The taking of property from the care and custody of a person by the threat of bodily harm.
D) The taking of property from within a locked safe or vault by a person of unlawful entry, as evidenced by visible signs to the safe or vault. It also means the removal of the safe from the premises. Ref. 7-10

32. All of the following are true of the Commercial Crime Coverage - Inside the Premises - Theft of Money and Securities EXCEPT:

A) It covers money and securities at a banking premises.
B) It covers money and securities at the insured premises.
C) It covers damage to the premises caused by an attempted theft.
D) It covers money and securities stolen by an employee. Ref. 7-12

33. All of the following are true of the Commercial Crime Coverage - Inside the Premises - Robbery and Safe Burglary of Other Property EXCEPT:

A) It covers money and securities inside the premises.
B) It covers property other than money and securities inside the premises.
C) It covers damage to the premises caused by an attempted robbery.
D) It covers precious metals, stones, and furs subject to a $5,000 limit.

Ref. 7-11 & 7-12

34. All of the following are true of the Commercial Crime Coverage - Outside Premises EXCEPT:

A) It covers money and securities in the care of a messenger.
B) It covers money and securities in the care of an armored motor vehicle company.
C) It covers other property in the care of a custodian.
D) It does not cover precious metals, stones and furs. Ref. 7-12

35. Which of the following is NOT true of Commercial Crime Coverage that is written on a Loss Sustained basis?

A) Retroactive dates are commonly used.
B) Coverage applies to losses sustained during the policy year.
C) Coverage applies to losses discovered within one year of policy expiration.
D) When coverage is renewed, the one year extended period to discover losses terminates. Ref. 7-11

36. All of the following are true of the Boiler and Machinery Coverage Part EXCEPT:

A) The coverage part contains a Boiler and Machinery Declarations Page.
B) The coverage part contains an Equipment Breakdown Protection Form.
C) The coverage part may include Business Interruption Coverage.
D) The coverage part may include Impaired Property Coverage. Ref. 7-15 & 7-18

37. Which of the following is true of the Equipment Breakdown Protection Form?

A) The form covers a breakdown to covered equipment.
B) Covered equipment is insured on an actual cash value basis.
C) Normal maintenance is covered.
D) Producers generally conduct boiler and machinery inspections. Ref. 7-16 & 7-17

38. All of following are commonly covered under the Equipment Breakdown Protection Form EXCEPT:

A) Mechanical failure caused by centrifical force.
B) Expediting expenses.
C) Property in the insured's care, custody and control.
D) Combustion explosion. Ref. 7-16 & 7-17

39. All of the following are optional endorsements that may be endorsed to the Equipment Breakdown Protection Form EXCEPT:

A) Refrigeration Interruption Coverage.
B) Turbine Units Explosion Coverage.
C) Pressure or Vacuum Equipment Coverage.
D) Product Recall Coverage. Ref. 7-18

40. All of the following are true of Transportation Coverage EXCEPT:

A) A common carrier offers their services to the public at large and is legally liable for damage to property being transported.
B) A contract carrier agrees to service specific clients based upon a prearranged agreement and are only liable when they are negligent.
C) A Released Bill of Lading is a contract between the common carrier and the shipper.
D) A common carrier cannot limit its liability. Ref. 7-30

41. All of the following are true of the Motor Truck Cargo Policies EXCEPT:

A) The Motor Truck Cargo Policy - Owner's Form provides coverage for property transported by a business using its own trucks.
B) The Motor Truck Cargo Policy - Trucker's Form provides liability coverage to common carriers who transport the goods of others for hire.
C) The Motor Truck Cargo Policy is an inland marine coverage.
D) The same coverage can be provided under the Crime Coverage Part. Ref. 7-28

42. All of the following are true of the Commercial Property Coverage Part EXCEPT:

A) The coverage part has limited flexibility.
B) There are eight coverage forms that may be included in the program.
C) There are four causes of loss forms.
D) It may be written as a monoline policy or as part of the CPP. Ref. 7-19

43. All of the following are true of the Building and Personal Property Coverage Form EXCEPT:

A) Coverage A applies to Buildings, Coverage B applies to Business Personal Property, Coverage C applies to Personal Property of Others.
B) Coverage B Business Personal Property is covered within 100 feet of the insured premises.
C) It is the preferred way to insure valuable business personal property.
D) Additional coverages and extensions of coverage are provided in the policy.
Ref. 7-20 & 7-21

44. All of the following are Additional Coverages under the Building and Personal Property Form EXCEPT:

A) Debris Removal.
B) Cost of extracting pollutants from land and water up to $10,000.
C) Fire department service charge up to $1,000.
D) Cost to repair or restore information. Ref. 7-21

45. Coverage extensions are provided under the Building and Personal Property Coverage Form if a coinsurance of at least 80% is shown in the declarations. All of the following are these coverage extensions EXCEPT:

A) Newly acquired or constructed property.
B) Personal effects and property of others.
C) Valuable papers.
D) Automobiles held for sale. Ref. 7-21

46. All of the following property are not covered under the Building and Personal Property Coverage Form EXCEPT:

A) Personal property used to service the premises such as fire extinguishers, outdoor furniture, floor coverings and appliances for cooking and refrigeration.
B) Accounts, bills and money.
C) Contraband.
D) Land. Ref. 7-20

47. Under the Building and Personal Property Coverage Form, which of the following is true?

A) Signs are not covered.
B) Signs are covered if attached to the building up to $1,000.
C) Signs are covered up to the Coverage A limit.
D) Signs are only covered by endorsement. Ref. 7-21

48. All of the following are optional coverages that may be endorsed to the Building and Personal Property Form EXCEPT:

A) Peak Season Endorsement.
B) Personal Liability.
C) Specialized Valuation Forms.
D) Ordinance or Law Endorsement. Ref. 7-26

49. All of the following are true of the Builders Risk Coverage Form EXCEPT:

A) Builders Risk Coverage is written to cover the exposure of buildings under construction.
B) It is the same coverage as the Building and Personal Property Form.
C) To address the unique features of Builders Risk exposure, coverage is provided for the foundation of the building, temporary structures used to construct the building if not insured elsewhere, and building materials within 100 feet of the premises.
D) Coverage may be written on a completed value or a reporting form basis. Ref. 7-22

50. All of the following are true of when coverage ceases under the Builders Risk Coverage Form EXCEPT:

A) Coverage ceases when the builder's interest is terminated.
B) Coverage ceases when the property is accepted by the purchaser.
C) Coverage continues indefinitely.
D) Coverage ceases if the builder/insurer abandons the construction with no intentions of completing the building. Ref. 7-22

51. All of the following are true of the Business Income Coverage Form EXCEPT:

A) Coverage applies to loss of business income sustained from a suspension of operations.
B) Coverage applies to extra expenses incurred by the insured in continuing operations.
C) Business income is a consequential loss exposure.
D) The insured must always comply with a coinsurance requirement. Ref. 7-23 & 7-24

52. All of the following are coverages under the Business Income Coverage Form EXCEPT:

A) Business Income.
B) Extra Expense Coverage.
C) Coverage for interruption by Civil Authority for up to two weeks.
D) Coverage for the installation of new glass due to vandalism.
E) Alterations and new buildings.
F) Extended business income for up to 30 days. Ref. 7-23 & 7-24

53. Which of the following is the correct coinsurance formula used in the Business Income Coverage Form?

A) Net income plus all expenses times coinsurance percentage equals insurance amount required to carry.
B) Gross income plus all expenses times coinsurance percentage equals insurance amount required to carry.
C) Gross profits plus all expenses times coinsurance percentage equals insurance amount required to carry.
D) None of the above. Ref. 7-23

54. All of the following are types of contingent or dependent locations that may be scheduled to the Business Income Form EXCEPT:

A) Contributing Locations.
B) All Type Locations.
C) Recipient Locations.
D) Leader Locations. Ref. 7-24

55. Which of the following Commercial Property Forms would best satisfy a business that specifically wanted coverage for extra expense?

A) Business Interruption Coverage Form.
B) Builders Risk Coverage Form.
C) Building and Personal Property Coverage Form.
D) Extra Expense Coverage Form. Ref. 7-25

56. Under both Farm Property and Livestock Coverage Forms, the term livestock includes all of the following EXCEPT:

A) Cattle.
B) Mules.
C) Sheep
D) Poultry.
E) Donkeys. Ref. 7-34

57. The Legal Liability Coverage Form:

A) Provides coverage arising out of loss or damage to property in the care, custody and control of the insured.
B) Is a form of commercial umbrella coverage.
C) Covers the named insured's personal property.
D) Is the preferred method to insure valuable items. Ref. 7-25

58. Under the Accounts Receivable Form, which of the following is NOT covered?

A) Uncollectible amounts.
B) Accounting mistakes.
C) Accountant fees to reestablish an account.
D) Interest on loans pending payment from the insurer. Ref. 7-28

59. The Causes of Loss - Special Form of a Building and Personal Property Form provides an important additional peril not covered under the Basic or Broad Forms. Which of the following is that important peril?

A) Dishonest acts of insureds and/or employees.
B) Water damage from broken pipes.
C) Earthquake.
D) Theft. Ref. 7-26

60. In which of the following instances would a Claims-made Commercial General Liability provide coverage:

A) The claim is made during the policy period regardless of when the claim occurred.
B) The claim occurs before the retroactive date and is reported during the policy period.
C) The claim occurs and is made before the retroactive date.
D) The claim occurs on or after the retroactive date and is made during the policy period. Ref. 7-6

61. If a farm building or structure is vacant or unoccupied:

A) Beyond 30 days no coverage applies.
B) Beyond 60 days no coverage applies.
C) Beyond 90 days coverage is reduced 15%.
D) Beyond 120 days coverage is reduced 50%. Ref. 7-36

62. A business which services the property of others would have a need for:

A) Wedding Presents Floater.
B) Personal Property Floater.
C) Bailees' Customers Form.
D) Bailors' Floater. Ref. 7-30

63. The Business Income Coverage Form's Option Coverage Monthly Limit of Indemnity:

A) Permits the insured to stack coverage.
B) Permits the insured to collect the amount of monthly loss as long as it does not exceed the total limit of indemnity.
C) Is of an unlimited duration.
D) Limits payment to the actual monthly loss of income not exceeding the monthly limit of indemnity. Ref. 7-24

64. All of the following are true of Commercial Inland Marine Coverage Part EXCEPT:

A) It is used to provide coverage that is limited under other forms.
B) Coverage provided is limited to a few named perils.
C) It may be written as a monoline policy.
D) Coverage is generally written on an Open Peril basis. Ref. 7-27 & 7-28

65. Which of the following Commercial Inland Marine Coverage Forms would provide coverage to an insured against the inability to collect monies due from customers because of the loss, damage or destruction of financial records?

A) Financial Paper Coverage.
B) Valuable Papers and Records.
C) Electronic Data Processing Coverage.
D) Accounts Receivable Coverage. Ref. 7-28

66. All of the following are true of the Condominium Coverage Form EXCEPT:

A) Its coverages address the unique conditions of condominium ownership.
B) Coverage may be provided for refrigeration and cooking equipment.
C) Condominium Association Form is similar to the Building and Personal Property Form.
D) Condominium Unit Owner's Form provides broad building coverages. Ref. 7-25

67. All of the following are true of the Commercial Farm Coverage Part EXCEPT:

A) It covers both personal property and commercial farm property.
B) It provides the same coverage as the Homeowners Policy.
C) The four farm coverage forms that may be written are Farm Property, Mobile Agricultural Machinery, Livestock and Farm Liability.
D) Coverage may be written as a separate policy or part of the CPP. Ref. 7-31

ANSWER KEY

1-C	2-B	3-D	4-B	5-D	6-A	7-C	8-B	9-B	10-B
11-D	12-C	13-D	14-D	15-D	16-B	17-B	18-A	19-B	20-C
21-A	22-D	23-C	24-D	25-D	26-B	27-A	28-D	29-C	30-B
31-C	32-D	33-A	34-D	35-A	36-D	37-A	38-D	39-D	40-D
41-D	42-A	43-C	44-D	45-D	46-A	47-B	48-B	49-B	50-C
51-D	52-D	53-A	54-B	55-D	56-D	57-A	58-B	59-D	60-D
61-D	62-C	63-D	64-B	65-D	66-D	67-B			

CHAPTER EIGHT

BUSINESSOWNERS POLICY

OVERVIEW

BUSINESSOWNERS 2002 POLICY

The Businessowners Policy (BOP) is used to insure the **small to medium sized business market**. It is an alternative to the more encompassing Commercial Package Policy which was reviewed in the preceding chapter. In fact, many of the CPP's coverages are identical to those in the BOP. The Businessowners Policy **is a replacement cost policy** and written on a **Special Form basis**. **Other features include** a built-in inflation guard, peak season coverage, business income and extra expense, business income from dependent properties, glass expense and fire extinguisher system recharge expense. **Optional coverages** are available for outdoor signs, crime coverage, employee dishonesty and mechanical breakdown.

BUSINESSOWNER ELIGIBILITY

Eligible risks under the Businessowners Policy includes:

- **Apartment Buildings** including residential or office condominium associations;
- **Office Buildings** not exceeding 6 stories or 100,000 square feet floor area;
- **Mercantile, Service or Processing Occupancies** (e.g., bakeries, funeral homes, printers, repair shops, etc.) if the total floor area of the building does not exceed 25,000 square feet nor annual gross sales of $3,000,000.
- **Motels** not exceeding 3 stories and not including a bar or a lounge.
- **Contractors** (e.g., carpenters, electricians, painters, plumbers, etc.)
- **Convenience Stores with Gasoline Pumps** - Gasoline sales limited to 75% of gross sales. No auto services, restaurant, or propane/kerosene filling permitted.
- **Restaurants** (e.g., cafes, sandwich shops, drug stores, pizza shops, etc.). Limited to fast food types up to 7,500 square feet. Only beer and wine sales are permitted subject to a limit of 25% of gross sales.
- **Laundries/Dry Cleaners** (limited to ones with less than three pickups per week).
- **Self-Storage Facilities** not exceeding 2 stories and not including industrial storage.
- **Wholesale Risks** limited to 25% annual gross sales from retail and 25% of total floor area open to the public.

INELIGIBLE RISKS under the Businessowners Program include:

- Automobile type businesses, garages, dealers and parking lots
- Bars, grills and restaurants (unless within eligibility guidelines)
- Contractors (unless within eligibility guidelines)
- Manufacturing or processing risks (unless within eligibility guideline)
- Household personal property
- One or two family dwellings
- Places of amusement
- Financial institutions (banks, savings & loans, credit unions, stockbrokers, etc.

POLICY STRUCTURE

The Businessowners Policy is composed of a Declarations Page, Special Property Coverage, Liability Coverage and applicable endorsements. The following chart and terms address these topics:

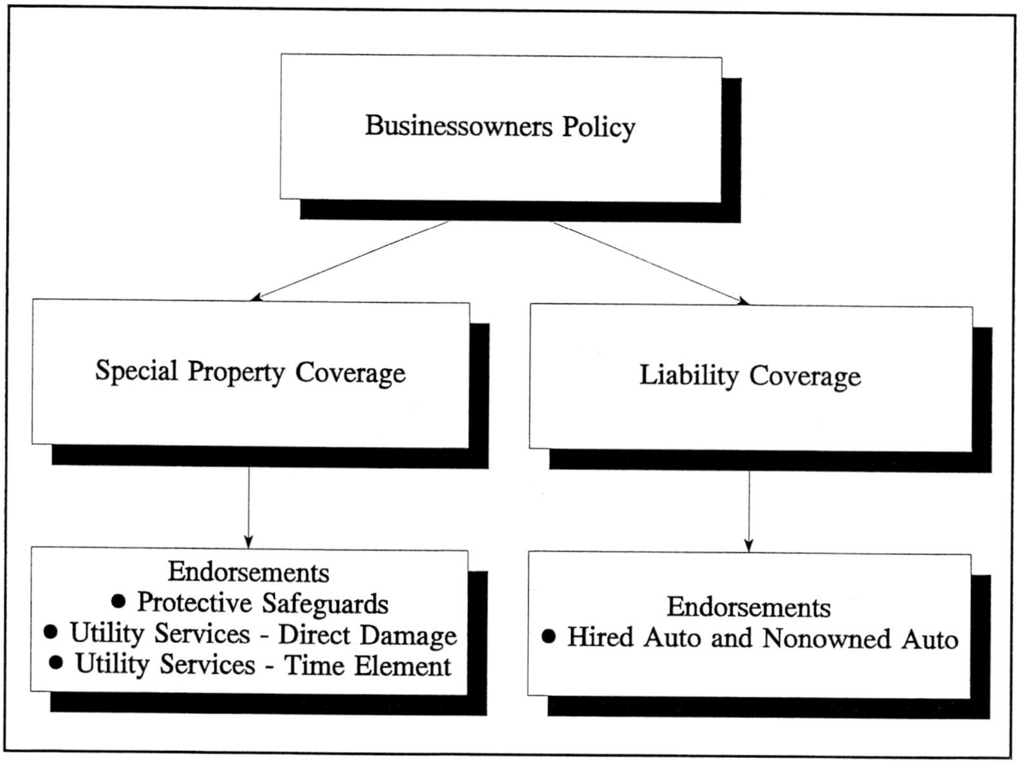

The Businessowners Policy is similar in may respects to the Commercial Package Policy. In fact may of the conditions, exclusions and limitations are the same. To assist in the study process, try to draw comparisons between the Businessowners Policy and the Commercial Package Policy.

COMMON POLICY CONDITIONS

The Businessowners Policy has eleven common policy conditions, six of which are identical to the Commercial Package Policy, and five are similar. The following are the eleven common policy conditions:

- **Changes** provision requires any policy change be made by endorsement.
- **Concealment, misrepresentation, fraud** permits the insurer to void the policy in the event of fraud or for a material concealment/material misrepresentation.
- **Examination of the Books** permits the insurance company the right to examine and audit books for up to three years from the date of policy expiration.
- **Inspections and Surveys** permits the insurance company the right to inspect and survey properties for underwriting purposes.

- **Two or More Coverages** limits the insurance company's exposure to the amount of damage in the event more than one coverage within the policy applies.
- **Liberalization** clause broadens current coverages to reflect the introduction of policy revisions when no additional premium is charged. This liberalization of coverage occurs during the policy term or within 45 days of inception.
- **Other Insurance** provides this coverage to be excess over other insurance.
- **Premiums** provision sets forth premium payment responsibilities.
- **Transfer of Rights of Recovery Against Others to Us** (Subrogation Provision)
- **Transfer of Rights and Duties Under this Policy** (Assignment Provision)
- **Cancellation** provision requires the insurer to give advance written notice. It specifically advises the insured that it may cancel for any of the following reasons:

    - Vacancy or unoccupancy of 60 days or more. This does not apply to seasonal unoccupancy or buildings in the course of construction. Buildings with 65% or more of the rental units or floor area vacant or unoccupied are considered unoccupied.
    - Failure to initiate permanent repairs to the building within 30 days of damage
    - If an order to vacate or demolish the building has been issued or a declaration that the building is unsafe by a governmental authority
    - Fixed and salvageable items are being removed from the building
    - Failure to furnish heat, water or electricity for more than 30 consecutive days
    - Failure to pay property taxes that have been outstanding for more than 1 year

These common policy conditions are similar to other policy conditions and are explained in full in Chapter Three. See SP-37 and SP-81 for policy language.

COMMON EXCLUSIONS

The following are exclusions common to the Businessowner Property Coverage Forms (see SP-52):

- **Ordinance or law**, including the cost of demolition and removal
- **Earth movement,** meaning earthquake, landslide, mine subsidence, etc.
- **Governmental Action**, meaning seizure of destruction of property
- **Nuclear hazard**
- **Power failure** off premises, however, if loss or damages caused by a covered cause of loss results, coverage applies
- **War and military action**
- **Water**, meaning flood, surface water, mudslide, sewers, etc.
- **Certain Computer-Related Losses** meaning computer failure or malfunctioning

Please note that these exclusions are almost identical to the general exclusions found in the Commercial Property Coverage Part of the CPP, the Dwelling Fire Policy and the Homeowners Policy.

BUSINESSOWNERS PROPERTY COVERAGE FORM (CAUSES OF LOSS)

The Businessowners Policy is written on a Special Form basis. This means coverage will be provided for risks of direct physical loss unless specifically excluded. The Businessowners Policy **specifically excludes losses** caused by any of the following:

- **Electrical apparatus**, meaning loss caused by artificially generated current
- **Consequential losses**, meaning loss of use or markets
- **Smoke, vapor, gas** from agricultural or industrial operations
- **Steam apparatus**, meaning an explosion of boilers, pipes, turbines owned or leased
- **Frozen plumbing**, unless the insured attempted to maintain heat
- **Dishonesty** by the insured, partner, trustee or representative
- **False pretense**, meaning any fraudulent scheme, trick or premise
- **Exposed property**, meaning damage while in the open by rain, ice or snow
- **Collapse**, except as provided in additional coverages for collapse
- **Pollution.** Limited coverage is provided for pollution clean-up
- **Neglect**, meaning using all reasonable means to save and protect property
- **Other Types of Loss**, meaning the following:
  - Wear and tear
  - Rust, corrosion, fungus, decay, deterioration, hidden or latent defect or any type of property that causes itself to destroy itself
  - Smog
  - Settling, cracking, shrinking or expansion
  - Insects, birds, rodents or other animals
  - Mechanical breakdown, including rupture by centrifugal force
  - Dampness, dryness, marring and scratching
- **Errors or Omissions** means computer errors or programming errors
- **Installation, Testing, Repair** means errors or deficiencies in computer design, installation, testing or repair.
- **Electrical Disturbances** meaning the erasure of electronic media or records
- **Weather conditions** if concurrent with any above occurrence
- **Acts or decisions** of any person, group or governmental body
- **Negligent work**, meaning faulty, inadequate or defective design

See SP-53 to SP-55 for exact policy language of BOP Special Form Exclusions.

Please note that unlike the Commercial Property Coverage Part, which may be written on a Basic, Broad or Special Form basis, the Businessowners Policy is only written on a Special Form Basis. Named peril coverage, similar to the Commercial Property Coverage Part's Basic Form may be provided under the Businessowners Policy by adding the Named Perils Endorsement.

COVERED PROPERTY

Covered property under the Businessowners Property Coverage is subject to the limit of insurance indicated on the Declarations Page. The following is an overview of the Businessowners Policy:

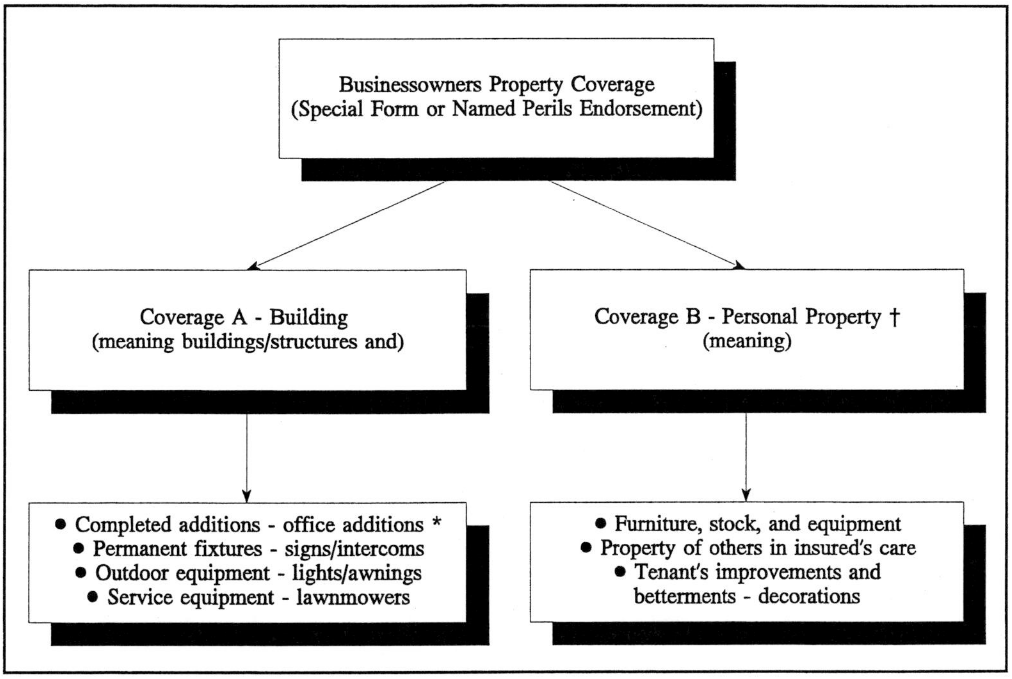

* **If not insured elsewhere**, coverage is provided for additions and alterations, while under construction, and materials, equipment, supplies and temporary structures on or within 100 feet of the described premises used for additions or alterations.

† Business personal property that is in or on the buildings at the described premises or in the open, or in a vehicle within 100 feet of the described premises.

COVERAGE A - BUILDINGS

Coverage A - Buildings of the Businessowners Policy covers the buildings, **meaning the buildings and structures described in the Declarations. It includes:**

- **Completed additions**, such as an office addition to a building.
- **Outdoor fixtures** such as lights, awnings, mailboxes, flag poles, etc.
- **Permanently installed fixtures and equipment**, such as signs, intercoms, blinds.
- **Personal property used as a landlord**, such as furnishings in an apartment.
- **Personal property used to service the business premises**, such as fire extinguishers, outdoor furniture, lawnmowers, snowplows, floor coverings, and appliances used for heating, refrigeration or ventilation.

If not insured elsewhere, coverage is provided for additions and alterations while under construction, and materials, equipment, supplies and temporary structures on or within 100 feet of the described premises used for additions or alterations.

COVERAGE B - BUSINESS PERSONAL PROPERTY

Coverage B - Business Personal Property includes:

- **Property owned by the insured and used in business**, such as furniture, fixtures, machinery or stock.
- **Property of others that is in the insured's care, custody and control**. This property is not covered for more than the amount the insured is legally liable.
- **Tenant's improvements and betterments**, such as the tenant's decorations of a store front or interior improvements.
- **Leased personal property** for which the insured is contractually responsible.
- **Exterior building glass** for which the insured owns or is responsible.

Business personal property that is in or on the buildings at the described premises or in the open, or in a vehicle within 100 feet of the described premises is covered as business personal property.

PROPERTY NOT COVERED

The following types of property are not covered or are limited in coverage:

- Aircraft or automobiles subject to motor vehicle registration.
- Bullion, money or securities. **Limited optional coverage is available.**
- Contraband or property in illegal transportation or trade.
- Land, water, growing crops or lawns.
- Outdoor fences, radio or television antennas including satellite dishes.
- Signs not attached to the building. **Optional coverage is available.**
- Trees or shrubs, except as provided in the coverage extension.
- Watercraft, including motors, equipment and accessories **while afloat.**
- Accounts, bills, food stamps, and evidence of debt
- Computers that are permanently installed in aircraft, watercraft or motor vehicles

ADDITIONAL COVERAGES

The Businessowners Policy provides the following additional coverages:

- **Debris Removal** up to 25% of direct loss and claimed within 180 days. An additional $10,000 limitation applies at each location if the 25% limit is exhausted.
- **Preservation of Property**, meaning coverage for property removed for protection from a covered cause of loss. This coverage applies for 30 days.
- **Fire Department Service Charge** up to $1,000 of liability.
- **Collapse** caused by hidden decay, insect, vermin, weight of people or property or use of defective materials or methods of construction **(Special Form Only).**
- **Water Damage** caused by accidental discharge or leakage. The repair cost of the plumbing equipment and/or appliance is excluded. **(Special Form Only).**
- **Business Income** meaning actual business losses that occur during the **period of restoration** which begins 72 hours after the time of direct physical loss and ends when the property can be repaired, replaced or rebuilt. Business income is net income and continuing normal operating expenses including payroll. Coverage applies for 12 consecutive months, however, ordinary payroll is limited to 60 days.

- **Extended Business Income** provides coverage for the readjustment period in considerations of loss customers. **It is provided for up to 30 days.**
- **Extra Expense** coverage is the extra expenses **incurred within 12 consecutive months after the date of direct physical loss**. Extra expense means expenses incurred to avoid or minimize the suspension of operations at the described location or replacement locations, including relocation expenses and costs to equip and operate the temporary location. **The 72 hour time deductible does not apply to extra expense losses.**
- **Pollutant Clean Up and Removal** provides coverage for the clean up of pollutants from land or water caused by a covered cause of loss, occurring during the policy period and reported within 180 days of loss, or the end of the policy period. **A $10,000 limit applies to each location**.
- **Civil Authority**, meaning prohibited by a civil authority to use the described premises as the result of a direct loss to property, other than at the described premises. For example, if an explosion occurred across the street from the insured premises, causing a civil authority (fire department) to close down the street, and causing the insured to have a loss of business income and/or extra expense, coverage would be provided. **Coverage is provided up to 3 consecutive weeks subject to the 72 hour time deductible.**
- **Money Orders and Counterfeit Paper Coverage**, meaning a loss that results from the good faith acceptance of U.S. and Canadian money orders or paper currency **subject to a $1,000 limitation.**
- **Forgery or Alteration** provides coverage for loss of money, resulting from the forgery or alteration of outgoing checks, drafts or promissory notes. A legal defense will also be provided in the event the insured is sued for his refusal to pay a check on the basis that it is a forged or altered document. **This coverage is subject to a $2,500 limitation.**
- **Increased Cost of Construction** *only* applies to buildings insured on a replacement cost basis. **It provides up to $5,000** in coverage for each described building **if a covered cause of loss creates an increase in construction costs mandated by a building ordinance or law.** Coverage does not apply to any cost due to an ordinance or law that the insured was required to and failed to comply with before the loss. For example, if the insured failed to install a fire escape that was required by the city, and a fire loss subsequently occurs, the insurer would not be obligated to pay the $5,000 limitation for the fire escape. Finally, this Additional Coverage will not apply to costs due to an ordinance or law which requires the insured or others to test, monitor or clean up or to assess the effects of pollutants.
- **Business Income from Dependent Properties** provides coverage for actual losses sustained by the insured due to the physical loss or damage at the premises of a dependent property.
- **Glass Expenses** pays the expenses incurred by the insured to put up temporary plates or board up openings. It also pays the cost to remove obstructions.
- **Fire Extinguisher Systems Recharge Expense** pays up to $5,000 to recharge a Fire Extinguisher System.

Additional coverages are paid beyond the principal policy coverages. For complete policy language see SP-43 to SP-50.

COVERAGE EXTENSIONS

In addition to the limits of insurance, coverage may be extended as follows (SP-50):

- **Buildings Newly Acquired or Constructed** covers newly acquired/constructed buildings **up to $250,000** on the described premises or at a new location.
- **Personal Property at Newly Acquired Premises** covers personal property **up to $100,000 at each newly acquired location**. This coverage applies until the policy expiration, 30 days, or when the values are reported, whichever comes first.
- **Personal Property Off Premises** covers personal property **other than money and securities up to $5,000**. This coverage applies to property that is *in transit* or temporarily at a location not owned, leased or occupied by the insured.
- **Outdoor Property** covers outdoor property including fences, trees, antennas and detached signs **for fire, lightning, explosion, riot and civil commotion and aircraft** subject to **$500 per tree or shrub, up to a maximum of $2,500.**
- **Valuable Papers and Records**, covers the cost to research and reconstruct loss records **up to $10,000** on premises and **$5,000** off premises. Examples include blueprints, deeds, maps, historical documents and general business records.
- **Personal Effects** covers business personal property owned by the named insured, officers, partners or employees. This extension does not apply to tools or equipment used in the named insured's business or to loss or damage by theft. **This coverage extension is limited to $2,500 at each described premises.**
- **Accounts Receivable** provides coverage in the event accounting records are destroyed due to a covered cause of loss, and because of this, the insured is unable to collect monies due. This form also covers the cost to reconstruct accounts receivable records, interest on loans resulting from the inability to collect accounts receivable and increased collection costs. **This coverage extension is limited to $5,000 on premises and $2,500 off premises.**

LIMITS, INCREASES AND DEDUCTIBLES

The Businessowners Policy provides the limits of insurance as indicated in the Declarations and including (SP-56):

- **Building Limit - Automatic Increase** coverage for buildings on a pro rata basis based upon the annual percentage indicated in the Declarations. For example, if 8% is indicated in the Declarations, a building insured for $100,000 on January 1, will increase on a daily basis to equal $108,000 on December 31.

- **Business Personal Property Limit - Seasonal Increase** coverage is automatically increased 25% to reflect seasonal variations of business personal property. This provision is only applicable if business personal property limits equal 100% of the previous 12 months' average values for business property are maintained.

The **standard deductible under the Businessowners Policy is $500**, however, no deductible applies to losses for fire department charges, business income and extra expense coverage. **Outdoor signs** that are attached to the building are limited to $1,000 per sign in any one occurrence.

PROPERTY LOSS CONDITIONS

The following Businessowners property loss conditions are similar to the previous-ly reviewed loss conditions (SP-57 to SP-61):

- **Abandonment** prohibits the insured from abandoning property as a total loss.
- **Appraisal** permits either insured or company to demand an appraisal of a loss.
- **Duties in the Event of Loss** means to notify the company, protect property, etc.
- **Legal Action Against Us** requires full compliance to policy provisions prior to the initiation of legal action and must be commenced within 2 years of the date of loss.
- **Limitations - Electronic Media and Records** limits loss of business income caused by damage or destruction to media after 60 days, or a reasonable time period.
- **Loss Payment** on buildings and business personal property at replacement cost without depreciation if at the time of loss property is 80% or more of the full replacement cost. *An ACV option is also available.* **Other categories of property are covered as follows:**
  - **Second-hand merchandise**, property of others, manuscripts, rare articles, works of art, pictures or statuary **at actual cash value**.
  - **Glass at the cost of replacement** with safety glazing material.
  - **Tenant's improvements and betterments at replacement cost** if repairs are made promptly.
  - **Valuable papers and records**, including electronic or magnetic media **at the cost of blank media and labor** to transcribe or copy the records. This does not apply to prepackaged software.
  - **Optional coverage money and securities. Money means at its face value** and **securities mean at their value at close of day the loss is discovered.**
- **Recovered Property** means that both insured and carrier must notify each other.
- **Resumption of Operation** permits reduction of payments under business income or extra expense to reflect resumption of operation.
- **Vacancy** beyond 60 days **excludes coverage caused by vandalism, sprinkler leakage, building glass breakage, water damage, theft or attempted theft**. In addition, all other covered perils are reduced by 15%. For example, if property was vacant beyond 60 days, no coverage would apply to loss caused by vandalism, sprinkler leakage, etc. All other covered losses would be reduced 15%.

PROPERTY GENERAL CONDITIONS

Property General Conditions address policy conditions. They include (SP-63):

- **Control of Property** means that any act or negligent conduct of others beyond the insured's control will not affect coverage.
- **Mortgage Holders** addresses the rights of the mortgage holder.
- **No Benefit to Bailee** prohibits assignment of benefits to a bailee.
- **Policy Period and Territory** means coverage will be provided if the loss occurs during the policy period and in the U.S., including its territories and possessions, Puerto Rico and Canada.

OPTIONAL COVERAGES

The Businessowners Policy **may be endorsed by indicating optional coverages forms with a limit of insurance on the policy Declarations Page**. The following provides a summary of these optional coverages (SP-62 to SP-64):

- **Outdoor Signs** coverage provides all risk type coverage for outdoor signs. This coverage is an important option since the base BOP limits coverage to $1,000 for attached outdoor signs and $2,500 for detached outdoor signs. This coverage is similar to the Commercial Inland Marine Sign Form.

- **Money and Securities** coverage pays the insured in the event a loss of money or securities is caused by theft, disappearance or destruction. **Money and Securities** is limited to $5,000 on premises and $2,000 off premises. **The off premises coverage is limited to loss at:** a savings institution; the named insured's or partners living quarters; or, while an employee is in transit between any of these places. This coverage is similar to the Commercial Crime Coverages Inside the Premises - Theft of Money and Securities and Outside the Premises coverage.

- **Employee Dishonesty** means loss to business personal property, including money and securities, caused by a dishonest employee discovered within one year from policy expiration. Coverage is excluded for named insureds and/or partners. This coverage is similar to the Commercial Crime Coverage - Employee Theft.

- **Mechanical Breakdown** provides coverage for direct damage to covered property caused by an accident to an object. An object means boilers, pressure vessels, steam heating tanks, etc. This coverage is similar to the Equipment Breakdown Coverage Form.

Please note the comparisons between the various BOP Optional Coverages and the corresponding CPP coverages of Chapter Seven are similar but not exact. See comparison at the end of this Chapter for an overview.

BUSINESSOWNERS LIABILITY COVERAGE

Businessowners Liability includes coverage in the following two areas:

1) **Business Liability** provides coverage for bodily injury and property damages to third parties that arise out of business activities for which the insured becomes legally liable. For example, if the insured failed to maintain his business premises in a safe manner (i.e., permitted broken steps or slippery floors on the premises) and a customer falls and is injured, the business liability will respond. Business liability also includes:

- **Personal injury**, and
- **Advertising injury.**

Supplementary Payments Coverage Extensions are also provided and they include (in addition to the Limit of Insurance) all expenses incurred by the company to defend the insured; up to $250 for bail bonds for traffic violations; the cost of bail bonds for release attachments; all reasonable expenses incurred by the insured to assist the claims process including loss of earnings, up to $250 per day; all costs taxed against the insured; and post-judgment interest.

2) **Medical Expenses** are the medical expenses incurred by third parties for bodily injury that is an accident, regardless of fault.

The Businessowners Liability Coverage is similar to the Commercial Liability Coverage Part, however, it **is only written on an occurrence basis**. Coverage is also provided for fire legal liability exposures as specified in the declarations. **Basic business liability** is $300,000, medical payments of $5,000 and fire legal liability of $50,000. These coverages may be increased. The following is an illustration of the Businessowners Liability Coverage.

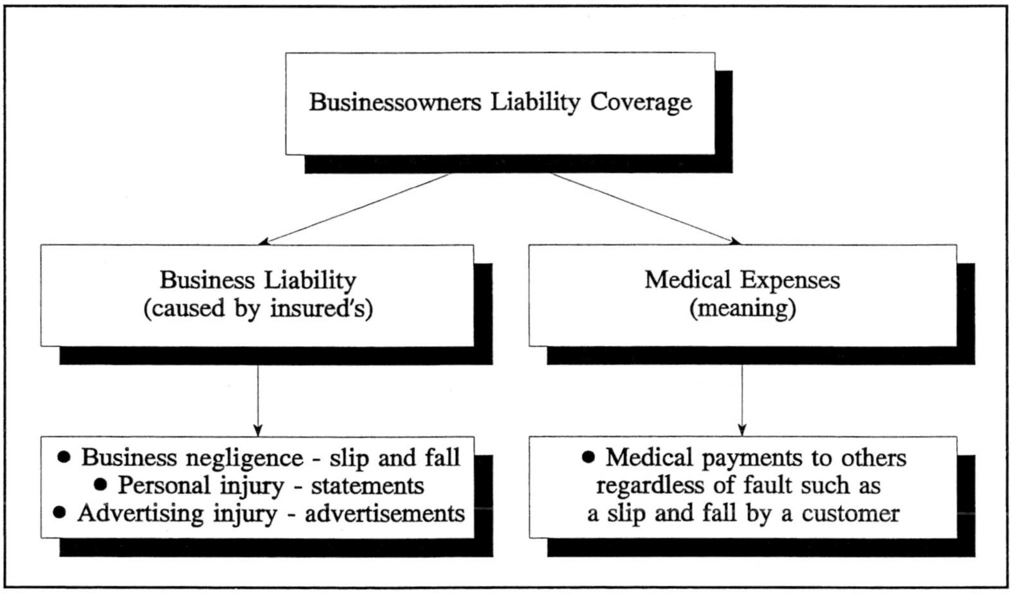

LIABILITY AND MEDICAL EXPENSE CONDITIONS

The Businessowners Policy includes the following general conditions that are applicable to the Liability Coverage:

- **Bankruptcy** means that bankruptcy of the insured does not void coverage
- **Duties in the event of occurrence, claim or suit** requires cooperation
- **Financial responsibility laws** means the policy will comply with state financial responsibility laws regarding motor vehicles
- **Legal action against us** means compliance with conditions prior to legal action
- **Separation of insureds** means each insured has a separate limit of liability

LIABILITY EXCLUSIONS

Liability exclusions under the Businessowners Policy **are similar to the Commercial General Liability Coverage**. These liability exclusions mean bodily in-jury and/or property damages:

- Expected or intended by the insured
- Arising out of contractual liability, except insured or incidental contracts
- Arising out of liquor liability **(host liquor liability is provided)**
- Arising out of Workers Compensation or similar law obligations
- Arising out of or in the course of employment
- Arising out of the release of pollutants
- Arising out of the ownership, maintenance, use or entrustment to others of any aircraft, auto or watercraft by or rented or loaded to any insured. **This exclusion does not apply to liability arising from:**
  - Watercraft on shore and on the insured's premises
  - Nonowned watercraft under 51 feet in length
  - Parking an auto not owned, rented or loaned to an insured on or next to the insured's own or rented premises
  - Liability assumed for any insured contract for the ownership maintenance or use of watercraft or aircraft
  - The operation of cherry pickers or similar devices, or,
  - The operation of air compressors, pumps or spraying and cleaning equipment
- Arising out of the transportation of mobile equipment
- Arising out of war, whether declared or undeclared
- Arising out of failure to render professional service including legal, accounting or advertising services; preparing maps, inspections or surveys; medical, surgical, dental or related health services; cosmetic, optical or ear piercing services; skin enhancement or hair replacement services; pharmacy practices
- To property owned or rented to, or in the care custody and control of the insured
- To the insured's product or impaired property
- For product recall or withdrawal from the market
- For personal and advertising injury if known to be false
- For advertising injury arising out of a breach of contract, product failure, wrong description or pricing or any offense committed by an insured whose business is advertising, broadcasting, publishing or telecasting

- For medical expenses for bodily injury to an insured, to a person hired by the insured or to a person taking part in athletics
- For medical expenses included within the products-completed operations hazard or excluded under business liability coverage or war.

Business liability and medical expenses resulting from hazardous properties of nuclear materials is also excluded.

DEFINITIONS

The following addresses several terms and definitions of the Businessowners Policy:

- **Advertisement** means a notice that is published to the general public or a specialized market about the insured's goods or services. It includes electronic media such as the Internet.
- **Advertising Injury** means injury arising out of oral or written publication that slanders or libels a person or organization, invades their privacy or infringes upon ideas, style, copyright, title or slogan.
- **Auto** means a land motor vehicle or trailer designed for travel on public roads and including equipment attached to the vehicle.
- **Bodily Injury** means bodily injury, sickness or disease including death.
- **Coverage Territory** means the United States including its territories and possessions, Puerto Rico and Canada. Coverage is provided worldwide for injury or damages arising out of the insured's goods or products, or while temporarily outside the described coverage territory.
- **Employee** includes a leased worker but not a temporary worker.
- **Executive Officer** means a person holding any officer positions created by the insured's charter, constitution, by-laws or similar document.
- **Hostile Fire** means one which becomes uncontrollable or breaks out from where it was intended to be.
- **Impaired Property** means tangible property, other than the insured's property, that cannot be used, or is less useful, because it incorporates the insured's product or work that is known or thought to be defective, deficient, inadequate or dangerous.
- **Insured Contract** means a lease of premises, a sidetrack agreement, an easement or license agreement, an elevator maintenance agreement or any agreement in which the insured assumes the tort liability of another to pay damages to third parties.
- **Leased Worker** means a person leased to the insured by a labor leasing firm.
- **Loading or Unloading** means the handling of property.
- **Mobile Equipment** means bulldozers, forklifts and related equipment.
- **Occurrence** means an accident, including continuous and repeated exposure to substantially the same general harmful conditions.
- **Personal and Advertising Injury** means false arrest, detention, malicious prosecution, wrongful entry, eviction, oral or written publications, use of another's advertising idea, copyright, trade dress or slogan.

- **Personal Injury** means false arrest, detention, malicious prosecution, wrongful entry, eviction and oral or written publications.
- **Products-Completed Operations Hazard** means bodily injury or property damage arising out of the insured's product.
- **Property Damage** means physical injury to tangible property resulting in loss.
- **Temporary Worker** means a person who is furnished to the insured to substitute for a permanent employee on leave or to meet seasonal or short-term workload.
- **Volunteer Worker** means a person who is not the insured's employee and donates his or her time (without compensation) under the insured's direction.
- **Your Product** means any product other than real property that is manufactured and/or sold by the insured.
- **Your Work** means work or operations performed by the insured, including materials, parts or equipment. Your work also includes warranties and representations.

ENDORSEMENTS

The Businessowners Policy may be endorsed as follows:

- **Protective Safeguards (BP 04 30)** endorsement adds a policy condition requiring the insured to maintain protective safeguards (e.g., automatic sprinkler system, automatic fire alarm system) as a condition for coverage. If an automatic sprinkler system is shut down due to breakage, leakage, freezing or opening of sprinkler heads, **the insured has 48 hours to restore the system before they must notify the insurer.**

- **Utility Services -- Direct Damage (BP 04 56)** endorsement covers the insured's property in the event of a direct physical loss to a utility service. The insured's covered property and utility service must be indicated in the endorsement. Utility services include water services, communication services and power supply services. If a limit of insurance is shown in the endorsement, that limit of insurance is not in addition to the limit of insurance stated in the Declarations.

- **Utility Services -- Time Element (BP 04 57)** endorsement covers the insured's business income loss in the event of a direct physical loss at a utility service. The insured's location and utility service must be indicated in the endorsement. Utility services include water services, communication services and power supply services. The most the insurer will pay for loss or damage in any one occurrence is the limit of insurance shown in the endorsement schedule.

- **Hired Auto and Nonowned Auto (BP 04 04)** provides liability coverage for business auto exposures. **Hired auto means any auto that is hired, rented, leased or borrowed by the business.** For example, a rented vehicle would be considered a hired auto. **Nonowned auto means any auto not owned, hired, leased or borrowed that is used in conjunction with the insured's business.** An example would be an employee using his personal auto for business. In both instances, coverage would be provided under this endorsement. This endorsement is typically added when the businessowner does not have a Business Auto Policy.

- **Pennsylvania Changes - Cancellation and Nonrenewal** is the state mandated endorsement requiring advance written notice. See page 7-38.

BUSINESSOWNERS 2002 POLICY SUMMARY		
NAMED PERILS	**Endorsement**	**Special**
Fire	●	●
Lightning	●	●
Explosion	●	●
Windstorm and Hail	●	●
Smoke	●	●
Aircraft and Vehicle	●	●
Riot and Civil Commotion	●	●
Vandalism	●	●
Sprinkler Leakage	●	●
Sinkhole Collapse	●	●
Volcanic Action	●	●
Transportation	●	●
Special Open Peril Coverage		●

ADDITIONAL COVERAGES (automatically provided at no additional premium)
Debris Removal up to 25% of loss (180 day limit). Add'l $10,000 after 25% is exhausted.
Preservation of Property, meaning protection up to 30 days when protecting property.
Fire Department Service Charge up to $1,000 of liability.
Collapse caused by hidden decay, insect, etc.
Water Damage excluding cost of the plumbing equipment.
Business Income, meaning actual business losses incurred up to 12 months.
Extended Business Income, meaning income for a readjustment period up to 30 days.
Extra Expense, meaning extra expenses incurred to continue operations up to 12 months.
Pollutants Clean Up & Removal up to $10,000 per location (180 day reporting applies).
Civil Authority, meaning being prohibited to use premises (72 hour deductible applies).
Money Orders and Counterfeit Paper Currency ($1,000 limitation applies).
Forgery and Alteration covers outgoing checks, etc. ($2,500 limitation applies).
Increase Cost of Construction (up to $5,000 if insured on a replacement basis).
Business Income from Dependent Properties
Fire Extinguisher Systems Recharge Expense

COVERAGE EXTENSIONS (automatically provided at no additional premium)
Buildings Newly Acquired or Constructed up to $250,000 at each location.
Personal Property at Newly Acquired Premises up to $100,000 at each location.
Personal Property Off Premises (other than money & securities) up to $5,000.
Outdoor Property (fences, trees, antennas, detached signs) up to $500/item and $2,500.
Valuable Papers & Records (maps, deeds) up to $10,000 on premises/$5,000 off premises.
Personal Effects up to $2,500.
Accounts Receivable up to $10,000 on premises and $5,000 off premises.

LIMITS, INCREASES AND DEDUCTIBLES (choice affects premium charged)
Building Limit - Automatic Increase coverage for buildings of up to 8%.
Business Property Seasonal Increase of 25% for seasonal variations.
Deductible Limits - Standard $500 property deductible.

OPTIONAL COVERAGES (choice affects premium charged)
Outdoor Signs - policy provides a limit of $1,000 attached and $2,500 detached.
Money & Securities for perils of Theft, Destruction & Disappearance.
Employee Dishonesty, meaning loss caused by dishonest employees.
Mechanical Breakdown, meaning direct damage to covered property.

PROPERTY NOT COVERED
Aircraft or automobiles subject to motor vehicle registration; Money or securities; Contraband/property in illegal transportation or trade; Land, water, growing crops or lawns; Outdoor fences, radio or TV antennas. Trees or shrubs except as provided in the coverage extension; Watercraft, including motors, equipment and accessories while afloat.

	COMMERCIAL PACKAGE POLICY v BUSINESSOWNERS POLICY	
	CPP	**BOP**
Eligibility	Used to insure larger commercial risks which are generally beyond the eligibility requirements of the Businessowners Policy. Eligible risks include: Service stations; auto repair facilities; auto, motor home or mobile home dealers; parking lots or garage operators; warehouses; office and apartment buildings; petrochemical plants; electric generating stations; and other large commercial exposures. The only type of risk prohibited under the CPP is the homeowner type exposure.	Use to small to medium "main street" type businesses. Eligible risks include: **Apartment Buildings** not exceeding 6 stories in height and 60 dwelling units; **Office Buildings** not exceeding 6 stories in height or 100,000 square feet in total floor area; **Mercantile, Service or Processing Occupancies** if total floor area of the building does not exceed 25,000 square feet nor annual gross sales of $3,000,000. **Motels** not exceeding 3 stories & not including a bar. **Contractors** (carpenters, painters, plumbers, etc.) **Convenience Stores with Gasoline Pumps** - Gasoline sales limited to 75% of gross sales. No auto services, restaurant, or propane/kerosene filling permitted. **Restaurants** (cafes, sandwich shops, drug stores, pizza shops, etc.). Limited to fast food types up to 7,500 square feet. Only beer and wine sales are permitted subject to a limit of 25% of gross sales. **Laundries/Dry Cleaners** (limited to less than 3 pickups per week). **Self-Storage Facilities** not exceeding 2 stories and not including industrial storage. **Wholesale Risks** limited to 25% annual gross sales from retail & 25% of total floor area open to the public.
Structure	Seven coverage parts with any two forming CPP. Insured must choose coverage parts and related forms to meet his or her needs.	Two coverage parts form the BOP in a "Homeowners Policy" approach to the small business market.
Property (1)	**Commercial Property Coverage Part** covers property exposures and includes 8 forms: 1) Building and Personal Property (BPP) 2) Builders Risk 3) Business Income 4) Extra Expense 5) Leasehold Interest 6) Legal Liability 7) Condominium Associations 8) Condominium Unit-owners	**Businessowners Property Coverage** covers property exposures. Similar to BOP's Property Coverage. N/A Similar to the BOP's Additional Coverages Business Income and Extra Expense. N/A N/A Similar if BOP's condominium endorsements are added.
	The Commercial Property Coverage Forms are written subject to one of three causes of loss forms. 1) Basic (11 perils) 2) Broad (14 perils), or 3) Special (open perils coverage)	The Businessowners Property Coverage is written subject to one cause of loss form: 1) Named Perils Endorsement is available 2) N/A 3) Special (open perils coverage)

	COMMERCIAL PACKAGE POLICY v BUSINESSOWNERS POLICY	
	CPP	**BOP**
Inland Marine Coverages (2)	**Inland Marine Coverage Part** covers property which is limited under the primary property coverage forms. It includes 6 forms:	Inland Marine coverage is provided under the BOP's Property Coverage, however it is in a more limiting form.
	1) Accounts Receivable	Similar to BOP's Coverage Extension. $10,000 on premises and $5,000 off premises limitation applies.
	2) Commercial Articles	N/A
	3) Equipment Dealers	N/A
	4) Jewelers Block	N/A
	5) Signs	Similar to BOP's Optional Coverage Outdoor Signs.
	6) Valuable Papers and Records	Similar to BOP's Coverage Extension Valuable Papers. $10,000 on premises and $5,000 off premises applies.
Crime Coverages (3)	**Commercial Crime Coverage Part** protects the business against burglary, safe burglary, robbery, extortion or theft. It includes 8 coverages and 5 endorsements:	Crime coverage is provided under the BOP's Property Coverage, however it is in a more limiting form than the Commercial Crime Part.
	1) Employee Theft	Similar to BOP's Optional Coverage Employee Dishonesty
	2) Forgery or Alteration	Similar to BOP's Additional Coverage Forgery and Alteration (limited to $2,500).
	3) Inside the Premises - Theft of Money/Securities	Covered under BOP's Optional Coverage.
	4) Inside the Premises - Robbery or Safe Burglary of Other Property	Covered under BOP's Special Form.
	5) Outside the Premises	Covered under the BOP's Special Form.
	6) Computer Fraud	N/A
	7) Fund Transfer Fraud	N/A
	8) Money Orders/Counterfeit Paper Currency	N/A
	9) Extortion	N/A
	10) Securities Deposited With Others	N/A
	11) Guests' Property	N/A
	12) Safe Depository	N/A
	13) Lessees of Safe Deposit Boxes	N/A
Boiler & Machinery Coverage (4)	**Boiler & Machinery Coverage Part** covers direct damage to property caused by an accident to an object. Written one form: 1) Equipment Breakdown Protection Form	Similar equipment breakdown coverage is provided under the Businessowners Property Coverage Optional Coverage Mechanical Breakdown.
Farm Coverage (5)	**Farm Coverage Part** covers farming exposures. It is written subject to 4 forms: 1) Farm Property Form 2) Farm Liability Form 3) Mobile Agricultural Equipment Form 4) Livestock Form	N/A
Liability Coverages (6)	**Commercial General Liability Coverage Part** (CGL) covers an insured's legal liability. Written on two forms: 1) Occurrence 2) Claims-made	**Businessowners Liability Coverage** is the same coverage as the CGL's occurrence form. The BOP does not offer a claims-made version.
Auto (7)	Commercial Auto Coverage Part covers businesses which own, use or service autos or trucks. It is written subject to 5 forms: 1) Business Auto 2) Business Auto Physical Damage 3) Garage 4) Truckers 5) Motor Carrier	Limited liability coverage for hired and nonowned auto may be endorsed to the businessowners liability coverage.

KEY TERMS AND CONCEPTS

The following terms were introduced in this chapter. You should know each word and concept and be able to apply them in everyday usage. To improve retention, it is recommended that you write out each key term and concept in your own words.

Accounts Receivable
Additional Coverages
Building Limits Increases
Business Liability
Businessowner Liability Coverage Form
Businessowners Policy
Common Policy Conditions
Coverage A - Buildings
Coverage B - Business Personal Property
Coverage Extensions
Coverage Territory
Covered Property
Deductible
Employee Dishonesty
Exclusions
General Property Conditions
Hired Auto and Nonowned Auto
Host Liquor Liability
Impaired Property
Ineligible Risks
Insured Contract
Liability Conditions
Liability Exclusions
Mechanical Breakdown
Medical Expenses
Mobile Equipment
Optional Coverages
Outdoor Property
Outdoor Signs
Personal Property at New Premises
Personal Property Off Premises
Property Loss Conditions
Property Not Covered
Seasonal Increases
Special Form
Valuable Papers and Records
Your Product
Your Work

REVIEW QUESTIONS

Before attempting to answer the end chapter practice questions, you should ask yourself if you can answer the following questions. It is recommended that you write out each review question in your own words. This exercise will help you apply the key terms and concepts that you've learned to form relationships with different topics.

1. Explain the types of businesses that would have a need for a Businessowners Policy. (8-1)

2. Identify 5 types of businesses that are ineligible for coverage under the Businessowners Policy. (8-1)

3. Identify and explain the 6 reasons an insurer may give to cancel a Businessowners Policy. (8-3)

4. The Businessowners Policy is written with what Property Coverage Form? (8-1 & 8-4)

5. Identify the 5 categories of property under Coverage A - Buildings. (8-5)

6. Identify the 5 categories of property under Coverage B - Business Personal Property (8-6)

7. Identify 8 types of property that are not covered under the Businessowners Policy. (8-6)

8. Identify 10 of the 15 Additional Coverages under the Businessowners Policy. (8-6 & 8-7)

9. Explain the Additional Coverage Debris Removal including the percentage and dollar limitations. (8-6)

10. Explain the Additional Coverage Pollutant Clean Up and Removal including both percentage and dollar limitations. (8-7)

11. Explain the Additional Coverage Money Orders and Counterfeit Paper Coverage including any dollar limitation. (8-7)

12. Explain the Additional Coverage Forgery and Alteration including any dollar limitation. (8-7)

13. Explain the Additional Coverage Increased Cost of Construction including any dollar limitation. (8-7)

14. Identify the 7 Coverage Extensions under the Businessowners Policy. (8-8)

15. Explain the Coverage Extension Personal Property at Newly Acquired Premises including any dollar or time limitation. (8-8)

16. Explain the Coverage Extension Personal Property Off Premises including any dollar limitation. (8-8)

17. Identify the six perils that cover outdoor property including any dollar limitations. (8-8)

18. Explain the Coverage Extension Valuable Papers and Records including any dollar limitation. (8-8)

19. Explain the Coverage Extension Personal Effects including any dollar limitation. (8-8)

20. Explain the Coverage Extension Accounts Receivable including any dollar limitations. (8-8)

21. Identify and explain the 2 increases in limits that may apply to property under the Businessowners. (8-8)

22. Explain the 2 limitations that apply to outdoor signs. (8-8)

23. Identify the 4 Optional Coverages of the Businessowners Policy. (8-10)

24. Identify and explain the 2 major coverages provided under the Businessowners Liability Coverage Part. (8-11)

25. Indicate the 3 basic limits of liability under the Businessowners Liability Coverage Part. (8-11)

26. Identify 10 Liability Exclusions of the Businessowners Policy. (8-12)

27. Identify and explain 5 exceptions to the Liability Exclusions of the Businessowners Policy. (8-12)

28. Identify 3 Endorsements that may be added to the Businessowners Policy. (8-14)

29. Explain the Protective Safeguards Endorsement including any time limitation. (8-14)

30. Explain the difference between the Utility Service - Direct Damage Endorsement and the Utility Service - Time Element Endorsement. (8-14)

31. Explain the Hired Auto and Nonowned Auto Endorsement. (8-14)

PRACTICE EXAM EIGHT

ON

BUSINESSOWNERS POLICY

1. **All of the following are policy components of a Businessowners Policy EXCEPT:**

   A) Declarations and common policy conditions.
   B) A Special Coverage Part.
   C) A Liability Coverage Part.
   D) A Schedule Coverage Part. Ref. 8-2

2. **A Businessowners Policy may be cancelled for all of following reasons EXCEPT:**

   A) When a building owner has failed to initiate permanent repairs within 30 days after a covered cause of loss.
   B) When a building owner has failed to maintain 100% occupancy in the building.
   C) When a building owner has failed to furnish heat, water or electricity for more than 30 consecutive days.
   D) When a building owner has failed to pay property taxes which have been outstanding for more than one year. Ref. 8-3

3. **The Businessowners Policy includes eleven conditions, many of which are common to other property policies. All of the following are Businessowners Policy conditions EXCEPT:**

   A) Cancellation and liberalization conditions.
   B) Concealment, misrepresentations and fraud condition.
   C) Additional coverage condition.
   D) Appraisal and subrogation conditions. Ref. 8-2 & 8-3

4. **The Businessowners Policy may be written on which of the following coverage forms:**

   A) Only on a Standard Coverage Form basis.
   B) Only on a Special Coverage Form basis.
   C) With a Special Coverage Form or a Named Perils Endorsement.
   D) On a Standard, a Broad or a Special Coverage Form basis. Ref. 8-1 & 8-4

5. **All of the following are eligible for coverage under the Businessowners Policy EXCEPT:**

   A) Bakery.
   B) Printer.
   C) Credit Union.
   D) Television repair shop. Ref. 8-1

6. **A retailer incurs a loss of income after a fire department blocks off a part of the city due to an explosion. Under a Businessowners Policy, the retailer's loss of income:**

A) Is only covered if the explosion peril physically damages the retailer's premises.
B) Is covered subject to a 72 hour deductible.
C) Is covered if loss of income is endorsed on to the policy.
D) Is covered in total. Ref. 8-7

7. **A Businessowner's employee is involved in an accident while driving his own auto on company business. In this example, the businessowner is:**

A) Automatically covered under the Businessowners Policy.
B) Not available.
C) Covered if the Hired Auto and Nonowned Auto is added to the Businessowners Policy.
D) Only provided under the Business Auto Form. Ref. 8-14

8. **The Businessowners Policy is a commercial policy that would provide coverage to which of the following exposures?**

A) Single Family residential structures.
B) Workers Compensation exposures.
C) Small to medium size apartment, office and retail buildings.
D) Automotive repair and service stations. Ref. 8-1

9. **All of the following are ineligible for coverage under the Businessowners Policy EXCEPT:**

A) Bars serving scotch.
B) Banks and financial institutions not associated with an insurance agency.
C) Condominiums.
D) Auto dealerships and garages. Ref. 8-1

10. **All of the following are covered causes of loss under the Businessowners Policy's Special Form EXCEPT:**

A) Vandalism damage.
B) Smoke damage.
C) Insect damage.
D) Sinkhole collapse damage. Ref. 8-4 & 8-15

11. **A businessowner moves business property after a fire loss. Under his Businessowners Policy:**

A) Coverage is not provided at the new location.
B) Coverage is provided at the new location until the building is completely repaired.
C) Coverage is provided at the new location for 5 days.
D) Coverage is provided at the new location for 30 days. Ref. 8-6

12. Under the Businessowners Policy, Forgery and Alteration coverage:

A) Is limited to $2,500.
B) Is limited to $5,000.
C) Is limited to $7,500.
D) Is unlimited if discovered within one year of the forgery or alteration.

Ref. 8-7

13. Under the Businessowners Policy, Extended Business Income coverage is:

A) Not included.
B) Only available by endorsement.
C) Included with a 12 month readjustment period.
D) Included with a 30 day readjustment period. Ref. 8-7

14. All of the following are Optional Coverages under the Businessowners Policy EXCEPT:

A) Outdoor Signs.
B) Employee Dishonesty.
C) Mechanical Breakdown.
D) Workers Compensation. Ref. 8-10

15. All of the following are specific types of property NOT covered in a Businessowners Policy EXCEPT:

A) Money located on the premises.
B) Watercraft while afloat.
C) Business personal property within 100 feet of described premises.
D) Automobiles parked in the businessowner's parking lot. Ref. 8-6

16. All of the following are exclusions in a Businessowners Policy EXCEPT:

A) Damage caused by a latent defect.
B) Loss of property caused by theft.
C) Damage to computer data caused by an electrical disturbance.
D) Loss of property caused by a fraudulent pretense. Ref. 8-4

17. Which of the following are the two major coverages provided under the Businessowners Liability Coverage?

A) Personal liability and business liability.
B) Business liability and medical expenses.
C) Personal liability and medical payments liability.
D) Commercial liability and fire legal liability. Ref. 8-8

18. The Businessowners Liability Coverage provides legal liability for bodily injury or property damage. All of the following are covered bodily injury and/or property damage coverages EXCEPT:

A) Personal injury and advertising injury.
B) Fire legal liability.
C) Professional liability.
D) Medical expenses to third parties. Ref. 8-11

19. All of the following are excluded under the Businessowners Liability Coverage EXCEPT:

A) An injury arising out of the sale of alcohol.
B) An injury arising out of a Workers Compensation Laws.
C) Damages sought by a third party as the result of an accounting error caused.
D) An injury arising out of a slip and fall by a customer due to a wet floor. Ref. 8-12 & 8-13

20. Which of the following is the Businessowners Coverage Extension that provides coverage for the inability to collect monies due from customers as the result of a covered peril?

A) Valuable Papers and Records.
B) Money and Securities.
C) Accounts Receivable.
D) Extortion. Ref. 8-8

21. Which of the following is a Businessowners Coverage Extension that provides coverage for loss or damage to manuscripts, deeds, drawings, films and mortgages?

A) Valuable Papers and Records.
B) Money and Securities.
C) Accounts Receivable.
D) Theft, Disappearance and Destruction. Ref. 8-8

22. Which of the following is NOT true of the Hired Auto and Nonowned Auto Liability endorsement of the Businessowners Policy?

A) It provides liability coverage for hired autos.
B) It provides liability coverage for nonowned auto.
C) It is typically endorsed to the BOP when the insured does not have a Business Auto Policy.
D) It is a common method of providing physical damage and liability coverage. Ref. 8-14

23. Under the Businessowners' Additional Coverage Business Income, ordinary payroll is:

A) Limited to 60 days.
B) Limited to 90 days.
C) Limited to 120 days.
D) Limited to 12 months. Ref. 8-6

24. If a businessowner maintains insurance equal to 100% of his inventory for the twelve months preceding loss, he may:

A) Receive a premium reduction of 15%.
B) Receive a premium increase of 15%.
C) Be paid up to an additional 25% above the amount indicated on the Declarations.
D) Be penalized up to 25% if a loss occurs. Ref. 8-8

ANSWER KEY

1-D	2-B	3-C	4-C	5-C	6-B	7-C	8-C	9-C	10-C
11-D	12-A	13-D	14-D	15-C	16-B	17-B	18-C	19-D	20-C
21-A	22-D	23-A	24-C						

CHAPTER NINE

WORKERS COMPENSATION

OVERVIEW

WORKERS COMPENSATION

Workers Compensation **provides coverage to employees for bodily injury that is accidental and/or occupational diseases that arise out of, or in the course of, employment.** Prior to the enactment of the Workers Compensation laws, employees would have to sue their employer and prove negligence to be reimbursed for injuries. Employers have a common law obligation to:

- **Provide a safe work place.**
- **Provide reasonably competent fellow employees.**
- **Provide safe tools and equipment.**
- **Enforce safety rules.**
- **Warn employees of dangers.**

Prior to the introduction of Workers Compensation, if an accident occurred, the employer would argue one or more of following common law defenses:

- **Assumption of Risk**.
- **Contributory Negligence**.
- **Fellow Servant Rule**, which barred recovery if the injury was caused by the negligence of a fellow employee.

Today, employees give up their right to sue in exchange for the Workers Compensation laws that guarantee medical, income, death and rehabilitation benefits. The cost incurred by the employer to provide Workers Compensation coverage is passed on to the public as a cost of doing business. In Pennsylvania, **Workers Compensation coverage is compulsory**.

WORKERS COMPENSATION LAWS

Workers Compensation laws are in effect in all 50 states, including the District of Columbia and U.S. territories. Coverage is provided through private insurers, the State Workers' Insurance Fund (SWIF) or a qualified self-insurer. Most states, including Pennsylvania, permit coverage to be obtained through either private or state markets. These states are termed **competitive**. A few states (North Dakota, Ohio, Washington, West Virginia, Wyoming) require coverage to be obtained exclusively through the state. These states are termed **monopolistic**. The following statutes address specific and unique areas of workers compensation coverage and law:

- **U.S. Longshore and Harbor Workers' Compensation Act** provides Workers Compensation to individuals who are employed on the navigable waterways of the U.S. or adjoining areas used to load, unload or repair marine vessels.

- **Jones Act**, also known as the Merchant Marine Act, permits **masters and crewmembers** of American vessels the **right to sue for negligence** in the event of bodily injury or death.
- **Federal Employer's Liability Act** protects **interstate railroad workers**. The Act (FELA) became effective prior to the enactment of Workers Compensation laws. It permits interstate railroad workers the **right to sue for negligence.**
- **Federal Employees Compensation Act** provides Workers Compensation to **civilian employees of the U.S. government** anywhere in the world.
- **Defense Base Act** provides Workers Compensation benefits to **civilian employees at any military, air or naval base**. Benefits under the Defense Base Act are similar to the U.S. Longshore and Harbor Workers Compensation Act.

POLICY STRUCTURE

The Workers Compensation Policy is composed of an **Information or Declarations Page,** which indicates the insurer's name, mailing address, etc.; a **General Section**, which defines policy provisions, such as, who an insured is, the Workers Compensation law, the state and the location; and six parts. Part I and Part II address the coverages and Parts III through VI address conditions and provisions. Endorsements alter the policy language and provide coverage for unusual exposures. The following is an overview of the Workers Compensation Policy.

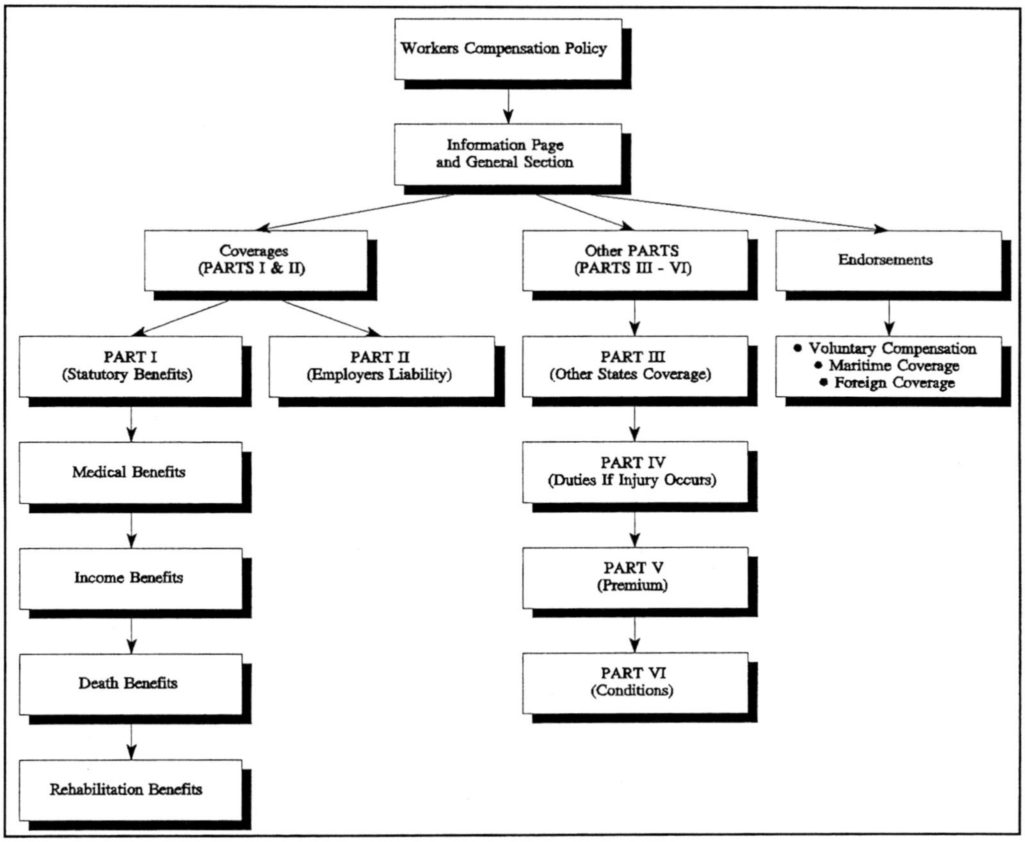

PART I - WORKERS COMPENSATION INSURANCE

Part I - Workers Compensation Insurance applies to the statutory law and mandates the following benefits:

1) **Unlimited Medical Benefits**, meaning all reasonable and necessary medical expenses due to work related injury or disease. Employers may provide a list of at least 6 health care providers for the injured employees to choose from for medical treatment. After 90 days of treatment following an injury, the employee may choose his own health care provider. The employee must give a 5 day notice if this option is elected. In the event the employer does not provide a list of physicians, the employee may choose any treatment provider.

2) **Income Benefits** of **66⅔% of average weekly earnings** subject to maximum and minimum weekly limits. Benefits begin after a 7 day waiting period and are retroactive if the disability continues beyond 14 days. Disability may be categorized as either:

   - **Total Disability**, meaning a disability that is permanent in nature causing the employee to be unable to work at all;
   - **Partial Disability**, meaning the person is able to do some work. It is any disability that is less than total disability. The extent of partial disability is measured by the loss of earning power. Partial income benefits restore a percent of the employee's wages. For example, an employer may have a **light duty return to work program** to help the employee get back to work. Benefit payments for partial disability may not exceed 500 weeks;
   - **Permanent Partial Disability**, meaning a disability which is partial but permanent. Examples include a loss of sight or hearing, or the loss a finger, hand or other limb. **Scheduled benefits** are provided for these permanent partial disabilities. In both partial and permanent partial disabilities, individuals may return to work and receive a reduced benefit; and,
   - **Temporary Disability**, meaning a disability which is a short time in duration. Examples include a sprained ankle or a broken arm.

   Individuals who are totally or temporarily disabled receive full income benefits. Individuals who are partially or permanently partially disabled and return to work receive a reduced benefit equal to a percentage of the wage loss.

3) **Death Benefits** of $3,000 as a burial allowance. Income benefits payable to surviving family members are provided as a percentage of the deceased worker's income subject to maximum and minimum weekly limits as follows:

   - **Family** *(spouse plus children)* at 66⅔%; **Family** *(spouse plus child)* at 60%; **Spouse only** at 51%; and **Child only** at 32%. Children's benefits are payable to age 18 and up to age 23 if in school. Spouse's benefits are payable for life, but in the event of remarriage, a two year lump sum benefit is provided.

4) **Rehabilitation Benefits**, meaning therapy and devices, such as wheelchairs, to assist in the rehabilitation process. *It also includes vocational training.*

PART II - EMPLOYERS LIABILITY

Part II - Employers Liability provides coverage for the employer for **legal actions that are not subject to Workers Compensation laws**. Under Workers Compensation, the employee gives up his or her common law right to sue, however, **third parties may bring legal actions**. For example, a spouse for loss of consortium. Employers Liability exclusions apply:

- To any condition covered by Workers Compensation or occupational disease law.
- To any unemployment compensation or similar law.
- To liability assumed under contract.
- To punitive damages if a worker is employed in violation of the law.
- For violation of any employment law with the insured's knowledge.
- To bodily injury claims occurring outside the United States, its territories or Canada. *Individuals temporarily outside these areas are covered.*
- To injury or damages arising out of wrongful discharge from employment, coercion, or discrimination that is in violation of the law.

Standard Limits for PART II - Employers Liability is $100,000 per accident for injuries, $100,000 per employee for disease, and $500,000 in the aggregate for disease.

PART III - Other States Insurance provides Workers Compensation coverage in additional states. For example, if a Pennsylvania firm operates in Maryland, that should be indicated on the Information Page of the Workers Compensation Policy.

PART IV - Duties if Injury Occurs addresses the duties of the insured to advise at once, and to give the insurer all information pertaining to injuries.

PART V - Premium addresses the calculation of premiums and the right to audit records.

PART VI - Conditions addresses the right of the company to conduct inspections, cancel the policy and prohibits the insured from assigning the policy.

OCCUPATIONS EXCLUDED

The Workers Compensation Law of Pennsylvania apply to practically all employees with the following exceptions:

- Domestic employees (e.g., maids, butlers and related employees).
- Outworkers (e.g., chauffeurs, gardeners and related employees).
- Casual workers (e.g., person who performs periodic services or repairs).
- Farm employees earning less than $1,200/year or working less than 30 days/year.
- Self employed (e.g., sole proprietor or partner in a partnership).
- Elected officers of the Commonwealth or any of its subdivisions.
- Executive officers **may elect** not to be an employee of the corporation.

Please note that federal employees, maritime workers and interstate railroad workers are covered under specific statutes as outlined earlier in this chapter.

SUBSEQUENT INJURY FUND

Pennsylvania's Subsequent Injury Fund **promotes the hiring of individuals who were previously injured** and who, because of this injury, new employers are reluctant to hire. For example, if an individual has a permanent disability, a new employer may fear a more serious disability and/or higher claims frequency if that individual is employed. **The subsequent injury fund would pay some or all of the additional compensation because of the second injury**. Most states have initiated subsequent injury funds to promote the hiring of the physically challenged.

SPECIAL CONSIDERATIONS FOR CONTRACTOR AND SUBCONTRACTOR

A situation that commonly develops on work projects is the use of subcontractors to complete specific jobs for the principal contractor. In these situations, it would be fairly easy to circumvent the intent of the Worker Compensation Law by hiring an uninsured subcontractor. To minimize this possibility, the principal contractor may not subcontract work on any contract unless the subcontractor has presented proof of Workers Compensation. Furthermore, in the event an uninsured employee of the subcontractor is injured, the principal contractor will be responsible for the compensation benefits.

SELECTED ENDORSEMENTS

The standard Workers Compensation Policy may be endorsed to cover various work related exposures. The following are several of these endorsements:

- **Voluntary Compensation** coverage may be provided to individuals who are not covered under the state's Workers Compensation Law. Examples include temporary workers, domestics, and outworkers. For example, if a domestic employee is injured while performing work for a homeowner, the only recourse the domestic employee would have is to sue the employer under the employer's Homeowner Policy. Under the voluntary compensation approach, the domestic employee is covered under a Workers Compensation Policy. In this case, a Voluntary Compensation and Employers Liability Coverage Endorsement (WC 00 03 11) is added to the policy providing the domestic employee statutory Workers Compensation benefits in return for the domestic employee giving up his common law right to sue.

  A similar example applies to individuals covered under the Jones Act. For example, a business which uses boats may also choose to cover its marine employees under the voluntary compensation approach. In this case, the Voluntary Compensation Maritime Coverage Endorsement (WC 00 02 03) is used. As with the domestic employee example, the crew member must give up his common law right to sue in return for statutory voluntary compensation benefits.

- **Foreign Coverage Endorsement** are available to cover incidental and unique foreign health exposures. For example, if an employee contracts an endemic disease (unique to a country) or is involved in a serious accident in a foreign country, exorbitant expenses (chartered plane, etc.) may be necessary in having the employee returned to the U.S. for treatment. These repatriation expenses may be covered under a Foreign Coverage Endorsement.

PREMIUM COMPUTATIONS

Workers Compensation rating is **developed by applying a rating bureau job classification loss cost (modified by the insurer's expense and profit elements in the form of a Loss Cost Multiplier) to each $100 of payroll**. Payroll means remuneration and includes salaries, wages, commissions, bonuses, non-cash compensation, vacation pay and sick leave. Jobs which are hazardous have a higher rate than non-hazardous jobs. For example, a roofer's rate may be $30.00 per $100.00 of payroll, whereas, a clerical employee's rate may be $0.50 per $100.00 of payroll. **Estimated payroll figures and job classifications are used when a policy is issued** and the final premium is determined by an audit. For example, if a business projects its payroll to be $1,000,000 for the policy term, and at the time of audit it is determined that the payroll was $1,200,000, the insured is charged an additional premium to reflect the additional $200,000 in payroll. Similarly, if the business' payroll was determined to be $800,000, the insured would receive a return premium to reflect the reduced $200,000 payroll figure. **Insurers may audit the records of a business up to 3 years after the expiration of the policy**. The following is an illustration of a workers compensation premium calculation:

ILLUSTRATION OF WORKERS COMPENSATION PREMIUM CALCULATION				
Pennsylvania Classification	Code No.#	Premium Basis Total Estimated Annual Remuneration	Rate Per $100 of Remuneration	Estimated Annual Premium
Salesmen	951	$300,000	1.04	$3,120
Clerical	953	$200,000	0.51	1,020
Engineer	955	$600,000	0.95	5,700
Standard Premium				9,840
Expense Constant †	0900			160
Annual Premium				$10,000
† Expense Constant is an additional charge on all policies to cover policy issue/auditing cost.				

LOSS COST RATING

Pennsylvania utilizes a loss cost rating system for Workers Compensation. Under this approach, rates are made up of two elements:

1) The **prospective loss costs element** (developed by PCRB), and
2) The **expense and profit element** (developed by each insurer as a LCM).

Under this method, the prospective loss costs element (1) is developed by the Pennsylvania Compensation Rating Bureau (PCRB) and the expense and profit element (2) is developed by individual insurers who apply their own specific expense/profit element (in the form of a loss cost multiplier) to arrive at the approved prospective rates. These **Loss Cost Multipliers (LCM)**, which are filed by the insurers, permit variation in rates from insurer to insurer. For example, a lost cost multiplier of 1.100 means that the insurer is charging 10% above the state loss costs. Alternatively, a loss cost multiplier of .900 means that the insurer is charging 10% below the loss cost projected by the state. A uniform classification and experience rating plan is maintained. The following addresses these topics:

- **Experience Rating** measures the **individual employer's loss experience against the average for its classification** and adjusts future premiums upon this loss experience. Under experience rating, the insured's expense modification factor for its current year is generally based upon its loss experience over three prior years. The **experience modification factor** which is based upon its payroll and its own losses is applied and results in either an increase or decrease in premium. *Experience rating takes the manual rate and modifies it by the insured's own loss experience.* **It tailors the state rates to reflect its experience.** It rewards businesses with lower premiums when claims are reduced. The experience modification is determined by the rating bureau and forwarded to the insurer.

- **Premium Discount** is a credit applied to the workers compensation premium. This is permitted when an insured owes a total standard premium of at least $5,000. The premium credit increases as the standard premium increases. The experience modification and premium discount are illustrated below.

ILLUSTRATION of EXPERIENCE MODIFICATION & PREMIUM DISCOUNT			
Higher Claims Average	Premium	Lower Claims Average	Premium
Payroll x Rate $1,100,000	$10,000	Payroll x Rate $1,100,000	$10,000
Experience Modification Premium before discount	1.100 $11,000	Experience Modification Premium before discount	.900 $9,000
Premium Discount ($6,000 x 10.9)† =	($654)	Premium Discount ($4,000 x 10.9)† =	($436)
Total Premium	$10,346	Total Premium	$8,564
† Premium discount factors are listed in the Workers Compensation Manual.			

- **Participating Dividend Plans** are programs where businesses with similar occupations are grouped together. In the event the group's loss experience is low, dividends are paid to participating members.

- **Retrospective Rating** is an optional rating program that may be used by mutual agreement between the insured and insurer. It measures the **individual employer's experience against its own loss history during the policy term**. An experience modification formula which is written into the policy, results in either an increase or decrease in premium. This type of rating is commonly elected by very large businesses with predictable loss experience.

OTHER SOURCES OF COVERAGE

In addition to private insurance, employers may secure coverage through either:

- **State Workers' Insurance Fund,** which is generally the insurer of last resort.

- **Qualified self-insurer**, which is an organization that meets certain minimum financial requirements including: considerations for make-up and size of group; joint and several liability; excess insurance; loss prevention and safety programs; and have adequate and competent administrative staff.

PENNSYLVANIA WORKERS' COMPENSATION ACT

On July 2, 1993, the Pennsylvania Workers' Compensation Act (Act 44 of 1993) was signed into law. Its primary purpose was to reduce the spiraling costs of Workers Compensation in the Commonwealth. On June 20, 1996, amendments to that law were signed into effect. The focus of these amendments centered on wage replacement issues. The Act is administered by the Department of Labor and Industry, Bureau of Occupational Injury and Disease Compensation. The following provides an overview of Act 44 of 1993 and the amendments which became effective on August 23, 1996.

COMPLIANCE

Workers Compensation is compulsory. Coverage may be secured through a licensed insurer, the State Workers' Insurance Fund (SWIF) or a qualified self-insurer. Any business which fails to secure Workers Compensation is punishable by a fine of between $500 and $2,000 per day and/or imprisonment for up to one year. The business may also be required to pay restitution to the injured employee.

NOTICE/RECORDING REQUIREMENTS

The following are required notice/recording requirements:

- **Employers must post** the notice "REMEMBER IT IS IMPORTANT TO TELL YOUR EMPLOYER ABOUT YOUR INJURY". This notice must be prominently displayed at the employer's place of business.
- **Employers may establish a list of at least 6 designated health care providers** for injured employees to choose from for medical treatment. In the event invasive surgery is recommended, the injured employee is entitled to a second opinion. **After 90 days** of treatment following an injury, the employee may choose his own health care provider. The employee must give a 5 day notice if this option is elected. In the event the employer does not provide a list of physicians, the employee may choose any treatment provider.
- **Employees must notify** their employer of injury within 21 days.
- **Employers must notify the Department of Labor and Industry** within 48 hours of any accident which results in death. All accidents which result in injury (except those resulting in injury of less than one day) must be filed within 7 days. A copy must be mailed to the employer's insurer.
- **Employers are required to record all injuries** by description and time of loss.
- **Notice of denial** must be sent to the employee and department within 21 days of notice of disability. If the claim is denied, the employee may request a hearing.

REDUCTION IN BENEFITS

Benefits will be reduced if an employee **receives unemployment benefits** other than death and scheduled injury benefits, such amount shall be credited against the amount of the award; **receives other benefits** under any state/federal law or from two or more employers; **is incarcerated in jail**, but only after conviction of the crime.

COMPENSATION EXCLUSIONS

No compensation will be paid if injury or death is:

- **Intentionally self-inflicted**;
- Caused by employees in violation of the law including, but not limited to, the **illegal use of drugs or consumption of alcohol**. For example, if an employee is injured while under the influence of illegal drugs or alcohol, workers compensation benefits can be denied. In these cases, the *employer must prove that the use of drugs and/or the consumption of alcohol caused the injury*; or
- Caused while an employee is **operating a motor vehicle** provided by the employer if the employee is **not in the course and scope of employment** at the time of injury. For example, if an employee is injured while using an employer provided motor vehicle outside the course of the employee's employment, Workers Compensation benefits can be denied.

PENALTIES

A person commits an offense if he knowingly and with the intent to defraud, does any of the following: presents any statement forming a part of, or in support of, a Workers Compensation claim that contains **false, incomplete or misleading information**; assists, solicits or conspires with another to prepare or make any statement that is intended to be presented to any insurer in connection with a Workers Compensation claim that contains false or misleading information. A person who violates this Act is guilty of a felony and subject to a fine of **$50,000 or double the amount of the fraud**, and/or imprisonment of up to seven years.

1996 AMENDMENTS TO THE WORKERS COMPENSATION ACT

The following is an overview of the amendments to the Workers Compensation Law which became effective on August 23, 1996. The focus of these amendments center on the following wage replacement cost issues.

- **Calculation of the average weekly wage** will be computed *using the amounts paid in the three highest of the prior four quarters*. The law also clarifies that certain fringe benefits (employee contributions to benefit plans) are not considered wages and that only tips or other gratuities that are reflected on the injured worker's tax return be considered in the calculation.
- **A benefit offset** reduces the wage loss benefits paid by Workers Compensation of up 50% if Social Security, pension and severance benefits are received. *The offset provision is not retroactive.*
- **Employee reporting requirement** mandating injured employees to report the receipt of Social Security, pension, severance benefits or new employment to their employers.
- **Medical evaluation requirement** mandating injured workers submit to a medical evaluation after the employee has received 104 weeks of benefits to determine the degree of impairment. It imposes a 500 week limit on indemnity benefits. This only applies to injured workers who are not severely disabled.
- **Employers may now utilize expert testimony** to demonstrate that an injured worker has earning capacity and therefor is entitled to a reduced benefit.

KEY TERMS AND CONCEPTS

The following terms were introduced in this chapter. You should know each word and concept and be able to apply them in everyday usage. To improve retention, it is recommended that you write out each key term and concept in your owns words.

Competitive
Death and Survivor Benefits
Defense Base Act
Employers Liability Exclusions
Employment Covered
Experience Modification Factor
Federal Employees Compensation Act
Federal Employer's Liability Act (FELA)
Foreign Coverage Endorsement
Income Benefits
Job Classifications
Jones Act
Loss Cost Rating
Monopolistic
Occupations Excluded
Part Five - Premium
Part Four - Duties If Injury Occurs
Part One - Workers Compensation
Part Six - Conditions
Part Three - Other States Insurance
Part Two - Employers Liability
Partial Disability
Participating (dividend plan)
Payroll
Permanent Partial Disability
Premium Discount
Rates
Remunerations
Retrospective Rating
Self-insured Employers
State Workers' Insurance Fund (SWIF)
Subsequent Injury Fund
Temporary Disability
Total Disability
U. S. Longshore & Harbor Worker's Act
Voluntary Compensation
Workers Compensation Law
Workers Compensation Policy

REVIEW QUESTIONS

Before attempting to answer the end chapter practice questions, you should ask yourself if you can answer the following questions. It is recommended that you write out each review question in your own words. This exercise will help you apply the key terms and concepts that you've learned to form relationships with different topics.

1. How does a monopolistic state differ from a competitive state? (9-1)

2. Identify and explain 5 Acts which address unique areas of Workers Compensation. (9-1)

3. Identify 2 Acts which permit injured workers the right to sue their employer for damages. (9-2)

4. Identify and explain the 4 major coverages of Workers Compensation. (9-3)

5. Identify the maximum percentage of income payable to injured workers including any waiting periods. (9-3)

6. Identify and explain the 4 types of disability. (9-3)

7. Identify the 4 percentage limitations payable to surviving family members in the event of a Workers Compensation related death. (9-3)

8. Identify 3 benefits available to injured workers under the Rehabilitation Benefit. (9-3)

9. Explain the coverage provided under Employers Liability. (9-4)

10. Identify 7 Employers Liability Exclusions. (9-4)

11. Identify the standards limits of liability under Employers Liability. (9-4)

12. Identify 7 categorizes of individuals that are exempt from Workers Compensation. (9-4)

13. Explain the Subsequent Injury Fund. (9-5)

14. What is the purpose of the Voluntary Compensation Endorsement? (9-5)

15. How is Workers Compensation rated? (9-6)

16. Identify 5 components of payroll. (9-6)

17. Explain the audit provision of the Workers Compensation Policy including any time limitation. (9-6)

18. Under Loss Cost rating, identify the 2 elements that make up a rate. (9-6)

19. Under Loss Cost rating, who files the Loss Cost Multipliers? (9-6)

20. What is the purpose of Loss Cost Multipliers? (9-6)

21. Explain experience rating. (9-7)

22. What is the purpose of an Experience Modification Factor? (9-7)

23. How does a Loss Cost Multiplier differ from an Experience Modification Factor? (9-7)

24. What is a premium discount and when does it apply? (9-7)

25. Identify 3 ways an employer can insure its workers compensation exposure. (9-7)

26. What is SWIF and explain its purpose? (9-7)

27. What penalties may be assessed against a businessowner which does not provide Workers Compensation for employees? (9-8)

28. Explain the Posting requirements under Workers Compensation. (9-8)

29. Explain the Designated Health Care Providers requirement under Workers Compensation. (9-8)

30. Explain the Notification to Employers of Injury requirement including time limitations under Workers Compensation. (9-8)

31. Explain the Notification by the Employer to the Department of Labor and Industry requirement including time limitations under Workers Compensation. (9-8)

32. What employer recording requirements are mandated by the Workers Compensation law? (9-8)

33. Explain the Notice of denial requirement including any time limitation under Workers Compensation. (9-8)

34. Explain 3 ways other than returning to work that an individual may have his or her benefits reduced. (9-8)

35. Identify and explain 3 activities that may cause an individual to have his or her Workers Compensation claim denied. (9-9)

36. What penalties may be assessed against an individual who provides false, incomplete or misleading information in relation to Workers Compensation claim? (9-9)

PRACTICE EXAM NINE

ON

WORKERS COMPENSATION

1. **All of the following are true of Workers Compensation Laws EXCEPT:**

   A) Workers Compensation Laws are in effect in all 50 states, the District of Columbia, and in U.S. Territories.
   B) It provides coverage for injuries occurred on the job.
   C) It may provide coverage to civilians working at military bases.
   D) It provides coverage for casual workers. Ref. 9-1

2. **Which of the following may exercise an option to be exempt from Workers Compensation:**

   A) Domestic employees.
   B) Outworkers.
   C) Certain corporate executive officers.
   D) Casual workers. Ref. 9-4

3. **Workers Compensation provides coverage for:**

   A) Bodily injury that is accidental.
   B) Occupational diseases that are unique to the occupation.
   C) Bodily injury that is intentional.
   D) Bodily injury that is accidental and occurs on the job, and occupational diseases that are unique to the occupation. Ref. 9-1

4. **Workers Compensation may be:**

   A) Purchased through private companies.
   B) Purchased through the state fund.
   C) Self-Insured.
   D) All of the above. Ref. 9-1

5. **Workers Compensation that must be obtained through the state is:**

   A) Competitive.
   B) Monopolistic.
   C) Private state.
   D) Public state. Ref. 9-1

6. **All of the following are benefits provided under Workers Compensation EXCEPT:**

   A) Medical benefits.
   B) Income benefits.
   C) Death benefits.
   D) Rehabilitation benefits. Ref. 9-3
   E) Occupation benefits.

7. **Pennsylvania's Workers Compensation Law provides medical benefits that are:**

A) Limited to $1,000,000.
B) Limited to one year after the accident.
C) Unlimited as to dollar amount and time period.
D) None of the above. Ref. 9-3

8. **Pennsylvania's Workers Compensation Law provides a disability income benefit of:**

A) 100% of average weekly wages subject to maximum and minimum limits.
B) 66⅔% of average weekly wages subject to maximum and minimum limits.
C) 50% of average weekly limits subject to maximum and minimum limits.
D) None of the above. Ref. 9-3

9. **All of the following are characteristics of Subsequent Injury Funds EXCEPT:**

A) Promotes the employment of the physically challenged.
B) Pays some or all of additional compensation required when a subsequent injury occurs.
C) Reduces an employer's cost exposure due to probability of increased claims frequency.
D) One does not exist in Pennsylvania. Ref. 9-5

10. **If an employee consumes alcohol, becomes intoxicated, and is injured at work, he is:**

A) Covered for Workers Compensation.
B) Covered for Workers Compensation if the intoxication occurred totally at work.
C) Not covered for Workers Compensation if proven the consumption of alcohol caused the injury.
D) Covered for Workers Compensation if approved by his supervisor. Ref. 9-9

11. **Which of the following provides coverage to workers in the ship building and ship repair occupations?**

A) The Jones Act.
B) The Defense Base Act.
C) The U.S. Longshore and Harbor Workers Compensation Act.
D) The Federal Employer's Liability Act (FELA). Ref. 9-1

12. **Under workers compensation, each job classification has:**

A) The same rate.
B) A rate reflective of its loss experience.
D) An experience modification factor.
C) A premium discount. Ref. 9-6

13. **Which of the following provides coverage to crew members under the Merchant Marine Act?**

A) The Jones Act.
B) The Defense Base Act.
C) The U.S. Longshore and Harbor Workers Compensation Act.
D) The Federal Employer's Liability Act (FELA). Ref. 9-2

14. Which of the following acts protects interstate railroad workers?

A) The Jones Act.
B) The Defense Base Act.
C) The U.S. Longshore and Harbor Workers Compensation Act.
D) The Federal Employer's Liability Act (FELA). Ref. 9-2

15. Coverage Parts I & II of the Workers Compensation Policy provide:

A) Statutory and property damage coverages.
B) Statutory and general liability coverages.
C) Statutory and employers liability coverages.
D) None of the above. Ref. 9-3 & 9-4

16. Part I of the Workers Compensation Policy will respond to:

A) Job related injuries.
B) Lawsuits against the employer arising out of employment.
C) Both of the above.
D) None of the above. Ref. 9-3

17. The annual premium of a Workers Compensation Policy is:

A) Always subject to a premium discount.
B) Developed by the Pennsylvania Compensation Rating Bureau.
C) Never subject to an experience modification.
D) Developed by applying a job classification rate to each $100 of remuneration.
Ref. 9-6 & 9-7

18. All of the following are exempt from Workers Compensation EXCEPT:

A) Sole proprietor.
B) Outworkers.
C) Casual workers.
D) Employees covered under labor contracts. Ref. 9-4

19. All of the following are true of partial disability EXCEPT:

A) It is any disability that is less than total disability.
B) The disabled individual may be involved in a light duty return to work program.
C) Benefit payments for partial disability are limited to 500 weeks.
D) Income received from employment has no effect on income benefits. Ref. 9-3

20. All of the following are included in the rehabilitation benefit EXCEPT:

A) Physical Therapy.
B) Durable equipment such as wheelchairs.
C) Medical expenses for acute care.
D) Vocational training. Ref. 9-3

21. In Pennsylvania, Workers Compensation coverage is:

A) Exclusive.
B) Monopolistic.
C) Compulsory.
D) Elective.

Ref. 9-1

22. The Workers Compensation Laws were developed upon the theory that:

A) Accidents are a part of the production process.
B) The cost should be passed on to society as a whole.
C) Coverage should be absolute.
D) All of the above.

Ref. 9-1

23. Workers Compensation income benefits are subject to a waiting period of:

A) No waiting period.
B) 7 Days.
C) 14 Days.
D) 30 days.

Ref. 9-3

24. In Pennsylvania, Workers Compensation coverage is:

A) Exclusive.
B) Monopolistic.
C) Competitive.
D) Elective.

Ref. 9-1

25. All of the following are exclusions under the Employers Liability part of the Workers Compensation Policy EXCEPT:

A) Liability assumed under contract.
B) Penalties for violation of employment law.
C) Consequential injury to a spouse or relative of an injured worker.
D) Injury to a worker while employed in violation of law with the insured's knowledge.

Ref. 9-4

26. Under a Voluntary Compensation Endorsement:

A) Compensation is paid based upon a negligence theory.
B) Individuals who accept voluntary compensation must give up their right to sue.
C) All employees are subject to voluntary compensation.
D) Only maritime employees are subject to voluntary compensation.

Ref. 9-5

ANSWER KEY

1-D	2-C	3-D	4-D	5-B	6-E	7-C	8-B	9-D	10-C
11-C	12-B	13-A	14-D	15-C	16-A	17-D	18-D	19-D	20-C
21-C	22-D	23-B	24-C	25-C	26-B				

CHAPTER TEN

OTHER COVERAGES AND OPTIONS

OVERVIEW

OTHER COVERAGES AND OPTIONS

Other coverages and options refers to the various insurance coverages and options that are written to complement the personal and commercial policies reviewed in Chapters One through Nine. The following is a description of these contracts:

COMPREHENSIVE PERSONAL LIABILITY (CPL) INSURANCE

Comprehensive Personal Liability Policies cover individuals for nonbusiness related liability. The CPL coverage is almost identical to the personal liability coverage provided under Section II of the Homeowners Policy and the Personal Liability Coverage L and M of the Dwelling Fire Program. The primary difference between a separate CPL and the Homeowner/Dwelling Policy liability insurance is the coverage limits. The CPL may be issued for amounts as low as $25,000. Because of the popularity of the Homeowner Policy, CPL's are seldom written.

PERSONAL UMBRELLA POLICY

Personal Umbrella Policies are written to provide **nonbusiness liability coverage in the following two areas**:

- **First**, *as excess coverage over the required underlying liability limits* of an individual's automobile and personal liability insurance. For example, if an insured maintained $300,000 of liability coverage under his Homeowners Policy, and $1,000,000 under his Umbrella Policy, and is found liable for damages of $700,000, the Personal Umbrella Policy would provide coverage in excess of the underlying Homeowner Policy limit up to the total Umbrella Policy limit. In this case, the umbrella would provide $400,000 of excess coverage above the homeowner limit. Failure to maintain the required underlying limit would result in the insured being responsible for the difference between the required amount and the umbrella's threshold.

- **Second**, *as additional coverage in certain situations where the underlying coverage does not respond.* For example, the unendorsed Homeowners Policy excludes liability for slander, libel and invasion of privacy. In the event a lawsuit was brought against the insured, the typical Personal Umbrella Policy would provide a legal defense and pay an amount up to the umbrella's limit of liability minus a self insured retention limit.

Please note that the self insured retention (SIR) is similar to a deductible and applicable to any loss excluded under the primary coverage. A typical SIR limit is $250. See page 10-13 for an illustration of the Personal Umbrella Policy.

COMMERCIAL UMBRELLA

Commercial Umbrella policies are written to provide **business liability coverage in the following two areas**:

- **First**, as excess coverage over the required underlying liability limits of the primary liability policy. For example, if an insured maintained $1,000,000 of liability coverage under his Commercial Liability Policy, he may purchase higher limits of coverage by securing an Umbrella Policy of $5,000,000. In this instance, the primary would provide coverage up to $1,000,000, with the Umbrella Policy providing excess coverage up to the additional $5,000,000 limit.
- **Second**, as additional coverage in certain situations where the underlying coverage does not respond. For example, a Commercial Liability Policy typically excludes coverage for foreign territorial claims.

The self insured retention on a commercial umbrella is usually a minimum of $10,000.

Please note that the Commercial Umbrella Policy is similar in policy structure, format and operation as the Personal Umbrella Policy that was discussed earlier. The primary difference between the two policies is that the Commercial Umbrella covers business exposures with higher limits and the Personal Umbrella covers personal exposures with lower limits.

SPECIALTY LIABILITY INSURANCE

Specialty liability insurance refers to the various specialty policies that are used to fill gaps caused by exclusions in the primary personal and commercial policies. These policies **provide coverage for legal liability resulting from the negligence, errors and omissions, or other aspects of rendering professional services**. Coverage is typically written on a claims made basis with fraud and related criminal acts excluded. Specialty Liability Policies that cover the medical field, such as hospitals, physicians, surgeons, dentists, opticians, chiropractors, veterinarians and nurses, are referred to as **malpractice insurance**. Nonmedical professional liability that is written to cover attorneys, accountants, architects, engineers, insurance agents and brokers is referred to as **errors and omissions insurance**. These policies, commonly referred to as Professional Liability Policies cover individuals who are rendering professional services. The following are some examples of common professional liability exposures:

- **Medical malpractice** refers to exposures that medical professionals face in their treatment of patients. For example, the failure to properly diagnose an illness or prescribe proper treatment.
- **Legal errors and omissions** refers to exposures that lawyers face in the services they render to clients. For example, the failure to provide competent legal advice or the failure to process legal papers as required by statute.
- **Agent's and broker's errors and omissions** refers to exposures that agents and brokers (i.e., producers) face in their service to their clients. For example, the failure to recommend proper coverage or the failure to process applications as required by each insurance company.

In addition to the professional liability policies cited on the preceding page, other specialty liability policies include:

- **Directors and officer's liability** refers to exposures directors and officers of corporations may become liable for in the event they fail to act in the corporation's best interest. For example, an individual stockholder, or more commonly a group of stockholders, may bring legal action against the directors and officers of a corporation because of alleged mismanagement. Similarly, creditors or competitors from outside the corporation may initiate legal action. A Director's and Officer's Liability Policy would provide a legal defense and protection in either of these instances. As with the professional liability policies indicated above, exclusions in other policies require the individuals acting as a director or officer to be covered under specific D & O insurance.

- **Fiduciary liability** refers to the exposure fiduciaries face in their service as an executor, administrator or trustee. For example, the failure of an executor to properly manage the financial affairs of the estate of the deceased.

- **Liquor liability** (also known as Dram Shop liability) refers to the exposure that restaurants, bars, beer distributors and other similar establishments face due to their selling or serving of alcoholic beverages. For example, if a restaurant serves a patron alcohol and that person causes an auto accident, the restaurant may be held legally liable.

- **Employment practices** refers to exposures employers face in their capacity as an employer. Examples of exposures covered under an **Employment Practices Liability Policy (EPL)** include liability arising from:

    1) Refusal to employ, termination of the person's employment, demotion or failure to promote, negative evaluation, reassignment, discipline, defamation or humiliation of the person based on discrimination;
    2) Work related sexual harassment; and
    3) Other work-related verbal, physical, mental, or emotional abuse directed at the person relating to race, color, national origin, gender, marital status, age, sexual orientation, physical or mental conditions or any other protected class or characteristic established by any federal, state or local law.

Each of the above liability policies provides coverage in the event the individual or business is found legally liable for their negligent actions. The need for this coverage is important for two specific reasons. **First**, professional and business liability coverage is excluded from all other primary personal and commercial insurance policies. **Second**, an increasingly common perception in today's litigious society is to place blame upon someone else for one's own misfortunes. For these reasons, practically everyone who provides services may become liable for their actions or inactions and should be properly insured.

SURPLUS LINES INSURANCE

Surplus lines insurers are nonadmitted or unauthorized companies that are permitted by the insurance department to transact business within the state. Surplus lines refers to the broad range of risk **exposures that are not available or cannot be procured through admitted or authorized markets**. Examples of risk that may fall into the surplus lines market vary depending upon the underwriting cycle, but they usually include amusement parks, asbestos or lead abatement contractors, demolition contractors, etc. **To secure coverage in the surplus lines market, the following conditions must be met:**

- The originating producer must make a **diligent effort** to place coverage in the standard market. **Three admitted carriers** must have previously rejected the risk.
- The accepting surplus lines agent must **maintain detailed records** by the number, type, name, address, and premium of policies issued. Furthermore, a 3% premium tax must be submitted to the state for the privilege of transacting business.

To act as a surplus lines agent, an individual must possess a producer license and pass a surplus lines examination.

SURETY BONDS

Surety bonds guarantee (**or make sure**) that specific obligations will be fulfilled. Unlike insurance, surety bond losses are not expected, however, they do occur. The surety bond is written **subject to a bond limit or "penalty"** which is similar to the limit of liability in an insurance policy. Surety bonds are generally in effect until the principal (responsible party) fulfills its obligation which may span a period of several years or longer.

SURETYSHIP is the practice of guaranteeing obligations through a three-party contract. This is in contrast to insurance policies which are two party contracts. The three parties to a surety bond include the:

1) **Principal**, who is the party **(i.e., contractor)** to fulfill the obligation. The principal purchases the bond and pays the premium as a requirement to perform certain projects;
2) **Obligee**, who is the party **(i.e., property owner)** to whose benefit the bond is written; and
3) **Surety or Guarantor**, who is the party **(i.e., usually an insurance company)** providing the bond for a fee.

To illustrate how a surety bond would apply consider the following: A property owner is planning construction of a new building and wants to make sure that the contractor will construct and complete the building in accordance with the contract. To protect itself, the property owner will require the contractor be bonded by an insurance company or surety company. Bonds are generally classified as either contract bonds (related to the construction business) or noncontract bonds (relating to other than the construction business).

BOND UNDERWRITING centers on three primary areas of concern:

- **Character**, which addresses the principal's character. The insurer is concerned with the traits of integrity, reliability and trustworthiness.
- **Capacity**, which addresses the principal's professional ability to meet commitments in regard to the work that is to be performed.
- **Capital**, which addresses the principal's financial resources. This not only includes existing cash, but accounts receivables, work in progress and the firm's line of credit. Please note that in some cases, the surety company may require collateral in the form of cash as a prerequisite to issuing the bond. In these cases, if the principal performs its obligations, the collateral will be returned. If however, the principal defaults (does not complete its obligations), the surety company will retain the collateral to offset its losses. The following address the three major categories of bonds:

CONTRACT BONDS are **used in the construction business** to ensure that contractors will carry out their contractual obligations. Examples include:

- **Bid Bonds**, which guarantees that if a bidder is awarded a contract, the bidder will sign the contract at the proposed price. Bid bonds protect the property owner against loss resulting from the failure of the bidder to accept the bid.
- **Performance Bonds**, which guarantees the owner that the contractor will complete the project in accordance with all of the terms and conditions of the contract.
- **Completion Bonds**, which guarantees the lender that the contractor will use borrowed funds to complete the project free of liens.

JUDICIAL BONDS are **used in the legal process**. Examples include:

- **Bail Bonds,** which guarantees a defendant will appear as required by the court.
- **Appeal Bonds**, which guarantees that a judgment will be paid if an appeal is upheld.
- **Attachment Bonds**, which indemnifies a party whose assets are wrongfully attached.
- **Injunction Bonds,** which indemnifies the party to whom the injunction applied, if it is found that the injunction was wrong.
- **Fiduciary Bonds**, which guarantees the faithful and honest performance of fiduciaries such as guardians or estate administrators.

MISCELLANEOUS BONDS are **used for other purposes**. Examples include:

- **License or Permit Bonds,** which authorize an individual to engage in a particular activity. Specific examples include licenses for **private detectives and funeral directors**, or permit bonds for the **sale of liquor, tobacco or gasoline**.
- **Workers Compensation Bond**, which guarantees a self insured Workers Compensation fund.
- **Motor Vehicle Bond**, which guarantees that an individual will respond to the financial responsibility requirements of a state.

OCEAN MARINE INSURANCE

Ocean marine insurance is one of the oldest forms of insurance and has evolved from a limited coverage form into today's modern Ocean Marine Policy. Although it is primarily an unregulated policy from a rate and policy form viewpoint, it typically is written with the following major four coverages:

1) **HULL COVERAGE**, which insures against damage to or loss of the ship itself. The standard hull insurance coverage includes collision liability or a "running down clause" which applies to damage to another ship or its cargo. No coverage is provided for damage to piers, wharves, other structures or loss of life. Hull coverage may be written on a **single vessel basis** or on a **fleet basis**.

2) **CARGO COVERAGE**, which insures against damage to the cargo and may be purchased on a **single trip policy**, a **voyage policy** or an **open cargo policy**, which is typically purchased by importers and exporters for longer terms. A **warehouse-to-warehouse clause** may be added to cover cargo both on sea and land.

   The need for cargo coverage, be it ocean going or over land, is governed by the terms upon which the goods are purchased or sold. The following are common terms used in transporting goods:

   - **Free Along Side (FAS)** meaning the seller is responsible for loss or damage until the time the goods have been delivered along side the vessel or the designated dock. Thereafter, the goods are the buyer's responsibility.

   - **Free On Board (FOB)** meaning the seller is responsible for loss or damage until the time the goods have been placed on board the vessel. Thereafter, the goods are the buyer's responsibility.

   - **Cost and Freight (C&F)** meaning the seller is responsible for goods until the time the goods enter the custody of the ocean carrier. Under C&F, the seller's price of the goods includes the cost of transportation to the named point. Thereafter, the goods are the buyer's responsibility.

   - **Cost, Insurance and Freight (CIF)** is the same as C&F with the addition that the seller provides marine insurance to a named point of destination. Under CIF, the seller's price includes the goods, marine insurance and transportation charges to the named destination point. Thereafter, the goods are the buyer's responsibility.

3) **FREIGHT COVERAGE** is an indirect loss coverage that reimburses the payor for loss of income that would be earned for moving the cargo. For example, a shipper of cargo would be exposed to the loss of freight charges if the voyage was interrupted. A similar exposure exists in transporting passengers in the event of voyage termination. **Passage money coverage** may be secured to cover the exposure of loss of passage money.

4) PROTECTION AND INDEMNITY (P&I)

Protection and Indemnity provides marine legal liability coverage and insures the shipowner against liability to:

- **Seamen** caused by the shipowner's negligence or general damages under the Jones Act. For example, if a seaman is injured while working on a ship, he may sue the shipowner to collect for lost wages, medical expenses, etc. Typically, workers are covered if injury occurs on the job, but a specific law (the Jones Act) applies to seamen and permits lawsuits.
- **Longshoremen and harbor workers**.
- **Loss of cargo** caused by the shipowner's negligence.
- Other vessels, piers, wharves and other structures caused by **collision**.

The protection and indemnity coverage may be written with other marine coverages or as a separate policy.

COVERAGE FORMS under ocean marine policies may be written on either an **All Risk** or **Named Peril** basis, with all risk coverage standard exclusions including loss due to war, strikers, riot, civil commotion, decay, deterioration and inherent vice. Named peril policies provide coverage for **perils of the sea** (wind, wave action, collision, stranding, sinking or capsizing) and **perils on the sea** (fire, lightning, earthquake, pirates and thieves, jettison, barratry or fraud and all other like perils, losses and misfortune)

IMPLIED WARRANTIES of ocean marine insurance require the vessel and its cargo to comply with certain standards. Specifically, the shipowner warrants the following conditions:

- **Seaworthy**, meaning the vessel is seaworthy with a competent captain and crew.
- **Condition of cargo**, meaning the cargo is properly packaged.
- **Legal**, meaning the venture is of legal purpose.
- **Not deviate in its voyage**, meaning the vessel must follow an agreed route.

The purpose of these warranties is to promote compliance with maritime practices. If any of the implied warranties are breached, coverage may be denied.

LOSS ADJUSTMENT under ocean marine losses are subject to the following loss adjustment provisions:

- **General Average**, meaning a partial loss which resulted from a voluntary and deliberate sacrifice that was made for the benefit of all concerned, and which must be shared by all parties in proportion to their interest. An example being the jettison of some cargo to save the ship from sinking. In these instances everyone shares in the loss.
- **Particular Average**, meaning a partial loss with no requirement to share the loss. In these instance, the loss is born entirely by the individual owner whose cargo was damaged or lost.

WATERCRAFT INSURANCE

Watercraft insurance is limited under the Homeowners Policy. Property coverage is provided up to $1,500 for watercraft and trailers and liability coverage is provided for owned watercraft up to 26 feet in length and/or 25 horsepower. Because of these limitations, individuals with watercraft exposures require additional protection. Watercraft coverage may be provided beyond the limited coverages of the Homeowners Policy through the following Boatowners/Yacht Policy.

BOATOWNERS/YACHT

Boatowners/Yacht insurance may be written to cover both physical damage and liability exposures. **Coverage applies to losses that occur within the navigational limits** as defined in the application and policy. Boatowner/yacht coverages include:

SECTION I - BOATOWNERS PROPERTY COVERAGE is generally written on an "All Risk" basis although named peril coverage is available. It includes:

- **Coverage A - Vessels** including horns, lights, mooring cleats and similar permanently attached items.
- **Coverage B - Outboard Motors** including fuel containers and start up equipment and controls supplied as integral equipment by the manufacturer.
- **Coverage C - Trailers** designed for and used to transport a vessel.
- **Coverage D - Miscellaneous Boating Equipment** meaning accessories which are used for the safety or operation of a covered vessel or motor. Examples include anchors, oars, life preservers, extra fuel tanks or batteries, motor covers, deck chairs, cook stoves, refrigerators, tools, fire extinguishers, ship-to-shore radios and similar equipment.

Property excluded includes hunting, fishing or other sporting equipment; water skiing, scuba or other equipment; photographic equipment; portable televisions sets, radios, etc.; food and beverages; clothing, jewelry and other personal effects; parasails, hang gliders, or other devices designed for flight. **Perils excluded** includes dishonest or illegal acts; mysterious disappearance; freezing; overheating of engines; corrosion or rust; weathering; marring, scratching; chipping, denting and deterioration. Boatowner policies generally include a **Lay-up Warranty** requiring boats that are located in cold waters to be out of use during the winter months. Rates charged reflect this lay-up period. Boatowner property losses are settled on an ACV basis with optional replacement cost coverage available.

SECTION II - BOATOWNERS LIABILITY COVERAGE pays all sums the insured is legally obligated to pay as damages due to bodily injury or property damage arising out of the ownership, maintenance or use of the described vessel. **Uninsured Boaters** coverage, which is similar to uninsured motorist coverage may also be included.

- **Coverage E - Vessel Liability**
- **Coverage F - Medical Payments**

Liability coverage is excluded while carrying persons or property for a fee, being rented, engaging in racing contests, being transported by a land vehicle, or while towing a parasail or hang glider.

AVIATION INSURANCE

Aviation insurance can be favorably compared to the commercial automobile coverage forms. Aviation insurance is commonly classified into the following two categories.

- **First**, insurance covering the aircraft itself (hull coverage and aircraft liability). This is similar to the Auto Policy's physical damage & liability insurance.

- **Second**, insurance covering airport operations (airport liability & hangarkeepers legal liability). This is similar to the Garage Policy and garagekeepers insurance. Coverages applying to aircraft may be written as individual coverage or packaged together. Aircraft insurance includes the following two primary coverage:

  1) **Hull coverage**, which is physical damage coverage for the hull of the aircraft. It includes equipment that is installed in the hull (e.g., navigational equipment). Hull coverage may be written on either an All Risk or Named Peril basis. Generally, two separate deductibles apply in hull coverage. One applies to **motion losses** and a second separate deductible applies to **not in motion losses**.

  2) **Aircraft liability**, which is liability coverage protecting the plane owner in the event of its negligent operation. Coverage is written on a **passenger basis** or on an **excluding passenger basis**. Separate limits may apply to each category. Aircraft liability coverage only applies to owned aircraft or for a temporary substitute.

Pilots who operate an aircraft must be certified by the Federal Aviation Agency (FAA) to operate an aircraft. In addition, **the aircraft policy excludes losses if the aircraft is:**

- Not registered as airworthy.
- Operated by someone other than the pilot named in the declarations page.
- Operated for a use not indicated in the declarations (e.g., business and pleasure; commercial; airline; industrial).
- Operated in violation of Civil Air Regulations.

Because of the catastrophic nature of the exposure, large aircraft are commonly insured through specialized aviation pools. **Endorsements** available include loss of use, automatic increase in value, foaming of runway costs, search and rescue costs, engine mechanical breakdown and nonowned liability. **Other coverages applying to airports include:**

- **Air meet liability**, which is liability coverage for air meets or air shows.
- **Airport liability**, which is liability coverage for premises and operations, products and completed operations and contractual liability. This coverage is similar to the Commercial General Liability Policy.
- **Hangarkeepers liability**, which provides coverage for products liability and hangarkeepers liability. This coverage is similar to the Garagekeepers Auto Form.

NATIONAL FLOOD INSURANCE PROGRAM (NFIP)

Flood insurance is underwritten by the federal government and administered by the Federal Insurance Administration. Its purpose is twofold. **First,** to provide coverage against the catastrophic effects of flood, which is excluded from both personal and commercial policies; and **secondly** as an incentive to local communities to improve land use by minimizing future flood losses and improving the quality of the community. **Any licensed insurance producer may make application for flood coverage to the Federal Insurance Administration or to any "Write Your Own" carrier.** A "Write Your Own" carrier writes and services flood policies in their name with underwriting losses retained by the government. Insurers who participate are paid an expense allowance.

Eligibility - National flood insurance may only be written in participating communities that agree to adopt flood control measures. A **30 day waiting period** applies for new applications and endorsements to increase coverage. An exception to this 30-day rule applies in the event the applicant is purchasing coverage prior to and/or in conjunction with a loan. **In this case there is no waiting period. Deductibles** may not be reduced mid-term unless required in writing by the mortgagee. Participating communities must agree to implement land use provisions to minimize flooding. During this initial period, the community qualifies for the NFIP Emergency Program. After the participating community has complied with the NFIP requirements, coverage limits are revised upward as follows:

Building Coverage	**Emergency**	**Regular**
Single Family Dwelling	$ 35,000	$250,000
2 - 4 Family Dwelling	100,000	250,000
Other Residential	100,000	250,000
Nonresidential or Small Business	100,000	500,000
Contents Coverage	**Emergency**	**Regular**
Residential	$10,000	$100,000
Nonresidential or Small Business	100,000	500,000

Perils covered - The Flood Policy covers direct loss by flood at the described location, and **includes overflow of tidal waters, runoff, surface water, mudslides and mudflows**. Almost any building that is walled, roofed, **principally above ground** and fixed to a permanent site is eligible.

Property not covered - The Flood Policy excludes the following: accounts, bills, currency, deeds, evidence of debt, money, securities, bullion and manuscripts; lawns, trees, shrubs, plants and livestock; fences, retaining walls, outdoor swimming pools, wharves, piers and docks; motor vehicles; underground structures such as septic tanks and wells. **Please note that basement coverage is limited to mechanicals (furnace, water tank) with no coverage for personal property.**

Loss settlement - Loss settlement of the Flood Policy provides for settlement on an ACV basis with optional replacement cost on principal residences. A standard $500 deductible applies separately to both building and content losses in all non-special flood hazard areas (e.g., Regular Program). A $1,000 deductible applies in all other areas (e.g., Emergency Program).

PERSONAL ARTICLE FLOATERS

Personal Article Floaters (PAFs), provide coverage to personal property for all risks of direct physical loss except war risks, nuclear hazards, wear and tear, deterioration and inherent vice, and insects or vermin. PAFs are a form of inland marine insurance. Coverage may be scheduled under a Homeowner Policy or written as a separate policy. Losses are adjusted on an ACV basis. **Other variations include:**

- **Personal Effects Floater** provides coverage to the personal property of tourists. Property excluded includes money, securities, tickets or household furniture.
- **Personal Property Floater** provides coverage to unscheduled personal property on a special form basis (e.g., wedding presents floater).

DIFFERENCE IN CONDITIONS (DIC)

Difference In Conditions (DIC) insurance is frequently written in conjunction with property policies to supplement and fill gaps in coverage. It is usually **written on an "All Risk" basis without a coinsurance clause and excludes coverages that are provided on the underlying policy**. Examples of DIC coverages include earthquake, flood, mysterious disappearance and weather conditions. DIC coverage is secured through the surplus lines market.

RESIDUAL MARKETS

FAIR (Fair Access to Insurance Requirements) PLAN is a state supervised pool. Coverages written through the FAIR Plan include fire, extended coverages and vandalism and malicious mischief. Typically, nonbound applications are submitted to the FAIR Plan, who in turn inspects the property and advises the producer of eligibility. Recommendations for improvements to the dwelling are sometimes required to **make the property insurable as a condition to policy issuance**. The Fair Plan generally insures risks that are marginal and not acceptable in the standard market. The Fair Plan considers the following exposures to be uninsurable:

- Property vacant and open to trespass;
- Property in violation of law or public policy;
- Property in violation of building codes;
- Property subject to poor housekeeping; and
- Fire damaged property which has not been repaired.

The Fair Plan **cannot refuse coverage because of environmental hazards beyond the control of the insured**. For example, if an applicant's property is adjacent to a land fill. All companies who write property insurance in the state are required to contribute to the FAIR Plan based upon the amount of fire business written.

MINE SUBSIDENCE INSURANCE covers **loss to buildings** that result from mine subsidence *or* which is caused by movement of the ground surface resulting from a surface discharge due to a **sudden and unexpected** breakout of water directly emanating from an underground mine. Coverage is limited to $250,000 with loss settlement on a replacement cost basis. No coverage applies to personal property, driveways, sidewalks, fences, swimming pools, septic tanks or loss of use.

ALTERNATIVE FUNDING MECHANISMS

Alternative funding mechanisms refers to alternative methods of treating loss exposures. This includes self-insuring, pooling, captive formation, and joining either risk retention or risk purchasing groups. These alternative mechanisms are generally utilized whenever a business believes it can reduce its insurance costs and/or is unable to secure coverage because of the nature of the loss exposure. The following addresses these alternative funding mechanisms.

- **Risk Retention Groups** grew out of the need for affordable product liability insurance in the late 1970's. The Product Liability Risk Retention Act which was passed by Congress in 1981, and amended in 1986, permitted **similar type businesses** to join together as risk retention groups and **write all kinds of commercial liability coverage, except Workers Compensation**. Once the risk retention group is chartered as an insurance company in a state, it may then operate in other states without being admitted or obtaining a company license. Risk retention groups must be controlled by its members.

- **Risk Purchasing Groups**, which are also covered under the Product Liability Risk Retention Act, enable **similar type businesses** to form a purchasing group to buy insurance at a premium savings. Like risk retention groups, purchasing groups may **write all kinds of commercial liability coverage, except Workers Compensation**. Purchasing groups are covered by insurance companies which must be licensed in each state the purchasing group has members. Purchasing groups buy insurance coverage for its members, whereas, risk retention groups, which were discussed above, retain risk and function as insurance companies.

- **Self-insured** means that a business has chosen to retain its loss exposures rather than transferring them through the purchase of insurance. Under a self-insured plan, a business will pay its losses and its claim administration expenses from either a funded reserve account or by expensing the losses as they come due. A typically self-insured plan will also have an excess policy in effect which will cover losses which exceed a predetermined dollar value. For example, a business may self-insure losses up to $1,000,000 and structure the excess policy to pay losses in excess of that amount. Advantages of self-insurance includes: improved cash flow through the elimination of insurance premiums; improved loss experience through more effective loss control; and produced savings through reduced administrative costs. Disadvantages include the possibility of losses and/or administrative costs beyond projected estimates.

- **Pooling** is an arrangement where a number of primary insurers agree to place a certain type of business into the pool. Each insurer receives a prearranged percentage of premiums and each insurer agrees to pay a prearranged percentage of losses. Aviation and nuclear exposures are typically handled in a pooling type arrangement.

- **Captives** are a formalized method of self-insuring and can be formed as either a pure captive or an association captive. A **pure captive** insures risks of its parent and affiliated companies. An **association captive** insures risks of the member organization of the association and their affiliated companies.

PERSONAL UMBRELLA ILLUSTRATION

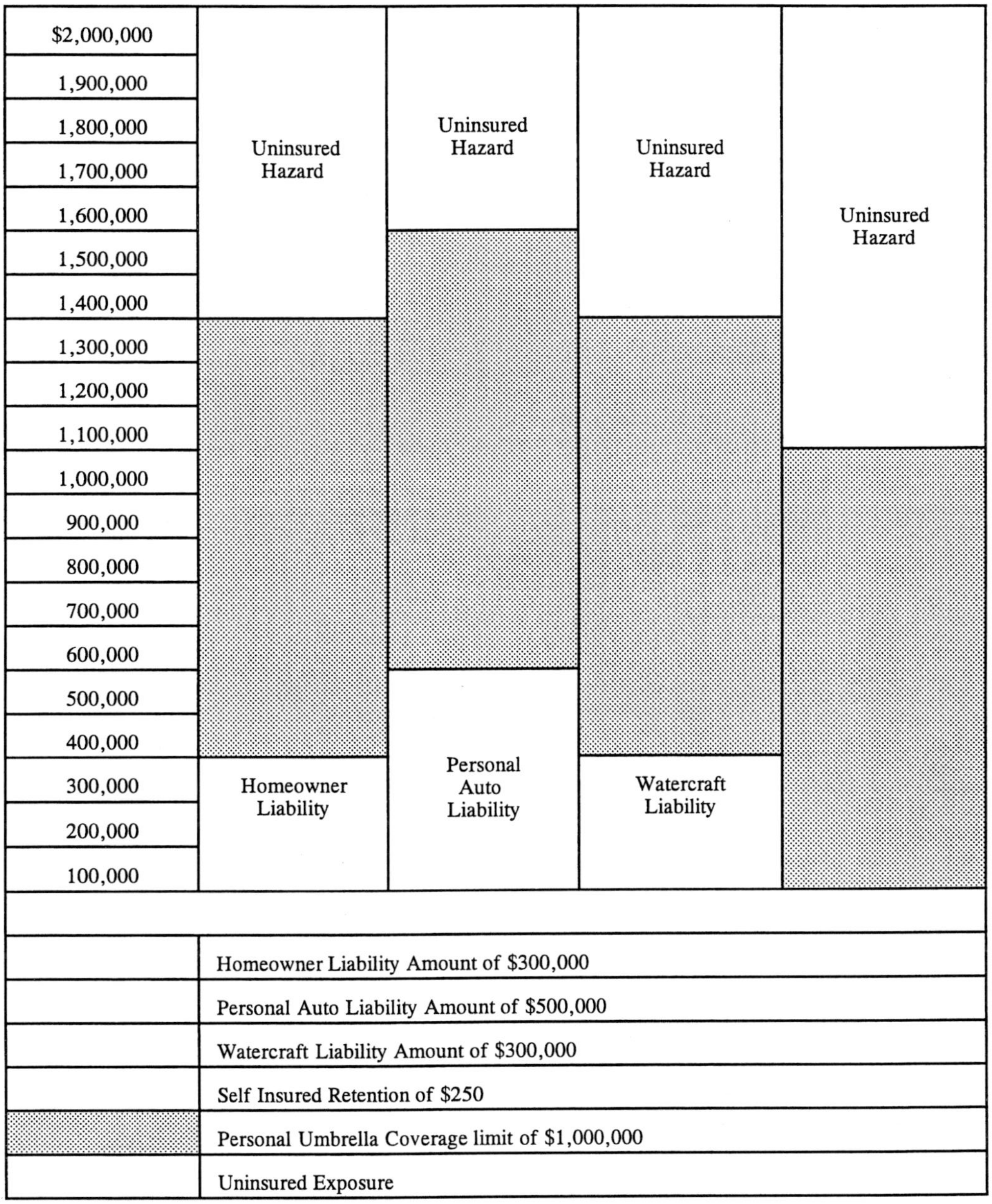

Personal Umbrella Policies are written to provide nonbusiness liability coverage in the following two areas:

First, as excess coverage over the required underlying liability limits of an individual's personal liability insurance. In the above example, if the insured maintains $300,000 of liability coverage under their Homeowners Policy, $500,000 under their Personal Auto Liability Policy, and $300,000 under their Watercraft Liability Policy, the $1,000,000 Personal Umbrella Policy will provide excess coverage beyond each individual underlying primary policy up to the umbrella's limit.

Second, as additional coverage in certain situations where the underlying coverage does not respond. For example, for slander, libel and invasion of privacy. In the event a law suit was brought against the insured, the Personal Umbrella Policy would provide a legal defense and pay an amount up to the umbrella's limit of liability minus a self insured retention limit, typically of $250.

KEY TERMS AND CONCEPTS

The following terms were introduced in this chapter. You should know each word and concept and be able to apply them in everyday usage. To improve retention, it is recommended that you write out each key term and concept in your own words.

Airport Liability
Aviation Insurance
Bid Bond
Boatowners Policy
Bonds
Captives
Cargo Coverage
Commercial Umbrella
Completion Bond
Comprehensive Personal Liability Insurance
Contract Bond
Court Bond
Difference in Conditions Policy
Difference In Conditions (DIC)
Directors and Officers Liability
Emergency v. Regular Flood Program
FAIR Plans
Fiduciary Liability
Floaters
Flood Insurance Policy
Flood Insurance Exclusions
Freight Coverage
General Average
Judicial Bond
Hangarkeepers Liability
Hull Coverage
License and Permit Bond
Legal Professionals
Liquor Liability
Medical Professionals
Miscellaneous Bonds
Ocean Marine
Particular Average
Personal Umbrella Policy
Performance Bond
Pooling
Premium Tax
Professional Liability Policies
Protection and Indemnity (P&I) Policy
Risk Purchasing Groups
Risk Retention Groups
Self-insured
Self Insured Retention (SIR)
Surety Bonds
Surplus Lines Insurance
Watercraft Insurance
Workers Compensation Bond

REVIEW QUESTIONS

Before attempting to answer the end chapter practice questions, you should ask yourself if you can answer the following questions. It is recommended that you write out each review question in your own words. This exercise will help you apply the key terms and concepts that you've learned to form relationships with different topics.

1. Identify and explain the 2 coverages provided under a Personal Umbrella Policy. (10-1)

2. Identify the required underlying coverages that an individual would be required to have before an Personal Umbrella Policy would be issued. (10-1 & 10-13)

3. Identify and explain 3 professional liability policies. (10-2)

4. Identify and explain 4 specialty liability policies. (10-2)

5. Identify 3 exposures that would cause a business to purchase an Employment Practices Liability Policy. (10-3)

6. What is Surplus Lines Insurance? (10-4)

7. What conditions must be met before business may be placed in the Surplus Lines market? (10-4)

8. What requirements are mandated before an individual can act as a Surplus Lines Agent? (10-4)

9. What requirements are mandated before an individual can place business with a Surplus Lines Agent? (10-4)

10. Identify and explain the 3 parties to a Surety Bond. (10-4)

11. What are the 3 primary areas of concern when underwriting a Bond? (10-5)

12. Identify and explain 3 types of Contract Bonds. (10-5)

13. Identify and explain 5 types of Judicial Bonds. (10-5)

14. Identify and explain 3 types of Miscellaneous Bonds. (10-5)

15. Identify and explain the 4 major coverages of an Ocean Marine Policy. (10-6)

16. Identify and explain the 4 terms upon which goods are purchased or sold. (10-6)

17. Identify 3 exposures that are covered under a Protection and Indemnity Policy. (10-7)

18. Identify and explain the 6 coverages provided under a Boatowners Policy. (10-8)

19. Give 5 examples of property that is covered under Coverage D - Miscellaneous Property of the Boatowners Policy. (10-8)

20. Give 5 examples of property that are not covered under Coverage D - Miscellaneous Property of the Boatowners Policy. (10-8)

21. Identify 5 property perils that are not covered under the Boatowners Policy. (10-8)

22. Identify the 2 major categories of aviation insurance. (10-9)

23. Identify and explain the 2 primary coverages of an Aircraft Insurance Policy. (10-9)

24. Identify 4 exclusions that apply to the operation activities under an Aircraft Policy. (10-9)

25. Identify 3 Endorsements that may be added to an Aircraft Policy. (10-9)

26. Identify the 2 ways an insurance produce may secure Flood Insurance. (10-10)

27. What is a "Write Your Own" carrier? (10-10)

28. Identify any time limitation(s) that apply to Flood Insurance. (10-10)

29. How does the Flood's Emergency Program differ from its Regular Program? (10-10)

30. Identify 4 occurrences that qualify as a flood under the Flood Policy. (10-10)

31. Give examples of 7 types of property that are not covered under the Flood Policy. (10-10)

32. How are losses settled under the Flood Policy? (10-10)

33. Identify 3 perils that are covered under a DIC Policy. (10-11)

34. What is the purpose of the FAIR Plan? (10-11)

35. Identify the 5 conditions that make a property ineligible for the FAIR Plan. (10-11)

36. Identify 2 Alternative Funding Mechanisms. (10-12)

37. How does a Risk Retention Group differ from a Risk Purchasing Group? (10-12)

38. What types of coverage may be insured in either a Risk Retention or Risk Purchasing Group? (10-12)

PRACTICE EXAM TEN

ON

OTHER INSURANCE COVERAGES AND OPTIONS

1. All of the following are true of Personal Umbrella Policies EXCEPT:

A) Provides excess liability coverage over underlying personal liability.
B) Provides errors and omissions coverage for a business.
C) May cover certain exposures not provided under primary layer.
D) May require the payment of a self insured retention. Ref. 10-1

2. Which of the following statements would be true if an insured failed to maintain the underlying liability limits as required by a Personal Umbrella Policy?

A) The insured would have to pay the self insured retention.
B) The insured would be responsible for the difference between the underlying amount and the amount required by the umbrella.
C) It would have no effect upon the umbrella coverage.
D) All coverages would be voided. Ref. 10-1

3. Which of the following is NOT covered under an Employment Practices Liability Policy:

A) Sexual harassment between employees.
B) Failure for hire a new applicant.
C) Failure to repurchase stock owned by shareholders.
D) Failure to promote a current employee. Ref. 10-3

4. All of the following would be covered property under the Boatowners Policy EXCEPT:

A) Trailer.
B) Hull.
C) Motors.
D) Water skis. Ref. 10-8

5. All of the following are true of Personal Articles Floaters EXCEPT:

A) Coverage may be provided under a Homeowner Policy.
B) Coverage is provided for direct physical loss unless specifically excluded.
C) Coverage may be provided under a separate Personal Articles Policy.
D) Provides coverage for valued articles regardless of the ACV. Ref. 10-11

6. **The National Flood Insurance Program is administered under what government department?**

A) Flood Insurance Administration.
B) Department of Education.
C) Department of Health, Education and Welfare.
D) Department of Insurance. Ref. 10-10

7. **All of the following are true of Flood Insurance EXCEPT:**

A) Maximum limits are available to communities immediately.
B) Participating communities must agree to implement certain land uses.
C) Flood Insurance provides coverage that is excluded from personal and commercial policies.
D) Implementation of the flood program promotes socio-economic goals. Ref. 10-10

8. **What is the waiting period for Flood Insurance?**

A) There is never a waiting period.
B) 3 days.
C) 30 days if not in conjunction with a loan.
D) 90 days. Ref. 10-10

9. **All of the following are excluded property under a Flood Insurance Policy EXCEPT:**

A) Accounts, bills and currency.
B) Lawns, trees and shrubs.
C) Educational books.
D) Motor vehicles. Ref. 10-10

10. **The standard deductible under the Flood Policy is:**

A) $100.
B) $250.
C) $500.
D) $750. Ref. 10-10

11. **Flood insurance is available through:**

A) An insurance producer.
B) A consultant.
C) A risk manager.
D) Only directly through the Flood Insurance Administration. Ref. 10-10

12. **In a Personal Umbrella, the amount paid by the insured for certain losses not covered under the primary coverage is called:**

A) The deductible.
B) Sole insurable retention.
C) Security insured retention.
D) Self insured retention. Ref. 10-1

13. All of the following are reasons for the use of alternative funding mechanisms EXCEPT:

A) Ability to secure coverage in standard markets.
B) Opportunity to save on insurance expenses.
C) Opportunity to secure difficult to place risks.
D) Inability to place coverage with standard insurance carriers. Ref. 10-12

14. All of the following are true of Surplus Lines Insurance EXCEPT:

A) To act as a surplus lines agent, an individual must possess a producer license and a surplus lines license.
B) Before coverage can be placed with a surplus lines company, a diligent effort must be made to place the business with at least three admitted companies.
C) Business written in a surplus lines company is subject to a 3% state premium tax.
D) Standard coverages are typically written in the surplus lines market. Ref. 10-4

15. Which of the following best defines Surplus Lines?

A) Lines of business that a producer is not licensed to write.
B) Business that cannot be placed with a producer's primary company.
C) Business that is in excess of a producer's binding authority.
D) Coverages that are not available or cannot be procured from authorized insurers within a state. Ref. 10-4

16. All of the following are true of Difference in Conditions (DIC) Policy EXCEPT:

A) DIC insurance is produced by admitted carriers and local producers.
B) DIC insurance may be used to fill gaps in coverage.
C) It typically excludes coverage provided under other property policies.
D) It typically provides coverage for earthquake and may act as excess over limited Flood Insurance. Ref. 10-11

17. The maximum available limit for a single family home under the National Flood Program is:

A) $100,000.
B) $150,000.
C) $250,000.
D) $500,000. Ref. 10-10

18. Under the National Flood Policy, deductibles apply:

A) Only to the building portion of the loss.
B) Only to the contents portion of the loss.
C) Only to the residential type losses.
D) Separately to both building and contents portions of the loss. Ref. 10-10

19. The maximum available limit for residential contents coverage under the National Flood Program is:

A) $ 35,000.
B) $ 50,000.
C) $ 75,000.
D) $100,000. Ref. 10-10

20. Under a Personal Umbrella Policy, the self insured retention:

A) Only applies to excess auto liability loss.
B) Only applies to excess homeowner premises liability losses.
C) Applies to certain losses which are not covered under the underlying primary policies.
D) Only applies to excess watercraft losses. Ref. 10-1

21. All of the following are true of Comprehensive Personal Liability (CPL) Policies EXCEPT:

A) It is a common method to insure personal liability exposures.
B) Its coverages are almost identical to Homeowner Policy's liability.
C) Its coverages are almost identical to personal liability coverages of the Dwelling Policy.
D) It may be issued in amounts as low as $25,000. Ref. 10-1

22. All of the following are covered perils under the National Flood Policy EXCEPT:

A) The overflow of tidal waters.
B) The rapid accumulation of runoff of surface water.
C) Mudslides caused by flooding.
D) Water spray. Ref. 10-10

23. Which of the following risks would be eligible for the Fair Plan:

A) Property vacant and open to trespass.
B) Property in violation of building codes.
C) Fire damaged property which is not repaired.
D) Property with potential environmental hazards. Ref. 10-11

24. An individual is involved in an auto accident after consuming alcohol at a local bar. Under these circumstances, the bar's:

A) Commercial Auto Policy will respond.
B) Liquor Liability Policy will respond.
C) Commercial General Liability Policy will respond.
D) Personal Umbrella Policy will respond. Ref. 10-3

25. Under the "Write Your Own" Flood Program:

A) Producers must make application through a local carrier.
B) Participating insurers have no underwriting exposure.
C) Producers are paid an expense allowance.
D) Limits are different under the "Write Your Own" Program. Ref. 10-10

26. All of the following are true of Professional Liability Policies EXCEPT:

A) It is also referred to as malpractice insurance or errors and omissions insurance.
B) It excludes coverage for fraud, dishonesty or criminal acts.
C) Similar coverage is also provided under the Commercial Liability Coverage Part.
D) A Professional Liability Policy would protect the insured against legal liability resulting from negligence, errors and omissions and other aspects of rendering, or failing to render, professional services. Ref. 10-2

27. All of the following are true of Professional Liability Policies EXCEPT:

A) It provides coverage for failure of an insured to act in a competent manner.
B) Examples of individuals who need professional liability coverage include insurance agents, lawyers, accountants, directors/officers of corporations, architects and engineers.
C) The need for this coverage has decreased in recent years.
D) Examples in the medical field who need professional liability coverage include hospitals, physicians, nurses, opticians, chiropractors and veterinarians. Ref 10-2

28. All of the following are true of Commercial Umbrella Policies EXCEPT:

A) It provides excess coverage over underlying liability coverage.
B) A self insured retention is typically higher than a Personal Umbrella.
C) It provides coverage only at the insured location as indicated in the declarations.
D) It provides excess coverage for business related exposures. Ref. 10-2

29. All of the following are true of Ocean Marine Coverage EXCEPT:

A) It provides coverage for ocean going vessels.
B) The underwriting of ocean marine is relatively new.
C) Hull and cargo coverage can be written on either a named peril or all risk basis.
D) The four major coverages of an ocean marine policy are hull coverage, cargo coverage, freight insurance and protection and indemnity (P&I). Ref. 10-6

30. Which of the following Ocean Marine Coverages provides marine legal liability insurance?

A) Hull coverage.
B) Cargo coverage.
C) Freight insurance.
D) Protection and indemnity (P&I). Ref. 10-6 & 10-7

31. **An attorney, who performs work out his home, makes a mistake in the preparation of a client's will and is subsequently sued because of this decision. Which of the following policies would protect against this exposure?**

A) L & O.
B) D & O.
C) Personal Liability.
D) Lawyers Professional Liability. Ref. 10-2

32. **All of the following are true of Aviation Insurance EXCEPT:**

A) Policies can be favorably compared in coverages to Automobile Policies.
B) Aviation insurance is not a specialized field.
C) The most common aviation coverages are bodily injury liability, property damage liability, medical payments and hull coverage.
D) Aviation liability coverage is typically written by an aviation pool. Ref. 10-9

33. **The "Penalty" of a bond is:**

A) The self insured retention.
B) The deductible.
C) The premium tax required.
D) Its limit of coverage. Ref. 10-4

34. **All of the following are true of Risk Retention Groups EXCEPT:**

A) Risk Retention Groups grew out of the need for affordable product liability insurance.
B) Similar type businesses may join together as a Risk Retention Group.
C) All kinds of commercial liability coverage, except Workers Compensation may be insured by the group.
D) The group buys insurance coverage for its members at a premium savings.
Ref. 10-12

35. **The type of Surety Bond which guarantees the lender that a contractor will use borrowed funds to complete the project free of liens is a:**

A) Bid Bond.
B) Completion Bond.
C) Fiduciary Bond.
D) Lien Bond. Ref. 10-4

36. **A person who is responsible for the administration of a decedent's estate would have a need for a:**

A) Fiduciary Bond.
B) Completion Bond.
C) Decedent's Bond.
D) Attachment Bond. Ref. 10-3

37. All of the following are true of a Surety Bond EXCEPT:

A) Surety Bonds guarantee that specific obligations will be fulfilled.
B) Surety Bonds are typically made up of two parties.
C) Surety Bonds contrast insurance in that losses are not expected.
D) Surety Bonds are typically made up of three parties. Ref. 10-4

38. All of the following are parties to a Surety Bond EXCEPT:

A) Insured.
B) Principal.
C) Obligee.
D) Surety. Ref. 10-4

39. Mr. Smith recently voted on a corporate merger and was subsequently sued for the decision. Which of the following policies would protect against this exposure?

A) Personal Umbrella Policy.
B) E & O Policy.
C) D & O Policy.
D) Commercial Umbrella Policy. Ref. 10-3

40. All of the following are true of the FAIR Plan EXCEPT:

A) Typically distressed property is written in the FAIR Plan.
B) FAIR Plans are state supervised insurance pools.
C) The property must be located in a high crime area.
D) The applicant must first attempt to secure coverage in the standard market. Ref 10-11

41. The ABC Corporation purchased a Commercial Umbrella Policy in the amount of $10,000,000. ABC is required to maintain an underlying limit of $1,000,000 on its primary liability coverages. ABC's Self Insured Retention is $10,000. A covered loss occurs in the amount of $1,000,000. The Commercial Umbrella will pay:

A) $ 0.
B) $ 1,000,000.
C) $10,000,000.
D) $11,000,000. Ref. 10-2 & 10-13

42. Using the same facts as in question above, what amount would the Commercial Umbrella Policy pay for a covered loss of $3,000,000:

A) $1,000,000.
B) $2,000,000.
C) $3,000,000.
D) $0. Ref. 10-2 & 10-13

43. The term Free On Board (FOB) means:

A) The buyer is responsible for goods until the time the goods enter the custody of the ocean carrier.
B) The seller is responsible for loss or damage until the time the goods have been delivered along side the vessel.
C) The seller is responsible for goods until the time the goods enter the custody of the ocean carrier.
D) The seller is responsible for loss or damage until the time the goods have been placed on board the vessel. Ref. 10-6

44. All of the following are characteristics of Ocean Marine Hull Coverage EXCEPT:

A) Coverage is provided for fixtures permanently attached to the ship.
B) Coverage includes collision liability.
C) Coverage is provided for damage to piers, wharves, other structures or loss of life.
D) Coverage may be written on a single vessel basis or on a fleet basis. Ref. 10-6

45. Which of the following watercraft would generally be covered under a Boatowners Policy?

A) A canoe.
B) A row boat powered by a 25 horsepower motor.
C) A wind ski.
D) A boat with an inboard-outdrive motor. Ref. 10-8

46. The primary purpose of a Surety Bond is to:

A) Eliminate loss possibilities.
B) Increase the contractor's credit line.
C) Make sure obligations are fulfilled.
D) Pay employer losses. Ref. 10-4

47. Surplus lines agents place coverage with:

A) Admitted companies only.
B) Non-admitted companies.
C) Domestic companies only.
D) Foreign companies. Ref. 10-4

ANSWER KEY

1-B	2-B	3-C	4-D	5-D	6-A	7-A	8-C	9-C	10-C
11-A	12-D	13-A	14-D	15-D	16-A	17-C	18-D	19-D	20-C
21-A	22-D	23-D	24-B	25-B	26-C	27-C	28-C	29-B	30-D
31-D	32-B	33-D	34-D	35-B	36-A	37-B	38-A	39-C	40-C
41-A	42-B	43-D	44-C	45-D	46-C	47-B			

SOME FINAL THOUGHTS

By this point in the study process, you should be completing your preparation for the state licensing exam, the content of which is fully explained throughout this manual. One can predict fairly easy your success. It requires some objective self analysis upon your part. Don't be fooled into believing that you will pass this exam because of prior experience at an agency or company or because you are taking a review course. Exam success is predicated upon one basic fact, your ability to master the examination outline. To assist in your preparation, I have prepared the following check list for you to review. Complete it objectively by asking yourself have I . . .

Objective	**Answer**	
Read the introduction pages located in the front of this manual	Yes	No
Reviewed the material prior to answering the chapter practice exams	Yes	No
Wrote out the key terms and review questions at the end of each chapter	Yes	No
Reviewed the glossary of terms located in the back of the book	Yes	No
Answered each chapter exam question.	Yes	No
Reviewed each incorrect chapter exam question	Yes	No
Taken the practice final exam under exam like conditions.	Yes	No
Reviewed each incorrect final exam question	Yes	No
Reviewed the state examination outline	Yes	No
Scored at least 85% on my practice exams	Yes	No
Reviewed the test taking strategies located in the front of the book	Yes	No
Reviewed the state licensing information bulletin	Yes	No
Used EXAM MASTER software in exam preparation	Yes	No

If you have answered yes to all of the above questions, you are ready to take your state examination.

Good luck and best of success!

George E. Krauss, CPCU, CLU

P.S. Practice exam end chapter and final exam scores will increase each time you retake an exam. Do not interpret this exam scoring improvement as an absolute indication that you know this material. The first time you take a practice exam is the best indicator of your mastery of this material.

SPECIAL NOTE

Questions which appear on your state licensing exam may indicate a specific ISO policy program (i.e., Homeowners 2000 Policy ('01 Edition), Dwelling 2002 Policy, Businessowners 2002 Policy or Personal Auto '05 Policy). ***Do not be confused by the inclusion of these numbers in your questions.*** They are stated in the exam questions to identify the specified ISO policy program which you are being tested on.

This manual addresses these ISO policy programs.

NOTES

Concealment, fraud. This entire policy shall be void if, whether before or after a loss, the insured has wilfully concealed or misrepresented any material fact or circumstance concerning this insurance or the subject thereof, or the interest of the insured therein, or in case of any fraud or false swearing by the insured relating thereto.

Uninsurable and excepted property. This policy shall not cover accounts, bills, currency, deeds, evidences of debt, money or securities; nor, unless specifically named hereon in writing, bullion or manuscripts.

Perils not included. This Company shall not be liable for loss by fire or other perils insured against in this policy caused, directly or indirectly, by: (a) enemy attack by armed forces, including action taken by military, naval or air forces in resisting an actual or an immediately impending enemy attack; (b) invasion: (c) insurrection; (d) rebellion; (e) revolution; (f) civil war; (g) usurped power; (h) order of any civil authority except acts of destruction at the time of and for the purpose of preventing the spread of fire, provided that such fire did not originate from any of the perils excluded by this policy; (i) neglect of the insured to use all reasonable means to save and preserve the property at and after a loss, or when the property is endangered by fire in neighboring premises; (j) nor shall this Company be liable for loss by theft.

Other Insurance. Other insurance may be prohibited or the amount of insurance may be limited by endorsement attached hereto.

Conditions suspending or restricting insurance. Unless otherwise provided in writing added hereto this Company shall not be liable for loss occurring
(a) while the hazard is increased by any means within the control or knowledge of the insured; or
(b) while a described building, whether intended for occupancy by owner or tenant, is vacant or unoccupied beyond a period of sixty consecutive days; or
(c) as a result of explosion or riot, unless fire ensue, and in that event for loss by fire only.

Other perils or subjects. Any other peril to be insured against or subject of insurance to be covered in this policy shall be by endorsement in writing hereon or added hereto.

Added provisions. The extent of the application of insurance under this policy and of the contribution to be made by this Company in case of loss, and any other provision or agreement not inconsistent with the provisions of this policy, may be provided for in writing added hereto, but no provision may be waived except such as by the terms of this policy is subject to change.

Waiver provisions. No permission affecting this insurance shall exist, or waiver of any provision be valid, unless granted herein or expressed in writing added hereto. No provision, stipulation or forfeiture shall be held to be waived by any requirement or proceeding on the part of this Company relating to appraisal or to any examination provided for herein.

Cancellation of policy. This policy shall be cancelled at any time at the request of the insured, in which case this Company shall, upon demand and surrender of this policy, refund the excess of paid premium above the customary short rates for the expired time. This policy may be cancelled at any time by this Company by giving to the insured a five days' written notice of cancellation with or without tender of the excess of paid premium above the pro rata premium for the expired time, which excess, if not tendered, shall be refunded on demand. Notice of cancellation shall state that said excess premium (if not tendered) will be refunded on demand.

Mortgagee interests and obligations. If loss hereunder is made payable, in whole or in part, to a designated mortgagee not named herein as the insured, such interest in this policy may be cancelled by giving to such mortgagee a ten days' written notice of cancellation.
If the insured fails to render proof of loss such mortgagee, upon notice, shall render proof of loss in the form herein specified within sixty (60) days thereafter and shall be subject to the provisions hereof relating to appraisal and time of payment and of bringing suit. If this Company shall claim that no liability existed as to the mortgagor or owner, it shall, to the extent of payment of loss to the mortgagee, be subrogated to all the mortgagee's rights of recovery, but without impairing mortgagee's right to sue; or it may pay off the mortgage debt and require an assignment thereof and of the mortgage. Other provisions relating to the interests and obligations of such mortagee may be added hereto by agreement in writing.

Pro rata liability. This Company shall not be liable for a greater proportion of any loss than the amount hereby insured shall bear to the whole insurance covering the property against the peril involved, whether collectible or not.

Requirements in case loss occurs. The insured shall give immediate written notice to the Company of any loss, protect the property from further damage, forthwith separate the damaged and undamaged personal property, put it in the best possible order, furnish a complete inventory of the destroyed, damaged and undamaged property, showing in detail quantities, costs, actual cash value and amount of loss claimed; **and within sixty days after the loss, unless such time is extended in writing by this Company, the insured shall render to this Company a proof of loss,** signed and sworn to by the insured, stating the knowledge and belief of the insured as to the following: the time and origin of the loss, the interest of the insured and of all others in the property, the actual cash value of each item thereof and the amount of loss thereto, all encumbrances thereon, all other contracts of insurance, whether valid or not, covering any of said property, any changes in the title, use, occupation, location, possession or exposures of said property since the issuing of this policy, by whom and for what purpose any building herein described and the several parts thereof were occupied at the time of loss and whether or not it then stood on leased ground, and shall furnish a copy of all the descriptions and schedules in all policies and, if required, verified plans and specifications of any building, fixtures or machinery destroyed or damaged. The insured, as often as may be reasonably required, shall exhibit to any person designated by this Company all that remains of any property herein described, and submit to examinations under oath by any person named by this Company, and subscribe the same; and, as often as may be reasonably required, shall produce for examination all books of account, bills, invoices and other vouchers, or certified copies thereof if originals be lost, at such reasonable time and place as may be designated by this Company or its representative, and shall permit extracts and copies thereof to be made.

Appraisal. In case the insured and this Company shall fail to agree as to the actual cash value or the amount of loss, then, on the written demand of either, each shall select a competent and disinterested appraiser and notify the other of the appraiser selected within twenty days of such demand. The appraisers shall first select a competent and disinterested umpire; and failing for fifteen days to agree upon such umpire, then, on request of the insured or this Company, such umpire shall be selected by a judge of a court of record in the state in which the property covered is located. The appraisers shall then appraise the loss, stating separately actual cash value and loss to each item; and, failing to agree, shall submit their differences, only, to the umpire. An award in writing, so itemized, of any two when filed with this Company shall determine the amount of actual cash value and loss. Each appraiser shall be paid by the party selecting him and the expenses of appraisal and umpire shall be paid by the parties equally.

Company's options. It shall be optional with this Company to take all, or any part, of the property at the agreed or appraised value, and also to repair, rebuild or replace the property destroyed or damaged with other of like kind and quality within a reasonable time, on giving notice of its intention so to do within thirty days after the receipt of the proof of loss herein required.

Abandonment. There can be no abandonment to this Company of any property.

When loss payable. The amount of loss for which this Company may be liable shall be payable sixty days after proof of loss, as herein provided, is received by this Company and ascertainment of the loss is made either by agreement between the insured and this Company expressed in writing or by the filing with this Company of an award as herein provided.

Suit. No suit or action on this policy for the recovery of any claim shall be sustainable in any court of law or equity unless all the requirements of this policy shall have been complied with, and unless commenced within twelve months next after inception of the loss.

Subrogation. This Company may require from the insured an assignment of all right of recovery against any party for loss to the extent that payment therefor is made by this Company.

STATE EXCEPTIONS

FLORIDA AND WISCONSIN: The words "five days'" in line 62 are changed to "ten days'."
IDAHO: The words "five days'" in line 62 are changed to "twenty days'."
KANSAS: The words "demand and" in line 58 and "on demand" in lines 65 and 67 are deleted. The words "twelve months" in line 161 are changed to "sixty months".
MAINE: The words "five days'" in line 62 are changed to "ten days'." The words "twelve months" in line 161 are changed to "two years".
NEW YORK: The words "twelve months" in line 161 are changed to "two years".
NORTH CAROLINA: The words "twelve months" in line 161 are changed to "three years".
NORTH DAKOTA: The words "twelve months" in line 161 are changed to "thirty-six months".
OREGON: The word "Noon" in the In Consideration provision is changed to "12:01 A.M."
WYOMING: The words "sixty days" in line 151 are changed to "forty-five days". The words "twelve months" in line 161 are changed to "four years".

HOMEOWNERS 3 – SPECIAL FORM

AGREEMENT

We will provide the insurance described in this policy in return for the premium and compliance with all applicable provisions of this policy.

DEFINITIONS

A. In this policy, "you" and "your" refer to the "named insured" shown in the Declarations and the spouse if a resident of the same household. "We", "us" and "our" refer to the Company providing this insurance.

B. In addition, certain words and phrases are defined as follows:

1. "Aircraft Liability", "Hovercraft Liability", "Motor Vehicle Liability" and "Watercraft Liability", subject to the provisions in **b.** below, mean the following:

a. Liability for "bodily injury" or "property damage" arising out of the:

(1) Ownership of such vehicle or craft by an "insured";

(2) Maintenance, occupancy, operation, use, loading or unloading of such vehicle or craft by any person;

(3) Entrustment of such vehicle or craft by an "insured" to any person;

(4) Failure to supervise or negligent supervision of any person involving such vehicle or craft by an "insured"; or

(5) Vicarious liability, whether or not imposed by law, for the actions of a child or minor involving such vehicle or craft.

b. For the purpose of this definition:

(1) Aircraft means any contrivance used or designed for flight except model or hobby aircraft not used or designed to carry people or cargo;

(2) Hovercraft means a self-propelled motorized ground effect vehicle and includes, but is not limited to, flarecraft and air cushion vehicles;

(3) Watercraft means a craft principally designed to be propelled on or in water by wind, engine power or electric motor; and

(4) Motor vehicle means a "motor vehicle" as defined in **7.** below.

2. "Bodily injury" means bodily harm, sickness or disease, including required care, loss of services and death that results.

3. "Business" means:

a. A trade, profession or occupation engaged in on a full-time, part-time or occasional basis; or

b. Any other activity engaged in for money or other compensation, except the following:

(1) One or more activities, not described in **(2)** through **(4)** below, for which no "insured" receives more than $2,000 in total compensation for the 12 months before the beginning of the policy period;

(2) Volunteer activities for which no money is received other than payment for expenses incurred to perform the activity;

(3) Providing home day care services for which no compensation is received, other than the mutual exchange of such services; or

(4) The rendering of home day care services to a relative of an "insured".

4. "Employee" means an employee of an "insured", or an employee leased to an "insured" by a labor leasing firm under an agreement between an "insured" and the labor leasing firm, whose duties are other than those performed by a "residence employee".

5. "Insured" means:

a. You and residents of your household who are:

(1) Your relatives; or

(2) Other persons under the age of 21 and in the care of any person named above;

b. A student enrolled in school full time, as defined by the school, who was a resident of your household before moving out to attend school, provided the student is under the age of:

(1) 24 and your relative; or

(2) 21 and in your care or the care of a person described in **a.(1)** above; or

c. Under Section **II:**

(1) With respect to animals or watercraft to which this policy applies, any person or organization legally responsible for these animals or watercraft which are owned by you or any person included in **a.** or **b.** above. "Insured" does not mean a person or organization using or having custody of these animals or watercraft in the course of any "business" or without consent of the owner; or

(2) With respect to a "motor vehicle" to which this policy applies:

(a) Persons while engaged in your employ or that of any person included in **a.** or **b.** above; or

(b) Other persons using the vehicle on an "insured location" with your consent.

Under both Sections **I** and **II,** when the word an immediately precedes the word "insured", the words an "insured" together mean one or more "insureds".

6. "Insured location" means:

a. The "residence premises";

b. The part of other premises, other structures and grounds used by you as a residence; and

(1) Which is shown in the Declarations; or

(2) Which is acquired by you during the policy period for your use as a residence;

c. Any premises used by you in connection with a premises described in **a.** and **b.** above;

d. Any part of a premises:

(1) Not owned by an "insured"; and

(2) Where an "insured" is temporarily residing;

e. Vacant land, other than farm land, owned by or rented to an "insured";

f. Land owned by or rented to an "insured" on which a one, two, three or four family dwelling is being built as a residence for an "insured";

g. Individual or family cemetery plots or burial vaults of an "insured"; or

h. Any part of a premises occasionally rented to an "insured" for other than "business" use.

7. "Motor vehicle" means:

a. A self-propelled land or amphibious vehicle; or

b. Any trailer or semitrailer which is being carried on, towed by or hitched for towing by a vehicle described in **a.** above.

8. "Occurrence" means an accident, including continuous or repeated exposure to substantially the same general harmful conditions, which results, during the policy period, in:

a. "Bodily injury"; or

b. "Property damage".

9. "Property damage" means physical injury to, destruction of, or loss of use of tangible property.

10. "Residence employee" means:

a. An employee of an "insured", or an employee leased to an "insured" by a labor leasing firm, under an agreement between an "insured" and the labor leasing firm, whose duties are related to the maintenance or use of the "residence premises", including household or domestic services; or

b. One who performs similar duties elsewhere not related to the "business" of an "insured".

A "residence employee" does not include a temporary employee who is furnished to an "insured" to substitute for a permanent "residence employee" on leave or to meet seasonal or short-term workload conditions.

11. "Residence premises" means:

a. The one family dwelling where you reside;

b. The two, three or four family dwelling where you reside in at least one of the family units; or

c. That part of any other building where you reside;

and which is shown as the "residence premises" in the Declarations.

"Residence premises" also includes other structures and grounds at that location.

DEDUCTIBLE

Unless otherwise noted in this policy, the following deductible provision applies:

Subject to the policy limits that apply, we will pay only that part of the total of all loss payable under Section **I** that exceeds the deductible amount shown in the Declarations.

SECTION I – PROPERTY COVERAGES

A. Coverage A – Dwelling

1. We cover:
   a. The dwelling on the "residence premises" shown in the Declarations, including structures attached to the dwelling; and
   b. Materials and supplies located on or next to the "residence premises" used to construct, alter or repair the dwelling or other structures on the "residence premises".
2. We do not cover land, including land on which the dwelling is located.

B. Coverage B – Other Structures

1. We cover other structures on the "residence premises" set apart from the dwelling by clear space. This includes structures connected to the dwelling by only a fence, utility line, or similar connection.
2. We do not cover:
   a. Land, including land on which the other structures are located;
   b. Other structures rented or held for rental to any person not a tenant of the dwelling, unless used solely as a private garage;
   c. Other structures from which any "business" is conducted; or
   d. Other structures used to store "business" property. However, we do cover a structure that contains "business" property solely owned by an "insured" or a tenant of the dwelling provided that "business" property does not include gaseous or liquid fuel, other than fuel in a permanently installed fuel tank of a vehicle or craft parked or stored in the structure.
3. The limit of liability for this coverage will not be more than 10% of the limit of liability that applies to Coverage **A.** Use of this coverage does not reduce the Coverage **A** limit of liability.

C. Coverage C – Personal Property

1. **Covered Property**

   We cover personal property owned or used by an "insured" while it is anywhere in the world. After a loss and at your request, we will cover personal property owned by:
   a. Others while the property is on the part of the "residence premises" occupied by an "insured"; or
   b. A guest or a "residence employee", while the property is in any residence occupied by an "insured".
2. **Limit For Property At Other Residences**

   Our limit of liability for personal property usually located at an "insured's" residence, other than the "residence premises", is 10% of the limit of liability for Coverage **C,** or $1,000, whichever is greater. However, this limitation does not apply to personal property:
   a. Moved from the "residence premises" because it is being repaired, renovated or rebuilt and is not fit to live in or store property in; or
   b. In a newly acquired principal residence for 30 days from the time you begin to move the property there.
3. **Special Limits Of Liability**

   The special limit for each category shown below is the total limit for each loss for all property in that category. These special limits do not increase the Coverage **C** limit of liability.
   a. $200 on money, bank notes, bullion, gold other than goldware, silver other than silverware, platinum other than platinumware, coins, medals, scrip, stored value cards and smart cards.
   b. $1,500 on securities, accounts, deeds, evidences of debt, letters of credit, notes other than bank notes, manuscripts, personal records, passports, tickets and stamps. This dollar limit applies to these categories regardless of the medium (such as paper or computer software) on which the material exists.

      This limit includes the cost to research, replace or restore the information from the lost or damaged material.

c. $1,500 on watercraft of all types, including their trailers, furnishings, equipment and outboard engines or motors.

d. $1,500 on trailers or semitrailers not used with watercraft of all types.

e. $1,500 for loss by theft of jewelry, watches, furs, precious and semiprecious stones.

f. $2,500 for loss by theft of firearms and related equipment.

g. $2,500 for loss by theft of silverware, silver-plated ware, goldware, gold-plated ware, platinumware, platinum-plated ware and pewterware. This includes flatware, hollow-ware, tea sets, trays and trophies made of or including silver, gold or pewter.

h. $2,500 on property, on the "residence premises", used primarily for "business" purposes.

i. $500 on property, away from the "residence premises", used primarily for "business" purposes. However, this limit does not apply to loss to electronic apparatus and other property described in Categories **j.** and **k.** below.

j. $1,500 on electronic apparatus and accessories, while in or upon a "motor vehicle", but only if the apparatus is equipped to be operated by power from the "motor vehicle's" electrical system while still capable of being operated by other power sources.

Accessories include antennas, tapes, wires, records, discs or other media that can be used with any apparatus described in this Category **j.**

k. $1,500 on electronic apparatus and accessories used primarily for "business" while away from the "residence premises" and not in or upon a "motor vehicle". The apparatus must be equipped to be operated by power from the "motor vehicle's" electrical system while still capable of being operated by other power sources.

Accessories include antennas, tapes, wires, records, discs or other media that can be used with any apparatus described in this Category **k.**

4. Property Not Covered

We do not cover:

a. Articles separately described and specifically insured, regardless of the limit for which they are insured, in this or other insurance;

b. Animals, birds or fish;

c. "Motor vehicles".

(1) This includes:

(a) Their accessories, equipment and parts; or

(b) Electronic apparatus and accessories designed to be operated solely by power from the electrical system of the "motor vehicle". Accessories include antennas, tapes, wires, records, discs or other media that can be used with any apparatus described above.

The exclusion of property described in **(a)** and **(b)** above applies only while such property is in or upon the "motor vehicle".

(2) We do cover "motor vehicles" not required to be registered for use on public roads or property which are:

(a) Used solely to service an "insured's" residence; or

(b) Designed to assist the handicapped;

d. Aircraft meaning any contrivance used or designed for flight including any parts whether or not attached to the aircraft.

We do cover model or hobby aircraft not used or designed to carry people or cargo;

e. Hovercraft and parts. Hovercraft means a self-propelled motorized ground effect vehicle and includes, but is not limited to, flarecraft and air cushion vehicles;

f. Property of roomers, boarders and other tenants, except property of roomers and boarders related to an "insured";

g. Property in an apartment regularly rented or held for rental to others by an "insured", except as provided in **E.10.** Landlord's Furnishings under Section **I** – Property Coverages;

h. Property rented or held for rental to others off the "residence premises";

i. "Business" data, including such data stored in:

(1) Books of account, drawings or other paper records; or

(2) Computers and related equipment.

We do cover the cost of blank recording or storage media, and of prerecorded computer programs available on the retail market;

j. Credit cards, electronic fund transfer cards or access devices used solely for deposit, withdrawal or transfer of funds except as provided in **E.6.** Credit Card, Electronic Fund Transfer Card Or Access Device, Forgery And Counterfeit Money under Section **I** – Property Coverages; or

k. Water or steam.

D. Coverage D – Loss Of Use

The limit of liability for Coverage **D** is the total limit for the coverages in **1.** Additional Living Expense, **2.** Fair Rental Value and **3.** Civil Authority Prohibits Use below.

1. Additional Living Expense

If a loss covered under Section **I** makes that part of the "residence premises" where you reside not fit to live in, we cover any necessary increase in living expenses incurred by you so that your household can maintain its normal standard of living.

Payment will be for the shortest time required to repair or replace the damage or, if you permanently relocate, the shortest time required for your household to settle elsewhere.

2. Fair Rental Value

If a loss covered under Section **I** makes that part of the "residence premises" rented to others or held for rental by you not fit to live in, we cover the fair rental value of such premises less any expenses that do not continue while it is not fit to live in.

Payment will be for the shortest time required to repair or replace such premises.

3. Civil Authority Prohibits Use

If a civil authority prohibits you from use of the "residence premises" as a result of direct damage to neighboring premises by a Peril Insured Against, we cover the loss as provided in **1.** Additional Living Expense and **2.** Fair Rental Value above for no more than two weeks.

4. Loss Or Expense Not Covered

We do not cover loss or expense due to cancellation of a lease or agreement.

The periods of time under **1.** Additional Living Expense, **2.** Fair Rental Value and **3.** Civil Authority Prohibits Use above are not limited by expiration of this policy.

E. Additional Coverages

1. Debris Removal

a. We will pay your reasonable expense for the removal of:

(1) Debris of covered property if a Peril Insured Against that applies to the damaged property causes the loss; or

(2) Ash, dust or particles from a volcanic eruption that has caused direct loss to a building or property contained in a building.

This expense is included in the limit of liability that applies to the damaged property. If the amount to be paid for the actual damage to the property plus the debris removal expense is more than the limit of liability for the damaged property, an additional 5% of that limit of liability is available for debris removal expense.

b. Fallen Trees

(1) If circumstances of a loss meet those specified in **(2)** below, we will pay your reasonable expense, up to $1000, for the removal from the "residence premises" of:

(a) Your tree(s) felled by the peril of Windstorm Or Hail or Weight Of Ice, Snow Or Sleet; or

(b) A neighbor's tree(s) felled by a Peril Insured Against under Coverage **C.**

The $1000 limit is the most we will pay in any one loss regardless of the number of fallen trees. No more than $500 of this limit will be paid for the removal of any one tree.

This coverage is additional insurance.

(2) Tree removal coverage as described in **b.(1)** above applies only if:

(a) The tree damages a structure covered under this policy;

(b) Windstorm or Hail or Weight of Ice, Snow or Sleet causes damage to a structure covered under this policy and the Pennsylvania Governor declares the area in which the "residence premises" is located to be a disaster area as a result of such weather conditions; or

(c) The tree does not damage a structure covered under the policy, but:

(i) Blocks a driveway on the "residence premises" which prevents a "motor vehicle", that is registered for use on public roads or property, from entering or leaving the "residence premises"; or

(ii) Blocks a ramp or other fixture designed to assist a handicapped person to enter or leave the dwelling building

2. Reasonable Repairs

a. We will pay the reasonable cost incurred by you for the necessary measures taken solely to protect covered property that is damaged by a Peril Insured Against from further damage.

b. If the measures taken involve repair to other damaged property, we will only pay if that property is covered under this policy and the damage is caused by a Peril Insured Against. This coverage does not:

(1) Increase the limit of liability that applies to the covered property; or

(2) Relieve you of your duties, in case of a loss to covered property, described in **B.4.** under Section **I** – Conditions.

3. Trees, Shrubs And Other Plants

We cover trees, shrubs, plants or lawns, on the "residence premises", for loss caused by the following Perils Insured Against:

a. Fire or Lightning;

b. Explosion;

c. Riot or Civil Commotion;

d. Aircraft;

e. Vehicles not owned or operated by a resident of the "residence premises";

f. Vandalism or Malicious Mischief; or

g. Theft.

We will pay up to 5% of the limit of liability that applies to the dwelling for all trees, shrubs, plants or lawns. No more than $500 of this limit will be paid for any one tree, shrub or plant. We do not cover property grown for "business" purposes.

This coverage is additional insurance.

4. Fire Department Service Charge

We will pay up to $500 for your liability assumed by contract or agreement for fire department charges incurred when the fire department is called to save or protect covered property from a Peril Insured Against. We do not cover fire department service charges if the property is located within the limits of the city, municipality or protection district furnishing the fire department response.

This coverage is additional insurance. No deductible applies to this coverage.

5. Property Removed

We insure covered property against direct loss from any cause while being removed from a premises endangered by a Peril Insured Against and for no more than 30 days while removed.

This coverage does not change the limit of liability that applies to the property being removed.

6. Credit Card, Electronic Fund Transfer Card Or Access Device, Forgery And Counterfeit Money

a. We will pay up to $500 for:

(1) The legal obligation of an "insured" to pay because of the theft or unauthorized use of credit cards issued to or registered in an "insured's" name;

(2) Loss resulting from theft or unauthorized use of an electronic fund transfer card or access device used for deposit, withdrawal or transfer of funds, issued to or registered in an "insured's" name;

(3) Loss to an "insured" caused by forgery or alteration of any check or negotiable instrument; and

(4) Loss to an "insured" through acceptance in good faith of counterfeit United States or Canadian paper currency.

All loss resulting from a series of acts committed by any one person or in which any one person is concerned or implicated is considered to be one loss.

This coverage is additional insurance. No deductible applies to this coverage.

b. We do not cover:

(1) Use of a credit card, electronic fund transfer card or access device:

(a) By a resident of your household;

(b) By a person who has been entrusted with either type of card or access device; or

(c) If an "insured" has not complied with all terms and conditions under which the cards are issued or the devices accessed; or

(2) Loss arising out of "business" use or dishonesty of an "insured".

c. If the coverage in **a.** above applies, the following defense provisions also apply:

(1) We may investigate and settle any claim or suit that we decide is appropriate. Our duty to defend a claim or suit ends when the amount we pay for the loss equals our limit of liability.

(2) If a suit is brought against an "insured" for liability under **a.(1)** or **(2)** above, we will provide a defense at our expense by counsel of our choice.

(3) We have the option to defend at our expense an "insured" or an "insured's" bank against any suit for the enforcement of payment under **a.(3)** above.

7. Loss Assessment

a. We will pay up to $1,000 for your share of loss assessment charged during the policy period against you, as owner or tenant of the "residence premises", by a corporation or association of property owners. The assessment must be made as a result of direct loss to property, owned by all members collectively, of the type that would be covered by this policy if owned by you, caused by a Peril Insured Against under Coverage **A,** other than:

(1) Earthquake; or

(2) Land shock waves or tremors before, during or after a volcanic eruption.

The limit of $1,000 is the most we will pay with respect to any one loss, regardless of the number of assessments. We will only apply one deductible, per unit, to the total amount of any one loss to the property described above, regardless of the number of assessments.

b. We do not cover assessments charged against you or a corporation or association of property owners by any governmental body.

c. Paragraph **P.** Policy Period under Section **I** – Conditions does not apply to this coverage.

This coverage is additional insurance.

8. Collapse

a. With respect to this Additional Coverage:

(1) Collapse means an abrupt falling down or caving in of a building or any part of a building with the result that the building or part of the building cannot be occupied for its current intended purpose.

(2) A building or any part of a building that is in danger of falling down or caving in is not considered to be in a state of collapse.

(3) A part of a building that is standing is not considered to be in a state of collapse even if it has separated from another part of the building.

(4) A building or any part of a building that is standing is not considered to be in a state of collapse even if it shows evidence of cracking, bulging, sagging, bending, leaning, settling, shrinkage or expansion.

b. We insure for direct physical loss to covered property involving collapse of a building or any part of a building if the collapse was caused by one or more of the following:

(1) The Perils Insured Against named under Coverage **C;**

(2) Decay that is hidden from view, unless the presence of such decay is known to an "insured" prior to collapse;

(3) Insect or vermin damage that is hidden from view, unless the presence of such damage is known to an "insured" prior to collapse;

(4) Weight of contents, equipment, animals or people;

(5) Weight of rain which collects on a roof; or

(6) Use of defective material or methods in construction, remodeling or renovation if the collapse occurs during the course of the construction, remodeling or renovation.

c. Loss to an awning, fence, patio, deck, pavement, swimming pool, underground pipe, flue, drain, cesspool, septic tank, foundation, retaining wall, bulkhead, pier, wharf or dock is not included under **b.(2)** through **(6)** above, unless the loss is a direct result of the collapse of a building or any part of a building.

d. This coverage does not increase the limit of liability that applies to the damaged covered property.

9. Glass Or Safety Glazing Material

a. We cover:

(1) The breakage of glass or safety glazing material which is part of a covered building, storm door or storm window;

(2) The breakage of glass or safety glazing material which is part of a covered building, storm door or storm window when caused directly by earth movement; and

(3) The direct physical loss to covered property caused solely by the pieces, fragments or splinters of broken glass or safety glazing material which is part of a building, storm door or storm window.

b. This coverage does not include loss:

(1) To covered property which results because the glass or safety glazing material has been broken, except as provided in **a.(3)** above; or

(2) On the "residence premises" if the dwelling has been vacant for more than 60 consecutive days immediately before the loss, except when the breakage results directly from earth movement as provided in **a.(2)** above. A dwelling being constructed is not considered vacant.

c. This coverage does not increase the limit of liability that applies to the damaged property.

10. Landlord's Furnishings

We will pay up to $2,500 for your appliances, carpeting and other household furnishings, in each apartment on the "residence premises" regularly rented or held for rental to others by an "insured", for loss caused by a Peril Insured Against in Coverage **C,** other than Theft.

This limit is the most we will pay in any one loss regardless of the number of appliances, carpeting or other household furnishings involved in the loss.

This coverage does not increase the limit of liability applying to the damaged property.

11. Ordinance Or Law

a. You may use up to 10% of the limit of liability that applies to Coverage **A** for the increased costs you incur due to the enforcement of any ordinance or law which requires or regulates:

(1) The construction, demolition, remodeling, renovation or repair of that part of a covered building or other structure damaged by a Peril Insured Against;

(2) The demolition and reconstruction of the undamaged part of a covered building or other structure, when that building or other structure must be totally demolished because of damage by a Peril Insured Against to another part of that covered building or other structure; or

(3) The remodeling, removal or replacement of the portion of the undamaged part of a covered building or other structure necessary to complete the remodeling, repair or replacement of that part of the covered building or other structure damaged by a Peril Insured Against.

b. You may use all or part of this ordinance or law coverage to pay for the increased costs you incur to remove debris resulting from the construction, demolition, remodeling, renovation, repair or replacement of property as stated in **a.** above.

c. We do not cover:

(1) The loss in value to any covered building or other structure due to the requirements of any ordinance or law; or

(2) The costs to comply with any ordinance or law which requires any "insured" or others to test for, monitor, clean up, remove, contain, treat, detoxify or neutralize, or in any way respond to, or assess the effects of, pollutants in or on any covered building or other structure.

Pollutants means any solid, liquid, gaseous or thermal irritant or contaminant, including smoke, vapor, soot, fumes, acids, alkalis, chemicals and waste. Waste includes materials to be recycled, reconditioned or reclaimed.

This coverage is additional insurance.

12. Grave Markers

We will pay up to $5,000 for grave markers, including mausoleums, on or away from the "residence premises" for loss caused by a Peril Insured Against under Coverage **C.**

This coverage does not increase the limits of liability that apply to the damaged covered property.

SECTION I – PERILS INSURED AGAINST

A. Coverage A – Dwelling And Coverage B – Other Structures

1. We insure against risk of direct physical loss to property described in Coverages **A** and **B.**

2. We do not insure, however, for loss:

a. Excluded under Section **I** – Exclusions;

b. Involving collapse, except as provided in **E.8.** Collapse under Section **I** – Property Coverages; or

c. Caused by:

(1) Freezing of a plumbing, heating, air conditioning or automatic fire protective sprinkler system or of a household appliance, or by discharge, leakage or overflow from within the system or appliance caused by freezing. This provision does not apply if you have used reasonable care to:

(a) Maintain heat in the building; or

(b) Shut off the water supply and drain all systems and appliances of water.

However, if the building is protected by an automatic fire protective sprinkler system, you must use reasonable care to continue the water supply and maintain heat in the building for coverage to apply.

For purposes of this provision a plumbing system or household appliance does not include a sump, sump pump or related equipment or a roof drain, gutter, downspout or similar fixtures or equipment;

(2) Freezing, thawing, pressure or weight of water or ice, whether driven by wind or not, to a:

(a) Fence, pavement, patio or swimming pool;

(b) Footing, foundation, bulkhead, wall, or any other structure or device that supports all or part of a building, or other structure;

(c) Retaining wall or bulkhead that does not support all or part of a building or other structure; or

(d) Pier, wharf or dock;

(3) Theft in or to a dwelling under construction, or of materials and supplies for use in the construction until the dwelling is finished and occupied;

(4) Vandalism and malicious mischief, and any ensuing loss caused by any intentional and wrongful act committed in the course of the vandalism or malicious mischief, if the dwelling has been vacant for more than 60 consecutive days immediately before the loss. A dwelling being constructed is not considered vacant;

(5) Mold, fungus or wet rot. However, we do insure for loss caused by mold, fungus or wet rot that is hidden within the walls or ceilings or beneath the floors or above the ceilings of a structure if such loss results from the accidental discharge or overflow of water or steam from within:

(a) A plumbing, heating, air conditioning or automatic fire protective sprinkler system, or a household appliance, on the "residence premises"; or

(b) A storm drain, or water, steam or sewer pipes, off the "residence premises".

For purposes of this provision, a plumbing system or household appliance does not include a sump, sump pump or related equipment or a roof drain, gutter, downspout or similar fixtures or equipment; or

(6) Any of the following:

(a) Wear and tear, marring, deterioration;

(b) Mechanical breakdown, latent defect, inherent vice, or any quality in property that causes it to damage or destroy itself;

(c) Smog, rust or other corrosion, or dry rot;

(d) Smoke from agricultural smudging or industrial operations;

(e) Discharge, dispersal, seepage, migration, release or escape of pollutants unless the discharge, dispersal, seepage, migration, release or escape is itself caused by a Peril Insured Against named under Coverage **C.**

Pollutants means any solid, liquid, gaseous or thermal irritant or contaminant, including smoke, vapor, soot, fumes, acids, alkalis, chemicals and waste. Waste includes materials to be recycled, reconditioned or reclaimed;

(f) Settling, shrinking, bulging or expansion, including resultant cracking, of bulkheads, pavements, patios, footings, foundations, walls, floors, roofs or ceilings;

(g) Birds, vermin, rodents, or insects; or

(h) Animals owned or kept by an "insured".

Exception To c.(6)

Unless the loss is otherwise excluded, we cover loss to property covered under Coverage **A** or **B** resulting from an accidental discharge or overflow of water or steam from within a:

(i) Storm drain, or water, steam or sewer pipe, off the "residence premises"; or

(ii) Plumbing, heating, air conditioning or automatic fire protective sprinkler system or household appliance on the "residence premises". This includes the cost to tear out and replace any part of a building, or other structure, on the "residence premises", but only when necessary to repair the system or appliance. However, such tear out and replacement coverage only applies to other structures if the water or steam causes actual damage to a building on the "residence premises".

We do not cover loss to the system or appliance from which this water or steam escaped.

For purposes of this provision, a plumbing system or household appliance does not include a sump, sump pump or related equipment or a roof drain, gutter, down spout or similar fixtures or equipment.

Section **I** – Exclusion **A.3.** Water Damage, Paragraphs **a.** and **c.** that apply to surface water and water below the surface of the ground do not apply to loss by water covered under **c.(5)** and **(6)** above.

Under **2.b.** and **c.** above, any ensuing loss to property described in Coverages **A** and **B** not precluded by any other provision in this policy is covered.

B. Coverage C – Personal Property

We insure for direct physical loss to the property described in Coverage **C** caused by any of the following perils unless the loss is excluded in Section **I** – Exclusions.

1. Fire Or Lightning

2. Windstorm Or Hail

This peril includes loss to watercraft of all types and their trailers, furnishings, equipment, and outboard engines or motors, only while inside a fully enclosed building.

This peril does not include loss to the property contained in a building caused by rain, snow, sleet, sand or dust unless the direct force of wind or hail damages the building causing an opening in a roof or wall and the rain, snow, sleet, sand or dust enters through this opening.

3. Explosion

4. Riot Or Civil Commotion

5. Aircraft

This peril includes self-propelled missiles and spacecraft.

6. Vehicles

7. Smoke

This peril means sudden and accidental damage from smoke, including the emission or puffback of smoke, soot, fumes or vapors from a boiler, furnace or related equipment.

This peril does not include loss caused by smoke from agricultural smudging or industrial operations.

8. Vandalism Or Malicious Mischief

9. Theft

a. This peril includes attempted theft and loss of property from a known place when it is likely that the property has been stolen.

b. This peril does not include loss caused by theft:

(1) Committed by an "insured";

(2) In or to a dwelling under construction, or of materials and supplies for use in the construction until the dwelling is finished and occupied;

(3) From that part of a "residence premises" rented by an "insured" to someone other than another "insured"; or

(4) That occurs off the "residence premises" of:

(a) Trailers, semitrailers and campers;

(b) Watercraft of all types, and their furnishings, equipment and outboard engines or motors; or

(c) Property while at any other residence owned by, rented to, or occupied by an "insured", except while an "insured" is temporarily living there. Property of an "insured" who is a student is covered while at the residence the student occupies to attend school as long as the student has been there at any time during the 60 days immediately before the loss.

10. Falling Objects

This peril does not include loss to property contained in a building unless the roof or an outside wall of the building is first damaged by a falling object. Damage to the falling object itself is not included.

11. Weight Of Ice, Snow Or Sleet

This peril means weight of ice, snow or sleet which causes damage to property contained in a building.

12. Accidental Discharge Or Overflow Of Water Or Steam

a. This peril means accidental discharge or overflow of water or steam from within a plumbing, heating, air conditioning or automatic fire protective sprinkler system or from within a household appliance.

b. This peril does not include loss:

(1) To the system or appliance from which the water or steam escaped;

(2) Caused by or resulting from freezing except as provided in Peril Insured Against **14.** Freezing;

(3) On the "residence premises" caused by accidental discharge or overflow which occurs off the "residence premises"; or

(4) Caused by mold, fungus or wet rot unless hidden within the walls or ceilings or beneath the floors or above the ceilings of a structure.

c. In this peril, a plumbing system or household appliance does not include a sump, sump pump or related equipment or a roof drain, gutter, downspout or similar fixtures or equipment.

d. Section **I** – Exclusion **A.3.** Water Damage, Paragraphs **a.** and **c.** that apply to surface water and water below the surface of the ground do not apply to loss by water covered under this peril.

13. Sudden And Accidental Tearing Apart, Cracking, Burning Or Bulging

This peril means sudden and accidental tearing apart, cracking, burning or bulging of a steam or hot water heating system, an air conditioning or automatic fire protective sprinkler system, or an appliance for heating water.

We do not cover loss caused by or resulting from freezing under this peril.

14. Freezing

a. This peril means freezing of a plumbing, heating, air conditioning or automatic fire protective sprinkler system or of a household appliance but only if you have used reasonable care to:

(1) Maintain heat in the building; or

(2) Shut off the water supply and drain all systems and appliances of water.

However, if the building is protected by an automatic fire protective sprinkler system, you must use reasonable care to continue the water supply and maintain heat in the building for coverage to apply.

b. In this peril, a plumbing system or household appliance does not include a sump, sump pump or related equipment or a roof drain, gutter, downspout or similar fixtures or equipment.

15. Sudden And Accidental Damage From Artificially Generated Electrical Current

This peril does not include loss to tubes, transistors, electronic components or circuitry that are a part of appliances, fixtures, computers, home entertainment units or other types of electronic apparatus.

16. Volcanic Eruption

This peril does not include loss caused by earthquake, land shock waves or tremors.

SECTION I – EXCLUSIONS

A. We do not insure for loss caused directly or indirectly by any of the following. Such loss is excluded regardless of any other cause or event contributing concurrently or in any sequence to the loss. These exclusions apply whether or not the loss event results in widespread damage or affects a substantial area.

1. Ordinance Or Law

Ordinance Or Law means any ordinance or law:

a. Requiring or regulating the construction, demolition, remodeling, renovation or repair of property, including removal of any resulting debris. This Exclusion **A.1.a.** does not apply to the amount of coverage that may be provided for in **E.11.** Ordinance Or Law under Section **I** – Property Coverages;

b. The requirements of which result in a loss in value to property; or

c. Requiring any "insured" or others to test for, monitor, clean up, remove, contain, treat, detoxify or neutralize, or in any way respond to, or assess the effects of, pollutants.

Pollutants means any solid, liquid, gaseous or thermal irritant or contaminant, including smoke, vapor, soot, fumes, acids, alkalis, chemicals and waste. Waste includes materials to be recycled, reconditioned or reclaimed.

This Exclusion **A.1.** applies whether or not the property has been physically damaged.

2. Earth Movement

Earth Movement means:

a. Earthquake, including land shock waves or tremors before, during or after a volcanic eruption;

b. Landslide, mudslide or mudflow;

c. Subsidence or sinkhole; or

d. Any other earth movement including earth sinking, rising or shifting;

caused by or resulting from human or animal forces or any act of nature unless direct loss by fire or explosion ensues and then we will pay only for the ensuing loss.

This Exclusion **A.2.** does not apply to loss by theft.

3. Water Damage

Water Damage means:

a. Flood, surface water, waves, tidal water, overflow of a body of water, or spray from any of these, whether or not driven by wind;

b. Water or water-borne material which backs up through sewers or drains or which overflows or is discharged from a sump, sump pump or related equipment; or

c. Water or water-borne material below the surface of the ground, including water which exerts pressure on or seeps or leaks through a building, sidewalk, driveway, foundation, swimming pool or other structure;

caused by or resulting from human or animal forces or any act of nature.

Direct loss by fire, explosion or theft resulting from water damage is covered.

4. Power Failure

Power Failure means the failure of power or other utility service if the failure takes place off the "residence premises". But if the failure results in a loss, from a Peril Insured Against on the "residence premises", we will pay for the loss caused by that peril.

5. Neglect

Neglect means neglect of an "insured" to use all reasonable means to save and preserve property at and after the time of a loss.

6. War

War includes the following and any consequence of any of the following:

a. Undeclared war, civil war, insurrection, rebellion or revolution;

b. Warlike act by a military force or military personnel; or

c. Destruction, seizure or use for a military purpose.

Discharge of a nuclear weapon will be deemed a warlike act even if accidental.

7. **Nuclear Hazard**

   This Exclusion **A.7.** pertains to Nuclear Hazard to the extent set forth in **M.** Nuclear Hazard Clause under Section **I** – Conditions.

8. **Intentional Loss**

   Intentional Loss means any loss arising out of any act an "insured" commits or conspires to commit with the intent to cause a loss.

   In the event of such loss, no "insured" is entitled to coverage, even "insureds" who did not commit or conspire to commit the act causing the loss.

9. **Governmental Action**

   Governmental Action means the destruction, confiscation or seizure of property described in Coverage **A, B** or **C** by order of any governmental or public authority.

   This exclusion does not apply to such acts ordered by any governmental or public authority that are taken at the time of a fire to prevent its spread, if the loss caused by fire would be covered under this policy.

B. We do not insure for loss to property described in Coverages **A** and **B** caused by any of the following. However, any ensuing loss to property described in Coverages **A** and **B** not precluded by any other provision in this policy is covered.

1. Weather conditions. However, this exclusion only applies if weather conditions contribute in any way with a cause or event excluded in **A.** above to produce the loss.
2. Acts or decisions, including the failure to act or decide, of any person, group, organization or governmental body.
3. Faulty, inadequate or defective:
   a. Planning, zoning, development, surveying, siting;
   b. Design, specifications, workmanship, repair, construction, renovation, remodeling, grading, compaction;
   c. Materials used in repair, construction, renovation or remodeling; or
   d. Maintenance;

   of part or all of any property whether on or off the "residence premises".

SECTION I – CONDITIONS

A. Insurable Interest And Limit Of Liability

Even if more than one person has an insurable interest in the property covered, we will not be liable in any one loss:

1. To an "insured" for more than the amount of such "insured's" interest at the time of loss; or
2. For more than the applicable limit of liability.

B. Duties After Loss

In case of a loss to covered property, we have no duty to provide coverage under this policy if the failure to comply with the following duties is prejudicial to us. These duties must be performed either by you, an "insured" seeking coverage, or a representative of either:

1. Give prompt notice to us or our agent;
2. Notify the police in case of loss by theft;
3. Notify the credit card or electronic fund transfer card or access device company in case of loss as provided for in **E.6.** Credit Card, Electronic Fund Transfer Card Or Access Device, Forgery And Counterfeit Money under Section **I** – Property Coverages;
4. Protect the property from further damage. If repairs to the property are required, you must:
   a. Make reasonable and necessary repairs to protect the property; and
   b. Keep an accurate record of repair expenses;
5. Cooperate with us in the investigation of a claim;
6. Prepare an inventory of damaged personal property showing the quantity, description, actual cash value and amount of loss. Attach all bills, receipts and related documents that justify the figures in the inventory;
7. As often as we reasonably require:
   a. Show the damaged property;
   b. Provide us with records and documents we request and permit us to make copies; and
   c. Submit to examination under oath, while not in the presence of another "insured", and sign the same;

8. Send to us, within 60 days after our request, your signed, sworn proof of loss which sets forth, to the best of your knowledge and belief:
   a. The time and cause of loss;
   b. The interests of all "insureds" and all others in the property involved and all liens on the property;
   c. Other insurance which may cover the loss;
   d. Changes in title or occupancy of the property during the term of the policy;
   e. Specifications of damaged buildings and detailed repair estimates;
   f. The inventory of damaged personal property described in **6.** above;
   g. Receipts for additional living expenses incurred and records that support the fair rental value loss; and
   h. Evidence or affidavit that supports a claim under **E.6.** Credit Card, Electronic Fund Transfer Card Or Access Device, Forgery And Counterfeit Money under Section **I** – Property Coverages, stating the amount and cause of loss.

C. Loss Settlement

In this Condition **C.,** the terms "cost to repair or replace" and "replacement cost" do not include the increased costs incurred to comply with the enforcement of any ordinance or law, except to the extent that coverage for these increased costs is provided in **E.11.** Ordinance Or Law under Section **I** – Property Coverages. Covered property losses are settled as follows:

1. Property of the following types:
   a. Personal property;
   b. Awnings, carpeting, household appliances, outdoor antennas and outdoor equipment, whether or not attached to buildings;
   c. Structures that are not buildings; and
   d. Grave markers, including mausoleums;

   at actual cash value at the time of loss but not more than the amount required to repair or replace.

2. Buildings covered under Coverage **A** or **B** at replacement cost without deduction for depreciation, subject to the following:
   a. If, at the time of loss, the amount of insurance in this policy on the damaged building is 80% or more of the full replacement cost of the building immediately before the loss, we will pay the cost to repair or replace, after application of any deductible and without deduction for depreciation, but not more than the least of the following amounts:
      (1) The limit of liability under this policy that applies to the building;
      (2) The replacement cost of that part of the building damaged with material of like kind and quality and for like use; or
      (3) The necessary amount actually spent to repair or replace the damaged building.

      If the building is rebuilt at a new premises, the cost described in **(2)** above is limited to the cost which would have been incurred if the building had been built at the original premises.
   b. If, at the time of loss, the amount of insurance in this policy on the damaged building is less than 80% of the full replacement cost of the building immediately before the loss, we will pay the greater of the following amounts, but not more than the limit of liability under this policy that applies to the building:
      (1) The actual cash value of that part of the building damaged; or
      (2) That proportion of the cost to repair or replace, after application of any deductible and without deduction for depreciation, that part of the building damaged, which the total amount of insurance in this policy on the damaged building bears to 80% of the replacement cost of the building.
   c. To determine the amount of insurance required to equal 80% of the full replacement cost of the building immediately before the loss, do not include the value of:
      (1) Excavations, footings, foundations, piers, or any other structures or devices that support all or part of the building, which are below the undersurface of the lowest basement floor;

(2) Those supports described in (1) above which are below the surface of the ground inside the foundation walls, if there is no basement; and

(3) Underground flues, pipes, wiring and drains.

d. We will pay no more than the actual cash value of the damage until actual repair or replacement is complete. Once actual repair or replacement is complete, we will settle the loss as noted in **2.a.** and **b.** above.

However, if the cost to repair or replace the damage is both:

(1) Less than 5% of the amount of insurance in this policy on the building; and

(2) Less than $2,500;

we will settle the loss as noted in **2.a.** and **b.** above whether or not actual repair or replacement is complete.

e. You may disregard the replacement cost loss settlement provisions and make claim under this policy for loss to buildings on an actual cash value basis. You may then make claim for any additional liability according to the provisions of this Condition **C.** Loss Settlement, provided you notify us of your intent to do so within 180 days after the date of loss.

D. Loss To A Pair Or Set

In case of loss to a pair or set we may elect to:

1. Repair or replace any part to restore the pair or set to its value before the loss; or
2. Pay the difference between actual cash value of the property before and after the loss.

E. Appraisal

If you and we fail to agree on the amount of loss, either may demand an appraisal of the loss. In this event, each party will choose a competent and impartial appraiser within 20 days after receiving a written request from the other. The two appraisers will choose an umpire. If they cannot agree upon an umpire within 15 days, you or we may request that the choice be made by a judge of a court of record in the state where the "residence premises" is located. The appraisers will separately set the amount of loss. If the appraisers submit a written report of an agreement to us, the amount agreed upon will be the amount of loss. If they fail to agree, they will submit their differences to the umpire. A decision agreed to by any two will set the amount of loss.

Each party will:

1. Pay its own appraiser; and
2. Bear the other expenses of the appraisal and umpire equally.

F. Other Insurance And Service Agreement

If a loss covered by this policy is also covered by:

1. Other insurance, we will pay only the proportion of the loss that the limit of liability that applies under this policy bears to the total amount of insurance covering the loss; or
2. A service agreement, this insurance is excess over any amounts payable under any such agreement. Service agreement means a service plan, property restoration plan, home warranty or other similar service warranty agreement, even if it is characterized as insurance.

G. Suit Against Us

No action can be brought against us unless there has been full compliance with all of the terms under Section **I** of this policy and the action is started within two years after the date of loss.

H. Our Option

We may repair or replace any part of the damaged property with material or property of like kind and quality if we give you written notice of our intention to do so within 15 working days after we receive your signed, sworn proof of loss.

I. Loss Payment

We will adjust all losses with you. We will pay you unless some other person is named in the policy or is legally entitled to receive payment. Loss will be payable 60 days after we receive your proof of loss and:

1. Reach an agreement with you;
2. There is an entry of a final judgment; or
3. There is a filing of an appraisal award with us.

J. Abandonment Of Property

We need not accept any property abandoned by an "insured".

K. Mortgage Clause

1. If a mortgagee is named in this policy, any loss payable under Coverage **A** or **B** will be paid to the mortgagee and you, as interests appear. If more than one mortgagee is named, the order of payment will be the same as the order of precedence of the mortgages.
2. If we deny your claim, that denial will not apply to a valid claim of the mortgagee, if the mortgagee:

   a. Notifies us of any change in ownership, occupancy or substantial change in risk of which the mortgagee is aware;

b. Pays any premium due under this policy on demand if you have neglected to pay the premium; and

c. Submits a signed, sworn statement of loss within 60 days after receiving notice from us of your failure to do so. Paragraphs **E.** Appraisal, **G.** Suit Against Us and **I.** Loss Payment under Section **I** – Conditions also apply to the mortgagee.

3. If we decide to cancel or not to renew this policy, the mortgagee will be notified at least 10 days before the date cancellation or nonrenewal takes effect.

4. If we pay the mortgagee for any loss and deny payment to you:

a. We are subrogated to all the rights of the mortgagee granted under the mortgage on the property; or

b. At our option, we may pay to the mortgagee the whole principal on the mortgage plus any accrued interest. In this event, we will receive a full assignment and transfer of the mortgage and all securities held as collateral to the mortgage debt.

5. Subrogation will not impair the right of the mortgagee to recover the full amount of the mortgagee's claim.

L. No Benefit To Bailee

We will not recognize any assignment or grant any coverage that benefits a person or organization holding, storing or moving property for a fee regardless of any other provision of this policy.

M. Nuclear Hazard Clause

1. "Nuclear Hazard" means any nuclear reaction, radiation, or radioactive contamination, all whether controlled or uncontrolled or however caused, or any consequence of any of these.

2. Loss caused by the nuclear hazard will not be considered loss caused by fire, explosion, or smoke, whether these perils are specifically named in or otherwise included within the Perils Insured Against.

3. This policy does not apply under Section **I** to loss caused directly or indirectly by nuclear hazard, except that direct loss by fire resulting from the nuclear hazard is covered.

N. Recovered Property

If you or we recover any property for which we have made payment under this policy, you or we will notify the other of the recovery. At your option, the property will be returned to or retained by you or it will become our property. If the recovered property is returned to or retained by you, the loss payment will be adjusted based on the amount you received for the recovered property.

O. Volcanic Eruption Period

One or more volcanic eruptions that occur within a 72 hour period will be considered as one volcanic eruption.

P. Policy Period

This policy applies only to loss which occurs during the policy period.

Q. Concealment Or Fraud

We provide coverage to no "insureds" under this policy if, whether before or after a loss, an "insured" has:

1. Intentionally concealed or misrepresented any material fact or circumstance;

2. Engaged in fraudulent conduct; or

3. Made false statements;

relating to this insurance.

R. Loss Payable Clause

If the Declarations show a loss payee for certain listed insured personal property, the definition of "insured" is changed to include that loss payee with respect to that property.

If we decide to cancel or not renew this policy, that loss payee will be notified in writing.

SECTION II – LIABILITY COVERAGES

A. Coverage E – Personal Liability

If a claim is made or a suit is brought against an "insured" for damages because of "bodily injury" or "property damage" caused by an "occurrence" to which this coverage applies, we will:

1. Pay up to our limit of liability for the damages for which an "insured" is legally liable; and

2. Provide a defense at our expense by counsel of our choice, even if the suit is groundless, false or fraudulent. We may investigate and settle any claim or suit that we decide is appropriate. Our duty to settle or defend ends when our limit of liability for the "occurrence" has been exhausted by payment of a judgment or settlement.

B. Coverage F – Medical Payments To Others

We will pay the necessary medical expenses that are incurred or medically ascertained within three years from the date of an accident causing "bodily injury". Medical expenses means reasonable charges for medical, surgical, x-ray, dental, ambulance, hospital, professional nursing and prosthetic devices. Medical expenses do not include expenses for funeral services. This coverage does not apply to you or regular residents of your household except "residence employees". As to others, this coverage applies only:

1. To a person on the "insured location" with the permission of an "insured"; or
2. To a person off the "insured location", if the "bodily injury":
   - **a.** Arises out of a condition on the "insured location" or the ways immediately adjoining;
   - **b.** Is caused by the activities of an "insured";
   - **c.** Is caused by a "residence employee" in the course of the "residence employee's" employment by an "insured"; or
   - **d.** Is caused by an animal owned by or in the care of an "insured".

SECTION II – EXCLUSIONS

A. "Motor Vehicle Liability"

1. Coverages **E** and **F** do not apply to any "motor vehicle liability" if, at the time and place of an "occurrence", the involved "motor vehicle":
   - **a.** Is registered for use on public roads or property;
   - **b.** Is not registered for use on public roads or property, but such registration is required by a law, or regulation issued by a government agency, for it to be used at the place of the "occurrence"; or
   - **c.** Is being:
     - **(1)** Operated in, or practicing for, any prearranged or organized race, speed contest or other competition;
     - **(2)** Rented to others;
     - **(3)** Used to carry persons or cargo for a charge; or
     - **(4)** Used for any "business" purpose except for a motorized golf cart while on a golfing facility.
2. If Exclusion **A.1.** does not apply, there is still no coverage for "motor vehicle liability" unless the "motor vehicle" is:
   - **a.** In dead storage on an "insured location";
   - **b.** Used solely to service an "insured's" residence;
   - **c.** Designed to assist the handicapped and, at the time of an "occurrence", it is:
     - **(1)** Being used to assist a handicapped person; or
     - **(2)** Parked on an "insured location";
   - **d.** Designed for recreational use off public roads and:
     - **(1)** Not owned by an "insured"; or
     - **(2)** Owned by an "insured" provided the "occurrence" takes place on an "insured location" as defined in Definitions **B.6.a., b., d., e.** or **h.;** or
   - **e.** A motorized golf cart that is owned by an "insured", designed to carry up to 4 persons, not built or modified after manufacture to exceed a speed of 25 miles per hour on level ground and, at the time of an "occurrence", is within the legal boundaries of:
     - **(1)** A golfing facility and is parked or stored there, or being used by an "insured" to:
       - **(a)** Play the game of golf or for other recreational or leisure activity allowed by the facility;
       - **(b)** Travel to or from an area where "motor vehicles" or golf carts are parked or stored; or
       - **(c)** Cross public roads at designated points to access other parts of the golfing facility; or
     - **(2)** A private residential community, including its public roads upon which a motorized golf cart can legally travel, which is subject to the authority of a property owners association and contains an "insured's" residence.

B. "Watercraft Liability"

1. Coverages **E** and **F** do not apply to any "watercraft liability" if, at the time of an "occurrence", the involved watercraft is being:
   - **a.** Operated in, or practicing for, any prearranged or organized race, speed contest or other competition. This exclusion does not apply to a sailing vessel or a predicted log cruise;

b. Rented to others;

c. Used to carry persons or cargo for a charge; or

d. Used for any "business" purpose.

2. If Exclusion **B.1.** does not apply, there is still no coverage for "watercraft liability" unless, at the time of the "occurrence", the watercraft:

a. Is stored;

b. Is a sailing vessel, with or without auxiliary power, that is:

(1) Less than 26 feet in overall length; or

(2) 26 feet or more in overall length and not owned by or rented to an "insured"; or

c. Is not a sailing vessel and is powered by:

(1) An inboard or inboard-outdrive engine or motor, including those that power a water jet pump, of:

(a) 50 horsepower or less and not owned by an "insured"; or

(b) More than 50 horsepower and not owned by or rented to an "insured"; or

(2) One or more outboard engines or motors with:

(a) 25 total horsepower or less;

(b) More than 25 horsepower if the outboard engine or motor is not owned by an "insured";

(c) More than 25 horsepower if the outboard engine or motor is owned by an "insured" who acquired it during the policy period; or

(d) More than 25 horsepower if the outboard engine or motor is owned by an "insured" who acquired it before the policy period, but only if:

(i) You declare them at policy inception; or

(ii) Your intent to insure them is reported to us in writing within 45 days after you acquire them.

The coverages in **(c)** and **(d)** above apply for the policy period.

Horsepower means the maximum power rating assigned to the engine or motor by the manufacturer.

C. "Aircraft Liability"

This policy does not cover "aircraft liability".

D. "Hovercraft Liability"

This policy does not cover "hovercraft liability".

E. Coverage E – Personal Liability And Coverage F – Medical Payments To Others

Coverages **E** and **F** do not apply to the following:

1. Expected Or Intended Injury

"Bodily injury" or "property damage" which is expected or intended by an "insured" even if the resulting "bodily injury" or "property damage":

a. Is of a different kind, quality or degree than initially expected or intended; or

b. Is sustained by a different person, entity, real or personal property, than initially expected or intended.

However, this Exclusion **E.1.** does not apply to "bodily injury" resulting from the use of reasonable force by an "insured" to protect persons or property;

2. "Business"

a. "Bodily injury" or "property damage" arising out of or in connection with a "business" conducted from an "insured location" or engaged in by an "insured", whether or not the "business" is owned or operated by an "insured" or employs an "insured".

This Exclusion **E.2.** applies but is not limited to an act or omission, regardless of its nature or circumstance, involving a service or duty rendered, promised, owed, or implied to be provided because of the nature of the "business".

b. This Exclusion **E.2.** does not apply to:

(1) The rental or holding for rental of an "insured location";

(a) On an occasional basis if used only as a residence;

(b) In part for use only as a residence, unless a single family unit is intended for use by the occupying family to lodge more than two roomers or boarders; or

(c) In part, as an office, school, studio or private garage; and

(2) An "insured" under the age of 21 years involved in a part-time or occasional, self-employed "business" with no employees;

3. **Professional Services**

"Bodily injury" or "property damage" arising out of the rendering of or failure to render professional services;

4. **"Insured's" Premises Not An "Insured Location"**

"Bodily injury" or "property damage" arising out of a premises:

a. Owned by an "insured";

b. Rented to an "insured"; or

c. Rented to others by an "insured";

that is not an "insured location";

5. **War**

"Bodily injury" or "property damage" caused directly or indirectly by war, including the following and any consequence of any of the following:

a. Undeclared war, civil war, insurrection, rebellion or revolution;

b. Warlike act by a military force or military personnel; or

c. Destruction, seizure or use for a military purpose.

Discharge of a nuclear weapon will be deemed a warlike act even if accidental;

6. **Communicable Disease**

"Bodily injury" or "property damage" which arises out of the transmission of a communicable disease by an "insured";

7. **Sexual Molestation, Corporal Punishment Or Physical Or Mental Abuse**

"Bodily injury" or "property damage" arising out of sexual molestation, corporal punishment or physical or mental abuse; or

8. **Controlled Substance**

"Bodily injury" or "property damage" arising out of the use, sale, manufacture, delivery, transfer or possession by any person of a Controlled Substance as defined by the Federal Food and Drug Law at 21 U.S.C.A. Sections 811 and 812. Controlled Substances include but are not limited to cocaine, LSD, marijuana and all narcotic drugs. However, this exclusion does not apply to the legitimate use of prescription drugs by a person following the orders of a licensed physician.

Exclusions **A.** "Motor Vehicle Liability", **B.** "Watercraft Liability", **C.** "Aircraft Liability", **D.** "Hovercraft Liability" and **E.4.** "Insured's" Premises Not An "Insured Location" do not apply to "bodily injury" to a "residence employee" arising out of and in the course of the "residence employee's" employment by an "insured".

F. Coverage E – Personal Liability

Coverage **E** does not apply to:

1. Liability:

   a. For any loss assessment charged against you as a member of an association, corporation or community of property owners, except as provided in **D.** Loss Assessment under Section **II** – Additional Coverages;

   b. Under any contract or agreement entered into by an "insured". However, this exclusion does not apply to written contracts:

      (1) That directly relate to the ownership, maintenance or use of an "insured location"; or

      (2) Where the liability of others is assumed by you prior to an "occurrence";

   unless excluded in **a.** above or elsewhere in this policy;

2. "Property damage" to property owned by an "insured". This includes costs or expenses incurred by an "insured" or others to repair, replace, enhance, restore or maintain such property to prevent injury to a person or damage to property of others, whether on or away from an "insured location";

3. "Property damage" to property rented to, occupied or used by or in the care of an "insured". This exclusion does not apply to "property damage" caused by fire, smoke or explosion;

4. "Bodily injury" to any person eligible to receive any benefits voluntarily provided or required to be provided by an "insured" under any:

   a. Workers' compensation law;

   b. Non-occupational disability law; or

   c. Occupational disease law;

5. "Bodily injury" or "property damage" for which an "insured" under this policy:

   a. Is also an insured under a nuclear energy liability policy issued by the:

      (1) Nuclear Energy Liability Insurance Association;

      (2) Mutual Atomic Energy Liability Underwriters;

(3) Nuclear Insurance Association of Canada;

or any of their successors; or

b. Would be an insured under such a policy but for the exhaustion of its limit of liability; or

6. "Bodily injury" to you or an "insured" as defined under Definitions **5.a.** or **b.**

This exclusion also applies to any claim made or suit brought against you or an "insured":

a. To repay; or

b. Share damages with;

another person who may be obligated to pay damages because of "bodily injury" to an "insured".

G. Coverage F – Medical Payments To Others

Coverage **F** does not apply to "bodily injury":

1. To a "residence employee" if the "bodily injury":

a. Occurs off the "insured location"; and

b. Does not arise out of or in the course of the "residence employee's" employment by an "insured";

2. To any person eligible to receive benefits voluntarily provided or required to be provided under any:

a. Workers' compensation law;

b. Non-occupational disability law; or

c. Occupational disease law;

3. From any:

a. Nuclear reaction;

b. Nuclear radiation; or

c. Radioactive contamination;

all whether controlled or uncontrolled or however caused; or

d. Any consequence of any of these; or

4. To any person, other than a "residence employee" of an "insured", regularly residing on any part of the "insured location".

SECTION II – ADDITIONAL COVERAGES

We cover the following in addition to the limits of liability:

A. Claim Expenses

We pay:

1. Expenses we incur and costs taxed against an "insured" in any suit we defend;

2. Premiums on bonds required in a suit we defend, but not for bond amounts more than the Coverage **E** limit of liability. We need not apply for or furnish any bond;

3. Reasonable expenses incurred by an "insured" at our request, including actual loss of earnings (but not loss of other income) up to $250 per day, for assisting us in the investigation or defense of a claim or suit; and

4. Interest on the entire judgment which accrues after entry of the judgment and before we pay or tender, or deposit in court that part of the judgment which does not exceed the limit of liability that applies.

5. Prejudgment interest awarded against an "insured" on that part of the judgment we pay. Any prejudgment interest awarded against an "insured" is subject to the applicable Pennsylvania Rules of Civil Procedure.

B. First Aid Expenses

We will pay expenses for first aid to others incurred by an "insured" for "bodily injury" covered under this policy. We will not pay for first aid to an "insured".

C. Damage To Property Of Others

1. We will pay, at replacement cost, up to $1,000 per "occurrence" for "property damage" to property of others caused by an "insured".

2. We will not pay for "property damage":

a. To the extent of any amount recoverable under Section **I;**

b. Caused intentionally by an "insured" who is 13 years of age or older;

c. To property owned by an "insured";

d. To property owned by or rented to a tenant of an "insured" or a resident in your household; or

e. Arising out of:

(1) A "business" engaged in by an "insured";

(2) Any act or omission in connection with a premises owned, rented or controlled by an "insured", other than the "insured location"; or

(3) The ownership, maintenance, occupancy, operation, use, loading or unloading of aircraft, hovercraft, watercraft or "motor vehicles".

This exclusion **e.(3)** does not apply to a "motor vehicle" that:

(a) Is designed for recreational use off public roads;

(b) Is not owned by an "insured"; and

(c) At the time of the "occurrence", is not required by law, or regulation issued by a government agency, to have been registered for it to be used on public roads or property.

D. Loss Assessment

1. We will pay up to $1,000 for your share of loss assessment charged against you, as owner or tenant of the "residence premises", during the policy period by a corporation or association of property owners, when the assessment is made as a result of:

   a. "Bodily injury" or "property damage" not excluded from coverage under Section **II** – Exclusions; or

   b. Liability for an act of a director, officer or trustee in the capacity as a director, officer or trustee, provided such person:

      (1) Is elected by the members of a corporation or association of property owners; and

      (2) Serves without deriving any income from the exercise of duties which are solely on behalf of a corporation or association of property owners.

2. Paragraph **I.** Policy Period under Section **II** – Conditions does not apply to this Loss Assessment Coverage.

3. Regardless of the number of assessments, the limit of $1,000 is the most we will pay for loss arising out of:

   a. One accident, including continuous or repeated exposure to substantially the same general harmful condition; or

   b. A covered act of a director, officer or trustee. An act involving more than one director, officer or trustee is considered to be a single act.

4. We do not cover assessments charged against you or a corporation or association of property owners by any governmental body.

SECTION II – CONDITIONS

A. Limit Of Liability

Our total liability under Coverage **E** for all damages resulting from any one "occurrence" will not be more than the Coverage **E** limit of liability shown in the Declarations. This limit is the same regardless of the number of "insureds", claims made or persons injured. All "bodily injury" and "property damage" resulting from any one accident or from continuous or repeated exposure to substantially the same general harmful conditions shall be considered to be the result of one "occurrence".

Our total liability under Coverage **F** for all medical expense payable for "bodily injury" to one person as the result of one accident will not be more than the Coverage **F** limit of liability shown in the Declarations.

B. Severability Of Insurance

This insurance applies separately to each "insured". This condition will not increase our limit of liability for any one "occurrence".

C. Duties After "Occurrence"

In case of an "occurrence", you or another "insured" will perform the following duties that apply. We have no duty to provide coverage under this policy if your failure to comply with the following duties is prejudicial to us. You will help us by seeing that these duties are performed:

1. Give written notice to us or our agent as soon as is practical, which sets forth:

   a. The identity of the policy and the "named insured" shown in the Declarations;

   b. Reasonably available information on the time, place and circumstances of the "occurrence"; and

   c. Names and addresses of any claimants and witnesses;

2. Cooperate with us in the investigation, settlement or defense of any claim or suit;

3. Promptly forward to us every notice, demand, summons or other process relating to the "occurrence";

4. At our request, help us:
   a. To make settlement;
   b. To enforce any right of contribution or indemnity against any person or organization who may be liable to an "insured";
   c. With the conduct of suits and attend hearings and trials; and
   d. To secure and give evidence and obtain the attendance of witnesses;
5. With respect to **C.** Damage To Property Of Others under Section **II** – Additional Coverages, submit to us within 60 days after the loss, a sworn statement of loss and show the damaged property, if in an "insured's" control;
6. No "insured" shall, except at such "insured's" own cost, voluntarily make payment, assume obligation or incur expense other than for first aid to others at the time of the "bodily injury".

D. Duties Of An Injured Person – Coverage F – Medical Payments To Others

1. The injured person or someone acting for the injured person will:
   a. Give us written proof of claim, under oath if required, as soon as is practical; and
   b. Authorize us to obtain copies of medical reports and records.
2. The injured person will submit to a physical exam by a doctor of our choice when and as often as we reasonably require.

E. Payment Of Claim – Coverage F – Medical Payments To Others

Payment under this coverage is not an admission of liability by an "insured" or us.

F. Suit Against Us

1. No action can be brought against us unless there has been full compliance with all of the terms under this Section **II.**
2. No one will have the right to join us as a party to any action against an "insured".
3. Also, no action with respect to Coverage **E** can be brought against us until the obligation of such "insured" has been determined by final judgment or agreement signed by us.

G. Bankruptcy Of An "Insured"

Bankruptcy or insolvency of an "insured" will not relieve us of our obligations under this policy.

H. Other Insurance

This insurance is excess over other valid and collectible insurance except insurance written specifically to cover as excess over the limits of liability that apply in this policy.

I. Policy Period

This policy applies only to "bodily injury" or "property damage" which occurs during the policy period.

J. Concealment Or Fraud

We do not provide coverage to an "insured" who, whether before or after a loss, has:

1. Intentionally concealed or misrepresented any material fact or circumstance;
2. Engaged in fraudulent conduct; or
3. Made false statements;

relating to this insurance.

SECTIONS I AND II – CONDITIONS

A. Liberalization Clause

If we make a change which broadens coverage under this edition of our policy without additional premium charge, that change will automatically apply to your insurance as of the date we implement the change in your state, provided that this implementation date falls within 60 days prior to or during the policy period stated in the Declarations.

This Liberalization Clause does not apply to changes implemented with a general program revision that includes both broadenings and restrictions in coverage, whether that general program revision is implemented through introduction of:

1. A subsequent edition of this policy; or
2. An amendatory endorsement.

B. Waiver Or Change Of Policy Provisions

A waiver or change of a provision of this policy must be in writing by us to be valid. Our request for an appraisal or examination will not waive any of our rights.

C. Cancellation

1. You may cancel this policy at any time by returning it to us or by letting us know in writing of the date cancellation is to take effect.

2. We may cancel this policy only for the reasons stated below by notifying the "insured" named in the Declarations in writing of the date cancellation takes effect. This cancellation notice may be delivered to or mailed to the "insured" named in the Declarations at the mailing address shown in the policy or at a forwarding address. Proof of mailing will be sufficient proof of notice.

   a. When this policy has been in effect for less than 60 days and is not a renewal with us, we may cancel for any reason by notifying the "insured" named in the Declarations at least 30 days before the cancellation takes effect.

   b. When this policy has been in effect for 60 days or more, or at any time if it is a renewal with us, we may cancel only for one or more of the following reasons by notifying the "insured" named in the Declarations at least 30 days prior to the proposed cancellation date:

      (1) This policy was obtained through material misrepresentation, fraudulent statements, omissions or concealment of fact material to the acceptance of the risk or to the hazard assumed by us;

      (2) There has been a substantial change or increase in hazard in the risk assumed by us subsequent to the date the policy was issued;

      (3) There is a substantial increase in hazard insured against by reason of willful or negligent acts or omissions by the "insured";

      (4) The "insured" has failed to pay the premium by the due date, whether payable to us or to our agent or under any finance or credit plan; or

      (5) For any other reason approved by the Pennsylvania Insurance Commissioner.

   This provision shall not apply if the named "insured" has demonstrated by some overt action to us or to our agent that the "insured" wishes the policy to be cancelled.

   Delivery of such written notice by us to the "insured" named in the Declarations at the mailing address shown in the policy or at a forwarding address shall be equivalent to mailing.

3. When this policy is canceled, the premium for the period from the date of cancellation to the expiration date will be refunded pro rata.

4. If the return premium is not refunded with the notice of cancellation or when this policy is returned to us, we will refund it within a reasonable time after the date cancellation takes effect.

D. Nonrenewal

We will not fail to renew this policy except for one of the reasons referred to in **C.** Cancellation above. We may refuse to renew for one of the listed reasons by mailing to the "insured" named in the Declarations at the mailing address shown in the policy or at a forwarding address, written notice at least 30 days prior to the expiration date of this policy.

This provision does not apply if:

1. We have indicated our willingness to renew and the "insured" has failed to pay the premium by the due date; or

2. The named "insured" has indicated to us or our agent that the "insured" does not wish the policy to be renewed.

Delivery of such written notice by us to the "insured" named in the Declarations at the mailing address shown in the policy or at a forwarding address shall be equivalent to mailing.

E. Assignment

Assignment of this policy will not be valid unless we give our written consent.

F. Subrogation

An "insured" may waive in writing before a loss all rights of recovery against any person. If not waived, we may require an assignment of rights of recovery for a loss to the extent that payment is made by us.

If an assignment is sought, an "insured" must sign and deliver all related papers and cooperate with us.

Subrogation does not apply to Coverage **F** or Paragraph **C.** Damage To Property Of Others under Section **II** – Additional Coverages.

G. Death

If any person named in the Declarations or the spouse, if a resident of the same household, dies, the following apply:

1. We insure the legal representative of the deceased but only with respect to the premises and property of the deceased covered under the policy at the time of death; and

2. Insurance under this policy will continue as provided in **a.** or **b.** below, whichever is later:
   a. For 180 days after your death regardless of the policy period shown in the Declarations, unless your premises and property, covered under the policy at the time of your death, is sold prior to that date; or
   b. Until the end of the policy period shown in the Declarations, unless your premises and property, covered under the policy at the time of your death, is sold prior to that date.

   Coverage during the period of time after your death is subject to all the provisions of this policy including payment of any premium due for the policy period shown in the Declarations and any extension of that period;

3. "Insured" includes:
   a. An insured who is a member of your household at the time of your death, but only while a resident of the "residence premises"; and
   b. With respect to your property, the person having proper temporary custody of the property until appointment and qualification of a legal representative.

PERSONAL AUTO POLICY

AGREEMENT

In return for payment of the premium and subject to all the terms of this policy, we agree with you as follows:

DEFINITIONS

A. Throughout this policy, "you" and "your" refer to:

1. The "named insured" shown in the Declarations; and

2. The spouse if a resident of the same household.

If the spouse ceases to be a resident of the same household during the policy period or prior to the inception of this policy, the spouse will be considered "you" and "your" under this policy but only until the earlier of:

1. The end of 90 days following the spouse's change of residency;

2. The effective date of another policy listing the spouse as a named insured; or

3. The end of the policy period.

B. "We", "us" and "our" refer to the Company providing this insurance.

C. For purposes of this policy, a private passenger type auto, pickup or van shall be deemed to be owned by a person if leased:

1. Under a written agreement to that person; and

2. For a continuous period of at least 6 months.

Other words and phrases are defined. They are in quotation marks when used.

D. "Bodily injury" means bodily harm, sickness or disease, including death that results.

E. "Business" includes trade, profession or occupation.

F. "Family member" means a person related to you by blood, marriage or adoption who is a resident of your household. This includes a ward or foster child.

G. "Occupying" means:

1. In;

2. Upon; or

3. Getting in, on, out or off.

H. "Property damage" means physical injury to, destruction of or loss of use of tangible property.

I. "Trailer" means a vehicle designed to be pulled by a:

1. Private passenger auto; or

2. Pickup or van.

It also means a farm wagon or farm implement while towed by a vehicle listed in **1.** or **2.** above.

J. "Your covered auto" means:

1. Any vehicle shown in the Declarations.

2. A "newly acquired auto".

3. Any "trailer" you own.

4. Any auto or "trailer" you do not own while used as a temporary substitute for any other vehicle described in this definition which is out of normal use because of its:

a. Breakdown;

b. Repair;

c. Servicing;

d. Loss; or

e. Destruction.

This Provision **(J.4.)** does not apply to Coverage For Damage To Your Auto.

K. "Newly acquired auto":

1. "Newly acquired auto" means any of the following types of vehicles you become the owner of during the policy period:

a. A private passenger auto; or

b. A pickup or van, for which no other insurance policy provides coverage, that:

(1) Has a Gross Vehicle Weight Rating of 10,000 lbs. or less; and

(2) Is not used for the delivery or transportation of goods and materials unless such use is:

(a) Incidental to your "business" of installing, maintaining or repairing furnishings or equipment; or

(b) For farming or ranching.

2. Coverage for a "newly acquired auto" is provided as described below. If you ask us to insure a "newly acquired auto" after a specified time period described below has elapsed, any coverage we provide for a "newly acquired auto" will begin at the time you request the coverage.

a. For any coverage provided in this policy except Coverage For Damage To Your Auto, a "newly acquired auto" will have the broadest coverage we now provide for any vehicle shown in the Declarations. Coverage begins on the date you become the owner. However, for this coverage to apply to a "newly acquired auto" which is in addition to any vehicle shown in the Declarations, you must ask us to insure it within 14 days after you become the owner.

   If a "newly acquired auto" replaces a vehicle shown in the Declarations, coverage is provided for this vehicle without your having to ask us to insure it.

b. Collision Coverage for a "newly acquired auto" begins on the date you become the owner. However, for this coverage to apply, you must ask us to insure it within:

   (1) 14 days after you become the owner if the Declarations indicate that Collision Coverage applies to at least one auto. In this case, the "newly acquired auto" will have the broadest coverage we now provide for any auto shown in the Declarations.

   (2) Four days after you become the owner if the Declarations do not indicate that Collision Coverage applies to at least one auto. If you comply with the 4 day requirement and a loss occurred before you asked us to insure the "newly acquired auto", a Collision deductible of $500 will apply.

c. Other Than Collision Coverage for a "newly acquired auto" begins on the date you become the owner. However, for this coverage to apply, you must ask us to insure it within:

   (1) 14 days after you become the owner if the Declarations indicate that Other Than Collision Coverage applies to at least one auto. In this case, the "newly acquired auto" will have the broadest coverage we now provide for any auto shown in the Declarations.

   (2) Four days after you become the owner if the Declarations do not indicate that Other Than Collision Coverage applies to at least one auto. If you comply with the 4 day requirement and a loss occurred before you asked us to insure the "newly acquired auto", an Other Than Collision deductible of $500 will apply.

PART A – LIABILITY COVERAGE

INSURING AGREEMENT

A. We will pay damages for "bodily injury" or "property damage" for which any "insured" becomes legally responsible because of an auto accident. Damages include prejudgment interest awarded against the "insured". We will settle or defend, as we consider appropriate, any claim or suit asking for these damages. In addition to our limit of liability, we will pay all defense costs we incur. Our duty to settle or defend ends when our limit of liability for this coverage has been exhausted by payment of judgments or settlements. We have no duty to defend any suit or settle any claim for "bodily injury" or "property damage" not covered under this policy.

B. "Insured" as used in this Part means:

   1. You or any "family member" for the ownership, maintenance or use of any auto or "trailer".
   2. Any person using "your covered auto".
   3. For "your covered auto", any person or organization but only with respect to legal responsibility for acts or omissions of a person for whom coverage is afforded under this Part.
   4. For any auto or "trailer", other than "your covered auto", any other person or organization but only with respect to legal responsibility for acts or omissions of you or any "family member" for whom coverage is afforded under this Part. This Provision **(B.4.)** applies only if the person or organization does not own or hire the auto or "trailer".

SUPPLEMENTARY PAYMENTS

We will pay on behalf of an "insured":

1. Up to $250 for the cost of bail bonds required because of an accident, including related traffic law violations. The accident must result in "bodily injury" or "property damage" covered under this policy.
2. Premiums on appeal bonds and bonds to release attachments in any suit we defend.
3. Interest accruing after a judgment is entered in any suit we defend. Our duty to pay interest ends when we offer to pay that part of the judgment which does not exceed our limit of liability for this coverage.

4. Up to $200 a day for loss of earnings, but not other income, because of attendance at hearings or trials at our request.
5. Other reasonable expenses incurred at our request.

These payments will not reduce the limit of liability.

EXCLUSIONS

A. We do not provide Liability Coverage for any "insured":

1. Who intentionally causes "bodily injury" or "property damage".
2. For "property damage" to property owned or being transported by that "insured".
3. For "property damage" to property:
   - **a.** Rented to;
   - **b.** Used by; or
   - **c.** In the care of;

   that "insured".

   This Exclusion **(A.3.)** does not apply to "property damage" to a residence or private garage.
4. For "bodily injury" to an employee of that "insured" during the course of employment. This Exclusion **(A.4.)** does not apply to "bodily injury" to a domestic employee unless workers' compensation benefits are required or available for that domestic employee.
5. For that "insured's" liability arising out of the ownership or operation of a vehicle while it is being used as a public or livery conveyance. This Exclusion **(A.5.)** does not apply to a share-the-expense car pool.
6. While employed or otherwise engaged in the "business" of:
   - **a.** Selling;
   - **b.** Repairing;
   - **c.** Servicing;
   - **d.** Storing; or
   - **e.** Parking;

   vehicles designed for use mainly on public highways. This includes road testing and delivery. This Exclusion **(A.6.)** does not apply to the ownership, maintenance or use of "your covered auto" by:
   - **a.** You;
   - **b.** Any "family member"; or
   - **c.** Any partner, agent or employee of you or any "family member".
7. Maintaining or using any vehicle while that "insured" is employed or otherwise engaged in any "business" (other than farming or ranching) not described in Exclusion **A.6.**

   This Exclusion **(A.7.)** does not apply to the maintenance or use of a:
   - **a.** Private passenger auto;
   - **b.** Pickup or van; or
   - **c.** "Trailer" used with a vehicle described in **a.** or **b.** above.
8. Using a vehicle without a reasonable belief that that "insured" is entitled to do so. This Exclusion **(A.8.)** does not apply to a "family member" using "your covered auto" which is owned by you.
9. For "bodily injury" or "property damage" for which that "insured":
   - **a.** Is an insured under a nuclear energy liability policy; or
   - **b.** Would be an insured under a nuclear energy liability policy but for its termination upon exhaustion of its limit of liability.

   A nuclear energy liability policy is a policy issued by any of the following or their successors:
   - **a.** Nuclear Energy Liability Insurance Association;
   - **b.** Mutual Atomic Energy Liability Underwriters; or
   - **c.** Nuclear Insurance Association of Canada.

B. We do not provide Liability Coverage for the ownership, maintenance or use of:

1. Any vehicle which:
   - **a.** Has fewer than four wheels; or
   - **b.** Is designed mainly for use off public roads.

   This Exclusion **(B.1.)** does not apply:
   - **a.** While such vehicle is being used by an "insured" in a medical emergency;
   - **b.** To any "trailer"; or
   - **c.** To any non-owned golf cart.
2. Any vehicle, other than "your covered auto", which is:
   - **a.** Owned by you; or
   - **b.** Furnished or available for your regular use.
3. Any vehicle, other than "your covered auto", which is:
   - **a.** Owned by any "family member"; or
   - **b.** Furnished or available for the regular use of any "family member".

However, this Exclusion (**B.3.**) does not apply to you while you are maintaining or "occupying" any vehicle which is:

a. Owned by a "family member"; or

b. Furnished or available for the regular use of a "family member".

4. Any vehicle, located inside a facility designed for racing, for the purpose of:

a. Competing in; or

b. Practicing or preparing for;

any prearranged or organized racing or speed contest.

LIMIT OF LIABILITY

A. The limit of liability shown in the Declarations for each person for Bodily Injury Liability is our maximum limit of liability for all damages, including damages for care, loss of services or death, arising out of "bodily injury" sustained by any one person in any one auto accident. Subject to this limit for each person, the limit of liability shown in the Declarations for each accident for Bodily Injury Liability is our maximum limit of liability for all damages for "bodily injury" resulting from any one auto accident.

The limit of liability shown in the Declarations for each accident for Property Damage Liability is our maximum limit of liability for all "property damage" resulting from any one auto accident.

This is the most we will pay regardless of the number of:

1. "Insureds";

2. Claims made;

3. Vehicles or premiums shown in the Declarations; or

4. Vehicles involved in the auto accident.

B. No one will be entitled to receive duplicate payments for the same elements of loss under this coverage and:

1. Part **B** or Part **C** of this policy; or

2. Any Underinsured Motorists Coverage provided by this policy.

OUT OF STATE COVERAGE

If an auto accident to which this policy applies occurs in any state or province other than the one in which "your covered auto" is principally garaged, we will interpret your policy for that accident as follows:

A. If the state or province has:

1. A financial responsibility or similar law specifying limits of liability for "bodily injury" or "property damage" higher than the limit shown in the Declarations, your policy will provide the higher specified limit.

2. A compulsory insurance or similar law requiring a nonresident to maintain insurance whenever the nonresident uses a vehicle in that state or province, your policy will provide at least the required minimum amounts and types of coverage.

B. No one will be entitled to duplicate payments for the same elements of loss.

FINANCIAL RESPONSIBILITY

When this policy is certified as future proof of financial responsibility, this policy shall comply with the law to the extent required.

OTHER INSURANCE

If there is other applicable liability insurance we will pay only our share of the loss. Our share is the proportion that our limit of liability bears to the total of all applicable limits. However, any insurance we provide for a vehicle you do not own, including any vehicle while used as a temporary substitute for "your covered auto", shall be excess over any other collectible insurance.

PART B – MEDICAL PAYMENTS COVERAGE

INSURING AGREEMENT

A. We will pay reasonable expenses incurred for necessary medical and funeral services because of "bodily injury":

1. Caused by accident; and

2. Sustained by an "insured".

We will pay only those expenses incurred for services rendered within 3 years from the date of the accident.

B. "Insured" as used in this Part means:

1. You or any "family member":

a. While "occupying"; or

b. As a pedestrian when struck by;

a motor vehicle designed for use mainly on public roads or a trailer of any type.

2. Any other person while "occupying" "your covered auto".

EXCLUSIONS

We do not provide Medical Payments Coverage for any "insured" for "bodily injury":

1. Sustained while "occupying" any motorized vehicle having fewer than four wheels.
2. Sustained while "occupying" "your covered auto" when it is being used as a public or livery conveyance. This Exclusion **(2.)** does not apply to a share-the-expense car pool.
3. Sustained while "occupying" any vehicle located for use as a residence or premises.
4. Occurring during the course of employment if workers' compensation benefits are required or available for the "bodily injury".
5. Sustained while "occupying", or when struck by, any vehicle (other than "your covered auto") which is:
   a. Owned by you; or
   b. Furnished or available for your regular use.
6. Sustained while "occupying", or when struck by, any vehicle (other than "your covered auto") which is:
   a. Owned by any "family member"; or
   b. Furnished or available for the regular use of any "family member".

   However, this Exclusion **(6.)** does not apply to you.
7. Sustained while "occupying" a vehicle without a reasonable belief that that "insured" is entitled to do so. This Exclusion **(7.)** does not apply to a "family member" using "your covered auto" which is owned by you.
8. Sustained while "occupying" a vehicle when it is being used in the "business" of an "insured". This Exclusion **(8.)** does not apply to "bodily injury" sustained while "occupying" a:
   a. Private passenger auto;
   b. Pickup or van; or
   c. "Trailer" used with a vehicle described in **a.** or **b.** above.
9. Caused by or as a consequence of:
   a. Discharge of a nuclear weapon (even if accidental);
   b. War (declared or undeclared);
   c. Civil war;
   d. Insurrection; or
   e. Rebellion or revolution.
10. From or as a consequence of the following, whether controlled or uncontrolled or however caused:
    a. Nuclear reaction;
    b. Radiation; or
    c. Radioactive contamination.
11. Sustained while "occupying" any vehicle located inside a facility designed for racing, for the purpose of:
    a. Competing in; or
    b. Practicing or preparing for;

    any prearranged or organized racing or speed contest.

LIMIT OF LIABILITY

A. The limit of liability shown in the Declarations for this coverage is our maximum limit of liability for each person injured in any one accident. This is the most we will pay regardless of the number of:

1. "Insureds";
2. Claims made;
3. Vehicles or premiums shown in the Declarations; or
4. Vehicles involved in the accident.

B. No one will be entitled to receive duplicate payments for the same elements of loss under this coverage and:

1. Part **A** or Part **C** of this policy; or
2. Any Underinsured Motorists Coverage provided by this policy.

OTHER INSURANCE

If there is other applicable auto medical payments insurance we will pay only our share of the loss. Our share is the proportion that our limit of liability bears to the total of all applicable limits. However, any insurance we provide with respect to a vehicle you do not own, including any vehicle while used as a temporary substitute for "your covered auto", shall be excess over any other collectible auto insurance providing payments for medical or funeral expenses.

PART C – UNINSURED MOTORISTS COVERAGE

INSURING AGREEMENT

A. We will pay compensatory damages which an "insured" is legally entitled to recover from the owner or operator of an "uninsured motor vehicle" because of "bodily injury":

1. Sustained by an "insured"; and

2. Caused by an accident.

The owner's or operator's liability for these damages must arise out of the ownership, maintenance or use of the "uninsured motor vehicle".

Any judgment for damages arising out of a suit brought without our written consent is not binding on us.

B. "Insured" as used in this Part means:

1. You or any "family member".

2. Any other person "occupying" "your covered auto".

3. Any person for damages that person is entitled to recover because of "bodily injury" to which this coverage applies sustained by a person described in **1.** or **2.** above.

C. "Uninsured motor vehicle" means a land motor vehicle or trailer of any type:

1. To which no bodily injury liability bond or policy applies at the time of the accident.

2. To which a bodily injury liability bond or policy applies at the time of the accident. In this case its limit for bodily injury liability must be less than the minimum limit for bodily injury liability specified by the financial responsibility law of the state in which "your covered auto" is principally garaged.

3. Which is a hit-and-run vehicle whose operator or owner cannot be identified and which hits:

a. You or any "family member";

b. A vehicle which you or any "family member" are "occupying"; or

c. "Your covered auto".

4. To which a bodily injury liability bond or policy applies at the time of the accident but the bonding or insuring company:

a. Denies coverage; or

b. Is or becomes insolvent.

However, "uninsured motor vehicle" does not include any vehicle or equipment:

1. Owned by or furnished or available for the regular use of you or any "family member".

2. Owned or operated by a self-insurer under any applicable motor vehicle law, except a self-insurer which is or becomes insolvent.

3. Owned by any governmental unit or agency.

4. Operated on rails or crawler treads.

5. Designed mainly for use off public roads while not on public roads.

6. While located for use as a residence or premises.

EXCLUSIONS

A. We do not provide Uninsured Motorists Coverage for "bodily injury" sustained:

1. By an "insured" while "occupying", or when struck by, any motor vehicle owned by that "insured" which is not insured for this coverage under this policy. This includes a trailer of any type used with that vehicle.

2. By any "family member" while "occupying", or when struck by, any motor vehicle you own which is insured for this coverage on a primary basis under any other policy.

B. We do not provide Uninsured Motorists Coverage for "bodily injury" sustained by any "insured":

1. If that "insured" or the legal representative settles the "bodily injury" claim and such settlement prejudices our right to recover payment.

2. While "occupying" "your covered auto" when it is being used as a public or livery conveyance. This Exclusion **(B.2.)** does not apply to a share-the-expense car pool.

3. Using a vehicle without a reasonable belief that that "insured" is entitled to do so. This Exclusion **(B.3.)** does not apply to a "family member" using "your covered auto" which is owned by you.

C. This coverage shall not apply directly or indirectly to benefit any insurer or self-insurer under any of the following or similar law:

1. Workers' compensation law; or

2. Disability benefits law.

D. We do not provide Uninsured Motorists Coverage for punitive or exemplary damages.

LIMIT OF LIABILITY

A. The limit of liability shown in the Declarations for each person for Uninsured Motorists Coverage is our maximum limit of liability for all damages, including damages for care, loss of services or death, arising out of "bodily injury" sustained by any one person in any one accident. Subject to this limit for each person, the limit of liability shown in the Declarations for each accident for Uninsured Motorists Coverage is our maximum limit of liability for all damages for "bodily injury" resulting from any one accident.

This is the most we will pay regardless of the number of:

1. "Insureds";
2. Claims made;
3. Vehicles or premiums shown in the Declarations; or
4. Vehicles involved in the accident.

B. No one will be entitled to receive duplicate payments for the same elements of loss under this coverage and:

1. Part **A** or Part **B** of this policy; or
2. Any Underinsured Motorists Coverage provided by this policy.

C. We will not make a duplicate payment under this coverage for any element of loss for which payment has been made by or on behalf of persons or organizations who may be legally responsible.

D. We will not pay for any element of loss if a person is entitled to receive payment for the same element of loss under any of the following or similar law:

1. Workers' compensation law; or
2. Disability benefits law.

OTHER INSURANCE

If there is other applicable insurance available under one or more policies or provisions of coverage that is similar to the insurance provided under this Part of the policy:

1. Any recovery for damages under all such policies or provisions of coverage may equal but not exceed the highest applicable limit for any one vehicle under any insurance providing coverage on either a primary or excess basis.
2. Any insurance we provide with respect to a vehicle you do not own, including any vehicle while used as a temporary substitute for "your covered auto", shall be excess over any collectible insurance providing such coverage on a primary basis.
3. If the coverage under this policy is provided:
   a. On a primary basis, we will pay only our share of the loss that must be paid under insurance providing coverage on a primary basis. Our share is the proportion that our limit of liability bears to the total of all applicable limits of liability for coverage provided on a primary basis.
   b. On an excess basis, we will pay only our share of the loss that must be paid under insurance providing coverage on an excess basis. Our share is the proportion that our limit of liability bears to the total of all applicable limits of liability for coverage provided on an excess basis.

ARBITRATION

A. If we and an "insured" do not agree:

1. Whether that "insured" is legally entitled to recover damages; or
2. As to the amount of damages which are recoverable by that "insured";

from the owner or operator of an "uninsured motor vehicle", then the matter may be arbitrated. However, disputes concerning coverage under this Part may not be arbitrated.

Both parties must agree to arbitration. If so agreed, each party will select an arbitrator. The two arbitrators will select a third. If they cannot agree within 30 days, either may request that selection be made by a judge of a court having jurisdiction.

B. Each party will:

1. Pay the expenses it incurs; and
2. Bear the expenses of the third arbitrator equally.

C. Unless both parties agree otherwise, arbitration will take place in the county in which the "insured" lives. Local rules of law as to procedure and evidence will apply. A decision agreed to by at least two of the arbitrators will be binding as to:

1. Whether the "insured" is legally entitled to recover damages; and
2. The amount of damages. This applies only if the amount does not exceed the minimum limit for bodily injury liability specified by the financial responsibility law of the state in which "your covered auto" is principally garaged. If the amount exceeds that limit, either party may demand the right to a trial. This demand must be made within 60 days of the arbitrators' decision. If this demand is not made, the amount of damages agreed to by the arbitrators will be binding.

PART D – COVERAGE FOR DAMAGE TO YOUR AUTO

INSURING AGREEMENT

A. We will pay for direct and accidental loss to "your covered auto" or any "non-owned auto", including their equipment, minus any applicable deductible shown in the Declarations. If loss to more than one "your covered auto" or "non-owned auto" results from the same "collision", only the highest applicable deductible will apply. We will pay for loss to "your covered auto" caused by:

1. Other than "collision" only if the Declarations indicate that Other Than Collision Coverage is provided for that auto.

2. "Collision" only if the Declarations indicate that Collision Coverage is provided for that auto.

If there is a loss to a "non-owned auto", we will provide the broadest coverage applicable to any "your covered auto" shown in the Declarations.

B. "Collision" means the upset of "your covered auto" or a "non-owned auto" or their impact with another vehicle or object.

Loss caused by the following is considered other than "collision":

1. Missiles or falling objects;

2. Fire;

3. Theft or larceny;

4. Explosion or earthquake;

5. Windstorm;

6. Hail, water or flood;

7. Malicious mischief or vandalism;

8. Riot or civil commotion;

9. Contact with bird or animal; or

10. Breakage of glass.

If breakage of glass is caused by a "collision", you may elect to have it considered a loss caused by "collision".

C. "Non-owned auto" means:

1. Any private passenger auto, pickup, van or "trailer" not owned by or furnished or available for the regular use of you or any "family member" while in the custody of or being operated by you or any "family member"; or

2. Any auto or "trailer" you do not own while used as a temporary substitute for "your covered auto" which is out of normal use because of its:

a. Breakdown;

b. Repair;

c. Servicing;

d. Loss; or

e. Destruction.

TRANSPORTATION EXPENSES

A. In addition, we will pay, without application of a deductible, up to a maximum of $600 for:

1. Temporary transportation expenses not exceeding $20 per day incurred by you in the event of a loss to "your covered auto". We will pay for such expenses if the loss is caused by:

a. Other than "collision" only if the Declarations indicate that Other Than Collision Coverage is provided for that auto.

b. "Collision" only if the Declarations indicate that Collision Coverage is provided for that auto.

2. Expenses for which you become legally responsible in the event of loss to a "non-owned auto". We will pay for such expenses if the loss is caused by:

a. Other than "collision" only if the Declarations indicate that Other Than Collision Coverage is provided for any "your covered auto".

b. "Collision" only if the Declarations indicate that Collision Coverage is provided for any "your covered auto".

However, the most we will pay for any expenses for loss of use is $20 per day.

B. Subject to the provisions of Paragraph **A.**, if the loss is caused by:

1. A total theft of "your covered auto" or a "non-owned auto", we will pay only expenses incurred during the period:

a. Beginning 48 hours after the theft; and

b. Ending when "your covered auto" or the "non-owned auto" is returned to use or we pay for its loss.

2. Other than theft of a "your covered auto" or a "non-owned auto", we will pay only expenses beginning when the auto is withdrawn from use for more than 24 hours.

Our payment will be limited to that period of time reasonably required to repair or replace the "your covered auto" or the "non-owned auto".

EXCLUSIONS

We will not pay for:

1. Loss to "your covered auto" or any "non-owned auto" which occurs while it is being used as a public or livery conveyance. This Exclusion **(1.)** does not apply to a share-the-expense car pool.
2. Damage due and confined to:
   a. Wear and tear;
   b. Freezing;
   c. Mechanical or electrical breakdown or failure; or
   d. Road damage to tires.

   This Exclusion **(2.)** does not apply if the damage results from the total theft of "your covered auto" or any "non-owned auto".
3. Loss due to or as a consequence of:
   a. Radioactive contamination;
   b. Discharge of any nuclear weapon (even if accidental);
   c. War (declared or undeclared);
   d. Civil war;
   e. Insurrection; or
   f. Rebellion or revolution.
4. Loss to any electronic equipment that reproduces, receives or transmits audio, visual or data signals. This includes but is not limited to:
   a. Radios and stereos;
   b. Tape decks;
   c. Compact disk systems;
   d. Navigation systems;
   e. Internet access systems;
   f. Personal computers;
   g. Video entertainment systems;
   h. Telephones;
   i. Televisions;
   j. Two-way mobile radios;
   k. Scanners; or
   l. Citizens band radios.

   This Exclusion **(4.)** does not apply to electronic equipment that is permanently installed in "your covered auto" or any "non-owned auto".
5. Loss to tapes, records, disks or other media used with equipment described in Exclusion **4.**
6. A total loss to "your covered auto" or any "non-owned auto" due to destruction or confiscation by governmental or civil authorities.

   This Exclusion **(6.)** does not apply to the interests of Loss Payees in "your covered auto".
7. Loss to:
   a. A "trailer", camper body, or motor home, which is not shown in the Declarations; or
   b. Facilities or equipment used with such "trailer", camper body or motor home. Facilities or equipment include but are not limited to:
      (1) Cooking, dining, plumbing or refrigeration facilities;
      (2) Awnings or cabanas; or
      (3) Any other facilities or equipment used with a "trailer", camper body, or motor home.

   This Exclusion **(7.)** does not apply to a:
   a. "Trailer", and its facilities or equipment, which you do not own; or
   b. "Trailer", camper body, or the facilities or equipment in or attached to the "trailer" or camper body, which you:
      (1) Acquire during the policy period; and
      (2) Ask us to insure within 14 days after you become the owner.
8. Loss to any "non-owned auto" when used by you or any "family member" without a reasonable belief that you or that "family member" are entitled to do so.
9. Loss to equipment designed or used for the detection or location of radar or laser.
10. Loss to any custom furnishings or equipment in or upon any pickup or van. Custom furnishings or equipment include but are not limited to:
    a. Special carpeting or insulation;
    b. Furniture or bars;
    c. Height-extending roofs; or
    d. Custom murals, paintings or other decals or graphics.

    This Exclusion **(10.)** does not apply to a cap, cover or bedliner in or upon any "your covered auto" which is a pickup.
11. Loss to any "non-owned auto" being maintained or used by any person while employed or otherwise engaged in the "business" of:
    a. Selling;
    b. Repairing;

c. Servicing;

d. Storing; or

e. Parking;

vehicles designed for use on public highways. This includes road testing and delivery.

12. Loss to "your covered auto" or any "non-owned auto", located inside a facility designed for racing, for the purpose of:

a. Competing in; or

b. Practicing or preparing for;

any prearranged or organized racing or speed contest.

13. Loss to, or loss of use of, a "non-owned auto" rented by:

a. You; or

b. Any "family member";

if a rental vehicle company is precluded from recovering such loss or loss of use, from you or that "family member", pursuant to the provisions of any applicable rental agreement or state law.

LIMIT OF LIABILITY

A. Our limit of liability for loss will be the lesser of the:

1. Actual cash value of the stolen or damaged property; or

2. Amount necessary to repair or replace the property with other property of like kind and quality.

However, the most we will pay for loss to:

1. Any "non-owned auto" which is a trailer is $1500.

2. Electronic equipment that reproduces, receives or transmits audio, visual or data signals, which is permanently installed in the auto in locations not used by the auto manufacturer for installation of such equipment, is $1,000.

B. An adjustment for depreciation and physical condition will be made in determining actual cash value in the event of a total loss.

C. If a repair or replacement results in better than like kind or quality, we will not pay for the amount of the betterment.

PAYMENT OF LOSS

We may pay for loss in money or repair or replace the damaged or stolen property. We may, at our expense, return any stolen property to:

1. You; or

2. The address shown in this policy.

If we return stolen property we will pay for any damage resulting from the theft. We may keep all or part of the property at an agreed or appraised value.

If we pay for loss in money, our payment will include the applicable sales tax for the damaged or stolen property.

NO BENEFIT TO BAILEE

This insurance shall not directly or indirectly benefit any carrier or other bailee for hire.

OTHER SOURCES OF RECOVERY

If other sources of recovery also cover the loss, we will pay only our share of the loss. Our share is the proportion that our limit of liability bears to the total of all applicable limits. However, any insurance we provide with respect to a "non-owned auto" shall be excess over any other collectible source of recovery including, but not limited to:

1. Any coverage provided by the owner of the "non-owned auto";

2. Any other applicable physical damage insurance;

3. Any other source of recovery applicable to the loss.

APPRAISAL

A. If we and you do not agree on the amount of loss, either may demand an appraisal of the loss. In this event, each party will select a competent and impartial appraiser. The two appraisers will select an umpire. The appraisers will state separately the actual cash value and the amount of loss. If they fail to agree, they will submit their differences to the umpire. A decision agreed to by any two will be binding. Each party will:

1. Pay its chosen appraiser; and

2. Bear the expenses of the appraisal and umpire equally.

B. We do not waive any of our rights under this policy by agreeing to an appraisal.

PART E – DUTIES AFTER AN ACCIDENT OR LOSS

We have no duty to provide coverage under this policy if the failure to comply with the following duties is prejudicial to us:

A. We must be notified promptly of how, when and where the accident or loss happened. Notice should also include the names and addresses of any injured persons and of any witnesses.

B. A person seeking any coverage must:

1. Cooperate with us in the investigation, settlement or defense of any claim or suit.

2. Promptly send us copies of any notices or legal papers received in connection with the accident or loss.

3. Submit, as often as we reasonably require:

a. To physical exams by physicians we select. We will pay for these exams.

b. To examination under oath and subscribe the same.

4. Authorize us to obtain:

a. Medical reports; and

b. Other pertinent records.

5. Submit a proof of loss when required by us.

C. A person seeking Uninsured Motorists Coverage must also:

1. Promptly notify the police if a hit-and-run driver is involved.

2. Promptly send us copies of the legal papers if a suit is brought.

D. A person seeking Coverage For Damage To Your Auto must also:

1. Take reasonable steps after loss to protect "your covered auto" or any "non-owned auto" and their equipment from further loss. We will pay reasonable expenses incurred to do this.

2. Promptly notify the police if "your covered auto" or any "non-owned auto" is stolen.

3. Permit us to inspect and appraise the damaged property before its repair or disposal.

PART F – GENERAL PROVISIONS

BANKRUPTCY

Bankruptcy or insolvency of the "insured" shall not relieve us of any obligations under this policy.

CHANGES

A. This policy contains all the agreements between you and us. Its terms may not be changed or waived except by endorsement issued by us.

B. If there is a change to the information used to develop the policy premium, we may adjust your premium. Changes during the policy term that may result in a premium increase or decrease include, but are not limited to, changes in:

1. The number, type or use classification of insured vehicles;

2. Operators using insured vehicles;

3. The place of principal garaging of insured vehicles;

4. Coverage, deductible or limits.

If a change resulting from **A.** or **B.** requires a premium adjustment, we will make the premium adjustment in accordance with our manual rules.

C. If we make a change which broadens coverage under this edition of your policy without additional premium charge, that change will automatically apply to your policy as of the date we implement the change in your state. This Paragraph **(C.)** does not apply to changes implemented with a general program revision that includes both broadenings and restrictions in coverage, whether that general program revision is implemented through introduction of:

1. A subsequent edition of your policy; or

2. An Amendatory Endorsement.

FRAUD

We do not provide coverage for any "insured" who has made fraudulent statements or engaged in fraudulent conduct in connection with any accident or loss for which coverage is sought under this policy.

LEGAL ACTION AGAINST US

A. No legal action may be brought against us until there has been full compliance with all the terms of this policy. In addition, under Part **A,** no legal action may be brought against us until:

1. We agree in writing that the "insured" has an obligation to pay; or

2. The amount of that obligation has been finally determined by judgment after trial.

B. No person or organization has any right under this policy to bring us into any action to determine the liability of an "insured".

OUR RIGHT TO RECOVER PAYMENT

A. If we make a payment under this policy and the person to or for whom payment was made has a right to recover damages from another we shall be subrogated to that right. That person shall do:

1. Whatever is necessary to enable us to exercise our rights; and

2. Nothing after loss to prejudice them.

However, our rights in this Paragraph **(A.)** do not apply under Part **D**, against any person using "your covered auto" with a reasonable belief that that person is entitled to do so.

B. If we make a payment under this policy and the person to or for whom payment is made recovers damages from another, that person shall:

1. Hold in trust for us the proceeds of the recovery; and

2. Reimburse us to the extent of our payment.

POLICY PERIOD AND TERRITORY

A. This policy applies only to accidents and losses which occur:

1. During the policy period as shown in the Declarations; and

2. Within the policy territory.

B. The policy territory is:

1. The United States of America, its territories or possessions;

2. Puerto Rico; or

3. Canada.

This policy also applies to loss to, or accidents involving, "your covered auto" while being transported between their ports.

TERMINATION

A. Cancellation

This policy may be cancelled during the policy period as follows:

1. The named insured shown in the Declarations may cancel by:

a. Returning this policy to us; or

b. Giving us advance written notice of the date cancellation is to take effect.

2. We may cancel by mailing to the named insured shown in the Declarations at the address shown in this policy:

a. At least 10 days notice:

(1) If cancellation is for nonpayment of premium; or

(2) If notice is mailed during the first 60 days this policy is in effect and this is not a renewal or continuation policy; or

b. At least 20 days notice in all other cases.

3. After this policy is in effect for 60 days, or if this is a renewal or continuation policy, we will cancel only:

a. For nonpayment of premium; or

b. If your driver's license or that of:

(1) Any driver who lives with you; or

(2) Any driver who customarily uses "your covered auto";

has been suspended or revoked. This must have occurred:

(1) During the policy period; or

(2) Since the last anniversary of the original effective date if the policy period is other than 1 year; or

c. If the policy was obtained through material misrepresentation.

B. Nonrenewal

If we decide not to renew or continue this policy, we will mail notice to the named insured shown in the Declarations at the address shown in this policy. Notice will be mailed at least 20 days before the end of the policy period. Subject to this notice requirement, if the policy period is:

1. Less than 6 months, we will have the right not to renew or continue this policy every 6 months, beginning 6 months after its original effective date.

2. 6 months or longer, but less than one year, we will have the right not to renew or continue this policy at the end of the policy period.

3. 1 year or longer, we will have the right not to renew or continue this policy at each anniversary of its original effective date.

C. Automatic Termination

If we offer to renew or continue and you or your representative do not accept, this policy will automatically terminate at the end of the current policy period. Failure to pay the required renewal or continuation premium when due shall mean that you have not accepted our offer.

If you obtain other insurance on "your covered auto", any similar insurance provided by this policy will terminate as to that auto on the effective date of the other insurance.

D. Other Termination Provisions

1. We may deliver any notice instead of mailing it. Proof of mailing of any notice shall be sufficient proof of notice.
2. If this policy is cancelled, you may be entitled to a premium refund. If so, we will send you the refund. The premium refund, if any, will be computed according to our manuals. However, making or offering to make the refund is not a condition of cancellation.
3. The effective date of cancellation stated in the notice shall become the end of the policy period.

TRANSFER OF YOUR INTEREST IN THIS POLICY

A. Your rights and duties under this policy may not be assigned without our written consent. However, if a named insured shown in the Declarations dies, coverage will be provided for:

1. The surviving spouse if resident in the same household at the time of death. Coverage applies to the spouse as if a named insured shown in the Declarations; and
2. The legal representative of the deceased person as if a named insured shown in the Declarations. This applies only with respect to the representative's legal responsibility to maintain or use "your covered auto".

B. Coverage will only be provided until the end of the policy period.

TWO OR MORE AUTO POLICIES

If this policy and any other auto insurance policy issued to you by us apply to the same accident, the maximum limit of our liability under all the policies shall not exceed the highest applicable limit of liability under any one policy.

COMMON POLICY DECLARATIONS

POLICY NO. ____________________

COMPANY NAME AREA	PRODUCER NAME AREA

NAMED INSURED ____

MAILING ADDRESS ____

____

POLICY PERIOD: From ____________________ **to** ____________________ **at 12:01 A.M. Standard Time at your mailing address shown above.**

BUSINESS DESCRIPTION ____

IN RETURN FOR THE PAYMENT OF THE PREMIUM, AND SUBJECT TO ALL THE TERMS OF THIS POLIC WE AGREE WITH YOU TO PROVIDE THE INSURANCE AS STATED IN THIS POLICY.

THIS POLICY CONSISTS OF THE FOLLOWING COVERAGE PARTS FOR WHICH A PREMIUM IS INDICATED. THIS PREMIUM MAY BE SUBJECT TO ADJUSTMENT.	PREMIUM
Boiler and Machinery Coverage Part	$ ________
Commercial Auto Coverage Part	$ ________
Commercial Crime Coverage Part	$ ________
Commercial General Liability Coverage Part	$ ________
Commercial Inland Marine Coverage Part	$ ________
Commercial Property Coverage Part	$ ________
Farm Coverage Part	$ ________
____________________________	$ ________
TOTAL	$ ________

Premium shown is payable: $ ____________ **at inception. $** ____________ ____________

____

____

Forms applicable to all Coverage Parts: ____
(Show numbers.)

____

____

COUNTERSIGNED ____________________ **BY** ____________________
(Date) **(Authorized Representative)**

NOTE: OFFICERS' FACSIMILE SIGNATURES MAY BE INSERTED HERE, ON THE POLICY COVER OR ELSEWHERE AT THE COMPANY'S OPTION

COMMERCIAL PROPERTY COVERAGE PART
DECLARATIONS PAGE

POLICY NO.

EFFECTIVE DATE ___/___/___

☐ *"X" IF SUPPLEMENTAL DECLARATIONS IS ATTACHED*

NAMED INSURED

DESCRIPTION OF PREMISES

PREM. NO.	BLDG. NO.	LOCATION, CONSTRUCTION AND OCCUPANCY

COVERAGES PROVIDED INSURANCE AT THE DESCRIBED PREMISES APPLIES ONLY FOR COVERAGES FOR WHICH A LIMIT OF INSURANCE IS SHOWN.

PREM. NO.	BLDG. NO.	COVERAGE	LIMIT OF INSURANCE	COVERED CAUSES OF LOSS	COINSURANCE*	RATES

* IF EXTRA EXPENSE COVERAGE, LIMITS ON LOSS PAYMENT

OPTIONAL COVERAGES APPLICABLE ONLY WHEN ENTRIES ARE MADE IN THE SCHEDULE BELOW

PREM. NO.	BLDG. NO.	AGREED VALUE EXPIRATION DATE	COVERAGE	AMOUNT	REPLACEMENT COST(X) BUILDING	PERSONAL PROPERTY	INCLUDING "STOCK"

INFLATION GUARD (Percentage) BUILDING	PERSONAL PROPERTY	*MONTHLY LIMIT OF INDEMNITY (Fraction)	*MAXIMUM PERIOD OF INDEMNITY (X)	*EXTENDED PERIOD OF INDEMNITY (Days)

* APPLIES TO BUSINESS INCOME ONLY

MORTGAGE HOLDERS

PREM. NO.	BLDG. NO.	MORTGAGE HOLDER NAME AND MAILING ADDRESS

DEDUCTIBLE

$250. EXCEPTIONS:

FORMS APPLICABLE

TO ALL COVERAGES:

TO SPECIFIC PREMISES/COVERAGES:

PREM. NO.	BLDG. NO.	COVERAGES	FORM NUMBER

BUSINESSOWNERS COVERAGE FORM

Various provisions in this policy restrict coverage. Read the entire policy carefully to determine rights, duties and what is and is not covered.

Throughout this Coverage Form the words "you" and "your" refer to the Named Insured shown in the Declarations. The words "we", "us" and "our" refer to the Company providing this insurance.

In **Section II – Liability,** the word "insured" means any person or organization qualifying as such under Paragraph **C** – Who Is An Insured.

Other words and phrases that appear in quotation marks have special meaning. Refer to Paragraph **H.** Property Definitions in **Section I – Property** and Paragraph **F.** Liability And Medical Expenses Definitions in **Section II – Liability.**

SECTION I – PROPERTY

A. Coverage

We will pay for direct physical loss of or damage to Covered Property at the premises described in the Declarations caused by or resulting from any Covered Cause of Loss.

1. Covered Property

Covered Property includes Buildings as described under Paragraph **a.** below, Business Personal Property as described under Paragraph **b.** below, or both, depending on whether a Limit of Insurance is shown in the Declarations for that type of property. Regardless of whether coverage is shown in the Declarations for Buildings, Business Personal Property, or both, there is no coverage for property described under Paragraph **2.** Property Not Covered.

a. Buildings, meaning the buildings and structures at the premises described in the Declarations, including:

(1) Completed additions;

(2) Fixtures, including outdoor fixtures;

(3) Permanently installed:

(a) Machinery; and

(b) Equipment;

(4) Your personal property in apartments, rooms or common areas furnished by you as landlord;

(5) Personal property owned by you that is used to maintain or service the buildings or structures or the premises, including:

(a) Fire extinguishing equipment;

(b) Outdoor furniture;

(c) Floor coverings; and

(d) Appliances used for refrigerating, ventilating, cooking, dishwashing or laundering;

(6) If not covered by other insurance:

(a) Additions under construction, alterations and repairs to the buildings or structures;

(b) Materials, equipment, supplies and temporary structures, on or within 100 feet of the described premises, used for making additions, alterations or repairs to the buildings or structures.

b. Business Personal Property located in or on the buildings at the described premises or in the open (or in a vehicle) within 100 feet of the described premises, including:

(1) Property you own that is used in your business;

(2) Property of others that is in your care, custody or control, except as otherwise provided in Loss Payment Property Loss Condition Paragraph **E.6.d.(3)(b);**

(3) Tenant's improvements and betterments. Improvements and betterments are fixtures, alterations, installations or additions:

(a) Made a part of the building or structure you occupy but do not own; and

(b) You acquired or made at your expense but cannot legally remove; and

(4) Leased personal property for which you have a contractual responsibility to insure, unless otherwise provided for under Paragraph **1.b.(2).**

(5) Exterior building glass, if you are a tenant and no Limit of Insurance is shown in the Declarations for Building property. The glass must be owned by you or in your care, custody or control.

2. Property Not Covered

Covered Property does not include:

a. Aircraft, automobiles, motortrucks and other vehicles subject to motor vehicle registration;

b. "Money" or "securities" except as provided in the:

(1) Money and Securities Optional Coverage; or

(2) Employee Dishonesty Optional Coverage;

c. Contraband, or property in the course of illegal transportation or trade;

d. Land (including land on which the property is located), water, growing crops or lawns;

e. Outdoor fences, radio or television antennas (including satellite dishes) and their lead-in wiring, masts or towers, signs (other than signs attached to buildings), trees, shrubs or plants, all except as provided in the:

(1) Outdoor Property Coverage Extension; or

(2) Outdoor Signs Optional Coverage;

f. Watercraft (including motors, equipment and accessories) while afloat.

g. Accounts, bills, food stamps, other evidences of debt, accounts receivable or "valuable papers and records"; except as otherwise provided in this policy.

h. "Computer(s)" which are permanently installed or designed to be permanently installed in any aircraft, watercraft, motortruck or other vehicle subject to motor vehicle registration. This paragraph does not apply to "computer(s)" while held as "stock".

3. Covered Causes Of Loss

Risks of direct physical loss unless the loss is:

a. Excluded in Paragraph **B.** Exclusions in Section **I;** or

b. Limited in Paragraph **4.** Limitations in Section **I.**

4. Limitations

a. We will not pay for loss of or damage to:

(1) Steam boilers, steam pipes, steam engines or steam turbines caused by or resulting from any condition or event inside such equipment. But we will pay for loss of or damage to such equipment caused by or resulting from an explosion of gases or fuel within the furnace of any fired vessel or within the flues or passages through which the gases of combustion pass.

(2) Hot water boilers or other water heating equipment caused by or resulting from any condition or event inside such boilers or equipment, other than an explosion.

(3) Property that is missing, where the only evidence of the loss or damage is a shortage disclosed on taking inventory, or other instances where there is no physical evidence to show what happened to the property. This limitation does not apply to the Optional Coverage for Money and Securities.

(4) Property that has been transferred to a person or to a place outside the described premises on the basis of unauthorized instructions.

(5) The interior of any building or structure caused by or resulting from rain, snow, sleet, ice, sand or dust, whether driven by wind or not, unless:

(a) The building or structure first sustains damage by a Covered Cause of Loss to its roof or walls through which the rain, snow, sleet, ice, sand or dust enters; or

(b) The loss or damage is caused by or results from thawing of snow, sleet or ice on the building or structure.

b. We will not pay for loss of or damage to fragile articles such as glassware, statuary, marbles, chinaware and porcelains, if broken, unless caused by the "specified causes of loss" or building glass breakage. This restriction does not apply to:

(1) Glass that is part of the exterior or interior of a building or structure;

(2) Containers of property held for sale; or

(3) Photographic or scientific instrument lenses.

c. For loss or damage by theft, the following types of property are covered only up to the limits shown:

(1) $2,500 for furs, fur garments and garments trimmed with fur.

(2) $2,500 for jewelry, watches, watch movements, jewels, pearls, precious and semi-precious stones, bullion, gold, silver, platinum and other precious alloys or metals. This limit does not apply to jewelry and watches worth $100 or less per item.

(3) $2,500 for patterns, dies, molds and forms.

5. **Additional Coverages**

a. **Debris Removal**

(1) Subject to Paragraphs **(3)** and **(4),** we will pay your expense to remove debris of Covered Property caused by or resulting from a Covered Cause of Loss that occurs during the policy period. The expenses will be paid only if they are reported to us in writing within 180 days of the date of direct physical loss or damage.

(2) Debris Removal does not apply to costs to:

(a) Extract "pollutants" from land or water; or

(b) Remove, restore or replace polluted land or water.

(3) Subject to the exceptions in Paragraph **(4),** the following provisions apply:

(a) The most that we will pay for the total of direct physical loss or damage plus debris removal expense is the Limit of Insurance applicable to the Covered Property that has sustained loss or damage.

(b) Subject to Paragraph **(a)** above, the amount we will pay for debris removal expense is limited to 25% of the sum of the deductible plus the amount that we pay for direct physical loss or damage to the Covered Property that has sustained loss or damage.

(4) We will pay up to an additional $10,000 for debris removal expense, for each location, in any one occurrence of physical loss or damage to Covered Property, if one or both of the following circumstances apply:

(a) The total of the actual debris removal expense plus the amount we pay for direct physical loss or damage exceeds the Limit of Insurance on the Covered Property that has sustained loss or damage.

(b) The actual debris removal expense exceeds 25% of the sum of the deductible plus the amount that we pay for direct physical loss or damage to the Covered Property that has sustained loss or damage.

Therefore, if Paragraphs **(4)(a)** and/or **(4)(b)** apply, our total payment for direct physical loss or damage and debris removal expense may reach but will never exceed the Limit of Insurance on the Covered Property that has sustained loss or damage, plus $10,000.

(5) **Examples**

Example #1

Limit of Insurance	$ 90,000
Amount of Deductible	$ 500
Amount of Loss	$ 50,000
Amount of Loss Payable	$ 49,500
	($50,000 – $500)
Debris Removal Expense	$ 10,000
Debris Removal Expense Payable	$ 10,000
($10,000 is 20% of $50,000)	

The debris removal expense is less than 25% of the sum of the loss payable plus the deductible. The sum of the loss payable and the debris removal expense ($49,500 + $10,000 = $59,500) is less than the Limit of Insurance. Therefore the full amount of debris removal expense is payable in accordance with the terms of Paragraph **(3).**

Example #2

Limit of Insurance	$ 90,000
Amount of Deductible	$ 500
Amount of Loss	$ 80,000
Amount of Loss Payable	$ 79,500
	($80,000 – $500)
Debris Removal Expense	$ 30,000
Debris Removal Expense Payable	
Basic Amount	$ 10,500
Additional Amount	$ 10,000

The basic amount payable for debris removal expense under the terms of Paragraph **(3)** is calculated as follows: $80,000 ($79,500 + $500) x .25 = $20,000; capped at $10,500). The cap applies because the sum of the loss payable ($79,500) and the basic amount payable for debris removal expense ($10,500) cannot exceed the Limit of Insurance ($90,000).

The additional amount payable for debris removal expense is provided in accordance with the terms of Paragraph **(4),** because the debris removal expense ($30,000) exceeds 25% of the loss payable plus the deductible ($30,000 is 37.5% of $80,000), and because the sum of the loss payable and debris removal expense ($79,500 + $30,000 =$109,500) would exceed the Limit of Insurance ($90,000). The additional amount of covered debris removal expense is $10,000, the maximum payable under Paragraph **(4).** Thus the total payable for debris removal expense in this example is $20,500; $9,500 of the debris removal expense is not covered.

b. Preservation Of Property

If it is necessary to move Covered Property from the described premises to preserve it from loss or damage by a Covered Cause of Loss, we will pay for any direct physical loss of or damage to that property:

(1) While it is being moved or while temporarily stored at another location; and

(2) Only if the loss or damage occurs within 30 days after the property is first moved.

c. Fire Department Service Charge

When the fire department is called to save or protect Covered Property from a Covered Cause of Loss, we will pay up to $1,000 for your liability for fire department service charges:

(1) Assumed by contract or agreement prior to loss; or

(2) Required by local ordinance.

d. Collapse

(1) With respect to buildings:

(a) Collapse means an abrupt falling down or caving in of a building or any part of a building with the result that the building or part of the building cannot be occupied for its intended purpose;

(b) A building or any part of a building that is in danger of falling down or caving in is not considered to be in a state of collapse;

(c) A part of a building that is standing is not considered to be in a state of collapse even if it has separated from another part of the building;

(d) A building that is standing or any part of a building that is standing is not considered to be in a state of collapse even if it shows evidence of cracking, bulging, sagging, bending, leaning, settling, shrinkage or expansion.

(2) We will pay for direct physical loss or damage to Covered Property, caused by collapse of a building or any part of a building that is insured under this policy, if the collapse is caused by one or more of the following:

(a) The "specified causes of loss" or breakage of building glass, all only as insured against in this policy;

(b) Decay that is hidden from view, unless the presence of such decay is known to an insured prior to collapse;

(c) Insect or vermin damage that is hidden from view, unless the presence of such damage is known to an insured prior to collapse;

(d) Weight of people or personal property;

(e) Weight of rain that collects on a roof;

(f) Use of defective material or methods in construction, remodeling or renovation if the collapse occurs during the course of the construction, remodeling or renovation. However, if the collapse occurs after construction, remodeling or renovation is complete and is caused in part by a cause of loss listed in Paragraphs **(a)** through **(e),** we will pay for the loss or damage even if use of defective material or methods in construction, remodeling or renovation, contributes to the collapse.

The criteria set forth in Paragraphs **(1)(a)** through **(1)(d)** do not limit the coverage otherwise provided under this Additional Coverage for the causes of loss listed in Paragraphs **(2)(a)**, **(2)(d)** and **(2)(e).**

(3) With respect to the following property:

(a) Awnings;

(b) Gutters and downspouts;

(c) Yard fixtures;

(d) Outdoor swimming pools;

(e) Piers, wharves and docks;

(f) Beach or diving platforms or appurtenances;

(g) Retaining walls; and

(h) Walks, roadways and other paved surfaces;

if the collapse is caused by a cause of loss listed in Paragraphs **(2)(b)** through **(2)(f),** we will pay for loss or damage to that property only if such loss or damage is a direct result of the collapse of a building insured under this policy and the property is Covered Property under this policy.

(4) If personal property abruptly falls down or caves in and such collapse is not the result of collapse of a building, we will pay for loss or damage to Covered Property caused by such collapse of personal property only if:

(a) The collapse was caused by a cause of loss listed in Paragraphs **(2)(a)** through **(2)(f)** of this Additional Coverage;

(b) The personal property which collapses is inside a building; and

(c) The property which collapses is not of a kind listed in Paragraph **(3)** above, regardless of whether that kind of property is considered to be personal property or real property.

The coverage stated in this Paragraph **(4)** does not apply to personal property if marring and/or scratching is the only damage to that personal property caused by the collapse.

Collapse of personal property does not mean cracking, bulging, sagging, bending, leaning, settling, shrinkage or expansion.

(5) This Additional Coverage, Collapse, will not increase the Limits Of Insurance provided in this policy.

e. Water Damage, Other Liquids, Powder Or Molten Material Damage

If loss or damage caused by or resulting from covered water or other liquid, powder or molten material damage loss occurs, we will also pay the cost to tear out and replace any part of the building or structure to repair damage to the system or appliance from which the water or other substance escapes.

We will not pay the cost to repair any defect that caused the loss or damage; but we will pay the cost to repair or replace damaged parts of fire extinguishing equipment if the damage:

(1) Results in discharge of any substance from an automatic fire protection system; or

(2) Is directly caused by freezing.

f. Business Income

(1) Business Income

(a) We will pay for the actual loss of Business Income you sustain due to the necessary suspension of your "operations" during the "period of restoration". The suspension must be caused by direct physical loss of or damage to property at the described premises. The loss or damage must be caused by or result from a Covered Cause of Loss. With respect to loss of or damage to personal property in the open or personal property in a vehicle, the described premises include the area within 100 feet of the site at which the described premises are located.

With respect to the requirements set forth in the preceding paragraph, if you occupy only part of the site at which the described premises are located, your premises means:

(i) The portion of the building which you rent, lease or occupy; and

(ii) Any area within the building or on the site at which the described premises are located, if that area services, or is used to gain access to, the described premises.

(b) We will only pay for loss of Business Income that you sustain during the "period of restoration" and that occurs within 12 consecutive months after the date of direct physical loss or damage. We will only pay for ordinary payroll expenses for 60 days following the date of direct physical loss or damage, unless a greater number of days is shown in the Declarations.

(c) Business Income means the:

(i) Net Income (Net Profit or Loss before income taxes) that would have been earned or incurred if no physical loss or damage had occurred, but not including any Net Income that would likely have been earned as a result of an increase in the volume of business due to favorable business conditions caused by the impact of the Covered Cause of Loss on customers or on other businesses; and

(ii) Continuing normal operating expenses incurred, including payroll.

(d) Ordinary payroll expenses:

(i) Mean payroll expenses for all your employees except:

i. Officers;

ii. Executives;

iii. Department Managers;

iv. Employees under contract; and

v. Additional Exemptions shown in the Declarations as:

- Job Classifications; or
- Employees.

(ii) Include:

i. Payroll;

ii. Employee benefits, if directly related to payroll;

iii. FICA payments you pay;

iv. Union dues you pay; and

v. Workers' compensation premiums.

(2) Extended Business Income

(a) If the necessary suspension of your "operations" produces a Business Income loss payable under this policy, we will pay for the actual loss of Business Income you incur during the period that:

(i) Begins on the date property except finished stock is actually repaired, rebuilt or replaced and "operations" are resumed; and

(ii) Ends on the earlier of:

i. The date you could restore your "operations", with reasonable speed, to the level which would generate the Business Income amount that would have existed if no direct physical loss or damage had occurred; or

ii. 30 consecutive days after the date determined in Paragraph **(a)(i)** above, unless a greater number of consecutive days is shown in the Declarations.

However, Extended Business Income does not apply to loss of Business Income incurred as a result of unfavorable business conditions caused by the impact of the Covered Cause of Loss in the area where the described premises are located.

(b) Loss of Business Income must be caused by direct physical loss or damage at the described premises caused by or resulting from any Covered Cause of Loss.

(3) With respect to the coverage provided in this Additional Coverage, suspension means:

(a) The partial slowdown or complete cessation of your business activities; and

(b) That a part or all of the described premises is rendered untenantable, if coverage for Business Income applies.

(4) This Additional Coverage is not subject to the Limits of Insurance of **Section I – Property.**

g. Extra Expense

(1) We will pay necessary Extra Expense you incur during the "period of restoration" that you would not have incurred if there had been no direct physical loss or damage to property at the described premises. The loss or damage must be caused by or result from a Covered Cause of Loss. With respect to loss of or damage to personal property in the open or personal property in a vehicle, the described premises include the area within 100 feet of the site at which the described premises are located.

With respect to the requirements set forth in the preceding paragraph, if you occupy only part of the site at which the described premises are located, your premises means:

(a) The portion of the building which you rent, lease or occupy; and

(b) Any area within the building or on the site at which the described premises are located, if that area services, or is used to gain access to, the described premises.

(2) Extra Expense means expense incurred:

(a) To avoid or minimize the suspension of business and to continue "operations":

(i) At the described premises; or

(ii) At replacement premises or at temporary locations, including relocation expenses, and costs to equip and operate the replacement or temporary locations.

(b) To minimize the suspension of business if you cannot continue "operations".

(c) To:

(i) Repair or replace any property; or

(ii) Research, replace or restore the lost information on damaged "valuable papers and records"

to the extent it reduces the amount of loss that otherwise would have been payable under this Additional Coverage or Additional Coverage **f.** Business Income.

(3) With respect to the coverage provided in this Additional Coverage, suspension means:

(a) The partial slowdown or complete cessation of your business activities; and

(b) That a part or all of the described premises is rendered untenantable, if coverage for Business Income applies.

(4) We will only pay for Extra Expense that occurs within 12 consecutive months after the date of direct physical loss or damage. This Additional Coverage is not subject to the Limits of Insurance of **Section I – Property.**

h. Pollutant Clean Up And Removal

We will pay your expense to extract "pollutants" from land or water at the described premises if the discharge, dispersal, seepage, migration, release or escape of the "pollutants" is caused by or results from a Covered Cause of Loss that occurs during the policy period. The expenses will be paid only if they are reported to us in writing within 180 days of the earlier of:

(1) The date of direct physical loss or damage; or

(2) The end of the policy period.

The most we will pay for each location under this Additional Coverage is $10,000 for the sum of all such expenses arising out of Covered Causes of Loss occurring during each separate 12 month period of this policy.

i. Civil Authority

We will pay for the actual loss of Business Income you sustain and necessary Extra Expense caused by action of civil authority that prohibits access to the described premises due to direct physical loss of or damage to property, other than at the described premises, caused by or resulting from any Covered Cause of Loss.

The coverage for Business Income will begin 72 hours after the time of that action and will apply for a period of up to three consecutive weeks after coverage begins.

The coverage for necessary Extra Expense will begin immediately after the time of that action and ends:

(1) 3 consecutive weeks after the time of that action; or

(2) When your Business Income coverage ends;

whichever is later.

The definitions of Business Income and Extra Expense contained in the Business Income and Extra Expense Additional Coverages also apply to this Civil Authority Additional Coverage. The Civil Authority Additional Coverage is not subject to the Limits of Insurance of **Section I – Property.**

j. Money Orders And Counterfeit Paper Currency

We will pay for loss resulting directly from your having accepted in good faith, in exchange for merchandise, "money" or services:

(1) Money orders issued by any post office, express company or bank that are not paid upon presentation; or

(2) "Counterfeit" paper currency that is acquired during the regular course of business.

The most we will pay for any loss under this Additional Coverage is $1,000.

k. Forgery Or Alteration

(1) We will pay for loss resulting directly from forgery or alteration of, any check, draft, promissory note, bill of exchange or similar written promise of payment in "money", that you or your agent has issued, or that was issued by someone who impersonates you or your agent.

(2) If you are sued for refusing to pay the check, draft, promissory note, bill of exchange or similar written promise of payment in "money", on the basis that it has been forged or altered, and you have our written consent to defend against the suit, we will pay for any reasonable legal expenses that you incur in that defense.

(3) The most we will pay for any loss, including legal expenses, under this Additional Coverage is $2,500, unless a higher Limit of Insurance is shown in the Declarations.

l. Increased Cost Of Construction

(1) This Additional Coverage applies only to buildings insured on a replacement cost basis.

(2) In the event of damage by a Covered Cause of Loss to a building that is Covered Property, we will pay the increased costs incurred to comply with enforcement of an ordinance or law in the course of repair, rebuilding or replacement of damaged parts of that property, subject to the limitations stated in Paragraphs **(3)** through **(9)** of this Additional Coverage.

(3) The ordinance or law referred to in Paragraph **(2)** of this Additional Coverage is an ordinance or law that regulates the construction or repair of buildings or establishes zoning or land use requirements at the described premises, and is in force at the time of loss.

(4) Under this Additional Coverage, we will not pay any costs due to an ordinance or law that:

(a) You were required to comply with before the loss, even when the building was undamaged; and

(b) You failed to comply with.

(5) Under this Additional Coverage, we will not pay any costs associated with the enforcement of an ordinance or law which requires any insured or others to test for, monitor, clean up, remove, contain, treat, detoxify or neutralize, or in any way respond to, or assess the effects of "pollutants".

(6) The most we will pay under this Additional Coverage, for each described building insured under **Section I – Property,** is $10,000. If a damaged building(s) is covered under a blanket Limit of Insurance which applies to more than one building or item of property, then the most we will pay under this Additional Coverage, for each damaged building, is $10,000.

The amount payable under this Additional Coverage is additional insurance.

(7) With respect to this Additional Coverage:

(a) We will not pay for the Increased Cost of Construction:

(i) Until the property is actually repaired or replaced, at the same or another premises; and

(ii) Unless the repairs or replacement are made as soon as reasonably possible after the loss or damage, not to exceed two years. We may extend this period in writing during the two years.

(b) If the building is repaired or replaced at the same premises, or if you elect to rebuild at another premises, the most we will pay for the Increased Cost of Construction is the increased cost of construction at the same premises.

(c) If the ordinance or law requires relocation to another premises, the most we will pay for the Increased Cost of Construction is the increased cost of construction at the new premises.

(8) This Additional Coverage is not subject to the terms of the Ordinance or Law Exclusion, to the extent that such Exclusion would conflict with the provisions of this Additional Coverage.

(9) The costs addressed in the Loss Payment Property Loss Condition in **Section I – Property** do not include the increased cost attributable to enforcement of an ordinance or law. The amount payable under this Additional Coverage, as stated in Paragraph **(6)** of this Additional Coverage, is not subject to such limitation.

m. Business Income From Dependent Properties

(1) We will pay for the actual loss of Business Income you sustain due to physical loss or damage at the premises of a dependent property caused by or resulting from any Covered Cause of Loss.

The most we will pay under this Additional Coverage is $5,000 unless a higher Limit of Insurance is indicated in the Declarations.

(2) We will reduce the amount of your Business Income loss, other than Extra Expense, to the extent you can resume "operations", in whole or in part, by using any other available:

(a) Source of materials; or

(b) Outlet for your products.

(3) If you do not resume "operations", or do not resume "operations" as quickly as possible, we will pay based on the length of time it would have taken to resume "operations" as quickly as possible.

(4) Dependent property means property owned by others whom you depend on to:

(a) Deliver materials or services to you, or to others for your account. But services does not mean water, communication or power supply services;

(b) Accept your products or services;

(c) Manufacture your products for delivery to your customers under contract for sale; or

(d) Attract customers to your business.

The dependent property must be located in the coverage territory of this policy.

(5) The coverage period for Business Income under this Additional Coverage:

(a) Begins 72 hours after the time of direct physical loss or damage caused by or resulting from any Covered Cause of Loss at the premises of the dependent property; and

(b) Ends on the date when the property at the premises of the dependent property should be repaired, rebuilt or replaced with reasonable speed and similar quality.

(6) The Business Income coverage period, as stated in Paragraph **(5)**, does not include any increased period required due to the enforcement of any ordinance or law that:

(a) Regulates the construction, use or repair, or requires the tearing down of any property; or

(b) Requires any insured or others to test for, monitor, clean up, remove, contain, treat, detoxify or neutralize, or in any way respond to, or assess the effects of "pollutants".

The expiration date of this policy will not reduce the Business Income coverage period.

(7) The definition of Business Income contained in the Business Income Additional Coverage also applies to this Business Income From Dependent Properties Additional Coverage.

n. Glass Expenses

(1) We will pay for expenses incurred to put up temporary plates or board up openings if repair or replacement of damaged glass is delayed.

(2) We will pay for expenses incurred to remove or replace obstructions when repairing or replacing glass that is part of a building. This does not include removing or replacing window displays.

o. Fire Extinguisher Systems Recharge Expense

(1) We will pay:

(a) The cost of recharging or replacing, whichever is less, your fire extinguishers and fire extinguishing systems (including hydrostatic testing if needed) if they are discharged on or within 100 feet of the described premises; and

(b) For loss or damage to Covered Property if such loss or damage is the result of an accidental discharge of chemicals from a fire extinguisher or a fire extinguishing system.

(2) No coverage will apply if the fire extinguishing system is discharged during installation or testing.

(3) The most we will pay under this Additional Coverage is $5,000 in any one occurrence.

6. Coverage Extensions

In addition to the Limits of Insurance of **Section I – Property,** you may extend the insurance provided by this policy as provided below.

Except as otherwise provided, the following Extensions apply to property located in or on the building described in the Declarations or in the open (or in a vehicle) within 100 feet of the described premises, unless a higher Limit of Insurance is shown in the Declarations.

a. Newly Acquired Or Constructed Property

(1) Buildings

If this policy covers Buildings, you may extend that insurance to apply to:

(a) Your new buildings while being built on the described premises; and

(b) Buildings you acquire at premises other than the one described, intended for:

(i) Similar use as the building described in the Declarations; or

(ii) Use as a warehouse.

The most we will pay for loss or damage under this Extension is $250,000 at each building.

(2) Business Personal Property

(a) If this policy covers Business Personal Property, you may extend that insurance to apply to:

(i) Business Personal Property, including such property that you newly acquire, at any location you acquire.

(ii) Business Personal Property, including such property that you newly acquire, located at your newly constructed or acquired buildings at the location described in the Declarations; or

(iii) Business Personal Property that you newly acquire, located at the described premises.

This Extension does not apply to personal property that you temporarily acquire in the course of installing or performing work on such property or your wholesale activities.

The most we will pay for loss or damage under this Extension is $100,000 at each premises.

(3) Period Of Coverage

With respect to insurance on or at each newly acquired or constructed property, coverage will end when any of the following first occurs:

(a) This policy expires;

(b) 30 days expire after you acquire the property or begin construction of that part of the building that would qualify as covered property; or

(c) You report values to us.

We will charge you additional premium for values reported from the date you acquire the property or begin construction of that part of the building that would qualify as covered property.

b. Personal Property Off Premises

You may extend the insurance that applies to Business Personal Property to apply to covered Business Personal Property, other than "money" and "securities", "valuable papers and records" or accounts receivable, while it is in the course of transit or at a premises you do not own, lease or operate. The most we will pay for loss or damage under this Extension is $5,000.

c. Outdoor Property

You may extend the insurance provided by this policy to apply to your outdoor fences, radio and television antennas (including satellite dishes), signs (other than signs attached to buildings), trees, shrubs and plants, including debris removal expense, caused by or resulting from any of the following causes of loss:

(1) Fire;

(2) Lightning;

(3) Explosion;

(4) Riot or Civil Commotion; or

(5) Aircraft.

The most we will pay for loss or damage under this Extension is $2,500, but not more than $500 for any one tree, shrub or plant.

d. Personal Effects

You may extend the insurance that applies to Business Personal Property to apply to personal effects owned by you, your officers, your partners or "members", your "managers" or your employees. This extension does not apply to:

(1) Tools or equipment used in your business; or

(2) Loss or damage by theft.

The most we will pay for loss or damage under this Extension is $2,500 at each described premises.

e. Valuable Papers And Records

(1) You may extend the insurance that applies to Business Personal Property to apply to direct physical loss or damage to "valuable papers and records" that you own, or that are in your care, custody or control caused by or resulting from a Covered Cause of Loss. This Coverage Extension includes the cost to research, replace or restore the lost information on "valuable papers and records" for which duplicates do not exist.

(2) This Coverage Extension does not apply to:

(a) Property held as samples or for delivery after sale;

(b) Property in storage away from the premises shown in the Declarations.

(3) The most we will pay under this Coverage Extension for loss or damage to "valuable papers and records" in any one occurrence at the described premises is $10,000, unless a higher Limit of Insurance for "valuable papers and records" is shown in the Declarations.

For "valuable papers and records" not at the described premises, the most we will pay is $5,000.

(4) Paragraph **B. Exclusions** in **Section I – Property** does not apply to this Coverage Extension except for:

(a) Paragraph **B.1.c.**, Governmental Action;

(b) Paragraph **B.1.d.**, Nuclear Hazard;

(c) Paragraph **B.1.f.**, War And Military Action;

(d) Paragraph **B.2.f.**, Dishonesty;

(e) Paragraph **B.2.g.**, False Pretense; and

(f) Paragraph **B.3.**

f. Accounts Receivable

(1) You may extend the insurance that applies to Business Personal Property to apply to accounts receivable. We will pay:

(a) All amounts due from your customers that you are unable to collect;

(b) Interest charges on any loan required to offset amounts you are unable to collect pending our payment of these amounts;

(c) Collection expenses in excess of your normal collection expenses that are made necessary by loss or damage; and

(d) Other reasonable expenses that you incur to re-establish your records of accounts receivable;

that result from direct physical loss or damage by any Covered Cause of Loss to your records of accounts receivable.

(2) The most we will pay under this Coverage Extension for loss or damage in any one occurrence at the described premises is $10,000, unless a higher Limit of Insurance for accounts receivable is shown in the Declarations.

For accounts receivable not at the described premises, the most we will pay is $5,000.

(3) Paragraph **B. Exclusions** in **Section I – Property** does not apply to this Coverage Extension except for:

(a) Paragraph **B.1.c.,** Governmental Action;

(b) Paragraph **B.1.d.,** Nuclear Hazard;

(c) Paragraph **B.1.f.,** War And Military Action;

(d) Paragraph **B.2.f.,** Dishonesty;

(e) Paragraph **B.2.g.,** False Pretense;

(f) Paragraph **B.3.**; and

(g) Paragraph **B.5.** Accounts Receivable Exclusion.

B. Exclusions

1. We will not pay for loss or damage caused directly or indirectly by any of the following. Such loss or damage is excluded regardless of any other cause or event that contributes concurrently or in any sequence to the loss. These exclusions apply whether or not the loss event results in widespread damage or affects a substantial area.

a. Ordinance Or Law

(1) The enforcement of any ordinance or law:

(a) Regulating the construction, use or repair of any property; or

(b) Requiring the tearing down of any property, including the cost of removing its debris.

(2) This exclusion, Ordinance Or Law, applies whether the loss results from:

(a) An ordinance or law that is enforced even if the property has not been damaged; or

(b) The increased costs incurred to comply with an ordinance or law in the course of construction, repair, renovation, remodeling or demolition of property or removal of its debris, following a physical loss to that property.

b. Earth Movement

(1) Earthquake, including any earth sinking, rising or shifting related to such event;

(2) Landslide, including any earth sinking, rising or shifting related to such event;

(3) Mine subsidence, meaning subsidence of a man-made mine, whether or not mining activity has ceased;

(4) Earth sinking (other than sinkhole collapse), rising or shifting including soil conditions which cause settling, cracking or other disarrangement of foundations or other parts of realty. Soil conditions include contraction, expansion, freezing, thawing, erosion, improperly compacted soil and the action of water under the ground surface.

But if Earth Movement, as described in Paragraphs **(1)** through **(4)** above, results in fire or explosion, we will pay for the loss or damage caused by that fire or explosion.

(5) Volcanic eruption, explosion or effusion. But if volcanic eruption, explosion or effusion results in fire, building glass breakage or volcanic action, we will pay for the loss or damage caused by that fire, building glass breakage or volcanic action.

Volcanic action means direct loss or damage resulting from the eruption of a volcano when the loss or damage is caused by:

(a) Airborne volcanic blast or airborne shock waves;

(b) Ash, dust or particulate matter; or

(c) Lava flow.

All volcanic eruptions that occur within any 168-hour period will constitute a single occurrence.

Volcanic action does not include the cost to remove ash, dust or particulate matter that does not cause direct physical loss of or damage to Covered Property.

c. Governmental Action

Seizure or destruction of property by order of governmental authority.

But we will pay for loss or damage caused by or resulting from acts of destruction ordered by governmental authority and taken at the time of a fire to prevent its spread, if the fire would be covered under this policy.

d. Nuclear Hazard

Nuclear reaction or radiation, or radioactive contamination, however caused.

But if nuclear reaction or radiation, or radioactive contamination, results in fire, we will pay for the loss or damage caused by that fire.

e. Power Failure

The failure of power or other utility service supplied to the described premises, however caused, if the failure occurs away from the described premises.

But if the failure of power or other utility service results in a Covered Cause of Loss, we will pay for the loss or damage caused by that Covered Cause of Loss.

This exclusion does not apply to loss or damage to "computer(s)" and "electronic media and records".

f. War And Military Action

(1) War, including undeclared or civil war;

(2) Warlike action by a military force, including action in hindering or defending against an actual or expected attack, by any government, sovereign or other authority using military personnel or other agents; or

(3) Insurrection, rebellion, revolution, usurped power, or action taken by governmental authority in hindering or defending against any of these.

g. Water

(1) Flood, surface water, waves, tides, tidal waves, overflow of any body of water, or their spray, all whether driven by wind or not;

(2) Mudslide or mudflow;

(3) Water that backs up or overflows from a sewer, drain or sump; or

(4) Water under the ground surface pressing on, or flowing or seeping through:

(a) Foundations, walls, floors or paved surfaces;

(b) Basements, whether paved or not; or

(c) Doors, windows or other openings.

But if Water, as described in Paragraphs **(1)** through **(4),** results in fire, explosion or sprinkler leakage, we will pay for the loss or damage caused by that fire, explosion or sprinkler leakage.

h. Certain Computer-Related Losses

(1) The failure, malfunction or inadequacy of:

(a) Any of the following, whether belonging to any insured or to others:

(i) "Computer" hardware, including microprocessors or other electronic data processing equipment as may be described elsewhere in this policy;

(ii) "Computer" application software or other "electronic media and records" as may be described elsewhere in this policy;

(iii) "Computer" operating systems and related software;

(iv) "Computer" networks;

(v) Microprocessors ("computer" chips) not part of any "computer" system; or

(vi) Any other computerized or electronic equipment or components; or

(b) Any other products, and any services, data or functions that directly or indirectly use or rely upon, in any manner, any of the items listed in Paragraph **(a)** above;

due to the inability to correctly recognize, distinguish, interpret or accept one or more dates or times. An example is the inability of computer software to recognize the year 2000.

(2) Any advice, consultation, design, evaluation, inspection, installation, maintenance, repair, replacement or supervision provided or done by you or for you to determine, rectify or test for, any potential or actual problems described in Paragraph **(1)** above.

However, if excluded loss or damage, as described in Paragraph **(1)** above results in a "Specified Cause of Loss" under **Section I – Property,** we will pay only for the loss or damage caused by such "Specified Cause of Loss".

We will not pay for repair, replacement or modification of any items in Paragraphs **(1)(a)** or **(1)(b)** to correct any deficiencies or change any features.

2. We will not pay for loss or damage caused by or resulting from any of the following:

a. Electrical Apparatus

Artificially generated electrical current, including electric arcing, that disturbs electrical devices, appliances or wires.

But if artificially generated electrical current results in fire, we will pay for the loss or damage caused by fire.

We will pay for loss or damage to "computer(s)" due to artificially generated electrical current if such loss or damage is caused by or results from:

(1) An occurrence that took place within 100 feet of the described premises; or

(2) Interruption of electric power supply, power surge, blackout or brownout if the cause of such occurrence took place within 100 feet of the described premises.

b. Consequential Losses

Delay, loss of use or loss of market.

c. Smoke, Vapor, Gas

Smoke, vapor or gas from agricultural smudging or industrial operations.

d. Steam Apparatus

Explosion of steam boilers, steam pipes, steam engines or steam turbines owned or leased by you, or operated under your control. But if explosion of steam boilers, steam pipes, steam engines or steam turbines results in fire or combustion explosion, we will pay for the loss or damage caused by that fire or combustion explosion. We will also pay for loss or damage caused by or resulting from the explosion of gases or fuel within the furnace of any fired vessel or within the flues or passages through which the gases of combustion pass.

e. Frozen Plumbing

Water, other liquids, powder or molten material that leaks or flows from plumbing, heating, air conditioning or other equipment (except fire protective systems) caused by or resulting from freezing, unless:

(1) You do your best to maintain heat in the building or structure; or

(2) You drain the equipment and shut off the supply if the heat is not maintained.

f. Dishonesty

Dishonest or criminal acts by you, anyone else with an interest in the property, or any of your or their partners, "members", officers, "managers", employees, directors, trustees, authorized representatives or anyone to whom you entrust the property for any purpose:

(1) Acting alone or in collusion with others;

(2) Whether or not occurring during the hours of employment.

This exclusion does not apply to acts of destruction by your employees; but theft by employees is not covered.

With respect to accounts receivable and "valuable papers and records", this exclusion does not apply to carriers for hire.

This exclusion does not apply to coverage that is provided under the Employee Dishonesty Optional Coverage.

g. False Pretense

Voluntary parting with any property by you or anyone else to whom you have entrusted the property if induced to do so by any fraudulent scheme, trick, device or false pretense.

h. Exposed Property

Rain, snow, ice or sleet to personal property in the open.

i. Collapse

Collapse, except as provided in the Additional Coverage for Collapse. But if collapse results in a Covered Cause of Loss, we will pay for the loss or damage caused by that Covered Cause of Loss.

j. Pollution

We will not pay for loss or damage caused by or resulting from the discharge, dispersal, seepage, migration, release or escape of "pollutants" unless the discharge, dispersal, seepage, migration, release or escape is itself caused by any of the "specified causes of loss". But if the discharge, dispersal, seepage, migration, release or escape of "pollutants" results in a "specified cause of loss", we will pay for the loss or damage caused by that "specified cause of loss".

k. Neglect

Neglect of an insured to use all reasonable means to save and preserve property from further damage at and after the time of loss.

l. Other Types Of Loss

(1) Wear and tear;

(2) Rust, corrosion, fungus, decay, deterioration, hidden or latent defect or any quality in property that causes it to damage or destroy itself;

(3) Smog;

(4) Settling, cracking, shrinking or expansion;

(5) Nesting or infestation, or discharge or release of waste products or secretions, by insects, birds, rodents or other animals;

(6) Mechanical breakdown, including rupture or bursting caused by centrifugal force.

This exclusion does not apply with respect to the breakdown of "computer(s)";

(7) The following causes of loss to personal property:

(a) Dampness or dryness of atmosphere;

(b) Changes in or extremes of temperature; or

(c) Marring or scratching.

But if an excluded cause of loss that is listed in Paragraphs **(1)** through **(7)** above results in a "specified cause of loss" or building glass breakage, we will pay for the loss or damage caused by that "specified cause of loss" or building glass breakage.

m. Errors Or Omissions

Errors or omissions in:

(1) Programming, processing or storing data, as described under "electronic media and records" or in any "computer" operations; or

(2) Processing or copying "valuable papers and records".

However, we will pay for direct physical loss or damage caused by resulting fire or explosion if these causes of loss would be covered by this coverage form.

n. Installation, Testing, Repair

Errors or deficiency in design, installation, testing, maintenance, modification or repair of your "computer" system including "electronic media and records".

However, we will pay for direct physical loss or damage caused by resulting fire or explosion if these causes of loss would be covered by this coverage form.

o. Electrical Disturbance

Electrical or magnetic injury, disturbance or erasure of "electronic media and records", except as provided for under the Coverage Extensions of **Section I – Property.**

However, we will pay for direct loss or damage caused by lightning.

3. We will not pay for loss or damage caused by or resulting from any of the following Paragraphs **a.** through **c.** But if an excluded cause of loss that is listed in Paragraphs **a.** through **c.** results in a Covered Cause of Loss, we will pay for the loss or damage caused by that Covered Cause of Loss.

a. Weather Conditions

Weather conditions. But this exclusion only applies if weather conditions contribute in any way with a cause or event excluded in Paragraph **B.1.** above to produce the loss or damage.

b. Acts Or Decisions

Acts or decisions, including the failure to act or decide, of any person, group, organization or governmental body.

c. Negligent Work

Faulty, inadequate or defective:

(1) Planning, zoning, development, surveying, siting;

(2) Design, specifications, workmanship, repair, construction, renovation, remodeling, grading, compaction;

(3) Materials used in repair, construction, renovation or remodeling; or

(4) Maintenance;

of part or all of any property on or off the described premises.

4. Business Income And Extra Expense Exclusions

a. We will not pay for:

(1) Any Extra Expense, or increase of Business Income loss, caused by or resulting from:

(a) Delay in rebuilding, repairing or replacing the property or resuming "operations", due to interference at the location of the rebuilding, repair or replacement by strikers or other persons; or

(b) Suspension, lapse or cancellation of any license, lease or contract. But if the suspension, lapse or cancellation is directly caused by the suspension of "operations", we will cover such loss that affects your Business Income during the "period of restoration".

(2) Any other consequential loss.

b. With respect to this exclusion, suspension means:

(1) The partial slowdown or complete cessation of your business activities; and

(2) That a part or all of the described premises is rendered untenantable, if coverage for Business Income applies.

5. **Accounts Receivable Exclusion**

The following additional exclusion applies to the Accounts Receivable Coverage Extension:

We will not pay for:

a. Loss or damage caused by or resulting from alteration, falsification, concealment or destruction of records of accounts receivable done to conceal the wrongful giving, taking or withholding of "money", "securities" or other property.

This exclusion applies only to the extent of the wrongful giving, taking or withholding.

b. Loss or damage caused by or resulting from bookkeeping, accounting or billing errors or omissions.

c. Any loss or damage that requires any audit of records or any inventory computation to prove its factual existence.

C. Limits Of Insurance

1. The most we will pay for loss or damage in any one occurrence is the applicable Limit of Insurance of **Section I – Property** shown in the Declarations.

2. The most we will pay for loss of or damage to outdoor signs attached to buildings is $1,000 per sign in any one occurrence.

3. The limits applicable to the Coverage Extensions and the Fire Department Service Charge and Pollutant Clean Up and Removal Additional Coverages are in addition to the Limits of Insurance of **Section I – Property.**

4. **Building Limit – Automatic Increase**

a. The Limit of Insurance for Buildings will automatically increase by the annual percentage shown in the Declarations.

b. The amount of increase will be:

(1) The Building limit that applied on the most recent of the policy inception date, the policy anniversary date, or any other policy change amending the Building limit, times

(2) The percentage of annual increase shown in the Declarations, expressed as a decimal (example: 8% is .08), times

(3) The number of days since the beginning of the current policy year of the effective date of the most recent policy change amending the Building limit, divided by 365.

Example:

If: The applicable Building limit is $100,000. The annual percentage increase is 8%. The number of days since the beginning of the policy year (or last policy change) is 146.

The amount of increase is

$100,000 x .08 x 146 ÷ 365 = $3,200.

5. **Business Personal Property Limit – Seasonal Increase**

a. The Limit of Insurance for Business Personal Property will automatically increase by 25% to provide for seasonal variations.

b. This increase will apply only if the Limit of Insurance shown for Business Personal Property in the Declarations is at least 100% of your average monthly values during the lesser of:

(1) The 12 months immediately preceding the date the loss or damage occurs; or

(2) The period of time you have been in business as of the date the loss or damage occurs.

D. Deductibles

1. We will not pay for loss or damage in any one occurrence until the amount of loss or damage exceeds the Deductible shown in the Declarations. We will then pay the amount of loss or damage in excess of the Deductible up to the applicable Limit of Insurance of **Section I – Property.**

2. Regardless of the amount of the Deductible, the most we will deduct from any loss or damage for Glass and under all of the following Optional Coverages in any one occurrence is the Optional Coverage/Glass Deductible shown in the Declarations:

a. Money and Securities;

b. Employee Dishonesty; and

c. Outdoor Signs.

But this Optional Coverage/Glass Deductible will not increase the Deductible shown in the Declarations. This Deductible will be used to satisfy the requirements of the Deductible in the Declarations.

3. No deductible applies to the following Additional Coverages:

a. Fire Department Service Charge;

b. Business Income;

c. Extra Expense;

d. Civil Authority; and

e. Fire Extinguisher Systems Recharge Expense.

E. Property Loss Conditions

1. Abandonment

There can be no abandonment of any property to us.

2. Appraisal

If we and you disagree on the amount of loss, either may make written demand for an appraisal of the loss. In this event, each party will select a competent and impartial appraiser. The two appraisers will select an umpire. If they cannot agree, either may request that selection be made by a judge of a court having jurisdiction. The appraisers will state separately the amount of loss. If they fail to agree, they will submit their differences to the umpire. A decision agreed to by any two will be binding. Each party will:

a. Pay its chosen appraiser; and

b. Bear the other expenses of the appraisal and umpire equally.

If there is an appraisal, we will still retain our right to deny the claim.

3. Duties In The Event Of Loss Or Damage

a. You must see that the following are done in the event of loss or damage to Covered Property:

(1) Notify the police if a law may have been broken.

(2) Give us prompt notice of the loss or damage. Include a description of the property involved.

(3) As soon as possible, give us a description of how, when and where the loss or damage occurred.

(4) Take all reasonable steps to protect the Covered Property from further damage, and keep a record of your expenses necessary to protect the Covered Property, for consideration in the settlement of the claim. This will not increase the Limits of Insurance of **Section I – Property.** However, we will not pay for any subsequent loss or damage resulting from a cause of loss that is not a Covered Cause of Loss. Also, if feasible, set the damaged property aside and in the best possible order for examination.

(5) At our request, give us complete inventories of the damaged and undamaged property. Include quantities, costs, values and amount of loss claimed.

(6) As often as may be reasonably required, permit us to inspect the property proving the loss or damage and examine your books and records.

Also permit us to take samples of damaged and undamaged property for inspection, testing and analysis, and permit us to make copies from your books and records.

(7) Send us a signed, sworn proof of loss containing the information we request to investigate the claim. You must do this within 60 days after our request. We will supply you with the necessary forms.

(8) Cooperate with us in the investigation or settlement of the claim.

(9) Resume all or part of your "operations" as quickly as possible.

b. We may examine any insured under oath, while not in the presence of any other insured and at such times as may be reasonably required, about any matter relating to this insurance or the claim, including an insured's books and records. In the event of an examination, an insured's answers must be signed.

4. Legal Action Against Us

No one may bring a legal action against us under this insurance unless:

a. There has been full compliance with all of the terms of this insurance; and

b. The action is brought within 2 years after the date on which the direct physical loss or damage occurred.

5. Electronic Media And Records Limitation

We will not pay for any loss of Business Income caused by direct physical loss of or damage to "electronic media and records" after the longer of:

a. 60 consecutive days from the date of direct physical loss or damage; or

b. The period, beginning with the date of direct physical loss or damage, necessary to repair, rebuild or replace with reasonable speed and similar quality, other property at the described premises due to loss or damage caused by the same occurrence.

Example #1

A Covered Cause of Loss damages a "computer" on June 1. It takes until September 1 to replace the "computer", and until October 1 to restore the data that was lost when the damage occurred. We will only pay for the Business Income loss sustained during the period June 1 – September 1. Loss during the period September 2 – October 1 is not covered.

Example #2

A Covered Cause of Loss results in the loss of data processing programming records on August 1. The records are replaced on October 15. We will only pay for the Business Income loss sustained during the period August 1 – September 29 (60 consecutive days). Loss during the period September 30 – October 15 is not covered.

6. Loss Payment

In the event of loss or damage covered by this policy:

a. At our option, we will either:

(1) Pay the value of lost or damaged property;

(2) Pay the cost of repairing or replacing the lost or damaged property;

(3) Take all or any part of the property at an agreed or appraised value; or

(4) Repair, rebuild or replace the property with other property of like kind and quality, subject to Paragraph **d.(1)(e)** below.

b. We will give notice of our intentions within 30 days after we receive the sworn proof of loss.

c. We will not pay you more than your financial interest in the Covered Property.

d. Except as provided in Paragraphs **(2)** through **(8)** below, we will determine the value of Covered Property as follows:

(1) At replacement cost without deduction for depreciation, subject to the following:

(a) If, at the time of loss, the Limit of Insurance on the lost or damaged property is 80% or more of the full replacement cost of the property immediately before the loss, we will pay the cost to repair or replace, after application of the deductible and without deduction for depreciation, but not more than the least of the following amounts:

(i) The Limit of Insurance under **Section I – Property** that applies to the lost or damaged property;

(ii) The cost to replace, on the same premises, the lost or damaged property with other property:

i. Of comparable material and quality; and

ii. Used for the same purpose; or

(iii) The amount that you actually spend that is necessary to repair or replace the lost or damaged property.

If a building is rebuilt at a new premises, the cost is limited to the cost which would have been incurred had the building been built at the original premises.

(b) If, at the time of loss, the Limit of Insurance applicable to the lost or damaged property is less than 80% of the full replacement cost of the property immediately before the loss, we will pay the greater of the following amounts, but not more than the Limit of Insurance that applies to the property:

(i) The actual cash value of the lost or damaged property; or

(ii) A proportion of the cost to repair or replace the lost or damaged property, after application of the deductible and without deduction for depreciation. This proportion will equal the ratio of the applicable Limit of Insurance to 80% of the cost of repair or replacement.

(c) You may make a claim for loss or damage covered by this insurance on an actual cash value basis instead of on a replacement cost basis. In the event you elect to have loss or damage settled on an actual cash value basis, you may still make a claim on a replacement cost basis if you notify us of your intent to do so within 180 days after the loss or damage.

(d) We will not pay on a replacement cost basis for any loss or damage:

(i) Until the lost or damaged property is actually repaired or replaced; and

(ii) Unless the repairs or replacement are made as soon as reasonably possible after the loss or damage.

However, if the cost to repair or replace the damaged building property is $2,500 or less, we will settle the loss according to the provisions of Paragraphs **d.(1)(a)** and **d.(1)(b)** above whether or not the actual repair or replacement is complete.

(e) The cost to repair, rebuild or replace does not include the increased cost attributable to enforcement of any ordinance or law regulating the construction, use or repair of any property.

(2) If the "Actual Cash Value – Buildings" option applies, as shown in the Declarations, Paragraph **(1)** above does not apply to Buildings. Instead, we will determine the value of Buildings at actual cash value.

(3) The following property at actual cash value:

(a) Used or second-hand merchandise held in storage or for sale;

(b) Property of others. However, if an item(s) of personal property of others is subject to a written contract which governs your liability for loss or damage to that item(s), then valuation of that item(s) will be based on the amount for which you are liable under such contract, but not to exceed the lesser of the replacement cost of the property or the applicable Limit of Insurance;

(c) Household contents, except personal property in apartments or rooms furnished by you as landlord;

(d) Manuscripts;

(e) Works of art, antiques or rare articles, including etchings, pictures, statuary, marbles, bronzes, porcelains and bric-a-brac.

(4) Glass at the cost of replacement with safety glazing material if required by law.

(5) Tenants' Improvements and Betterments at:

(a) Replacement cost if you make repairs promptly.

(b) A proportion of your original cost if you do not make repairs promptly. We will determine the proportionate value as follows:

(i) Multiply the original cost by the number of days from the loss or damage to the expiration of the lease; and

(ii) Divide the amount determined in **(i)** above by the number of days from the installation of improvements to the expiration of the lease.

If your lease contains a renewal option, the expiration of the renewal option period will replace the expiration of the lease in this procedure.

(c) Nothing if others pay for repairs or replacement.

(6) Loss or damage to "valuable papers and records" will be valued at the cost of restoration or replacement, including the cost of data entry, re-programming, computer consultation services and the media on which the data or programs reside. To the extent that the contents of the "valuable papers and records" are not restored, the "valuable papers and records" will be valued at the cost of replacement with blank materials of substantially identical type.

(7) Applicable only to the Optional Coverages:

(a) "Money" at its face value; and

(b) "Securities" at their value at the close of business on the day the loss is discovered.

(8) Applicable only to Accounts Receivable:

(a) If you cannot accurately establish the amount of accounts receivable outstanding as of the time of loss or damage:

(i) We will determine the total of the average monthly amounts of accounts receivable for the 12 months immediately preceding the month in which the loss or damage occurs; and

(ii) We will adjust that total for any normal fluctuations in the amount of accounts receivable for the month in which the loss or damage occurred or for any demonstrated variance from the average for that month.

(b) The following will be deducted from the total amount of accounts receivable, however that amount is established:

(i) The amount of the accounts for which there is no loss or damage;

(ii) The amount of the accounts that you are able to re-establish or collect;

(iii) An amount to allow for probable bad debts that you are normally unable to collect; and

(iv) All unearned interest and service charges.

e. Our payment for loss of or damage to personal property of others will only be for the account of the owners of the property. We may adjust losses with the owners of lost or damaged property if other than you. If we pay the owners, such payments will satisfy your claims against us for the owners' property. We will not pay the owners more than their financial interest in the Covered Property.

f. We may elect to defend you against suits arising from claims of owners of property. We will do this at our expense.

g. We will pay for covered loss or damage within 30 days after we receive the sworn proof of loss, provided you have complied with all of the terms of this policy, and

(1) We have reached agreement with you on the amount of loss; or

(2) An appraisal award has been made.

7. Recovered Property

If either you or we recover any property after loss settlement, that party must give the other prompt notice. At your option, you may retain the property. But then you must return to us the amount we paid to you for the property. We will pay recovery expenses and the expenses to repair the recovered property, subject to the Limits of Insurance of **Section I – Property.**

8. Resumption Of Operations

We will reduce the amount of your:

a. Business Income loss, other than Extra Expense, to the extent you can resume your "operations", in whole or in part, by using damaged or undamaged property (including merchandise or stock) at the described premises or elsewhere.

b. Extra Expense loss to the extent you can return "operations" to normal and discontinue such Extra Expense.

9. Vacancy

a. Description Of Terms

(1) As used in this Vacancy Condition, the term building and the term vacant have the meanings set forth in Paragraphs **(a)** and **(b)** below:

(a) When this policy is issued to a tenant, and with respect to that tenant's interest in Covered Property, building means the unit or suite rented or leased to the tenant. Such building is vacant when it does not contain enough business personal property to conduct customary operations.

(b) When this policy is issued to the owner or general lessee of a building, building means the entire building. Such building is vacant unless at least 31% of its total square footage is:

(i) Rented to a lessee or sub-lessee and used by the lessee or sub-lessee to conduct its customary operations; and/or

(ii) Used by the building owner to conduct customary operations.

(2) Buildings under construction or renovation are not considered vacant.

b. Vacancy Provisions

If the building where loss or damage occurs has been vacant for more than 60 consecutive days before that loss or damage occurs:

(1) We will not pay for any loss or damage caused by any of the following even if they are Covered Causes of Loss:

(a) Vandalism;

(b) Sprinkler leakage, unless you have protected the system against freezing;

(c) Building glass breakage;

(d) Water damage;

(e) Theft; or

(f) Attempted theft.

(2) With respect to Covered Causes of Loss other than those listed in Paragraphs **(1)(a)** through **(1)(f)** above, we will reduce the amount we would otherwise pay for the loss or damage by 15%.

F. Property General Conditions

1. Control Of Property

Any act or neglect of any person other than you beyond your direction or control will not affect this insurance.

The breach of any condition of this Coverage Form at any one or more locations will not affect coverage at any location where, at the time of loss or damage, the breach of condition does not exist.

2. Mortgageholders

a. The term "mortgageholder" includes trustee.

b. We will pay for covered loss of or damage to buildings or structures to each mortgageholder shown in the Declarations in their order of precedence, as interests may appear.

c. The mortgageholder has the right to receive loss payment even if the mortgageholder has started foreclosure or similar action on the building or structure.

d. If we deny your claim because of your acts or because you have failed to comply with the terms of this policy, the mortgageholder will still have the right to receive loss payment if the mortgageholder:

(1) Pays any premium due under this policy at our request if you have failed to do so;

(2) Submits a signed, sworn proof of loss within 60 days after receiving notice from us of your failure to do so; and

(3) Has notified us of any change in ownership, occupancy or substantial change in risk known to the mortgageholder.

All of the terms of this policy will then apply directly to the mortgageholder.

e. If we pay the mortgageholder for any loss or damage and deny payment to you because of your acts or because you have failed to comply with the terms of this policy:

(1) The mortgageholder's rights under the mortgage will be transferred to us to the extent of the amount we pay; and

(2) The mortgageholder's right to recover the full amount of the mortgageholder's claim will not be impaired.

At our option, we may pay to the mortgageholder the whole principal on the mortgage plus any accrued interest. In this event, your mortgage and note will be transferred to us and you will pay your remaining mortgage debt to us.

f. If we cancel this policy, we will give written notice to the mortgageholder at least:

(1) 10 days before the effective date of cancellation if we cancel for your nonpayment of premium; or

(2) 30 days before the effective date of cancellation if we cancel for any other reason.

g. If we elect not to renew this policy, we will give written notice to the mortgageholder at least 10 days before the expiration date of this policy.

3. No Benefit To Bailee

No person or organization, other than you, having custody of Covered Property will benefit from this insurance.

4. Policy Period, Coverage Territory

Under **Section I – Property:**

a. We cover loss or damage commencing:

(1) During the policy period shown in the Declarations; and

(2) Within the coverage territory or, with respect to property in transit, while it is between points in the coverage territory.

b. The coverage territory is:

(1) The United States of America (including its territories and possessions);

(2) Puerto Rico; and

(3) Canada.

G. **Optional Coverages**

If shown as applicable in the Declarations, the following Optional Coverages also apply. These coverages are subject to the terms and conditions applicable to property coverage in this policy, except as provided below.

1. **Outdoor Signs**

   a. We will pay for direct physical loss of or damage to all outdoor signs at the described premises:

      (1) Owned by you; or

      (2) Owned by others but in your care, custody or control.

   b. Paragraph **A.3., Covered Causes Of Loss,** and Paragraph **B., Exclusions** in **Section I – Property,** do not apply to this Optional Coverage, except for:

      (1) Paragraph **B.1.c.,** Governmental Action;

      (2) Paragraph **B.1.d.,** Nuclear Hazard; and

      (3) Paragraph **B.1.f.,** War And Military Action.

   c. We will not pay for loss or damage caused by or resulting from:

      (1) Wear and tear;

      (2) Hidden or latent defect;

      (3) Rust;

      (4) Corrosion; or

      (5) Mechanical breakdown.

   d. The most we will pay for loss or damage in any one occurrence is the Limit of Insurance for Outdoor Signs shown in the Declarations.

   e. The provisions of this Optional Coverage supersede all other references to outdoor signs in this policy.

2. **Money And Securities**

   a. We will pay for loss of "money" and "securities" used in your business while at a bank or savings institution, within your living quarters or the living quarters of your partners or any employee having use and custody of the property, at the described premises, or in transit between any of these places, resulting directly from:

      (1) Theft, meaning any act of stealing;

      (2) Disappearance; or

      (3) Destruction.

   b. In addition to the Limitations and Exclusions applicable to **Section I – Property,** we will not pay for loss:

      (1) Resulting from accounting or arithmetical errors or omissions;

      (2) Due to the giving or surrendering of property in any exchange or purchase; or

      (3) Of property contained in any "money"-operated device unless the amount of "money" deposited in it is recorded by a continuous recording instrument in the device.

   c. The most we will pay for loss in any one occurrence is:

      (1) The limit shown in the Declarations for Inside the Premises for "money" and "securities" while:

         (a) In or on the described premises; or

         (b) Within a bank or savings institution; and

      (2) The limit shown in the Declarations for Outside the Premises for "money" and "securities" while anywhere else.

   d. All loss:

      (1) Caused by one or more persons; or

      (2) Involving a single act or series of related acts;

      is considered one occurrence.

   e. You must keep records of all "money" and "securities" so we can verify the amount of any loss or damage.

3. **Employee Dishonesty**

   a. We will pay for direct loss of or damage to Business Personal Property and "money" and "securities" resulting from dishonest acts committed by any of your employees acting alone or in collusion with other persons (except you or your partner) with the manifest intent to:

      (1) Cause you to sustain loss or damage; and also

      (2) Obtain financial benefit (other than salaries, commissions, fees, bonuses, promotions, awards, profit sharing, pensions or other employee benefits earned in the normal course of employment) for:

         (a) Any employee; or

         (b) Any other person or organization.

   b. We will not pay for loss or damage:

      (1) Resulting from any dishonest or criminal act that you or any of your partners or "members" commit whether acting alone or in collusion with other persons.

(2) Resulting from any dishonest act committed by any of your employees (except as provided in Paragraph **a.**), "managers" or directors:

(a) Whether acting alone or in collusion with other persons; or

(b) While performing services for you or otherwise.

(3) The only proof of which as to its existence or amount is:

(a) An inventory computation; or

(b) A profit and loss computation.

c. The most we will pay for loss or damage in any one occurrence is the Limit of Insurance for Employee Dishonesty shown in the Declarations.

d. All loss or damage:

(1) Caused by one or more persons; or

(2) Involving a single act or series of acts;

is considered one occurrence.

e. If any loss is covered:

(1) Partly by this insurance; and

(2) Partly by any prior cancelled or terminated insurance that we or any affiliate had issued to you or any predecessor in interest;

the most we will pay is the larger of the amount recoverable under this insurance or the prior insurance.

We will pay only for loss or damage you sustain through acts committed or events occurring during the Policy Period. Regardless of the number of years this policy remains in force or the number of premiums paid, no Limit of Insurance cumulates from year to year or period to period.

f. This Optional Coverage is cancelled as to any employee immediately upon discovery by:

(1) You; or

(2) Any of your partners, "members", "managers", officers or directors not in collusion with the employee;

of any dishonest act committed by that employee before or after being hired by you.

g. We will pay only for covered loss or damage sustained during the policy period and discovered no later than one year from the end of the policy period.

h. If you (or any predecessor in interest) sustained loss or damage during the policy period of any prior insurance that you could have recovered under that insurance except that the time within which to discover loss or damage had expired, we will pay for it under this Optional Coverage, provided:

(1) This Optional Coverage became effective at the time of cancellation or termination of the prior insurance; and

(2) The loss or damage would have been covered by this Optional Coverage had it been in effect when the acts or events causing the loss or damage were committed or occurred.

i. The insurance under Paragraph **h.** above is part of, not in addition to, the Limit of Insurance applying to this Optional Coverage and is limited to the lesser of the amount recoverable under:

(1) This Optional Coverage as of its effective date; or

(2) The prior insurance had it remained in effect.

4. Mechanical Breakdown

a. We will pay for direct damage to Covered Property caused by an Accident to an Object. The Object must be:

(1) Owned by you or in your care, custody or control; and

(2) At the described premises.

b. Accident means a sudden and accidental breakdown of the Object or a part of the Object. At the time the breakdown occurs, it must manifest itself by physical damage to the Object that necessitates repair or replacement.

c. None of the following is an Accident:

(1) Depletion, deterioration, corrosion or erosion;

(2) Wear and tear;

(3) Leakage at any valve, fitting, shaft seal, gland packing, joint or connection;

(4) Breakdown of any vacuum tube, gas tube or brush;

(5) Breakdown of any "computer", including "computer(s)" used to operate production type machinery or equipment;

(6) Breakdown of any structure or foundation supporting the Object or any of its parts;

(7) The functioning of any safety or protective device; or

(8) The explosion of gases or fuel within the furnace of any Object or within the flues or passages through which the gases of combustion pass.

d. Object means any of the following equipment:

(1) Boiler and Pressure Vessels:

(a) Steam heating boilers and condensate return tanks used with them;

(b) Hot water heating boilers and expansion tanks used with them;

(c) Hot water supply boilers;

(d) Other fired or unfired vessels used for maintenance or service of the described premises but not used for processing or manufacturing;

(e) Steam boiler piping, valves, fittings, traps and separators, but only if they:

(i) Are on your premises or between parts of your premises;

(ii) Contain steam or condensate of steam; and

(iii) Are not part of any other vessel or apparatus;

(f) Feed water piping between any steam boiler and a feed pump or injector.

(2) Air Conditioning Units – Any air conditioning unit that has a capacity of 60,000 Btu or more, including:

(a) Inductors, convectors and coils that make use of a refrigerant and form part of a cooling, humidity control or space heating system;

(b) Interconnecting piping, valves and fittings containing only a refrigerant, water, brine or other solution;

(c) Vessels heated directly or indirectly that:

(i) Form part of an absorption type system; and

(ii) Function as a generator, regenerator or concentrator;

(d) Compressors, pumps, fans and blowers used solely with the system together with their driving electric motors; and

(e) Control equipment used solely with the system.

e. Object does not mean:

(1) As Boiler and Pressure Vessels:

(a) Equipment that is not under internal vacuum or internal pressure other than weight of contents;

(b) Boiler settings;

(c) Insulating or refractory material; or

(d) Electrical, reciprocating or rotating apparatus within or forming a part of the boiler or vessel.

(2) As Air Conditioning Units, any:

(a) Vessel, cooling tower, reservoir or other source of cooling water for a condenser or compressor, or any water piping leading to or from that source; or

(b) Wiring or piping leading to or from the unit.

f. We will not pay for an Accident to any Object while being tested.

g. **Suspension**

Whenever an Object is found to be in, or exposed to, a dangerous condition, any of our representatives may immediately suspend the insurance against loss from an Accident to that Object. This can be done by delivering or mailing a written notice of suspension to:

(1) Your last known address; or

(2) The address where the Object is located.

If we suspend your insurance, you will get a pro rata refund of premium. But the suspension will be effective even if we have not yet made or offered a refund.

H. Property Definitions

1. "Computer" means:

a. Programmable electronic equipment that is used to store, retrieve and process data; and

b. Associated peripheral equipment that provides communication, including input and output functions such as printing and auxiliary functions such as data transmission.

"Computer" does not include those used to operate production type machinery or equipment.

2. "Counterfeit" means an imitation of an actual valid original which is intended to deceive and to be taken as the original.

3. "Electronic media and records" means the following, if owned by you or licensed to you and used in your business:

   a. Media, meaning disks, tapes, film, drums, cells or other media which are used with electronically controlled equipment.

   b. Data, meaning information or facts stored on media described in Paragraph **a.** above. Data includes "valuable papers and records" converted to data.

   c. "Computer" program, meaning a set of related electronic instructions which direct the operations and functions of a "computer" or a device connected to it, which enable the "computer" or device to receive, process, restore, retrieve or send data.

   d. Software, including systems and applications software.

4. "Manager" means a person serving in a directorial capacity for a limited liability company.

5. "Member" means an owner of a limited liability company represented by its membership interest, who also may serve as a "manager".

6. "Money" means:

   a. Currency, coins and bank notes in current use and having a face value; and

   b. Travelers checks, register checks and money orders held for sale to the public.

7. "Operations" means your business activities occurring at the described premises.

8. "Period of restoration":

   a. Means the period of time that:

      (1) Begins:

         (a) 72 hours after the time of direct physical loss or damage for Business Income Coverage; or

         (b) Immediately after the time of direct physical loss or damage for Extra Expense Coverage;

         caused by or resulting from any Covered Cause of Loss at the described premises; and

      (2) Ends on the earlier of:

         (a) The date when the property at the described premises should be repaired, rebuilt or replaced with reasonable speed and similar quality; or

         (b) The date when business is resumed at a new permanent location.

   b. Does not include any increased period required due to the enforcement of any ordinance or law that:

      (1) Regulates the construction, use or repair, or requires the tearing down of any property; or

      (2) Requires any insured or others to test for, monitor, clean up, remove, contain, treat, detoxify or neutralize, or in any way respond to or assess the effects of "pollutants".

   The expiration date of this policy will not cut short the "period of restoration".

9. "Pollutants" means any solid, liquid, gaseous or thermal irritant or contaminant, including smoke, vapor, soot, fumes, acids, alkalis, chemicals and waste. Waste includes materials to be recycled, reconditioned or reclaimed.

10. "Securities" means negotiable and non-negotiable instruments or contracts representing either "money" or other property and includes:

   a. Tokens, tickets, revenue and other stamps (whether represented by actual stamps or unused value in a meter) in current use; and

   b. Evidences of debt issued in connection with credit or charge cards, which cards are not issued by you;

   but does not include "money".

11. "Specified Causes of Loss" means the following:

   Fire; lightning; explosion; windstorm or hail; smoke; aircraft or vehicles; riot or civil commotion; vandalism; leakage from fire extinguishing equipment; sinkhole collapse; volcanic action; falling objects; weight of snow, ice or sleet; water damage.

   a. Sinkhole collapse means the sudden sinking or collapse of land into underground empty spaces created by the action of water on limestone or dolomite. This cause of loss does not include:

      (1) The cost of filling sinkholes; or

      (2) Sinking or collapse of land into man-made underground cavities.

   b. Falling objects does not include loss of or damage to:

      (1) Personal property in the open; or

      (2) The interior of a building or structure, or property inside a building or structure, unless the roof or an outside wall of the building or structure is first damaged by a falling object.

c. Water damage means accidental discharge or leakage of water or steam as the direct result of the breaking apart or cracking of any part of a system or appliance (other than a sump system including its related equipment and parts) containing water or steam.

12. "Stock" means merchandise held in storage or for sale, raw materials and in-process or finished goods, including supplies used in their packing or shipping.

13. "Valuable papers and records" means:

a. Inscribed, printed or written:

(1) Documents;

(2) Manuscripts; and

(3) Records;

including abstracts, books, deeds, drawings, films, maps or mortgages; and

b. "Electronic media and records".

But "valuable papers and records" does not mean "money" or "securities".

SECTION II – LIABILITY

A. Coverages

1. Business Liability

a. We will pay those sums that the insured becomes legally obligated to pay as damages because of "bodily injury", "property damage" or "personal and advertising injury" to which this insurance applies. We will have the right and duty to defend the insured against any "suit" seeking those damages. However, we will have no duty to defend the insured against any "suit" seeking damages for "bodily injury", "property damage" or "personal and advertising injury", to which this insurance does not apply. We may at our discretion, investigate any "occurrence" and settle any claim or "suit" that may result. But:

(1) The amount we will pay for damages is limited as described in Paragraph **D** – Liability And Medical Expenses Limits Of Insurance in **Section II – Liability;** and

(2) Our right and duty to defend end when we have used up the applicable limit of insurance in the payment of judgments or settlements or medical expenses.

No other obligation or liability to pay sums or perform acts or services is covered unless explicitly provided for under Paragraph **f.** Coverage Extension – Supplementary Payments.

b. This insurance applies:

(1) To "bodily injury" and "property damage" only if:

(a) The "bodily injury" or "property damage" is caused by an "occurrence" that takes place in the "coverage territory";

(b) The "bodily injury" or "property damage" occurs during the policy period; and

(c) Prior to the policy period, no insured listed under Paragraph **C.1.** Who Is An Insured and no "employee" authorized by you to give or receive notice of an "occurrence" or claim, knew that the "bodily injury" or "property damage" had occurred, in whole or in part. If such a listed insured or authorized "employee" knew, prior to the policy period, that the "bodily injury" or "property damage" occurred, then any continuation, change or resumption of such "bodily injury" or "property damage" during or after the policy period will be deemed to have been known before the policy period.

(2) To "personal and advertising injury" caused by an offense arising out of your business, but only if the offense was committed in the "coverage territory" during the policy period.

c. "Bodily injury" or "property damage" which occurs during the policy period and was not, prior to the policy period, known to have occurred by any insured listed under Paragraph **C.1.** Who Is An Insured or any "employee" authorized by you to give or receive notice of an "occurrence" or claim, includes any continuation, change or resumption of "bodily injury" or "property damage" after the end of the policy period.

d. "Bodily injury" or "property damage" will be deemed to have been known to have occurred at the earliest time when any insured listed under Paragraph **C.1.** Who Is An Insured or any "employee" authorized by you to give or receive notice of an "occurrence" or claim:

(1) Reports all, or any part, of the "bodily injury" or "property damage" to us or any other insurer;

(2) Receives a written or verbal demand or claim for damages because of the "bodily injury" or "property damage"; or

(3) Becomes aware by any other means that "bodily injury" or "property damage" has occurred or has begun to occur.

e. Damages because of "bodily injury" include damages claimed by any person or organization for care, loss of services or death resulting at any time from the "bodily injury".

f. Coverage Extension – Supplementary Payments

(1) In addition to the Limit of Insurance of **Section II – Liability** we will pay, with respect to any claim we investigate or settle, or any "suit" against an insured we defend:

(a) All expenses we incur.

(b) Up to $250 for cost of bail bonds required because of accidents or traffic law violations arising out of the use of any vehicle to which Business Liability Coverage for "bodily injury" applies. We do not have to furnish these bonds.

(c) The cost of bonds to release attachments, but only for bond amounts within our Limit of Insurance. We do not have to furnish these bonds.

(d) All reasonable expenses incurred by the insured at our request to assist us in the investigation or defense of the claim or "suit", including actual loss of earnings up to $250 a day because of time off from work.

(e) All costs taxed against the insured in the "suit".

(f) Prejudgment interest awarded against the insured on that part of the judgment we pay. If we make an offer to pay the Limit of Insurance, we will not pay any prejudgment interest based on that period of time after the offer.

(g) All interest on the full amount of any judgment that accrues after entry of the judgment and before we have paid, offered to pay, or deposited in court the part of the judgment that is within our Limit of Insurance.

(2) If we defend an insured against a "suit" and an indemnitee of the insured is also named as a party to the "suit", we will defend that indemnitee if all of the following conditions are met:

(a) The "suit" against the indemnitee seeks damages for which the insured has assumed the liability of the indemnitee in a contract or agreement that is an "insured contract";

(b) This insurance applies to such liability assumed by the insured;

(c) The obligation to defend, or the cost of the defense of, that indemnitee, has also been assumed by the insured in the same "insured contract";

(d) The allegations in the "suit" and the information we know about the "occurrence" are such that no conflict appears to exist between the interests of the insured and the interests of the indemnitee:

(e) The indemnitee and the insured ask us to conduct and control the defense of that indemnitee against such "suit" and agree that we can assign the same counsel to defend the insured and the indemnitee; and

(f) The indemnitee:

(i) Agrees in writing to:

i. Cooperate with us in the investigation, settlement or defense of the "suit";

ii. Immediately send us copies of any demands, notices, summonses or legal papers received in connection with the "suit";

iii. Notify any other insurer whose coverage is available to the indemnitee; and

iv. Cooperate with us with respect to coordinating other applicable insurance available to the indemnitee; and

(ii) Provides us with written authorization to:

i. Obtain records and other information related to the "suit"; and

ii. Conduct and control the defense of the indemnitee in such "suit".

(3) So long as the conditions in Paragraph **2.** are met, attorneys' fees incurred by us in the defense of that indemnitee, necessary litigation expenses incurred by us and necessary litigation expenses incurred by the indemnitee at our request will be paid as Supplementary Payments. Notwithstanding the provisions of Paragraph **B.1.b.(2)** Exclusions in **Section II – Liability,** such payments will not be deemed to be damages for "bodily injury" and "property damage" and will not reduce the limits of insurance.

Our obligation to defend an insured's indemnitee and to pay for attorneys' fees and necessary litigation expenses as Supplementary Payments ends when:

(a) We have used up the applicable limit of insurance in the payment of judgments or settlements; or

(b) The conditions set forth above, or the terms of the agreement described in Paragraph **2.f.** above are no longer met.

2. Medical Expenses

a. We will pay medical expenses as described below for "bodily injury" caused by an accident:

(1) On premises you own or rent;

(2) On ways next to premises you own or rent; or

(3) Because of your operations;

provided that:

(a) The accident takes place in the "coverage territory" and during the policy period;

(b) The expenses are incurred and reported to us within one year of the date of the accident; and

(c) The injured person submits to examination, at our expense, by physicians of our choice as often as we reasonably require.

b. We will make these payments regardless of fault. These payments will not exceed the Limits of Insurance of **Section II – Liability.** We will pay reasonable expenses for:

(1) First aid administered at the time of an accident;

(2) Necessary medical, surgical, x-ray and dental services, including prosthetic devices; and

(3) Necessary ambulance, hospital, professional nursing and funeral services.

B. Exclusions

1. Applicable To Business Liability Coverage

This insurance does not apply to:

a. Expected Or Intended Injury

"Bodily injury" or "property damage" expected or intended from the standpoint of the insured. This exclusion does not apply to "bodily injury" resulting from the use of reasonable force to protect persons or property.

b. Contractual Liability

"Bodily injury" or "property damage" for which the insured is obligated to pay damages by reason of the assumption of liability in a contract or agreement. This exclusion does not apply to liability for damages:

(1) That the insured would have in the absence of the contract or agreement; or

(2) Assumed in a contract or agreement that is an "insured contract", provided the "bodily injury" or "property damage" occurs subsequent to the execution of the contract or agreement. Solely for the purposes of liability assumed in an "insured contract", reasonable attorney fees and necessary litigation expenses incurred by or for a party other than an insured are deemed to be damages because of "bodily injury" or "property damage", provided:

(a) Liability to such party for, or for the cost of, that party's defense has also been assumed in the same "insured contract"; and

(b) Such attorney fees and litigation expenses are for defense of that party against a civil or alternative dispute resolution proceeding in which damages to which this insurance applies are alleged.

c. Liquor Liability

"Bodily injury" or "property damage" for which any insured may be held liable by reason of:

(1) Causing or contributing to the intoxication of any person;

(2) The furnishing of alcoholic beverages to a person under the legal drinking age or under the influence of alcohol; or

(3) Any statute, ordinance or regulation relating to the sale, gift, distribution or use of alcoholic beverages.

This exclusion applies only if you are in the business of manufacturing, distributing, selling, serving or furnishing alcoholic beverages.

d. Workers' Compensation And Similar Laws

Any obligation of the insured under a workers' compensation, disability benefits or unemployment compensation law or any similar law.

e. Employer's Liability

"Bodily Injury" to:

(1) An "employee" of the insured arising out of and in the course of:

(a) Employment by the insured; or

(b) Performing duties related to the conduct of the insured's business; or

(2) The spouse, child, parent, brother or sister of that "employee" as a consequence of Paragraph **(1)** above.

This exclusion applies:

(1) Whether the insured may be liable as an employer or in any other capacity; and

(2) To any obligation to share damages with or repay someone else who must pay damages because of the injury.

This exclusion does not apply to liability assumed by the insured under an "insured contract".

f. Pollution

(1) "Bodily injury" or "property damage" arising out of the actual, alleged or threatened discharge, dispersal, seepage, migration, release or escape of "pollutants":

(a) At or from any premises, site or location which is or was at any time owned or occupied by, or rented or loaned to, any insured. However, this subparagraph does not apply to:

(i) "Bodily injury" if sustained within a building and caused by smoke, fumes, vapor or soot from equipment used to heat that building;

(ii) "Bodily injury" or "property damage" for which you may be held liable, if you are a contractor and the owner or lessee of such premises, site or location has been added to your policy as an additional insured with respect to your ongoing operations performed for that additional insured at that premises, site or location and such premises, site or location is not and never was owned or occupied by, or rented or loaned to, any insured, other than that additional insured; or

(iii) "Bodily injury" or "property damage" arising out of heat, smoke or fumes from a "hostile fire";

(b) At or from any premises, site or location which is or was at any time used by or for any insured or others for the handling, storage, disposal, processing or treatment of waste;

(c) Which are or were at any time transported, handled, stored, treated, disposed of, or processed as waste by or for:

(i) Any insured; or

(ii) Any person or organization for whom you may be legally responsible; or

(d) At or from any premises, site or location on which any insured or any contractors or subcontractors working directly or indirectly on any insured's behalf are performing operations if the "pollutants" are brought on or to the premises, site or location in connection with such operations by such insured, contractor or subcontractor. However, this subparagraph does not apply to:

(i) "Bodily injury" or "property damage" arising out of the escape of fuels, lubricants or other operating fluids which are needed to perform the normal electrical, hydraulic or mechanical functions necessary for the operation of "mobile equipment" or its parts, if such fuels, lubricants or other operating fluids escape from a vehicle part designed to hold, store or receive them. This exception does not apply if the "bodily injury" or "property damage" arises out of the intentional discharge, dispersal or release of the fuels, lubricants or other operating fluids, or if such fuels, lubricants or other operating fluids are brought on or to the premises, site or location with the intent that they be discharged, dispersed or released as part of the operations being performed by such insured, contractor or subcontractor;

(ii) "Bodily injury" or "property damage" sustained within a building and caused by the release of gases, fumes or vapors from materials brought into that building in connection with operations being performed by you or on your behalf by a contractor or subcontractor; or

(iii) "Bodily injury" or "property damage" arising out of heat, smoke or fumes from a "hostile fire".

(e) At or from any premises, site or location on which any insured or any contractors or subcontractors working directly or indirectly on any insured's behalf are performing operations if the operations are to test for, monitor, clean up, remove, contain, treat, detoxify or neutralize, or in any way respond to, or assess the effects of, "pollutants".

(2) Any loss, cost or expense arising out of any:

(a) Request, demand, order or statutory or regulatory requirement that any insured or others test for, monitor, clean up, remove, contain, treat, detoxify or neutralize, or in any way respond to, or assess the effects of, "pollutants"; or

(b) Claim or "suit" by or on behalf of a governmental authority for damages because of testing for, monitoring, cleaning up, removing, containing, treating, detoxifying or neutralizing, or in any way responding to, or assessing the effects of, "pollutants".

However, this paragraph does not apply to liability for damages because of "property damage" that the insured would have in the absence of such request, demand, order or statutory or regulatory requirement or such claim or "suit" by or on behalf of a governmental authority.

g. Aircraft, Auto Or Watercraft

"Bodily injury" or "property damage" arising out of the ownership, maintenance, use or entrustment to others of any aircraft, "auto" or watercraft owned or operated by or rented or loaned to any insured. Use includes operation and "loading or unloading".

This exclusion applies even if the claims allege negligence or other wrongdoing in the supervision, hiring, employment, training or monitoring of others by an insured, if the "occurrence" which caused the "bodily injury" or "property damage" involved the ownership, maintenance, use or entrustment to others of any aircraft, "auto" or watercraft that is owned or operated by or rented or loaned to any insured.

This exclusion does not apply to:

(1) A watercraft while ashore on premises you own or rent;

(2) A watercraft you do not own that is:

(a) Less than 51 feet long; and

(b) Not being used to carry persons or property for a charge;

(3) Parking an "auto" on, or on the ways next to, premises you own or rent, provided the "auto" is not owned by or rented or loaned to you or the insured;

(4) Liability assumed under any "insured contract" for the ownership, maintenance or use of aircraft or watercraft; or

(5) "Bodily injury" or "property damage" arising out of the operation of any of the following equipment:

(a) Cherry pickers and similar devices mounted on automobile or truck chassis and used to raise or lower workers; and

(b) Air compressors, pumps and generators, including spraying, welding, building cleaning, geophysical exploration, lighting and well servicing equipment.

h. Mobile Equipment

"Bodily injury" or "property damage" arising out of:

(1) The transportation of "mobile equipment" by an "auto" owned or operated by or rented or loaned to any insured; or

(2) The use of "mobile equipment" in, or while in practice for, or while being prepared for, any prearranged racing, speed, demolition or stunting activity.

i. War

"Bodily injury" or "property damage" due to war, whether or not declared, or any act or condition incident to war. War includes civil war, insurrection, rebellion or revolution. This exclusion applies only to liability assumed under a contract or agreement.

j. Professional Services

"Bodily injury", "property damage", "personal and advertising injury" caused by the rendering or failure to render any professional service. This includes but is not limited to:

(1) Legal, accounting or advertising services;

(2) Preparing, approving, or failing to prepare or approve maps, drawings, opinions, reports, surveys, change orders, designs or specifications;

(3) Supervisory, inspection or engineering services;

(4) Medical, surgical, dental, x-ray or nursing services treatment, advice or instruction;

(5) Any health or therapeutic service treatment, advice or instruction;

(6) Any service, treatment, advice or instruction for the purpose of appearance or skin enhancement, hair removal or replacement or personal grooming;

(7) Optometry or optical or hearing aid services including the prescribing, preparation, fitting, demonstration or distribution of ophthalmic lenses and similar products or hearing aid devices;

(8) Body piercing services; and

(9) Services in the practice of pharmacy.

k. Damage To Property

"Property damage" to:

(1) Property you own, rent or occupy, including any costs or expenses incurred by you, or any other person, organization or entity, for repair, replacement, enhancement, restoration or maintenance of such property for any reason, including prevention of injury to a person or damage to another's property;

(2) Premises you sell, give away or abandon, if the "property damage" arises out of any part of those premises;

(3) Property loaned to you;

(4) Personal property in the care, custody or control of the insured;

(5) That particular part of real property on which you or any contractor or subcontractor working directly or indirectly on your behalf is performing operations, if the "property damage" arises out of those operations; or

(6) That particular part of any property that must be restored, repaired or replaced because "your work" was incorrectly performed on it.

Paragraphs **(1)**, **(3)** and **(4)** of this exclusion do not apply to "property damage" (other than damage by fire or explosion) to premises, including the contents of such premises, rented to you for a period of 7 or fewer consecutive days. A separate limit of insurance applies to Damage To Premises Rented To You as described in Paragraph **D.** Liability And Medical Expenses Limit Of Insurance in **Section II – Liability.**

Paragraph **(2)** of this exclusion does not apply if the premises are "your work" and were never occupied, rented or held for rental by you.

Paragraphs **(3)**, **(4)**, **(5)** and **(6)** of this exclusion do not apply to liability assumed under a sidetrack agreement.

Paragraph **(6)** of this exclusion does not apply to "property damage" included in the "products – completed operations hazard".

l. Damage To Your Product

"Property damage" to "your product" arising out of it or any part of it.

m. Damage To Your Work

"Property damage" to "your work" arising out of it or any part of it and included in the "products – completed operations hazard".

This exclusion does not apply if the damaged work or the work out of which the damage arises was performed on your behalf by a subcontractor.

n. Damage To Impaired Property Or Property Not Physically Injured

"Property damage" to "impaired property" or property that has not been physically injured, arising out of:

(1) A defect, deficiency, inadequacy or dangerous condition in "your product" or "your work"; or

(2) A delay or failure by you or anyone acting on your behalf to perform a contract or agreement in accordance with its terms.

This exclusion does not apply to the loss of use of other property arising out of sudden and accidental physical injury to "your product" or "your work" after it has been put to its intended use.

o. Recall Of Products, Work Or Impaired Property

Damages claimed for any loss, cost or expense incurred by you or others for the loss of use, withdrawal, recall, inspection, repair, replacement, adjustment, removal or disposal of:

(1) "Your product";

(2) "Your work"; or

(3) "Impaired property";

if such product, work or property is withdrawn or recalled from the market or from use by any person or organization because of a known or suspected defect, deficiency, inadequacy or dangerous condition in it.

p. Personal And Advertising Injury

"Personal and advertising injury":

(1) Caused by or at the direction of the insured with the knowledge that the act would violate the rights of another and would inflict "personal and advertising injury";

(2) Arising out of oral or written publication of material, if done by or at the direction of the insured with knowledge of its falsity;

(3) Arising out of oral or written publication of material whose first publication took place before the beginning of the policy period;

(4) Arising out of a criminal act committed by or at the direction of any insured;

(5) For which the insured has assumed liability in a contract or agreement. This exclusion does not apply to liability for damages that the insured would have in the absence of the contract or agreement;

(6) Arising out of a breach of contract, except an implied contract to use another's advertising idea in your "advertisement";

(7) Arising out of the failure of goods, products or services to conform with any statement of quality or performance made in your "advertisement";

(8) Arising out of the wrong description of the price of goods, products or services stated in your "advertisement";

(9) Committed by an insured whose business is:

(a) Advertising, broadcasting, publishing or telecasting;

(b) Designing or determining content of web-sites for others; or

(c) An Internet search, access, content or service provider.

However, this exclusion does not apply to Paragraphs **14.a., b.** and **c.** of "personal and advertising injury" under Paragraph **F.** Liability And Medical Expenses Definitions.

For the purposes of this exclusion, the placing of frames, borders or links, or advertising, for you or others anywhere on the Internet, by itself, is not considered the business of advertising, broadcasting, publishing or telecasting.

(10) Arising out of the actual, alleged or threatened discharge, dispersal, seepage, migration, release or escape of "pollutants" at any time.

(11) With respect to any loss, cost or expense arising out of any:

(a) Request, demand or order that any insured or others test for, monitor, clean-up, remove, contain, treat, detoxify or neutralize or in any way respond to, or assess the effects of, "pollutants"; or

(b) Claim or "suit" by or on behalf of a governmental authority for damages because of testing for, monitoring, cleaning up, removing, containing, treating, detoxifying or neutralizing or in any way responding to, or assessing the effects of, "pollutants".

(12) Arising out of an electronic chatroom or bulletin board the insured hosts, owns or over which the insured exercises control.

(13) Arising out of the infringement of copyright, patent, trademark, trade secret or other intellectual property rights.

However, this exclusion does not apply to infringement, in your "advertisement", of copyright, trade dress or slogan.

(14) Arising out of the unauthorized use of another's name or product in your e-mail address, domain name or metatags, or any other similar tactics to mislead another's potential customers.

Exclusions **c., d., e., f., g., h., i., k., l., m., n.** and **o.** in **Section II – Liability** do not apply to damage by fire or explosion to premises while rented to you, or temporarily occupied by you with permission of the owner. A separate Damage To Premises Rented To You Limit of Insurance applies to this coverage as described in Paragraph **D.** Liability And Medical Expenses Limits of Insurance in **Section II – Liability.**

2. Applicable To Medical Expenses Coverage

We will not pay expenses for "bodily injury":

a. To any insured, except "volunteer workers".

b. To a person hired to do work for or on behalf of any insured or a tenant of any insured.

c. To a person injured on that part of premises you own or rent that the person normally occupies.

d. To a person, whether or not an "employee" of any insured, if benefits for the "bodily injury" are payable or must be provided under a workers' compensation or disability benefits law or a similar law.

e. To a person injured while taking part in athletics.

f. Included within the "products – completed operations hazard".

g. Excluded under Business Liability Coverage.

h. Due to war, whether or not declared, or any act or condition incident to war. War includes civil war, insurrection, rebellion or revolution.

3. Applicable To Both Business Liability Coverage And Medical Expenses Coverage – Nuclear Energy Liability Exclusion

This insurance does not apply:

a. Under Business Liability Coverage, to "bodily injury" or "property damage":

(1) With respect to which an insured under the policy is also an insured under a nuclear energy liability policy issued by the Nuclear Energy Liability Insurance Association, Mutual Atomic Energy Liability Underwriters or Nuclear Insurance Association of Canada, or would be an insured under any such policy but for its termination upon exhaustion of its limit of liability; or

(2) Resulting from the "hazardous properties" of "nuclear material" and with respect to which:

(a) Any person or organization is required to maintain financial protection pursuant to the Atomic Energy Act of 1954, or any law amendatory thereof; or

(b) The insured is, or had this policy not been issued would be, entitled to indemnity from the United States of America, or any agency thereof, under any agreement entered into by the United States of America, or any agency thereof, with any person or organization.

b. Under Medical Expenses Coverage, to expenses incurred with respect to "bodily injury" resulting from the "hazardous properties" of "nuclear material" and arising out of the operation of a "nuclear facility" by any person or organization.

c. Under Business Liability Coverage, to "bodily injury" or "property damage" resulting from the "hazardous properties" of the "nuclear material"; if:

(1) The "nuclear material":

(a) Is at any "nuclear facility" owned by, or operated by or on behalf of, an insured; or

(b) Has been discharged or dispersed therefrom;

(2) The "nuclear material" is contained in "spent fuel" or "waste" at any time possessed, handled, used, processed, stored, transported or disposed of by or on behalf of an insured; or

(3) The "bodily injury" or "property damage" arises out of the furnishing by an insured of services, materials, parts or equipment in connection with the planning, construction, maintenance, operation or use of any "nuclear facility"; but if such facility is located within the United States of America, its territories or possessions or Canada, this Exclusion **(3)** applies only to "property damage" to such "nuclear facility" and any property thereat.

d. As used in this exclusion:

(1) "By-product material" has the meaning given it in the Atomic Energy Act of 1954 or in any law amendatory thereof;

(2) "Hazardous properties" include radioactive, toxic or explosive properties;

(3) "Nuclear facility" means:

(a) Any "nuclear reactor";

(b) Any equipment or device designed or used for:

(i) Separating the isotopes of uranium or plutonium;

(ii) Processing or utilizing "spent fuel"; or

(iii) Handling, processing or packaging "waste";

(c) Any equipment or device used for the processing, fabricating or alloying of "special nuclear material" if at any time the total amount of such material in the custody of the insured at the premises where such equipment or device is located consists of or contains more than 25 grams of plutonium or uranium 233 or any combination thereof, or more than 250 grams of uranium 235;

(d) Any structure, basin, excavation, premises or place prepared or used for the storage or disposal of "waste";

and includes the site on which any of the foregoing is located, all operations conducted on such site and all premises used for such operations;

(4) "Nuclear material" means "source material", "special nuclear material" or "by-product material";

(5) "Nuclear reactor" means any apparatus designed or used to sustain nuclear fission in a self-supporting chain reaction or to contain a critical mass of fissionable material;

(6) "Property damage" includes all forms of radioactive contamination of property.

(7) "Source material" has the meaning given it in the Atomic Energy Act of 1954 or in any law amendatory thereof;

(8) "Special nuclear material" has the meaning given it in the Atomic Energy Act of 1954 or in any law amendatory thereof;

(9) "Spent fuel" means any fuel element or fuel component, solid or liquid, which has been used or exposed to radiation in a "nuclear reactor";

(10) "Waste" means any waste material:

(a) Containing "by-product material" other than the tailings or wastes produced by the extraction or concentration of uranium or thorium from any ore processed primarily for its "source material" content; and

(b) Resulting from the operation by any person or organization of any "nuclear facility" included under Paragraphs **(a)** and **(b)** of the definition of "nuclear facility".

C. Who Is An Insured

1. If you are designated in the Declarations as:

a. An individual, you and your spouse are insureds, but only with respect to the conduct of a business of which you are the sole owner.

b. A partnership or joint venture, you are an insured. Your members, your partners and their spouses are also insureds, but only with respect to the conduct of your business.

c. A limited liability company, you are an insured. Your members are also insureds, but only with respect to the conduct of your business. Your managers are insureds, but only with respect to their duties as your managers.

d. An organization other than a partnership, joint venture or limited liability company, you are an insured. Your "executive officers" and directors are insureds, but only with respect to their duties as your officers or directors. Your stockholders are also insureds, but only with respect to their liability as stockholders.

2. Each of the following is also an insured:

   a. Your "volunteer workers" only while performing duties related to the conduct of your business, or your "employees", other than either your "executive officers" (if you are an organization other than a partnership, joint venture or limited liability company) or your managers (if you are a limited liability company), but only for acts within the scope of their employment by you or while performing duties related to the conduct of your business. However, none of these "employees" or "volunteer workers" are insureds for:

      (1) "Bodily injury" or "personal and advertising injury":

         (a) To you, to your partners or members (if you are a partnership or joint venture), to your members (if you are a limited liability company), or to a co-"employee" while in the course of his or her employment or performing duties related to the conduct of your business, or to your other "volunteer workers" while performing duties related to the conduct of your business;

         (b) To the spouse, child, parent, brother or sister of that co-"employee" as a consequence of Paragraph **(a)** above;

         (c) For which there is any obligation to share damages with or repay someone else who must pay damages because of the injury described in Paragraphs **(a)** or **(b)**; or

         (d) Arising out of his or her providing or failing to provide professional health care services.

      (2) "Property damage" to property:

         (a) Owned, occupied or used by,

         (b) Rented to, in the care, custody or control of, or over which physical control is being exercised for any purpose by

      you, any of your "employees", "volunteer workers", any partner or member (if you are a partnership or joint venture), or any member (if you are a limited liability company).

   b. Any person (other than your "employee" or "volunteer worker"), or any organization while acting as your real estate manager.

   c. Any person or organization having proper temporary custody of your property if you die, but only:

      (1) With respect to liability arising out of the maintenance or use of that property; and

      (2) Until your legal representative has been appointed.

   d. Your legal representative if you die, but only with respect to duties as such. That representative will have all your rights and duties under this policy.

3. With respect to "mobile equipment" registered in your name under any motor vehicle registration law, any person is an insured while driving such equipment along a public highway with your permission. Any other person or organization responsible for the conduct of such person is also an insured, but only with respect to liability arising out of the operation of the equipment, and only if no other insurance of any kind is available to that person or organization for this liability. However, no person or organization is an insured with respect to:

   a. "Bodily injury" to a co-"employee" of the person driving the equipment; or

   b. "Property damage" to property owned by, rented to, in the charge of or occupied by you or the employer of any person who is an insured under this provision.

No person or organization is an insured with respect to the conduct of any current or past partnership, joint venture or limited liability company that is not shown as a Named Insured in the Declarations.

D. Liability And Medical Expenses Limits Of Insurance

1. The Limits of Insurance of **Section II – Liability** shown in the Declarations and the rules below fix the most we will pay regardless of the number of:

   a. Insureds;

   b. Claims made or "suits" brought; or

   c. Persons or organizations making claims or bringing "suits".

2. The most we will pay for the sum of all damages because of all:

   a. "Bodily injury", "property damage" and medical expenses arising out of any one "occurrence"; and

b. "Personal and advertising injury" sustained by any one person or organization;

is the Liability and Medical Expenses limit shown in the Declarations. But the most we will pay for all medical expenses because of "bodily injury" sustained by any one person is the Medical Expenses limit shown in the Declarations.

3. The most we will pay under Business Liability Coverage for damages because of "property damage" to premises while rented to you or temporarily occupied by you with permission of the owner, arising out of any one fire or explosion is the Damage To Premises Rented To You limit shown in the Declarations.

4. **Aggregate Limits**

The most we will pay for:

a. All "bodily injury" or "property damage" that is included in the "products-completed operations hazard" is twice the Liability and Medical Expenses limit; and

b. All:

(1) "Bodily injury" or "property damage" except damages because of "bodily injury" and "property damage" included in the "products-completed operations hazard";

(2) Plus medical expenses;

(3) Plus all "personal and advertising injury" caused by offenses committed;

is twice the Liability and Medical Expenses limit.

This Aggregate Limit does not apply to "property damage" to premises while rented to you or temporarily occupied by you with the permission of the owner, arising out of fire or explosion.

The Limits of Insurance of **Section II – Liability** apply separately to each consecutive annual period and to any remaining period of less than 12 months, starting with the beginning of the policy period shown in the Declarations, unless the policy period is extended after issuance for an additional period of less than 12 months. In that case, the additional period will be deemed part of the last preceding period for purposes of determining the Limits of Insurance.

E. Liability And Medical Expenses General Conditions

1. Bankruptcy

Bankruptcy or insolvency of the insured or of the insured's estate will not relieve us of our obligations under this policy.

2. Duties In The Event Of Occurrence, Offense, Claim Or Suit

a. You must see to it that we are notified as soon as practicable of an "occurrence" or an offense which may result in a claim. To the extent possible, notice should include:

(1) How, when and where the "occurrence" or offense took place;

(2) The names and addresses of any injured persons and witnesses; and

(3) The nature and location of any injury or damage arising out of the "occurrence" or offense.

b. If a claim is made or "suit" is brought against any insured, you must:

(1) Immediately record the specifics of the claim or "suit" and the date received; and

(2) Notify us as soon as practicable.

You must see to it that we receive written notice of the claim or "suit" as soon as practicable.

c. You and any other involved insured must:

(1) Immediately send us copies of any demands, notices, summonses or legal papers received in connection with the claim or "suit";

(2) Authorize us to obtain records and other information;

(3) Cooperate with us in the investigation, or settlement of the claim or defense against the "suit"; and

(4) Assist us, upon our request, in the enforcement of any right against any person or organization that may be liable to the insured because of injury or damage to which this insurance may also apply.

d. No insured will, except at that insured's own cost, voluntarily make a payment, assume any obligation, or incur any expense, other than for first aid, without our consent.

3. Financial Responsibility Laws

a. When this policy is certified as proof of financial responsibility for the future under the provisions of any motor vehicle financial responsibility law, the insurance provided by the policy for "bodily injury" liability and "property damage" liability will comply with the provisions of the law to the extent of the coverage and limits of insurance required by that law.

b. With respect to "mobile equipment" to which this insurance applies, we will provide any liability, uninsured motorists, underinsured motorists, no-fault or other coverage required by any motor vehicle law. We will provide the required limits for those coverages.

4. Legal Action Against Us

No person or organization has a right under this policy:

a. To join us as a party or otherwise bring us into a "suit" asking for damages from an insured; or

b. To sue us on this policy unless all of its terms have been fully complied with.

A person or organization may sue us to recover on an agreed settlement or on a final judgment against an insured; but we will not be liable for damages that are not payable under the terms of this policy or that are in excess of the applicable limit of insurance. An agreed settlement means a settlement and release of liability signed by us, the insured and the claimant or the claimant's legal representative.

5. Separation Of Insureds

Except with respect to the Limits of Insurance of **Section II – Liability,** and any rights or duties specifically assigned in this policy to the first Named Insured, this insurance applies:

a. As if each Named Insured were the only Named Insured; and

b. Separately to each insured against whom claim is made or "suit" is brought.

F. Liability And Medical Expenses Definitions

1. "Advertisement" means a notice that is broadcast or published to the general public or specific market segments about your goods, products or services for the purpose of attracting customers or supporters. For the purposes of this definition:

a. Notices that are published include material placed on the Internet or on similar electronic means of communication; and

b. Regarding web-sites, only that part of a web-site that is about your goods, products or services for the purposes of attracting customers or supporters is considered an advertisement.

2. "Auto" means a land motor vehicle, trailer or semitrailer designed for travel on public roads, including any attached machinery or equipment. But "auto" does not include "mobile equipment".

3. "Bodily injury" means bodily injury, sickness or disease sustained by a person, including death resulting from any of these at any time.

4. "Coverage territory" means:

a. The United States of America (including its territories and possessions), Puerto Rico and Canada;

b. International waters or airspace, but only if the injury or damage occurs in the course of travel or transportation between any places included in Paragraph **a.** above; or

c. All other parts of the world if the injury or damage arises out of:

(1) Goods or products made or sold by you in the territory described in Paragraph **a.** above;

(2) The activities of a person whose home is in the territory described in Paragraph **a.** above, but is away for a short time on your business; or

(3) "Personal and advertising injury" offenses that take place through the Internet or similar electronic means of communication;

provided the insured's responsibility to pay damages is determined in a "suit" on the merits in the territory described in Paragraph **a.** above or in a settlement we agree to.

5. "Employee" includes a "leased worker". "Employee" does not include a "temporary worker".

6. "Executive officer" means a person holding any of the officer positions created by your charter, constitution, by-laws or any other similar governing document.

7. "Hostile fire" means one which becomes uncontrollable or breaks out from where it was intended to be.

8. "Impaired property" means tangible property, other than "your product" or "your work", that cannot be used or is less useful because:

a. It incorporates "your product" or "your work" that is known or thought to be defective, deficient, inadequate or dangerous; or

b. You have failed to fulfill the terms of a contract or agreement;

if such property can be restored to use by:

(1) The repair, replacement, adjustment or removal of "your product" or "your work"; or

(2) Your fulfilling the terms of the contract or agreement.

9. "Insured contract" means:

   a. A contract for a lease of premises. However, that portion of the contract for a lease of premises that indemnifies any person or organization for damage by fire to premises while rented to you or temporarily occupied by you with permission of the owner is not an "insured contract";

   b. A sidetrack agreement;

   c. Any easement or license agreement, except in connection with construction or demolition operations on or within 50 feet of a railroad;

   d. An obligation, as required by ordinance, to indemnify a municipality, except in connection with work for a municipality;

   e. An elevator maintenance agreement;

   f. That part of any other contract or agreement pertaining to your business (including an indemnification of a municipality in connection with work performed for a municipality) under which you assume the tort liability of another party to pay for "bodily injury" or "property damage" to a third person or organization. Tort liability means a liability that would be imposed by law in the absence of any contract or agreement.

      Paragraph **f.** does not include that part of any contract or agreement:

      (1) That indemnifies a railroad for "bodily injury" or "property damage" arising out of construction or demolition operations, within 50 feet of any railroad property and affecting any railroad bridge or trestle, tracks, road beds, tunnel, underpass or crossing;

      (2) That indemnifies an architect, engineer or surveyor for injury or damage arising out of:

         (a) Preparing, approving or failing to prepare or approve maps, drawings, opinions, reports, surveys, change orders, designs or specifications; or

         (b) Giving directions or instructions, or failing to give them, if that is the primary cause of the injury or damage; or

      (3) Under which the insured, if an architect, engineer or surveyor, assumes liability for an injury or damage arising out of the insured's rendering or failure to render professional services, including those listed in Paragraph **(2)** above and supervisory, inspection or engineering services.

10. "Leased worker" means a person leased to you by a labor leasing firm under an agreement between you and the labor leasing firm, to perform duties related to the conduct of your business. "Leased worker" does not include a "temporary worker".

11. "Loading or unloading" means the handling of property:

   a. After it is moved from the place where it is accepted for movement into or onto an aircraft, watercraft or "auto";

   b. While it is in or on an aircraft, watercraft or "auto"; or

   c. While it is being moved from an aircraft, watercraft or "auto" to the place where it is finally delivered;

   but "loading or unloading" does not include the movement of property by means of a mechanical device, other than a hand truck, that is not attached to the aircraft, watercraft or "auto".

12. "Mobile equipment" means any of the following types of land vehicles, including any attached machinery or equipment:

   a. Bulldozers, farm machinery, forklifts and other vehicles designed for use principally off public roads;

   b. Vehicles maintained for use solely on or next to premises you own or rent;

   c. Vehicles that travel on crawler treads;

   d. Vehicles, whether self-propelled or not, on which are permanently mounted:

      (1) Power cranes, shovels, loaders, diggers or drills; or

      (2) Road construction or resurfacing equipment such as graders, scrapers or rollers;

   e. Vehicles not described in Paragraphs **a.**, **b.**, **c.** or **d.** above that are not self-propelled and are maintained primarily to provide mobility to permanently attached equipment of the following types:

      (1) Air compressors, pumps and generators, including spraying, welding, building cleaning, geophysical exploration, lighting and well servicing equipment; or

(2) Cherry pickers and similar devices used to raise or lower workers;

f. Vehicles not described in Paragraphs **a., b., c.** or **d.** above maintained primarily for purposes other than the transportation of persons or cargo.

However, self-propelled vehicles with the following types of permanently attached equipment are not "mobile equipment" but will be considered "autos":

(1) Equipment designed primarily for:

(a) Snow removal;

(b) Road maintenance, but not construction or resurfacing; or

(c) Street cleaning;

(2) Cherry pickers and similar devices mounted on automobile or truck chassis and used to raise or lower workers; and

(3) Air compressors, pumps and generators, including spraying, welding, building cleaning, geophysical exploration, lighting and well servicing equipment.

13. "Occurrence" means an accident, including continuous or repeated exposure to substantially the same general harmful conditions.

14. "Personal and advertising injury" means injury, including consequential "bodily injury", arising out of one or more of the following offenses:

a. False arrest, detention or imprisonment;

b. Malicious prosecution;

c. The wrongful eviction from, wrongful entry into, or invasion of the right of private occupancy of a room, dwelling or premises that a person occupies, committed by or on behalf of its owner, landlord or lessor;

d. Oral or written publication, in any manner, of material that slanders or libels a person or organization or disparages a person's or organization's goods, products or services;

e. Oral or written publication, in any manner, of material that violates a person's right of privacy;

f. The use of another's advertising idea in your "advertisement"; or

g. Infringing upon another's copyright, trade dress or slogan in your "advertisement".

15. "Pollutants" mean any solid, liquid, gaseous or thermal irritant or contaminant, including smoke, vapor, soot, fumes, acids, alkalis, chemicals and waste. Waste includes materials to be recycled, reconditioned or reclaimed.

16. "Products – completed operations hazard":

a. Includes all "bodily injury" and "property damage" occurring away from premises you own or rent and arising out of "your product" or "your work" except:

(1) Products that are still in your physical possession; or

(2) Work that has not yet been completed or abandoned. However, "your work" will be deemed completed at the earliest of the following times:

(a) When all of the work called for in your contract has been completed.

(b) When all of the work to be done at the job site has been completed if your contract calls for work at more than one job site.

(c) When that part of the work done at the job site has been put to its intended use by any other person or organization other than another contractor or subcontractor working on the same project.

Work that may need service, maintenance, correction, repair or replacement, but which is otherwise complete, will be treated as completed.

The "bodily injury" or "property damage" must occur away from premises you own or rent, unless your business includes the selling, handling or distribution of "your product" for consumption on premises you own or rent.

b. Does not include "bodily injury" or "property damage" arising out of:

(1) The transportation of property, unless the injury or damage arises out of a condition in or on a vehicle not owned or operated by you, and that condition was created by the "loading or unloading" of that vehicle by any insured; or

(2) The existence of tools, uninstalled equipment or abandoned or unused materials.

17. "Property damage" means:

a. Physical injury to tangible property, including all resulting loss of use of that property. All such loss of use shall be deemed to occur at the time of the physical injury that caused it; or

b. Loss of use of tangible property that is not physically injured. All such loss of use shall be deemed to occur at the time of the "occurrence" that caused it.

For the purposes of this insurance, electronic data is not tangible property.

As used in this definition, electronic data means information, facts or programs stored as, created or used on, or transmitted to or from computer software, including systems and applications software, hard or floppy disks, CD-ROMs, tapes, drives, cells, data processing devices or any other media which are used with electronically controlled equipment.

18. "Suit" means a civil proceeding in which damages because of "bodily injury", "property damage", "personal and advertising injury" to which this insurance applies are alleged. "Suit" includes:

a. An arbitration proceeding in which such damages are claimed and to which the insured must submit or does submit with our consent; or

b. Any other alternative dispute resolution proceeding in which such damages are claimed and to which the insured submits with our consent.

19. "Temporary worker" means a person who is furnished to you to substitute for a permanent "employee" on leave or to meet seasonal or short-term workload conditions.

20. "Volunteer worker" means a person who is not your "employee", and who donates his or her work and acts at the direction of and within the scope of duties determined by you, and is not paid a fee, salary or other compensation by you or anyone else for their work performed for you.

21. "Your product":

a. Means:

(1) Any goods or products, other than real property, manufactured, sold, handled, distributed or disposed of by:

(a) You;

(b) Others trading under your name; or

(c) A person or organization whose business or assets you have acquired; and

(2) Containers (other than vehicles), materials, parts or equipment furnished in connection with such goods or products.

b. Includes:

(1) Warranties or representations made at any time with respect to the fitness, quality, durability, performance or use of "your product"; and

(2) The providing of or failure to provide warnings or instructions.

c. Does not include vending machines or other property rented to or located for the use of others but not sold.

22. "Your work":

a. Means:

(1) Work or operations performed by you or on your behalf; and

(2) Materials, parts or equipment furnished in connection with such work or operations.

b. Includes:

(1) Warranties or representations made at any time with respect to the fitness, quality, durability, performance or use of "your work"; and

(2) The providing of or failure to provide warnings or instructions.

SECTION III – COMMON POLICY CONDITIONS (APPLICABLE TO SECTION I – PROPERTY AND SECTION II – LIABILITY)

A. Cancellation

1. The first Named Insured shown in the Declarations may cancel this policy by mailing or delivering to us advance written notice of cancellation.

2. We may cancel this policy by mailing or delivering to the first Named Insured written notice of cancellation at least:

a. 5 days before the effective date of cancellation if any one of the following conditions exists at any building that is Covered Property in this policy.

(1) The building has been vacant or unoccupied 60 or more consecutive days. This does not apply to:

(a) Seasonal unoccupancy; or

(b) Buildings in the course of construction, renovation or addition.

Buildings with 65% or more of the rental units or floor area vacant or unoccupied are considered unoccupied under this provision.

(2) After damage by a covered cause of loss, permanent repairs to the building:

(a) Have not started, and

(b) Have not been contracted for,

within 30 days of initial payment of loss.

(3) The building has:

(a) An outstanding order to vacate;

(b) An outstanding demolition order; or

(c) Been declared unsafe by governmental authority.

(4) Fixed and salvageable items have been or are being removed from the building and are not being replaced. This does not apply to such removal that is necessary or incidental to any renovation or remodeling.

(5) Failure to:

(a) Furnish necessary heat, water, sewer service or electricity for 30 consecutive days or more, except during a period of seasonal unoccupancy; or

(b) Pay property taxes that are owing and have been outstanding for more than one year following the date due, except that this provision will not apply where you are in a bona fide dispute with the taxing authority regarding payment of such taxes.

b. 10 days before the effective date of cancellation if we cancel for nonpayment of premium.

c. 30 days before the effective date of cancellation if we cancel for any other reason.

3. We will mail or deliver our notice to the first Named Insured's last mailing address known to us.

4. Notice of cancellation will state the effective date of cancellation. The policy period will end on that date.

5. If this policy is cancelled, we will send the first Named Insured any premium refund due. If we cancel, the refund will be pro rata. If the first Named Insured cancels, the refund may be less than pro rata. The cancellation will be effective even if we have not made or offered a refund.

6. If notice is mailed, proof of mailing will be sufficient proof of notice.

B. Changes

This policy contains all the agreements between you and us concerning the insurance afforded. The first Named Insured shown in the Declarations is authorized to make changes in the terms of this policy with our consent. This policy's terms can be amended or waived only by endorsement issued by us and made a part of this policy.

C. Concealment, Misrepresentation Or Fraud

This policy is void in any case of fraud by you as it relates to this policy at any time. It is also void if you or any other insured, at any time, intentionally conceal or misrepresent a material fact concerning:

1. This policy;

2. The Covered Property;

3. Your interest in the Covered Property; or

4. A claim under this policy.

D. Examination Of Your Books And Records

We may examine and audit your books and records as they relate to this policy at any time during the policy period and up to three years afterward.

E. Inspections And Surveys

1. We have to right to:

a. Make inspections and surveys at any time;

b. Give you reports on the conditions we find; and

c. Recommend changes.

2. We are not obligated to make any inspections, surveys, reports or recommendations and any such actions we do undertake relate only to insurability and the premiums to be charged. We do not make safety inspections. We do not undertake to perform the duty of any person or organization to provide for the health or safety of workers or the public. And we do not warrant that conditions:

a. Are safe and healthful; or

b. Comply with laws, regulations, codes or standards.

3. Paragraphs **1.** and **2.** of this condition apply not only to us, but also to any rating, advisory, rate service or similar organization which makes insurance inspections, surveys, reports or recommendations.

4. Paragraph **2.** of this condition does not apply to any inspections, surveys, reports or recommendations we may make relative to certification, under state or municipal statutes, ordinances or regulations, of boilers, pressure vessels or elevators.

F. Insurance Under Two Or More Coverages

If two or more of this policy's coverages apply to the same loss or damage, we will not pay more than the actual amount of the loss or damage.

G. Liberalization

If we adopt any revision that would broaden the coverage under this policy without additional premium within 45 days prior to or during the policy period, the broadened coverage will immediately apply to this policy.

H. Other Insurance

1. If there is other insurance covering the same loss or damage, we will pay only for the amount of covered loss or damage in excess of the amount due from that other insurance, whether you can collect on it or not. But we will not pay more than the applicable Limit of Insurance of **Section I – Property.**
2. Business Liability Coverage is excess over:
   a. Any other insurance that insures for direct physical loss or damage; or
   b. Any other primary insurance available to you covering liability for damages arising out of the premises or operations for which you have been added as an additional insured by attachment of an endorsement.
3. When this insurance is excess, we will have no duty under Business Liability Coverage to defend any claim or "suit" that any other insurer has a duty to defend. If no other insurer defends, we will undertake to do so; but we will be entitled to the insured's rights against all those other insurers.

I. Premiums

1. The first Named Insured shown in the Declarations:
   a. Is responsible for the payment of all premiums; and
   b. Will be the payee for any return premiums we pay.
2. The premium shown in the Declarations was computed based on rates in effect at the time the policy was issued. On each renewal, continuation or anniversary of the effective date of this policy, we will compute the premium in accordance with our rates and rules then in effect.
3. With our consent, you may continue this policy in force by paying a continuation premium for each successive one-year period. The premium must be:
   a. Paid to us prior to the anniversary date; and
   b. Determined in accordance with Paragraph **2.** above.

   Our forms then in effect will apply. If you do not pay the continuation premium, this policy will expire on the first anniversary date that we have not received the premium.
4. Undeclared exposures or change in your business operation, acquisition or use of locations may occur during the policy period that are not shown in the Declarations. If so, we may require an additional premium. That premium will be determined in accordance with our rates and rules then in effect.

J. Premium Audit

1. This policy is subject to audit if a premium designated as an advance premium is shown in the Declarations. We will compute the final premium due when we determine your actual exposures.
2. Premium shown in this policy as advance premium is a deposit premium only. At the close of each audit period we will compute the earned premium for that period and send notice to the first Named Insured. The due date for audit premiums is the date shown as the due date on the bill. If the sum of the advance and audit premiums paid for the policy period is greater than the earned premium, we will return the excess to the first Named Insured.
3. The first Named Insured must keep records of the information we need for premium computation, and send us copies at such times as we may request.

K. Transfer Of Rights Of Recovery Against Others To Us

1. Applicable to Businessowners Property Coverage:

   If any person or organization to or for whom we make payment under this policy has rights to recover damages from another, those rights are transferred to us to the extent of our payment. That person or organization must do everything necessary to secure our rights and must do nothing after loss to impair them. But you may waive your rights against another party in writing:
   a. Prior to a loss to your Covered Property.
   b. After a loss to your Covered Property only if, at time of loss, that party is one of the following:
      (1) Someone insured by this insurance;
      (2) A business firm:
         (a) Owned or controlled by you; or
         (b) That owns or controls you; or
      (3) Your tenant.

   You may also accept the usual bills of lading or shipping receipts limiting the liability of carriers.

   This will not restrict your insurance.

2. Applicable to Businessowners Liability Coverage:

   If the insured has rights to recover all or part of any payment we have made under this policy, those rights are transferred to us. The insured must do nothing after loss to impair them. At our request, the insured will bring "suit" or transfer those rights to us and help us enforce them. This condition does not apply to Medical Expenses Coverage.

L. Transfer Of Your Rights And Duties Under This Policy

Your rights and duties under this policy may not be transferred without our written consent except in the case of death of an individual Named Insured.

If you die, your rights and duties will be transferred to your legal representative but only while acting within the scope of duties as your legal representative. Until your legal representative is appointed, anyone having proper temporary custody of your property will have your rights and duties but only with respect to that property.

A

A. M. Best Company - Insurance industry advisory organization used by regulators, insurers, producers and the public to appraise the financial strength of insurers. 2-7

Abandonment (general) - Common policy condition that prohibits an insured from deserting a property and claiming a total loss. 3-17

Accidental Death Insurance (auto) - Optional first party benefit coverage of Pennsylvania's Motor Vehicle Financial Responsibility Law. 6-2

Accounts Receivable - Inland Marine Coverage Form that covers uncollectible monies due the insured as the result of a covered loss, damage or destruction to accounts receivable records. 7-27

Act 6 - 1990 Amendment to the Pennsylvania Motor Vehicle Financial Responsibility Law. Purpose was to reduce auto insurance costs. 6-1

Actual Cash Value (ACV) - Basic valuation provision found in property policies. Determined by subtracting depreciation from the property's replacement value. 3-7

Additional Insured (general) - Individual or business not listed as named insured in declarations, but added by endorsement. Examples include contractors or distributors. 3-9

Additional Insured -- Lessor Endorsement (CA 20 01) - Commercial Auto Endorsement used when a vehicle is under a long term lease. 6-21

Additional Coverages (general) - Coverages included in property policies that extend beyond the principal policy coverages. Examples include: debris removal; reasonable repairs; fire department service charge. 3-8

Additional Residence Rented To Others (HO 24 70) - Homeowner Endorsement that extends the Homeowner Section II - Liability coverage to additional residences rented to others. 5-17

Adhesion (general) - Insurance policy characteristic requiring ambiguous policy language to be interpreted in favor of the insured. 2-13

Admitted or Authorized Companies - Insurance companies that are authorized by the insurance department to conduct business. Must file detailed financial documents and are under the jurisdiction of the insurance department. 2-6

Adverse Selection - Process of being selected against. A risk that has a greater bias to an exposure than the average risk. It is the tendency of poorer risks to seek insurance. 2-3

Advertising Injury - Injury arising out of oral or written publication that slanders or libels a person or organization, invades their privacy or infringes upon ideas, style, copyright, title or slogan. Coverage is provided under CGL Policy and the Businessowners Policy. 8-12

Affirmative Warranty - Type of warranty requiring certain facts to be affirmed or true at policy inception. 2-14

Agency Billed Policies - Premium collection method whereby the agent bills the insured for gross premium, subtracts commissions and remits the net amount to insurance company. Used in some commercial policy transactions. 2-11

Agency - Legal relationship that exists when one party acts on behalf of another party (i.e., agent acting for company; employee acting for agency). 2-10

Agent (producer) - Individual, partnership or corporation authorized by a company to solicit risks, collect premiums or countersign policies. Agents represent companies. 1-1

Agent License (Producer License) - Insurance Department document that indicates an agent's licensing powers. 1-5

Aggregate Limits (general) - Maximum overall limit of liability for a policy period. 3-15

Agreement (Offer and Acceptance) - Element of a contract that refers to the offer by one party and the acceptance by a second party. 2-12

Agreed Value Approach - Property valuation method whereby insurer and insured agree to coverage amount. In these cases the coinsurance requirement is waived. 3-7

Aleatory Contracts - Insurance policy characteristic of unequal bargaining value (premium payment v. loss settlement) and based upon a future unknown event. 2-13

Alien Company - Company domiciled outside the United States (e.g., Nippon Life in Japan; Allianz in Germany). 2-6

Apparent Authority - Type of authority the public perceives an agent to have based upon his actions. 2-8

Appraisal Condition (general) - Common property insurance policy provision that provides that in the event the insured and insurer cannot agree to the value of the damaged property, either party may make a demand for appraisal. 3-17

Arbitration Condition (general) - Common liability insurance policy provision that provides that in the event the insured and insurer cannot agree on the amount of loss, either party may make a demand for arbitration. 3-17

Assigned Risk Plan (auto) - Residual market for individuals who are unable to secure insurance through the voluntary auto market. Also known as Automobile Insurance Plan. 6-14

Association Captive - Alternative financing mechanism. Type of captive that insures risks of its members and their affiliated companies. 10-12

Assuming Company - Reinsurance company that assumes the exposure from the ceding company. 2-4

Assumption of Risk - Common law defense that bars or reduces recovery to an injured person if that person knew of the consequences and assumed the risk. 3-14

Auto - Land motor vehicle or trailer designed for travel on public roads and includes equipment attached to the vehicle. Requires motor vehicle registration. 8-12

Automatic Increase - Endorsement that provides for increases in coverage amounts to reflect increases in inflation. 4-10

B

Bailee - An individual or business that accepts property from another (e.g., dry cleaner, laundry, furniture refinisher, etc.). 7-29

Bailees Customers Form - An Inland Marine Form used to cover a bailee for property in his possession. 7-29

Bailor - An individual or business that transfers their property for service. 7-29

Bill of Lading - A contract between the common carrier and the shipper evidencing title and responsibilities. 7-29

Binders - Temporary insurance contracts that may be made orally or in writing, for a period of not more than 30 days. 3-20

Blanket Insurance - Single amount of insurance that is provided to all locations. 3-5

Boatowners Form - Coverage Form that provides property damage to the boat, outboard motors, trailer and miscellaneous boating equipment and boatowners liability caused by the insured's negligence. 10-7

Bodily Injury (general) - Bodily harm, sickness, disease, including death. 6-6

Bodily Injury Liability (auto) - Pays others when the insured is responsible for causing injuries and includes medical and rehabilitation expenses and noneconomic damages such as pain and suffering. 6-1

Boiler and Machinery Coverage Part - Commercial Property Part used to cover steam boilers, pressure vessels, air conditioning equipment, air compressors, turbines and other similar types of machinery for breakdown. 7-15

BOP - Abbreviation for Businessowners Policy. 8-1

Broad Form Nuclear Energy Exclusion Endorsement - Commercial General Liability Endorsement that specific-ally excludes coverage for bodily injury or property damage caused by nuclear materials at a nuclear facility. 7-3

Broad Form Products Endorsement (CA 25 01) - Garage Policy Endorsement that covers property damage to the insured's (garage owner) defective product. 6-21

Broker - An individual, partnership or corporation, not an officer or agent of a company, who for compensation, acts or aids in any manner in obtaining insurance for a person other than himself. A broker represents the insured. 1-1

Broker's License - Insurance Department document that indicates a broker's licensing powers. Retired in 2003. 1-5

Building Limit - Automatic Increase - BOP Endorsement that increases coverage for buildings on a pro rata basis. 8-7

Builders Risk Form - Commercial Property Coverage Form that provides coverage to buildings under construction. 7-22

Building and Personal Property Form - Commercial Form used to insure various types of commercial property. 7-19

Building Ordinance or Law Coverage (HO 04 77) - Homeowner Endorsement that provides additional coverage if at the time of loss stricter building ordinances require construction different than originally designed. 5-16

Business Income Form - Commercial Property Coverage Form that provides income due to the interruption or suspension in business. Business interruption must be caused by a covered direct loss. 7-23

Business Personal Property Limit - Seasonal Increase - BOP coverage that automatically increases business personal property an additional 25% to reflect seasonal increases. 8-8

Business Pursuits (HO 24 71) - Homeowners Endorsement that covers occupational liability of those who are employed by others (e.g., teachers, messengers). 5-16

Business Liability (BOP) - Provides coverage for bodily injury and property damages to third parties that arise out of business activities for which the insured becomes legally liable. 8-10

Business Auto Coverage Form - Commercial Form used to cover owned, leased, hired or borrowed business autos. 6-16

Businessowners Policy (BOP) - Commercial Policy used to insure small to medium sized businesses. Includes a wide range of property and liability coverages. 8-1

C

Camera and Musical Instrument Form - Inland Marine Coverage Form that covers a dealer's stock in trade, such as cameras and musical instruments and for property in their care, custody and control.

Captives - Alternative risk mechanism that is a formalized method of self-insuring. Can be formed as either a pure or association captive. 10-12

Cargo Coverage - Ocean Marine Policy coverage that insures against damage to the cargo on a ship. 10-5

Causes of Loss (general) - The perils of a policy (e.g., fire, lightning, windstorm, etc.). 3-4

Ceding Company - Reinsurance term meaning the original insurer that reinsures its loss exposures. 2-4

Certified Insurance Counselor (CIC) - Designation administered by the Society of Certified Insurance Counselors requiring the passing of 5 examinations on various insurance subjects. 1-4

CGL - Abbreviation for Commercial General Liability policy.

Chartered Property Casualty Underwriter (CPCU) - Designation administered by the American Institute for CPCU requiring the passing of 8 national examinations on various insurance subjects. 1-4

Claims-Made Coverage - CGL Coverage Form that applies to claims made after the retroactive date and during the claims made policy period, regardless of when the injury or damage occurred. 7-4

Coinsurance (property) - Common property provision that requires an insured to carry insurance coverage equal to a specified percentage of a property's actual cash value in return for a reduced rate. 3-12

Collision Insurance (auto) - Auto coverage that insures an auto for a collision with another object or vehicle. 6-5

Combined Ratio - Ratio used to determine profitability of an insurance company. It is the combination or sum of the loss and expense ratios. 3-2

Combined Single Limit (CSL) - Combines both bodily injury liability and property damage liability into one single limit of protection. 3-15

Commercial Articles Form - Inland Marine Coverage Form that covers property such as cameras, musical instruments and related equipment that is used commercially. 7-28

Commercial Auto Policy - Commercial Policy that provides coverage for businesses that own, use or service automobiles or trucks. 6-15

Commercial Carriers Regulations - Federal regulation requiring commercial carriers to carry minimum limits of liability and prove financial responsibility. 6-20

Commercial Crime Coverage - Commercial Policy that provides coverage in the event property is taken by burglary, safe burglary, robbery, extortion or theft. 7-9

Commercial General Liability Coverage - Commercial coverage that covers an insured's legal liability arising out of injuries or damages suffered by the public, tenants and/or customers. 7-3

Commercial Umbrella - Commercial liability policy that provides coverage in two areas: first, for losses in excess of the required underlying limits, and second, for other coverages not provided under underlying policies (e.g., extra territorial coverage). 10-2

Common Carrier - Carriers who offer their services to the public at large and are legally liable for damage to property they are transporting (e.g., UPS, FEDEX). 7-28

Common Law Defenses - Defenses that were developed through judicial case decisions and based upon precedent or custom (i.e., Assumption of Risk, Intervening Cause). 3-14

Comparative Negligence - Statutory defense which compares actions and apportions negligence between all parties. 3-14

Compensatory Damages - Damages which consist of both general and special damages. 3-14

Comprehensive Insurance - Auto coverage which insures an auto for fire, theft, earthquake, flood, vandalism, etc. Also known as Other Than Collision. 6-5

Comprehensive Personal Liability (CPL) Insurance - Covers individuals for nonbusiness related liability. Similar to Section II - Liability of the Homeowners Policy. 10-1

Computer Fraud Coverage - Commercial Crime Coverage which covers all types of property against loss caused by computer fraud from inside an insured's premises or a banking premises. 7-12

Concealment - Failure to disclose a fact. If the concealment is material to the application, coverage may be voided. 2-10

Conditions (general) - Insurance policy component which sets forth the rules, duties, provisions and obligations of the insured and the insurance company. 3-8

Conditional Contracts - Contracts which are contingent upon certain acts by the insured and/or claimant. 2-13

Condominium Association Form - Commercial Property Coverage Form which provides coverage for the building which houses condominium units. 7-25

Condominium Unit Owner's Form - Commercial Property Coverage Form which provides coverage for the unit owners of commercial condominiums. 7-25

Consequential or Indirect Loss - Losses that are the result of a direct loss (i.e., Business Interruption, Extra Expense). 3-5

Consideration - Bargaining elements of a contract. The insured's consideration is the premium payment and statements contained in the application. The insurer's consideration is the promise to pay claims in accordance with policy provisions. 2-10

Continuing or Promissory Warranty - Type of warranty contained in an insurance contract which requires certain facts to be promised and continued during the policy term. 2-14

Contract Bonds - Bonds which are used in the construction business. 10-4

Contract Carrier - Carriers who agree to service specific clients based upon a prearranged agreement and are only liable when they are negligent. 7-28

Contractors Equipment Form - Inland Marine Coverage Form which covers various types of equipment used by contractors such as bulldozers, backhoes, tractors, cranes, etc. 7-29

Contributing Locations - A business location which the insured depends upon for materials and services. One of four dependent properties for which a Business Income Policy may be written. 7-24

Contribution by Equal Shares - Form of proportional coverage where the loss is paid equally until one policy is exhausted, whereby the other policy pays alone. 3-11

Contributory Negligence - Common law defense which bars recovery to the injured person if that injured person contributed to the accident, even if in the slightest degree. 3-14

Countersignature - Pennsylvania regulation that requires that policies placed by resident producers be countersigned. Limited exceptions apply. 3-21

Coverage For Damage To Your Auto - Part D - Auto Coverage that provides coverage for direct and accidental physical damage to your covered auto. It includes the payment of applicable sales tax for stolen or damaged property. Also referred to as physical damage coverage. 6-10

D

Declarations (general) - Insurance policy component that indicates the named insured and address, policy term, the amount of insurance, policy forms, deductible, premium and related information that is specific to the insured. 3-8

Deductibles (general) - The initial amount, or the first dollar cost paid or absorbed by the insured in the event of a loss. 3-10

Deductible Liability Coverage Endorsement (CA 03 02) - Commercial Auto Endorsement that allows the insured to elect deductibles for bodily injury and property damage either separately or combined. 6-21

Defense Base Act - Federal Regulation that provides Workers Compensation benefits to civilians employed at any military, air or naval base. 9-2

Definitions (general) - Insurance policy component that clarifies terms as used in the policy. 3-8

Difference In Conditions (DIC) - Insurance frequently written to supplement and fill gaps in property policies. Examples of DIC coverage include flood and earthquake. 10-11

Direct Loss - Losses that are the direct physical result of an insured peril. 3-5

Direct Billed Policies - Premium collection method whereby premiums are billed directly to the insured and collected by the insurance company. 2-11

Direct Writer System - Distribution system comprised of insurance agents who are employees of the insurance company they represent and market the products of that one company (e.g., USAA and GEICO). 2-8

Directors and Officers Insurance - Specialty liability policy that provides coverage for the directors and officers of a corporation who may become liable for failure to act in the corporation's best interest. 10-3

Dollar Deductible (general) - Deductible expressed in a dollar amount. 3-10

Domestic Company - Company domiciled in your state. (e.g., CIGNA, Erie and Harleysville are domiciled in the state of Pennsylvania). 2-6

Domicile - Legal address of a company. Generally the place where the company's home office is located. 2-6

Drive Other Car Coverage Endorsement (CA 99 10) - Commercial Auto Endorsement that extends business auto coverage to nonbusiness (personal) exposures of named individuals who may not own an automobile. Also referred to as DOC coverage. 6-22

Duty to Defend - Policy provision that requires the insurance company to investigate and defend any claim or lawsuit brought against an insured. 3-18

Dwelling Policy - Provides insurance coverage for residential rental properties up to four units, or occupied by no more than five roomers or boarders. Typically written on property that does not qualify for a Homeowners Policy. 4-1

Dwelling Policy Basic Form (DP 00 01) - Dwelling Policy Form that provides basic form named peril coverage on both the building and contents. Losses are adjusted on an actual cash value basis. 4-7

Dwelling Policy Broad Form (DP 00 02) - Dwelling Policy Form that provides broad form named peril coverage on both the building and contents. Building losses are adjusted on a replacement cost basis and contents are adjusted on an actual cash value basis. 4-8

Dwelling Policy Special Form (DP 00 03) - Dwelling Policy Form that provides special form coverage on the building and named peril coverage on the contents. Building losses are adjusted on a replacement cost basis and contents are adjusted on an actual value basis. 4-9

Dwelling Under Construction Endorsement - Dwelling Policy Endorsement that provides coverage for the named insured for dwellings under construction and permits the naming of additional insureds, such as contractors. 4-10

E

Earned Premiums - Portion of the policy premium that has been used in the course of a policy term. 2-11

Earthquake Endorsement (HO 04 54) - Homeowner Endorsement that provides coverage in the event an earthquake causes loss to the dwelling. 5-17

Electronic Data Processing Form - Inland Marine Coverage Form that insures electronic data processing equipment, data processing media and extra expenses and business interruption incurred in the loss of media. 7-29

Employees As Insureds Endorsement (CA 99 33) - Commercial Auto Endorsement that extends business auto coverage to employees who use their personal auto in the course of business. 6-22

Employee Theft - Commercial Crime Coverage that covers losses resulting from employee dishonesty. It covers all types of property. 7-11

Endorsements (general) - Insurance policy component used to change a policy's original terms, conditions or coverages. 3-9

Equipment Dealers Form - Inland Marine Coverage Form that covers a dealer's stock in trade, such as construction, agricultural and other mobile equipment. 7-29

Errors and Omissions Insurance - Liability insurance covering professionals for negligent acts. (i.e., Agent and Brokers E & O Insurance). 10-2

Estoppel (general) - Legal doctrine that prohibits or stops a company from citing its standard policy defenses because of the actions or inactions of the company and/or its agents. 2-14

Exclusions (general) - Insurance policy component that eliminates coverage for specific occurrences that are deemed uninsurable or not calculated in the policy premium (i.e., intentional acts, war, nuclear radiation, smog). 3-9

Exclusive Agency System - Distribution system comprised of insurance agents who are independent contractors but agree to market the products of one exclusive company (e.g., State Farm, Nationwide and Allstate). 2-8

Expense Ratio - Ratio used to determine profitability of an insurance company. It is the ratio of expenses incurred by the company in producing the business to premiums earned. 3-2

Express Authority - Specific authority that may be either verbal or written. 2-10

Extended Non-Owner Liability - Personal Auto Policy Endorsement issued to individuals who do not own a personal auto but have personal auto exposures. 6-13

Extended Reporting Periods - CGL - Claims-made policy provision used to provide coverage for claims that may be reported after the end of a claims-made policy period. 7-4

Extortion Coverage - Commercial Crime Coverage Form that covers all types of property when surrendered away from the premises as the result of threat to an insured, employee or family member. 7-12

Extra Expense Form - Commercial Property Coverage Form that provides coverage to an insured for the extra expenses incurred from a direct loss. 7-25

Extraordinary Medical Benefits (auto) - Optional first party benefit coverage. Permits the insured the option of buying additional medical and rehabilitation limits. 6-2

F

Facultative Reinsurance - Type of reinsurance that requires an individual reinsurance agreement of each risk. 2-4

False Pretense Coverage Endorsement (CA 25 03) - Commercial Auto Endorsement that provides coverage in the event the garage releases a vehicle under false pretense. 6-22

Fair Credit Reporting Act - Federal Act that protects consumers from unfair and inaccurate information contained in the files of credit reporting agencies. 1-12

FAIR Plans - State supervised pools that provide a market to individuals who are unable to secure coverage through standard insurance carriers. 10-10

Farm Coverage Part - Commercial Policy that insures the unique exposures of farming type risks. May include a Property Form, Liability Form, Mobile Agricultural Form and/or a Livestock Form. 7-31

Federal Employees Compensation Act - Federal act that affords Workers Compensation to civilian employees of the U.S. government anywhere in the world. 9-2

Federal Employer's Liability Act (FELA) - Federal act that permits interstate railroad workers the right to sue for benefits for negligence. 9-2

Fiduciary Liability - Specialty liability policy that covers liability exposures fiduciaries face in their service as an executor, administrator or trustee. 10-3

Film Form - Inland Marine Coverage Form that covers motion pictures, video tapes or sound tracks developed by commercial production companies.

Financial Responsibility - The ability to respond to liability on accounts of accidents arising out of the maintenance or use of a motor vehicle. 6-1

First Party Benefits (auto) - Benefits that are payable to an insured. 6-2

First Named Insured (general) - The individual named in a commercial policy who is responsible for carrying on the day-to-day functions of the insured, such as paying premiums and/or reporting losses. 3-9

Flood Insurance - Federal program that provides coverage for flood. May be purchased directly through the government or through an agent. 10-9

Floor Plan Form - Inland Marine Coverage Form that covers merchandise for sale that is financed through a lending institution.

Foreign Company - Companies domiciled outside the Commonwealth of Pennsylvania. (e.g., Prudential is domiciled in New Jersey, Metropolitan in New York and Aetna, Travelers and Hartford are in Connecticut). 2-5

Forgery or Alteration Coverage - Commercial Crime Coverage that covers the insured worldwide for loss of money resulting from forgery and alteration of outgoing checks, drafts or promissory notes. 7-12

Fraud - Deliberate deceit with the intent to take property of another. 2-14

Freight Coverage - Ocean Marine Policy Coverage that reimburses the payor for loss of income that would be earned for moving the cargo. 10-6

Friendly Fire - Deliberately ignited flame or glow that stays within its intended confines (i.e., fire within heating, cooking or lighting units). 3-23

Full Tort (auto) - Tort option that permits an insured to sue for specific damages plus noneconomic damages such as pain and suffering regardless if the injury was serious or not.6-2

Full Reporting (honesty clause) - Reporting form feature requiring full disclosure on values. Losses are adjusted on the prorated portion of the reported values to the actual values. 3-6

Functional Replacement Cost - Basic valuation provision that permits the insurer to replace damaged property with a functional equivalent. Used with older properties. 3-7

Funeral Benefits (auto) - Optional first party benefit coverage that pays the funeral, burial or cremation expenses if an insured dies in a car crash within 24 months from the date of the accident. 6-2

G

Garage Form - Commercial Auto Form that covers garage operations of service stations, auto dealers, parking garages, repair shops and similar type risks. 6-18

Garagekeepers - Garage Form Coverage that provides legal liability for damage to a customer's auto or property in the insured's care, custody and control while the insured is attending, servicing, parking or storing the property. May be written on a primary or excess basis. 6-18

General Damages - The natural, necessary and usual result of the wrongful act or occurrence in question (i.e., compensation for pain and suffering, disfigurement, loss of limbs, sight or hearing, and the loss of the ability to bear children). 3-14

Guests' Property Coverage - Commercial Crime Coverage that covers an innkeeper for loss to guest's property caused by that innkeeper's negligence. 7-13

H

Hazards (general) - Condition or exposure that increases the possibility of loss (poor housekeeping, bad wiring, etc.). 3-3

Hired Auto and Non-Owned Auto (BP 04 04) - Businessowners Endorsement that provides liability coverage for businessowner auto exposures. Typically written when a businessowner does not have a Business Auto Policy. 8-13

Home Day Care Coverage Endorsement (HO 04 97) - Homeowners Endorsement that provides liability coverage for a home day care business on the residence premises. 5-17

Homeowners Form HO 00 02 - Homeowner Policy that provides broad form named peril coverage on the building and contents. Building losses are adjusted on a replacement cost basis and contents on an actual cash value basis. Covers owner occupied one or four family dwellings. 5-6

Homeowners Form HO 00 03 - Homeowner Policy that provides special form coverage on the building and named peril coverage on the contents. Building losses are adjusted on a replacement cost basis and contents on an actual cash value basis. Covers owner occupied one or four family dwellings. 5-6

Homeowners Form HO 00 04 - Homeowner Policy that provides broad form named peril contents coverage for tenant occupants of apartments. Contents losses are adjusted on an actual cash value basis. 5-6

Homeowners Form HO 00 05 - Homeowner Policy that provides special form coverage on the building contents. Building losses are adjusted on a replacement cost basis and contents on an actual cash value basis. Covers owner occupied one to four family dwellings. 5-6

Homeowners Form HO 00 06 - Homeowner Policy that provides broad form named peril contents coverage to owner occupants of condominiums. Limited building coverage is provided. Losses are adjusted on an actual cash value basis. 5-7

Homeowners Form HO 00 08 - Homeowner Policy that provides modified named peril coverage to owner occupants of one and four family dwellings. Dwelling losses are adjusted on a functional replacement cost basis and contents at actual cash value. 5-7

Hostile Fire - Fire that escapes its intended confines (i.e., a log rolling out of a fireplace). 3-23

Hull Coverage - Ocean Marine Policy coverage that insures against damage to or loss of a ship. 10-5

I

Implied Authority - Authority not specifically defined in the agent's agreement, but is an extension of an agent's standard duties. 2-10

Implied Warranty - Type of warranty contained in most sales contracts that indicates that the product is legal, merchantable and fit for public use. 2-14

Income Loss Benefits (auto) - Optional first party benefit coverage that pays for lost income due to injuries that prevent an insured from working. Limited to 80% of loss of gross income up to $2,500 per month. 6-2

Indemnity (general) - Principle of restoring or reimbursing one to the extent of his loss. 2-13

Independent Agency System - Distribution system comprised of insurance agents who are independent contractors who enter into agency and marketing arrangements with various insurance companies. 2-8

Inflation Guard Endorsement (HO 04 66) - Homeowners Endorsement that increases Coverages A, B, C & D to reflect the increase in costs due to inflation. 5-16

Inland Marine Coverage Forms - Coverage Forms that are written to provide coverage for virtually any type of risk that may be transported. 7-27

Installation Floaters Form - Inland Marine Coverage Form that insures property such as turbines, transformers and air conditioning equipment during transit or installation at the construction or installation site. 7-29

Insurable Interest (general) - The interest one has in life or property that may cause one the possibility of financial loss. In property and casualty insurance it is required at the time of loss. 3-1

Insurance (general) - Risk transfer technique accomplished by the collecting and pooling of premiums to pay future losses. 2-2

Insured (general) - Anyone who may be covered by the policy. May include individuals who are not named in the policy, such as resident relatives or minor children. 3-9

Insuring Agreement (general) - The contractual clause of the policy setting forth the agreement between the insured and the insurance company. It provides coverage for the insured in return for the premium and compliance with all applicable policy provisions. 3-8

Intentional Torts/Intentional Acts - Acts that are carried out with purpose and knowledge of their consequences. Generally not covered. 3-13

Intervening Cause - Common law defense that bars or reduces recovery to an injured person if an intervening cause interrupted the chain of events and sets in motion a new chain of events. 3-14

J

Jewelers Block Form - Inland Marine Coverage Form that covers the jeweler's stock in trade, such as jewelry, precious and semi-precious stones and precious metals. 7-29

Joint Ownership Coverage Endorsement - Personal Auto Endorsement that modifies the policy language to permit coverage for joint owners in nontraditional households. 6-13

Jones Act - Federal Act that permits masters and crew-members of American vessels the right to sue for negligence in the event of bodily injury or death. Also known as the Merchant Marine Act. 9-2

Judicial Bonds - Bonds that are used in the legal process.10-5

L

Laser Beam Endorsement - General Liability Policy Endorsement that may be added to exclude coverage for specific accidents, products, work or locations. 7-5

Law of Large Numbers - Basic principle of insurance in that predictability increases when larger numbers of occurrences are exposed to a similar type of exposure. 2-2

Leader Locations - A business that attracts customers to the insured's business location. One of four dependent properties for which a Business Income Policy may be written. 7-24

Leasehold Interest Form - Commercial Property Coverage Form that protects the lessee from loss in the event the business has a favorable lease arrangement that cannot be reproduced. 7-25

Legal Liability Form - Commercial Property Coverage Form that protects the insured against legal liability due to the damage of property of others in the insured's care, custody and control. 7-25

Legal Errors and Omissions Insurance - Professional liability policy that covers liability exposures that lawyers face in the services they render to clients. 10-2

Lessees of Safety Deposit Boxes - Commercial Crime Coverage that covers securities for theft, disappearance and destruction at the depository premises and property other than money and securities from within a safety deposit box for burglary or robbery. 7-13

Liability Coverage - Part A (auto) - Auto Coverage that provides coverage for bodily injury or property damage up to the limit of liability for which an insured becomes legally responsible because of an auto accident. 6-7

Liberalization Clause (general) - A common insurance policy condition that provides that in the event the insurer broadens coverage without an additional premium charge, the broadened coverage will apply to all insureds immediately. 3-17

Limited Tort - Auto tort option that limits the insured's right to sue to specific out-of-pocket expenses, except in cases involving serious injury or death. 6-2

Liquor Liability - Specialty liability policy that covers liability exposures that restaurants, bars, beer distributors and other similar establishments face due to their selling or serving of alcoholic beverages. 10-3

Livestock Coverage Form - Farm Property Coverage Form that provides coverage for livestock. 7-33

Lloyds - Association or group of individuals who share in the making of insurance contracts (e.g., Lloyd's of London). 2-4

Loss Cost Rating - Rating method that utilizes loss costs published by an advisory rating organization (e.g., I.S.O., Pennsylvania Compensation Rating Bureau) permitting insurers to apply their own expense costs. 3-2, 9-6.

Loss Payable Clause (general) - Basic policy provision that reflects the legitimate interest that a finance company has in personal property in that it has a financial interest. 3-20

Loss Ratio - Ratio used to determine profitability of an insurance company. It is the ratio of losses incurred to premiums earned. 3-2

Loss - Reduction in the value of an asset. 2-1

M

Mail Order System - Distribution system that markets its products through the mail, television, radio or magazines (e.g., Colonial Penn). 2-8

Mail Form - Inland Marine Coverage Form that covers valuable shipments of mail forwarded by first class mail, certified mail, or registered mail (e.g., stock certificates, bonds, postage stamps and travelers checks).

Management General Agency System - Distribution system comprised of insurance agencies that perform many of the functions of the branch office system. Generally have a specialized knowledge of products or markets. 2-9

Manufacturing Locations - A business that manufactures products for customers under a sales agreement. One of four dependent properties for which a Business Income Policy may be written. 7-24

Market Value - The price one would pay based upon free market conditions. 3-7

Maximum Period of Indemnity (BIC) - Optional Business Income coverage that limits the loss period to 120 days immediately after loss. 7-24

Medical Malpractice Insurance - Professional liability policy that covers liability exposures that medical professionals face in their treatment of patients. 10-2

Medical Payments Coverage - Part B (auto) - Auto coverage that provides reasonable and necessary medical and funeral expenses resulting from accidental bodily injury. 6-8

Mini Tail (CGL) - Covers claims reported within 60 days of policy termination. 7-4

Midi Tail (CGL) - Covers claims reported within 5 years of policy termination provided the occurrence is reported within 60 days of termination of the coverage part. 7-4

Miscellaneous Type Vehicles Endorsement - Personal Auto Endorsement that alters the definition of a covered auto to include motorcycles, dune buggies, golf carts and motor homes. 6-13

Misrepresentation (general) - Statements made by an applicant or insured that are not true. If a misrepresent-ation is material (i.e., insurer would not have written coverage knowing that fact), coverage may be voided. 2-11

Mobile Agricultural Machinery/Equipment Form - Farm Property Coverage Form that open peril" coverage to mobile agricultural machinery and equipment. 7-33

Mobile Equipment Endorsement (CA 20 15) - Commercial Auto Endorsement that provides auto coverage to mobile equipment. 6-22

Mobilehome (MH 40 01) - Endorsement used to modify Homeowner Forms HO 00 02 and HO 00 03. Requires year round living and must be at least 10 feet wide and 40 feet long. 5-17

Monthly Limits of Indemnity (BIC) - Optional Business Income coverage. Limits BI losses to each 30 consecutive day period. Fractional options for 3, 4 or 6 months. 7-24

Motor Carrier - A person or organization providing transportation by auto in the furtherance of a commercial enterprise. 6-20

Motor Carrier Form - Commercial Auto Coverage Form that insures common and private motor carriers. 6-20

Motor Truck Cargo Policy - Owner's Form - Transportation Policy used to cover the truckowner's cargo while being transported in their own truck. 7-30

Motor Truck Cargo Policy - Shipper's Form - Transportation Policy used by shippers to cover property that they own and ship. 7-30

Motor Truck Cargo Policy - Trucker's Form - Transportation Policy that provides liability coverage to cover cargo of others which is being transported for hire by a common carrier. 7-30

Mutual Companies - Companies owned by the policyholders who have voting rights and share in the profits in the form of dividends (e.g., Prudential and State Farm). Mutuals are classified as either assessment mutuals or nonassessment mutuals. 2-4

N

Named Non-Owner Endorsement (auto) - Personal Auto Policy Endorsement used to insure individuals who do not own an auto but have personal auto exposures. 6-13

Named Insured (general) - The individual or business named in the policy declarations. 3-9

Named Peril Policy - Policy that specifically lists the perils insured against in the policy. 3-4

National Association of Insurance Commissioners (NAIC)- Organization of Insurance Commissioners from each state. 2-7

National Flood Insurance - Federal program that provides flood coverage. May be secured directly through the Flood Insurance Administration or through a "Write Your Own" insurance company. 10-9

Negligence - Failure to exercise the care that a reasonable or prudent person would under similar circumstances. 3-13

Non-admitted or Unauthorized Companies - Company that is not authorized or admitted by the state insurance department to conduct business. 2-6

Nonconcurrency - Situation that arises when policies are written on the same property, but not on the same coverage basis. 3-10

O

Occurrence (general) - An accident, including continuous or repeated exposure to substantially the same general harmful conditions that result, during the policy period, in bodily injury or property damage. 5-1

Occurrence Coverage - CGL Coverage Form that applies to injury or damage that occurs during the policy period, regardless of when the claim is reported to the company. 7-4

Ordinance or Law Coverage (HO 04 77) - Homeowners Endorsement that provides additional coverage if, at the time of loss, stricter building ordinances require construction different than originally designed. 5-17

Other Than Collision (OTC) - Auto coverage that insures theft or damage to an insured's car from hazards including fire, flood or vandalism. Also known as Comprehensive Insurance. 6-5

Other Insurance (general) - Policy provision that addresses the apportionment of coverage in the event more than one policy is written on the same risk at the time of loss. 3-10

Owners and Contractor Protective Liability Policy (OCP)- Policy that protects an owner, operator or contractor against loss caused by the negligence of a hired contractor or subcontractor. 7-9

P

Parol Evidence Rule - Legal rule that limits a contract to its written terms. 2-13

Peak Season Endorsement (CP 12 30) - Commercial Property Endorsement that increases business property during specific periods. 7-26

Pennsylvania Insurance Guaranty Association Act - State association that pays certain covered claims of insolvent admitted insurers. Limited to $300,000 per claim. 3-21

Percentage Deductible - Deductible expressed as a percent of the amount of insurance, the value of the insured property, or the amount of loss. 3-10

Per Person Limits - Limits the amount of coverage for each person, regardless of the overall or aggregate limit. 3-15

Per Occurrence Limits - Limits the amount of coverage for each occurrence, regardless of the number of persons injured. 3-15

Peril - A cause of loss (i.e., fire, lightning, theft, etc.). 2-1

Permitted Incidental Occupancies (HO 00 42) - Homeowner Endorsement that provides liability coverage for business activities such as an office or studio on the residence premises. 5-16

Personal Contracts - Refers to the personal nature between parties requiring the highest degree of good faith. 2-13

Personal Injury Endorsement - Homeowner Endorsement that modifies the bodily injury definition to include libel, slander, malicious prosecution and invasion of privacy. 5-17

Personal Umbrella Policy - Personal liability policy that provides coverage in two areas: first, for losses in excess of the required underlying limits, and second, for other coverages not provided under underlying policies (i.e., personal injury, slander). 10-1

Personal Article Floaters - Inland Marine Coverage that insures personal property for all risks of direct physical loss except for war risks, nuclear hazards, wear and tear, deterioration, inherent vice, insects or vermin. 10-10

Personal Property Replacement Cost (HO 04 90) - Homeowner Endorsement that provides full replacement cost coverage on personal property in place of actual cash value coverage. 5-17

Personal Auto Policy (PAP) - Provides liability and physical damage coverages for an insured vehicle. 6-6

Physicians and Surgeons Equipment Form - Inland Marine Coverage Form that covers medical and dental equipment and related furniture and supplies used by physicians in their practice.

Policy Period (general) - Time period as indicated in the declarations page during which coverage will be provided. 3-10

Policy Conditions (general) - Sets forth the rules, duties, provisions and obligations of the insured and the insurance company. 3-8

Policy Forms - Documents that make up a policy. Must be filed with the insurance department prior to their introduction. 1-9

Policy Limits (general) - The maximum amount of money the insured can recover in the event of a loss. 3-11

Policy Territory - (general) - Defines the location where coverage will be provided. 3-10

Pollution Liability - Broadened Coverage For Covered Autos (CA 99 48) - Commercial Auto Endorsement that provides coverage for bodily injury or property damage resulting from the transportation, handling, storage or disposal of pollutants. 6-23

Pollution Liability - Broadened Coverage For Covered Autos (CA 99 55) - Commercial Auto Garage Policy endorsement that provides coverage for bodily injury or property damage resulting from the transportation, handling, storage or disposal of pollutants. 6-23

Pooling - Arrangement where a number of primary insurers agree to place a certain type of business into a pool. Each insurer receives a prearranged percentage of premiums and each insurer agrees to pay a prearranged percentage of losses (i.e., aviation pools, nuclear liability pools). 10-12

Premises and Operations - Liability terms meaning the insured location and its operations. Liability policies generally cover these exposures. 7-3

Premium Financing - Agreement between insured and financing company whereby the financing company pays the insured's premium in a lump sum and the insured makes installment payments to the finance company. These installment payments include interest charges. 2-11

Presumption of Agency - Belief by insured that agent has authority to function in the capacity he is representing. 2-7

Primary Coverage - Policy that pays first. 3-7

Pro Rata Cancellation - Cancellation requested by the insurer. The actual proportion of the unearned premium will be returned to the insured. 3-21

Producers - Individuals who sell insurance to the public.

Products and Completed Operations (CGL) - Liability term addressing the exposure caused by the manufacturing of products and/or the completion of operations away from the insured location. 7-3

Professional Liability Policies - Policies that provide coverage against legal liability resulting from the negligence, errors and omissions, or other aspects of rendering professional services. 10-2

Property Damage - Physical injury to tangible property resulting in loss. 8-11

Property Damage Liability (auto) - Pays others when the insured is responsible for damaging their property. 6-1

Punitive Damages - Damages levied over and above general damages to punish the negligent party for their wanton, reckless or malicious actions. 3-14

Purchasing Groups - Alternative funding mechanism whereby similar type businesses form a purchasing group to buy insurance at a premium savings. 10-11

Pure Captives - Alternative financing mechanism. Type of captive that insures risks of its parent and their affiliated companies. 10-11

Pure Risk - Risk that has two outcomes, loss and no loss. 2-1

R

Rating - Process by which a company determines a price for the exposure it is underwriting. 3-2

Reasonable Expectations - Legal doctrine that states that an insured is entitled to the coverage under a policy that he or she might reasonably expect it to provide. 2-13

Rebating - Illegal practice of giving back to an insured a part of the policy commission or other consideration as an inducement to purchase insurance. 1-11

Recipient Locations - A business that accepts the insured's products or services. One of four dependent properties for which a Business Income Policy may be written. 7-24

Reciprocals - Unincorporated associations in which members, called subscribers, insure one another. Managed by an attorney-in-fact who solicits new subscribers, collects premiums, adjusts losses, and manages administrative functions (e.g., Erie Insurance Exchange). 2-4

Redlining - Illegal practice of discrimination against insureds based upon location. 1-11

Reinsurance - Contractual process whereby an insurance company purchases insurance to protect itself from losses. 2-3

Rental Reimbursement (auto) - Auto coverage that reimburses the insured for automobile rental costs in the event an insured auto is stolen or damaged. 6-10

Replacement Cost - Basic valuation provision that replaces old damaged property with new replacement property at today's replacement cost, without any deduction for depreciation. 3-7

Reporting Forms - Method of reporting property values. Reports can be filed daily, weekly, monthly, quarterly or by policy year. Requires full and complete reporting (honesty clause). Losses are adjusted subject to 100% coinsurance requirement. Used to vary the amount of coverage in force to reflect fluctuations in property. 3-6 & 7-26

Representations - Oral or written statements made by the applicant with the intention of securing insurance coverage. 2-14

Resident Producer - Individual who has either a business or legal address in the Commonwealth of Pennsylvania. 1-2

Restoration of Limits (general) - Provision that automatically restores a property policy's limits after a loss. 3-11

Retention - The exposure retained by the ceding company in a reinsurance transaction. May be expressed as a dollar amount, a percentage of the original amount of insurance, or as a combination of both. It is also the amount retained by an individual or business under an umbrella policy. 2-4

Retroactive Date - Determines or defines when coverage begins under a claims made policy. 7-4

Retrocession - Process of reinsuring reinsurance. 2-4

Risk Management - Process of treating and managing loss exposures. 2-2

Risk Retention Groups - Alternative funding mechanism whereby similar type businesses form a risk retention group to write all kinds of commercial liability coverage, except Workers Compensation. 10-11

S

Safe Depository Coverage - Commercial Crime Coverage that covers an individual's property against loss caused by the depository's negligence. 7-13

Salvage - Process in which damaged property is taken by the insurer to reduce its loss after a claim is paid. A dollar amount for salvage value is paid to the insured. 3-18

Scheduled Personal Property Endorsement (HO 04 61) - Homeowner Endorsement that provides coverage for personal property that have values in excess of the policy limits. 5-16

Securities Deposit With Others Coverage - Commercial Crime Coverage that covers securities for theft, disappearance and destruction when deposited with a custodian, such as a bank or broker. 7-13

Self-insured - Alternative funding mechanism whereby a business chooses to retain its loss exposures rather than transferring them through the purchase of insurance. 10-11

Short Rate Cancellation - A cancellation requested by the insured. A penalty will be charged against the return premium. 3-21

Sign Form - Inland Marine Coverage Form that covers signs including automatic and/or neon types. 7-29

Sinkhole Collapse - Dwelling Policy Endorsement that provides coverage for sudden settlement or collapse of the earth supporting the property if caused by subterranean voids created by the action of water on limestone or similar rock formation. 4-11

Special Damages - The natural, but not the necessary and inevitable results of the wrongful act (i.e., hospital expenses, doctor expenses and ambulance charges). 3-14

Special Form Coverage - Type of policy that lists the exclusions from coverage. 3-4

Specialty Liability Insurance - Various specialty policies that are used to fill gaps caused by exclusions in the primary personal and commercial policies. 10-2

Specific Insurance - Single amount of insurance for a specific location. 3-5

Speculative Risk - Type of risk which has three outcomes, loss, no loss and financial gain. Insurance underwriters seek to avoid speculative risk. 2-1

Split Limits - Specifies different amounts of coverage for different types of losses. 3-15

Spoilage Coverage Endorsement - Optional Endorsement that provides coverage for loss to perishable stock located at the described premises. 7-26

Stacking (auto) - Procedure whereby an insured can add together the limits of the uninsured or underinsured motorist coverage limits for all autos insured under a policy. 6-5

Stacking Waiver (auto) - Waiver required to be signed by the insured that rejects the stacking benefit. A premium savings results. 6-5

Standard Fire Policy - Standard policy developed by the fire insurance industry as a means of providing uniform fire coverages. Provided in a 165 line format. 3-22

Standard Mortgage Clause - Basic policy provision that reflects the legitimate interest that mortgage holders have in real property in which they have a financial interest. 3-20

Stated Amount - Valuation provision that establishes coverage amounts on property at policy inception and pays the full amount regardless of actual cash value. 3-7

Statute of Limitations - Statutory defense that sets a time limit in which an injured party may bring legal action against an individual. 3-14

Statutory Defenses - Defenses that are the written laws as enacted by the legislature. 3-14

Stock Companies - Type of company owned by stockholders who have the usual rights of ownership, including the right of voting and incurring profits or losses. (e.g., Travelers, Aetna and Allstate). 2-4

Strict Liability - Liability that is imposed without the need to prove fault or negligence. 3-15

Subrogation - Legal process that permits the insurance company to subrogate against third parties who, because of their negligence, cause the company to pay a claim. 2-13

Supplemental Extended Reporting Periods (SERP) - Extends the CGL reporting period indefinitely. Requires the payment of an additional premium. 7-4

Supplementary Payments (general) - Provides coverage beyond the principal policy coverages (i.e., claim expense, first aid, loss assessment). 3-8

Surety Bonds - Type of bond that guarantees that a specific obligation will be fulfilled. 10-4

Surplus Lines - Broad range of risk exposures that are not available or cannot be procured through admitted or authorized markets (i.e., Lloyds of London). 10-3

T

Temporary License - License issued without examination to certain individuals (i.e., spouse of a deceased agent, agent serving in the military). Issued for a period of 180 days. 1-3

Theatrical Property Form - Inland Marine Coverage Form that covers scenery, costumes and related property for theatrical productions.

Theft Coverage Endorsement - Dwelling Policy Endorsement that provides coverage for theft, attempted theft and vandalism and malicious mischief damage resulting from the theft act. 4-10

Time Deductible - Deductible expressed in a number of days that must elapse prior to coverage being afforded. 3-10

Time Element Coverage - Insurance that covers indirect losses (i.e., business income and extra expenses). 3-21

Total Loss - Loss in which the cost of repairs plus salvage value (value remaining in the vehicle after a total loss) equals or exceeds the vehicle's ACV. 3-18

Towing and Labor Endorsement - Personal Auto Endorsement that provides coverage limits of $25, $50, or $75 for towing and labor costs incurred each time an auto becomes disabled. 6-13

Transfer of Rights and Recovery (Subrogation) - Policy provision that permits the insurance company to subrogate against third parties who, because of their negligence, cause the insurance company to pay a claim. 3-18

Trailer Interchange Coverage - Commercial Auto Endorsement that covers the insured's legal liability for loss or damage to nonowned trailers and equipment. 6-19

Transfer of Rights and Duties (Assignment) - Policy provision that prohibits the insured from transferring or assigning the policy to another individual without the written consent of the insurer. 3-16

Transportation Policy - Annual Form - Inland Marine Form used by businesses to cover incoming and outgoing goods on an annual basis. 7-30

Transportation Policy - Trip Transit Form - Inland Marine Form used by businesses to cover goods that are shipped for one specific trip. 7-30

Treaty Reinsurance - Contractual arrangement whereby the ceding company agrees to cede business to the reinsurer, who in turn agrees to accept the risks. 2-4

Truckers Form - Commercial Auto Form that covers trucking operations. 6-19

Truckers - Insurance for Non-trucking Use Endorsement (CA 23 09) - Commercial Auto Endorsement that provides coverage to independent truck owners who are hired by truckers to move goods. Also known as Bobtail Liability. 6-22

Twisting - Illegal practice of misrepresenting policy provisions, or the making of incomplete comparisons as an inducement to terminate, lapse, forfeit or surrender one's policy for another of similar risks. 1-11

U

U.S. Longshore and Harbor Workers Comp Law - Law that covers individuals who are employed on the navigable waterways of the U.S. or adjoining areas used to load, unload or repair marine vessels. 9-1

Underinsured Motorists Insurance (auto) - Auto coverage that protects the auto owner in the event a negligent motorist causes an accident and carries limits that are too low to pay what the insured is due. 6-4

Underwriting - The broad range of duties and functions performed by agents and company underwriters during risk selection (i.e., completing applications, inspections, etc.). 3-1

Unearned Premiums - The portion of the policy premium that has not been used in the course of the policy term. 2-11

Unfair Insurance Practices Act - Act that regulates trade practices (twisting, rebating, misrepresentations) in the business of insurance by defining practices in this state that constitute unfair methods of competition or unfair or deceptive acts or practices. 1-12

Unfair Claim Settlement Practices - Act that regulates claim settlement activities (i.e., failure to pay claims promptly or failure to acknowledge a claim). 1-10

Uninsured Motorists Insurance (auto) - Auto coverage that protects the auto owner in the event an irresponsible driver (one driving without insurance) causes an accident. 6-4

Unintentional Torts (general) - Failure to exercise the care that a reasonable or prudent person would under similar circumstances. 3-13

Unoccupancy (general) - The absence of people from the insured home or building. Generally will not affect a claim settlement. 3-19

Utmost Good Faith - Dealing in accordance with standards of honesty and sincerity. Insurance is a contract of utmost good faith. 2-13

V

Vacancy (general) - The absence of both people and furniture from the insured home or building. Vacancy will affect a claim settlement if the building is vacant beyond 30 days for personal policies and 60 days for commercial policies. 3-19

Valuable Papers and Records Form - Inland Marine Coverage Form that covers the reconstruction cost to generate records such as blueprints, deeds or historical records that were destroyed due to a covered loss. 7-29

Valued Policies (general) - Basic valuation provision that establishes coverage amounts on personal or business property at policy inception and pays the full amount regardless of actual cash value.

Vandalism or Malicious Mischief (VM&M) - The willful and malicious damage or destruction to property. 4-8

Vicarious Liability - Liability that is imputed from one to another (i.e., employee to employer, son to parent). 3-15

W

Waiver - Voluntary relinquishment of a known right. 2-4

Warranty - Guarantees or promises contained in an insurance contract that would void the policy if untrue. 2-14

Watercraft Insurance - Provides coverage for watercraft exposures limited under the Homeowners Policy. 10-7

Watercraft Liability (HO 24 75) - Homeowners Endorsement that provides coverage for scheduled watercraft with inboard or inboard-outboard power outboard motors in excess of 25 HP, or any sailing vessel in excess of 26 feet. 5-17

Workers Compensation - Mandatory coverage required to be carried by all employers. Provides coverage to employees for bodily injury that is accidental, and/or occupational diseases that arise out of, or in the course of, employment. 9-1

Workers Compensation Law (Act 44) - 1993 Act that amended the Pennsylvania Workers Compensation Law. Its purpose was to reduce the increase costs of workers compensation premiums. 9-8

Wrongful Death Statutes - Statutes that preserve the right of deceased to bring legal actions against negligent parties. 3-15
Inherent vice - A natural condition of property that leads to its self-destruction (e.g., iron rusts, food spoils, flowers die). Inherent vice is a common property exclusion. 3-9

INDEX

A

A.M. Best Company . . . 2 .. 7
Abandonment . . . 3 .. 17
Accident Insurance Policies . . . 1 .. 17
Accidental Death Benefits . . . 6 .. 2
Accounts Receivable Form . . . 7 .. 28
Actual Cash Value . . . 3 .. 7
Additional Coverage and Supplemental Payments . 3 .. 8
Additional Coverages - Businessowners Policy . . . 8 .. 6
Additional Coverages - Commercial Property . . . 7 .. 21
Additional Coverages - Farm Coverage Part . . . 7 .. 36
Additional Coverages - Section I - Homeowners . . 5 .. 11
Additional Coverages - Section II - Homeowners . . 5 .. 6
Additional Insured - Lessor (CA 20 01) . . . 6 .. 21
Additional Insureds . . . 3 .. 9
Additional Residence Rented to Others (HO 24 70) 5 .. 15
Adhesion . . . 2 .. 13
Admitted or Authorized Companies . . . 2 .. 6
Advantages of Policy Package Concept-Commercial 7 .. 2
Adverse Selection - General . . . 2 .. 3
Affirmative Warranty . . . 2 .. 14
Agency Appointments . . . 1 .. 9
Agency Billed Policies . . . 2 .. 11
Agency - General . . . 2 .. 10
Agents and Brokers Errors and Omissions . . . 10 .. 2
Agents - Definition . . . 2 .. 9
Aggregate Limits . . . 3 .. 15
Agreed Value . . . 3 .. 7
Agreed Value Approach . . . 7 .. 24
Air Meet Liability . . . 10 .. 9
Airport Liability . . . 10 .. 9
Aleatory Contracts . . . 2 .. 13
Alien Company . . . 2 .. 6
Alterations and New Buildings . . . 7 .. 23
Alternative Funding Mechanisms . . . 10 .. 21
Ambiguities . . . 2 .. 13
Amendments of Policy Provisions - Pennsylvania . 6 .. 14
Apparent Authority . . . 2 .. 10
Appraisal . . . 3 .. 17
Arbitration . . . 3 .. 17
Assigned Risk Plan . . . 6 .. 14
Assuming Company . . . 2 .. 4
Assumption of Risk . . . 3 .. 14
Automatic Increase In Insurance - Dwelling . . . 4 .. 10
Aviation Insurance . . . 10 .. 9

B

Bailees' Customers Form . . . 7 .. 29
Basic, Broad and Special Form Analysis . . . 5 .. 7
Basic Form - Building & Personal Property . . . 7 .. 26
Basic Form - Farm Coverage Part . . . 7 .. 31
Basic Property Ins-Death of the Named Insured . . 3 .. 21
Basic Types of Construction . . . 3 .. 6
Bid Bonds . . . 10 .. 5
Bill of Lading . . . 7 .. 30
Binders . . . 3 .. 20
Blanket Insurance - General . . . 3 .. 5
Blanket v. Specific Insurance . . . 3 .. 5
Boatowners . . . 10 .. 8
Bodily Injury and Property Damage - Personal Auto 6 .. 7
Bodily Injury Liability - Auto . . . 6 .. 1
Boiler and Machinery Coverage Part . . . 7 .. 15
Boycott and Coercion . . . 1 .. 11
Branch Office System . . . 2 .. 9
Breakdown - Definition . . . 7 .. 16
Broad Form - Building and Personal Property . . . 7 .. 26
Broad Form - Farm Coverage Part . . . 7 .. 34
Broad Form Products (CA 25 01)-Commercial Auto 6 .. 21
Broker - Definition . . . 2 ... 9
Broker . . . 1 ... 2
Builders Risk Form - Commercial . . . 7 ... 22
Building and Personal Property Form . . . 7 ... 19
Building Limit - Automatic Increase - BOP . . . 8 ... 8
Building Ordinance and Law Coverage - Dwelling . . 4 ... 10
Building Ordinance or Law Coverage - Homeowners 5 ... 16
Business Auto Coverage Form . . . 6 ... 16
Business Income - BOP . . . 8 ... 6
Business Income - Commercial Property . . . 7 ... 23
Business Income From Dependent Properties . . . 7 ... 24
Business Liability . . . 8 ... 11
Business Personal Property Limit-Seasonal Increase . 8 ... 8
Business Property Coverage Forms - Causes of Loss 8 ... 3
Business Pursuits (HO 24 71) . . . 5 ... 14
Businessowner Liability Coverage Form . . . 8 ... 11
Businessowners Policy . . . 8 ... 1
Businessowners Policy Practice Exam . . . 8 ... 21
Businessowners Policy Summary . . . 8 ... 15
Businessowners Policy . . . SP .. 41

C

Cancellation and Nonrenewal - BOP . . . 8 ... 14
Cancellation and Nonrenewal - Commercial . . . 7 ... 38
Cancellation and Nonrenewal - Commercial Auto . . 6 ... 23
Cancellation and Nonrenewal - Dwelling Policy . . . 4 ... 11
Cancellation Methods . . . 3 ... 21
Captive Agents or Exclusive Agents . . . 2 ... 9
Captives . . . 10 .. 12
Cargo Coverage - Ocean Marine Insurance . . . 10 .. 6
Causes of Loss - Building and Personal Property . . . 7 ... 26
Causes of Loss - Farm Coverage Part . . . 7 ... 34
Causes of Loss - General . . . 3 ... 4
Ceding Company . . . 2 ... 4
Certificate of Qualification Requirements . . . 1 ... 1
Change, Sale or Dissolution of an Agency . . . 1 ... 3
Civil Authority . . . 7 ... 23
Claim Settlement Options . . . 3 ... 18
Claims Made Coverage . . . 7 ... 4
Claims-Made v. Occurrence . . . 7 ... 4
Clerical Activities Not Requiring Licensure . . . 1 ... 2
Co-mingling of Funds . . . 1 ... 3
Coinsurance . . . 3 ... 12
Collapse - Businessowners . . . 8 ... 6
Collision Coverage . . . 6 ... 17
Collision - Definition . . . 6 ... 10
Collision Insurance . . . 6 ... 5
Combined Ratio . . . 3 ... 2
Combined Single Limit . . . 3 ... 15
Commercial Articles Form . . . 7 ... 28
Commercial Auto Coverage Part . . . 7 ... 38
Commercial Auto Endorsements . . . 6 ... 21
Commercial Auto Policy . . . 6 ... 15
Commercial Carrier Regulation . . . 6 ... 20
Commercial Crime Coverage Forms . . . 7 ... 11
Commercial Crime Coverage Part . . . 7 ... 9
Commercial General Liability (CGL) Coverage Part . 7 ... 3
Commercial General Liability Coverages . . . 7 ... 6
Commercial Package Policy (CPP) Format . . . 7 ... 1
Commercial Package Policy Common Conditions . . SP .. 39
Commercial Package Policy Overview . . . 7 ... 1
Commercial Package Policy Declarations . . . SP .. 38
Commercial Package Policy Summary . . . 7 ... 39
Commercial Property Conditions . . . SP .. 41
Commercial Property Coverage Declarations Page . . SP .. 40
Commercial Property Coverage Part . . . 7 ... 19
Commercial Umbrella Policy . . . 10 .. 2

Commissions . . . 1 . . 12
Common Carriers . . . 7 . . 30
Common Law Defenses . . . 3 . . 14
Common Law v. Statutory Law . . . 3 . . 13
Common Policy Conditions - BOP . . . 8 . . 2
Common Policy Conditions - CPP . . . 7 . . 2
Company Certification . . . 1 . . 6
Company Regulation . . . 1 . . 9
Company Representatives . . . 2 . . 10
Company Solvency . . . 1 . . 9
Comparative Negligence . . . 3 . . 14
Comparison of Dwelling Fire and Homeowners . . 5 . . 18
Compensatory Damages . . . 3 . . 14
Competent Parties . . . 2 . . 12
Completion Bonds . . . 10 . . 5
Compliance - Workers Compensation . . . 9 . . 8
Comprehensive Coverage . . . 6 . . 17
Comprehensive Insurance . . . 6 . . 5
Comprehensive Personal Liability Insurance . . . 10 . . 1
Computer Fraud . . . 7 . . 12
Concealment . . . 2 . . 14
Conditional Contracts . . . 2 . . 13
Conditions - Businessowners Policy . . . 8 . . 12
Conditions - Commercial General Liability . . . 7 . . 7
Conditions - Definition . . . 3 . . 8
Conditions - Dwelling Policy . . . 4 . . 6
Conditions - Farm Coverage Part . . . 7 . . 36
Conditions - General . . . 3 . . 23
Conditions - Section I - Property . . . 5 . . 9
Conditions - Section II - Liability . . . 5 . . 11
Condominium Association Coverage Form . . . 7 . . 25
Condominium Forms . . . 7 . . 25
Condominium Unit Owner's Coverage Form . . . 7 . . 25
Consequential or Indirect Losses . . . 3 . . 5
Consideration . . . 2 . . 12
Considerations for Contractor and Subcontractor . . 9 . . 5
Continuing Education Requirements . . . 1 . . 6
Continuing or Promissory Warranty . . . 2 . . 14
Contract Bonds . . . 10 . . 5
Contract Carriers . . . 7 . . 30
Contract Elements . . . 2 . . 12
Contractor's Equipment Form . . . 7 . . 29
Contractual Relationship . . . 1 . . 2
Contributing Locations . . . 7 . . 24
Contribution By Equal Shares . . . 3 . . 11
Contributory Negligence . . . 3 . . 14
Conviction or No Contest Plea . . . 1 . . 4
Coordination of Benefits . . . 6 . . 3
Cost and Freight (C&F) . . . 10 . . 6
Cost, Insurance and Freight (CIF) . . . 10 . . 6
Countersignature . . . 3 . . 21
Court Bonds . . . 10 . . 4
Coverage A - Bodily Injury/Property Damage . . 7 . . 6
Coverage A - Buildings - Building/Personal Property 7 . . 20
Coverage A - Buildings - Businessowners . . . 8 . . 5
Coverage A - Dwelling Amount - Dwelling . . . 4 . . 2
Coverage A - Dwelling Amount - Homeowners . . 5 . . 2
Coverage B - Business Personal Property . . . 7 . . 20
Coverage B - Business Personal Property - BOP . . 8 . . 6
Coverage B - Other Structures - Dwelling . . . 4 . . 2
Coverage B - Other Structures - Homeowners . . . 5 . . 3
Coverage B - Personal & Advertising Injury . . . 7 . . 6
Coverage C - Medical Payments - CGL . . . 7 . . 7
Coverage C - Personal Property - Dwelling . . . 4 . . 2
Coverage C - Personal Property - Homeowners . . 5 . . 3
Coverage C - Personal Property of Others . . . 7 . . 20
Coverage D - Fair Rental Value - Dwelling . . . 4 . . 3
Coverage D - Loss of Use - Homeowners . . . 5 . . 4
Coverage E - Additional Living Expenses - Dwelling 4 . . 3
Coverage E - Personal Liability - Homeowners . . . 5 . . 11
Coverage Extensions - BOP . . . 8 . . 8
Coverage Extensions - BPP . . . 7 . . 21
Coverage F - Medical Payments - Homeowners . . 5 . . 11
Coverage Forms - CGL . . . 7 . . . 4
Coverage Forms - Dwelling . . . 4 . . . 7
Coverage Forms - Homeowners . . . 5 . . . 6
Coverage Forms - Ocean Marine Policy . . . 10 . . 7
Coverage H - BI/PD - Farm . . . 7 . . . 33
Coverage I - Personal & Advertising Injury - Farm . 7 . . . 33
Coverage J - Medical Payments - Farm Coverage . . 7 . . . 34
Coverages A-E - Farm Property Coverage Form . . . 7 . . . 32
Coverages F-G - Farm Property Coverage Form . . . 7 . . . 33
Covered Property - BOP . . . 8 . . . 5
Crime Coverage - BOP . . . 8 . . . 10
Crime General Conditions . . . 7 . . . 10
Crime General Definitions . . . 7 . . . 10
Crime General Exclusions . . . 7 . . . 10
Criminal Conduct Reporting . . . 1 . . . 4

D

Damages - General . . . 3 . . . 14
Death Benefits - Workers Compensation . . . 9 . . . 3
Debris Removal - BOP . . . 8 . . . 6
Declarations Page - General . . . 3 . . . 8
Deductible Liability Coverage (CA 03 02) . . . 6 . . . 21
Deductibles - Auto . . . 6 . . . 10
Deductibles - General . . . 3 . . . 10
Defamation of Insurer . . . 1 . . . 11
Defense Base Act . . . 9 . . . 2
Definitions - BOP . . . 8 . . . 13
Definitions - Commercial Auto . . . 6 . . . 15
Definitions - General . . . 3 . . . 8
Definitions - Homeowners . . . 5 . . . 1
Definitions - Personal Auto . . . 6 . . . 6
Difference In Conditions (DIC) . . . 10 . . 11
Direct Billed Policies . . . 2 . . . 11
Direct Loss . . . 3 . . . 5
Direct Response System . . . 2 . . . 8
Direct Writer System . . . 2 . . . 8
Directors and Officer's Liability . . . 10 . . 3
Disciplinary Actions . . . 1 . . . 7
Disciplinary Procedures . . . 1 . . . 8
Discovery Form - Crime . . . 7 . . . 11
Distinct Characteristics of Insurance Contracts . . . 2 . . . 13
Doctrine of Insurable Interest . . . 2 . . . 3
Dollar Deductible . . . 3 . . . 10
Domestic Company . . . 2 . . . 6
Domicile . . . 2 . . . 6
Dram Shop Liability . . . 10 . . 3
Drive Other Car Coverage (CA 99 10) . . . 6 . . . 22
Duties After Loss . . . 3 . . . 16
Duty To Defend . . . 3 . . . 18
Dwelling Policy . . . 4 . . . 1
Dwelling Policy Basic Form DP 00 01 . . . 4 . . . 7
Dwelling Policy Broad Form DP 00 02 . . . 4 . . . 8
Dwelling Policy Coverages & Loss Settlement . . . 4 . . . 9
Dwelling Policy Program Comparison . . . 4 . . . 12
Dwelling Policy Special Form DP 00 03 . . . 4 . . . 9
Dwelling Under Construction . . . 4 . . . 10

E

Each Occurrence Limit . . . 7 . . . 8
Earned Premiums . . . 2 . . . 11
Earthquake Endorsement (HO 04 54) - Homeowners 5 . . . 16
Earthquake Form - BPP . . . 7 . . . 26
Electronic Data Processing Form . . . 7 . . . 29
Elements of an Insurable Risk . . . 2 . . . 3
Eligibility - National Flood Program . . . 10 . . 10
Eligible Risks - BOP . . . 8 . . . 1
Eligible Vehicles Under the Personal Auto Policy . . 6 . . . 6
Emergency v. Regular - Flood Insurance . . . 10 . . 6
Employee Dishonesty . . . 8 . . . 10
Employee Theft . . . 7 . . . 11
Employees as Insureds (CA 99 33) . . . 6 . . . 22

Employment Practices Liability (EPL) . . . . 10 . . 3
Endorsements - BOP . . . . 8 . . 13
Endorsements - Commercial Auto . . . . 5 . . 21
Endorsements - Commercial Property . . . . 7 . . 26
Endorsements - Dwelling . . . . 4 . . 10
Endorsements - Homeowners . . . . 5 . . 16
Endorsements - Personal Auto . . . . 6 . . 13
Equipment Breakdown Protection Form . . . . 7 . . 16
Equipment Breakdown Protection - Exclusions . . . 7 . . 17
Equipment Breakdown Protection - Limitations . . . 7 . . 17
Equipment Breakdown Protection - Valuation . . . . 7 . . 17
Equipment Breakdown Protection - Deductibles . . . 7 . . 18
Equipment Dealers Form . . . . 7 . . 29
Estoppel . . . . 2 . . 14
Ethics . . . . 1 . . 18
Examination of Books and Records . . . . 1 . . 13
Exclusions - BOP . . . . 8 . . 4
Exclusions - Definition . . . . 3 . . 9
Exclusions - Farm Coverage Part . . . . 7 . . 36
Exclusions From Benefits - Auto . . . . 6 . . 3
Exclusions - Personal Auto . . . . 6 . . 11
Exclusive Agency or Captive Agency System . . . . 2 . . 8
Expense Ratio . . . . 3 . . 2
Experience Rating . . . . 9 . . 7
Exposure . . . . 2 . . 1
Express Authority . . . . 2 . . 10
Extended Business Income . . . . 7 . . 23
Extended Nonowned Coverage-Named Individuals . 6 . . 13
Extended Period of Indemnity . . . . 7 . . 24
Extended Reporting Periods (ERP) . . . . 7 . . 4
Extensions - Farm Coverage Part . . . . 7 . . 33
Exterior Glass - BOP . . . . 8 . . 6
Extortion . . . . 7 . . 12
Extra Expense - BOP . . . . 8 . . 7
Extra Expense - Business Income . . . . 7 . . 23
Extra Expense Coverage Form . . . . 7 . . 25
Extraordinary Medical Benefits . . . . 6 . . 2

F

Facultative Reinsurance . . . . 2 . . 4
Fair Access to Insurance Requirements (FAIR Plans) 10 . . 11
Fair Credit Reporting Act . . . . 1 . . 15
False Advertising . . . . 1 . . 11
False Pretense Coverage (CA 25 03) . . . . 6 . . 22
Farm Coverage Part . . . . 7 . . 31
Farm Liability Coverage Form . . . . 7 . . 33
Farm Property Coverage Form . . . . 7 . . 31
Federal Employees Compensation Act . . . . 9 . . 2
Federal Employer's Liability Act . . . . 9 . . 2
Fees . . . . 1 . . 12
Fictitious or Assumed Name . . . . 1 . . 4
Fiduciary Capacity . . . . 1 . . 3
Fiduciary Liability . . . . 10 . . 3
Field Underwriting . . . . 3 . . 1
Financial Status . . . . 2 . . 6
Fire Damage Limit . . . . 7 . . 8
Fire Department Service Charge . . . . 8 . . 6
First Named Insureds . . . . 3 . . 9
First Party Benefits - Auto . . . . 6 . . 2
First Party Benefits Coverage - Pennsylvania - Auto 6 . . 14
First Party Benefits/Priority of Payments - Auto . . 6 . . 3
Foreign Company . . . . 2 . . 6
Foreign Coverage Endorsement . . . . 9 . . 5
Forgery or Alterations . . . . 7 . . 12
Frame Construction . . . . 3 . . 6
Fraternal Associations . . . . 2 . . 5
Fraud . . . . 2 . . 14
Free Along Side (FAS) - Ocean Marine Insurance . 10 . . 6
Free On Board (FOB) - Ocean Marine Insurance . . 10 . . 6
Freight Coverage - Ocean Marine Insurance . . . . . 10 . . 6
Friendly Fire v. Hostile Fire . . . . 3 . . 23
Full Reporting (Honesty Clause) . . . . 3 . . 6
Full Tort . . . . 6 . . . 2
Functional Replacement Cost . . . . 3 . . . 7
Funds Transfer Fraud . . . . 7 . . . 12
Funeral Benefits - Auto . . . . 6 . . . 2

G

Garage Coverage Form . . . . 6 . . . 18
Garage Liability Exclusions . . . . 6 . . . 18
Garagekeepers Exclusions . . . . 6 . . . 18
General Aggregate Limit . . . . 7 . . . 8
General Damages . . . . 3 . . . 14
General Exclusions - Dwelling . . . . 4 . . . 5
Gramm-Leach-Bliley Act (GLBA) . . . . 1 . . . 13
Guest's Property . . . . 7 . . . 13

H

Hangerkeepers Liability . . . . 10 . . 9
Hazard . . . . 2 . . . 1
Hazards . . . . 3 . . . 3
Health Insurance Policies . . . . 1 . . . 17
Hired Auto and Nonowned Auto (BP 04 04) - BOP . 8 . . . 14
Hired Autos Specified as Owned Autos (CA 99 16) . 6 . . . 22
Home Day Care Coverage Endorsement (HO 04 97) 5 . . . 17
Homeowner Coverage & Loss Settlement Comp . . . 5 . . . 10
Homeowner Form HO 00 02 . . . . 5 . . . 7
Homeowner Form HO 00 03 . . . . 5 . . . 7
Homeowner Form HO 00 04 . . . . 5 . . . 7
Homeowner Form HO 00 05 . . . . 5 . . . 7
Homeowner Form HO 00 06 . . . . 5 . . . 7
Homeowner Form HO 00 08 . . . . 5 . . . 7
Homeowner Policy Program . . . . 5 . . . 6
Homeowner Policy Structure . . . . 5 . . . 2
Homeowners Policy . . . . 5 . . . 1
Homeowners Policy Comparison . . . . 5 . . . 19
Hull Coverage - Ocean Marine Insurance . . . . 10 . . 6

I

Illegal Inducements . . . . 1 . . . 11
Illustration - Additional Living Expenses . . . . 4 . . . 3
Illustration - Boiler and Machinery Coverage Part . . 7 . . . 15
Illustration - Businessowners Policy Structure . . . . 8 . . . 2
Illustration - Businessowners Property Part . . . . . 8 . . . 5
Illustration - Claims-Made Coverage Form . . . . . . 7 . . . 5
Illustration - Coinsurance Formula and Examples . . 3 . . . 12
Illustration - Coinsurance Requirements . . . . 7 . . . 23
Illustration - Commercial Auto Policy . . . . 6 . . . 15
Illustration - Commercial Cancellation Requirements 7 . . . 38
Illustration - Commercial Crime Coverages . . . . . . 7 . . . 14
Illustration - Commercial General Liability Coverage 7 . . . 3
Illustration - Commercial General Liability Limits . 7 . . . 8
Illustration - Commercial Inland Marine Coverage . 7 . . . 27
Illustration - Commercial Package Policy Format . . . 7 . . . 2
Illustration - Commercial Property Coverage Part . . 7 . . . 19
Illustration - Crime Coverage Part Format . . . . 7 . . . 10
Illustration - Dwelling Policy Cancellation - PA . . . 4 . . . 11
Illustration - Dwelling Policy Coverage Forms . . . . 4 . . . 1
Illustration - Experience Modification . . . . 9 . . . 7
Illustration - Farm Coverage Part . . . . 7 . . . 31
Illustration - Financial Responsibility . . . . 6 . . . 21
Illustration - Homeowner Policy Structure . . . . 5 . . . 2
Illustration - Major Distribution Systems . . . . 2 . . . 8
Illustration - Named Peril v. Special Form . . . . . . 3 . . . 5
Illustration - Overview of Unoccupancy and Vacancy 3 . . . 19
Illustration - PA Cancellation/Nonrenewal . . . . . . 3 . . . 22
Illustration - PA Homeowner Cancellation . . . . 5 . . . 15
Illustration - PA Motor Vehicle Responsibility Law . 6 . . . 5
Illustration - Personal Auto Cancellation . . . . 6 . . . 12
Illustration - Personal Auto Policy Structure . . . . . . 6 . . . 6
Illustration - Personal Umbrella Policy . . . . 10 . . 13
Illustration - Underinsured Motorist Coverage . . . . 6 . . . 9

Illustration - Workers Compensation Policy ..... 9 .. 2
Implied Authority .... 2 .. 10
Implied Warranties - Ocean Marine Insurance ... 10 .. 7
Implied Warranty .... 2 .. 14
Income Benefits - Workers Compensation ...... 9 .. 3
Income Loss Benefits - Auto .... 6 .. 2
Indemnity .... 2 .. 13
Independent Agency System .... 2 .. 8
Independent Agents .... 2 .. 9
Independent Rating Services .... 2 .. 7
Individual Named Insureds (CA 99 17) .... 6 .. 22
Individual or Judgment Rating .... 3 .. 2
Ineligible Claimants - Auto .... 6 .. 3
Ineligible Risks - BOP .... 8 .. 1
Inflation Guard Endorsement (HO 04 66) ...... 5 .. 16
Inland Marine Conditions .... 7 .. 28
Inland Marine Coverage Forms .... 7 .. 28
Inland Marine Coverage Part .... 7 .. 27
Inland Marine Exclusions .... 7 .. 28
Inside Premises - Robbery or Safe Burglary ..... 7 .. 12
Inside Premises - Theft of Money & Securities ... 7 .. 12
Ins. Commissioner's General Duties and Powers .. 1 .. 9
Installation Floater Form .... 7 .. 29
Instrumentations of Transportation/Communication 7 .. 28
Insurable Interest .... 3 .. 1
Insurance .... 2 .. 2
Insurance Agreement .... 3 .. 23
Insurance Concepts .... 2 .. 1
Insurance Consultation Services Exemption Act ... 3 .. 21
Insurance Department Examinations .... 2 .. 7
Insurance Fraud Regulation .... 1 .. 14
Insurance Regulations Practice Exam .... 1 .. 23
Insured .... 3 .. 9
Insured Status .... 3 .. 9
Insured's Provisions Or Duties .... 3 .. 16
Insurer's Provisions or Duties .... 3 .. 17
Insuring Agreement .... 3 .. 8
Intentional Torts/Intentional Acts .... 3 .. 13
Intervening Cause .... 3 .. 14
Introduction and Exam Strategies .... xvii xx

J

Jewelers Block Form .... 7 .. 29
Joint Ownership Coverage .... 6 .. 13
Joint Underwriting Association .... 10 .. 11
Jones Act .... 9 .. 2
Judicial Bonds .... 10 .. 5

L

Laser Beam Endorsement .... 7 .. 5
Law of Large Numbers .... 2 .. 3
Leader Locations .... 7 .. 24
Leasehold Interest Coverage Form .... 7 .. 25
Legal Errors and Omissions .... 10 .. 2
Legal Interpretations Affecting Insurance Contracts 2 .. 13
Legal Liability Coverage Form .... 7 .. 25
Legal Purpose .... 2 .. 12
Lessees of Safe Deposit Boxes .... 7 .. 13
Liability Coverage Extensions - Commercial Auto . 6 .. 17
Liability Coverage Section II - Homeowner ..... 5 .. 11
Liability Exclusions - BOP .... 8 .. 11
Liability Exclusions - Commercial Auto .... 6 .. 17
Liability Exclusions - Personal Auto .... 6 .. 8
Liability Insurance .... 3 .. 13
Liberalization Clause .... 3 .. 17
License or Permit Bond .... 10 .. 5
License Restrictions Placed on Producers ...... 1 .. 6
Licensing Application Procedures .... 1 .. 1
Life Insurance Policies .... 1 .. 16
Limitations - BOP .... 8 .. 6
Limitations of License .... 1 .. 6
Limited Tort .... 6 ... 2
Limited Tort Alternative Information Notice - PA .. 6 ... 14
Limits of Insurance .... 7 ... 21
Limits of Liability - CGL .... 7 ... 8
Limits Of Liability - General .... 3 ... 15
Liquor Liability .... 10 .. 3
Livestock Coverage Form .... 7 ... 34
Lloyds .... 2 ... 5
Loss .... 2 ... 2
Loss Adjustment - Ocean Marine .... 10 .. 7
Loss Cost Rating .... 3 ... 2
Loss Cost Rating - Workers Compensation ..... 9 ... 6
Loss Payable Clause .... 3 ... 20
Loss Ratio .... 3 ... 2
Loss Sustained From - Crime .... 7 ... 11
Loss Valuation .... 3 ... 7

M

Maintenance of Producer License .... 1 ... 7
Major Distribution Systems .... 2 ... 8
Management of Distribution Systems .... 2 ... 9
Managing General Agency System .... 2 ... 9
Manual or Class Rating .... 3 ... 2
Manufacturing Locations .... 7 ... 24
Market Value .... 3 ... 7
Masonry Construction .... 3 ... 6
Material Fact .... 3 ... 23
Maximum Period of Indemnity .... 7 ... 24
MCS-90 Endorsement for Motor Carriers ...... 6 ... 21
Mechanical Breakdown .... 8 ... 10
Medical Benefits - Auto .... 6 ... 2
Medical Expense Limit - CGL .... 7 ... 8
Medical Expenses - BOP .... 8 ... 11
Medical Malpractice Insurance .... 10 .. 2
Merit Rating .... 3 ... 2
Mini/Midi tail .... 7 ... 4
Mine Subsidence Insurance .... 10 .. 11
Miscellaneous Bonds .... 10 .. 5
Miscellaneous Type Vehicles .... 6 ... 13
Misrepresentations - Regulations .... 1 ... 11
Misrepresentations - General .... 2 ... 14
Mobile Agricultural Machinery & Equipment Form . 7 ... 34
Mobile Equipment (CA 20 15) .... 6 ... 22
Mobilehome Endorsement (HO 40 01) .... 5 ... 17
Money Orders and Counterfeit Paper .... 7 ... 12
Monthly Limit of Indemnity .... 7 ... 24
Moral Hazard .... 3 ... 3
Morale Hazard .... 3 ... 3
Motor Carrier Form .... 6 ... 20
Motor Truck Cargo Policy - Owner's Form ..... 7 ... 30
Motor Truck Cargo Policy - Shipper's Form .... 7 ... 30
Motor Truck Cargo Policy - Trucker's Form .... 7 ... 30
Motor Vehicle Bond .... 10 .. 5
Motor Vehicle Financial Responsibility Law .... 6 ... 1
Motor Vehicle Fraud .... 6 ... 5
Mutual Companies .... 2 ... 5

N

Name Restrictions on License .... 1 ... 4
Named Insured .... 3 ... 9
Named Nonowner Endorsement .... 6 ... 13
National Assn of Insurance Commissioners (NAIC) . 2 ... 7
National Flood Insurance Program .... 10 .. 10
Negligence .... 3 ... 13
No Benefit to Bailee .... 3 ... 20
Nonadmitted or Unauthorized Companies .... 2 ... 6
Nonconcurrency .... 3 ... 10
Nonowned Aircraft - Aviation Insurance .... 10 .. 9
Nonresident Producer .... 1 ... 3
Nonresident Applicant .... 1 ... 3
Notice/Recording Requirements .... 9 ... 8

O

Occupations Excluded - Workers Compensation . . 9 . . 4
Occurrence Coverage . . . . 7 . . 4
Ocean Marine Insurance . . . . 10 . . 6
Offer & Acceptance . . . . 2 . . 12
Offset of Benefits - Workers Compensation . . . . . 9 . . 9
Optional Coverages - BOP . . . . 8 . . 10
Optional Coverages - Business Income . . . . 7 . . 24
Ordinance or Law - BPP . . . . 7 . . 26
Ordinance or Law - Homeowners . . . . 5 . . 17
Other Categories of Construction . . . . 3 . . 6
Other Coverages and Options . . . . 10 . . 1
Other Coverages and Options Practice Exam . . . . 10 . . 17
Other Coverages - Dwelling . . . . 4 . . 3
Other Inland Marine Coverages . . . . 7 . . 29
Other Insurance . . . . 3 . . 10
Other Perils or Subjects . . . . 3 . . 25
Other Provisions - Personal Auto . . . . 6 . . 5
Other Risk Management Concepts . . . . 2 . . 2
Other Sources of Coverage - Workers. Comp. . . . 9 . . 7
Other Than Collision (OTC) - Auto . . . . 6 . . 10
Outdoor Property . . . . 8 . . 8
Outdoor Signs . . . . 8 . . 10
Outside The Premises . . . . 7 . . 12
Owners & Contractors Protective Liability Policy . 7 . . 9

P

Part A - Liability Coverage - Personal Auto . . . . . 6 . . 7
Part B - Medical Payments - Personal Auto . . . . . 6 . . 8
Part C - Uninsured Motorists Coverage . . . . 6 . . 8
Part D - Coverage For Damage To Your Auto . . . 6 . . 10
Part E - Duties After Accident/Loss - Personal Auto 6 . . 11
Part F - General Provisions - Personal Auto . . . . . 6 . . 12
Part Five - Premium - Workers Compensation. . . . 9 . . 4
Part Four - Duties If Injury Occurs - Workers Comp 9 . . 4
Part One - Workers Compensation Insurance . . . . 9 . . 3
Part Six - Conditions - Workers Comp . . . . 9 . . 4
Part Three - Other States Insurance - Workers Comp 9 . . 4
Part Two - Employers Liability - Workers Comp . 9 . . 4
Part-Time Agents or Brokers . . . . 1 . . 2
Partial Disability . . . . 9 . . 3
Participating Dividend Plans . . . . 9 . . 7
Parties to a Surety Bond . . . . 10 . . 5
Partnerships - Licensing . . . . 1 . . 1
Payment of Benefits . . . . 6 . . 3
Peak Season Endorsement . . . . 7 . . 26
Penalties - Workers Compensation . . . . 9 . . 8
Pennsylvania Insurance Guaranty Association Act . 3 . . 21
Pennsylvania Notice . . . . 4 . . 11
Per Occurrence Limits . . . . 3 . . 15
Per Person Limits . . . . 3 . . 15
Percentage Deductible . . . . 3 . . 10
Performance Bonds . . . . 10 . . 5
Peril . . . . 2 . . 2
Perils Covered - Flood Insurance . . . . 10 . . 9
Perils Insured Against - Homeowners . . . . 5 . . 5
Permanent Partial Disability . . . . 9 . . 3
Permitted Incidental Occupancies (HO 00 42) . . . . 5 . . 16
Personal and Advertising Injury . . . . 7 . . 8
Personal Article Floaters . . . . 10 . . 11
Personal Auto Policy . . . . SP . 26
Personal Auto Policy . . . . 6 . . 6
Personal Contracts . . . . 2 . . 13
Personal Effects Floaters . . . . 10 . . 11
Personal Injury (HO 24 82) . . . . 5 . . 17
Personal Liability . . . . 4 . . 11
Personal Producing General Agency System . . . . . 2 . . 9
Personal Property at Newly Acquired Premises . . . 8 . . 8
Personal Property Floaters . . . . 10 . . 10
Personal Property Not Covered - Homeowners . . . 5 . . 3
Personal Property Off Premises - BOP . . . . 8 . . 8
Personal Property Replacement Cost (HO 04 90) . . . 5 . . . 17
Personal Umbrella Policy . . . . 10 . . 1
Persons to be Licensed . . . . 1 . . . 2
Physical Damage Coverage Extensions - Auto . . . . 6 . . . 17
Physical Damage Exclusions - Auto . . . . 6 . . . 17
Physical Hazard . . . . 3 . . . 3
Policy Forms . . . . 1 . . . 9
Policy Limits . . . . 3 . . . 11
Policy Period . . . . 3 . . . 10
Policy Structure . . . . 3 . . . 8
Policy Territory . . . . 3 . . . 10
Pollutants Clean Up and Removal . . . . 8 . . . 7
Pollution Liability . . . . 7 . . . 9
Pollution Liability Coverage for Covered Autos . . . 6 . . . 23
Pollution Liability Coverage Form . . . . 7 . . . 9
Pollution Liability Extension Endorsement . . . . 7 . . . 9
Pollution Liability Limited Coverage Form . . . . . . 7 . . . 9
Pooling . . . . 10 . . 12
Potential Agent Liabilities and Exposures . . . . 2 . . . 12
Premises and Operations . . . . 7 . . . 3
Premium Computations - Workers Compensation . . 9 . . . 6
Premium Discount - Workers Compensation . . . . . 9 . . . 7
Premium Financing . . . . 2 . . . 11
Preservation of Property . . . . 8 . . . 6
Presumption of Agency . . . . 2 . . . 10
Primary and Excess . . . . 3 . . . 11
Principle of Indemnity . . . . 2 . . . 3
Priority of Recovery . . . . 6 . . . 4
Privacy of Consumer Information Regulation . . . . . 1 . . . 13
Private Insurers v. Government Insurers . . . . 2 . . . 5
Pro Rate . . . . 3 . . . 21
Producer Regulation . . . . 1 . . . 11
Producer Powers . . . . 1 . . . 6
Producers . . . . 2 . . . 9
Producer's Collection and Financial Responsibilities . 2 . . . 11
Producer's Responsibilities to the Insured . . . . 2 . . . 11
Producer's Responsibility to the Insurance Company 2 . . . 11
Products and Completed Operations . . . . 7 . . . 3
Products/Completed Operations Aggregate . . . . 7 . . . 8
Professional Designations . . . . 1 . . . 5
Professional Liability Policies . . . . 10 . . 2
Profitability . . . . 3 . . . 2
Property Casualty Insurance Basics Practice Exam . . 3 . . . 27
Property Coverages - Section I - Homeowners . . . . 5 . . . 2
Property Damage Liability - Auto . . . . 6 . . . 1
Property Excluded - Watercraft Insurance . . . . 10 . . 8
Property General Conditions - BOP . . . . 8 . . . 9
Property Insurance v. Liability Insurance . . . . 3 . . . 3
Property Loss Conditions - BOP . . . . 8 . . . 9
Property Not Covered - BOP . . . . 8 . . . 6
Property Not Covered - BPP . . . . 7 . . . 20
Property Not Covered - Flood Insurance . . . . 10 . . 10
Protection and Indemnity (P&I) . . . . 10 . . 7
Protective Safeguards (BP 40 39) . . . . 8 . . . 14
Proximate Cause . . . . 3 . . . 13
Punitive Damages . . . . 3 . . . 14
Purchasing Groups . . . . 10 . . 12
Purpose of Licensing . . . . 1 . . . 1
Purpose of Reinsurance . . . . 2 . . . 4

R

Rate Regulation . . . . 1 . . . 9
Rating . . . . 3 . . . 2
Reasonable Expectations . . . . 2 . . . 13
Rebating . . . . 1 . . . 11
Recipient Locations . . . . 7 . . . 24
Reciprocals . . . . 2 . . . 5
Redlining . . . . 1 . . . 11
Reduction in Benefits - Workers Compensation . . . . 9 . . . 9
Referral Fees . . . . 1 . . . 12
Rehabilitation Benefits - Workers Compensation . . . 9 . . . 3
Reinsurance . . . . 2 . . . 4

Related Pennsylvania Regulations . . . . 3 . . 21
Released Bill of Lading . . . . 7 . . 30
Remittance of Premiums . . . . 2 . . 11
Rental Vehicles . . . . 6 . . 4
Replacement Cost . . . . 3 . . 7
Reporting Forms . . . . 3 . . 6
Representations . . . . 2 . . 14
Reserves . . . . 1 . . 12
Restoration of Limits . . . . 3 . . 11
Restrictions on License Transfer . . . . 1 . . 4
Retention . . . . 2 . . 4
Retroactive Date . . . . 7 . . 4
Retrocession . . . . 2 . . 4
Retrocessionaire . . . . 2 . . 4
Retrospective Rating . . . . 9 . . 7
Risk . . . . 2 . . 1
Risk Management . . . . 2 . . 1
Risk Retention Groups . . . . 10 . . 12
Running Down Clause . . . . 10 . . 6

S

Safe Depository . . . . 7 . . 13
Salvage . . . . 3 . . 18
Scheduled Insurance . . . . 3 . . 5
Scheduled Personal Property Form HO 04 61 . . . . 5 . . 16
Section I - Boatowners Property Coverage . . . . . . 10 . . 8
Section I - Covered Autos - Business Auto . . . . . 6 . . 16
Section I - Covered Autos - Garage Coverage Form 6 . . 18
Section I - Covered Autos - Motor Carrier Form . . 6 . . 20
Section I - Homeowners Property Exclusions . . . . 5 . . 9
Section II - Boatowners Liability Coverage . . . . . 10 . . 8
Section II - Business Auto Liability Coverage . . . . 6 . . 16
Section II - Garage Liability - Garage Coverage . . 6 . . 18
Section II - Liability/Medical Payments Exclusions 5 . . 12
Section II - Motor Carrier Liability Coverage Form 6 . . 20
Section II - Truckers Liability Coverage . . . . 6 . . 20
Section III - Garagekeepers Coverage . . . . 6 . . 18
Section III - Physical Damage Coverage . . . . 6 . . 17
Section III - Trailer Interchange Coverage . . . . . . 6 . . 20
Section IV - Business Auto Conditions . . . . 6 . . 17
Section V - Business Auto Definitions . . . . 6 . . 17
Securities Deposited with Others . . . . 7 . . 13
Self-insured . . . . 10 . . 12
Short Rate . . . . 3 . . 21
Signs Form . . . . 7 . . 29
Sinkhole Collapse - Dwelling . . . . 4 . . 11
Special Damages . . . . 3 . . 14
Special Form - BOP . . . . 8 . . 4
Special Form - BPP . . . . 7 . . 26
Special Form - Farm Coverage Part . . . . 7 . . 35
Specific Insurance . . . . 3 . . 5
Specific Perils Coverage - Business Auto . . . . . . 6 . . 17
Split Limits . . . . 3 . . 15
Spoilage Coverage Endorsement . . . . 7 . . 26
Stacking . . . . 6 . . 4
Standard Deductible . . . . 8 . . 8
Standard Fire Policy (165 Lines) . . . . SP . 1
Standard Fire Policy Endorsement . . . . 4 . . 11
Standard Mortgage Clause . . . . 3 . . 20
State Regulations . . . . 1 . . 8
State Worker's Insurance Fund (SWIF) . . . . 9 . . 7
Stated Amount . . . . 3 . . 7
Statute of Limitations - General . . . . 3 . . 14
Statutory Defenses . . . . 3 . . 14
Stock Companies . . . . 2 . . 5
Strict or Absolute Liability . . . . 3 . . 15
Subrogation . . . . 2 . . 13
Subsequent Injury Fund . . . . 9 . . 5
Supplemental Coverage Extensions - BOP . . . . . . 8 . . 11
Supplemental Extended Reporting Periods (SERP) . 7 . . 4
Supplemental Payments - CGL . . . . 7 . . 7
Supplementary Payments - Personal Auto . . . . . . 6 . . 7
Surety Bonds . . . . 10 . . 5
Surplus Lines Insurance . . . . 10 . . 4
Suspension and Revocation . . . . 1 . . . 7
Suspension Provision . . . . 7 . . . 17

T

Temporary Disability . . . . 9 . . . 3
Temporary License . . . . 1 . . . 3
Terrorism Risk Insurance Act (TRIA) . . . . 3 . . . 21
Theft Coverage . . . . 4 . . . 10
Time Deductible . . . . 3 . . . 10
Timely Reporting and Full Reporting . . . . 3 . . . 6
Tort Concepts . . . . 3 . . . 13
Tort Options . . . . 6 . . . 2
Total Disability . . . . 9 . . . 3
Towing and Labor . . . . 6 . . . 13
Transfer of Rights and Duties (Assignment) . . . . . . 3 . . . 16
Transfer of Rights of Recovery (Subrogation) . . . . . 3 . . . 18
Transportation Coverages . . . . 7 . . . 30
Transportation Expense . . . . 6 . . . 10
Transportation Policy - Annual Form . . . . 7 . . . 30
Transportation Policy - Trip Transit Form . . . . . . 7 . . . 30
Treaty Reinsurance . . . . 2 . . . 4
Truckers Coverage Form . . . . 6 . . . 19
Truckers Insurance for Non-Trucking Use . . . . 6 . . . 22
Twisting . . . . 1 . . . 11
Types of Authority . . . . 2 . . . 10
Types of Insurers . . . . 2 . . . 5

U

Underinsured Motorists Insurance . . . . 6 . . . 4
Underwriting . . . . 3 . . . 1
Unearned Premiums . . . . 2 . . . 11
Unfair Claims Settlement Practices . . . . 1 . . . 10
Unfair Discrimination . . . . 1 . . . 11
Unfair Insurance Practices Act . . . . 1 . . . 12
Unfair Trade Practices . . . . 1 . . . 11
Uniformity of Licenses . . . . 1 . . . 4
Unilateral Contracts . . . . 2 . . . 13
Uninsurable and Excepted Property . . . . 3 . . . 25
Uninsured Motorists Insurance . . . . 6 . . . 4
Unintentional Torts . . . . 3 . . . 13
Unlimited Medical Benefits - Workers Compensation 9 . . . 3
Unoccupancy and Vacancy . . . . 3 . . . 19
US Longshore and Harbor Workers Comp Law . . . 9 . . . 1
Utility Service - Direct Damage (BP 04 56) . . . . . 8 . . . 14
Utility Service - Time Element (BP 04 57) . . . . . . 8 . . . 14
Utmost Good Faith . . . . 2 . . . 14

V

Valuable Papers and Records Form - Inland Marine . 7 . . . 29
Valuation Clause - Inland Marine . . . . 7 . . . 13
Value Reporting Form . . . . 7 . . . 26
Vicarious Liability . . . . 3 . . . 15
Voluntary Compensation . . . . 9 . . . 5

W

Waiver . . . . 2 . . . 14
Waiver of Examination . . . . 1 . . . 5
Waiver of Subrogation . . . . 3 . . . 18
Warranty . . . . 2 . . . 14
Water Backup and Sump Overflow - Dwelling . . . . 4 . . . 11
Water Damage - BOP . . . . 8 . . . 6
Watercraft Endorsement (HO 24 75) - Homeowners . 5 . . . 17
Watercraft Insurance . . . . 10 . . 8
Workers Compensation (Act 44 of 1993) . . . . 9 . . . 8
Workers Compensation (1996 Amendments) . . . . . . 9 . . . 9
Workers Compensation Law . . . . 9 . . . 1
Wrongful Death Statutes . . . . 3 . . . 15